MMOs FROM THE INSIDE OUT

THE HISTORY, DESIGN, FUN, AND ART OF MASSIVELY-MULTIPLAYER ONLINE ROLE-PLAYING GAMES

Richard A. Bartle

Apress®

ISBN-13 (pbk): 978-1-4842-1723-8

ISBN-13 (electronic): 978-1-4842-1724-5

Managing Director: Welmoed Spahr
Lead Editor: Ben Renow-Clarke
Editorial Board: Steve Anglin, Pramila Balen, Louise Corrigan, Jim DeWolf, Jonathan Gennick,
    Robert Hutchinson, Celestin Suresh John, Michelle Lowman, James Markham,
    Susan McDermott, Matthew Moodie, Jeffrey Pepper, Douglas Pundick,
    Ben Renow-Clarke, Gwenan Spearing
Coordinating Editor: Melissa Maldonado
Copy Editors: Kezia Endsley, Patrick Meador
Compositor: SPi Global
Indexer: SPi Global
Artist: SPi Global

Distributed to the book trade worldwide by Springer Science+Business Media New York, 233 Spring Street, 6th Floor, New York, NY 10013. Phone 1-800-SPRINGER, fax (201) 348-4505, e-mail orders-ny@springer-sbm.com, or visit www.springeronline.com. Apress Media, LLC is a California LLC and the sole member (owner) is Springer Science + Business Media Finance Inc (SSBM Finance Inc). SSBM Finance Inc is a Delaware corporation.

For information on translations, please e-mail rights@apress.com, or visit www.apress.com.

Apress and friends of ED books may be purchased in bulk for academic, corporate, or promotional use. eBook versions and licenses are also available for most titles. For more information, reference our Special Bulk Sales–eBook Licensing web page at www.apress.com/bulk-sales.

Any source code or other supplementary materials referenced by the author in this text is available to readers at www.apress.com. For detailed information about how to locate your book's source code, go to www.apress.com/source-code/.

MMOs FROM THE INSIDE OUT

THE HISTORY, DESIGN, FUN, AND ART OF MASSIVELY-MULTIPLAYER ONLINE ROLE-PLAYING GAMES

Richard A. Bartle

Apress®

ISBN-13 (pbk): 978-1-4842-1723-8

ISBN-13 (electronic): 978-1-4842-1724-5

Managing Director: Welmoed Spahr
Lead Editor: Ben Renow-Clarke
Editorial Board: Steve Anglin, Pramila Balen, Louise Corrigan, Jim DeWolf, Jonathan Gennick,
    Robert Hutchinson, Celestin Suresh John, Michelle Lowman, James Markham,
    Susan McDermott, Matthew Moodie, Jeffrey Pepper, Douglas Pundick,
    Ben Renow-Clarke, Gwenan Spearing
Coordinating Editor: Melissa Maldonado
Copy Editors: Kezia Endsley, Patrick Meador
Compositor: SPi Global
Indexer: SPi Global
Artist: SPi Global

Distributed to the book trade worldwide by Springer Science+Business Media New York, 233 Spring Street, 6th Floor, New York, NY 10013. Phone 1-800-SPRINGER, fax (201) 348-4505, e-mail orders-ny@springer-sbm.com, or visit www.springeronline.com. Apress Media, LLC is a California LLC and the sole member (owner) is Springer Science + Business Media Finance Inc (SSBM Finance Inc). SSBM Finance Inc is a Delaware corporation.

For information on translations, please e-mail rights@apress.com, or visit www.apress.com.

Apress and friends of ED books may be purchased in bulk for academic, corporate, or promotional use. eBook versions and licenses are also available for most titles. For more information, reference our Special Bulk Sales–eBook Licensing web page at www.apress.com/bulk-sales.

Any source code or other supplementary materials referenced by the author in this text is available to readers at www.apress.com. For detailed information about how to locate your book's source code, go to www.apress.com/source-code/.

MMOs FROM THE INSIDE OUT

THE HISTORY, DESIGN, FUN, AND ART OF MASSIVELY-MULTIPLAYER ONLINE ROLE-PLAYING GAMES

Richard A. Bartle

Apress®

MMOs from the Inside Out

Copyright © 2016 by **Richard A. Bartle**

ISBN-13 (pbk): 978-1-4842-1723-8

ISBN-13 (electronic): 978-1-4842-1724-5

Managing Director: Welmoed Spahr
Lead Editor: Ben Renow-Clarke
Editorial Board: Steve Anglin, Pramila Balen, Louise Corrigan, Jim DeWolf, Jonathan Gennick,
    Robert Hutchinson, Celestin Suresh John, Michelle Lowman, James Markham,
    Susan McDermott, Matthew Moodie, Jeffrey Pepper, Douglas Pundick,
    Ben Renow-Clarke, Gwenan Spearing
Coordinating Editor: Melissa Maldonado
Copy Editors: Kezia Endsley, Patrick Meador
Compositor: SPi Global
Indexer: SPi Global
Artist: SPi Global

Distributed to the book trade worldwide by Springer Science+Business Media New York, 233 Spring Street, 6th Floor, New York, NY 10013. Phone 1-800-SPRINGER, fax (201) 348-4505, e-mail orders-ny@springer-sbm.com, or visit www.springeronline.com. Apress Media, LLC is a California LLC and the sole member (owner) is Springer Science + Business Media Finance Inc (SSBM Finance Inc). SSBM Finance Inc is a Delaware corporation.

For information on translations, please e-mail rights@apress.com, or visit www.apress.com.

Apress and friends of ED books may be purchased in bulk for academic, corporate, or promotional use. eBook versions and licenses are also available for most titles. For more information, reference our Special Bulk Sales–eBook Licensing web page at www.apress.com/bulk-sales.

Any source code or other supplementary materials referenced by the author in this text is available to readers at www.apress.com. For detailed information about how to locate your book's source code, go to www.apress.com/source-code/.

To those who would make worlds

Contents

About the Author

Dr. Richard A. Bartle has been playing and designing MMOs longer than anybody. In 1978, he co-wrote MUD, the progenitor of the entire genre. His famous Player Types model has seen widespread adoption by the MMO industry and beyond, and the online test bearing his name has been taken more than 800,000 times. His first book, *Designing Virtual Worlds*, is the classic text on the subject, and he is an influential writer on all aspects of online game design. In 2010, he was the first recipient of the prestigious Game Developers Choice award of Online Game Legend. He is an honorary professor of computer game design at the University of Essex, England, where it all began. He's also innumerable characters in MMOs.

Acknowledgments

This book would not have been written were it not for:

Ben Renow Clarke at Apress, who decided to take on a project so unlike other Apress projects that I can only guess at how many favors he had to call in to get it green-lit.

The army of editors who swarmed over my text to convert it from British English to American English in time to meet the publication deadline.

My wife, Gail Bartle, who isn't a gamer but understands.

I'd also like to thank the hundreds of students, blog readers, e-mail correspondents, game designers, journalists (whether clueless or clueful), academics (likewise), and players who have given me cause to think about MMOs over the years. This is where you get to wish you hadn't.

Introduction

In 1978, I bought a book.

I'd been a student for only a few weeks. The book cost £5.95—more money than my weekly food budget—and it was piled high and neglected in the campus bookshop because it wasn't on any reading list. Nevertheless, because I'd been recommended it by some of my new friends, I dusted off the top copy (literally, as it was covered in dust) and had a look inside.

Ten minutes later, I had handed over the cash and was carrying the second-from-top copy (hey, who wants a dusty book?) back to my student accommodations. In so doing, I had tacitly accepted that although I had gone to university to study mathematics, my future lay in computer science.

The book in question was *Computer Lib*, by Ted Nelson.

It was also *Dream Machines*, by Ted Nelson.

If you held the book with *Computer Lib* as the front cover, then flipped it between your fingers away from you so you should be looking at the back cover upside-down, you'd find you were actually looking at the front cover of *Dream Machines* right-way-up. Flip it again and you were back to *Computer Lib*. This was two books in one, with the text from each meeting in the middle.

Computer Lib had the subtitle, *You Can and Must Understand Computers NOW*. It was for people who wanted to know more about this obscure technology that promised (or threatened) to change the world. *Dream Machines* was for programmers themselves, laying out the power and wondrous potential they held in their hands.

To an 18-year-old boy from nowhere, it was an inspiration.

It was still an inspiration back in 2007, when I decided to write a book of my own. What *Computer Lib/Dream Machines* had done for me, I wanted to do for MMO designers (and for the players who are to become designers). Computer games in general, and MMOs in particular, are vehicles of tremendous power—far more power than their designers realize. They could be so much more than they are. They're being held back, though, their potential kept in check. They could change the real world. They could supersede the real world. They could liberate imagination and make it manifest. They could free humanity. They have it in their purview to grant anyone the gift of being ... well, of simply being. Oh, and "they" here doesn't mean the MMOs, it means the people who would create MMOs. It means you.

The working title for this book was *MMOs FTW!* (I even bought the domain name). It's the equivalent of *Dream Machines*—a celebration of what MMOs are, what they could be, what they should be, and what some day they will be, written for the people who make them or want to make them. Its companion volume, the Computer Lib-equivalent that looks at how the real world sees MMOs, was *MMOs WTF?*. Sadly, those aren't titles acceptable to book publishers (for "those won't come up in any search for books on game design" reasons), but by the time I'd put together all the material I'd planned to include in them it was clear there would be too many pages to do the *Computer Lib/ Dream Machines* novelty two-books-in-one flip trick anyway.

You may have noticed that there's some temporal distance between when I started to write this book and when I finished. It took me eight years to complete. The reason for this is that the nature of the content is non-standard. Rather than the usual narrative format, I went with something closer to a game-like, episodic experience that the reader could drop into or out of at will. The result is a set of several hundred articles, inter-related to greater or lesser degrees, some threaded together with others, some stand-alone but resonating with the ongoing theme. I did it this way because I wanted to disrupt the narrative in order to give the reader time to think—to disagree. If I'd collected all the narrative threads and ordered them serially (which would have been much easier than what I did do), okay, you'd have got the same content but it wouldn't have left you time to reflect. It would have been like when you watch a movie and it's only afterward on the way back to the car that you think "Wait! If Qui-Gon can't use his mind control powers on Watto to accept 20,000 Republic Dataries as currency, why doesn't he use them on someone else to buy something expensive that he can then sell for a currency Watto will accept?". By giving you threads piecemeal, interspersed with other articles talking about related topics from different angles, you have a chance to think "Wait!" before the thread is over. This means you get to be critical of the next article in the thread as you read it. It becomes fuel for your fire, not fuel for your fuel tank.

You're a gamer. In games, you can think while you're playing. This is the closest I could get to that in book form.

As for the articles themselves, well, they come from numerous sources. Some are adapted from blog posts, some from e-mails, some from lectures and talks, some from academic papers, some from forum discussions, and some from recollections of conversations. Mostly, though, they're written from scratch. Whether you like them or dislike them; whether you find them topical or passé; whether they're insightful or humdrum; whether they're right or wrong; I don't mind. What matters isn't what I write, but what you do.

The purpose of this book is merely to encourage you to do it.

Have fun!

Richard A. Bartle

December, 2015

On History

CompSoc

In the late 1970s, students at Essex University wishing to use its DECsystem-10 mainframe for academic work were allocated a project-programmer number (PPN). Mine was [4011,4243]. This came with a fixed set of resources that allowed roughly two hours at a terminal each week.

If you wanted to do non-academic work on the computer, that meant joining the Computer Society. Actually, its name might have been the Computing Society; we just called it *CompSoc* the whole time.

CompSoc made resources available for non-academic use; indeed, if you used your CompSoc PPN for assignments, you would lose it and get zero marks for those assignments. It was solely for play: it could only be used in the evenings and on weekends, when the mainframe wasn't running to full capacity and so would otherwise have stood partly idle.

Programmers today might have a hard time imagining what this meant for coding. When you have only limited face time on the computer, you have to maximize it. We used to print off listings of our programs and write on them all the changes we were going to make. Because printing also cost resources, sometimes we'd write on printouts that already had writing on them from earlier alterations. We'd make the changes using a text editor, either logged in (which ate up precious time) or via a punched-card batch job that would be run when there was next free capacity. We'd test our programs the same way. As a result, all programmers from that era have a great appreciation for planning out their code, which is not the rather gung-ho, experimental approach that many modern programmers seem to think we had.

Most of the better programmers at Essex University joined CompSoc. I myself signed up because I enjoyed getting computers to do things: I'd learned BASIC at school using a 110-baud modem connected to a computer run by BP as part of a public relations exercise (BP had a chemical works in the area). So it was that once I was at Essex University, I would—through CompSoc—inevitably come to meet other students who were interested in programming for fun.

The Chairman of CompSoc was a second-year student named Nigel Roberts. The secretary was his best friend, Roy Trubshaw.

Did You Know?

Golf was invented in China[1], where it was known as *Chuiwan* ("hitting ball"). There is evidence from the *Dongxuan Records*[2] that it was played as early as the year 945. A Ming dynasty scroll in the National Museum of China[3], *The Autumn Banquet*, depicts a man swinging something having the appearance of a golf club at something having the appearance of a golf ball, with the apparent goal of hitting it into something having the appearance of a golf hole.

Players and Playing

These are a couple of terms I use in this book:

- **Player:** A person controlling an in-world character.
- **Playing:** Engaging in an MMO.

I've used them for decades, but worry that the colors in them have run so much that it's hard to tell what they mean any more.

[1]Ling Hongling: Verification of the Fact that Golf Originated from Chuiwan. Bulletin for the Australian Society for Sports History v14 pp 12-23, 1991. http://www.aafla.org/SportsLibrary/ASSH%20Bulletins/No%2014/ASSHBulletin14c.pdf#search=%22dongxuan%20records%22
[2]Wei Tei: Dongxuan Records v12. Song Dynasty (960-1279).
[3]The Autumn Banquet. Ming Dynasty (1368-1644). http://www.heritagemuseum.gov.hk/archive//eng/exhibitions/exhibition_highlights/ex38_5en.htm

Dr. Toddystone

In my early teens, back in the days when children had spare time, I invented role-playing games.

They'd already been invented by other people, of course—I'm not suggesting I got the jump on Gygax and Arneson—but the point is that I didn't know about them at the time. It wouldn't have surprised me to learn of their existence, though—I didn't think I was doing anything unusual. As far as I was concerned, I was simply using games to tell myself stories.

I had three major (what we'd nowadays call) role-playing campaigns, of which the purest in terms of role-playing (because I didn't have to pretend to be multiple characters) was called *Dr. Toddystone*. I was maybe about 12 or 13 when I first played it, hence the embarrassing name; however, in my defense, I wasn't expecting to tell anyone else about it, except my brother (with whom I discussed game ideas), because it was written for one person and one person only: me.

So, I'll explain how *Dr. Toddystone* worked.

Back in the early 1970s, ISO 216 for paper sizes hadn't officially been adopted in the UK (it had been introduced in 1959, but hadn't yet achieved critical mass), so I used to make my games using sheets from pads of writing paper that I bought at the local newsagent's. These measured something like 4½ inches by 6 inches and there were anything between 80 and 140 in a pad, depending on how much profit the manufacturers wanted to make. The pads cost 11p in 1971, immediately after decimalization, but were 14p by the time they stopped selling them in about 1977. I must have bought 50 or more of them in that time.

Anyway, for *Dr. Toddystone* I took a pad and removed all the sheets. I stuck these together using sticky tape on what was to be the back, as you can't use felt tips or pencils on sticky tape. I always taped the sheets so the edges were aligned like a grid, as it's easier to fold everything up that way. The overall shape of my construction was important: sometimes it was long and snaking; sometimes it was bulgy with bits coming off it. The biggest ones (I did this 5 or 6 times in all) were maybe 10 or 12 feet long.

The conceit was that this was an unknown continent, and that *Dr. Toddystone* was a Victorian-era explorer who was going to explore it.

In laying out the paper, I gave myself ideas of how the geography would go. For example, if I left a sheet out of the middle, that would obviously be a place where I was going to put an inland sea. The paper was only a crude topographical constraint, though: the next step involved actually creating the continent by drawing a map on the paper. This would take hours—days—as I built coastlines, incorporated bays and small islands, river deltas, mangrove swamps, and more. I put in mountain ranges and ran rivers from them to the coast, adding lakes and waterfalls and mosquito-infested marshes. As I did this, my imagination was envisioning the features (even today, writing this, I couldn't help but add "mosquito-infested" just then). In the process of building up the continent, I got a real feel for the place—its jungles, plains, tundra in the south, mist-shrouded hills, and strange-calling birds in the north.

I populated the continent with various native villages and a few coastal "European" colonies to use as a base. Again, the more I added, the more I understood the place. I knew which tribes were friendly and which weren't; which were at war and which weren't; what resources they needed; what strange cultures they exhibited. Some of these promised to be exciting and I hoped *Dr. Toddystone* would get to encounter them, yet I could never be sure if he would or not.

I won't pretend that the continents I built were realistic. They made sense to me, but I was only 12 or 13 so I didn't have all that detailed knowledge of how geographical features actually fit together. In later worlds made for my personal amusement, I'd run some tectonics to get the basic setup and play a game to create a history, but I didn't do that here. I knew about volcanoes and where they went, so I had those. I didn't know about volcanic calderas, though, so I didn't have those.

I should mention that the first time I did this, that's all I was intending to do: build a continent. It's fun creating worlds, and so that was my aim. It's just that, having constructed the world, I was brimming with ideas. It was full of potential; all it took was for someone to go in and release all that penned-in narrative energy. This person was *Dr. Toddystone*.

Yeah, I'll tell you about him later.

The Lord of the Rings

Of all the sources that fed into the design of today's MMOs, the most important is J. R. R. Tolkien's *The Lord of the Rings*. The influence of this astonishing work extends not only to fantasy books and all role-playing games, but also to movies and wider culture. Much to the annoyance of literature snobs, it's consistently voted the UK's favorite novel, winning the BBC's huge "The Big Read" survey in 2003 (Jane Austen's *Pride and Prejudice* came second)[4]. The only novel in the English language that has sold more copies is *A Tale of Two Cities* by Charles Dickens.

It's my favorite book, too.

The Lord of the Rings has influenced MMO development in three major ways:

- **Concept**: It showed that the creation of a believable, consistent, self-contained, imaginary world was possible. All children make up their own, pretend worlds. Tolkien demonstrated what could be achieved when adults did the same thing.

- **Content**: The world that Tolkien describes, Middle Earth, is richly detailed and realized. Generations of MMO designers have plundered it for ideas, whether first-hand from the book itself or second-hand through other Tolkien-influenced works (particularly *Dungeons & Dragons*). *The Lord of the Rings Online* uses the content of the book directly.

---

[4]BBC: The Big Read. 2003. http://www.bbc.co.uk/arts/bigread/top100.shtml

- **Culture**: The players of MMOs bring into the virtual world their experiences from the real world. *The Lord of the Rings* has had such an impact on popular culture that it created the paradigm that is fantasy. There were fantasy stories before Tolkien (Robert E. Howard's *Conan* novelettes, for example), but there was no fantasy *genre* until Tolkien.

The reason I like *The Lord of the Rings* myself has nothing to do with the story or the writing, which is turgid at times and has Tom Bombadil in it. The only bit of action I really enjoy re-reading is when Éowyn kills the Witch-King of Angmar, and even that's tainted by Merry's involvement. No, the reason that I read it three times in my teens and have read it at least once every decade since is because of the first point: the concept. I'd always designed worlds; *The Lord of the Rings* was the proof that such designs could be beautiful.

Oh, the reason that there's no spoiler alert here, despite my mentioning Éowyn and the Witch-King of Angmar, is that if you think reading *The Lord of the Rings* is less important than reading what I'm writing about it, you have really messed-up priorities.

MUD

I'll be mentioning *MUD* shortly. Once, it needed no introduction; now, because most MMO players will never have heard of it, it does. Here are the main facts you need to know about it to set the context:

- *MUD*, an acronym for *Multi-User Dungeon*, is generally recognized as being the common ancestor of today's MMOs.

- *MUD* was written by Roy Trubshaw and Richard Bartle (that's me, in case you don't read book covers). Roy began it; I joined him soon after.

- *MUD* was developed in England. Roy and I are both English. Colour, defence, centre. See?

- *MUD* was a textual world, not a graphical world. Graphics weren't widely available back then.

- *MUD* is now often referred to as *MUD1*, because MUD was later used to refer to the whole genre. Yes, *MUD* was a MUD.

Because I co-wrote *MUD* and have remained working in (what's now called) the MMO industry ever since, I have some vague name recognition among old-timers. Most players and developers are not old-timers by the definition of "old" you'll be seeing here; hence, this explanation.

Virtual Whats?

MMOs are virtual worlds. Academics who don't recklessly invent their own names for them tend to default to "virtual worlds," and won't call them MMOs unless one of the following conditions holds:

- They specifically mean game worlds, as opposed to social worlds.

- They are new academics and barely remember *Second Life* and its ilk.

- They wish to impress non-gamer academics with their grasp of gamer jargon.

- They are clueless.

- They hope to sell a book to people who call them MMOs.

The "world" part of "virtual world" means an environment, the inhabitants of which treat as being self-contained. The "virtual" part means something imaginary that has the form or effect of being real. Together, put more poetically: virtual worlds are places that exist where the real meets the imaginary.

Yes, this does mean they're not necessarily games. What you *do* in them can make them games, in which case they're MMOs. Most virtual worlds were indeed designed to have gameplay and are therefore MMOs, but there are some avowedly non-game virtual worlds: *Second Life* is probably the best-known example.

Normally, the terminology I use would be *virtual world* for virtual worlds in general, *social worlds* for ones along the lines of *Second Life* with no built-in gameplay, and *game-like worlds* for the ones along the lines of *World of Warcraft* that are played as games by most of the people who use them. However, just for you (because I'm using the last bullet from the above list), I'll generally use *MMO* in this book rather than "game-like worlds". Except I might call them virtual worlds anyway, or *game worlds* when contrasting them with social worlds, or even *games* if some point I wish to make isn't MMO-specific.

Oh, and even for social worlds I call the users *players*. They don't always like the term, because they don't feel that they're "playing".

Well, they are—because if they're not, they damned well should be.

High and Low

The architecture of the DECsystem-10 was such that when you ran a program it was split into two parts, a *high segment* and a *low segment*, so-called because of which half of memory they each addressed. The former was for program code; the latter for local data.

The high segment was shared. Thus, if 20 people were using, say, the same editor, there would be only one copy of the code in memory (in the high segment) but 20 individual low segments storing each user's local data (the text being edited, in this example).

Because the high segment was shared, normally you didn't want anyone writing to it. A change to the executable code for one user would be a change for everyone else running that program, too. You could load data in the high segment, but it was effectively constant because the high segment wasn't writeable. All users could access it; they just couldn't change it.

The ability to store shared data in the high segment is what Roy Trubshaw took advantage of when he wrote *MUD*. Indeed, it's what initially inspired him to write *MUD*. He encountered an operation called SETUWP ("set user write protect") that enabled him make the high segment both shareable *and* writeable. Instantly, he saw that it could be used to keep a single, shared copy of a virtual world that was the same for every player and could be changed by every player.

It wasn't the only way to do it: communication through files or through device assignment would also have worked. He was never called upon to think "what can I do with files and device assignment," though. He *was* called upon to think "what can I do with SETUWP," so he did it.

Only?

In 2015, the UK Minister for Culture, Ed Vaizey, told the Develop Conference in Brighton that video games are as important to British culture as cinema.

What? *Only* as important as cinema?

Dungeons & Dragons

The most venerable role-playing game, progenitor of the whole genre, is *Dungeons & Dragons* (*D&D* for short).

It's hard to imagine today the impact that *D&D* had on gamers when it came out. It was liberating. It was all about imagination—about sharing a world, about consensus, about living the adventure. People came together to play and could define the boundaries of that play for themselves. They could create their own worlds, their own personalities; they could be the masters of their own destinies; they could make their intelligence count.

The origins of *D&D* were in miniature wargaming. The way these worked, players would set up armies of hand-painted figures and recreate historical battles such as Waterloo and Gettysburg. The Lake Geneva Tactical Studies Group in Wisconsin developed a set of rules, *Chainmail*, for mass battles set in the medieval period. One of its authors, Gary Gygax, wrote a 14-page fantasy supplement for it. The fantasy units were like regular ones, but with special abilities—dragons could breathe fire, heroes took four simultaneous hits to kill, wizards could cast fireballs and lightning bolts, and so on. Magical weapons were also present.

Other groups had also created fantasy rules. After all, a dragon in a medieval setting is basically just a World War I bomber with a different name. The crucial addition of a role-playing element came when Dave Arneson took the *Chainmail* rules and adapted them for his fictional world, called Blackmoor. Instead of controlling armies, players controlled individuals. Gygax saw the potential of this, and he and Arneson collaborated to design *D&D*. It was first published in 1974 and took the gamer community by storm.

I clubbed together with my brother and a friend and bought my copy on 6th May, 1976. Yes, I still have the receipt. *D&D* wasn't the first role-playing game I'd played, but it *was* the first I'd played with other people. We played it a lot, too, this being an era when homework wasn't made of open-ended project work.

The original game came as three booklets: *Men and Magic*; *Monsters and Treasure*; *Underworld and Wilderness Adventures*. These rules were serviceable, but had gaping holes in them; it wasn't until the *Greyhawk* supplement arrived that the sweet spot was reached. It had enough extra detail to fill in the gaps and spark ideas, but not so many that it tied the players down.

In 1977, the D&D rules were cleaned up and presented in a more readable fashion as the *Dungeons & Dragons Basic Set*. We weren't impressed: they only covered character levels 1 to 3 and seemed to us to be patronizing.

When *Advanced Dungeons & Dragons* came out in 1978, I was initially enthusiastic. However, the rules for AD&D were far more prescriptive than those of the original *D&D*, with less scope for improvisation. In my view, the preponderance of rules detracted from the imaginative aspect of play. I still liked it, though, and ran a campaign one summer while I was a student, albeit heavily modifying the system. Several times, we played all through the day, all through the night, and some way through the next day too, all without sleep.

More editions followed, each getting further away from the original. I bought the rule books and read them, but didn't play them. The second edition of *AD&D* went with a toned-down concept of fantasy, to address the worries of concerned parents who thought the real deal would turn their children into devil-worshippers. It was less sword-and-sorcery and more of a hotchpotch of myth-and-medieval. More rules were added.

The third edition introduced the d20 concept and was a much less haphazard affair. The rules actually seemed to have been designed with consistency in mind, rather than as an accretion of independent ideas. The fourth edition streamlined the rules, but the result felt more like a tabletop equivalent of MMOs. It polarized player opinion: you either loved it or hated it (most hated it). The fifth edition streamlined the rules still further and went back to a more classic feel. It's very polished and seems to have reinvigorated the game, which has to be a good thing.

Much has been written about the influence of *D&D* on computer games, including on MMOs. You have to remember a key point, though: *D&D* was and remains a magnificent game *in its own right*. You can't play a computer game that descends from *D&D* and expect to understand *D&D* as a result: you have to play *D&D* itself. Face-to-face role-playing games, moderated by a person rather than a computer, are limitless. *D&D* isn't just some mere waypoint on the road to computer games, it's a highway to its own destination.

Oh, and it's fun, too!

ADVENT

Adventure, also known as *Colossal Cave* and *Colossal Cave Adventure,* was the 1976 progenitor of the genre of computer games that bears its name: adventures. It was designed and implemented by Will Crowther, based on parts of the longest underground cave system in the world, Mammoth Cave in Kentucky. Fantasy elements and more rooms were added by Don Woods in 1977, leading to the game as it is known today.

At Essex University, because file names were limited to six upper-case characters or numbers, we called it *ADVENT.*

So, *ADVENT* was a text adventure. Players typed one- or two-word commands at a prompt that either queried the world state or made changes to it. For example, INVENTORY would list what you were carrying and TAKE LAMP would add the lamp to your inventory. Movement was primarily achieved using compass directions, plus some relational options such as LEAVE HOUSE and limited teleportation. Some commands could be abbreviated, and indeed some had to be: the parser only looked at the first five characters of a word, so NORTHEAST and NORTH became NE and N.

When you played the game, the world from your perspective was described, then you typed something at the prompt. You received feedback from your command, then if the world or your perspective on it changed as a result you got a new description. Here's a fragment:

```
YOU ARE IN A 20-FOOT DEPRESSION FLOORED WITH BARE DIRT. SET INTO THE DIRT
IS A STRONG STEEL GRATE MOUNTED IN CONCRETE. A DRY STREAMBED LEADS INTO THE
DEPRESSION.
THE GRATE IS LOCKED

>OPEN GRATE
THE GRATE IS NOW UNLOCKED.

>DOWN
YOU ARE IN A SMALL CHAMBER BENEATH A 3X3 STEEL GRATE TO THE SURFACE. A LOW
CRAWL OVER COBBLES LEADS INWARD TO THE WEST.
THE GRATE STANDS OPEN.
```

This doesn't look especially complicated, but if you bear in mind that nothing like it had been written before, you can perhaps appreciate how impressive it seemed to computer users of the era. Programmers were even more impressed, as it was written in FORTRAN.

Many players were inspired by *ADVENT* to write their own games along similar lines. A decade after *ADVENT,* text adventures dominated the home computer games market. It was not to last, however: the audience for home computers changed; improved graphics made textual interfaces less attractive; the puzzles in the games became so complicated that they put players off.

Adventure games may now be niche. However, the influence they had on games lives on.

Did You Know?

Golf was invented in France[5], where it was known as *Palle Mail*. Tax records from 1292 show that makers of clubs and balls had to pay a toll to sell their goods to nobles anywhere outside Paris. A c1540 devotional book in the British Library[6], *Les Heures de la Duchesse de Bourgogne*, depicts a man swinging something having the appearance of a golf club at something having the appearance of a golf ball, having the apparent goal of hitting it into something having the appearance of a golf hole.

1978

Back in 2005, the tradeoff between effort and irritation finally tipped: I modified a page on Wikipedia that had been bugging me for ages. Okay, so it was the entry for me, but still.

What I changed was the date of the first MUD. It said 1979; I changed it to 1978. To be fair, the 1979 date was quoting from a Usenet posting that I myself had written in 1990, so you can't blame anyone for thinking that it was correct. The Usenet posting is wrong, though: it gives the date of the first MUD as Spring 1979 because that was the earliest date I had on a printout of it. Actually, it was more like October 1978.

When I went to Essex University, I signed up to do Mathematics. However, because it had a common first year, I also took Computer Science and Physics. Being a campus university, Essex boasted a thriving collection of student societies, but at the Societies' Bazaar I somehow missed the one for CompSoc.

---

[5]Michael Flannery and Richard Leech: *Golf Through the Ages: 600 Years of Golfing Art*. Golf Links Press: Fairfield, Iowa. 2003. http://www.golfspast.com/golfthroughtheages/
[6]*Les Heures de la Duchesse de Bourgogne*, September. France. *circa* 1500 http://www.bl.uk/manuscripts/Viewer.aspx?ref=add_ms_24098_fs001r

I kept hearing from other students taking the Computer Science course that CompSoc was worth joining because you got free computer time to do anything non-academic that you wanted, so I went to see the chairman, Nigel Roberts, to sign up. He suggested that we talk while standing in line for the free tickets that the Student Union was giving out for a Lindisfarne *Rock Goes to College* gig. If we were going to be talking anyway we may as well do it in a queue and kill two birds with one stone.

We got there fairly early (we were within 20 people of the front). Nigel and I are both from the north of England, so it's natural for us to join queues 45 minutes before the doors open and then complain about the wait. As it was, we also chatted about the kind of things that CompSoc did. I wanted to know if it allowed games, and Nigel said yes, it did. I described to him a transcript of a computer game I'd seen in a postal games magazine called *Bellicus*. "That's *ADVENT*," said Nigel. "You should speak to Roy about *MUD*".

I vaguely recall that Roy did show up briefly to give Nigel his registration card so he could get him a Lindisfarne ticket too, but he was in a hurry to get over to the Open Shop (our one and only computer lab) and would meet us there later.

After we picked up the tickets, we went over to the Open Shop to look for Roy. He wasn't there—he'd gone back to his flat to pick up some program listings—but a third-year undergraduate friend of his and Nigel's, Keith Rautenbach, was mooching around. Keith was interested at a technical level in what Roy had done, and had been commenting and making some minor adjustments to Roy's code. An almost commemorative printout of his final version is the oldest artefact from *MUD* in existence; it currently resides in the History of Science and Technology Collections at Stanford University, and it's from this that the 1979 date came (because that's when I found it on a tape and printed it off).

Anyway, Keith showed me *MUD* in action, commandeering three or four teletypes (yes, teletypes) to do so. Keith envisaged *MUD* as a game in which you told characters to do something on your behalf; you didn't enter the game world yourself, you controlled an ostensibly independent entity ("I am the genie of the watering can"). This was probably due in part to how *ADVENT* introduced itself. I didn't see it that way at all, though. I saw it as a way for *me* to enter a completely new world. Better, I saw it as a way for me to create worlds for *other* people to enter.

Roy finally showed up, carrying the familiar wad of 11x15-inch green-screen paper under his arm that was the then sign of a programmer. He explained that he'd given Keith the old code to comment and play with because he himself was now working on *MUD* version 2. Version 1 was merely a proof of concept; he was going to turn it into a full-fledged game. I sought reassurances that it would refer to the player as "you" rather than "I," and Roy confirmed that of course it would.

So, he asked: did I know anything much about games, then?

1978.

All Programs

At heart, all programs are either a compiler or a database.

— Roy Trubshaw, January 1980

After rewriting the core of *MUD*:

Or an operating system.

— Roy Trubshaw, April 1980

Criteria

What do I mean when I refer to something as an "MMO"?

Well, I mean a virtual world with gameplay.

Didn't help, huh? Okay, well I dare say I'll get around to explaining "gameplay" later, but for the moment, what do I mean by "virtual world"?

Secretly, what I mean by it is anything that descends from the first MUD, but I can hardly say that in public. Besides, I do have a more usable and less self-serving definition.

A virtual world is something with the following characteristics:

- It operates using an underlying automated rule set—its *physics*.

- Each player represents an individual "in" the virtual world—that player's *character*.

- Interaction with the world takes place in *real time*—if you do something, it happens pretty much when you do it.

- The world is *shared*—other people can play in the same world at the same time as you.

- The world is *persistent*—it's still there when you're not.

I suppose to be *entirely* accurate I should add another clause:

- It's not the real world.

Only if *all* these criteria are satisfied do you have a virtual world. If even *one* of them is missing, you don't. Thus, when I read academic texts explaining that the "first virtual worlds" were cave paintings, or oral folk tales, or peyote-inspired dances, or the *I Ching*, or theatre, or prayer books, or novels, or telephones, or flight simulators, I sigh.

Let's put it this way: if you want to call any of those things "virtual worlds," please supply a new term to describe what objects the six conditions above identify, because whatever objects they *do* identify, they're different, they're special, and they give human beings freedoms and a sense of self that they have never had before in their 30,000-year history unless they were either very rich or were being shot at.

Taking this long view, virtual worlds (and therefore MMOs) are something new and unique. Nothing that has gone before them has delivered what *they* can deliver. They have *so much* potential.

I just hope I live long enough to see some of it fulfilled.

Why "World"?

Virtual world is an umbrella term covering both game worlds (MMOs), such as *Star Wars: the Old Republic*, and social worlds, such as *Habbo*. Why is the word "world" used there and not, say, "universe" or "space" or "environment"?

Well, as I'm responsible for it, I guess I should explain.

A world in this context is a self-contained environment, the inhabitants of which treat as if it were whole. It's that notion of self-containment—that the environment is set apart from other environments—that rules out the word "environment" itself.

The word "space" fails because it's too general: if you were to talk about a "social space" then you could include spaces such as Facebook. Facebook is indeed a space, but it has no connotations of place. It's the difference between "the world of high finance" and "the space of high finance": a world is instantiated, whereas a space is where instantiations form.

As for "universe," well, that would be to imply that there was nothing beyond it. I'm comfortable with calling an MMO set in Colditz Castle a "virtual world," but a "virtual universe" is overstating its boundaries somewhat. Likewise, if I saw a commercial for a collection of country music pieces, I wouldn't be surprised if it said "welcome to the world of country music". I would be surprised if it said "welcome to the universe of country music". The latter has completely different overtones (and I don't mean the ones that make your ears throb).

Dinos

People who played textual worlds in the early 1990s were called *dinos* by later generations (short for "dinosaurs"). Those of us who had been around for 10 or 12 years before the earliest dinos appeared were, of course, amused by this.

Ironically, only people who are themselves now dinosaurs would ever recall the term "dinos" these days.

Versions

As with all software, *MUD* went through several versions before settling down. It managed four in all, which I'll describe here not because I want to bore you (although I'm sure I'll succeed at that), but because later I'll be mentioning the historical context of MMOs and you may develop a sufficient glimmer of interest to wish to disambiguate between them.

The versions followed (indeed, still follow) the DECsystem-10 naming system. This starts with an integer that indicates the number of times the code has been written from scratch. This is followed by a letter that indicates any major changes that didn't involve rewrites from scratch but are still rewrites (ports to other operating systems or transliterations into other languages, for example). Following this, in parentheses, is the sub-version integer that indicates the number of releases this version hashad.

So, version 1A(1) was called *MUD*. It was conceived and written by Roy Trubshaw, with helpful programming suggestions by Nigel Roberts and Keith Rautenbach. Roy wrote it without commenting the code (taking the traditional hacker line that the code is its own comment), but it was later commented by Keith as a tool to help him to understand what it was doing. This explains why its main comment said "MUDD—MULTI-USER GAME OF ADVENTUROUS ENDEAVOUR"—it was Keith making a typing error (the file it was in was MUD.MAC—the .MAC meaning it was written in MACRO-10 assembly language).

Version 1A was not programmed as a playable game: it was a test to see whether the shared memory system that Roy envisaged would work (it did).

Version 2A was also called *MUD*, and its opening comment expanded the acronym into "Multiple User Dungeon"; the more informal multi- was always used, though, and this became the standard in version 3A. As with version 1A, version 2A was coded in the MACRO-10 assembly language entirely by Roy; its content was run-time programmable by suitably *privved* (privileged) players. Nigel Roberts and I were privved, and aside from making suggestions actually created some rooms/objects for it. The ox, which is still in the game today, snuck in that way—it was my first *MUD* creation.

This real-time programmability approach, while common nowadays, used too much computer memory for 1978. Furthermore, as it was written in an assembly language, the code for version 2A itself became increasingly unwieldy. After a year or so, Roy snapped and rewrote the game in BCPL (an ancestor of C) as version 3A. He designed a separate language for defining *MUD*'s world, which he called MUDDL ("*MUD* Definition Language"), based loosely on *ADVENT*'s data format. MUDDL was compiled externally rather than interpreted, then loaded into the *MUD* engine.

Roy only managed to write perhaps 25% of version 3A's code (the hardest 25%!) before his final-year exams loomed so close that even he had to pay attention to them, so he handed it over to me to finish. I added the remaining 75% incrementally over the next three years. Fellow CompSoc members Brian Mallett and Ronan Flood each provided some useful hacks to the low-level code that improved its performance (mainly by stopping it from crashing). Although version 3A was begun in 1979, it wasn't in a playable state until Easter 1980 when I took it over, and therefore this later date is often quoted with regard to the program's beginnings. I had to recode it as version 3B in 1986 so it could run on the U.S. online service CompuServe, where it was known as *British Legends*.

MUDDL eventually proved too inexpressive for what I wanted to say, so in 1985 I began work on version 4A using a new *MUD* definition language that I had designed: MUDDLE. This version of *MUD* went through four rewrites for various platforms before finally launching as version 4E, which is the one that still runs today. Roy Trubshaw wrote the system tools that accompanied it.

Important! In the 1980s, players of worlds that descended from *MUD* collectively adopted the name "MUD" as an umbrella term for the entire genre. To avoid confusion, they took to calling *MUD* itself *MUD1*. However, *MUD1* was *not* version 1 of *MUD*: it was version 3. *MUD2* is version 4.

Still awake?

Liar!

Exactly When?

I've been asked many times for the *exact* date that the very first version of *MUD* was written. Yes, it was 1978—but *when* in 1978?

Okay, so the short answer is that I don't know the exact date. However, I can make a fair stab at pinning it down.

My first contact with *MUD*, as I've just described, followed my standing in line with Nigel for tickets to a BBC-sponsored Lindisfarne concert. The concert is widely reported as having been broadcast in December 1978, but the date of the recording was 17th November. We obtained our tickets maybe a month before then.

So, this would only be two or three weeks into term, which at Essex traditionally starts in October. My best guess is that I queued up with Nigel probably in the fourth week, so Roy would have written *MUD* in the third week. But *when* in the third week?

All origin stories have inconsistencies. I was once told by another CompSoc member who'd been present when Roy wrote his first (test) version of *MUD* that there were half a dozen or so hackers sitting around talking code at the time. They'd had this collective idea for writing to shared memory; Roy was merely the first to a keyboard. He got the basic mechanism working fairly quickly with the group's help, then developed this into version 1 of *MUD* after about two hours more of programming on his own.

Okay, well I know this story isn't *quite* right, because Roy had been trying to get the necessary user privileges to play with inter-process communications for a while. His request had been turned down, so he was actively looking for something that could do the job instead. It's more likely that the group of hackers was scanning through manuals together and proposing solutions to Roy's problem, which is why when one of them (Roy himself, I believe) discovered the legendary SETUWP call, he was the one who got to program with it.

Anyway, the thing was, I was given the impression that this happened in the evening, rather than during daytime. I doubt it would have been on a Saturday, because there would have been a Film Society movie on that day and Roy wouldn't have missed it.

So, taking all this into account, I'd say that the chances are Roy wrote the first version of *MUD* one evening between Monday 16th and Friday 20th October, 1978. Of these, I'd rate the Friday as being the most probable.

The smart thing to do would be to ask Roy, of course, but I did that and he couldn't remember the date he did it either.

Lines of Code

I once heard that the average number of lines of fully-debugged code the average programmer produces in one day is 60. Blank lines and comments are excluded from the count. Interestingly, the figure of 60 is supposedly independent of programming language.

The code size for the classic version of *MUD* known as *MUD1* was:

- MUDDL code defining the world: 10,347 lines.

- Loader code, to parse MUDDL into usable data: 2,723 lines

- *MUD* code, to handle I/O and interpret MUDDL data: 9,580 lines

Total: 22,650 lines.

This suggests that *MUD* had around 377.5 days of work done on it, or just over a man-year.

Actually, though, it didn't have that much. Both Roy Trubshaw and I are very fast coders and we average over 100 lines of code a day (more when we're not writing to specification, which was the case for *MUD*), so at most it would have taken us 7.5 man-months of work to create *MUD* if we'd been paid to do it.

Elapsed time was longer, of course, because development was spread over a couple of actual years; we had other things to do apart from program *MUD*.

The First Age—1978 to 1985

For the first seven years of the history of virtual worlds, there was only one: *MUD*.

Well, actually, no—there were several. *MUD* was one, yes, but there was also *Sceptre of Goth* (1978), *Avatar* (1979), *Island of Kesmai* (1981), and *Habitat* (1985).

Those are just the ones that were invented independently during that period; there were others around that were directly inspired by some of them—*PIGG* (1980), for example, was sparked by *MUD*. Indeed, the existence of a bunch of are-they-aren't-they proto-worlds on a system called PLATO (more later) means that, depending on how far you want to stretch your definition of "virtual world," there could even have been some around *before* 1978. (I personally don't think they qualify as virtual worlds, but then I wouldn't, would I?).

What this tells you is the *context* of the era. Lots of people had the idea to create what we would later call MMOs, and half a dozen of them successfully built such worlds.

However, only one of these virtual worlds had any meaningful impact on the development of MMOs *as MMOs* today. The effects of the others endure only as faint echoes, if indeed they endure at all. If we're talking *history* and not context, there really was only one virtual world from 1978 to 1985: *MUD*.

Well, except that *Aradath*, a 1984 world inspired by *Sceptre of Goth*, has a tree of direct descendents that includes modern MMOs such as *Camelot Unchained*. Then again, the influence of *MUD*'s descendents on *Camelot Unchained* is probably greater than *Aradath*'s.

I hope you get the picture that I'm trying to paint here: this is a distant and ambiguous time, and just because a consensus has coalesced to form a clean, accepted canon, that doesn't mean it's the whole story.

Nevertheless, whenever the present looks back to the past, it inevitably wants a story, whole or not, and the fact is that *MUD* really was the progenitor of today's MMOs. There was nothing like it that its designers had seen before, and there is overwhelming evidence showing how its family tree developed to become the MMOs of today. Any of the virtual worlds I mentioned earlier could have been the one that struck lucky; it happened to be *MUD*.

We could go back further than 1978, though. I've read histories of MMOs that began with prehistoric art, drug-induced shamanistic trances, the Egyptian Book of the Dead, and more besides. It's only a matter of time before we get one claiming it all started with the possible worlds that came into being during the Planck Epoch (the first 10^{-43} seconds after the Big Bang). Yes, they're part of the causal chain that led to the creation of *MUD*, but so what?

Less speculative, but still fanciful, histories begin with *The Lord of the Rings*, *ADVENT*, *Spacewar!*, PLATO, and *D&D*. All of these are indeed important in defining the context, and three (*The Lord of the Rings*, *ADVENT*, and *D&D*) were directly influential in the creation of *MUD* to greater or lesser degrees. None of them were virtual worlds, though. They're *prehistory*, but not history; they may be direct ancestors along other dimensions (for example role-play), but they had no "virtual worldliness" dimension. If you want a history of today's MMOs in terms of what makes them MMOs (as opposed to anything else), you have to follow their ancestry back until you come to the species line. Continuing further gives you more ancestors, yes, but not ones that are virtual worlds.

So, do that, and the place you'll stop is *MUD*.

Yes, I am aware that "stick in the mud" is an appropriate pun here.

I'm also aware that, because I co-wrote *MUD*, all this is going to look like boastfulness and conceit. It does to me, and I'm the one writing it. To be frank, I find it painfully embarrassing to say all this—so much so that I almost didn't put *anything* historical in this book, in order to avoid my having to say it at all. However, history is important, as we shall see time and time again, so I bit the bullet. Neither you nor I have to like it, but the history of MMOs as virtual worlds began with *MUD*; or, as it's now known, *MUD1*.

So that's why the First Age of MMOs starts in 1978. The reason it ends in 1985 is because, from a revolutionary (rather than evolutionary) perspective, it wasn't until then that anything else remotely of significance took place.

People played *MUD*, they liked it, and they figured they could do the same thing only better.

Some could, too.

Great Interfaces of Our Time—Text

Textual worlds describe the environment in words and accept commands in words. Even the most hard-core graphical 3D worlds will still generally have a text box to them for inputting all that tricky freeform speech (although the use of voice, phones, and consoles could eventually change this).

Textual interfaces are the simplest to implement of all MMO-related interfaces, because you can use a general-purpose program such as Telnet as a client.

Here's an example of a text interface (from *MUD*):

```
Road opposite cottage.
You are standing on a badly paved road with a cemetery to the north and the
home of a grave-digger to the south. An inscription on the cemetery gates
reads, "RESTING PLACE OF LOST SOULS".
*s
Path.
You are standing on a path which leads off a road to the north, to a cottage
south of you. To the west and east are separate gardens.
*w
Flower garden.
You are in a well-kept garden. There is an unexpectedly sweet smell here and
you notice lots of flowers. To the east across a path there is more garden.
A curious herb gives off a sweet odour nearby.
*g herb
Wolfsbane taken.
*
```

Text is a very flexible interface, and it benefits greatly from the fact that the form of input is the same as the form of output: words. People think in words, so text is incredibly immersive. As we'll see later, it has a number of other impressive advantages, too.

Today, however, text is only niche. I don't need to explain why: nine out of ten of the people reading that transcript from *MUD* will have already made their mind up never to try it, so they already know the answer.

Happy to read a book, though, eh?

Memories of Memory

So, I went into the attic to try to find my copy of *Neuromancer*. I didn't find it, but I *did* find a box containing the three albums of photographs I took at university while I was an undergraduate.

They're not wonderful photos. My camera wasn't good, it had no flash, the prints are decades old and they've picked up ink from the photos facing them (when I say "albums," I mean "scrap books I glued photos into").

Here's a typical example: a photo of Roy Trubshaw in the Open Shop (more shortly). The photo is too dark, it's grainy, its yellows have darkened, and it had bits of scrapbook paper on it until I brushed them off:

My friends in CompSoc thought I was odd for taking photographs of them. Why bother, when we all knew what we looked like? Yet today, students probably take more photos in a week than I took during my entire undergraduate career.

Society back then wasn't as it is today, because technology back then wasn't as it is today.

There are 340,690 bytes in that image, or 2,725,520 bits. *MUD*, the program that Roy and I wrote, was 70k of 36-bit words, or 2,580,480 bits. There are more bits in that image of Roy than there were in *MUD*'s code.

Those machines behind Roy are teletypes.

Wizzes

In modern MMOs, when you reach the level cap you're stuck there until the next expansion. In *MUD1*, when you reached the level cap the game was over.

MUD1 was (well, is, as it's still extant) a world, though, not a game. The *game* was over, but *play* wasn't. Players who reached the level cap were given vast powers and administrator status. They ran the game for the benefit of the players who hadn't reached the level cap.

MUD1 levels all had names. You could tell what level a player was because they had the level name appended to their own name—Polly the legend, for example. The level at which points and progress stopped was *wizard* for male characters and *witch* for female characters. The collective name for such a character was *wiz* (meaning witches and wizards).

Later MUDs would call these characters *admins* or *gods*. Modern MMOs don't routinely appoint players to positions of power at all, so their equivalent is the Customer Service Representative, or CSR. CSRs don't run the world in the same sense that wizzes or admins did, though; they're more like social workers and police officers than the all-seeing, capricious, supernatural beings of yore.

In *MUD1*, we also had *arch-wizzes*, whose relationship to wizzes was roughly equivalent to the wizzes' relationship to non-wizzes (known as *mortals*). Arch-wizzes rarely had to do anything, but we had them because if we hadn't had them we'd have needed them. They started out as being implementers (Roy Trubshaw and I), but later we added other people on the grounds that they knew *MUD* better than we did.

Did You Know?

Golf was invented in the Netherlands, where it was known as *Kolf*[7]. Because of the danger to pedestrians and windows, in 1480 it was prohibited in the Amsterdam street known as Nes[8]. A 1755 drawing in the Amsterdam Municipal Archive[9] by Nicolaas Aartman of the course behind the Stadlander Inn depicts a man swinging something having the appearance of a golf club at something having the appearance of a golf ball, with the apparent goal of hitting it onto something having the appearance of a post.

AAA

In the vernacular, AAA (pronounced "triple A") means something of the highest quality. It's the same with computer games, but when the term is not qualified it specifically refers to *production* quality, not gameplay quality.

A AAA MMO could absolutely suck in terms of gameplay, yet a cheap-and-cheerful one could be brilliant.

---

[7]Geert & Sara Nijs: *From Colf to Kolf: The Same Word, a World of Difference.*
http://www.ancientgolf.dse.nl/pdfs/colf%20to%20kolf.pdf
[8]Amsterdam Municipal Archives. http://stadsarchief.amsterdam.nl/schatkamer/
300_schatten/sport/kolfen/
[9]Amsterdam Municipal Archives, catalogue number 010097000035

ADVENT and MUD

Given that Roy Trubshaw had played *ADVENT* (he was the first at Essex University to get its notoriously non-obvious last point), it seems fairly clear that *ADVENT* was a direct ancestor of *MUD*. It could be argued that merely adding a multi-player dimension to the concept was no different from adding a graphical element to MUDs. In other words, if *EverQuest* is just a graphical MUD then *MUD* was just a multi-player *ADVENT*. After all, the D in *MUD* stands for "Dungeon" in part because Roy thought that the genre would be called "dungeons" after *Zork* rather than "adventures" after *ADVENT*.

This is a reasonable view, although the true relationship is less clear-cut than it might seem at first glance. Roy definitely based *MUD*'s interface on *ADVENT*'s, but as all computers back then all had command-line interfaces the idea itself wasn't new; indeed, it's hard to envisage how else he might have done it. As for the command set itself, he went with his own but included synonyms for *ADVENT*'s commands in order that *ADVENT*'s players wouldn't have to learn new ones. *MUD* used GET but *ADVENT*'s TAKE also worked, for example.

Roy definitely based *MUD*'s data format loosely on that of *ADVENT*, so you can certainly contend with some justification that *MUD* inherited the idea of having a game-specific programming language from it. That has nothing to do with *MUD*'s virtual worldliness, though. Also, Roy was already familiar with the idea of application-specific languages, having worked with a bespoke, macro-based word-processing program we had at Essex University called *FORM*. He adapted *ADVENT*'s format because it best suited his needs, not because he didn't know about language design and implementation.

ADVENT's opening instructions began:

SOMEWHERE NEARBY IS COLOSSAL CAVE, WHERE OTHERS HAVE FOUND FORTUNES IN
TREASURE AND GOLD, THOUGH IT IS RUMORED THAT SOME WHO ENTER ARE NEVER SEEN
AGAIN. MAGIC IS SAID TO WORK IN THE CAVE. I WILL BE YOUR EYES AND HANDS.
DIRECT ME WITH COMMANDS OF 1 OR 2 WORDS.

Looking at this, you can see that *ADVENT* did not take a first-person perspective: you were controlling your *representative* in its world, you weren't there *yourself*. Now although Roy's initial, test implementation of *MUD* took the same approach—mainly at the behest of his watching friends—he'd already dropped it by the time I met him. Like me, he wanted players to be *in* the world, not observers of it.

A key innovation was that *MUD* was open-ended in a way that *ADVENT* wasn't (and adventure games today still aren't). *MUD* was about freedom; *ADVENT* was about puzzle-solving. Although *MUD* did feature some *ADVENT*-style puzzles, they were less constrained and more non-linear. This wasn't just for philosophical reasons, either: in practical terms, if one object (such as *ADVENT*'s lamp) was the key to advancing, then whoever got it first would lock up the game for everyone else. I suspect that this is why a multi-player version of *Zork* that was mentioned in the December 1980 issue of *Byte* magazine came to nothing.

To summarize: *ADVENT* is undeniably one of several sources that Roy drew on for *MUD*, but it *didn't* give him the idea to write *MUD*. For me, this marks a clear separation between the two; for you, well, you can make up your own mind.

XP

XP is a shorthand for *experience points*, or simply *points*. Tabletop role-playing games tend to call them EPs (which has the benefit of being an actual acronym) or *experience*.

I put experience points into *MUD* because I wanted to reward players for their actions in such a way that the accumulation of these rewards would give them goals and commensurate status. I took the idea from wargames and from *Dungeons & Dragons* (which also took the idea from wargames).

Experience points have been in MMOs ever since. They don't *have* to be, but few designers seem to give much thought to that.

Open Shop

Here's another photo of the Open Shop at Essex University where Roy and I first worked on *MUD*:

The machines in the foreground are teletypes. They printed onto paper (in capital letters only) at 110 baud. I can type faster than a teletype can show what I'm typing.

Next to the teletypes are wooden boxes. They're useful as desks, but their main purpose was to hold stocks of paper for the teletypes.

Beyond the teletypes are the punched card machines. You queued, you typed, and you took your cards to the reader. The person manning it fed them in, you waited 15 minutes, and you got your printout. That's unless there was a Hollerith error because a card didn't punch properly. You used punched cards because there was no clock ticking on them, unlike the teletypes.

Beyond the punched card machines is a wall with baskets. When you sent something to the lineprinter from a teletype, or submitted a card job for batch processing overnight, it would appear in the basket with your project programmer number on it.

This, boys and girls, is why we had no graphics in *MUD1*. Our state-of-the-art lab looks as old to you today as today's computer labs will look 40 years from now.

NOSMOKING was the password to COMPSOC 1, the Computer Society's master login.

ARPA

When I was an undergraduate, the Internet hadn't yet been invented. What there was instead was ARPAnet, operated by the U.S. Advance Research Projects Agency. There were only a handful of institutions on it, almost all (unsurprisingly) in the United States.

However, Essex University is located only a 40-minute drive from what at the time was the Post Office Research Centre at Martlesham Heath in Suffolk (it's now British Telecom's Adastral Park science campus); the boffins there were working on what they called the Experimental Packet-Switching Service, or EPSS. Because Essex University's Computer Science department had a long-standing research relationship with them, it was possible for ultra-keen students (such as those in CompSoc) to get access to an EPSS account. Using that, we could hop through a gateway at the University of Kent over to the Stanford Research Institute's systems. From SRI we could access other universities and research labs using public logins (which was all above board—we weren't breaking any rules by doing this). I remember visiting BBN, MIT, Stanford proper, Carnegie Mellon, RAND, and UCLA this way.

The CompSoc leadership, Roy Trubshaw and Nigel Roberts, played *Zork* at MIT and *Haunt* at Stanford; *Zork* and *Haunt* were the only two adventure games around at the time apart from *Adventure* itself (*ADVENT* to us), of which we had a local copy.

The Stanford login procedure required us to state our own name, the name of the person we were "hacking for," and a short description. We didn't know this beforehand, so when Roy connected to Stanford for the first time (*circa* 1979), we had to think of answers quickly before the link timed out. I suggested the description of "You haven't lived until you've died in *MUD*," which was to become our slogan.

From an historical perspective, it would turn out not to be all that important that we could occasionally get through to overseas computers over what was to become the Internet. What transpired to be the bigger deal was that people from overseas computers could get through to ours.

Sceptre of Goth

Around the same time Roy Trubshaw began work on *MUD*, Alan Klietz (his surname rhymes with "beats") independently began work on *Sceptre of Goth*. *Sceptre of Goth* wasn't always its name—it was also known as *Milieu*, *E*M*P*I*R*E* and *Ghost*—but *Sceptre of Goth* is how it's remembered today because that was the name its commercial version used. I'll call it *Sceptre* for short, as that's what its players called it.

Klietz developed *Sceptre* for the Minnesota Educational Computer Consortium (MECC) mainframe. Unlike *MUD*, his game was fundamentally inspired by both *ADVENT* and *Dungeons & Dragons*, as he says himself:

> I wondered how to make ADVENT multiplayer. How would interaction work? There needed to be some sort of rule system, one that was simple enough to program into the computers of the day. A student named Mike Pritchard wrote ... a 'Talk' program ... and it all clicked. I could write a 'super Talk' too, have it show prompts like ADVENT, but be multiplayer using the AD&D rule-set.[1]

Because of this, *Sceptre* played far more like the much later *DikuMUD* than it did *MUD*. It became the most popular game on the MECC system—so much so that Klietz had to shut it down between midnight and 5am following complaints from the parents of some of its players. Note that these same hours were roughly the only ones that *MUD* was *allowed* to be played by people off-campus, at least on weekdays.

In perhaps the earliest example of what would later be called *MUDflation*, *Sceptre* characters obtained gold pieces faster than they could spend them. Klietz decided to reset the database, and built a fiction around why this happened: high-level players would face a series of difficult challenges to obtain the Sceptre of Goth; success would invoke the database-resetting cataclysm. It proved to be a popular idea, too.

When the MECC system was closed down in 1983, Klietz formed a company, GāmBit, with Bob Alberti and two others to commercialize *Sceptre*. He rewrote the game in C (the original had been in Multi-Pascal) to run on an 8088 (that's a CPU chip, youngsters). By 1985, GāmBit was grossing $70,000 a year—comparable to what the UK's top MUDs were making.

Klietz had always been careful with his code. There were no anti-piracy laws at the time, and he didn't want people ripping off his work (which, his being first class programmer, was frighteningly good). Unfortunately, his fears were soon to be realized.

Maintaining and updating *Sceptre* was a lot of work, so GāmBit made some hires. The first programmer, hired in late 1984, copied all the system's software and attempted to sell it through GāmBit's own chat room. When caught red-handed and fired in early 1985, he immediately used the stolen software to set up a competing system at the rate of $10/month (in contrast with GāmBit's approximately $2/hour rate.)[10]

Players flocked to the cheaper system, leading to a collapse of the original's subscriber base. GāmBit hit back by franchising *Sceptre*. Soon, there were *Sceptre* operations in 13 cities (at $10,000/year each). The company was a success, but its principals didn't really enjoy running a business. They accepted a buy-out offer from a Virginian company called InterPlay (not to be confused with the venerable Californian developer, Interplay Entertainment).

Unfortunately, InterPlay subsequently collapsed, taking *Sceptre* with it. Had *Sceptre* not fallen victim to this fate, the course of MMO history would surely have been changed in a profound way. As it was, *Sceptre* was stopped in its tracks and today's MMOs are almost all direct descendents of *MUD* instead.

Note that word "almost".

Choosing a Genre

If you're an indie MMO developer and can't afford to sell an MMO on the strength of its budget alone, what genre do you go for?

Well, you need something that:

- Lots of people like.
- Isn't available anywhere else at the moment.
- Doesn't have fans that will be avidly playing something else already.

It's a set of possibilities that's getting smaller.

---

[10]Bob Alberti: *Scepter of Goth History*. Program for Individualized Learning 3251, University of Minnesota. 2010. http://www.scribd.com/doc/205379306/Scepter-of-Goth-history

2011

The mere existence of CompSoc meant that when it came to people who programmed for the sheer joy of it, Essex University offered a much more supportive environment than did most other UK universities.

Actually, that's not all that impressive when you realize that most other UK universities back then didn't have a computer unless they were rich or needed one for research.

The Computing Service, which operated the DEC-10, was of the collective opinion that people should be *encouraged* to play with computers if they wanted to do so, because then they would learn more. They therefore allocated CompSoc off-peak resources to use—despite the outrage of the majority of academic departments, which regarded the move a waste of precious computing power. A number of times, some of these departments tried to get the concept of off-peak usage scrapped, so that that they could run SPSS ("Statistical Package for the Social Sciences") data-crunching batch jobs overnight and have them finish a few seconds earlier the next morning. Others were just annoyed because CompSoc had more resources available to it than they did; it wasn't that the History Department had much *use* for computers—it was the principle! However, the Computing Service, especially its head, Charles Bowman, resisted all these attempts to prevent us from having fun; for this, I shall always be grateful.

Ironically, in 2011, I was present at a staff meeting in the School of Computer Science and Electronic Engineering, during which a call was made that the School should reserve its computer labs for people working on assignments only. Encouragingly, I wasn't the only old-timer to jump down the throat of the person who was fool enough to make the suggestion.

2011 was the project number shared by all CompSoc users. COMPSOC 1, the master account, was [2011,2011] (pronounced "two oh one one squared").

Okay, so that 2011 was in octal, but still...

PIGG

Having seen our work with *MUD*, one of my fellow students at Essex University, Stephen Murrell, was inspired to write *PIGG* ("because it's a pig to program").

I mention this not because Stephen Murrell is a *bona fide* genius (although he is—he was in the *Guinness Book of Records* at the time for getting the most grade As at A-level in one examination period), nor because *PIGG* inspired other people to write their own games (it didn't). I mention it because it used a different method for creating a shared world.

In *MUD*, multiple people ran separate copies of the same program. This program maintained the virtual world in writeable, shared memory. In *PIGG*, people assigned their input device (teletype or, later, VDU—"Visual Display Unit") to one program, which then controlled it along with those of all the other players.

The difference between these two approaches is that in a shared memory system like *MUD*'s, the virtual world is updated asynchronously. Any copy of the program running can access the shared memory, so there has to be a system of locks in place for when changes are being made. If there's only one copy of the program running, as with *PIGG*, you don't have to lock parts of memory because there's no competition to access it anyway.

Modern MMOs work in a similar manner to *PIGG*: the client software connects to a server, which then treats it as an input/output device. There's no need for any fancy code to make sure that only one command is accessing the world model at once, because there's only one copy of the program accessing it anyway.

PIGG's device-assigning idea wasn't new to members of Essex University's student Computer Society. Why, then, had no one thought of using it to create a virtual world years earlier? It was only when Roy Trubshaw discovered the writeable, shared memory technology that we got a virtual world.

Well, the solution might have been in plain sight the whole time, but the problem it solved was not. Discovering the writeable, shared memory technique is itself what sparked Roy to make a writeable, shared world.

Island of Kesmai

Another of the (what we'd now call) MMOs created independently of *MUD* was *Island of Kesmai*, by Kelton Flinn and John Taylor at the University of Virginia.

IoK was not the first multiplayer game the pair had written. Before it came:

- *Air*, an aerial warfare game featuring 3D "graphics" rendered in ASCII characters. This was the foundation upon which Kesmai (the name they gave their company) later built its seminal multiplayer graphical dogfight game, *Air Warrior*.

- *S*, an eight-player space colonization game. It would become the basis for Kesmai's hit, *MegaWars III*.

- *Dungeons of Kesmai*, a combat-oriented text adventure inspired by *ADVENT* and *Zork*.

It could be argued that *Air* qualifies as an MMO, but it didn't really have the real-time component nailed. Likewise, *S* didn't have the playing-as-an-individual-in-the-game-world element. The most interesting case is *Dungeons of Kesmai*. It's clear from *Air* and *S* that Kelton and John could do multiplayer, and clear from *Dungeons of Kesmai* that they could do text adventures. Why, for their next project, did they not combine the two and invent MUDs?

Well, for input they did use an *ADVENT*-like command-line interface—better, in fact, because you could do things such as OPEN BALM AND DRINK IT. For output, though, they went with the ASCII graphics they'd toyed with in the other two games. Eschewing the 3D look, which was not a success, *IoK* adopted *S*'s tessellation approach: the world was made up of squares, each of which was represented on screen by two fixed-width ASCII characters (~~ meant water, for example). Thus, although it didn't use graphics, you could probably call *IoK* a graphical game; it's not a huge jump to put a square of water texture on the screen instead of ~~. That wouldn't have helped back when *IoK* was launched in 1981, though, as most computers could only display fixed-width ASCII characters and no bitmaps anyway.

Although histories tend to discuss *IoK* only in terms of its pre-graphics graphics, this is somewhat unfair. *IoK* was an excellent game in its own right. It ran on CompuServe, alongside *MUD*, and there was a significant player overlap between the two. Although it clearly drew much more on *Dungeons & Dragons* than did *MUD* (it had D&D's character attributes and alignment system), it also had plenty of differences.

For example, its fights were fairly tactical affairs. Movement speed was important, as was positioning. You could be stunned, you could be poisoned, you
could fumble your weapon (and have to re-equip it before you could use it
again), and your hits could be blocked by armor. Spells had to be "warmed"
before casting. This entailed typing a unique incantation (for example, asak
nungi irrga luubluyi), unfortunately giving an advantage to players who
had communications software with a hotkey capability.

IoK engendered an air of realism: things that "should be" different in small ways
were indeed different, and when you tried something because it "ought to"
work, it probably would work. Okay, so no one drinks balm in real life (they
rub it on), and something like TAKE BERRIES FROM SACK AND EAT IT reads
as if you want to eat the sack, but the world itself aimed for verisimilitude.
For example, person-to-person communication over arbitrary distances was
missing because you can't do that in real life (unlike in *MUD*, which did have it).

Bearing this in mind, it should not come as a surprise to learn that in *IoK* your
character could die permanently. This didn't happen right away, but each time
your character was killed there was a chance that some permanent damage to
its stats would be done. Once your constitution fell below the minimum, that
character was not coming back.

IoK featured many staples of today's MMOs, such as a bank, shops that buy
anything off you, recall rings and character classes. Then again, other *D&D*-
inspired games did too. By the end of the 1980s, *IoK* was fairly average in that
regard; however, it was tuned to perfection and complex enough to merit a
160-page manual.

Oh, there's one final nice touch I'd like to mention. The players of MMOs have
always regarded their world's designers as the gods of the game's reality. In
IoK they were called *ghods*, so as not to offend religious people and to spare
Kelton and John embarrassment. I always thought that this was rather classy
of them—and so much better than *MUD*'s wizzes.

What Isn't a Virtual World?

I said earlier that a virtual world has the following properties:

- The world has an underlying, automated physics.
- Players represent virtual characters "in" the world.
- Interaction with the world takes place in real time.
- The world is shared.
- The world is, to at least some degree, persistent.
- The world isn't the real world.

What this means:

- The world is computer-moderated. *Dungeons & Dragons* is not a virtual world.

- Players identify with and control a single in-world character when playing. *Pillars of Eternity* is not a virtual world.

- When you do something, you get a response in a time commensurate with what you're doing. You issue a movement command, and you move. *Planetarion* is not a virtual world.

- You and your fellow players are in the same virtual world, not in separate copies of it. What one does, the other sees. *The Sims* is not a virtual world.

- The world continues to exist in your absence. When the server is rebooted, some things carry over from before the reboot. *Counter-Strike* is not a virtual world.

- The town or city you live in, which satisfies all the above criteria, is not a virtual world. It's part of the real world.

What this doesn't mean:

- *Players have to be able to build.* They don't. Killing a monster changes the world; you don't have to be able to construct a house.

- *Players can't have more than one character.* They can. They can even play them separately on two computers if they like. Just because the server doesn't know you're not two people, that doesn't stop it from being a virtual world. The point is, you're not a party of characters or some strings-pulling remote actor. As for interaction, well yes, you can use VoIP to speak and you can debate on a web site forum, but while in the virtual world it's all done modulo your character.

- *Having multiple servers means you don't have a virtual world.* What it means is that you have several running copies of a virtual world, but each one of those copies is itself a distinct virtual world in its own right.

- *If you kill a creature, it's dead forever.* Nah, they can respawn.

MMOs are virtual worlds with a game element built into them. A lot of what's said about MMOs applies to virtual worlds in general, but not all of it. Some virtual worlds aren't games, they're just social spaces.

Exercise: Why isn't *League of Legends* a virtual world?

Did You Know?

Golf was invented in Greece[11], where it was known as *Keritizin*. A marble relief[12], dated around 510BC-500BC, found on the base of a funerary *kouros* embedded in the Themistokleian wall of the Kerameikos (the cemetery of ancient Athens), depicts a man swinging something having the appearance of a golf club at something having the appearance of a golf ball, with the apparent goal of ... well, of getting it off some other man doing the same thing. This relief has also been used to suggest that *Hockey* was invented in Greece[13].

Dr. Toddystone

The character of Dr. Toddystone was, of course, based on Dr. Livingstone. I'd played no games that involved the exploration of an unknown (to the explorer—obviously the natives knew about their part of it) continent, but I'd read about Dr. Livingstone and the opening up of Africa. I wasn't especially a fan of Livingstone's, but as I'd just built something that was a bit like Africa and was now looking for a means to explore it, well, it was the obvious mechanism to do so. I'd spent so long making such a huge map, had created so many possibilities for exciting things, and had given myself so many ways they could unfold, that I wanted to see what was going to happen there! Dr. Toddystone, as an outsider exploring the continent, was my way to visit the world I had created.

---

[11]*The Complete History of Golf.* http://www.golf-information.info/golf-history.html
[12]The National Archaeological Museum of Athens, catalogue number 3477. This image from Wikimedia Commons, under attribution to Han borg. http://upload.wikimedia.org/wikipedia/commons/7/7c/Antiek_hockey.JPG
[13]Norman Walker: *A History of Hockey.* http://home.alphalink.com.au/~hockeyv/history.htm

I made myself a compass. No, not *that* kind of compass, *this* kind of compass: I took two pins, separated the points by 30mm, and used sticky tape to hold the other ends together. This compass represented how far Dr. Toddystone could travel in a single day, with 1mm representing 1 mile (how's that for mixing units?). Given that Dr. Toddystone travelled on foot with bearers and pack mules, 30 miles per day is probably a bit too optimistic, but, as I said, I was 12 or 13. I knew how long it took me to walk a mile (15–20 minutes) and worked out Dr. Toddystone's range from that, factoring in some time for sleeping. Also, it was the absolute maximum distance, so if the terrain was rough he wouldn't actually go that far (unless I had something special going on, such as a trip down a river by canoe). Sometimes, if he was in a friendly native village or a cave, he wouldn't move at all.

Finally, I could play. Here's what I did.

I wrote a diary. Dr. Toddystone began in some outpost of empire and headed off inland. Maybe he was aiming for that mountain in the distance, or perhaps he was following the river, or he could just have been attempting to find where those elephants that occasionally wandered nearby were coming from (he *was* a scientist, after all). Whatever, he wrote his thoughts down in his diary and then he moved. At the end of the day, he recounted his adventures, then the next morning he'd move again; and so it continued. I recorded his route on the map, wiggling it around if he got lost, making it straight if it were plain sailing or he was attempting to escape from pursuers. He recorded his discoveries, noted his concerns and suspicions, made plans, sought out supplies, followed legends—it was stirring, adventurous stuff! I was experiencing all of it myself, using Dr. Toddystone as my conduit. He *wasn't* me—he did things I would never have done—but he *was* me, in that I was visiting my own, constructed world through being him. It was straight down the line role-playing.

The way the story came out was not always how I had intended or hoped; this is why I thought of it first and foremost it as a game, rather than as anything else. There may have been some particular area where ancient forests grew and where natives spoke in hushed tones of strange, primitive life forms, which I desperately wanted Dr. Toddystone to visit, but he couldn't because some of his bearers had gone down with a fever and he'd had to head off in a different direction to get the berries he needed to cure them; or perhaps he'd inadvertently offended members of the tribe that lived nearby and couldn't risk their wrath. There were so many things that could happen, yes, but they *interacted*. That's what made it so exciting: I knew what *could* happen, but not what *would* happen. The world had a life of its own. I could have cheated, yes, of course, but who cheats at patience?

As soon as I finished the first game, which took me several days (he went from one side of the continent to the other), I started another one on the same map. I did perhaps three or four journeys on that; I could probably have continued with it for another few, but by then I was itching to create a new continent, so I did. I think I undertook fewer discrete journeys on that one—two or three—but they were longer.

Did I re-read the diaries, once I'd written them down? Actually, I don't believe I did. I used them as reference material, but I didn't read them as a novel. The purpose of the diary was to realize (*i.e.*, make real) what otherwise was only a mass of interacting possibilities. It constituted a story, but I wasn't doing it so I'd have a story to *read*: I was doing it so I could *live* the story.

The Second Age—1985 to 1989

During the First Age of virtual worlds, the concept was independently invented at least five times. For three of these (*Sceptre of Goth, Island of Kesmai,* and *Habitat*), the resulting game was exploited commercially; the developers kept their code and practices secret. For the other two (*MUD* and *Avatar*—plus a latecomer, *Monster*, in 1989), the game was made available for free by enlightened academic institutions and old-era hacker-mentality designers. These games' developers opened up their code and offered help to anyone who asked.

In *MUD*'s case, anyone could play if they were able to connect to the Essex University mainframe by whatever means. In *Avatar*'s case, anyone could play if they had a PLATO console and a direct connection to the PLATO system (which, sadly for *Avatar*, no members of the general public did).

So it was that the vast, vast majority of people who picked up the idea of virtual worlds and ran with it were *MUD* players. These started to appear in 1985, and so began the Second Age of MMO history.

First out were Neil Newell's *Shades*, Ben Laurie's *Gods,* and Mike Blandford's *AMP*. They were shortly followed by Pip Cordrey *et al*'s *MirrorWorld*, Alan Lenton's *Federation II* (there was no *Federation I*, it started at *II*), and my and Roy Trubshaw's *MUD2*. The number of people exposed to the concept of (what were by then being called) MUDs increased, and as a consequence yet more designers-to-be were inspired to write their own. Because these individuals had to code their own programs from scratch (earlier games tending to be customized for particular hardware), they were able to give full vent to their imagination. The result was a wondrous—and as-yet unparalleled—flowering of ideas, as people pushed at the boundaries of what was possible. It was a very exciting period to be an MMO designer.

It was also almost a dead end.

This was all going on in the UK. In the United States, *Avatar* was trapped in its gilded cage, and the other "seed" worlds (*Sceptre, IoK,* and *Habitat*) were commercial ventures with jealously-guarded code and no cross-pollination. The ongoing evolution of virtual worlds was thus entirely a British thing. This would have been fine if Britain was a comms-friendly environment, but it wasn't. In the United States, people could make local telephone calls effectively for free; in the UK, local calls cost 40p/hour (in 1986, about £1 an hour in today's money). Long distance calls cost far, far more. People complained about the price of going online not because the games were expensive (most were free), but because the phone calls were expensive. Some people were racking up bills of £1,000 a month—at a time when the average salary was £750 a month.

With this kind of overhead burdening players, British MUDs had major difficulties attracting newbies who could afford to play. As a result, most commercial MUDs struggled and withered away. Indeed, almost all of them are little more than footnotes when it comes to the history of MMOs, as they had barely any influence on the games we see today. There are exceptions (*Avalon* is a direct ancestor of both *Puzzle Pirates* and *Earth Eternal*, for example), but most of them are of scant lasting significance in and of themselves.

This is something of a shame, in both intellectual and practical terms. Intellectually, because of the sheer inventiveness that was lost; practically, because all the key issues were nailed down in this period but not all were carried through to the Third Age—they had to be (re)discovered anew.

The influence of *MUD* and its progeny on the history of MMOs could easily have hit a wall at this point. Some commercial MUDs did make the jump to the United States and beyond—most notably *MUD1* itself and *Federation II*—but that fact alone would merely have put them in the same position as *IoK* and *Aradath* in terms of their potential for future impact. That's not what happened, though.

Home computer enthusiasts weren't the only people who wrote their own MUDs from scratch: so did students, using university machines. Some of these students were aware of, and part of, the wider MUD programming community. Some of them were at sufficiently progressive institutions that they were able to make their games available to the public and other students for free. Some of them wrote portable code that would run on different hardware. Some of them wrote portable code which they *gave away*.

One of the worlds so created was *AberMUD*.

MUDTXT.MAS

Here's a photograph of a printout of *MUD1* dated June 12th, 1985. I think it's probably the oldest copy in my possession; as I alluded to earlier, I gave my oldest ones to Stanford University Library (they were the first to ask).

The .MAS extension is because it contains a bunch of files combined into one. A program called SUBFIL on the Essex University DEC-10 was used to collect files and create one big file with the sub-files in it; the same program could also split them apart. It's a bit like a ZIP file, except without the encryption (because if it were encrypted, you couldn't print it out).

As for why we *wanted* to package files like this, well the main reason was because each individual file came with an overhead of three blocks (each block being half a kilobyte of 36-bit words). If you had lots of files, those blocks added up and you could easily exceed your storage limit. We therefore preferred to keep our files in .MAS format rather than as lots of smaller files. To this day, I still don't like creating programs that have separate files for each individual class or function or whatever.

Oh, the reason the job name is THIRD is because it contains the MUDDL code (MUD.TXT) that defines the virtual world's content. Prior to that, I also printed out the *MUD* engine code itself and the MUDLIB library that interfaced it to the operating system. These were FIRST and SECOND. If I'd called the jobs anything that looked like MUD, the operators would have spotted what I was printing and told me off for wasting paper.

Also oh, "operators" were the university employees who were allowed to touch the computer and its major peripherals. It took three of them per shift to keep the mainframe and its related hardware up and running. I thought I'd better mention it because it's not a term you hear a lot nowadays.

The Lessons of *Dr. Toddystone*

From playing *Dr. Toddystone*, I learned a great deal. I discovered the power of role-playing—how, by pretending to be someone else, you can be yourself. I understood how games turn a space of potential narratives into actual, personal stories (or "histories," to be strictly accurate); I picked up some knowledge of geography and cultures, and how they interact, from reading library books for research; and I gained some insight into the nature of imperialism.

Above all, though, I learned what game design is *about*. It's about building potentials for players to turn into actualities, and it's about saying something you can't say any other way.

I could have written a story instead of drawing a map. I wrote stories all the time; it wouldn't have been out of character. However, I did draw a map. I did draw a map, because what I wanted to say—"there are so many wonderful things that can happen"—I couldn't say any other way. I could build the world and write a story set in it, or I could build it and *play* it.

Following *Dr. Toddystone*, my future creative direction was never in doubt. I was always, always going to create worlds that people could *visit*.

Avatar

Avatar was an impressive virtual world written in 1979 by Bruce Maggs, Andrew Shapira, and David Sides for the ground-breaking PLATO system operated by the University of Illinois. Here's a screenshot:

From this, you can see why *Avatar* lays claim to being the first graphical virtual world (and hence, if your definition of MMO insists on graphics, the first MMO).

Avatar was actually but the latest of a long line of role-playing games on the PLATO system, which included *Mines of Moria, Orthanc, Oubliette,* and a handful inspired by *Dungeons & Dragons—dnd* and *The Dungeon* being foremost among them. *The Dungeon* is better known as *pedit5,* the name its executable file was given so that PLATO's administrators wouldn't notice it. The earlier games tended to use a top-down perspective; *Oubliette* (1977) introduced a first-person perspective, as adopted in the *Avatar* screenshot (yes, that collection of lines in the middle at the top).

Avatar was a complex game, with challenging gameplay—which is just what PLATO users wanted. It was a roaring success, accounting for 600,000 hours of play from its launch until May, 1985 (about 6% of all PLATO usage for the period)[14]. Even by today's standards, it's impressive; to the players of the early 1980s, it was staggeringly so.

---

[14]David R. Woolley: *PLATO: The Emergence of Online Community.* http://www.thinkofit.com/plato/dwplato.htm

It's worth asking why, if *Avatar* was based on *Oubliette*, which itself descended via *Mines of Moria* from *pedit5*, *Avatar* counts as an MMO when the others don't. Well, the answer is that some of these others might, too—it really depends on your definition. *Avatar* does by mine, but *Oubliette* and its ancestors don't. Your definition may be more accepting.

In a sense, it doesn't really matter, though: *Avatar*'s influence on today's MMOs is barely perceptible. Even the fact that the term "Avatar" is used to describe the visualization of characters in MMOs isn't due to *Avatar*, it's just a lifting from the same source (Hinduism). *Avatar* and some of its ancestors anticipated what we'd see in MMOs, but didn't determine anything about them except possibly their graphics (as one of the first commercial games to use a first-person perspective, *Wizardry*, was directly inspired by *Oubliette*).

Avatar was ahead of its time, but trapped in the walled garden of PLATO that gifted it its expressiveness. You couldn't play *Avatar* without a PLATO terminal. That was then, though; this is now. Today's computers are easily powerful enough to emulate the PLATO system, and the Cyber1 project does just that. Head on over to http://www.cyber1.org/, where perhaps you can try it out for yourself.

AberMUD

AberMUD was written in 1987 by Alan Cox, Jim Finnis, Leon Thrane, and Richard Acott; Rich Salz and Brian Preble further enhanced it. Cox was the primary programmer, his having started work on *AberMUD* after playing *MUD*. The name comes from where it was written: the University of Wales at Aberystwyth.

AberMUD was rather rough around the edges. Its architecture owed much to *Lance*, a MUD being written by Leon Thrane, and its content was a mixture of parodies of other MUDs of the era plus TV shows and stand-alone surreal scenes. On the face of it, then *AberMUD* was nothing special. However...

In 1988 Cox rewrote the game in C to run on Southampton University's new Unix machine. This made it portable to any other Unix machine—of which there were hundreds (if not thousands) in U.S. universities. As a result, *AberMUD* was to become one of the key MUDs in the whole family tree.

ROCK, MIST, BLUD, and UNI

MUD1 needed a lot of memory by the standards of the day to run. Essex University's Computing Service put limits on the amount of memory that individual programs were allowed to use during the busiest period (*prime time*), and *MUD1* came to exceed these limits. This meant you could still play during the evening and at weekends, but not during the day. "During the day" still applied in summer, when the mainframe was largely idle.

To give diehards something to while away their Resource Control Units when most people were back at home, I wrote a smaller database in MUDDL that conformed to the memory constraints. I called this *VALLEY*. To create it, I had to go through the *MUD* database and extract into shared files the pieces that I wanted in both. Having done so, I let other students have access to them so they could write their own MUDs using MUDDL and the *MUD1* engine. The four that were actually completed were *ROCK, MIST, BLUD,* and *UNI*.

ROCK was the first one written. It was based on the Muppet spin-off, *Fraggle Rock*, and was a proper, self-contained game. It had no particular angle, being programmed by a bunch of CompSoc *MUD1* players for fun. It was fairly good, with some puzzles that stretched MUDDL further than I thought it could go (assembling a drill from components, for example: "There is a bit here").

MIST was a different world altogether. It was very easy to make wiz through scoring points, so a "game" evolved which was basically all politics. *MIST* became the personal fiefdom of one of the major figures in the Second Age of virtual worlds, Michael Lawrie (LORRY—he would eventually be responsible for introducing *AberMUD* to the United States). LORRY would regularly wipe the persona file, dewiz people, promote complete newbies, and so on. Its players loved the sheer anarchy of it.

BLUD was for killing. It wasn't a game where you could expect to keep a character for very long. Even if the other players didn't get you, the monsters certainly would. *BLUD* was written by a single undergraduate in the Computer Science department, although I have a vague recollection that he may have had some link to the Electronics department, too.

UNI was written by a later group of CompSoc members. It started out being a straight implementation of the layout of the Computer Science building, but then parody monsters were added to represent members of staff and it gained a following. *UNI* was the weakest of the MUDDL worlds, though: as with any in-joke, it only really appeals to those who are in on the joke.

As all professional game designers know deep down, basing a game world on a familiar real-world location for no good reason, as *UNI* did, smacks of laziness. *UNI* wasn't the first world coded in MUDDL to do this, though. Roy Trubshaw based the house in *MUD1* itself on the house he used to live in. When I put it to him that this was lazy design, his reply was: "Well yes, I'm lazy".

MUA

AberMUD was, for a while, known as *AberMUG*. The reason it was known as *AberMUG* was that I persuaded its author, Alan Cox, that if he didn't rename it then people would think "MUD" was a generic term rather than a particular world.

The players just kept on calling it *AberMUD*.

I myself used to use MUA ("Multi-User Adventure") as the generic term, on the grounds that this is what Roy Trubshaw would have called *MUD* if he'd known that adventure games would wind up being called adventure games and not dungeon games.

Needless to say, MUA didn't catch on despite my efforts, and MUD did become the generic term. The virtual world Roy and I wrote was itself renamed *MUD1* (by its players, not by us) to avoid confusion.

When there's a consensus among players what a word means, they're going to use it regardless of your wish that they wouldn't.

And the Winner Is...

Text beats graphics as an interface in every major respect except one: immediacy.

That one difference is enough to consign textual worlds to the margins of history.

Adventure '89

Adventure '89 was a gathering in the UK of independent MUD designers/developers that took place, unsurprisingly, in 1989. The event was a showplace for ideas, with perhaps 20 worlds on display, all of them different. I still have some of the fliers I picked up at the event:

When I say that the worlds were different, I mean it. These were some of the genres:

- *Federation II*—space opera
- *The Zone*—adult ("score to score")
- *Dark City*—cyberpunk
- *Strat*—holiday on the moon
- *Trash*—"fire-breathing cabbages and inflatable hover-cars"
- *Void*—magical adult
- *Prodigy*—ancient Britain
- *Empyrion*—underwater city
- *Spacers*—generation spaceship

Even the fantasy worlds weren't all the same:

- *Gods*—end game players can create objects using points given by worshippers
- *MirrorWorld*—rolling resets (see later)
- *Avalon*—grid-based in places
- *Bloodstone*—object decomposition (humans made of 260 parts)
- *AMP*—objects with shape
- *Strata*—internal currency
- *Warlord*—highly combat-intensive

These game worlds were as different as *WoW* and *EVE* (although *Void* was a social world, perhaps closer to *Second Life*). Why can't we have equally different worlds now? Where's the *variety*?

Three Girls

When Alice arrived in Wonderland, her first words were:

> *Curiouser and curiouser.*[15]

When Dorothy arrived in Oz, her first words were:

> *We will go to the Emerald City and ask the Great Oz how to get back to Kansas again.*[16]

When Wendy arrived in Neverland, her first words were:

> *I wish I had a pretty house,*
>
> *The littlest ever seen,*
>
> *With funny little red walls*
>
> *And roof of mossy green.*[17]

All three girls found themselves in strange and wondrous worlds, but each behaved differently when she got there.

Anarchy

If the name of *AberMUD*'s designer, Alan Cox, rings a bell, it may be because you're a Linux user. Alan was for many years the maintainer of the main 2.2 branch of the Linux kernel. He's an outspoken advocate of free software and argues strongly against software patents. So, he's one of the good guys, then.

In 2013, Alan was awarded an honorary fellowship by the University of Wales. It's probably because of all his other achievements, but I like to think that *AberMUD* might have been a factor.

---

[15]Lewis Carroll: *Alice's Adventures in Wonderland*. Macmillan: London. 1865.
http://www.gutenberg.org/files/11/11-h/11-h.htm
[16]L. Frank Baum: *The Wonderful Wizard of Oz*. George M. Hill: Chicago. 1900.
http://www.gutenberg.org/files/55/55-h/55-h.htm
[17]James M. Barrie: *Peter and Wendy*. Hodder & Stoughton: London. 1911.
http://www.gutenberg.org/files/26654/26654-h/26654-h.htm

Decus et Tutanem

Back in the late 1970s, there were basically two main networks for software distribution among the kind of academics who wrote computer games: DECUS and PLATO.

The Digital Equipment Corporation, DEC, was a company that made mini-computers and mainframes. These were very popular in Computer Science departments, in part due to their elegant design and in part due to the fact that DEC wasn't IBM. DECUS was the Digital Equipment Corporation User Society; it was funded by DEC but run by volunteers, and it distributed software via magnetic tape.

PLATO was a more integrated system, running on Control Data Corporation machines. It was way ahead of its time, having vector graphics as standard when almost everyone else still relied on teletypes. Users accessed a large time-sharing system from pretty well identical terminals, meaning it was relatively easy for someone to write a game in one physical location that could be played by people in other physical locations.

In terms of application software, PLATO was a hotbed of innovation. It can claim to be where message boards, paint programs, instant messaging, and touchscreens first made an appearance. It also saw several multiplayer games, the most celebrated of which, *Avatar*, would today be regarded as an MMO. As I mentioned earlier, depending on how slack you make your definition of "MMO" and the degree to which you believe Wikipedia, some PLATO games prior to *Avatar* could be called MMOs, too.

DEC users didn't have the universal graphics terminals that PLATO users had, so few of their games were graphical. PLATO ultimately gave us *Freecell*, *Battlezone,* and *Microsoft Flight Simulator*; DECUS gave us *Hunt the Wumpus*, *Adventure,* and *Zork*.

DECUS also gave us MUDs.

It didn't do so directly. It *might* have done if I'd sent them a copy of *MUD1*, but I didn't—I was just a student and had no means to put *MUD1* onto the DECUS tapes. When someone who could do it submitted a version without asking me, they took a copy I was working on that had debugging print statements in it and wasn't really playable. The upshot of all this, then, was that if people wanted a local *MUD1*-like game, they had to write their own.

This was not without significance.

MUD1 and *Avatar* were written within a year of each other. That being so, how come today's virtual worlds descend almost universally from *MUD1*, with none of them owing a jot of their virtual worldliness to *Avatar*?

There are two primary reasons.

First, PLATO was effectively an island. Its graphical capability was too far in advance of what was available elsewhere for its games to escape into the environment. All the games written for PLATO were stuck on PLATO until the rest of the world caught up with its graphics.

Second, *MUD1* generated more evolutionary pressure than *Avatar*. On PLATO, the only reason to write your own game was if you were a designer with an idea. Although this was also true in general of DECUS games, in *MUD1*'s case there was an additional problem: limited access. There was only one instantiation of *MUD1* (at least initially), and more people wanted to play it than there were resources available to allow them. Rather than sit around complaining about Essex University's lack of modems, people went off and wrote their own MUD instead. *Shades, Gods,* and *AberMUD* appeared this way, along with dozens more.

The resulting cocktail of competition, inspiration, and experiment led to rapid innovation, both in technology and world design. Thus, when the Internet finally became established, it was *MUD1*'s descendents that were better positioned to propagate, not *Avatar*'s (because it didn't really have any). Later, when commercial developers looked for people with experience in creating virtual worlds, they had thousands of *MUD1*-descended designers to choose from and only trace numbers of *Avatar* designers.

So it is, as with much else in history, the way things are with MMOs today is largely to do with blind chance.

LOL

LOL originally meant "laugh out loud"; ROFL was "roll on floor, laughing". I first encountered them on CompuServe in the 1980s. LOL was something you said (well, wrote—you just regarded it as speech) if you thought something was really funny; ROFL was for if you thought it was utterly hilarious. ROFLMAO was for if you wanted everyone to think you were a superficial jerk.

These days, the usage of LOL has changed. No longer does it mean that you think something is actually laugh-out-loud amusing; rather, it's a way to acknowledge that you recognize someone's attempt at humor had vague merit to it. It can also be used to flag that what immediately precedes it isn't meant to be serious, or that it is but please don't hit me for saying it.

LOL has proven to be real-world extensible, in that some people now actually use it in everyday conversation. Normally, words such as LOL are present in virtual environments to represent an act of communication that can be expressed in real life but not easily in text (MUAHAHAHA, for maniacal laughter, is like this); however, occasionally one of them fills a linguistic gap that's present in spoken language as well as written language. LOL is such a term—evidenced by the fact that some people write it as "lawl" (North Americans—it would be more like "loll" in my accent).

Personally, I don't use LOL or ROFL as I consider both terms dangerously new-fangled. I don't use smileys either, for the same reason.

Yes, this is indeed a form of snobbery.

Alice

Alice's view of Wonderland was just that: a land of wonder. She went where fancy took her, with no initial goal save that of satisfying her curiosity.

Alice was engaged on a personal journey of self-discovery. She wasn't so much curious about the wonders around her as curious about herself. She had to find her own direction in life; Wonderland was the metaphorical place where she did that.

1985 Wish List

Back in 1985, I was asked to do some market research prior to setting up a company to develop *MUD2*.

To this end, I asked a bunch of senior *MUD1* players what might influence their choice of which MUD to play. I sorted these out into categories and got a list of 24. Some of these were features; some were forms of recommendation. I then put this list to the player base in general, asking them to rank each one between -5 (hate) and 5 (love). The resulting average scores were then multiplied by 5 for no good reason and rounded to the nearest integer to avoid decimal places.

Here is the result:

25	Intelligent mobiles
22	Conversing with mobiles
21	More magic
19	Cheap per hour to play
19	Regularly improved
15	Messages to pick up later
14	Lots of rooms
13	Different start locations
13	Reputation of author
13	Higher access speed
12	Cheap registration fee
12	Friend's recommendation
11	Understand complex sentences
11	Lots of players
10	Increased speed of response
10	Free sample game
9	Long textual descriptions
9	Never crashes
9	Special offers for cheap time
6	International game
5	Lots of books/documentation
3	What magazines said
-3	Built-in adverts
-3	Graphics

Moral: never entirely believe your players when they tell you what they want.

The Third Age—1989 to 1995

The third age is when the ascent of MUDs became unstoppable. However, it's also the time of a monumental event in design terms, the consequences of which are still with us.

In the First Age, the concept of a virtual world was invented (multiple times). In the Second Age, it was taken up and developed, but because of the prevailing conditions of the time (economic and technical), it didn't achieve critical mass. In the Third Age, it achieved critical mass—and then exploded.

AberMUD was one of the more game-oriented MUDs around in the late 1980s. It wasn't particularly *avant garde*, but as I mentioned earlier, its designer (Alan Cox) made the critical decision to rewrite it in C. C ran under Unix, the main operating system used by American universities. A strong advocate of free software, Cox released the game onto the nascent Internet. It spread like a rash, and within a year was installed on thousands of Unix systems worldwide.

For the vast majority of players, this was the first MUD they'd seen. In the same way that Second Age MUDs had been inspired by First Age MUDs, *AberMUD* inspired a new (and larger) generation of designer-programmers to write MUDs of their own; thus, the Third Age came into being.

If that were all there was too it, there wouldn't be much point in calling this period "the Third Age". As I've described it, it's basically just more of the Second Age; sure, the dam that was holding back virtual worlds burst, but that alone doesn't really qualify as an inflexion point. Yet the Third Age is probably the most important period in MMO history to date; what happened then fixed how MMOs are now. Without it, even the concept of an MMO (as distinct from virtual worlds in general and social worlds in particular) would not exist.

The inflexion point was the Great Schism.

The Origins of MUDDLE

To recapitulate: *MUD1* hard-coded most of the physics of the game in BCPL (a beautiful language that remains my favorite to this day); the world objects and non-general verbs were defined separately in a data file using a language of Roy Trubshaw's own design called MUDDL. MUDDL was okay to begin with, but it wasn't expressive enough to handle many of the concepts we wanted. I kept having to extend it in a series of hacks, until eventually it reached its limit. Every time I wanted to do anything more sophisticated, I had had to code it in BCPL rather than MUDDL; this meant that it was forced on all other uses of the *MUD1* game engine (*ROCK, MIST*, etc.), not just my own *MUD* and *VALLEY*.

I therefore decided to rewrite *MUD* from scratch. I had to determine early on how much to code in C (or, as it turned out, Pascal—thanks, British Telecom) and how much to put into a data file. The more I thought about it, the more obvious it became that *everything* should go in the data file. If I wanted a generic virtual world engine, how could it be otherwise?

Thus, I created MUDDLE. MUDDLE is data for the *MUD2* engine, but code insofar as its programmer is concerned. In other words, it's a *domain-specific* language. Whether you want to call it a scripting language or a programming language is up to you; I see it as a programming language, and even have a MUDDLE-to-C compiler for it.

It's not perfect, though. For one thing, it still leaves too much to the run-time system (e.g., command parsing is done in C, which means that if you want to write a virtual world with no command parsing, or a non-English one, you can't do it just with MUDDLE).

I'd thoroughly recommend writing a domain-specific language for MMO coding, though. If nothing else, it means you have to understand what it is you need to be able to say in your virtual world design, rather than just trying to say it and then finding out you can't.

Dorothy

Dorothy's view of Oz was as a place where she didn't want to be. She followed a predetermined path—the yellow brick road—to get back to her home.

Dorothy was engaged on a personal journey of self-discovery. She wasn't so much trying to find the Great Oz as to find herself. She had to follow her own path in life; Oz was the metaphorical place where she did that.

Narrow Road Between Lands

When you entered *MUD1*, this is the first room description that you saw (cut and pasted from the source file):

```
Narrow road between lands.
You are stood on a narrow road between The Land and whence you came. To the
north and south are the small foothills of a pair of majestic mountains,
with a large wall running round. To the west the road continues, where in
the distance you can see a thatched cottage opposite an ancient cemetery.
The way out is to the east, where a shroud of mist covers the secret pass by
which you entered The Land.
```

I had it printed on some sweatshirts in the 1980s. Here's one of them:

That block of text on the front is strangely compelling; the players who bought one would say that they were often "read" by strangers while on the tube or waiting in a queue.

One player, Sue the Witch, complained that the words "majestic mountains" appeared right across her, well, majestic mountains. As the first-known example of cross-gender trickery, she later turned out to be a guy named Steve; you have to admire his attention to detail.

I lost about 50p on each sweatshirt, yet people still said I was ripping them off.

Pairs Game

Virtual worlds were independently invented at least six times. See if you can match the inventors to the virtual world they designed:

Bartle and Trubshaw	Sceptre of Goth
Farmer and Morningstar	*Avatar*
Flinn and Taylor	*Habitat*
Skrenta	*Island of Kesmai*
Klietz	*Monster*
Maggs, Shapira, and Sides	MUD

I've put one in to start you off...

MicroMUD

There was a version of *MUD* written for the Commodore 64 that simulated being an online world. It featured other "player characters," but they were controlled by the computer. They would "log in" while you yourself were playing. To some degree, they could do most of the things real players could do—even communicate—and they had different personalities. Some would attack you, some would try to help you, some would ignore you, and some hated each other.

Unfortunately, in the time it took for *MicroMUD* to be implemented the market for text games crashed. Nevertheless, the idea of a single-player version of an MMO remains intriguing.

Would you play a *MicroWoW*?

The Great Schism

In the first two ages, MUDs had been played both by people who saw them as games and by people who saw them as worlds. The two groups lived happily alongside each other and were mutually supportive. Yes, there were philosophical clashes, but in general each group kept the worst excesses of the other in check; virtual worlds were all the better for it.

AberMUD leaned more toward the game side than the social side. There *were* MUDs around that were more game-oriented, but overall most had a much stronger social component than did *AberMUD*. So it was that when *AberMUD* hit the Internet, not all the social players liked what they saw. They liked they *concept*, just not the execution.

With *TinyMUD*, they broke ranks. Written by James Aspnes in 1989, *TinyMUD* was, as its name suggests, a MUD; however, it also drew from another game, Rich Skrenta's *Monster*. *Monster* had gameplay, but it also allowed player-created content. The second version of *MUD* had featured this (if you remember, I added an ox to it that way), and so had some Second Age MUDs (*MirrorWorld* founder Pip Cordrey pushed the idea hard). However, *AberMUD* didn't have it, therefore the idea didn't propagate to the Third Age. The reason that virtual worlds such as *Second Life* have user-created content is because *Monster* had it, not because *MUD* or the games on Pip Cordrey's IOWA system had it.

TinyMUD was, also as its name suggests, not very large. To make anything of it, people had to take the basic code and extend it with content of their own. This introduced one of the defining features of the Third Age, the *codebase*. Anyone with modest (or in some cases, no) programming skills could take a codebase and tailor it to make their own MUD.

The viability of this idea was confirmed by Lars Pensjö with *LPMUD*. *LPMUD* featured a powerful scripting language, LPC, that enabled people to create sophisticated objects and environments on the fly. Designed to be flexible, *LPMUD* was used for implementing a wide range of very different, bespoke MUDs. It suffered, however, in that social-oriented players found LPC too much of a chore to learn and game-oriented players didn't like the fiction-breaking that invariably occurred when other players created content. *LPMUD* was probably the best codebase of the era for designers, but few players are designers.

TinyMUD wasn't itself all that impressive, but it did inspire another designer to develop two codebases that *were* impressive. In 1990, Stephen White improved *TinyMUD*'s functionality to create *TinyMUCK*, which he rapidly followed with *MOO* ("MUD, Object-Oriented"). Like *LPMUD*, *MOO* incorporated a full-power scripting language; unlike *LPMUD*, it was presented in a relatively intuitive way. *MOO* became the default codebase for non-game worlds of the textual era, and was the basis of perhaps the most famous of all Third Age virtual worlds, Pavel Curtis's *LambdaMOO*.

Surprisingly, *TinyMUCK* wasn't entirely superseded by *MOO* and developed a strong following of its own. Furthermore, it moved Larry Foard to write *TinyMUSH*, which became popular among role-players. By the end of 1990, this made a total of three major social-world codebases (MUCKs, MUSHes, and MOOs), plus one flying the flag for traditional mixed game/social worlds (LPMUDs). The social players had successfully cast off their chains.

This, however, meant that the gamers no longer had to concern themselves with the non-gaming elements of MUDs; they could go as hard-core as they liked. So they did.

DikuMUD was written solely to be a better *AberMUD*. Although formally a codebase, it came with sufficient content to run as a stand-alone game, and was trivial to install: anyone with access to a Unix (or, by extension, Linux) system could be playing it within minutes of obtaining a copy. Most important, though, was its gameplay: it was utterly compelling. All today's major MMOs use the *DikuMUD* gameplay paradigm, which has become so ingrained that at times it's hard to remember that other approaches do exist.

DikuMUD took the gaming MUD community by storm. With it, the gamers successfully cast off *their* chains. The social players tried to distance themselves from what was in their eyes a heinous development; the gamers didn't care, so long as they didn't have crafters in their midst mewling about being ignored.

Social worlds went one way; game worlds went another. This was the Great Schism that rent the concept of virtual worlds in two, and—sadly in my view—persists to this day.

DikuMUD

I mention a lot of historical MMOs in this book, some of which have had a bigger influence on today's MMOs than others. However, with the possible exception of *MUD* itself, the one to which current MMO design owes the greatest debt is *DikuMUD*.

DikuMUD was a textual world written in 1990 by a group of friends (Katja Nyboe, Tom Madsen, Hans Henrik Staerfeldt, Michael Seifert, and Sebastian Hammer) at the Computer Science department at the University of Copenhagen (*Datalogisk Institut Københavns Universitet* in Danish, hence the name). It was conceived as an improved *AberMUD*, but whereas other MUDs of its era were going in the direction of providing greater in-world creation facilities, *DikuMUD* went in the opposite direction: it hard-coded almost everything.

It hard-coded it well, too: it was easy to install, but any moderately competent C programmer could easily customize it. Many did, and as a result a slew of codebases were created with *DikuMUD* at their root. There were well over a thousand viable *DikuMUDs* running in the mid-1990s, with several hundred derivatives, too. Eventually, scripting was also introduced, which resulted in a further flurry of content-creation.

The most important thing about *DikuMUD* from a modern perspective, however, is not its popularity: rather, it's the gameplay and other design elements that it pioneered or popularized. Most of the developers of early (graphical) MMOs had played a *DikuMUD* or derivative, and they took what they learned with them into the commercial environment. To this day, the gameplay of MMOs is very strongly reminiscent of *DikuMUD*'s gameplay, and even some "new" ideas are merely reinventions of what *DikuMUD* did years earlier.

Here are some of the things you see in modern MMOs for which you can thank (or curse!) *DikuMUD* or its derivatives (collected by Raph Koster[18]):

- Characters:
  - Classes
  - Races
  - Pets
  - Quests (once scripting came in)

---

[18]Raph Koster: *What is a Diku?*. January, 2009. http://www.raphkoster.com/2009/01/09/what-is-a-diku/

- Combat:
  - Procs
  - Cooldowns
  - Aggro
  - Stuns
  - Respawn timers
  - Corpse runs
  - The trinity (tank, healer, and DPS)
- Grouping:
  - Battlefields
  - Raids (sort of)
  - Public quests
- World:
  - Zones
  - Banks
  - Auction houses
  - Housing
  - Instancing

Not everything transported from *DikuMUD* into modern MMOs lasted. Its death penalties included XP and probable gear loss, for example, which *EverQuest* had but today's MMOs don't. Other ideas such as combat stances, character moods, "rent" for logging off, and admin status for people who "won" the game didn't stand the test of time either.

Some attractive aspects of *DikuMUD* have yet to appear in modern MMOs. Procedural content generation is much easier in a textual world than in a graphical world, for example, so DikuMUDs are still ahead there. Also, modern MMO design hasn't exactly stood still, and concepts such as crafting are done better today than they were in *DikuMUD*. Furthermore, although the overall hack-and-slash *feel* of modern MMOs is basically still that of *DikuMUD*, they don't simply do in graphics what *DikuMUD* did in text—they do more besides.

Oddly, despite the fact that *DikuMUD* influenced the design of modern MMOs a great deal, it wasn't itself particularly innovative. It drew a lot from *Dungeons & Dragons* and it drew a lot from earlier MUDs (especially *AberMUD*). Its contemporary, *LPMUD*, was far more ground-breaking. However, what it did do was bring all the essential features together and package them in such a way that people could pick them up and run with them. One day, we'll surely have graphical worlds that afford this kind of creative opportunity to players and would-be designers.

One day...

MUDDL to MUDDLE

This is an extract from *MUD1*, in MUDDL:

```
feed nanny victuals       destroy second 682 0
feed nanny antidote       destroy second 682 0
feed nanny flower         destroy second 682 0
feed nanny herring        destroy second 682 0
feed nanny nut            destroy second 682 0
feed nanny pen            destroy second 682 0
feed nanny parachute      destroy second 682 0
feed nanny money          destroy second 682 0
feed nanny gem            destroy second 682 0
feed nanny liquid         destroy second 682 0
feed nanny medication     destroy second 682 0
feed nanny book           destroy second 682 0
feed nanny biscuit        destroy second 682 0
feed nanny paper          destroy second 682 0
feed nanny map            destroy second 682 0
feed nanny tome           destroy second 682 0
feed nanny limb           null    null   684 0
feed nanny corpse         null    null   684 0
feed nanny frog           null    null   684 0
feed nanny bird           null    null   684 0
feed nanny birdofprey     null    null   684 0
feed nanny rodents        null    null   684 0
feed nanny bunny          null    null   684 0
feed nanny vermin         null    null   684 0
feed nanny familiar       null    null   684 0
feed nanny serpent        null    null   684 0
feed nanny none           null    null   687 0
```

Here's what it would be in MUDDLE:

```
{ feed goat edible }:
$(   !! "The goat eats it.*N"
     destroy(second)
$)
{ feed goat animal }:
     !? "It's not a carnivore.*N"
{ feed goat }:
     !? "The goat won't eat.*N"
```

The nanny goat was what finally made me snap and rewrite *MUD* from scratch as *MUD2*.

Lost Worlds

Every once in a while, someone proposes that we create an online museum of virtual worlds, so that future generations can wander around and marvel at how we ever thought they were cool.

I recall a proposal for this in the early 1990s for textual worlds—which should surely have been an easier task than it would be for graphical worlds. The idea was that in order to preserve the past, a meta- world would be created, modeled as a park that included segments of interesting earlier virtual worlds as offshoots. As with real-world archaeology, only the structures would be there, not the functionality.

I was asked to send (and did send) some *MUD1* rooms for permanent display in this museum. My aim was to encourage others to donate parts of their MUDs, too; I believed (and still believe) it was important that evidence of the tremendous creativity that went on in MUDs should be preserved before such content was lost forever.

Unfortunately, it's not just game worlds that fade away when people move on. The museum world itself inevitably succumbed to the same fate as most of the worlds it was trying to archive.

Oh, how the gods of irony must smile.

The Flowering

Instead of asking why we don't have such a variety of MMOs today as we had in Adventure '89, perhaps the better question to ask is why did we have it back then? Was it always going to happen? What factors enabled it? Perhaps if we understand the history, we might have a better understanding of what conditions would allow it to repeat in the future.

Okay, so it *was* always going to happen:

- People saw was possible
- Development costs came down
- There was money to be made
- There were no decent engines available so people had to write their own
- Designing virtual worlds is fun

Do these same conditions apply today?

MMO DSL

A *domain-specific language* is a programming language designed for one kind of application only. It contrasts with a *general-purpose language*, which can be used for many applications. DSLs are better than GPLs for the purpose they're designed for, but they're not a lot of use for anything other than that purpose.

When designing an MMO, you want some things to be expressed in directly-executable code and some things to be expressed in data for that code. As a general rule, if it changes from run to run, it should be data; if it stays the same, it should be code. For most applications this distinction is fine, but sometimes "from run to run" becomes fuzzy. If, for example, you're writing a program that is only ever going to be used for one MMO, you could happily hard-code the lot and only save state data (such as whether an individual mob is alive or dead). If, on the other hand, you want your program to work for many different MMOs, you'd want to put a lot more into data.

This leads to a recursion. Here's how:

1. You can, if you want, hard-code your entire MMO in C++. This is bad, because it means you need to recompile it if you want to change any data (e.g., how much damage a sword does).

2. You separate your implementation into code (written in C++) and data (written in some format of your own devising). Now you can change the data without changing the program. However, anything that involves execution is still hard-coded; this means if you want to add a new command to your virtual world, you have to code it in C++.

3. You create a way of describing commands and store it as data. Now, when you want to add a new command, you only need to modify the data, not the code. You don't need to recompile the program, because you now have a *scripting language* that is interpreted on the fly. Some important application-specific functions are still defined in C++, though, and you realize that if you want to use your program for more than one MMO then these should be soft-coded as data, too.

4. Your data is now used to define all the functionality of the MMO. The only things left in the C++ are either used by all virtual worlds (e.g., input/output) or they support the interpretation of your data. Your data format is effectively a new, stand-alone domain-specific language for writing MMOs. Let's call it MMODSL.

5. You notice that if you want to make any changes to your data, you have to change your MMODSL code. This is bad, because it means you need to reload it every time you change your data. Now, we're back at Step 1, except with MMODSL in the position that C++ was in.

There are three main ways out of this.

One way is to decide that yes, you are going to put your data in your code, but you don't care because you do so at the point where your (C++ or MMODSL) code really *is* only going to be used for one virtual world. I did this with MUDDLE.

Another way is to separate the scalar data from your MMODSL code (at Step 2 of the second iteration) but take it no further. You can do this because the MMODSL you designed is sufficiently expressive that you never *need* to put commands into a new data format. Although the data may differ between shards of an MMO, the MMODSL code is the same for all of them. This is how LPMUDs do it.

Finally, you can make the code self-modifiable (*i.e.*, interpreted rather than executed directly), but only modify the *data* used by MMODSL, not the MMODSL code itself. This means you can make changes to the code but you don't need to recompile it—you just dump it to disc every so often. This is how MOOs do it.

If you have a DSL for MMOs, you won't code any quicker in it than if you used a GPL instead. However, each line would carry more expressive power, so you'd be able to achieve more in fewer lines. This is why DSLs are so useful: they let you speak in the language of the application's design.

Four Uses

In textual non-game worlds such as MOOs and Tiny*s, here's what people tended to do to occupy themselves:

- Make stuff, either for fun or as conversation pieces.
- Politick about resource allocation.
- Create games.
- Indulge in virtual sex.

The only thing that surprised me about the vibrant sex scene in *Second Life* was that other people were surprised it sprang up (er, so to speak).

Stock MUD Syndrome

The first virtual worlds—the text MUDs of the First and Second Ages—were written from scratch and were entirely different from each other judged by the standards of today. Yes, the Second Age MUDs drew their inspiration and basic concepts from *MUD1*, but they headed off in a compass-full of different directions.

Some of them shared code, too. For example, most of the MUDs on the IOWA ("Input/Output World of Adventure") system were written using a definition language called Slate, for which licenses were available (and actually sold!) at £3,000 each. *MUD1*'s definition language, MUDDL, was also successfully used to write a succession of fully-fledged MUDs (*ROCK, MIST, BLUD,* and *UNI,* as I mentioned earlier). Sharing code did not mean that these MUDs were all the same, though; although some of the concepts were fixed (the IOWA worlds all used *rolling resets,* for example, which is now the standard for MMOs), the results were all strikingly different from each other. This is because although the definition language was made available, the descriptions of the virtual worlds in this language were not made available (because then people would read them to cheat).

Things began to change in the Third Age, with the appearance of codebases. Codebases all incorporated sample world definitions to get potential developers up and running. Some, most notably *DikuMUD*, came with a full-blown virtual world that was immediately playable. By downloading a codebase and modifying it, many more people could develop MUDs than at any time previously—surely a good thing?

Well, yes, it *was* a good thing, but it wasn't without its downside. See, if people have a choice between writing their own games and modding a ready-made game, many of them will take the latter approach because it's just easier. They don't acquire a strong understanding of design fundamentals this way. Also, if large numbers of people downloaded a codebase to mod and then never really put a lot of effort into modding it, the result would be a great wodge of virtual worlds that all looked like the sample one that came with the installation.

Back in the 1990s, this is indeed what happened. Of the several thousand DikuMUDs that were up and running, I'd guess that around three quarters were pretty well clones of one another—a bit like the way today's MMOs have parallel servers all running the same world. The players and administrators are different, but the rest is the same. For a DikuMUD, as soon as you entered and saw that the main town was called Midgaard, you knew what was coming.

The other quarter of DikuMUDs did take things in different directions; many of these worlds remain unmatched by today's graphical MMOs for their depth, complexity, range, inventiveness, and gameplay. Yes, I do mean *unmatched*—and by a considerable margin, too. It doesn't matter, of course, I know. You're not going to play them no matter how good they are, because they don't have purdy pictures.

Most DikuMUDs, though, were not like this. Most were clones, plain and simple. They were repetitive, they crowded out the rest, and although the first one you played would be tremendous fun, the second and subsequent ones would be just more of the same. The barrenness of invention was the stuff of despair for players and designers alike.

From this, we got the term *Stock MUD Syndrome*. This is a play on the psychological phenomenon of the Stockholm Syndrome, in which people who are held captive come to feel they're on their captives' side. People who are imprisoned by identical MMOs with identical gameplay come to feel they're on their captives' sides, too, and will often defend them against the slightest hint that they may in some small way be, you know, not perfect.

Tools are good. The more tools we have, the more MMOs we'll have. Sure, if people can pick up a fully-integrated system for next to nothing, the less likely they are to do anything original with it; however, the more people overall will do *something* with it, and therefore in absolute terms the number of people who *do* use it to make something dazzling is going to be larger.

On that basis, I guess I'm okay with them.

Genres and Settings

Currently, the top five most popular MMO genres are:

- Fantasy
- Science fiction
- More fantasy
- Fantasy plus some horror
- Even more fantasy

Okay, so those are fairly broad. Superhero worlds and post-apocalypse worlds are both SF, for example, but as you can see, fantasy dominates. Even something like *The Secret World* has magic in its modern setting.

I once had a consultancy job in which I was asked to produce genre/setting ideas for particular audiences. Here's the result:

- Legendary
    - Robin Hood
    - Wild West Outlaws
    - 1001 Arabian Nights
- Historical
    - London, 1966
    - Korean war (*MASH*)
    - Ancient Rome
    - Age of Exploration
    - Renaissance Europe
    - Colonization of North America (from point of view of natives)
    - Casanova's Venice
- Victorian
    - Age of Imperialism (Flashman)
    - Grand Tours of Europe
    - Victorian vampires
    - Steampunk
- Action
    - Spy fiction (James Bond)
    - Escapist adventure (Indiana Jones)
    - World War I espionage (*Riley, Ace of Spies*)
- Inaction
    - Lazy Students

- Science Fiction
  - Escape from Jurassic Park
  - Rampaging Japanese Monsters
  - Asimov's *Foundation* series
  - 1950s Science fiction (bug-eyed monsters)
- Crime
  - Hardboiled detective (Sam Spade)
  - Gangsters/FBI (1920s Chicago)
  - Gangs (*Warriors*)
  - Pimps and Prostitutes
- Modern
  - Cruise Ship
  - Millionaire Street

These are just the ones that matched the target groups—there are hundreds of others I or anyone else can think up.

In terms of genre, much more can be done for MMOs than straight fantasy/SF (or modern for social worlds, or cutesy for kids' worlds). Historical settings in particular look ripe for exploitation.

A change of fiction isn't just good for the *feel* of a world, either: it can suggest new gameplay ideas. If you look at areas where there is no existing paradigm, you have to come up with solutions yourself—you have the freedom to escape from the penitentiary of player expectations as to what a world of that genre "should" look like.

It's not a case of evolution *or* revolution, here: you can have both.

Hmm, I suspect my argument might be stronger if I gave an example or two.

Pairs Game—the Answers

Here's the solution to the pairs game I gave you earlier.

- *Avatar* was designed and written by Bruce Maggs, Andrew Shapira, and David Sides.

- *Habitat* was designed and written by Randy Farmer and Chip Morningstar.

- *Island of Kesmai* was designed and written by Kelton Flinn and John Taylor.

- *Monster* was designed and written by Rich Skrenta.

- *MUD* was designed and written by Richard Bartle <wave> and Roy Trubshaw.

- *Sceptre of Goth* was designed and written by Alan Klietz.

If *you* don't remember, who will?

Threading

MUD1 was implemented using a mechanism we'd now call *threading*. Each player ran their own peer process, which communicated with other processes through shared memory. The operating system's timesharing mechanism switched between processes, which gave the effect of parallel processing; furthermore, as the CPU was dual-processor; it was possible that *actual* parallel processing could take place, too. Programmatically, Roy Trubshaw and I therefore took the abstract view and treated each process as if it were running on its own, separate processor.

This being the case, we had to have a lot of signal/wait locking code to prevent memory blocks from being accessed simultaneously by two processes. Otherwise, it would have been possible for one process to start to move an object, then another process to come in and move it somewhere else, then the first process to continue moving it as if it were still where it thought it was. That way lie crashes.

This was something of a pain to program. We had to put in the memory locks manually, as MUDDL was too tied to its interpreter for us to have it insert them automatically. We also had a lingering suspicion that having a sequence of locks on parts of memory ran slower overall than if we'd just locked the entire shared memory each time we had a command to execute.

MUD2 switched to a non-threaded model. As a programmer, this allows you to mess about with objects without the worry that someone else might mess about with them at the same time. The result worked out much faster overall, but it did mean that if one player's command took inordinately long to execute then everyone else's commands would have to wait and there could be noticeable server lag as a result. In other words, the game itself was faster but the players occasionally perceived it to be slower.

As it happens, MUDDLE doesn't really care how it's implemented, so its runtime system could switch to a threaded model if that improved performance. It's certainly easier to program MMO content without having to think about threading, though.

Genre Example I

Many retired people have Internet access. They would be attracted to a genre that isn't violent, relies on brains rather than brawn, and will attract other retired people. Other criteria that might also work are a hankering for an idyllic past and an opulent or rural setting.

So, that's an Agatha Christie world, then!

Now if you wanted to make an Agatha Christie MMO, one way to do it would simply be to reskin regular MMO features to fit:

- **Tank**: The interrogator who has to keep suspects distracted using tools such as small talk, flirting, discussion of their interests, and perhaps physical presence.

- **DPS**: The investigator looking for clues while the suspect is distracted.

- **Healer**: The person whose frowns and tut-tuts stop the suspect from doing anything socially gauche (such as breaking off conversation with the tank).

- **Rogue**: The gentleman/woman thief who breaks into houses, desks, safes, cars, and so on, with only charisma as a defense should servants witness the action.

Okay, so that's not too bad. It's already slightly different from the norm in that the healer works by containing the enemy rather than by repairing the tank. However, the setting's fiction naturally suggests some new gameplay possibilities:

- It would be case-based rather than quest-based. This implies some procedural generation of cases, and that many such cases would be instanced.

- The social world of the 1930s as a backdrop could introduce a contextual social world that could become the preferred experience for some people.

- Having it skill-based or reputation-based, rather than level/class-based, would be more natural. Perhaps introducing social XP leading to social levels would work?

- Espionage could be the end game?

By changing the genre to something a little different, new gameplay ideas soon follow. Rather than trying to find a genre that fits the gameplay, designers should create gameplay to fit the genre.

The Fourth Age—1995 to 1997

Of all the Ages of MMOs, the Fourth is the shortest—but for those involved, the most exciting. It's the period in which virtual worlds proved their commercial viability.

In the days before regular people had access to the Internet, they used "online services," also known as "information providers". The biggest of these, CompuServe, had *MUD1* and *Island of Kesmai*, plus a few other multiplayer games. They did not, however, make a big deal of them; then as now, parents feared that games might turn their children into axe murderers.

Other big rivals to CompuServe—Prodigy, Delphi, The Source—took a similar view. However, there were exceptions. Most prominent of these was GEnie, under the visionary leadership of Bill Louden. Its first major virtual world offering was *GemStone][* in 1988, which became *GemStone III* in late 1989; it was followed in 1990 by *Dragon's Gate* and the proven UK classic, *Federation II*.

GemStone had been written by David Whatley and his company, Simutronics, in 1987. It was an inspired-by descendant of the First Age virtual world, *Sceptre of Goth*—indeed, following *Sceptre's* demise five people who used to work on *Sceptre* were hired by Simutronics to create content for *GemStone][* (including Scott Hartsman, who later went on to become Technical Director for *EQ2*-makers SOE, then later Chief Executive Officer of *Rift*-makers Trion Worlds). The *GemStone* games were extremely well received, and despite its textual nature *GemStone IV* is still thriving today.

Dragon's Gate was designed by Mark Jacobs, who had written the First Age MMO, *Aradath*. It was programmed by Darrin Hyrup, who previously had been lead programmer for a Simutronics game, *Orb Wars*. Jacobs had tried to get *Aradath* onto QuantumLink (which was later to become AOL) but was turned down. *Dragon's Gate* was in part his response to this.

So, in order to follow what happened, you need to know something about the way these online services worked.

Basically, they charged users for the time they were connected. Back when computers were monstrous machines housed in rooms the size of a tennis court, if you wanted to use computer time you went to a computer bureau and paid for the time you used. It was natural that the online companies that grew out of this tradition should use the same pricing strategy.

It also made sense to pay the developers of products for online services a royalty. These were invariably miserable ("How do you expect us to run a service when we only keep 92% of the income *our* customers generate?"—that kind of miserable). Access to such services was expensive ($12.50/hour for CompuServe in 1990), so per-user profit was good; however, the high price deterred many potential users in the first place, so overall income was merely modest.

Then, along came the World Wide Web. Suddenly, lots of people wanted to access the Internet. A price war between the big online services in 1993 meant that now they could afford to, too. They flocked to the service providers, seeking things to do, and found, oh, look—games!

AOL noticed a sudden boost in player numbers for its innovative-but-flawed MMO *Neverwinter Nights*, and realized what was going on. It quickly lured *GemStone III, Dragon's Gate,* and *Federation II* into the AOL fold, by the simple technique of offering their developers a fair royalty. As the newbie hordes poured through the gates, usage rose spectacularly.

Thousands of players, a good royalty, per-hour charging—these were the ingredients that stoked the fires of the Fourth Age. Even the "failing" *Neverwinter Nights*, capped at 500 simultaneous users, grossed $5m in 1996.

For the 18 glorious months of the Fourth Age, the developers of AOL's MMOs wore money hats. Then, it all fell apart. Smaller companies started charging flat rates for Internet access and in late 1996 AOL had to follow suit. They couldn't keep paying royalties on a per-hour basis, and by mid-1997 the show was over. Nevertheless, *GemStone III* still managed to gross $10m from 2,500 to 3,000 simultaneous users that year.

The Fourth Age of MMO development may have been short, and it may have only involved a handful of MUDs, but it left one, lasting legacy without which we wouldn't have the MMOs of today: it caused the regular game industry to notice virtual worlds.

Wendy

Wendy's view of Neverland was as a place of fantasy—her own. She made up the world herself, instantiating her imagination by telling stories.

Wendy was engaged on a personal journey of self-discovery. She wasn't so much envisioning Neverland as envisioning herself. She had to find out who she was in life; Neverland was the metaphorical place where she did that.

Great Interfaces of Our Time—Text with Fixed Graphics

The general-purpose comms programs that players used to connect to MUDs didn't support graphics. However, if you wrote your own client (or *front end*, as they were known), you *could* add graphics to it.

Gemstone III took this approach. Here's a screenshot that appeared in some 1993 GEnie advertising material (yes, I *do* keep this stuff for decades):

As you can see, there's an illustration of a forest in the top-right corner; this would change for other types of terrain. The rest of the title bar shows health and mana bars that would be familiar to players of today's MMOs, plus other useful at-a-glance stats.

The rest of the screen is text. I nearly wrote "just text," but there was no "just" about it: this was a quality game. Check out *Gemstone IV* to see what I mean.

Originality

What color are health and mana bars?

In general, health bars are red or green (or both if you're color-blind) and mana bars are blue. If there's no mana bar, the health bar will be green but get yellow then red as damage is taken.

Why is this? They don't *have* to be colored this way. Neither do they have to fill up left-to-right, nor even be bars in the first place. Aren't designers capable of originality?

Well yes, of course they are. They deliberately follow the herd, however, because that's easier on the players. If a user interface item works and the players understand it, you need a *very* good reason to make them learn a new one.

Originality purely for originality's sake is not always a great idea. Good designers know this.

PvP v PvE

In MMOs, players sometimes compete against other players and sometimes compete against the environment. The former is PvP (player *versus* player); the latter is PvE (player *versus* environment).

Although, strictly speaking, PvP and PvE can cover all manner of activities, combat is the usual differentiator. If you spend your time fighting other player characters, that's PvP; if you spend your time fighting computer-controlled enemies, that's PvE. A server that allows PvP combat is called a *PvP server*; one that doesn't is called a *PvE server*.

Some people love PvP and some people hate it. The same can be said of PvE. It's very hard for designers to balance an MMO for both of them. It's not easy for designers to balance an MMO at all, come to that.

Client/Server

Most MMOs use a *client/server* architecture. In this, the players connect their computers (the clients) to another computer (the server). Both these terms (client and server) can refer either to the hardware or software involved. Either way, the key to this architecture is that the server alone makes all the gameplay-critical decisions, leading to what is called a *centralized* system.

Here's what one looks like (or did when we used CRT monitors):

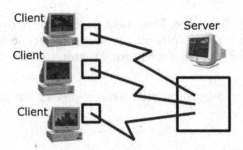

The server reflects the true state of the game world; the clients perform input/output for the server, and at best each client can only show what *was* true when the server last told it anything.

This architecture shares *some* load, but for a regular MMO the server will have to be many times more powerful than the disparate computers that are being used as clients. Indeed, for most modern virtual worlds the server isn't itself a single computer but a cluster or (for very large worlds) a grid or cloud. In any event, from the server's point of view, there's a huge bandwidth cost in dealing with all those incoming connections—far more than in a distributed system.

In other words, it's expensive.

Given this, then, why does almost every MMO out there nevertheless use a client/server architecture?

There are some legal and business reasons for it, to do with controlling the code and providing workable customer service, but what about the *gameplay* reasons?

Well, it's very hard for players to cheat on a client/server system unless the developers are naïve or foolish enough to allow the client to make authoritative decisions. When you remember that "cheat" here can mean "steal all your players," that's an important factor.

This approach is also highly resilient to client-side crashes; yes, if the *server* goes down then that's it for everyone, but if my PC dies then it's only me who's affected. The server for a well-maintained client/server system can persist indefinitely (we're already talking decades in some cases).

The fact that client/server is far easier to program than any of the alternatives is merely a happy coincidence.

ADVENT Coda

I mentioned earlier than although *ADVENT* was an influence on Roy Trubshaw when he created *MUD*, it wasn't an inspiration. His inspiration was the coming-together of a number of factors at the nexus that was his discovery of the SETUWP operating system call.

Roy wasn't the only person who wrote *MUD*, though. I co-wrote it with him. It's reasonable, therefore, to ask if I was inspired by *ADVENT* in a way that Roy wasn't, as this would add weight to the suggestion that *MUD* could be regarded as the spiritual child of *ADVENT*.

When I was at school, well before I came across *ADVENT*, I wrote a program in BASIC called *TALKER* that tried to hold a conversation with the user. It essentially worked using keyword recognition; appropriate responses were composed from canned, pre-written fragments. It was hard-coded and naïve, but surprising effective for about a minute or so. I did have a notion that I could make the computer interlocutor act as the gamesmaster of a role-playing game, but could see it would take up more computer time than we were allowed.

When I first came across a page-long transcript of *ADVENT* I was moderately pleased: it showed that what I'd imagined could be done could indeed be done. That's why I described the transcript to Nigel Roberts while waiting for free tickets to see a folk/progressive rock band in October 1978, and why he suggested I should speak to Roy Trubshaw about *MUD*.

So no, it wasn't an inspiration for me; it was more a proof of concept.

Genre Example 2

> Female, divorced, mid-30s, two
> children, WLTM new MMO.
> Highly literate, good education,
> comfortable with technology. Not
> fond of violence but is OK if
> it's cartoony. Loves history,
> finds elves so-so. GSOH.
> Serious enquiries only.

Suppose you wanted to create an MMO for the above person.

Okay, so she aches for what once was and hopes for what could once more be; she prefers mind over muscle, the subtle over the crass. The key word for her is *intrigue*. That says something like the *Scarlet Pimpernel* era, or Eleanor of Acquitaine, or the Doge of Venice.

In an historical context, gender usually plays a larger part than in SF or fantasy. Assuming we didn't want to take that particular bull by the horns, we might perhaps consider the revolutionary France setting: we could use the *liberté, égalité, fraternité* ideology as cover to give female characters on the revolutionary side freedom of action; on the aristocratic side, the privileges of wealth would achieve the same objective. Okay, so let's go with that, then.

The gameplay could involve either freeing aristocrats or imprisoning them. There might be some fancy swordplay (although never ending in death or injury; people still had *standards* back then), but there could also be some rather-more-unusual verbal battles.

Verbal battles have the potential to introduce some new techniques to combat. For example, if you say something that embarrasses your opponent, the damage it does is relative to how many people they have on their side. If they came with a lot of friends, the damage to their ego will be much worse than if only you and they heard the remark. Sarcasm works as a good riposte to bombast, but a muted one to earlier sarcasm. A joke will hurt, but only if it's not been used much before; otherwise, it could backfire and hurt you instead. There's a lot that could be done here: rudeness, playing dumb, accusations, laughing remarks off, impregnable logic, breaking down in tears; I'm sure you can think of more. Regular MMO combat has a background stream of damage that is then modulated by individual commands performed independently and simultaneously by the combatants. A damage meter is reduced until it reaches zero for one side, whereupon combat is over. The amount by which a meter is reduced is determined by a rotation of the commands available to a player: 3 clicks of this then 1 click of that, then back to 3 of this, maybe 1 of those if it comes off cooldown—all the while not standing in the fire.

What we have here with verbal battles is much the same, except it uses a turn-based approach in which what you respond is based on what your opponent just said. You have to choose from the possible things you *could* say to counter what they said, while guarding that you're not going to give them an opening to say something devastating in response.

There are plenty of games that have this kind of system in place (not necessarily for verbal combat), but it's not exactly common in MMOs. That's not what I'm getting at here, though. The point is, this came from the choice of genre. Switching from fantasy to France, 1789, naturally led to a different combat mechanic.

Genre change can do that, because it brings with it new fiction that has different requirements to traditional fictions. However, this does mean that you have to uphold the integrity of the fiction rather more than designers tend to do when it comes to fantasy.

Tanks

Yes, you know what the term *tank* means: it refers to the person who stands there taking all the damage while the healer clears it and the DPS deals it to the opponent.

What you might not know is that originally it referred to the kind of overpowered character you got in some classless systems, who could take damage, heal damage, and deal damage all at the same time. People would argue against classless systems "because then you get tanks".

Oh, how times and terms change.

Berserkers

Some of the things I added to *MUD1* I later took out. Primary among these was the *berserker* character option.

There was a command you could use to make your character a berserker. As a berserker, you got a special prompt (a > instead of a *) and double points for killing other player characters. However, you couldn't flee fights and you could never become a wiz (that is, a witch or a wizard—the game's administrators).

Berserkers were a failed experiment. They were out-and-out killer characters, and they exerted influence way beyond their number. The problem wasn't so much with the mortals who ran berserkers (they kept to the "no bullying" rules), but with the wizzes who were supposed to come down hard on mortal excesses. See, then as now, wizzes had secondary characters (*alts*, we'd call them today) and some wizzes made a berserker. When *these* berserkers misbehaved, wizzes were reluctant to interfere: they knew that the player running them would log back immediately on their wiz and argue about it.

I didn't really expect berserkers to be a success when I implemented them. It's not that I deliberately *programmed* them to fail or anything; rather, I was fairly certain that they would be abused. It turned out I was right. In that case, why did I add them in the first place?

Well, I added them for two reasons: to undermine any notion that *D&D*-style character classes should be introduced into *MUD1*; to make clear to wizzes what constituted responsible behavior on their part. I never really needed the former argument, but I often used the second one. Eventually, we wrote a document—the *Good Wiz Guide*—that formalized how wizzes should use their powers; it's still in use today.

Interestingly, *Sceptre of Goth* had a berserker-like "barbarian" class that was eventually restricted for similar reasons: it was over-powered, and when groups of barbarians came together they could (and therefore did) defeat anything that stood against them. In that respect, they were rather like real barbarians.

Great Interfaces of Our Time—Graphics Made of Text

When you're using a connection that can carry ASCII characters at a rate of about 30 per second, maximum, there isn't a great deal of scope for graphics. If potential players of your virtual world only have general-purpose client software (and we're talking raw text terminal protocols here, not even Telnet), then what can you do?

Well, you can use ASCII characters to draw your virtual world.

Island of Kesmai, by Kelton Flinn and John Taylor, did just this. Here's a screenshot (missing two lines of stats at the bottom that would mean I'd have to shrink everything so small to fit them in that you couldn't read any of it without the aid of an optical instrument):

```
[][][][]--[] orc  sword  shield  chain
[]A     S [] 1 A Jennie.c
/ >  ++++ [] 2 A 2 skeletons
[]   ++++ [] 3 B trolls
[]B    dn []
[][][][][][]
Swing hits with moderate damage
Skeleton is slain
Orc is blocked by your armour
Troll: kia ardata luuppatar ne
>throw bottle at troll
```

As you can see, the display had a map of cells (squares, but *IoK* called them hexes), each one comprising two fixed-width ASCII characters. [ ] was a wall, for example. Labels were used to refer to the contents of squares, so we can see that A contains Jennie.c and two skeletons (probably bad news for the skellies, as Jennie.c was one of the top players).

IOK was written in 1981, completely independently of *MUD*. It was a big hit on CompuServe, even though to play there at 30 characters per second (300 baud) would have cost you $6 per hour in the late 1980s—and more than double that if you used a "fast," 1200-baud modem.

Designing Is Fun

The main factor that made the Adventure '89 flowering of creativity inevitable was that designing MMOs is *fun*. Indeed, if you think about it, it's the only reason anyone *would* design them—they're not something the real world needs. As we'll see later, though, "fun" can mean different things to different people.

Of course, it isn't just *anyone* who'd design and implement an MMO: it takes a special kind of person to do it. First and foremost, the people who attended Adventure '89 wanted to create worlds. Sure, many wanted to make money, too, but that was basically an excuse: the prospect of gold raining from above was how they rationalized spending their time creating worlds. Really, though, they created worlds simply because for some people creating worlds is fun.

They were those kind of people. Are you?

Genre Example 3

How about an MMO in which the aim was to escape from a prisoner of war camp?

This would attract some of the more explorative and crafting-oriented players who are ill-served by today's combat-focused MMOs. The bulk of the gameplay would concern sneaking and hiding and distracting, rather than combat, because the guards have guns and you don't. So, we're talking a stealth MMO (without zombies, for a change).

Interestingly, when you reach Blighty, it's game over for that character. There's no endgame: you can play another character or leave on a high.

Again, see how a simple change of setting brings with it implications from the fiction that affect the gameplay.

There's no design law that says MMOs *have* to play exactly the same way.

The Tragedy of Geography

MMOs (in the form of MUDs) were invented in the UK, but we don't have many major MMO developers here. Why is that?

Well, it's because no one with money in the UK at the time MUDs made a splash believed in the concept (or, if they did, they made themselves so difficult to find that I never came across them). The underlying reason for this is the financial conservatism of the UK's banks and other investment organizations, which are famously reluctant to put money into new ventures unless you can prove categorically that you don't need it. Had MMOs been invented pretty well anywhere else in the developed world, they would have been given a much better reception than they were in England.

The thing is, though, that when they *were* (re)invented anywhere else, they never became strong enough to last. Almost every virtual world in existence can trace its genealogy directly to *MUD1*, not to other first-generation worlds. This is in part *because* of the very forces of financial conservatism that stopped us from commercializing MUDs in the first place: we were free to do whatever we liked with them. In the United States, designers spent time writing worlds they could sell; in the UK, we knew we hadn't a hope of doing that so we wrote them for fun instead. The art trumped the commerce, at least until the commerce could afford to brush aside the art.

So it is that we conformed to the traditional British stereotype of being great at inventing things but hopeless at exploiting them afterward.

Adding Coffee to Tea

If you add a drop of coffee to a cup of tea, few people will be able to taste it. If you add a couple of drops more, suddenly everyone can taste it. This is fine if you like coffee, but not so fine if you paid to drink tea.

Add too much of the real world to an MMO, and you've got the same situation.

Creating Realities

People have always created their own realities. What makes MMOs different is that now, for the first time, other people can *enter* those realities.

Great Interfaces of Our Time—Tile-Based Graphics

With your own client software and computers that can display graphics, it's not hard to see how *Island of Kesmai* could easily have been converted to use images for each square instead of ASCII characters.

Or, if the Kesmai Corporation is being slow about it, you could write your own *IOK*-like world and beat them to the punch.

Here's *Neverwinter Nights*, as it looked in AOL's advertisements in 1992:

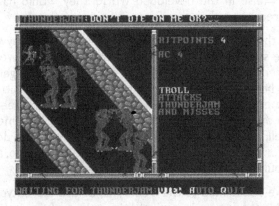

No, this isn't the *NWN* released by BioWare in 2002, nor the *Neverwinter* MMO developed by Cryptic in 2013; this is the Stormfront *NWN* from 1991 designed by Don Daglow, which I mentioned earlier when describing the Fourth Age of MMOs.

You'll notice that although the map is actually a flat tessellation of squares, some effort has been expended to give an appearance of perspective. While not entirely convincing, *NWN* was better at this than most of the other attempts that appeared at around the same time. Here, for example, is *Kingdom of Drakkar* from some 1993 MPG-NET publicity matter:

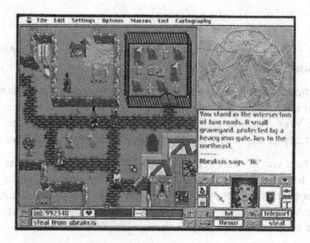

The mixture of oblique-projection walls and side-on animals and player-characters is a little, well, unimmersive.

The big filler image at the top of the right panel was for further details. If you examined your inventory, for example, you'd get this kind of thing:

Note that the command line at the bottom still uses text (it was the top line for *NWN*), and there's a separate panel for incoming messages. Even though *KoD* appeared only a year or so later than *NWN*, its interface is a lot more detailed and fussy—showing how quickly things began to move once home computers were capable of displaying half-decent artwork.

There is a modern take on this kind of thing with voxel-based worlds such as *Minecraft*. These use cubes instead of squares but otherwise work on similar principles except that no one in them looks if they're lying on their back unless they are, in fact, lying on their back.

Genre X

Suppose you're fabulously wealthy and decide to create an MMO. What genre would you choose?

Let's say you choose genre X. Of all the genres you *could* have gone for, you went for X. You don't need the money (you're fabulously wealthy), so why did you choose X? Well, X must enable you to say something that you can't say as well (or perhaps at all) in any other genre. Otherwise, you'd have chosen Y.

Designing a virtual world is an art: there are thousands of decisions you have to make, some for gameplay reasons, some for fiction reasons, some for business reasons, but ultimately they all depend on a handful of key decisions that you make because the solution "feels" right. Those are the ones that make you a designer—an artist, rather than a crafter.

Why would you choose your genre X? Seriously, why *would* you?

The Old Times

On occasion, people ask me questions about the history of MMOs. Some of these are a touch endearing.

> Q: Why did you write *MUD* as a text game instead of using graphics?
>
> A: We didn't have graphics.
>
> Q: Do you have any screenshots from *MUD*'s early days?
>
> A: We didn't have screens.
>
> Q: Were there communities on the Internet before *MUD*?
>
> A: There was no Internet.

Technology has moved on so quickly, it's hard to appreciate exactly what we had to deal with back then.

Did You Know?

Golf was invented in Egypt[19], where whatever it was known as hasn't made it to the present day. The rock tomb of Kheti at Beni Hasan[20] is adorned with paintings showing scenes of Egyptian life, its east wall focusing on sports. One vignette depicts a man swinging something having the appearance of a golf club at something having the appearance of a golf ball, with the apparent goal of ... well, much the same as whatever it was the guys in the Greek relief were aiming to do.

This painting has also been used to suggest that *Hockey* was invented in Egypt, although it might have got there from Sumeria where it was called *Pukku-Mikku*[21]. Except the Sumerians used a ring, not a ball[22].

[19]*The Complete History of Golf.* http://www.golf-information.info/golf-history.html
[20]Beni Hasan tomb BH17. This image from Wikimedia Commons, under attribution to Kurohito. https://commons.wikimedia.org/wiki/File:EgypteBH167.jpg
[21]George and Darril Fosty: *Splendid is the Sun: the 5,000 Year History of Hockey.*
[22]Society of North American Hockey Historians and Researchers: *The History of Hockey.*

Permadeath

Permadeath is a portmanteau word meaning *permanent death*. It describes the situation in which, when your character dies, it stays dead—obliterated from the database.

It's hard for modern MMO players to get their heads around the concept of permadeath (or PD as it's sometimes known). They can't really grasp the idea that a character is actually >GONE< when it's killed. Even designers don't always get it. They'll come up with ways around it, such as having clones or fighting your way out of the underworld. That's not permadeath, though. With permadeath, your character Does Not Come Back, Ever.

When the concept has sunk in, today's players tend to be aghast at the very idea. Their characters can die 10 or 15 times a night when learning a boss fight, and as for PvP, well it doesn't bear thinking about. How could they play if they kept having to restart from scratch every time their character died?!

What they don't necessarily realize is that in an MMO with permadeath *that doesn't happen*. We had permadeath in *MUD1*, and people could and did play for months without dying. They *fled* from fights they thought they were going to lose. The only times their characters did get killed were when they:

- Left it too long before fleeing

- Attacked some mobile so far out of their league that it one-shotted them

- Were set upon by so many enemies that they fled from one straight into another

Permadeath is a superb mechanic, because it adds *meaning*. Fights aren't necessarily more exciting when they involve PD, but people who enter fights knowing their character could suffer PD are of a different order compared to those who will only do it if the worse they can suffer is a wuss slap.

If you can't lose something, you don't value it. MMOs are about identity. You only really come to understand how much your character is *you* when it's in danger of extinction. *Then* you know.

Permadeath is never seen in modern AAA MMOs. Although the gameplay payload it delivers is vast, players detest it when it happens to them. That's the point of it, of course, but it's also its fatal weakness.

Real life, you may have heard, has permadeath.

MUD's Setting

Hard though it may seem to believe today, there wasn't really such a thing as fantasy back when Roy Trubshaw and I wrote *MUD*.

There was *D&D*, of course, which explicitly talked about "fantasy campaigns," drawing its sword-and-sorcery setting from the writings of Tolkien, Howard, Lieber, and (for the magic system) Vance. However, the only other games I'd played that had what we'd now call a fantasy component to them were ones I'd invented myself. As far as the general public was concerned, this was *fairytale* territory—and fairytales were regarded as being for young children.

As it happened, for *MUD*'s rewrite as *MUD1* I looked at a number of other potential genres. I ultimately went for the one I did (which I thought of as folklore) because it delivered what I wanted in terms of message: I knew that I could *speak* through it. Although I was only in my late teens, I was fully aware of what this setting could offer because of a board game I'd designed a few years earlier, *Wizards & Heroes*. I distanced myself from Gygax and Arneson's interpretation, not because I didn't like it but because they were saying different things for different reasons.

As it happened, the genre I chose was also the one that would be most enduring. There's a reason for that: the question, "why fantasy?" has an answer.

Cut from the Same Cloth

On the whole, the argument that 3D graphical worlds are somehow a different species from textual or non-3D graphical worlds is an overstatement. They *are* certainly different, in the same way that movies with sound are different from movies without sound, but underneath there are so many similarities that they can't be considered apart. There is such a large intersection between the processes involved in designing and playing both kinds of world that they *must* be regarded as essentially the same thing.

Great Interfaces of Our Time—2D Profile

IOK, NWN, and *KoD* displayed their worlds in 2D from an overhead (rendered as near-overhead) perspective. This is not the only way you can display 2D images, though. If you're going to remove a dimension, it doesn't have to be height—it could be depth.

The first virtual world to do this was Lucasfilms' *Habitat,* by F. Randall Farmer and Chip Morningstar. Here's what it looked like on a Commodore 64:

To go somewhere, you used your joystick (yes, joystick) to move your cursor over where you wanted to go, then you pressed and held the button and moved the joystick forward (the command for "go"). Then, you released the button. The screen didn't scroll: if you wanted to move to the region next door, you pointed to the appropriate edge.

By the way, the image above comes from a famous paper[23] that Chip and Randy wrote documenting their experiences with *Habitat.* You should read it, if you haven't already. It's immensely perspicacious, and has probably had more influence on MMO designers than *Habitat* itself.

Habitat was innovative but somewhat separate from the virtual world mainstream, which didn't catch up with the idea of profile-view worlds until much later. Here's a screenshot from the next one to appear, Steve Nichols' *The Realm Online* (launched late 1996). Here's a screenshot courtesy of Mobygames.com:

---

[23]Chip Morningstar and F. Randall Farmer: *The Lessons of Lucasfilm's Habitat.* First International Conference on Cyberspace, University of Texas at Austin, 1990. http://www.fudco.com/chip/lessons.html

In *The Realm*, each room is a square on a map. You can wander around freely within it, but when you leave you go to the adjacent square (left, right, up, or down—curiously *not* north, south, east, and west). Again, there's no scrolling.

Given that *The Realm* launched just nine months before *Ultima Online*, which proceeded to wipe the floor with it, you might be forgiven for thinking that this was the end for side-view worlds. Well yes, it pretty well was until *MapleStory* came along in 2003. Here's a screenshot, courtesy of Nexon.net:

MapleStory is a Korean MMO with a side-scrolling, platformer kind of movement to it. By April 2006, it had 44 million players worldwide (including 1 in 7 of the population of Taiwan). Okay, so it's "free," so those players are "players," but still!

The Fifth Age—1997 to 2012

The Fourth Age of MMOs was important not because it introduced any new design paradigms to MUDs—it didn't—but because it showed there was money to be made from them. Almost all virtual world development up until this point had been undertaken by strongly motivated amateurs making up in enthusiasm what they lacked in resources. The regular computer game industry, while aware of MUDs, regarded them as a niche genre; what the Fourth Age showed them was that okay, niche they may be, but HOLY COW, LOOK AT THEIR PROFITS!

MUDs of this era were almost all text-based. It wasn't that people hadn't thought of doing (what were at the time called) *graphical MUDs*, it was that they lacked the money to pay for the artists—and even the computers—necessary to develop them. Text adventures, which had been dominant in the mid-1980s (*The Hobbit* sold over a million copies), had completely evaporated when graphics came along. Everyone making text MUDs knew they would go the same way once someone was able to get the funding to make a decent graphical one. As it happened, we got three.

The three in question were worked on simultaneously by teams aware of each other's existence. In order of release, they were: *Meridian 59*, *Ultima Online*, and *EverQuest*.

M59 came out first primarily because it *wanted* to come out first. It launched in September 1996 in order to claim the title of the world's first graphical MUD. Nowadays, it is indeed often called the world's first 3D MMO, although actually it was only 2½D (i.e., it looked 3D but had to fake caves and bridges). Sadly, in its rush to be first, it rather hurt itself: too few people had an Internet connection or a good enough computer to run it, and those who did found a game still very thin on content.

M59 was designed by Mike Sellers, Steve Sellers, and John Hanke. It was inspired partially by *Sceptre of Goth* and partially by the *MUD1* line. Its gameplay was certainly in tune with the times, though, thanks to the influence of a new hire, Damion Schubert. Schubert had been employed on the recommendation of Raph Koster, whom *M59* had approached but were too late to sign up: by then, he'd agreed to design a different MMO.

This different MMO was *Ultima Online*, with which the Fifth, graphical, Age of MMOs truly dawned in September 1997. It needed to attract 20,000 subscribers to break even; in their wildest dreams, the developers speculated that it might get up to 40,000. It garnered 100,000 in its first six months, and over a quarter of a million at its peak. Published by Origin Systems, using Richard Garriott's much-loved *Ultima* milieu, its success established MMOs at the forefront of the computer game industry. 100,000 people paying $9.95 a month, *none* of which was going to retailers? It's hard today to imagine the impact this revelation had on games publishers.

UO didn't have true 3D graphics either. It, too, had a 2½D "height map" world, this time rendered in an isometric perspective—a trend followed in Korea by *Lineage* and still very popular in the Far East to this day. It looked gorgeous, however, and could have held onto its preeminent position had not a combination of circumstances brought it low at just the wrong time. Essentially, it was a victim of its own success: it had more players than it could deal with, both in terms of the demands on its technology and of its customer service. A big change to its PvP system proved deeply unpopular and lots of bad publicity ensued; then just at the worst possible moment, in the Spring of 1999, *EverQuest* finally launched.

EverQuest, designed by Steve Clover, Brad McQuaid, and Bill Trost, was essentially a rewritten *DikuMUD* with a graphics engine bolted on. *UO* had tried (with mixed results) to innovate with new gameplay, but *EQ* stayed with what had proven most popular in text MUDs—and so struck gold. Within six months it had overtaken *UO*'s player numbers, and it went on to double them. *EQ*'s graphics were perhaps more in line with what players of the day expected of a computer game, but it was its combination of visuals with *DikuMUD* gameplay that made it a winner. Almost all major MMOs launched since *EQ* have followed the same formula.

The Fifth Age of MMOs was where we were while MMOs strode majestically across the computer game landscape. All that was to change, however, with a simple adjustment to the revenue model.

Ultima Online

Although *Meridian 59* was released a full year before *Ultima Online*, it was the latter rather than the former that kicked off the MMO genre in earnest.

At a time when it wasn't clear whether (what would soon be called) MMORPGs could be profitable or not, the development of *UO* was a gamble. The *Ultima* series of single-player role-playing games was much-loved and respected, so the brand had a good chance of attracting players; however, if it flopped then its developer, Origin Systems, would have taken a big financial hit. Its core team was Richard Garriott (*Ultima*'s creator), Starr Long (producer), Rick Delashmit (lead programmer), and very soon afterward Raph Koster (lead designer).

UO used a 2D isometric viewpoint, as had its recent predecessors in the *Ultima* series—particularly *Ultima VIII*. This meant that some existing code and graphics could be re-used to keep costs down. The world was expansive and looked great, too (at least to 1997 eyes).

As I mentioned just now, the developers had figured they would need perhaps 20,000 players to break even and secretly hoped they might be able to manage 40,000. I myself, when asked at a conference how many players I thought *UO* would get, was ridiculed for answering "at least 60,000". We were all way off: it was the first MMO to rack up 100,000 players, and it peaked at around 270,000 in 2003.

Other developers were electrified by *UO*'s achievement: 100,000 people were paying close to $10 *every month* to play the game. Whereas before *UO*, graphical MUDs (as they were called) were all potential, *UO* realized that potential and opened the gates to riches.

Although its roots were in MUDs, *UO* brought in innovation after innovation of its own. It had skill-based combat and crafting systems that were components of a vast and complicated economic system. An archetypal sandbox game, *UO* gave its players enormous freedom to act.

Being a pioneer, though, *UO* had some unexpected problems. Although it was known from text MUDs that macros could be an issue, the scale of UO meant that macro-ing went on at an industrial rate. Likewise, although griefers in a 2,000-player MUD were controllable, they were not controllable in a world with 50 times that number of players.

The size of the world was also problematic. It was large enough to accommodate (literally, in the case of player housing) the *expected* number of players, but not the number that actually arrived. Although the economy didn't care how many players there were, it too suffered: players didn't behave as expected, leading to resource shortages that seized up part of it entirely. Dupe bugs that allowed players effectively to print their own money didn't help, either.

Penalties for character death in *UO* were stiff by modern standards (that is, it had them). Characters had to remain dead for a while or suffer stat loss to come back straight away. Players would probably find their characters' corpses looted when they got back to them, too. Given that this was a world in which player-versus-player combat was unrestricted, characters tended to die often. A reputation system called *notoriety* was introduced to warn decent players who were the bad guys, but it gave too many false positives and could itself be used for griefing purposes.

EverQuest came out at a bad time for *UO*, giving players who were complaining about the effects of unrestricted PvP somewhere else to play instead. In response, Origin created two versions ("facets") of *UO*: Felucca was the original; Trammel was the same but with only consensual PvP. Travel between the two was possible, but over 90% of the players decamped to Trammel and stayed there, leaving Felucca practically deserted. This signaled the beginning of *UO*'s decline. It lost the exhilarating, Wild West atmosphere which was central to its design, and along with it part of its soul.

UO remains to this day a remarkable and influential MMO; there's still nothing quite like it out there. Its depth and richness, its verisimilitude and its open-worldliness, are matched only perhaps by *EVE Online*; its inventiveness by nothing. It's looked back on with great affection by most of those who played it—and indeed those who are still playing it. It's a true classic; today's MMOs would not be what they are without it.

D&D and MMOs

A falsehood I often see expressed as if it were a statement of truth is that MMOs are modeled on *Dungeons & Dragons*.

Well, they're not.

D&D is but one influence among many on the design of virtual worlds, although of course some MMOs were influenced by it more than others. For example, *Ultima Online*'s fiction (but not gameplay) owes a debt to *D&D*, and the *DikuMUD*s from which most of today's MMOs descend consciously adopted several *D&D* tropes—character classes and races in particular. However, they also made wholesale use of some non-*D&D* ideas, such as a mana system for spells instead of the traditional *D&D* one-off nuclear option. They weren't modeled on *D&D*; rather, they plundered it for ideas.

Even *MUD1* did this. It had two specific *D&D* elements in it: experience points and levels. I looked at a number of possible ways to implement what I wanted to say, and chose the *D&D* mechanism for character leveling as it was the best fit. The gameplay of *MUD1* and the "virtual worldliness" of it were nothing like *D&D*, and neither were a number of other key features such as character stats and combat. Taking a handful of mechanics doesn't mean you have a clone.

So *D&D* did have some influence on *MUD1*, yes, but nowhere near as much as, say *The Lord of the Rings* (which also influenced *D&D*). I used many more ideas from role-playing games of my own invention than I did from *D&D*, and Roy Trubshaw had never even played it. Few other early virtual world developers had played it, either.

The assertion that MMOs are just computerized *D&D* does *not* come from *D&D* old-timers trying to rewrite history: they know the score. *D&D* is something special—a fictional form in its own right that isn't merely a step along the path to computerized role-playing. No, the problem comes from clueless journalists and academics trying to bluff us into believing they're competent—or from angry players who wish to belittle designers.

D&D is a wondrous game. Treating it as mere step along the way to MMOs insults it.

Why Fantasy?

Around 70% of MMOs are sword and sorcery fantasy. Around 15% are science fiction. The remaining 15% are assorted others (superhero, pirate, horror, modern warfare, whatever). Why is this?

It's actually better than it was when text MUDs were in their prime, because when we had stock MUD syndrome anyone with access to a Unix box and the Internet could download a ready-made MUD and just run it. The easiest to install and get running were *DikuMUD* and its offspring, which were almost all fantasy. This meant that perhaps 95% of Third Age text MUDs were therefore fantasy worlds.

It was a different story in the Second Age. Back then, people wrote MUDs mainly for fun, and fewer than half went with fantasy. The mix was rather eclectic, with all manner of idiosyncratic worlds. The fantasy ones tended to attract more players, though, so by the early 1990s, fantasy was dominant. It wasn't the designers who brought this about, however, it was the players.

Why, though?

Paradigm Consolidation

I wrote this in an e-mail in 2002:

> *That's one of my concerns about EverQuest's being a paradigm: people will come to think that the EQ way of doing things is "right," even though many of the early changes they made were knee-jerk on behalf of jittery management.*

Unfortunately, my concern was justified.

Great Interfaces of Our Time—2D Isometric

Even with pretend perspective, a top-down world view like *Neverwinter Nights'* or *Kingdom of Drakkar's* is still basically flat. However, if you were to give each square a height, rotate the map so you looked at the squares corner-first, and lower the viewing angle somewhat, you could get something far more persuasive.

That's what *Ultima Online* did, and here's what it looked like in contemporary publicity material:

Behind the scenes, this is still a tessellated 2D squares approach, of course, with a human-size granularity.

Lineage, which was the first behemoth of Korean MMOs, also uses an isometric perspective. It lowers the viewing angle further, which means that in theory if your character is inside a building, you might not be able to see them. However, the client helpfully makes intervening walls transparent so your view is not obscured.

Isometric interfaces to virtual worlds have many attractions, not least that you can make absolutely *enormous* landscapes quickly and comparatively cheaply. The first one I came across was *DragonSpires* in 1994, which was developed by just two people (programmer Dr. Cat and artist Manda, both of whom had worked on the single-player *Ultima* games); they followed it up with the December 1996 launch of *Furcadia*—a social world in which characters are anthropomorphic animals that's still going strong almost two decades later.

Isometric worlds can look absolutely beautiful. However, they demand a third-person perspective, which can engender an unfortunate feeling of disconnection with your character when you first start: one more obstacle to surmount when striving for immersion.

Legend

December, 2006: I pick up a copy of *Games*™, one of the more in-depth UK games magazines, and there's an article on "The Videogame Legends". Number five is Richard Garriott.

Now as far as I'm concerned Richard Garriott is indeed a videogame legend. I played *Ultimas* IV to VI and enjoyed them thoroughly.

Bizarrely, though, the write-up barely mentions the *Ultima* series. It's all-out *Ultima Online*:

> **Richard Garriott.** The so-called "Father of MMOs," Richard Garriott is responsible for introducing the world to the Massively Multiplayer RPG. Although the genre had technically existed prior to his Ultima Online, he is the man who brought the MMO template to the masses. Ultima Online, and indeed Ultima before it, proved an unbelievable success— more than outselling all its predecessors combined—and established a market that the likes of World of Warcraft, City of Heroes and Guild Wars have since exploited to the max.

When the history of virtual worlds is written, Richard Garriott is going to be regarded as their majesterial inventor, and even those who insist that the first virtual world was *Maze War* will be unable to do anything about it.

I blame his publicists.

Rank and File

Here's something you don't see a lot of nowadays.

Some of the old *Star Trek* MUDs had a system in which players took on the roles of officers on the bridges of spaceships. There would be one person controlling navigation, another monitoring communications, another in charge of the ship's systems, another on weapons, another on security duty, and a captain. There'd also be someone down in the engine room to tell you what the warp drive will and willnae take.

When you logged in, you came out of suspended animation and took your place aboard the ship. You could well find yourself as acting captain if the other senior officers were still in bed, and therefore mount away missions or change the ship's destination if you wanted. Of course, that could mean demotion if the actual captain found out and disapproved.

This mechanism integrates a number of MMO concepts in interestingly different ways. Those officer stations are basically character classes; the ship is a guild fragment; away missions are instance groups; ship-on-ship combat is a PvP raid. There's great potential to do a lot more, here.

Oh, and if you think this kind of thing is fine for small, hundreds-of-players textual worlds but that it would never scale to a tens-of-thousands-of-players graphical world, check out *Puzzle Pirates* and change your mind.

D&D Differences

In *Dungeons & Dragons*, interaction goes through the players; in MMOs, it goes through the characters.

In *Dungeons & Dragons*, people see the player first and only experience the character through the player's actions; in MMOs, people see the character first and only experience the player through the character's actions.

If you like wearing a mask, play MMOs; if you don't, play *D&D*.

Six Months of Effort

Typical anti-permadeath reaction: "You mean I could lose my character that I've spent six months of effort working on?!".

Formal response: "No, because you'll have already lost it several times so you won't *have* any characters that you've spent six months of effort working on".

Permadeath is a hard sell.

Mouse Mat

I found this old mouse mat in my almost-as-old laptop case:

It dates from about 2000 and is a screenshot of *MUD2* as it looked in the client developed for the Wireplay dial-up service. Sadly, the people who wrote this client only provided an executable and they closed their company down shortly afterward, so no one uses it today. They don't use Wireplay, either, come to that.

The mouse mat was one of two batches we had made (the first sold out). I kept this one because it wasn't printed properly—there's a white line down the left edge where it doesn't align—so I couldn't really sell it.

I'd eBay it as important MMO historical ephemera, except I get annoyed when things cost more to post than they're worth.

Why Fantasy

Science fiction is "about" ideas; westerns are "about" the loner; Greek myth is "about" power; non-game virtual worlds are "about" the community. For some people, those are also fine things for an MMO to be about, but more are attracted to the worlds in which they can become and *be* heroes than to the ones where they can't. Fantasy is "about" identity.

It doesn't matter how much wonder, optimism, iconography, ease-of-implementation, and romance an MMO has, if it's not about the character then it's not about the player. Only if it's about the player can an individual truly feel *part* of the virtual world.

That's why fantasy.

When Today Was the Future

Here's something I wrote in September, 2001:

> In 1912, the Motion Picture Patents Company was a consortium that held all the major movie-related patents. It controlled over half the 10,000 Nickelodeons in the USA and was the only organization other than Pathé in France licensed to use Eastman filmstock.
>
> This consortium held all the aces, but none of the founding companies survived the 1920s. They were geared to produce 1- and 2-reel movies only. Independents borrowed the concept of "feature" films from French and Italian film-makers and cleaned up.
>
> Are new games [MMOs] dumping outmoded ideas and forging ahead with something that has the potential to turn the market on its head?

My short answer was no, they're not.

Damn, sometimes it sucks to be right.

Great Interfaces of Our Time—2½D

Imagine a *Chess* board. Now imagine that the squares aren't flat, but are blocks of different heights. Imagine you're a pawn, standing on one of the lower such blocks, and what you'd see.

That's a 2½D world.

Okay, so any virtual world based on a tessellation of squares with a height map is, strictly speaking, 2½D. *Ultima Online* and the other isometric viewpoint worlds are all 2½D. However, they use a third-person viewpoint. The first MMO to give you a first-person view of a 2½D world—a pawn's eye view rather than a *Chess* player's eye view—was 3DO's *Meridian 59*, launched in September 1996. Here's how the Badlands area of it looks with its original rendering engine, courtesy of Brian Green:

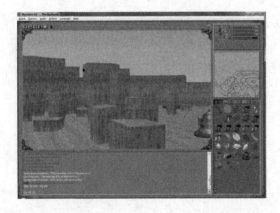

Hmm, now you *may* be thinking "hey, that looks 3D, what's with this 2½D stuff?".

Ah, well that's the thing: it *looks* 3D, but it's not. Remember the *Chess* board? Each square has a height, so you get contours, but what if you wanted, say, a cave at the bottom of a cliff and another directly above it at the top? How would you do that? You'd need for a square to have a height with a gap in it. For similar reasons, you can't have proper bridges, either.

So, the world is 2D, but the client renders it to make it look 3D: that makes it 2½D.

MUD's Combat System

This is the story of how MUD's combat system developed.

Reminder: the program known as MUD1 was actually MUD version 3. MUD version 1 was a proof-of-context written by Roy Trubshaw in October 1978 that he discarded as soon as it ran; it was replaced by MUD version 2 which was playable a few weeks later (before the end of November 1978); MUD version 3 was started in late 1979 when version 2 got too unwieldy, and I took it over from Roy around Easter 1980.

Okay, so obviously version 1 didn't have anything you could call combat in it. Version 2 sort of did: Roy had planned the too-and-fro exchange of blows that we know and love in today's MMOs, but he was so busy implementing other components that he didn't get around to it. I therefore added it myself using MUDDL, the content-creation language that Roy had built into the world. The result was pretty simple, though—basically decided on the flip of a weighted coin. If you lost, you died (permadeath); this didn't really matter, though, because there was no character advancement in version 2.

When it came to combat in version 3, the way Roy originally saw it was like this: I try to hit you, then you try to hit me, then I try to hit you, and so on, until one of us made contact and killed the other. Yes: one hit and you'd be dead. This is actually a reasonable approximation of how armed combat works in the real world: a succession of minor cuts and bruises you can shrug off until there's one, incapacitating blow. However, while discussing this design, Roy mused that he did think it was perhaps a *little* harsh, and that maybe he should give characters a number of lives—3, 5 or 10, say—so they could flee before they got killed forever.

I suggested that we should go with something more fine-grained. Give characters 100 lives, only don't call them "lives," call them "stamina". Give them another property, "dexterity," to determine their chance to hit and a third property, "strength," to decide how many stamina points they'd knock off their opponent should they succeed (affected by weapon used). Put in some randomness and some scaling, and the fights would be more exciting: if you were on low stamina then you wouldn't know for sure if you'd be hit, nor whether that hit would kill you, so you might hang on in the hope your opponent would chicken out first, or you might not risk it.

Now it's often assumed that MUD's combat system came out of Dungeons & Dragons, but it didn't. In D&D back then, characters rolled a number of dice to calculate how many "accumulative hits" they had at their level, e.g., a level 1 "fighting-man" would get one six-sided die plus 1, giving a total number of "hit points" between 2 and 7; a "super hero" would get eight six-sided dice plus 2. In combat, the way you calculated whether you hit your opponent or not was embodied in a table that cross-indexed your level and your opponent's armor class (from 2 to 9) to give a number; this number was what you needed to roll on a 20-sided die to hit. For example, a level 1-3 fighting-man against an armor class 2 opponent needed to roll 17 or more to hit, but against an armor class

9 opponent would only need a 10 or more. As for how much damage each weapon did, well it was the same for all weapons: 1 point. This changed with the arrival of the first supplement, *Greyhawk*, which modified the chance to hit by weapon type against each armor class and gave a table for damage inflicted by each weapon. Players were horrified to discover that a sword would do 1-8 damage, especially as the dice rolled to determine your hit points had also been altered (8-sided for what were now called fighters, 6-sided for clerics, and only 4-sided for magic-users and the new "thieves" they'd introduced).

So that's how *D&D* combat went. It's not how *MUD* combat went. Even today, the core of MMO combat is closer to that of *MUD* than it is *D&D*—large numbers of hit points chipped away at by variable amounts in an automated exchange, with individual commands woven in.

Interestingly, it's the same in most other computer RPGs, too. As these aren't descended from *MUD*, all the indications are that it's just one of those ideas that several people had independently. In *D&D* it would have been a pain stopping combat to calculate what 16 points off your 73-point total came to, but computers are built to do that stuff.

I sometimes wonder if the concept of permadeath would still be in use if we'd stuck with Roy's original framing of (what we now call) hit points as "lives".

Beautiful Architecture

Here's a screenshot of *Meridian 59* extracted from an early magazine review (I believe in *Computer Games Strategy Plus*, but could be wrong):

Note the caption.

This is just a sample of the beautiful architecture found in Ko'catan

However beautiful your graphics, they're always going to look poor alongside what comes out later.

Lifespans

I once suggested to MMO veteran Jess Mulligan that characters could have a finite lifetime. This would address many of the issues that would otherwise take permadeath to solve, but would wouldn't be anywhere near as painful as permadeath.

Jess's response, mimicking a player, was: "So why would I want to play your game when I know my character is going to be dead after two years no matter what I do?".

Better in relative terms can still be bad in absolute terms.

Did You Know?

Golf was invented in Rome, where it was known as *Paganica*.

Golf was invented in England, where it was known as *Cambuca*.

Golf was invented in Ireland, where it was known as *Camanachd*.

Golf was invented in Laos, where it was known as *Khi*.

Hitting a ball into a hole with a stick is an utterly *obvious* idea. Why wouldn't golf-like games be invented independently in different countries at different times?

Likewise, having a computer simulate an imaginary world is also an utterly *obvious* idea. Virtual worlds have been invented independently at least six times: *MUD*, *Sceptre of Goth*, *Avatar*, *Island of Kesmai*, *Habitat*, and *Monster*. We were *always* going to get them.

Nevertheless, it remains the case that the modern game of *Golf* is entirely the product of Scotland. Follow the audit trail back from the U.S. Masters and it ends at Scotland. That's just how it happened.

Similarly, follow the audit trail back from *WildStar* or *Guild Wars 2* and it ends at *MUD*. That, too, is just how it happened. Writing *MUD* was not an act of genius.

Okay, so I *am* a genius, but this isn't evidence of it.

Evolutionary Arguments

One of the arguments in favor of privileging graphics over text is that humans have evolved to process three-dimensional visual information efficiently.

That's true, they have; on the whole, men more so than women.

It's also true that humans have evolved to process linguistic information efficiently; on the whole, women more so than men.

Great Interfaces of Our Time—3D

Yay! At last, I've got around to talking about the predominant interface of today's virtual worlds, 3D.

Aww, you know what they look like anyway, but here's a screenshot from Sony Interactive Studios' November 1997 pre-alpha footage of *EverQuest*, which was the progenitor of fully-3D MMOs:

Okay, so the first thing to point out is that although 3D virtual worlds are 3D internally, they're not usually 3D on your screen. Your screen is only 2D (unless you're very rich and don't mind migraine-category striations across your field of view) (or you're from the future). A 3D world rendered on a 2D screen is a 2D image. MMO clients can and do present stereoscopic images, which give depth of field on the right hardware; head-mounted displays are still some way away from being a mass-market success, though.

The second thing to point out is that in 3D worlds (and *M59*-style 2½D worlds, come to that), you can move the camera around fairly freely—as much as the designer decides to allow. This means you can go with one of three basic viewpoints:

- **First-person:** See the world through your character's eyes.

- **Second-person:** See the world, including the back of your character, from a short distance behind your character.

- **Third-person:** See your character from some distance away, with other characters around having reasonably equal prominence.

"Second-person" here is actually just a short-distance "third-person". Interestingly, though, the scenery in textual worlds was actually described in formal second-person language ("You are in a vaguely circular room with a high ceiling").

The third thing to point out is that although you can indeed do caves and bridges in this 3D landscape, the vast majority of it is actually only 2½D. The tools to create the world are mainly about raising and lowering land and populating it with buildings, vegetation, and watercourses. When you do get a cave or a multi-story building, it's often a prefabricated structure (which is why so many of them have the same layout) or it's a hand-crafted set piece. This will change as the tools improve, but quite when that will be is another matter.

Of all the ways of representing a virtual world, 3D is the most costly. This is because you need a small army of developers to create it. It's to be hoped that sometime soon we'll get a critical mass of free or ultra-cheap 3D models and animations that anyone can use for their virtual worlds, so anyone *will* use them for their virtual worlds and people can concentrate on improving the way their world *is*, rather than the way it *looks*.

It might be a while yet before that happens, though.

Question Me

It's June 18th, 2015, the 200th anniversary of the Battle of Waterloo, and I am looking through the examination papers at Lincoln University in my capacity of External Examiner for their computer game modules. The following question catches my eye:

Richard Bartle famously worked on which pioneering game at Essex University?

- MUD
- Pong
- Donkey Kong
- Tetris

That's ... scary.

I was so taken aback, it was only hours later that I realized the game names hadn't been italicized.

EverQuest

Although *Meridian 59* (1996) and *Ultima Online* (1997) were both published before *EverQuest* (1999), it is nevertheless through *EverQuest* that the thread of MMO history most strongly runs. There are three reasons for this.

First, it was in the right place at the right time. *M59* was in the right place at the wrong time, coming out before the Internet was ready for it.

Second, it only innovated in one area: its graphics. *UO* also innovated in its gameplay, some of which paid off and some of which didn't. *EQ* went with straight, long-proven *DikuMUD* gameplay that was known to work.

Third, it was a good game that was well put-together. Designed by Steve Clover, Brad McQuaid, and Bill Trost from an idea by John Smedley, it was extensive and enthralling. All four had been players of text MUDs, most notably *TorilMUD* and *Sojourn* (which were set in the *Forgotten Realms* universe of D&D); they learned well from this, constructing the richly-detailed world of Norrath as their setting.

Even by the standards of 1999, *EQ*'s graphics weren't great: they were low-resolution, and the windows for chat, character stats, inventory, and the like weren't transparent. Here's a contemporary screenshot (with no windows open) courtesy of Mobygames.com:

Nevertheless, in combination with *DikuMUD's* gameplay, these graphics were still more than sufficient to attract players to *EQ*—430,000 at its peak.

Norrath was a tough environment—too tough for many of those who tried it. To advance with any speed, you needed to group with other players: this meant it needed levels of commitment that are today only occasionally present in the hardest-core MMO endgames. This gave *EQ* a high turnover of players, but while large numbers of newbies were still flocking to the game it wasn't perceived to be an issue.

EverQuest inspired a generation of MMO designers, and its most famous immediate descendant, *World of Warcraft*, inspired a generation more. *EQ* graduates now work throughout the MMO industry. Despite the fact that *EQ* has its own sequels—*EverQuest II* (2004) and *EverQuest Next Landmark* (which entered closed beta in March, 2014), the original *EQ* is still going strong. Its 20th expansion, *Call of the Forsaken*, appeared in October 2013.

As with text MUDs, we were always going to get 3D graphical MUDs: it was just a question of when. That doesn't mean that the ones we did get aren't important, though. If someone other than the *EQ* team had developed a graphical *DikuMUD*, today's MMOs would look radically different from what they do today. After all, we know today that the MMOs of tomorrow will be played using brain-computer interfaces, but someone still has to make the archetype of those worlds.

The place that *EQ* occupies among the pantheon of great MMOs is deserved. Time may have moved on, but class is permanent.

Dingday

In the old days, people remembered when they reached the top level in an MMO and would celebrate it a year on as like a birthday. This wasn't just a textual world thing, it was the case with *Ultima Online* and *EverQuest* as well.

Nowadays, who remembers when they reached the top level in the MMO they play? Who even plays one for long enough to celebrate more than one anniversary anyway?

Why is this?

Remember, we had *more* choice of what to play back in the text world days, so "next big shiny" shouldn't be a factor.

Twink

Here's a term you don't hear very often these days. A *twink* is a low-level character geared up with high-level equipment. They were more often a feature of PvP environments than PvE ones, because they looked to be easy prey when they weren't.

Twinks were invariably secondary characters (or *alts* as they are known these days—short for "alternate character," as opposed to *main* for your primary character). They were common in the past, peaking in popularity in *EverQuest*. Since then, however, level constraints on items have been introduced and twinks have all but died out. They've been replaced by hordes of alts imbued with account-specific perks that enable them to breeze through content to reach the joyous raid-and-reputation grind of the elder game that much more quickly.

Of course, if you play the right MMO then you can just *buy* a high-level character and never have to touch earlier content again. Or, indeed, never touch it in the first place.

Recovering from Death

If you don't want your MMO to have permadeath, which these days is almost certainly the case, then you have to accept that whatever fiction you come up with in the context of the MMO to rationalize *why* you don't have it is going to feel false unless it somehow explains that player characters *are* actually immortal. That is possible, of course: characters in *Asheron's Call* are brought back to life by artefacts created by Asheron, for example, and characters in the *The Secret World* recover because they, er, swallowed a bee. However, if you do take this approach then your story can't treat character death as in any way meaningful—because it's clearly not.

What you shouldn't do is waste time trying to think of ever-more-subtle refinements that get closer to permadeath without actually being permadeath, because you're never going to get close enough unless you actually *have* permadeath.

The Lion, the Corpse, and the Scratched Box

I wasn't impressed by the party composition in *The Lion, The Witch, and the Wardrobe*[24].

Had *I* been organizing the party, I would have gone for a different make-up. Lucy is a fair enough healer, but Susan makes a dismal rogue: she shoots arrows, but that's it; she's more of a ranger than a rogue. She should maybe have chosen a magic-user, she has enough attitude that I'm sure she could hurl the odd fireball if she tried. Peter's okay as a fighter, perhaps as a paladin if Edmund was also a fighter. However, I'd have maybe made Edmund be a rogue, given his sneakiness, or perhaps have him as a ranger and make Susan dual class rogue/MUser if she bucked her ideas up.

Nah, she has the bow, she should be a ranger/MUser elf; Edmund can be the rogue.

These fantasy authors know nothing about how things work. Sometimes, I think they just make it all up.

---

[24]C. S. Lewis: *The Lion, the Witch and the Wardrobe*. Geoffrey Bles: London. 1950.

MUD and Social Networks

I was once asked by a journalist what debt social networks owe *MUD*.

You know how astronomers point telescopes to far distant points in the universe and pick up radiation from the big bang that's still there but is only really noticeable if you specifically look for it? That's *MUD's* relationship to social networks.

There are so many factors involved in the creation of social networks that calling their relationship to *MUD* a "debt" is wild overstatement. There are plenty of things that MUDs can still teach social networks, but I'd have to be extremely vain to claim that today's social networks owe *MUD* or MUDs anything whatsoever.

Why MMO?

Okay, so they're currently called *MMOs*, but they weren't in the past and they won't be for much more of the future. Here's a history lesson for you that won't necessarily make a lot of sense right now, but hey, you could tell this was going to be that kind of book when you dipped inside the covers, right?

So, originally we had *MUD. MUD* stood for "Multi-User Dungeon," and it was the name of the great-great-grandfather of today's virtual worlds. Other pieces of software inspired by it were collectively called MUDs. Some of *MUD's* immediate followers used *MUG* instead of MUD, for "Multi-User Game". That never really took off, though, not least because it was too general—even something like soccer is a "multi-user game".

Around 1989/90 there was the Great Schism in virtual world development. We got a split between social worlds and game worlds. The gamers still used MUD to mean all virtual worlds, but the socials used it to mean just the game worlds, referring to the non-game worlds by whatever codebase they used (MOO, MUSH, MUCK, whatever). They used *MU** to refer to all virtual worlds, including game worlds—except for those who only used it to mean social virtual worlds.

MUD still held on as the dominant umbrella term until the arrival of *Meridian 59*. Most virtual worlds before then were textual rather than graphical; there were some with graphics, but these were called *graphical MUDs* rather than anything special. What *M59* brought (or was expected to bring) that made a difference was not the graphics *per se* but the players attracted by the graphics. Thus, we got "Massively Multiplayer Online Role-Playing Games," or *MMORPGs* for short (well, less long).

Now you might be wondering where this mouthful comes from, and because not many people actually know, I'm going to tell you.

Well no, not quite yet, obviously. That would be undramatic.

Public Quests

Public quests are quests that any player in the vicinity can join in when they appear. They were a big selling point of *Warhammer Online* and a central feature of *Rift*. They are integrated into the very gameplay of *Realm of the Mad God*. What's interesting about them is that they weren't present in *DikuMUD*; therefore, their appearance in modern MMOs is a new development.

Well, not so much "development" as "redevelopment". *DikuMUD* didn't have them, but some non-Diku text MUDs did. My own *MUD2*, for example, has an event called a "mobile bash," the aim of which is for the players to kill all the mobs in the game world within a single reset (*i.e.*, a fixed time period). The main problem with such cooperative quests lies in fairly rewarding participation. They can be a heck of a lot of fun, though!

Public quests in a modern MMO do have some issues we didn't in the old days, though, primarily because of the size of their player base. For a public quest to work, there actually has to be a public. There usually is one when a server first opens and a bulge of players works its way through the content. However, if you start six months behind everyone else then you're going to have fewer people in areas when a public quest starts. The same applies if you're running an alt. When there's only you there, this is likely to compromise your ability to complete the quest (unless there's some ghastly AI balancing system going on, in which case a passer-by or someone who comes to watch can make it worse). In other words, these things are great fun when there are lots of people running around joining in, but frustrating and samey when there are too few people to complete them.

I do agree that putting public quests into a *DikuMUD* format that has no tradition of them is a good idea, though. That's if you want formal quests at all, of course.

Peer to Peer

Most MMOs use a client/server architecture, but that's not the only way you can link computers together. The main alternative is peer-to-peer, which is the LAN game tradition.

As the name suggests, all the computers in a peer-to-peer system are equal—they all have the same responsibilities for running the game. Here's what a peer-to-peer architecture looks like:

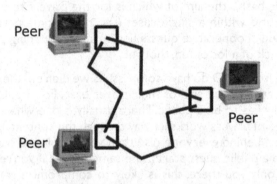

Peer-to-peer is good for multiplayer games, but not for massively-multiplayer games. It's a *distributed* architecture, which means work is shared between the computers: you don't need an expensive server to run a P2P game. Instead, it works by each computer taking it in turn to have control. What you see on your screen reflects the exact state of the game world, because your computer got to decide what that state was at the time it displayed it.

P2P games are easy to set up, and they're particularly good for people playing on the same nice, fast network.

They have some disadvantages when it comes to massively multiplayer games, though:

- Players need computers that are vaguely similar if no one is to be at a disadvantage.

- If one computer crashes, there can be technical or game-play issues as a result.

- Games stop when the players stop playing, with no saved state; there's an inherent lack of persistence.

- Because gameplay-critical decisions are made on computers controlled by the players, the software/data/datastream are open to being hacked. You have to be able to trust your fellow players.

All of these issues can be handled, mainly by massive redundancy—making decisions multiple times on different peers simultaneously talking to multiple other peers. So why don't we see P2P MMOs?

Well, there's one more disadvantage to mention:

- You only get to charge people money for P2P software once.

Why Tolkien?

Fantasy as the genre it is today owes its popularity primarily to J. R. R. Tolkien. There were other authors who wrote sword-and-sorcery before Tolkien— Robert E. Howard, Fritz Leiber, C. L. Moore, and Clark Ashton Smith spring to mind—but it is Tolkien who defined it. He created a vast, deep, and self-consistent world—exactly what MMO designers also want to do. Is it any wonder that so many MMOs are fantasy?

Well, it's not quite that simple. There are other vast, deep, self-consistent worlds out there. The *1,001 Nights* are very well-known, and have more magic in them than Tolkien; Robert E. Howard was partly inspired by these stories. Myths from Ancient Greece are also well-known, and are packed full of the kind of things that could make a wonderfully rich and exciting MMO.

Why, then, does Tolkien have such influence? And why is his work still so important for MMOs when they have fireballs and his books don't?

Different Attitudes

For some people, 80 hours of leveling in an MMO is worth paying $25 to avoid. For others, it's worth paying $25 to experience.

Sworn Statement

The developers of *EverQuest* openly admitted to having based it on *DikuMUD*. That's fine for gameplay (which can't be copyrighted, let alone patented), but not so fine for code. Even though *DikuMUD* was open source, that didn't mean its code could be used in a commercial product. Members of the *DikuMUD* community therefore sought assurances from *EQ*'s developers that they hadn't used any of *DikuMUD*'s code in *EQ*.

Here's the result[25]:

> As programmer on the server side of EverQuest on we hereby declare that:
>
> EverQuest was not based on DIKU MUD source code, nor is there any DIKU MUD source code in EverQuest. EverQuest is not a derivative of DIKU MUD. The EverQuest source code was built from the ground up. EverQuest has not, in whole or in part, infringed on any copyrighted DIKU MUD material.
>
> I hereby declare that the above is the full truth.
>
> Mr. Brad McQuaid
>
> Mr. Steve Clover
>
> Mr. Roger Uzun

With its assorted errors of grammar, punctuation, and nomenclature, this doesn't strike me as a great piece of legalistic text; however, the *DikuMUD* people were happy to accept it and that's all that matters.

The rumors alleging that *EQ* contained some of the same spelling mistakes present in *DikuMUD* continued for a while afterward, though.

---

[25]Brad McQuaid, Steve Clover, and Roger Uzun: *Sworn Statement*. March 17th, 2000.

Tolkien and *MUD*

I didn't base *MUD* on Tolkien. There isn't an orc or an elf in there, and the dwarfs are dwarfs, not dwarves. I wanted a world that everyone was bound to, deep-down, that was open-ended, that had mystery and mystique, that was known and unknown, that gave a strong sense of place, that was consistent, that had its own identity. I considered a number of possibilities, but went with what best reflected what I wanted to say: it was fundamentally Northern English, anachronistic and joyous. I used tropes that were straight out of the folk story tradition of my part of the world, because they gave me the symbols with which I wanted to create, to carry meaning. *MUD*'s "fantasy world" only aligns with Tolkien's where he used related sources.

This wasn't a genre I was unfamiliar with, either. As I mentioned in passing earlier, I (and initially two of my school friends) had designed a board game called *Wizards and Heroes*, which went through several iterations and was very unTolkien. It was pre-*D&D*, so when *D&D* came out I *D&D*ized it to see what would happen; it wasn't a success, so the next iteration I de*D&D*ized it (except I kept the priest class, which allowed for more balanced three-player games). The original character of the game, which it retained, was at times evocative of *Conan, 1,001 Nights,* and Greek myth, and from it I gained a strong idea of the match between the personality of the game world and that of the designer. Thus, when it came to *MUD*, I sought something that *felt* right. An author seeks an authorial voice; a virtual world designer seeks an authorial world. *MUD* was me, not Tolkien.

The Lord of the Rings was a big influence on *MUD*, it's true, but because of its world design, not its content: it showed what was possible. It was the sheer *scope* of it that was inspiring, not the genre nor the fantasy (as opposed to "high fantasy") aspects. For those, *MUD* owes far more to the children's worlds of Enid Blyton and *Rupert the Bear*. Also, my mother used to make up fairy stories for my brother and me when we were young, which gave both of us an enduring sense of wonder that I tried to infuse into *MUD*.

Gamer dad, fairytale-writing mum; I was doomed from the start.

Whence the Trinity?

So, combat in *MUD1* was pretty much the same as it is in today's MMOs. There were basically two ways we could have done it: automatically (you start a fight and then it continues by itself until someone dies or flees) or manually (you type a command, it does a hit, then you type another command and it does another hit, and so on). Although Roy Trubshaw and I had discussed the mechanics of individual hits, we didn't really discuss which of the two combat methods to use—Roy simply implemented the automatic version just before he handed over the program to me. I'm not sure he even considered the hit-by-hit version. I combined the two so that individual commands during combat could be used to mitigate events and thereby add some skill to the proceedings. Fights were a stream of automated events handling the main exchange of blows, but the fun came from doing other things while this was happening so as to increase your chances of winning (casting spells, shouting for help, trying to disarm your opponent, and so on).

This is how combat in MMOs still works, albeit with more spells, more buffs/ debuffs, larger fights, but perhaps fewer opportunities to interfere in creative ways with your opponent's ability to fight (such as trying to weigh them down, or trying to set fire to things in their inventory). That's at the abstract level, though: obviously, modern MMOs are a lot more sophisticated in other ways and there is some variety among them. One major paradigm-level difference from *MUD1* is the fact that today there are character classes that perform different functions—the first MUDs didn't have character classes.

Now if, back in 1978, you'd told me that there were going to be three main character classes in future MMOs, I would probably have assumed some kind of rock/paper/scissors relationship among them for reasons of balance. Archers beat infantry, cavalry beat archers, infantry beat cavalry—that sort of thing. I don't believe for a moment I'd have gone with what we have, which is the "trinity" of tank, heals, and DPS (short for "damage *per* second"—although DD for "damage dealer" is gaining increasing currency). The tank takes all the damage issued by the opponent, the healer undoes this damage, and the DPS gives damage to the opponent. This doesn't make a great deal of sense in gameplay terms: the healer is redundant (they're basically just armor for the tank), the premise is unrealistic ("I'll hit the guy in the metal suit who isn't hurting me, rather than the ones in the cloth robes who are burning my skin off"), it doesn't work for player *versus* player combat (because players *don't* go for the guy in the metal suit), and it doesn't scale (a battle with 1,000 fighters on either side—how many tanks do you need?). Don't get me wrong, it can be a lot of fun, but it's a dead end in design terms.

So how did this trinity come about?

Low Levels

MMOs today normally launch with 50 or more levels. Early MUDs had far fewer. The reason for this was because with permanent death you don't need this many.

As the effects of character "death" gradually diminished over time, we saw a rise in the number of levels that characters could achieve. The points-between-levels began to shorten, too, so that whereas in *MUD1* the points you needed to get to level *N* were double those you needed to get to level *N-1*, later games had a more logarithmic relationship between their levels. However, overall the number of points you needed to get to the highest levels were far, far more than in the earlier game worlds that had permadeath.

The end result was that in absolute terms, the number of experience points required to go up levels got astronomically larger. In *MUD1* you needed 102,400 points to reach the highest level, but eventually we saw textual worlds where the points had to be stored in floating-point number format.

Many concepts are tied to levels. What monsters drop, how much damage weapons do, how much health heals heal, how much armor blocks—they're all dictated by character levels and they all have to scale accordingly. Basically, when you're playing at one non-introductory level, it's pretty much the same as at any other non-introductory level except that all the numbers are slightly bigger.

This is where the "level inflation" we see today ultimately comes from, and why it is that a level 1 character can hit a compliant level 50 character with an axe in perpetuity without causing injury.

Second Life

Given that this is a book about MMOs, and *Second Life* is not an MMO, it does seem to get mentioned rather more than you might expect.

Well, there's a reason for that.

MMOs are game worlds, with actual built-in gameplay. *Second Life* is an example of a social world, with no gameplay. Game worlds and social worlds are subtypes of virtual worlds. Some things about virtual worlds apply to both game worlds and social worlds—their underlying technology is the same, for example. It therefore makes sense at times to talk about virtual worlds, rather than specifically about game worlds or social worlds.

Okay, so the real world occasionally makes decisions about virtual worlds. These could be cultural ("they're turning our children into flesh-eating monsters!") or legal ("they must keep a record of every player's /tell commands because they could be terrorists") or critical ("they're not as good as movies") or commercial ("they're exceedingly good value for money")—whatever. Anyway, the thing is, if you're making decisions about virtual worlds and you know little about them, you need an exemplar. For many people, that exemplar is *Second Life*.

Now you may ask why anyone would choose *Second Life* as an exemplar; after all, it's not a game. Well, there are two main reasons. First, it received a lot of publicity in its heyday and as a result is the only virtual world to have reached the consciousness of many opinion-formers and people in power. Second, as I said, it's not a game.

Oh, uniformed prejudice.

So what is *Second Life*, then? It's a first/third-person 3D world much like any other, but with no game mechanics and no underlying fiction. In their stead, it has the ability for players to create *and program* their own in-world objects. These objects are constructed from atomic entities called *prims* (short for "primitives"). Prims come in a variety of shapes (boxes, cylinders, spheres, prisms, rings, and so on) and materials (metal, stone, glass, flesh, wood, plastic, rubber, whatever). There's an in-world editor to help players cut them up, reshape them, and stick them together. Scripts can be attached to prims to give them functionality.

Now most players of *Second Life* (or *SL* for short) don't actually make anything. It's time-consuming, you need a certain amount of technical and artistic skill, and once you *have* made something it's only the reaction of the other players that determines whether you've wasted your time or not.

What most players of *Second Life* do do is socialize. They hang out together, consume indigenous *SL* content together, consume content streamed from outside *SL* together; they organize, they debate, they educate, they protest, they show off—they do all the things that they might want to do in the real world but can't because it's real.

So, just like an MMO, then, *SL* is first and foremost a place. Okay, so it happens to be one that most of the people who tried it found too boring to want to invest time in, but those who do like it tend to like it *a lot*.

When its star was in the ascendant, *SL* attracted a great deal of academic research. As a result, many of the paradigms that different academic disciplines have established with regards to virtual worlds in general came out of research into *SL*. This makes it important for MMOs, especially as a lot of that research was by legal scholars whose work informs lawmakers.

Nowadays, heavy projects dependent on building virtual constructs tend to be done in *OpenSimulator* (or *OpenSim*, as it's usually known), which is an open-source virtual world platform that's compliant with the *SL* client. *SL* itself is declining as technology and fashion overtake it; people new to virtual worlds who like the idea of making things play *Minecraft* instead. It used to have problems retaining players and making money from them; now it has problems attracting them, too.

Despite all this, *SL* is still the dominant social world, and is frequently used as a cipher to stand for all of them (much as *World of Warcraft* is often used as the canonical example of an MMO). It's already more than established itself a place in the MMO history books—a significant feat for a virtual world that specifically defines itself as *not* being an MMO.

High = Low x 1.05

High-level content isn't better than low-level content. It's the same as low-level content, except the numbers have been multiplied by a factor greater than 1.

Big N Worlds

The first textual worlds were written by players of *MUD1*. The big three were *MUD1*, *Shades*, and *Gods*, becoming the big four with *MirrorWorld*, then the big five with *Federation II*. None of these actually *were* big compared to what was to come, of course.

The first graphical worlds were written by players of textual worlds. The big three were *Ultima Online*, *EverQuest*, and *Asheron's Call*, becoming the big four with *Anarchy Online*, then the big five with *Dark Age of Camelot*. None of these actually *were* big compared to what was to come, of course.

Big N worlds show what's feasible; in the minds of the imaginative, they also show what's possible. All players want to be designers ("how hard can it be?"), but only a few actually *are* designers—most just want to play their designs. However, when you get a critical mass of design talent, you have the right conditions for a flowering such as we saw at Adventure '89.

Dimensions of Inheritance

When constructing game design family trees, you have to decide which primary dimension your tree follows.

For example, consider *Ultima Online*. This was clearly a direct descendent of Richard Garriott's *Ultima I: The First Age of Darkness*, both in terms of the fiction and in terms of the display (*UO* used basically the same engine and assets as *Ultima VIII*). However, it was also a direct descendant of *MUD1* via *LegendMUD, DikuMUD,* and *AberMUD*. So which is it to be? Is *Ultima Online* properly thought of as a descendent of *MUD1* or of *Ultima I*?

Both views are valid. In one, it's the *Ultima* universe with the addition of a new bit of technology; in the other, it's a virtual world with the addition of a particular piece of IP. Which to go with depends on the dimension of interest to you. If you're talking MMOs, then *UO* descends (directly) from *MUD1*; if you're talking RPGs, it descends (directly) from *U1*.

It would be wrong, though, to call a single-player spin-off from *UO* a descendant of *MUD1*, or to call an MMO written by *UO* designers a descendant of *U1*: the dimensions of inheritance are different.

The Elder Game

When you play an MMO, the "game" you're playing subtly changes. The core gameplay loop may be much the same at the end as it is at the start (albeit with added complexity), but your goals will have changed. This may or may not be reflected in the design of the MMO, but you yourself will certainly feel it.

The classic point at which there's a significant change for players is when they reach the game's level cap. They've effectively won the *leveling game* they were playing (gaining experience points to go up levels), so what do they now do instead?

Well, that's up to the individual player (quitting is a definite option!), but the MMO's design will usually incorporate some activities to keep the players in a kind of holding pattern until the next expansion is released and they can start leveling again. These post-leveling, pre-expansion activities form the *elder game*. It will usually involve some or all of: raiding, instance-running, resource-gathering, PvP or RvR. Naturally, any gains from these will be rendered obsolete the moment the next expansion comes out.

This is the classic form of the elder game, but other elder games are possible. In text MUDs, for example, the elder game could involve being given administrator powers. In *EVE Online*, the elder game comes up gradually, with individual players themselves making the decision to change their goals to ones that were always there but now seem more possible. Some MMOs in the

Far East don't have an elder game *per se*: the developer releases new games (rather than expansions), whereupon people leave the now-superseded MMO they were playing to try the new one, regardless of how far they'd got in the old one.

Note that although the terms "elder game" and "end game" are often used interchangeably, there is (strictly speaking) a difference: the former suggests that the player consuming the content will carry on playing; the latter suggests that the player is close to finishing. An elder game can have an end game, but an end game can't have an elder game.

Should all MMOs have an end game, or only an elder game?

Why MMO

In the mid-1990s, "multiplayer" was something of a selling point for computer games. Developers were slapping the label on anything that could cope with more than one player. This meant that calling a graphical MUD a "multiplayer online RPG" was no big deal—pretty well all online games were multiplayer.

So, there was a UK company called On-Line that developed and operated online games. It started with *Federation II*, added a dogfight flight simulator kind of game by Kesmai called *Air Warrior*, plus its own submarine combat game and at one point *MUD2*. Its managing director, Clement Chambers, said—well, why don't I let him tell you in his own words?

> Back in the day, Total Entertainment Network and Heat.net came out. They were leveraging the success of Doom, and marketing themselves as multi-player games networks providing LAN games over WLAN.
>
> This troubled me because 8-player Doom was not the kind of multiplayer game we were running. TEN and Heat had millions to spend on marketing and were miseducating people to what a multiplayer game was and could be.
>
> I thought we needed a differentiator, as they were 8 players and we were hundreds. The solution in my mind was to tag on Massively to the "multi-player". MMP was bigger, brighter and better than MP. This of course sounded grand and hit back at the 8-playerness of these new networks.
>
> I put it into a press release and after that, the massively-multiplayer nomenclature got picked up almost immediately.

I know this because Clem used the term "massively multiplayer" on me around two weeks later and, kinda liking it, I asked him where it came from. The above is a recent quote because I didn't actually remember his original answer and had to e-mail to ask.

Now that sounds cut and dried, but I've also heard persuasively that the term originated in a meeting between the developers of *Kingdom of Drakkar* and those of *Legends of Kesmai*. Perhaps, as with "newbie," it's a word that has been coined independently multiple times.

Anyway, MMORPGs as a term beat another newcomer, *Persistent Worlds*, to become the most widely-accepted. MUDs became relegated to meaning just textual worlds. Indeed, it's rare that people today believe they even qualify as being MMORPGs (which is a bit rich, given that even today the biggest textual worlds have more players than some of the graphical ones) (check out `http://mudstats.com/Browse`).

You noticed MMORPG was unpronounceable? This eventually became something of an issue. The more tongue-friendly *MMOG* appeared, but didn't really catch on for much the same reasons as MUG hadn't two decades earlier. We then got MMO, which to the untrained eye might appear even more general than MMOG, but as it's actually an abbreviation of MMORPG (rather than an acronym in its own right), this isn't the case.

Even MMO isn't going to last, though. You only have to look it up in Wikipedia, see the legion of definitions of MMO-prefixed terms that some obsessive has defined, and you'll realize its days are numbered.

For the moment, though, *you* know what MMO means and *I* know what it means, and that's all that we really need from it.

Half a Million Players

From the heyday of *EverQuest*: "half a million players can't be wrong!".

Those wouldn't include the more-than-half a million who tried it and decided it wasn't for them?

Whenever people criticize a popular game, the same old "<number> players can't be wrong!" argument is trotted out in its defense.

Yes, actually: they can be wrong. Thus, in *EverQuest*'s case, *World of Warcraft*.

Bandwidth

Ultima Online used to have more external bandwidth than all of the city of New York. *Meridian 59* used to have more than all of Silicon Valley.

Limbo

We had a place in *MUD1* called Limbo, where wizzes (administrators) put recalcitrant players to cool down. The description read:

> Everything around you is a glowing white, and there
> are no walls you can focus on. You feel as if you are
> floating on air. You are.

People in Limbo could talk to other people in Limbo (typically the wiz who put them there), but they couldn't do anything else. It had no exits, magic didn't work, and shouts didn't work. Pretty well all they could do was stew until a wiz released them. They couldn't even quit, although they could disconnect the phone to get out that way.

As far as I know, no other MMOs (apart from *MUD2*) implemented the Limbo concept, which I guess suggests that their designers were sufficiently well-behaved never to see the place. Years later, however, *Second Life* loudly reinvented the concept with its "corn field". If you hear of something like this in a future MMO, the idea will almost certainly have come from *SL*, not *MUD1*—if it hasn't been reinvented yet again (which it may have been for *EverQuest 2*'s Drunder "prison server").

First doesn't always mean progenitor.

If the Elder Game Is So Good...

Why bother with the leveling game?

We see from the traffic in top-level characters that players are eager to get to the point "where the game really begins". So why not start there? Why waste time and money implementing a leveling game if people only race through it to reach the elder game as soon as possible? You only need have one level—the "top level"—that applies to everyone. Problem solved!

If the elder game is *so good* that everyone wants it, why not give it from the beginning?

Can we all go home now?

Grinding

Grinding is when you do the same boring thing over and over again in order to reach the point where you don't have to do it.

Some players seem to think that grindy content has been put in on purpose to pad out play, with the additional effect that once you've been through it you won't want to quit because then you'd be throwing away all that work. I suppose there could be cynical MMO designers out there who might consider creating grindy content deliberately, but in the past it merely happened by accident. The designers believed that the what-turned-out-to-be grindy content was good content that people would enjoy.

Actually, they could well be right. For long-established MMOs, some of what is now considered grind content used to be "best content" when it was high-end; adding new content beyond it reduced its appeal. This seems to suggest that the best content is merely the content found where all the players are, which is to say the top-most level content. Its actual intrinsic fun value need not necessarily be all that high, but even if it is that won't save it.

Today's jewels are tomorrow's grind. It was ever thus.

The Indie Spirit

Indies shouldn't try to break into the big N comfort zone, as they can't compete on polish or content. Someone with $25,000,000 to spend developing an MMO could compete in those areas, but because they can't afford to slip up they can't compete on innovation.

The less you have, the less you have to lose. Indies can take risks. Big N gives evolution; independents give revolution.

In history-of-MMOs terms, I'm a dinosaur who isn't yet extinct. By now I really should be extinct. I *want* to be extinct! I want to be *surprised* for once! That's why I put my faith in indies: it will be an independent designer who takes MMOs in a new, undreamt-of direction.

Oh, to visit such worlds...

Two Unknowns

June 23rd, 2007. Following a ludium (that's a special conference-as-a-game thing, etymology fans) at Indiana University, I go into downtown Bloomington and seek out the local games shop. Inside, I find Randy Farmer, who has done the same thing. I buy a game he recommends, *Trains Europe*, and while I am paying for it Randy picks up a box of *World of Warcraft* collectable cards next to the checkout desk. "Molten Core Expansion Set," he reads, then adds, "I've never been to Molten Core". The lad on the till seems pleasantly pleased to find that these gray-haired guys play *WoW*.

Here's roughly how the conversation goes:

```
        LAD
You play World of Warcraft?


        RANDY
Well, I have a level 65, but I've
never been to MC as I'm not in a
raid guild.


        ME
I've pugged it a few times. I have
three 70s, a 60, and a 20-something.


        LAD
I have two 70s. Hey, I think it's
really great that people of all
ages play WoW.


        ME
Well, we have been playing this
kind of game for a while...
Randy glances at me with an "are you going to do it?" look.
        ME
What was World of Warcraft based on?
What game did the developers looked
at and think, "we can do that, only
better"?
        LAD
Er, was it called EverQuest?


        ME
That's right. Do you know what EverQuest
was based on?


        LAD
No, but I think there was some guy at
IU who gave a talk...
```

ME
EverQuest was based on DikuMUD,
which was a textual world developed
at the Datalogisk Institut Kobenhavns Universitet in Denmark. DikuMUD
was based on AberMUD, written at
the University of Wales in Aberystwyth.
AberMUD was based on MUD, written at the University of Essex in England. MUD
wasn't based on anything. I co-wrote it.

LAD
(with disbelief)
You wrote it?

ME
The first graphical virtual world was
Habitat, written in 1985 by—who
wrote Habitat, Randy?

RANDY
Randy Farmer and Chip Morningstar.

ME
We've been writing and playing these
games since before you were born.

I wouldn't normally do this kind of thing as it's boastful, but with Randy and me both there together it was just too sweet to pass up.

Making the Impossible Possible

I'm indebted to Mike Rozak for pointing out these promotional screenshots he came across.

So, this detail is from *Chronicles of Chronia: Renaissance*:

See how those windows cut right across the support beams holding up the walls?

This detail is from *SystemHolic Online Rohan*:

I love this kind of thing: the pride shown in the texture-mapping of the stones and the modeling of the statues. These are images released to impress the viewer. They largely succeed.

Except, how do those portcullises go up and down?

This is what comes of letting artists build structures in a world that has feeble physics.

Zerging

Zerging is using large numbers of weak characters to overcome a small number of powerful ones. Although the concept has a long history in MMOs, the term itself derives from *StarCraft*, which features a Zerg Swarm race designed to be used with this tactic.

In real life, zerging isn't a great approach: you only have to watch the movie *Zulu* to see why. In human combat, people are alive, wounded, or dead. If they're wounded or dead, they can't zerg; if they're wounded or alive, they can defend themselves. If they have vastly superior technology or a very strong defensive position, you have to break them by siege or go around them (which is what the Zulus eventually did at Rorke's Drift).

In MMOs, there's no "wounded" or "dead". Even dragons can be chipped away at in a death-by-a-thousand-cuts zerg attack until they eventually succumb. Players whose zerging characters are killed in such a fight just step up with their next piece of cannon fodder (which could conceivably be the one that was just killed) and join in again.

Zerging is usually considered as a dubious but begrudgingly accepted tactic in PvP; it's slightly more respectable in PvE, but not by much. It does have its positive side, in that it can be good for building a sense of community. Participating players may pay for this in self-esteem, though. The group may be strong but the individuals who comprise it, through accepting that they have to be members of the group in order to succeed, are admitting to themselves that they are weak. This can be depressing in a world built to be competitive.

Tibia

Tibia is an MMO released in January 1997, a full eight months before *Ultima Online*. It's still running. The reason it doesn't have much of a profile is that it was developed by a German company, CipSoft, and players from Brazil, Sweden, Poland, and Mexico account for half its player base. Nevertheless, it completed its first decade with around 300,000 active players, which is more than *UO* managed.

As you might expect from a product of its era, *Tibia* has 2D graphics. These don't stack up well against today's 3D graphical extravaganzas, but they did mean that *Tibia* (in the form of *TibiaME*, where the ME stands for "Micro Edition") was the first MMO to be playable on a mobile phone. Here's a screenshot from the *TibiaME* web site:

I mention *Tibia* because so few developers and historians have heard of it. It's another example of an underrated virtual world that came chronologically before its more famous peers, yet didn't have much impact at all on what came after. *Sigh*.

Victorious Factions

Most realm *versus* realm, faction *versus* faction combat never ends. One side can't completely obliterate the other.

I personally rather like the idea that one side *can* completely obliterate another. It frequently happens in real life, and in game balance terms it works so long as there's disintegration pressure on the winning side so it will be riven with internal divisions and eventually split in a civil war. That's how it happens with *EVE Online*, which allows players to form their own factions. The other obvious way to do it, espoused by *Crowfall*, is to have the conquered land itself disappear after a while so you have to conquer new lands from scratch.

Of course, letting one faction succeed isn't always going to be commercially wise. If Mordor takes over Middle Earth, all that fancy Elf and Hobbit artwork is going to be redundant.

Sixteen Permutations

Speaking of Middle Earth:

1 Aragorn

2 Arragorn

3 Araggorn

4 Arraggorn

5 Aragorrn

6 Arragorrn

7 Araggorrn

8 Arraggorrn

9 Aragornn

10 Arragornn

11 Araggornn

12 Arraggornn

13 Aragorrnn

14 Arragorrnn

15 Araggorrnn

16 Arraggorrnn

Hmm, this makes the Arraggornn my daughter saw in *Lord of the Rings Online* the twelfth least-imaginative Aragorn fan on her server.

The Elroond and Elrroond in her kinship (guild) got along famously.

Alice, Dorothy, and Wendy

Initially, we had Alice worlds. The designers of early MUDs took a *sandbox* approach—an open-ended world that encouraged players to explore both their new environment and themselves. You were given an ultimate objective (to rack up enough experience points to "win"), but as for how you achieved that, well, it was up to you. The journey was more important than the destination.

The Great Schism gave us Dorothy and Wendy worlds, and left Alice worlds behind.

The designers of Dorothy worlds took a *theme park* approach—a more closed world that encouraged players to progress through their environment while progressing as individuals. You were given signposts to follow, with all roads eventually leading to a satisfactory conclusion. The destination was more important than the journey.

The designers of Wendy worlds took a *content-free* approach—a framework world in which players could create new sub-worlds and new sub-selves (and therefore selves). You were given no objective, because people can never fully buy into a fiction that they themselves create. The creation of a destination was itself their journey.

Following the Great Schism, we arrived at the situation that still pertains today: a large number of Dorothy (game) worlds played by a large number of players; a smaller number of Wendy (social) worlds played by a smaller number of players; a *much* smaller number of Alice (balanced) worlds played by a man, a woman, and their pet dog.

Interestingly, these three world types (plus the empty world) are the very ones predicted to exist by Player Type theory, about which I'll say more later.

"Interestingly" isn't really enough, though. Can we somehow turn it into "usefully"?

Silent Movies

Interface aside, textual and graphical worlds are one and the same thing, in the same way that today's movies are in essence the same thing as silent movies but a different thing from photographs.

Of course time moves on. Fundamentally, though, all virtual worlds have a "virtual worldiness" to them that separates them from other forms of computer software. In the same way that *Casino Royale* and *Fahrenheit 9/11* can both be considered movies, WoW and SL can both be considered virtual worlds. Yes, the film shoots for a feature and (let's call it) a documentary are different, and there are subsequent design differences, but there's something about the medium itself which is inviolate and which has been there since before Charlie Chaplin made his name.

So it is with MMOs. Yes, graphical worlds do have different considerations from textual ones, but they're all part of the same medium. Those design differences don't go near the heart of what it is for something to be a virtual world; they leave it intact. Modern MMOs may ultimately have got their graphics from *Maze* or from *Spacewar!*, but they didn't get their virtual worldliness from there. They got that mainly from *MUD1* and (to a lesser extent) *Sceptre of Goth*.

Reboot

It's getting so that the development of MMOs is so expensive and risky that investors won't touch them.

It's not just "art house" or back-to-their-roots MMOs that don't get made, it's all the rest, too. For every MMO that staggers blinking into the daylight, there are hundreds that die in production—and most of the few that do appear can't be regarded as having lived up to their promise.

MMOs need a reboot.

Evolution of the Trinity

In text MUD days, physical locations were represented as *rooms*. These could be of any size, from cupboard to mountain (in the same MMO—scale wasn't constant, as it didn't have to be). Rooms were just nodes in a graph. If there were several of you in the same room, then there was no positional relationship between you, you were all just "there," milling around.

This situation worked well enough for one-on-one fights, but if there were lots of players attacking a single enemy it meant that any one (or indeed all) of them could be hit. This suggested that everyone had to be heavily armored to dull any blows against them, which reduced the ability of players to specialize. Ranged combat or backstabbing-style melée were risky options.

The way such specialization were implemented in *Dungeons & Dragons*, following the convention of miniature wargames, was based on what would happen in real life: the guys in the best armor would physically block access to the less well-armored characters by using their own bodies. This approach couldn't work in a world with the room granularity that MUDs had, though, because there was no "space" between the characters and opponents sharing a room.

The solution, which was popularized (and possibly invented) in *DikuMUD*, was to have taunting commands act to cause the opponent to attack one character in preference to others. Threat-management became a substitute for access-containment. This performed well enough under the circumstances, and added a lot to the gameplay (especially for boss fights); it was a bit of a hack, though. Nevertheless, so it was that the tank was born.

With the tank came the trinity.

When the *DikuMUD* gameplay was adopted by *EverQuest*, the trinity came with it. It turned out that players would employ physical blocking to grief one another (e.g., standing in a doorway and not budging), but using the trinity avoided that problem. Almost all of the big MMOs that came after followed EQ's lead (rather than *Ultima Online*'s, which was more hard-core), and that's why we still have the trinity today.

We don't *have* to have it, though. There have already been some experiments in allowing physical blocking, most notably in *Age of Conan*: the grief-your-own-side aspect of it was solved by only performing collision-detection between you and your enemies. However, it wasn't done in concert with any other trinity-busting activities so it wasn't as effective as it might have been in plowing a new furrow.

Physical blocking isn't the only way to replace the trinity with something more flexible and interesting, of course; there are many ways to do it. Hit location would be one way (DPS the legs and it doesn't move); speed would be another (if it can't catch you, it can't hit you); proximity check would be a third (if you're standing close to someone in armor, they're deemed to be defending you so they take the hits aimed at you). There's lots you can do. I personally *like* physical blocking, but then I also like area of effect spells to damage friend and foe equally, so I'm probably a bit too traditional for most of today's MMO players.

Anyway, I thought I'd mention this, just so that the generation of players who think their games owe nothing to text MUDs can see evidence of how the latter's legacy continues (albeit, perhaps, incongruously).

Oh, and just so you don't think I'm trying to harken back to the halcyon days of yore, I'm not: I want things to *advance*, not to go backward. If you don't know where you've been, though, advancing is that much harder.

General Ignorance

From *The Independent*, August 9th, 2006:

World of Warcraft
Said to have more than six million players worldwide, this is the grandfather of all role-playing MOGs. It was developed by Blizzard Entertainment.
www.wow-europe.com/en/

Grandfather? Two years after it launched?

Well, that's got the family tree sorted, then.

The Sixth Age—2012 to Present

The idea of using microtransactions to fund MMOs is quite an old one. In the West, it was pioneered by textual worlds, in particular *Achaea*; in the far East, it grew out of gold farming in an "if you can't beat 'em, join 'em" way. It took off quickly in South Korea and then in China. It didn't take off in the West, though.

For many years, microtransactions—or *free-to-play* as the revenue model became known—were rejected in the West. When they were tried, players avoided those MMOs. At the time, this was put down to cultural differences between the West's focus on individualism and the Far East's on collectivism.

Although cultural differences were indeed probably important, there were other factors at work. The main one arose from the fact that the longer people play MMOs, the more likely their ideas of what is fun about them are to change. They eventually drift away from the game side of things and toward the social side of things. Thus, whereas in the past they might have regarded paying real money for experience-point boost potions as being cheating, now they no longer necessarily felt that way.

The first mainstream MMO to try switching from a subscription revenue model to free-to-play was *Dungeons & Dragons Online*. It was decried and derided for doing so, but the results spoke for themselves: revenue more than doubled almost overnight.

Other MMOs followed suit, until in 2012 the dam burst and a whole cascade of virtual worlds dropped subscriptions and started charging real money for certain virtual items. Most of their players now played for free, but some were prepared to pay a little. Crucially, some of the very wealthy players were prepared to pay a *mint*.

The switch in revenue model brought with it a sea change in design requirements. New MMOs were no longer being created with the aim of giving players lots to do so they would spend lots of (subscription) time doing it. Instead, they were being constructed with the intention of being reasonably playable without payment but with lots of temptations and pressures to spend. The character of MMOs changed as a result, with most old-timers embracing the change but significant numbers—especially those self-identifying as *gamers*—leaving in dismay at what they regarded as institutionalized unfairness.

The Sixth Age of Virtual Worlds is where we are right now. As to how long we'll stay in it, well, that remains to be seen. We don't yet know how the Sixth Age will pan out, nor what will follow it; we can't even assume it will be welcome. Not all of what's on the horizon necessarily augurs well for today's MMO players (or indeed yesterday's). The Sixth Age, as with any of its forebears, could end in the death of the MMO as a viable concept or in its spectacular rebirth.

Enjoy while you can?

Chain Mail

You have to attach the loose chain vest because that makes this a proper "chain letter".

Droppable Objects

Objects in MMOs didn't used to work the way they do now. MMOs had wacky physics models in which dropping an object *wouldn't* cause it to evaporate on contact with the ground. Other people could even pick up stuff that *you* had dropped. Imagine what kind of a crazy universe you'd have to live in if that were possible in real life!

Okay, so this is indeed how the real world (let's call it *Reality*) works. Textual worlds worked the same way, because if you want to make players feel that the virtual world is real, it's easier if said players don't come across unrealistic behaviors. It's bad enough that they have to will themselves to believe that magic works; if they also have to will themselves to believe that the world's mundane physics is magical then that's unimmersive.

It's fine for textual worlds to have objects lying around on the ground, but for graphical worlds it's costly. First of all, you have to store in your run-time database the locations of whatever trash people have discarded, which clogs it up in a way that doesn't happen if you have a node-based world (as text worlds generally do). Second, someone has to create a model of the object so that you can see it on the ground (at least for 3D worlds).

Both of these are tractable problems. The first one can be solved by having objects despawn after a few minutes. The second one can be solved by having objects that are retexturings of one other or by hiring more artists. At a pinch, you can just have a "there's something here" symbol that people click on to see (as a 2D icon) what it is.

Being able to drop objects on the ground in textual worlds wasn't just for reasons of verisimilitude—it had gameplay potential. You could use objects as markers to map mazes, for example, or as traps or bait. If you're being chased by a wolf, then throwing a dead chicken on the ground might distract it (I know it would distract me!).

Nevertheless, for 3D graphical worlds, the cost of creating models for everything you want players to be able to hold in their inventory is large, so the movement away from being able to drop them was inevitable. Bonus: If you can't see that the giant moth you just killed was carrying a shield, you're less likely to think it's as ridiculous as it actually is.

Importance

MUD is not important because of its commercial success, which was only modest (some $5,000,000 a year into the coffers of CompuServe). *MUD* is important because of its ideas—because it showed what was possible, because it inspired others, because Roy and I knew what we wanted to see. *MUD* didn't take us where we wanted to go (we never expected it would), but it charted the course. I'm disappointed that none of today's virtual worlds take us where we wanted to go either, but they're further along the way. One day they'll arrive, perhaps, although I doubt I'll live to see it.

People still watch silent movies, but the only reason to make one these days is for artistic or comedic reasons. Nevertheless, the early silent movie makers were pioneers, and their influence is seen everywhere in today's movies. So it is with MMOs: Roy, I, and others in the 1980s pioneered them, but once civilization arrives then pioneers become unnecessary.

MMOs are to MUDs as talkies are to silent movies, but they're still in the equivalent of black-and-white. I don't know what will equate to color, but I do know it'll come.

Many-Tentacled Beast

There are many MMOs in the Far East. They feel somewhat different from the ones in the West. Surely *they* don't descend from *MUD1*?

Well, they do.

Most modern Oriental MMOs descend from the seminal *Lineage*, designed by Jake Song. *Lineage* is the offspring of his earlier MMO, *Nexus, Kingdom of the Winds*, which itself descends from *Baramue Nara*, which descends from *Jyuragi Gongwon* ("Jurassic Park MUD"), which descends from *LPMUD* and thence from *MUD1*.

So yes, all those MMOs in South Korea and China do indeed descend from *MUD1*. MMO history is a many-tentacled beast.

Quiz Quests

One of the innovations introduced by *The Secret World* is a real-world component to investigative quests. The idea behind this is to support *TSW* (which has a present-day setting) by seeping some *Reality* into it and seeping some of it into *Reality*. An example of the former would be a quest requiring you to know who composed *The Four Seasons*; an example of the latter would be one in which you need to discover the name of the wife of a fictional *TSW* character, to be found on his fictional *TSW* employer's actual real-world web site.

Of course, the problem with quiz quests is that as soon as one person has the answer, everyone has the answer. *TSW*'s in-game browser (a nice idea, as they can track your search queries and mine them for problems) will let you Google the question, but (for *TSW*-bleeding-into-real-world quests in particular) what Google returns first is likely to be a walk-through for the very quest chain you're following, rather than a reference to whatever information you're seeking.

Innovation is a matter of context, of course, and needless to say we had some of these out-of-game elements in *MUD1*. I was against them as a concept, as I didn't want the real world coming in to the Land (the name of *MUD1*'s world). Also, puzzles have no replay value: you need to solve one only once then any "fun" from solving it is gone. Furthermore, their answers would soon get around. I might as well just put in a lever saying "pull for treasure" for all the gameplay they added. Still, people did keep asking and asking for puzzles, so eventually I created some just to show how awful the game would be if it were filled to the brim with them. To isolate them from the rest of the Land, I put them in a single, small area: the mausoleum.

The mausoleum had eight doors off it. One was the entrance door and the rest led to tombs. Six had puzzles on them and the remaining (northeast) door was what opened if you got the wrong answer to a puzzle door (the northeast tomb contained a very nasty skeleton by way of disincentive). In *MUD2*, I added some extra puzzles and randomized which ones appeared so that people couldn't just go in and press a macro key to open all the puzzle doors at once.

Now the puzzles I came up with to put on the doors were quite varied. Here's an example:

- ls b sp cl h tcr oc bs ma lg q nhg hp sb wc ea na wa ?

The answer is eb, because those are the initials of tube stations on London's Central Line going west from Liverpool Street (ls).

Here's another along similar lines:

- AnEbArPrAyUnJl?

Months of the year without their first letter.

Some puzzles were straight arithmetic, which back in 1980 you had to write a program to solve because the numbers were too big for calculators:

- 2 to the power of 60

- The square root of 6023921858319047472771 6922039 36249

- The 142,812nd prime number

Enjoy.

Some puzzles were in code. This one is easy:

- 1854   151811475   25512121523   7185514   212215 91449715?

It's a straight letters-for-numbers thing: 18=R, 5=E, 4=D. It's the colors of the rainbow.

Temporarily diverting though such puzzles may be, the majority of players don't like them. They find it irritating to be blocked by a smug problem that they know *how* to solve but which will take them ages. It's even worse when the answer is obvious once you "get it," but you don't get it and there's no clue anywhere that would hint at it.

Such players' objection is ultimately the same as mine, in that you need *outside knowledge* to solve these wretched things. Outside knowledge of a kind is needed in MMOs anyway; there's a difference, though, between assuming that players know a key will open a locked thing and assuming that they can solve a random second-order differential equation. You can work around most normal MMO problems, but you can't work around a combination lock with a sequence based on the treble scores on a dartboard cubed or the initials of streets on a *Monopoly* board converted into numbers in base 16. Logic puzzles and quiz quests are brittle that way.

I kept all the answers to my old mausoleum puzzles. I just wish I'd written down all the reasons why the answers *are* the answers.

Timelines and Pedigrees

Internet history is often presented as a timeline.

Timelines work well when there are rich, causal connections such that everything affects everything else. In such cases, you can be reasonably sure that anything shown later in the timeline is more or less dependent on everything shown before it.

Timelines are not good when no such causal connections are in place. If you present events chronologically in these cases, you need an audit trail to be able to tie things together in a meaningful manner. A timeline is not a pedigree: merely having been first to the cut doesn't mean there was automatic influence on what followed.

The concept of the MMO has been invented independently at least six times. However, most of these inventions had little or no impact on the future development of the concept. Therefore, when it comes to understanding MMO history, the important question is not so much which one came first as which of the several ones that came first (as far as their designers were aware) produced offspring that lead to the virtual worlds we have today.

The PLATO games, for example, were certainly prototype MMOs and, depending on your definition of "MMO" and your loyalty to PLATO, some could be regarded as actual MMOs. What influence did they have on the development of today's virtual worlds, though? Almost none—they're like Chinese golf.

The second version of *MUD* had the facility for users to create new objects and commands within the game; that was indeed how new objects and commands were added to it. However, we took that out for the third version (the one that came to be known as *MUD1*). When Rich Skrenta wrote *Monster* almost a decade later (without knowing about MUDs), he incorporated the ability to add content from within the game while playing it. This feature was then picked up by James Aspnes when he wrote *TinyMUD*. If you were to look at a timeline, you would think that *TinyMUD* got its object-creation system from *MUD* because *MUD* had it first; however, the truth is that *TinyMUD* got it from the much later *Monster*.

Beware of timelines. Beware of pedigrees too, but timelines are especially good at making it easy to draw false conclusions.

Looking the Same in the Dark

For modern MMOs (ho boy, is *that* going to sound twee 50 years from now), the virtual world itself is maintained on a *server*. Players connect to it through a *client*. The client shows the virtual world to the player from the perspective of his or her character, and allows the player to issues commands for the server to execute on behalf of said character.

Or, if you're in no mood for stilted, formal language, the client is the player's window on the player's character's world.

Now, many players will look at a client and assume that this *is* the virtual world. It's not. It's just a *view* of the virtual world. Virtual worlds are maintained on the server, and they're pretty much the same in terms of how they work irrespective of what their view is like. Most famously, as I mentioned earlier, *EverQuest* replicated parts of the *DikuMUD* codebase so closely that its programmers had to sign an affidavit swearing they didn't include any *DikuMUD* code in *EverQuest*. I assume that also means they didn't use any code from the Sequent codebase, which was the heavily-modified DikuMUD derivative used for *Sojourn MUD*—the particular virtual world *EQ* designer Brad McQuaid played.

Thus, although today's players of 3D extravaganzas may look snootily down on 2½D, isometric, 2D, and textual worlds, actually all these worlds are very similar behind the scenes. 3D clients merely look prettier and give you better motion sickness.

MMO Print Magazines

There are commercially viable newsstand magazines for people who paint wargames miniatures; have blonde hair; collect diecast model cars; fly gliders; own a dairy herd; study the Wild West; are female poker players; want cannabis legalized; keep koi carp; do cross-stitching.

There are millions of MMO players out there. If the cross-stitchers have half a dozen or more magazines to choose from (and they do), why aren't there half a dozen MMO print magazines vying for our attention? It's not as if there aren't free cross-stitch sites online, just as there are free MMO sites.

The first issue of *Massive Online Gaming* came out in the Fall of 2002. The second issue didn't come out at all. The first issue of *Massive* came out in September 2006. Six months and three issues later, it closed down.

Online is best for news, because print takes time. However, a magazine doesn't have to be a news source. There are magazines for antiques, but it's not as if there are any new antiques being made. There are plenty of things you can put in a magazine about MMOs. Off the top of my head:

- Comparing the animation styles of *WildStar* and *World of Warcraft*.
- The newbie experience in today's *UO*.
- What makes *RvR* tick in *Dark Age of Camelot*.
- A look at Korean MMOs.
- The free-to-play debate.
- An analysis of tank builds in *The Secret World*.
- Maps, walkthroughs.
- Interviews with designers.
- How to run a guild.
- Your first raid.
- Children who play.
- Telegraphs: good, bad, or ugly?
- Convention reports.
- Merchandise reviews (books, games, action figures, and so on).
- How to write add-ons.

The reasons that *Massive Online Gaming* and *Massive* failed were to do with funding, not the subject matter—and certainly not the quality of writing.

The first issue of *Beckett Massive Online Gamer* came out in May 2006; the final one in January 2012. Faith can pay off.

A Brief History

MCV ("market for home computing and video games") is the weekly UK trade magazine for people on the business side of video games (mainly in marketing). You have to be in the industry to receive it, and since I am, I do. Well, I did—it's all online now,

On Friday, November 26th, 2010, it had a special, multi-page feature on MMOs. This is how the article began its history of the genre:

> **MMOs: A BRIEF HISTORY**
>
> *1975*—*The first widely used MUD (multi-user dungeon) adventure game, Colossal Cave Adventure, arrives.*
>
> *1986*—*Kesmai's Air Warrior for the GEnie online service becomes the first graphical MMOG. The firm's Gemstone II, the first MMORPG, follows two years later.*
>
> *1991*—*Neverwinter Nights debuts on AOL. It is the first MMORPG to feature graphics. 50 players can log in at once—that rises to a then-impressive 500 within four years.*
>
> *1996*—*Meridian 59 is released. The game is often credited as being the first MMO with 3D graphics.*
>
> *1996*—*Ultima Online debuts, following a series of PC RPGs.*
>
> *1999*—*EverQuest arrives.*

Well, that's my lack of a place in history assured.

I keep telling people in other countries that as far as the UK game industry is concerned, Roy Trubshaw and I never existed. They don't believe me.

Here's your evidence, folks.

Trickle-Down

Although droppable-and-pick-uppable-again objects became unfashionable in MMOs, the ability to trade items remained important. Trade, whether through a trade window or through an auction house, is vital if you want your game to have an economy—which you generally do, although they're not actually essential.

Historically the ability to transfer objects between players was still regarded as being A Good Thing even in MMOs without a complex economy. It meant that low-level characters could have access to better items when high-level characters upgraded. You would sell your +4 sword once you got your +5 sword, so a lower-level character could use it. This was called *trickle-down*, and was seen as a way of redistributing wealth.

It wasn't without problems, though.

30 Up

October 20th, 2008: *MUD's* official 30th anniversary.

It was reached without causing a ripple of interest. There were no articles in newspapers, no radio interviews, no podcasts, no blogs: the only people who noticed were the players of *MUD2* (who held a MUDmeet).

Why was this so?

Well, the mainstream media have no interest in anything but the new. That's why they call them *new*spapers. Computer games are new, MMOs are newer, so a reminder that they were invented 30 years earlier didn't sit well with the narrative.

As for the game industry, well, some old-timers know the history of MMOs and whence they came, but most of today's developers haven't a clue, nor do they feel the need to get one. They can always reinvent anything old and they see no reason to know *why* things are the way they are, just that they *are* the way they are. The ones coming out of college know all about *Pong* and Atari, but MMOs are just niche insofar as history goes. Also, they were unfashionably invented in the UK, not the United States or Japan, so don't slot neatly into a timeline (and even when they are included, there'll be 50 entries ahead of *MUD*).

MMO players themselves were unaware that it was 30 years since their hobby began. I occasionally ask those I meet in-world if they know its development history. Few are even able to cite *EverQuest* as an influence, although occasionally someone will have a stab at "Ultimate Online". With even the graphical worlds of the early 2000s forgotten, what hope do their textual precursors have? Older players have sometimes played MUDs, and recognize the connection between those worlds and today's MMOs; few know which one started it all off, though.

It's easy for me, who every once in a while is lauded as the father/grandfather/great-grandfather of MMOs (which I'm not—you want Roy Trubshaw, not me), to get the impression that MMOs are a major cultural influence of the 21st Century and that I'm a minor celebrity. In truth, though, neither they nor I are anything of the sort. MMOs will, I believe, finally reach their potential—but they haven't yet. As for me, well as I've said before, the idea of having a computer simulate an imaginary world is obvious—we were *always* going to get them. The fact that almost all today's MMOs descend directly from *MUD1* rather than *Sceptre of Goth*, *Avatar*, *Island of Kesmai*, *Habitat*, or *Monster* is mostly a right place, right time accident.

So standing back and looking at it, the answer as to why there was not a lot of fuss over *MUD*'s 30th anniversary is that in the great scheme of things, it *wasn't actually important*. The mainstream wasn't interested because MMOs haven't had much impact; developers weren't interested because the paradigm is obvious; players weren't interested because knowing doesn't add anything to their play experience; academics *might* have been interested in the historical facts, but anniversaries don't figure in their analyses.

The only people who could be expected to be interested were those who played *MUD2*, because *MUD* is their world. As their celebratory MUDmeet showed, they were indeed interested. Almost everyone else may be playing worlds that *descend* directly from *MUD*, but they're not playing *MUD*; their worlds have gone in different directions.

Which, in the end, is as it should be.

PLATO Revisionism

Every once in a while, I'll be contacted by someone I've never heard of before who is writing a book or article on the history of computer games. I'm happy to cooperate, because so much is misreported about their history that it's possible for an entirely false picture to be built up if people don't do their research. Providing that the person asking doesn't want so much information that I may as well be writing the piece myself, I'm glad to help.

Occasionally, however, the people who contact me aren't trying to obtain or verify information, they're aiming to fit an agenda. For some reason, authors writing about the early and highly influential PLATO system at the University of Illinois are the most revisionist in this regard. The vast majority of game historians obviously *aren't* revisionist, but of the ones who are, most in my experience have been writing about PLATO.

I believe the reason for this is that PLATO was the root of so many advances in computers (plasma displays, touchscreens, message boards, flight simulators, *Freecell*) that it's easy to assume it to be the root of everything. It certainly had more influence on computer games than one might expect, because of its use of graphics at a time when everyone else was using text. However, its influence on MMOs is minimal.

I do know some industry old-timers who cut their teeth on PLATO and who have influenced MMO development for the better; in particular, Gordon Walton, David Shapiro (Dr. Cat), and Andy Zaffron have made big contributions. Overall, however, the PLATO system had only a drop-in-the-ocean effect. Today's MMOs are descendents of the textual worlds invented in the late 1970s and the 1980s—primarily *MUD1* and to some degree *Sceptre of Goth*. PLATO did have its own (what we'd now call an) MMO, *Avatar*, but despite its huge popularity on PLATO it never jumped species to propagate outside of PLATO; any evolutionary path that derived from it was ultimately moribund.

I do get the impression that some ex-PLATO people (none of those mentioned above, I hasten to add!) can't quite get over the fact that there are some aspects of computer game history that *don't* have PLATO as their starting point. They like PLATO and they want it credited for its many numerous achievements, which is fair enough; it's not fair, though, when they start claiming credit for things it didn't pioneer (or, if it did pioneer them, they fell by the wayside). MMOs are one such thing.

There was a game on PLATO called *Oubliette*, which predates *MUD1* by about a year. A while back, I managed to play this on a PLATO simulator. In terms of its "virtual worldliness," I wasn't impressed: its inter-player communication was extremely limited, its inter-character interaction was nominal, and its world persistence was zero. It was close, but not close enough for me (*you* might be more forgiving, of course). In my view, it's a multi-player game, but not quite a virtual world. *Avatar*, on the other hand, is definitely a virtual world by any standards. Both, however, fall into the "golf was invented in China" category when it comes to MMO history.

If you think I'm being unreasonable, here's what the opening of the "history" section for the definition of MMORPG in Wikipedia used to say:

> The beginning of the MMORPG genre can be traced back to non-graphical online Multi-User Dungeon (MUD) games such as those developed in the late-1970s for the PLATO system. Earlier games such as *pedit5*, *dnd*, *Dungeon*, *orthanc*, *baradur*, *bnd*, and *sorcery* were multi-user games, but the players could not interact with one another. Subsequent games on PLATO, including *oubliette*, *avathar* (later renamed *avatar*), *emprise*, and *moria* allowed players to interact, including helping each other in battle and trading equipment.

You can probably trace *Avatar* back to *pedit5*, but *Avatar*'s and *World of Warcraft*'s paths don't cross. Given that most players can't even trace *World of Warcraft*'s lineage even as far back as *EverQuest*, though, does it matter if it's traced back to *pedit5* instead of *MUD1*?

Well, if history matters, it matters. If history doesn't matter, it doesn't. If it *didn't* matter, though, why would some people wish to change it?

Trickle-Down Problems

I mentioned that trickle-down as a concept had problems, which is why we don't see it advocated much today. Four in particular are worth examining.

First, it was possible to give extremely powerful objects to low-level characters (the *twinks* I described earlier). They could cut down monsters that were supposed to be challenging as if they were made of butter. What's more, they could do the same to other characters of their own level in PvP. The solution adopted for this was to put limits on what objects players could use, so a sword intended for level 50 content couldn't be wielded until you were level 40, say.

I personally don't like this approach: if you can wield a sword, you can wield a sword—the level of the sword shouldn't make much difference. What *does* make a difference is your degree of skill. I'd have liked instead for a level 10 person wielding a level 50 sword to get only a minor advantage (because it's sharper, say, but they're not skilled enough to exploit this properly). However, by this point in MMO history the ill-conceived shift of stats from character to equipment was well established, so my preferred solution wasn't an option. If you're only as good as your gear, then to stop people from becoming too good you have to limit their access to too-good gear.

The second problem with trickle-down arose because characters accumulate at the high end. This meant there were more players selling high-level things than there were buyers for them. Coupled with the inflation that typically accompanies levels (1 GP at level 20 could seem a fortune, but at level 60 could seem a pittance), this meant the higher-level objects were practically given away. Those high-level players who felt that their uber-elite armor ought to be worth more than next-to-nothing were annoyed by this. Anyone could have over-powered gear if they sought it out.

To fix this properly, gear should have been damaged more in combat (it's usually combat gear we're talking about here) and have a half life before it disintegrates beyond repair. You can imagine how popular that would have been among the players, though. The introduction of *bind-on-equip* and *bind-on-use* mitigated this by allowing players to sell stuff they found but didn't need, while preventing them from selling things they had used but no longer needed. It's a hack, though.

The third problem with trickle-down was that sometimes it was trickle-up. In worlds with meaningful penalties for getting killed, why would you send your main character into a dangerous zone when you could send in an alt whom you didn't mind getting killed? Having died on your alt a few times obtaining something stealthily, you could then pass what you got on to your main. This doesn't happen so much now, though, as MMOs have relaxed death penalties to slap-on-the-wrist level.

The fourth and final problem with trickle-down was trickle-sideways. Some objects in MMOs will be very powerful and rare. You can only get a shot at obtaining them every few days; success is not guaranteed, and even if after four hours you down the boss that *may* drop what you want, there's a good chance it won't. Ah, but what if someone *else* already has the item you want? They could give it to you! Hmm, but why would they do that if it's so powerful? Well, they might exchange it for *real* money.

What happened, then, was that people started to farm rare items in order to sell them to other players. This increased the supply of the rare items (adding some imbalance, although not show-stopping amounts) and also introduced competition to fight the bosses that dropped those items. There could be scores of people camping a location, waiting for a boss to appear so that they could attack it. Most of those people would be farmers, who were in effect imposing a toll on the regular players: if you want this rare object, that you could get far more easily if we weren't here, you'll have to pay us for it. Shifting the bosses to instanced content removed this camping aspect of the problem, but it meant that farmers no longer had to compete with each other—each group could have its own, private boss to kill. This greatly increased the supply of rare objects, which then sometimes *did* create imbalance by a show-stopping amount.

Sceptre of Goth Alumni

I always say that "almost all" today's MMOs are directly descended from *MUD*, because if I said "all" it would be untrue. A good few are direct descendents of *Sceptre of Goth*, and some former *Sceptre* players are among the most influential in the MMO industry.

Perhaps the most famous of these is Mark Jacobs. As a young, ardent *Sceptre* player, he applied for a job at InterPlay but was turned down. When InterPlay then closed his local *Sceptre* franchise he snapped and set up his own company, Adventures Unlimited Software Inc., to create a rival game that became *Aradath*. Following *Aradath*, Mark designed *Dragon's Gate*, one of the big-hitters of the Fourth Age of MMOs. He went on to design *Dark Age of Camelot* and *Warhammer: Age of Reckoning* among other titles. He's a towering figure among MMO designers, hugely respected for his passionate support of the ordinary player.

Matt Firor and Rob Denton had tried to buy a *Sceptre* franchise, but InterPlay's collapse stymied them. They set up a company, Interesting Systems Inc., which later merged with Mark Jacobs' AUSI to form Mythic Entertainment. Electronic Arts acquired Mythic in 2006 and merged it with Bioware in 2009.

- Firor left in 2006 to become president of ZeniMax Online, developers of The Elder Scrolls Online.

- Jacobs left in 2009 and set up a new company, City State Entertainment, to develop Camelot Unchained.

- Denton stayed on as Mythic's General Manager and headed up Broadsword Online Games, a studio created to develop, support, and operate DAoC and UO for EA.

Game designer and *Sceptre* player David Whatley set up Simutronics in the aftermath of the demise of InterPlay, along with former InterPlay vice-president Tom Zelinski. Simutronics enjoyed great success with its *GemStone* series of textual worlds, which still operate today. Simutronics is not just about text, though: its Hero Engine is widely admired and was chosen by Bioware for developing *Star Wars: the Old Republic*.

Scott Hartsman played on the Milwaukee *Sceptre* franchise. He was one of several ex-*Sceptre* players to work on *GemStone* for Simutronics. Scott later moved on to Sony Online Entertainment, becoming *EverQuest*'s technical director, then senior producer and creative director for *EverQuest 2*. He finally hit pay dirt as CEO of Trion Worlds, the developer of *Rift*; I have to say, it couldn't have happened to a nicer guy.

The list goes on. Andrew and Chris Kirmse formed Archetype Interactive to develop *Meridian 59*. Both were former *Sceptre* players. Wolfpack Studios, which developed *Shadowbane*, was set up by several *Sceptre* veterans, including Todd Coleman (who went on to make *Crowfall*). Brett Vickers, the lead programmer for *Guild Wars 2*, cut his teeth on *Sceptre*.

I'm telling you all this for three reasons.

First, it shows that the history of MMOs does not just begin with *MUD*. Had InterPlay not gone under, we could now be calling old textual worlds Sceptres. I greatly dislike it when people try to take credit that is not their due, but I dislike it more when people are not given credit that *is* their due; credit is due *Sceptre*'s pioneers, so I'm making sure you know that.

Second, if you know the names of designers, you know that MMOs are designed. You understand that each designer is different, with a different background and different things to say. You appreciate that MMO design is an art form.

Third, the reason these people are the important figures they are today is that they were so driven by a desire to create their own worlds that they made it happen. Sure, you may rather like the idea of building your own MMO, but do you want to do it so badly that you're prepared to throw away a promising career in law and learn programming from scratch to realize your ambition? Mark Jacobs did.

That almost all today's MMOs are directly descended from *MUD* is in part down to luck. That doesn't mean that if luck doesn't favor you, you can't make it to the top anyway, though.

Avast, Tharr, ye Avatars!

In 2001, I did some consultancy sessions for a pirates MMO (it was canned, so I'm allowed to talk about it). The idea was, the player took on the role of a ship's captain, controlling the ship while at sea but the character while ashore. This meant the player was represented by an avatar while wandering around the pirate towns, but as a ship while on the high seas.

An interesting thing about this was that although you could sink ships, the captain (that is, you) always managed to escape. Thus, although your character could never suffer permanent death, many of the beneficial effects of PD were nevertheless present if your ship-you was at the bottom of the ocean. You had to do the start-from-scratch thing, but didn't have that "oh god oh god oh god I'm DEAD" moment that can make PD so inordinately distressing.

Players of the space opera *EVE Online* will recognize this mechanism, as it's employed there. You'll generally survive as an individual (in an escape pod, or, if that gets shot up too, as a clone), but the material costs of defeat are somewhat more biting than in the likes of *WoW*.

The usual way to avoid implementing PD is to state that a character is dead when it isn't. "He killed me!," yeah, right. As *EVE* shows, though, you can also avoid it by doing the complete opposite: state that a character *isn't* dead when it *is*.

Ever Forward

What I want is for MMOs to become what they have the potential to become, not to rebecome what they once were. When I started on *MUD*, back in the late 1970s, I had to look forward because there *was* no backward to look; I still look forward, and I always *will* look forward.

When people today take a backward step, I point out what they've just lost. This may appear to be nostalgia for past glories, but I don't see it that way. For me, it's trying to drag MMOs kicking and screaming into the future, not miring them once more in the past.

BOA Constriction

In response to the problems that item-farmers introduced into MMOs, highly-desirable objects were made bind-on-pickup.

The idea was that BOP items couldn't be traded. If someone had one, the only way they could have got it was to have killed the boss that dropped it. This restored the supply to its intended levels and removed at a stroke the quite legitimate complaints coming from some players that other players were buying success.

Bind-on-account was an innovation that allowed players to transfer goods to their own twinks, but not to those of other players. It breaks the fiction of a world even more than BOP does, as an account is a concept from a reality external to that of the virtual world itself, and is therefore not something meaningful within it. You do occasionally get some scant cover, such as the legacy system in *Star Wars: the Old Republic*, but it's never natural.

My own view is that bind-on-pickup/equip/use are necessary evils in the current MMO paradigm, but that the current MMO paradigm is in dire need of an overhaul. Putting the equivalent of biometric passwords on swords makes no sense. Putting it on armor makes more sense because properly, any given piece of armor should only fit people who are roughly the same size. The way it's implemented at the moment, though, armor either fits you so well that you can't even give it to someone else (BOP) or it will fit them even if they're a female gnome and you're a male orc (because BOE makes it conform to the shape of the first being to don it).

If you want to visit another reality, it has to *feel* like a reality. It has to make sense. BOP, BOE, BOU, and especially BOA interfere with this, which is why ultimately I'd like to see them all go.

It's going to take a paradigm shift, though.

Prompt Response

MUD1 was textual in nature, which meant you typed your commands at a keyboard. Trust me, graphics don't work at all well on a 110-baud teletype printing uppercase letters onto fanfold paper.

For those of you who have never used a command line, the way it works is that the system prints a prompt to let you know it's ready to accept input. You can usually type ahead (very handy during periods of heavy use when you're watching output appear at six characters per second), but if you do then you can't see what you're typing—or you can, but it's interspersed with the output. You might therefore want to wait until there's no more output pending before you start your next command. The appearance of the prompt tells you it's okay to go ahead: the system is waiting for a command.

Different programs used different prompts. The TOPS-10 operating system upon which *MUD1* was developed used a dot prompt, for example; the BASIC programming language interpreter used the word READY.

When you're writing for a teletype, you really don't want a long prompt, so *MUD1* used a single character, a star: *. It had a different prompt when you were in wizard mode, though, to remind you that you *were* in wizard mode. Players might get upset if you forgot and attacked their character, as it would lead to its instant and permanent death.

The wizard mode prompt was the same as the regular prompt, except it was preceded by four minus signs. This meant it looked like a magic wand (on a teletype at least).

This is why, when I wrote this book, I used ----* to separate the articles. You can thank the copy editor for being spared the result.

Elder Game Emptiness

At the moment, the MMO paradigm is to have two games: the *leveling game* and the *elder game*.

As I've already explained, the leveling game is where you rack up experience points for doing stuff, causing you to go up levels and gain new abilities. Eventually, you reach the level cap. The "game" ought to stop there, but it doesn't because developers are scared that they'll lose players if they let them feel they've "finished". Thus, we get the elder game.

The elder game itself can involve many activities, but primarily comes in two flavors: the raiding game and PvP/RvR.

In the raiding game, you and your guildies spend a week in an instance dancing with buggy bosses for a shot at the last piece of top-of-the-range gear you need to complete a set that will be superseded in the next major patch.

In PvP/RvR, you spend your time fighting other players for tokens that you can cash in for gear that will enable you at last to beat the people who, if they hadn't beaten you, you would have got tokens for beating. There's a PvE variant where you collect tokens to cash in for tokens that help you collect tokens better.

Neither of these elder game alternatives has much at all to do with the leveling game. Both only put the player on hold ready for the next leveling game, which they will then consume like locusts until they're back at the elder game and are bored again.

I asked earlier why, if the elder game is so good, do we need the leveling game? Well, it's because actually the elder game *isn't* good. Raid content is fixed and too samey. Realm *versus* Realm is never resolved and is therefore pointless. PvP has a positive feedback loop, so the worse you are, the harder it is to catch up.

What we need is an elder game that is meaningful, in which players can decide for *themselves* what's fun instead of passively expecting designers to identify it for them.

Something that could help sort that out would be interesting. More than that, it would be *useful*.

Indie Development Costs

The development of early textual worlds was hindered because mainframes cost more than ocean liners. Only when PCs came out could home users think of writing MMOs. Costs were still high, but by 1989 they were tantalizingly within reach. Here's a clip from an Adventure '89 advertising flier:

> The MUG is now run on a customised 386 PC running at between 6 and 7 MIPS. The computer is estimated to have cost over £20,000.

The development of early graphical worlds was also hindered by cost: hardware, bandwidth, and artwork were the main worries. They remain expensive, to run as well as to develop, but their costs are nevertheless tantalizingly within reach. You'll make it all back once you launch, right?

Back in 1989, even small-scale textual worlds made money. Here's why (from a *MUD2* flier I handed out at the same event):

> *MUD's pricing structure is based around the "credit". Credits are units of time on the game (each one represents 12 minutes). As you play, your credit total is automatically reduced, five per hour. Credits are bought in advance. The more you buy, the less they cost. The cheapest rate works out at 50p an hour and the most expensive is £1 an hour.*

£1 of 1989 money is over £2 of today's money. Imagine if nowadays you could charge players £2 an hour—or even $2 an hour—to play an MMO! Back then, people figured that these game worlds would make money enough to fill several barns. Indeed, some actually *did* make life-changing amounts of money, but most just about broke even. Developers innocently believed that their *game* was their product, whereas actually it's the *company* that is the product; the game is merely what the company sells in order for it (the company) to be worth something.

Assuming you have a brilliant idea for an MMO that everyone will want to play, there are two ways to make eye-boggling amounts of money from it:

1. Spend eye-boggling amounts of money on development.

2. Be lucky. Indies tend to aim for this one.

For indies, it's easy to persuade yourself that just because you build an MMO, players will come, and that originality means success. Unfortunately, the stark truth is that if you aim for half a million players you will not get them. That's *not*. You can regard 100,000 as a cause for unfettered celebration and 40,000 as a major achievement; after all, you probably "only" need 20,000 to 30,000 to break even.

However, you don't actually care, do you?

Indies don't develop MMOs to make money. They develop them because they *have* to—it's their medium of expression. It's who they are. This is why if you don't *aim* for half a million users, you can still wind up with many times *more* than that number, as happened with *Minecraft* and *DayZ*.

Indie development costs, but it also rewards.

Type Systems

Type systems in programming languages are supposed to empower programmers with the ability to portray abstractions, protect them from making mistakes, help with optimization, and assist in documentation.

Speaking as an old-time hacker, this is depressing stuff. For me, type systems limit programmers their ability to portray abstractions, prevent them from making mistakes they were never going to make, help optimize code that might have run faster if the programmer could have had stronger control in the first place, and assist in documentation no more than might a decent choice of variable names.

You can say anything you like in an untyped language. In a typed language, you can only say what it allows you to say. Never mind modern languages such as C# and C++; to me, even their common ancestor, C, is over-typed. I grew up with BCPL, which is typeless (or, if you like, it has one type, the word; or, if you really like, it has an infinite number of types, just no coercion).

What's needed is data *structuring*, not data typing.

What You Need to Know to Write an MMO (1978)

Memory is made of soft-iron toroidal cores suspended across a grid of wires, with a diagonal sense/inhibit wire to read/write them.

Circuits are made of wires and gates. An *and* gate is like two switches in series; an *or* gate is like two switches in parallel. By combining and gates and (rather trickier) *not* gates, you can make *nand* gates, from which you can construct any logic circuit. One such circuit is a *flip-flop*, which has two stable states and so works as another (more power-hungry) form of memory. You can connect flip-flops in a chain to make a *register*. By passing the inputs to these flip-flops through a set of gates, you can effect operations—shifting a register's bit settings all to the left, for example (which is the same as multiplying the number the register represents by 2). Another arrangement of gates makes a circuit called a *half-adder*; combining multiple half-adders will allow you to add the contents of two registers together.

In order to decide which operation to perform on an *accumulator* register, you have a special *instruction register*. By using gates to detect combinations of bits in the instruction register, the operation it identifies can be determined. Instructions are stored in memory, and the address of the next instruction to fetch is kept in a register called a *program counter*. Having fetched an instruction, it is executed, and then the program counter is incremented so the next operation can be fetched. Operations on the program counter, such as addition, implement concepts such as jumps.

A set of panel switches load initial values into registers. This is tedious, so just enough are loaded to enable further instructions to be read from paper tape. These allow many more instructions to be loaded into memory from a magnetic tape. The program loaded from the magnetic tape is the *operating system*, which will administer the computer (for example, manage the devices that application programs run).

User programs are kept on disc packs, cards, paper tape, and magnetic tape. To write a program, you use a programming language. The first programs are entered using the panel switches; they ultimately create a program called an *assembler*, which converts human-readable *assembly language* into the binary that the computer actually executes. Assembly language is used to write the makings of a *compiler* for a high-level language. Compilers take programs written in high-level languages and drop either assembler or direct binary. Just enough of the compiler is written in assembler that the rest of it can be written in the compiler's language itself, a piece at a time across multiple iterations.

High-level languages can be used to write general-purpose programs. Almost every program is some combination of the activities performed by a compiler, a database, and/or an operating system. You need to be fluent in a high-level language before you can program much in it, but they're all basically the same when it comes down to it. Choice of language is a balance between speed of execution, speed of writing, and speed of maintenance.

To create a virtual world, you need to design your own *data definition language* to specify the virtual world. You write your own compiler to convert it into assembly language plus some intermediate code that you can *interpret* (that is, execute in software rather than in hardware). You store details about the players and the world itself in a database, which you also write yourself. When the virtual world runs, it acts like an operating system—continually processing until it is stopped, crashes, or exits gracefully.

If, when you create your virtual world, you don't know the whole story from memory cores (or their transistor equivalent) right the way up to write-your-own-compiler level, you won't be able to tweak every bit, stretch every instruction, pack every data structure or take every shortcut; less of your world will fit in the (in *MUD1*'s case) 70K of memory you get in evenings and weekends on the local timesharing system. You need to know all this if you're going to do it.

Oh, you also need that little bit at the end where you design the game world itself.

Company Organization

Regular non-game software engineering companies are usually organized along functional lines:

- Company leadership
- Sales and marketing
- Finance and accounting
- Software development, support, and quality assurance
- Operations and IT
- Human resources

There are variations of course; for example, there may be both a sales department and a marketing department, but the above structure is fairly typical.

Software development creates the products; the other divisions support the sale of these products and the running of the company itself. There won't usually be a group for product specification, though—the specification task falls to whoever sources the software. For large companies (such as banks) that have in-house programming sections, there will probably be a business development unit that does the specification.

Regular game software engineering companies (which the industry calls *developers*, or more formally, *development studios*) have a modified version of this standard organization:

- Add an art and animation section
- Add audio (music and sound effects)
- Expand quality assurance and separate it from software development
- Include a small design group

There is variation here, too; audio may be outsourced, for example.

Regular MMO software engineering companies take the modified game developer model and refine it further:

- Expand the operations section
- Expand the design group
- Greatly expand the support section and separate it from software development
- Reabsorb quality assurance into this new support section

Variation here includes combining operations and support, and some differences in the make-up of the individual sections.

Setting Up a Wargames Campaign

This is my 2nd edition (1973) copy of, well, you can see for yourself:

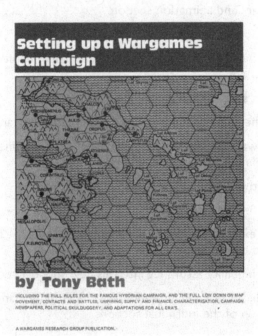

I read this cover to cover (which sounds impressive but it only has 79 pages) and used its advice to set up my own wargames campaign.

It was a time-consuming task in the days when we didn't have computers—I had to create individual slips of paper for every unit in the game, and there were hundreds of them. I worked on it on and off for several years, just about finishing it over the summer break before I went to university. This was in the belief that I'd be able to run it as a student, which unfortunately did not turn out to be the case. Maybe one day...

I mention this now to reiterate the point that I'd made many worlds before I began working on *MUD*. My wargames campaign was but one of them (albeit an alarmingly detailed one), my *D&D* campaign was another, *Dr. Toddystone* was a third, and there were others besides (at least one of which was even more detailed than any of those mentioned here).

If you want to make worlds, you can't help it: you make worlds.

Gameaholics

Every once in a while a batch of near-identical articles shows up in my Internet vanity search. They're on different sites and purport to be written by different people, but they're basically all the same. They contain a particular phrase that makes them easily recognizable: "gameaholics named Richard Bartle and Roy Trubshaw". There were close to 2,400 of these articles last time I looked (*i.e.*, just now), but the number goes up and down. Sometimes it's close to 5,000; sometimes it's in the low hundreds.

This is the kind of phrase I remember, because Roy Trubshaw wasn't and isn't a gameaholic by any stretch of the imagination, so it's basically bad journalism—or at least it's based on what was originally bad journalism. The surrounding text changes a little: sometimes we're "two" gameaholics, sometimes we're "a couple of" gameaholics, sometimes we're "a pair of" gameaholics, but the gist is always the same. These articles have been appearing for years—well over a decade.

It's clear that they go through some kind of synonym-processing to make them look superficially different while actually being the same. One of the words in their dictionary has a mistaken form, too, as can be seen in another sentence in the articles (the one preceding the one that mentions Roy's and my names). Some of the many variations of this include:

- "Whilst these types of games are widely well-known nowadays, they in fact have been in existence for quit some time"

- "Whilst these types of games are widely well-known nowadays, they actually have been in existence for quit some time"

- "While these kinds of online games are widely popular these days, they actually have been in existence for quit some time."

- "While these online games are widely popular today, they in fact have been alive for several years"

- "Whilst these sorts of games have been at large obvious nowadays, they essentially have been in life for give up the little time".

As you can see from the last one, this synonym system doesn't always work. It would still have been wrong even if they'd spelled "quite" properly in the source document.

I guess the reason they do this is in order that the pages look valid to search engines so as to give the links on the page credence, the aim being to boost their profile. Whatever, it doesn't work: as I said, I've been seeing these articles for well over 10 years, but only the newer ones show up in Google; presumably the earlier ones were detected by Google as being fraudulent and removed.

Every once in a while, though, along comes another batch.

Oh, for a Toolkit

The current vagaries of the MMO implementation process mean we have unitary, inflexible worlds that need to try to be as many things to as many people as they can be if they're to recover their development costs.

If the effort involved in developing a 3D graphical MMO dropped to that involved in developing a text MUD (i.e., roughly on a par with writing a novel) then you could make your own. If you could build your own MMO as a hobbyist; you could charge whatever you liked for people to play; you could obliterate the accounts of miscreants on a whim; you could change the physics of the world to reflect your preferred playing style—in short, you could do what the MUD community has been doing for decades.

Does it really matter that only 1,000 people are ever going to see your MMO if it's fun for *you?*

The Development Process

The development of regular computer games has three phases:

- Pre-production
- Production
- Roll-out

MMOs have a fourth phase:

- Operation

Pre-production is where the concept evaluation and project planning is done. It greatly reduces the risk of making mistakes in later phases, and therefore reduces the chance that Things Will Go Expensively Wrong. It's the most exciting part of development (especially for designers), despite the lack of resources and the time pressure that traditionally accompany it.

Pre-production normally lasts no more than six months, although for very well-funded MMOs it could be longer (I know of one that took 18 months). It results in a set of deliverables in various states of completion. These will usually include a design document, a technical design review, an art bible, a pro-duction management assessment, assorted prototypes, plus sets of incoherent notes presented in smart binders.

The production phase is where the game is actually made. This takes around 18 months for a AAA console product, and up to three years for an MMO (although this is falling). Code is created (for the game itself and for develop-ment tools), artwork is executed (object models, texture maps, sundry images, whatever), level design is undertaken (dialogue written, behaviors scripted, 240 kinds of weapon specifications specified) and the result is something playable.

Roll-out consists of two testing phases. *Alpha testing* is a form of system testing undertaken in-house by the people making the game plus senior quality assur-ance personnel. *Beta testing* is performed by trusted people from outside the team, including hard-core players from related games.

MMOs have two types of beta tests. *Closed beta* comes first, and is invitation-only. This aims to test the MMO's functionality and basic playability. It's fol-lowed by *open beta*, which allows pretty well anyone in. This further tests playability, and allows for flood testing (*i.e.*, can you *really* handle those 6,000 players per server that you think you can?); it's also seen as a marketing tool, although this can easily backfire (there are many cases where MMOs had more beta-testers than they ever got post-launch).

The operation phase (or *exploitation* phase if you don't mind the negative overtones) begins when people start being able to pay to play. Most MMO developers will take the original development team off the project at this point and switch to a *live team* (I've no idea why—developers such as Mythic and CCP, who don't do this, have much better continuity and consistency). The live team's duties include:

- Feature development
- Responding to acts of player cunning
- Network and server maintenance
- Customer and community support
- Keeping pace with technology (new hardware, new ver-sions of middleware, and so on)

Regular AAA games are also increasingly getting an operation phase, to man-age forum communities and check out user-created mods, but they're tiny by MMO standards—just one or two people normally. In contrast, an MMO that has a development team of 30 at the end of its first year (5 designers, 10 programmers, and 15 artists) will probably begin the operation phase with a live team three or four times larger than that, mainly through the addition of 100 or more customer service representatives.

Not that the players will notice any of this, of course...

Change <player>

MUD1 had a spell that would change the sex of player characters; this enabled people to do both of the (what would now be called) quests that were gender-specific, instead of just one.

I deliberately made the spell easy to cast, so that people would be tempted to use it to annoy one another. Except, because there was no real difference between the sexes, I was using it to say there was *nothing to be annoyed about*. I put in the spell and the two quests entirely so as to make a political statement about gender.

As to what the politics of that statement were, well, if I could say it in words I wouldn't have had to implement it in *MUD1*, would I?

What You Need to Know to Write an MMO (Today)

First you need to decide which kits, tools, libraries, and middleware you're going to buy in to get the following functionality:

- 3D/graphics engine/renderer
- AI engine
- Animation package
- Art package
- Asset management software
- Audio package
- Back-end billing system
- Community management tools
- Compiler/development environment
- Database
- Load-balancing system
- Network library
- Object modeling/specification system
- Patching software
- Physics engine
- Project development tools

- Security system
- Vegetation-creation tools
- Web-creation tools

Having bought them, you and your team of programmers need to know how to sew the executable ones together with your own program code, then how to code the game mechanics on top of that, plus all the project-specific tools you require, while your vast army of artists are creating the graphics you've specified.

To do this, you must have knowledge of every API (application programming interface) for every kit, tool, library, and middleware you're using.

If, when you create your virtual world, you don't know the whole story from audio package right the way up to write-your-own-planet creation tools, you won't be able to tweak every object, stretch every script, pack every data structure, or take every shortcut; less of your world will appear in the three-year window you get for its construction. You need to know all this if you're going to do it.

Oh, you also need that little bit at the end where you design the game world itself.

Trains to the Wilderness

When you start off in a new MMO, it's like arriving at a foreign railway station on a backpacking trip. With classes and "races," the designers have provided trains that are guaranteed to go to interesting places. You want to shoot fireballs? Board the mage train! Quests are the engines that pull the carriages along.

However, trains run on rails. If you want to disembark somewhere other than at a station, well, you can't. The design philosophy is all about controlling the player experience, and this same philosophy is applied for newbies and oldbies alike. It's consistent—but players themselves *aren't* consistent. Sure, when they started out they might have wanted to board the mage train, but if after watching the scenery for five months they wish to get out and explore the village of Melée Magic, they can't. There isn't a train from here that goes there.

Not all MMOs are like that, though. Some are more like hiking in the wilderness. There are few paths, and those there are often run out before reaching anywhere. You don't know to start with whether you want to climb the mage mountain or cross the healing river or cut through the forest of swords. You might even want some of all three. You will, however, find a place that's *exactly* right for you, eventually.

That's *eventually*.

The MMOs that have this design philosophy are all about emergent content, but again they apply it consistently to newbies and oldbies alike. It's great once you get into it, but you *do* have to get into it.

Ideally, MMOs should begin on rails, because most players really don't know what's ahead of them when they start out. They really do need guidance. However, after riding the train for a while they should be able to leave the rails and head off into the wilderness, because by then they have tastes too nuanced for crude character classes to capture.

In short, what we want here is for Alice and Dorothy to play together.

"I Want To Be a Lead Designer"

The lead designer is the person who is Keeper of the Vision™. Lead designers design the games.

They start off with the initial *treatment* (or vision document), and once it's accepted by whoever green-lights the project they'll develop this into a full-blown design document. They will usually keep notes to explain why they made their various decisions, but these are invariably incomprehensible to everyone, including the lead designer.

A lead designer may be the *only* designer for some games, but for MMOs they'll usually head up a team of designers.

When lead designers come from a non-programming background (e.g., they have a history degree), they will consult with the project's software planner (usually the lead programmer) to ensure that everything they want to have is programmable. The software planner will customarily lie in response, so as to make their programmers' lives easier.

This may be why many designers do, in fact, have a programming background.

What You Need to Know to Write an MMO (Tomorrow)

That little bit at the end where you design the virtual world itself.

Floral Spaghetti Strap Dress

The Secret World has a cornucopia of art bugs. I particularly like this one:

You buy a sleeveless dress, you get a sleeveless dress.

DAMN YOU

As far as playing MMOs is concerned, I'm pretty well incognito. People who know who I am in real life can find out who I play as, and people who know who I play as could find out who I am in real life, but neither group has any particular incentive to do either.

Hmm, I'm sure some of those instances of "who" there should have been "whom".

So, back in 2010, I was doing some wretched Valentine's Day quest in WoW to get a pretty frock or something and I received a tell from one of the very few players who did know my name: "Did you see that?".

"See what?" I replied.

"The shout!"

Okay, so I'd installed an add-on to filter out shouts and non-trade trade channel messages, in order not to have to subject myself to whatever conversations the resident 15-year-olds might wish to share with me; consequently, I hadn't seen any shout. However, I checked the add-on's equivalent of the Deleted Items folder and found this:

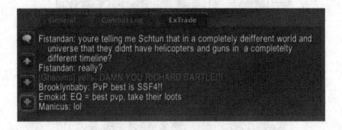

I'm almost certain that whoever it was who shouted those words had no idea that Richard Bartle was playing on that very server at that very moment, so it must have been that they were taking my name in vain because they actually felt I was in some small way responsible for whatever it was that was annoying them.

That's kinda cool, actually! Except, of course, it should have been DAMN YOU RICHARD BARTLE AND ROY TRUBSHAW!!!

What You Need to Know About What You Needed to Know to Write an MMO (1978)

Only having read what I've written do I now realize how arcane what I wrote must seem to most of the readers of this book. It's like something out of *Finnegans Wake*. Words with Chinese-whisper meanings drift gloriously between structural ones that convey form but not content.

In MMO terms, no one needs to know any of this, but someone *needs to have known it*. It's a "deeper magic from before the dawn of time," that informs all but has lost its meaning.

Rather like me, really.

So much knowledge, so little use.

DIY Options

If you're thinking of making your own MMO, you basically have five options:

- Write everything from first principles.
- Use a commercial MMO engine.
- Use an MMO software development kit.
- Use an integrated creation and hosting solution.
- Embed it within a host virtual world.

Writing from first principles gives the most control, but involves a great deal of effort, which costs a great deal of money. It is in attempting to avoid this expense that the other options have arisen.

We got all of these options with textual worlds, but with graphical worlds only the first has resulted in commercial success. The rest have been tried, but none have yet taken off.

So, there's a bit of will-the-future-repeat-the-past? for you to ponder on.

Alice and Dorothy Play Together

The central design philosophy of Dorothy worlds is one of direction: Dorothy is wary of the new world she finds herself in and wants a path she can follow to get through it. She's about *structure*. She represents modern game worlds epitomized by *World of Warcraft*.

The central design philosophy of Alice worlds is one of being: Alice finds merely existing in the new world interesting. She's about *freedom*. She represents old-style balanced worlds such as *MUD1*.

The central design philosophy of Wendy worlds is one of expression: Wendy wants to live in the personal fantasy that she has created. She's about *statement*. She represents the modern social worlds such as *Second Life*.

Because of the Great Schism, Wendy worlds define themselves as *not* being Alice or Dorothy worlds. Dorothy worlds define themselves as *not* being Alice or Wendy worlds. Alice worlds look on both as estranged children. History has locked Wendy and Dorothy worlds into design philosophies that concern what these worlds *aren't* almost as much as what they *are*.

Alice worlds are newbie-unfriendly but provide the depth and freedom that oldbies crave. Dorothy worlds are very newbie-friendly but oldbies who don't want their hands held feel disenchanted. So, why not start off as a Dorothy world and then switch to Alice for the elder game? These decades-old philosophical differences have to persist no longer!

How this would work: you'd start off using a character pack optimized for one kind of experience (say, mage). You can diverge from it any time you like, but are given advice so you can't do it without knowing what you're letting yourself in for. Quests will initially be hand-crafted, but the more you play then the more will emerge from player interactions (such as putting want ads in an auction house, but potentially much more complex than this). Eventually, you'll segue into a freeform game.

Alice and Dorothy can play together because they both have the conceit that they're separated from *Reality*. This is possible because both are in worlds not of their own making. Sadly, Wendy *is* in a world of her own making. She can build Alice and Dorothy their own Wendy houses to play *in*, but she can't play *with* them. They can still be friends, of course, they just can't play together.

Today's MMOs are victims of their own orthodoxies. They operate within artificial boundaries for obscure historical reasons few people are aware of any more. Players and designers sense there's *something* wrong, but not quite *what*. Fortunately, by understanding the cause, the effect is easily removed.

As a final word of caution here, I'm not saying that how things once were means that's how they should be. History can inform the present and the future, but it shouldn't dictate it. Times change.

Nevertheless, Alice and Dorothy *can* play together, and we'd get better MMOs if they did.

"I Want To Be a Level Designer"

No, you *actually* want to be a *lead* designer; you're only a level designer because that's one of the steps on the ladder.

Level designers create episodic gameplay experiences within the framework of the overall design. The name "level designer" comes from the practice of assigning the creation of self-contained game levels in early games to junior designers. Nowadays, it just means a junior designer (but is still hanging on as an authentic job title).

Level designers often work with tools created by the programming team specifically for them. For example, a level designer for an MMO might have the job of creating monsters. Said designer will find out from the senior designers (the *content* team—that's content as in "contained by," not as in "at peace with the world") what monsters are allowed that will fit the fiction and animation, then having chosen one he or she will design its properties and behaviors by filling in fields in a design tool's window.

Level designers can also write a lot of scripts. This is another reason why it's useful for designers to have programming experience.

"I Want To Be a Lead Programmer"

Why?

The lead programmer (who will often double as the software planner *and* the lead architect) is basically responsible for the integrity of the project's software. They monitor the other programmers to make sure they're doing what they're supposed to be doing and are on schedule. If they find any problems, they'll set the producer on the offenders.

Almost always, the lead programmer will be the most technically able programmer on the team. The role therefore carries much kudos among programmers. However, because they have to manage the other programmers, lead programmers typically only spend half to three quarters of their time actually programming, which is a clear waste of their skills that developers nevertheless seem happy to accept.

Given that programmers program because they like programming, though, why would they *want* to be a lead programmer if that means giving up time they could spend programming?

Hmm, well, they are *paid* more than regular programmers.

Plodding

In the text MUD days, we regarded time as a poor substitute for skill. If you could get to the top through time alone, with little or no skill, we called it *plodding*; it was regarded as A Bad Thing.

Today's MMOs actually protect plodding as a leveling strategy. Spend enough time trying to get to the level cap and you will indeed get to the level cap. There's nothing to stop you. Worse, you actually *need* to spend the time to get there, rather than blitzing your way through because you're skillful.

The fact that plodders outnumber non-plodders probably explains this.

Back from the Mists of Time

Every so often, I receive invitations to attend industry conferences ("a whole day for only £816.63!") sent by people whose actual understanding of the industry is so limited that they don't know why they shouldn't be sending such invitations to me. These conferences invariably include perennially favorite topics such as "the importance of community," "multi-player management," and "business models" that were old when I went to the predecessors of these conferences in 1995.

I don't know whether this is a good thing or a bad thing. I don't know whether to be amused or disgruntled.

I must be getting old when not only do I have a sense of *déjà vu*, but I have a particular sense of *déjà vu* that I feel I've had once before.

Wow!

Look at the size of this Defias Thug's weapon!

World of Warcraft's collision detection is deliberately turned off for interactions between pretty well anything that moves. This saves on all those tedious calculations, but it can lead to unfortunate comedic experiences.

Criteria for a Name

On the assumption that we won't be able to call MMOs MMOs for much longer, and that the umbrella term *virtual worlds* has already almost slipped from our grasp, how should we go about creating a new term that is built to last?

What we need from such a term is:

- **Pronounceability:** No acronyms you have to spell out.

- **Unclaimed:** Someone already staked out Virtual Reality. The acronym for Virtual Worlds is used by Volkswagen.

- **Inclusive:** If it mentions games, the *Second Life* crowd won't like it; if it mentions user-created content, the *World of Warcraft* crowd won't like it.

- **Exclusive:** Bingo is a "massively multiplayer online game" when you break the terms down and see if they apply.

- **Future-proof:** Does it fall prey to a distinction between free-to-play and pay-to-play worlds, say? Would it still work if stereoscopic 3D head-mounted graphics became nearly universal?

- **Neutral:** Sorry, Persistent Environment Games, but your acronym is too smutty.

- **Descriptive:** It should at least hint as to what it refers. If only "Those Online Things" were acceptable.

This is why I expect to go to my grave without there being a commonly-accepted and long-lasting term for (what we currently call) MMOs.

What's in a Name?

Most people probably aren't aware that memory sticks are so called because that's what Sony called its flash memory product in 1998. However, if you were to set up as a manufacturer of flash memory, it's something you really ought to know. You wouldn't even consider calling your product "memory stick".

July 28th, 2015: Pure Bang Games get their project greenlit on Steam. It's "an open-world exploration and survival game, inspired by old school M.U.D.s and Minecraft." Their game is called *MUD*.

That's the trouble with history; it's all in the past.

"I Want To Be a Lead Artist"

The lead artist is (as I'm sure will not come as a surprise) the person in charge of ensuring that all artists working on a project are producing output that is consistent with the Vision, and with the work of each other.

As with lead programmers, this means that the best artist has to give up time doing what they do well (in this case, art) to perform a task to which they may be ill-suited (monitoring other people). However, lead artists only tend to spend maybe 10%-20% of their time looking at what the art team produces, because it's so much easier to see flaws with art—poor work is obvious at a glance.

The lead artist will usually be the person who creates the *look* of the game and the rules that the art team will follow (compiled as the *art bible*). This will have been done in consultation mainly with the lead designer, but also (for animation) the lead programmer. MMOs have a long shelf life, which can mean state-of-the-art, er, art at launch looks old and jaded five years later; art bibles should therefore be strong enough to be dusted off and re-used by possibly a new team several years away.

For a large art team, there may be sub-leads with responsibility for specific areas of artwork—static or animated, for example.

Large developers sometimes pool their artists, so any individual artist could be working on several different projects at once. This is because the requirement for artwork can come in ebbs and flows. For consistency, lead artists will remain with one project, however. Needless to say, this can lead to strife when two leads from different projects tell the same artist that they want a ton of work produced RIGHT NOW.

Artists in general are renowned for not getting along with technology and for being independent free-thinkers who don't take well to being bossed around. Artists who work on computer games are no exception. If you find a project for which all artwork is reliably logged in the asset management system, watch out: it means the producer has a taser hidden somewhere.

"I Want To Be a CS Lead"

Customer service is an important part of MMO operation (not that this is reflected in the salaries of those working in it). Also known as *community management*, it's basically the player-facing part of an MMO development team, handling pretty well anything that involves speaking to the customer base. This includes fielding general queries, fire-fighting forum flare-ups, managing the web site, judging competitions, banning people for misbehaving, dealing with billing enquiries, preliminary bug investigating, reporting to the appropriate local agency people threatening suicide, telling players what they would have known if only they'd read the manual, and so on and so forth.

CS representatives (or CSRs) are, in common with quality assurance technicians, prone to burning out. Their job is dealing with problems that to those concerned are very often regarded as emergencies. As a result, most players they deal with are uptight and pushing for answers or action, which leads to a lot of pressure.

The CS lead has the doubly tricky job of training and managing the CSRs while fending off the rest of the company's attempts to talk to players directly. One misplaced word from a programmer can lead to the dissipation of months of carefully-managed player expectations. One premature press release by the marketing section can cause a storm surge on the forums as people weigh in with awkward questions and indignant complaints.

Good CS leads are hard to find, but they do exist, and they do emerge from the pool of CSRs. It's the kind of job which can often be very rewarding (people are *genuinely happy* if you solve their problem for them), but also a little frustrating ("oh look, another death threat made it through my spam filter").

In the early days, when MMOs (in the form of text MUDs) were relatively small, they were usually managed by senior players answering to the designer/programmer. As such, I personally acted as CS lead for *MUD1/MUD2* for over 20 years. This experience means I'm surprisingly good at it, but I have to say I don't *like* doing it at all—it's hassle, hassle, hassle, all the way. CS leads, who have chosen this as their career path, have my undying admiration. I *know* how tough their job is.

Engines of Creation

Most independent MMO developers don't use a commercial MMO engine, they write their own. Okay, so they may use Unity or something for the graphics, but the rest of the system will be bespoke. The reason for this is that commercial engines are too expensive, they don't do what you want, and you can write something better anyway ("and sell it").

This situation won't last, as off-the-shelf engines are becoming more and more powerful and attractive (that is, free). It *is* how things are right this moment, though.

Now although indie developers may not like the extra work, it turns out that programming a hand-crafted engine is exceptionally good for creativity. The more you write in-house, the more different your world will be to everyone else's—there's a much greater possibility for divergence. This is why there was such a variety of worlds at Adventure '89.

It won't be like this for ever, though. With textual worlds, it went:

- 1989 *TinyMUD*
- 1989 *LPMUD*
- 1990 *DikuMUD*
- 1990 *MOO*
- 1990 *TinyMUCK*
- 1991-present One of the above

The capacity for innovation is *reduced* once game engines become a viable option. People take the short cut then have to rely on features that if they'd implemented them on their own would be entirely different. The physics, the combat system, the economy—you get the idea.

Any new medium only gets one window of exuberant creative expression. For graphical worlds, we're beginning it right now.

At least, I hope we are. If we've already been into it and come out the other side, we've got depressingly little to show for it.

Benefits of a Federation

Here's a set of notes I composed with regard to setting up a federation of MMO developers. My guess is that I wrote it around 1987:

> BENEFITS OF A FEDERATION
>
> (IN NO PARTICULAR ORDER!)

- Consistency across games for similar commands.

- Guardian of standards in the face of PD [public domain, *i.e.*, free] MUDs.

- Coordination of press releases.

- Organize conventions.

- Joint stands at shows.

- A common method of rating games for sex/violence, like with films.

- Better we do it than amateurs!

- Founder members get a say in organizing it, rather than taking what comes in the inevitable federation that will arise instead.

- Stand up to large competitors (e.g., Fujitsu).

- Stand up to large companies (e.g., BT, CompuServe).

- Common legal contracts to use, e.g., non-disclosure agreements, royalty agreements.

- Central mailing list.

- Blacklist (optional) for eternal troublemakers.

- Joint protocols for graphics, *etc.*, so can share FEs [front ends, *i.e.*, client software].

- Focal point for media interest in these games in general.

- Code of conduct, to protect us from "on-line porn available" charges in *NOTW* [*News of the World*, a now-defunct sensationalist newspaper].

- Guidelines for charging strategies.

- Newsletter.

- Pressure group *v* e.g., BT, government.

- (Members would be commercial systems, affiliates for amateurs)
- "Commercial" needs a definition!
- Companies are members, not individuals?
- Example: Government decides to ban MUAs because "they're the same thing as chatlines". What can we do unless we've organized beforehand?
- Contact list for e.g., U.S. companies
- Name? Awkward, because there is no common term for these games.
- Soc. of Multi-User Adv. games—SMAUG
- Society? Federation? Organization? Foundation? Association?
- Independent?
- International?
- The games themselves—Multi-User Adventure Games?
- Multi-/Many- User/Player
- Adventures?
- Role-playing?
- Text-based?
- Virtual/Alternate realities?

Entirely unsurprisingly, we're no closer to the "inevitable" federation now than we were then.

Falling Proud

A question I'm something asked by interviewers is "Which of *MUD*'s achievements are you most proud of?".

Why would I be proud of any of them?

It's all lost opportunities from my point of view. I see unreached potential, I see glorious possibilities, I see liberty, I see the ability to BE! Then I look at what we have, and I despair.

The gifts that *MUD* held forth and promised, humanity *will* eventually obtain; however, it will be from a reinvention of the concept, not a rediscovery.

I'm not proud of *MUD*'s achievements, I'm frustrated by them.

Reading Matter

It used to be that I'd read every academic paper about MMOs because I'd written them.

Then, other people started writing on the subject. I eagerly tracked down and read every single piece of work I could find. Even in the late 1990s, it was possible to do this: a newcomer to the field could sit down for three or four weeks and read in full pretty well every major article on the topic.

Well, in English, anyway—I had some foreign-language papers too but I couldn't make head nor tail of those.

MMO books started to come out. I bought and read each and every one I could find. Every couple of months, I would spend a few hours in the largest London bookshops looking through the indexes of anything promising, to see if there was a mention of MUDs, MOOs, or (sometimes) me.

By the time my book *Designing Virtual Worlds* came out in 2003, things were starting to change. I could keep up with the books, but I had a backlog of papers starting to build up, mainly because of a few lengthy MA and Ph.D. theses that took ages to read.

Shortly after, I started to discover areas of research that, worryingly, I hadn't come across before—whole seams of it, waiting to be mined. The reason I hadn't heard of it earlier was because the researchers involved hadn't heard about MMOs. They had their own names for what at the time we were calling "virtual worlds," and were put out that no one would adopt their terminology.

In about 2005, the floodgates started to open. Partly because academics were writing more papers, but mainly because *Second Life* and *World of Warcraft* garnered so much attention, papers started to appear faster than I could read them. Some areas, such as Serious Games, really rocketed. The quality of the papers went down, though; I was reading material that treated what we'd known for years as if it were a new discovery, or that made big claims on flimsy evidence, or that had poor scholarship, or that misinterpreted facts, or that was just plain wrong. My pile of papers to read got higher and higher. I started to get a pile of books, too.

Still, I kept collecting every article on virtual worlds that I could find. If I couldn't read it right away, I might get time later. Often, I did get time later. Whenever I came across a bunch of papers, I would print them off and put them in my pile to read. The pile just seemed to get taller and taller, though.

On August 26th, 2010, I received a link to a journal in my e-mail. It wasn't anything out of the ordinary—*Learning, Media and Technology vol. 35(2)*—and it included some papers that I did actually want to read (and indeed did go on to read). However, through no fault of its own, it was the straw the broke the camel's back. I lost the will to print off every single paper in it to add to my repository. Merely being *about* virtual worlds wasn't enough of a reason to collect papers any more. There were just too many.

I do try to get hold of books still, but not for archival purposes; I get them because I want to read them. Twenty years from now, there'll be no need for someone to have collected any of them, because they'll all have been digitized (and, most probably, neglected). A couple of hundred years from now, historians will simply search for articles ("sources") that support whatever point they are trying to make; they won't know the good papers from the bad—and they won't necessarily *care*, either, so long as what they find substantiates their argument.

Still, I wasn't ever collecting papers for posterity, I was collecting them to read. It took a while, but I finally had to recognize what had been obvious for some time. I don't have the time to read everything, and a good deal of what's out there isn't worth reading anyway. I have to be selective instead.

Besides, I've run out of shelf space in my office at the university.

As You Are Now, So Once Was I

Of course things have changed since virtual worlds went graphical. The main change isn't so much the graphics itself as the fact that there are orders of magnitudes more players in single incarnations of MMOs as a result of the introduction of said graphics.

As I've suggested before, the difference between textual and graphical virtual worlds is like the difference between silent movies and talkies. Once sound came out, it killed the talkies pretty well stone dead. That didn't mean knowledge gained in making silent movies was suddenly inapplicable "because some people like movie stars for the way they talk". Neither did it mean that people who grew up making silent movies were incapable of accepting progress.

There is exciting and innovative work going on in textual worlds, but this doesn't alter the fact that they're a dated form. You can legitimately refer to them as old hat because frankly, yes, the concept itself *is* old hat. You would be wrong, however, to dismiss as flotsam what has been discovered through these worlds.

Look into the future when the virtual world equivalent of color in the movies comes along—virtual reality hardware, say, or voice synthesis, or believable artificial intelligence. You, an expert in black-and-white talkie worlds, may be very keen to encourage this exciting phenomenon—imagine the possibilities! It's going to come as a bit of a jolt, therefore, when you discover that people new to the field start dismissing as evolved-away all the work that you and others have done on black-and-white MMOs, not even caring to look at it before making their judgment. Indeed, they may want *not* to look at it.

So, if you want to ignore the past, that's your right. However, bear in mind that the present will, in time, itself become the past. If you can't believe that all *your* knowledge of MMOs will be irrelevant to the MMOs of the future, at least afford the same acknowledgement to the players and designers of the MMOs that came before yours.

"I Want To Be a QA Lead"

Quality assurance (known universally as QA—so much so that there are probably people working in QA right now who don't know what the acronym expands to) is basically about testing. The QA lead supervises the people who do this testing, telling them what to test.

There are two main types of testing that need to be done: technical and gameplay. Technical testing is done by QA technicians, and is focused on the software. All the code paths, no matter how trivial, are investigated to see whether they do what they're supposed to do (nothing more, nothing less). Gameplay testing is done by playtesters: they check that the game plays well, that it has no exploits, and that it's balanced. They don't check that it's fun, because nothing is fun if you spend eight hours a day doing it for months on end.

"QA technician" and "playtester," while formally separate roles, are often used synonymously. It depends on whether you want to give the impression of respecting those who do it or of disrespecting them.

The QA lead, in collaboration with the producer, determines what needs to be tested. It's usually better to leave the other leads (designer, programmer, and artist) out of it, because it's their work that's being tested. Oh, and yes, artwork and modeling *is* tested: if you like the idea of walking your avatar into every single wall in an MMO to make sure it functions as a wall, QA is your field.

The QA lead draws up the test plans and assigns different areas to different QA technicians. QA technicians are not, however, easy to manage, because most are not there out of a love for testing: they either want to get a foot in the door as a designer, or they have the naïve idea that playing games for a living would be paradise. It's also possible that they want *your* job, in order to get the producer's. Most QA technicians burn out within two years, but some few do find they have a genuine aptitude for the work. These are the ones who will go on to be QA leads.

QA has the lowest-paid positions in game development, but a good QA lead is so hard to find, and the consequences of bad QA are so expensive, that talented people are rewarded well.

Personally, I'd be burnt out in under a month.

The Personality of a World

One of the legacies of *MUD* that has reached today's MMOs is its playful spirit. I don't know whether today's designers generally consider that their MMOs have a personality, but I certainly did for *MUD* and designed it accordingly.

I used to run my own postal games fanzine in my teens (called *Sauce of the Nile*) (I did say it was in my teens). People would subscribe to several such fanzines, and I realized that readers interacted with each one differently by projecting personalities onto them. This was mainly because *Sauce of the Nile* had a number of subzines that had different personalities, making the clashing contrast rather irritatingly obvious.

I wrote *MUD* with a single voice in mind, in the hope that players would find it amusing, engaging, affable, and likeable. I wanted them to feel that it—the virtual world—was in some sense a friend. I say "voice" here, but the language it spoke in wasn't English (although as a textual world, obviously it *used* English); the language it spoke in was the make-up of the virtual world itself. If I wanted the players to like the world, then the world was my medium; the text was merely a means of bringing *MUD*'s world to life, as graphics are today. Playing *MUD* was meant to be a playful activity, so the world itself had to be playful.

In the main, today's MMOs still have that aesthetic. I'd like to think it's because the designers of today were the players of yesterday, and they picked up on the idea either consciously or subconsciously and went with it after some thought. However, I suspect that in the majority of cases, few designers have given the matter much consideration and have just carried on with what they know works as part of the paradigm.

Nevertheless, I still have the vague feeling that whenever anyone sits down to play an MMO, in some tenuous sense I'm there playing with them.

"I Want To Be a Producer"

A producer is the project manager for a development team. Indeed, "project manager" may be their job title.

The producer plans the overall development schedule and keeps everything on track. They badger leads when their groups fall behind, and they badger management when the leads need more resources (which is not quite the same as when the leads *say* they need more resources).

The producer's job is more onerous than this sounds, to the extent that on big teams they may have one or more assistant producers to help them.

As you can no doubt deduce, producers annoy management by asking for more money/people/time to complete the project, and they annoy developers when management says they can't have it. Thus, they are hated by all. This perhaps in part explains why they get paid more than anyone else in the core team except the elitest of programmers.

Design by Committee

There is reluctance among some game developers to accept design as a skill. I have in my time come across several companies that design games by committee. They get everyone in the company together and brainstorm ideas. It's like a badge of pride for them that "even the receptionist" helps design games.

No!

No one writes a novel, paints a picture, or composes a symphony by committee. Well, they do, but the results suck. It's the same for games.

Most of the companies that practice design by committee seem to make serious games, by the way, rather than commercial games. That probably explains it.

On Design

Four of Clubs?

Go into the street with a pack of playing cards and a clipboard. Tell passers-by that you're doing an experiment about the prevalence of psychic powers (the clipboard is just to add an air of authenticity to this assertion). When you have assembled a small group of people, shuffle the pack and take out a card at random. Ask one person from your audience to guess what the card is.

Most people will guess wrong. However, 1 in 52 will guess right. If they don't know that you've been soliciting guesses all day, it's not difficult to imagine how they might believe that they actually do have nascent psychic powers. In truth, all they have is luck.

It's the same with many game designs. The reason they're successful is not because they're any good, but because they aren't so bad that when they happened to be in the right place at the right time they flopped.

This happens often in game design, or indeed anything else that involves a lot of luck. People end up being supremely confident of their abilities while not really having the talent they think they have. Obviously, some people *do* know what they're doing, and their good luck is of their own making; yet others are clueless while believing they're experts. It's possible to build a career on the strength of an initial hit followed by a series of mediocre misses.

Don't believe that game designers with big reputations deserve those reputations unless you've studied their designs. Conversely, don't believe that game designers with tiny reputations deserve those reputations unless you've studied their designs. Make up your own mind.

That applies to me, too, and to anything you read in this book. Don't take what I say as gospel: *make up your own mind*.

Games, Education

Whenever I hear "games" and "education" in the same phrase, it's always about using games to help in education. Why does it never mean using education to help in games?

Most Useful

Which of the following would be of most use to an MMO design team?

- An economist
- A social historian
- A design technologist
- An ex-army officer
- A technical author
- An applied mathematician
- An advertising executive
- An anthropologist

No, I'm not going to tell you what I think. I'm asking that *you* think about it.

Oh, and don't try to get out of it by giving a clever answer such as "the woman".

No Gophers

The film industry has gophers ("go for this; go for that"). They're not paid a lot, but they have a foot on the movie-making ladder.

The game industry doesn't have gophers. If it did, that would mean there would have to be a wage that was lower than what the developers were getting.

Why Designers?

Everyone who works for a computer games company thinks they can design:

- Coders can code *and* design
- Artists can draw *and* design
- Animators can animate *and* design
- Playtesters can playtest *and* design
- Producers can put together boring production schedules *and* design

Given this, why do we need designers?

We need them because designers actually *can* design.

Because People Ask

I'm asked maybe once or twice a year what people should study if they want to be a game designer.

They should study game design.

Game design is a form of art; for game designers, game design is their medium of expression. You can't *want* to be a game designer, you just *are* one whether you like it or not. You can aspire to have a *job* as a game designer, but that's not the same as *being* a game designer. Some people who have a career as successful game designers are actually hacks; some people who design brilliant, awe-inspiring games never see them made. It's like *any* art form in that regard. Great artists aren't always successful; successful artists aren't always great.

As to why you should study game design, as opposed to anything else, well you can't be *taught* to be a designer any more than you can be *taught* to be a novelist. However, you *can* be taught some of the things you would otherwise have to figure out for yourself, so you don't have to learn them the hard way. You can hit the ground running. Some skill-based and technique-based teaching is going to be essential, but the end result you are really aiming for is to understand the rules of game design.

Then, and *only* then, you can break them.

Vision *versus* Look and Feel

The vision is the designer's unifying sense of how they envisage their game to be.

Look and feel is the same thing from the players' point of view.

They don't always line up.

Zimmerman's Game

Here's a game I call *Zimmerman's Game*, because game designer Eric Zimmerman told me it. There may be an official name, but I'd rather call it *Zimmerman's Game* so people will remember who invented it.

Okay, so it's a game for two players. Here's how it goes: players take turns saying words, no repeats, and whoever first says a word ending in Y or M loses.

Hmm. Not much fun, right? Let's try again: players take turns saying words from the same category (maybe animals), no repeats, and whoever first says a word ending in Y or M loses.

Not much better, is it? Okay, how about this: players take turns saying words from the same category (maybe city names), no repeats, where each word starts with the letter that ended the previous word, and whoever first says a word ending in Y or M loses.

So:

- You: London

- Me: Newcastle

- You: Exeter

- Me: Rochester

- You: Ripon

- Me: Notti—ah, no, that ends in M—er, Newark

- You: Kingston

- Me: Blast and damn it, er …

- Someone else: Northampton!

- Me: Northampton!

- You: Nelson

- Me: That's a person, not a place

- You: It's in Lancashire

- Me: Hmm, do we have to have UK cities or can they be anywhere?

- Etc.

Okay, so suddenly we have a game.

The thing is, we *had that game at the beginning*. That exact conversation could have taken place under the first set of rules, but it didn't. The third game was identical to the first two, except with *more rules*. Yet the third one was fun and the first two were no fun.

This paradox lies at the heart of all games. You willingly pay for the freedom to play by constraining your freedom to act.

Designing to Context

When designing a game to a context (that is, to match a particular subject domain—dinosaurs, pirates, medieval warfare, the novels of Jules Verne, whatever), you have to understand the context. This means you need to research it. Understanding is not your only goal, though: you actually have four.

- Understand the context
- Identify the central, must-have concepts
- Figure out how the context works as a system
- Have gameplay ideas

Note: All this comes naturally to designers. They don't have to think about the means by which they identify the must-have concepts; it just comes to them as they do the research.

Once you have the system and the gameplay ideas, you can strip out the context and concentrate on the mechanics.

That's if you want to do so.

What Designers Design

You may have noticed that when I talk about "designers" in this book, I'm a little vague as to what it is they design. Sometimes I'll say "MMO designers," sometimes "game designers," and sometimes neither. If I'm writing about MMOs, why am I mentioning non-MMOs at all?

The thing is, most MMO designers are also game designers; MMOs are game worlds, therefore MMOs need gameplay, therefore their designers need to be able to design games. Actually, it's more than that: their designers *need* to design games, in the same way that an author *needs* to write. It's what they *do*.

MMOs are the particular kind of game that an MMO designer finds gives them the best canvas to express their souls, but that doesn't mean they won't be active in other areas. Picasso painted, sculpted, and drew; MMO designers design game worlds, but they also design games, mini-games, and worlds in general. Furthermore, they also write stores, poetry, film scripts, music, and do all the other creative things they did before they came to game design.

Scunthorpe

Scunthorpe is a steel-making town in Lincolnshire, England. If you lived in Scunthorpe in the 1990s and wanted to use AOL, you couldn't. Well, you could, but you had to say you lived in Scanthorpe.

Helpfully, AOL had implemented profanity-checking software to protect its younger users from foul language. The second-to-fifth letters in Scunthorpe triggered the profanity filter. Therefore, if you wanted to use the name of the town, you had to modify it so the filter didn't object to it.

It took a lot of lobbying by the residents of Scunthorpe, but finally AOL relented and allowed users who lived there to call it by its official name. Immediately, other AOL users began using it as a swearword (putting the second-to-fifth letters in uppercase to remove any doubt as to what they meant).

The point is, whatever you do in an MMO that has a profanity filter, people will find a way to get round it. All you can do is block out casual usage. Yes, the initial letters of the paragraphs for this article are indeed not arranged that way by accident.

Training and Education

Training is the acquisition of skills and knowledge as a result of being taught. It's good for preparing you for known situations. It's often focused for a particular vocation.

Education is the acquisition of skills and knowledge as a result of learning. It's good for preparing you for unknown situations. It aims for a more rounded, think-for-yourself ideal.

Respecs

The question isn't whether players should be able to re-spec their characters. The question is whether characters should have specs to re.

Procedural or Declarative?

Theoretical computer scientists use formal mathematics to describe programs, in order that they can reason about them. There are several different approaches, but at heart they're usually either *declarative* or *procedural*.

A declarative semantics describes programs as a set of statements in some logic. Given the entire such semantics for a program, you can prove it does what it's supposed to do (which may be useful if it, say, controls nuclear weapons). You can also use declarative semantics to generate programs automatically.

A procedural semantics describes programs as an ordered collection of executable fragments. What this comes down to is that program code is its *own* proof—the semantics are used to help make statements about this code.

Computer science theoreticians can get somewhat heated about which approach is better, but for the rest of us it's interesting to note that there's actually a relationship between the two. A program is a specification in code of a process. A declarative semantics reduces this to a non-executable set of facts; however, if you're to use these facts to prove something, you have to construct a series of deductive steps in order—which is once again a process. Likewise, if you use a procedural semantics, you're mapping from one process (that described by the program code) to another process (that described by the procedural semantics); however, when it comes to saying something about the process, the result is a statement, not a process. So you use statements to say things about processes, and processes to say things about statements.

They're two sides of the same coin.

Rules and Instantiations

There's a difference between "*Chess*" and "the particular game of *Chess* we played last week". Which of these is truly *Chess*?

Is the *design* of an MMO truly that MMO, or is the *playing* of the MMO truly that MMO?

Everyone's a Designer

Everyone who plays MMOs for fun thinks they're a designer.

If you play MMOs, *you* think you're a designer. You have views on why some things are wrong, how other things could be improved with just a few tweaks here and there, what's engaging and what's not, and how the MMO *ought* to be. If *you* were in charge, well, things would be like *this*!

Of course, if were to I ask you, you'd say that no, of course you're not a designer, you're a player. Then, in your very next breath, you'd tell me why PvP is unbalanced, or how one if the instance end-bosses is over-powered, or why people shouldn't be allowed to buy in-game pets for real money, or that some random class needs to be nerfed *right now*. You'd profess not to be a designer, but then proceed to act as if you believed you were one.

The thing is, unless you actually *are* a designer, or at least a designer-in-the-making, you're not *thinking* like a designer here. What you really want is an MMO that you, personally, would wish to play.

Designers don't create MMOs that they, personally, wish to play; they create virtual worlds that *people* wish to play.

Amazing

One of the things that players and developers of social worlds often say is that their players (or "users" or "residents," or whatever they choose to call them that doesn't sound as if it's to do with games) are *amazing*. They're so incredibly creative!

It's true, they are. However, that's because people *in general* are amazing.

Resets

Today's MMOs stay running until either they are taken down for maintenance or the server crashes.

Early virtual worlds didn't used to do that.

When a mobile was killed in *MUD1*, that was it; it was dead. It didn't respawn 10 minutes later; it was *gone*. Large changes to the game world would take place: doors would be smashed down, much-desired treasures were cast into a swamp, scrolls and books were burned. After a few hours or so, the game world was markedly different than what it had been earlier.

Then, it would reset. The players would be kicked out for a few seconds, and everything would be returned to its starting state. The players would then return, and the creatures, doors, treasure, and everything else would be ready for playing with again.

This is known as a *sudden reset* or *Groundhog Day* approach. If you can cope with having everyone thrown out every few hours, it gives you a lot more scope for making things happen. In a *rolling reset* (spawn-based) world, you can only make limited changes because each component has to be undone individually and people can be caught between the effects. If the rocket has launched, then you can't respawn it if someone is still in it. Sudden resets are a very powerful technique. For this reason, some early MMOs such as *Island of Kesmai* used both: some objects were individually respawned, then every 60 days or so the whole game world reset.

Today's MMOs have more structured content than those of the past, which means players can embark on activities that could take up an entire evening. This is not compatible with everyone being thrown out every few hours, which is why nowadays sudden resets only happen for scheduled maintenance and crashes. Their functionality lives on in instances and phases, though.

So, when an MMO does reset (for whatever reason), what survives the reboot?

This is actually an important question.

The Magic Circle

All games have a set of rules that players willingly obey together in order to gain some perceived benefit (e.g., fun!). While all players follow these rules, you have a game.

This "social contract" between players is called the *magic circle*, a term used in 1938 by the Dutch historian Johan Huizinga but coined by Katie Salen and Eric Zimmerman in their book, *Rules of Play*. Deciding to enter into the social contract entails adopting what's called a *lusory attitude*. Breaking the social contract while continuing to play is called *cheating*.

A magic circle allows a set of consenting individuals to gain freedoms they couldn't have had otherwise. What it basically comes down to is that people in a group willingly agree to limit their behavior (i.e., conform to a set of rules) in order to gain an experience they wouldn't have got if they didn't all do that.

For example, if you and I are playing *Chess*, I could physically take your king with my queen immediately with my first move, but I don't because that would break the rules. I don't want to break the rules, because the fun from *Chess* goes away if there are no rules. You, my opponent, have the same point of view. You want to do all the planning and counter-planning and pattern-recognition that make *Chess* enjoyable. You also want to win, and are willing to follow the rules for a shot at that. Therefore, even though in practice either one of us could take the other's king, snap its head off, and hurl it across the room into a fire, we don't. We're limiting our behavior in order to gain an experience we couldn't have if we didn't limit it.

That is what the magic circle is: an arena of behavior sustained by the consent of those within it.

No magic circle, no game.

Do You Know This Game?

Okay, this is a game called *3-to-15*, designed by Marc LeBlanc (formerly of Looking Glass Studios). It's for two players.

Write out the numbers 1 to 9 in a line. Players take turns crossing off one of the numbers and writing it down in front of them. Players can't cross off a number that's already been crossed-off. When three of the numbers that one of the players has written down add up to 15, that player wins.

Easy!

So, do you know that game? It sounds like one of those mathematical ones that have a special trick to them which, if you know it, means you can always win (or at least avoid defeat). Okay, that being so, what's the trick?

Let's have a run through it:

- I pick 5.
- You pick 7.
- I pick 2.
- You pick 8 (because otherwise I'd pick it next time to have three numbers add up to 15).
- I pick 4.
- You pick 6 (to stop 4+5+6=15).
- I pick 9. 4+9+2=15—I win!

Seem familiar?

I'll let you think about it for a while.

Games You Can't Win

Some games, you can't win. You can lose them, but you can't win them.

Take *Dungeons & Dragons*, for example. What's the outcome of a game of *D&D*? No one gets to win. The person behind the screen never even gets to lose. People play for the *journey*, not for the destination. A game of *D&D* ends either when an entire party wipes or when the magic circle breaks (i.e., people stop playing).

It's still a game, though.

In Defense of Suits

The suits who run large MMO development companies are necessary, because where else are you going to get the money to develop a AAA MMO? However, they can be a pain—especially when they start believing they're designers. The best suits will keep out of the creative process as much as they can, but of course designers do still have to work to their specifications.

For example, when *EverQuest 2* was green-lighted by Sony Online Entertainment, the marketing types had done their due diligence and concluded that what they wanted was *EQ1* with better graphics, better gameplay, the *EQ* brand name, and a costly differentiator from potential competitors (which came in the form of 700 hours of voice acting). This therefore set the business parameters within which the designers were to work.

The designers duly went about creating what they had been tasked to create, and the project was delivered on time, on budget, and reasonably to spec. The launch was the second-best of any MMO of the period, and *EQ2* was set to become the first virtual world to break the million-subscribers barrier. Indeed, I was expecting it to hit 2 million. The suits had given the designers business-only constraints within which to work, and the designers had exercised their creative freedom admirably. This is a great example of how the creatives and non-creatives in a company can toil together for the betterment of the product.

Sadly for SOE, however, the game that had the first-best launch of any MMO of the period, *World of Warcraft*, came from nowhere and ate its lunch. However, because it had been done right, *EQ2* still gained player numbers that would have been highly respectable in pre-*WoW* days; it didn't sink without trace.

You can make your own mind up about *EQ Next*.

Two Games

Nomic is a game by Peter Suber, created to illustrate flaws in self-amending systems (previously only obvious to people who had come across Gödel's Incompleteness theorem) (and yes some of us game designers had indeed come across it before). Here is a (somewhat abridged) version of *Nomic*'s rules:

- Players take turns in clockwise order.

- In your turn, you propose a change in rules that all the other players then vote on.

- You roll a die to determine the number of points you add to your score.

- First to 100 points wins.

- If your proposed change is passed, it comes into immediate effect.

- Any rule can be changed, including this one.

Okay, that's *Nomic*.

Mornington Crescent was designed as a parody of snobbish games such as *Chess* and *Bridge*. Here are the rules in their entirety:

- Players take turns naming London Underground stations.

- The first to say "Mornington Crescent" wins.

In considering (written) game rules, *Nomic* and *Mornington Crescent* are at different extremes of the spectrum. *Mornington Crescent* is the game of playing until the precise moment that playing is no longer fun. *Nomic* is the game of creating any other game in existence (which includes *Mornington Crescent*).

So, I assert the following: If at any point during a game of *Nomic* it becomes impossible for it ever to become *Mornington Crescent*, that's when that game of *Nomic* ends. This is because it can only happen under one of two conditions:

- It has entirely lost its ability to change.

- It has ceased to be a game at all.

In the former case, if it can't change then it's not *Nomic* anymore but the game into which it has metamorphosed.

In the latter case, it's because *Mornington Crescent* is the magic circle incarnate.

No magic circle, no game.

The *Cluedo* Example

Suppose you're playing *Cluedo* (or *Clue*, as it's known in the United States). Your fellow players are a man and a woman. You're getting close to figuring out who did it when suddenly the man leans over to the woman and whispers something in her ear. She shows him her cards. He announces that Colonel Mustard did it with the candlestick in the hall.

You probably wouldn't be happy with that. The reason you wouldn't be happy is because the man has brought something into the game that ought not to be there. He might have been bribing the woman, threatening her, calling in a favor—you don't know. What you do know is that the game was over the moment the woman showed him her cards—not the two seconds later when the man announced whodunit. You're not going to play *Cluedo* with either of them ever again if you can help it.

All games have a magic circle. MMOs are not games for all their players, but all their players do have the same lusory attitude that requires play to be separate from real life. If you bring in real life, you end play.

Universal Flawed Design

Who in their right mind would create a universe that contains both matter and anti-matter? That's just asking for trouble! The matter and anti-matter could eliminate each other, leaving you with nothing. All that effort you spent universe-creating is just *wasted*.

If a game designer had created our universe out of nothing, they wouldn't have split the nothing into two, they'd have split it into three. Rock-matter would eliminate scissors-matter, scissors-matter would eliminate paper-matter, paper-matter would eliminate rock-matter. They'd also increase the mass of the winning matter by the mass of the eliminated matter, give or take some energy. That way, regardless of how much elimination goes on, you've always got some matter.

Next time *you* create a universe, don't make the same mistakes that were made when this one was created.

Early Lesson

When I was about seven years old, I made a board game. I'd made them before, but for this one I had constructed pieces out of Plasticine and my dad saw them. He asked if he could play the game with me and my brother. This was the first game I'd made that he'd asked to play, so I was really pleased.

The board had an outer track and an inner map. You took turns rolling dice to move round the outer track, picking up different resources when you landed on different squares. For one particular kind of square, if you felt you had enough resources then you could move to the inner map. On the map, you moved your piece from a starting edge to one of three designated locations (changing your mind and going for a different one was one of your options), while other players could use their resources to try to stop you.

I was fairly pleased with the design, as it got exciting when you were close to one of the target locations and you had to decide how many resources to gamble on attack and defense. My dad liked it too, except…

…except, well, I've told you what the basic mechanics were, but not the dressing. The game was about collecting bombs to supply your zeppelin for it to drop on British cities. When you're aged seven, zeppelins are cool. My dad pointed out that there might not be many people who would want to play a game in which the aim was to rain death and destruction on undefended cities. He said that the way the game played, it didn't feel as if it should be about aerial warfare at all. It felt as if it should be about travel or exploration.

I was disappointed in this, mainly because I'd put quite some effort into my Plasticine zeppelins. However, it did make me realize for the first time that there was a relationship between the subject matter of a game and the (what I would now call) gameplay. If the two aren't in unison, then the game will feel wrong. If you *wanted* it to feel wrong for some reason, well that would be okay. However, you should *think* about whether you want it to feel right or wrong before you do that.

Not a bad lesson for a juvenile game designer to learn.

Oh, I also learned that Lego makes better pieces than Plasticine.

You Do Know This Game

Hey, you've heard of magic squares, right? They're these grids of consecutive numbers muddled up so the columns, rows, and diagonals all add up to the same total.

Here's a simple 3x3 magic square:

4	9	2
3	5	7
8	1	6

This particular one is the "Lo Shu" square, which dates back to 650BC China. All its columns, rows, and diagonals add up to 15.

So, remember that *3-to-15* game I asked you about earlier? The one in which you write down the numbers from 1 to 9 and take turns crossing one off; the first to get three that total 15 wins? Okay, so play the same game, but instead of crossing off the numbers from a list, cross them off from the above magic square.

Yes, it's *Noughts and Crosses*, or, if you prefer your etymology to be more mystifying, *Tic-Tac-Toe*.

Sometimes, a cunning change of context can obscure even the simplest of mechanics.

Mechanics

I keep mentioning mechanics, so perhaps ought to say what I mean by the term. Okay, so strip away the context from a game design and the mechanics are what's left.

Warning: much of the enjoyment of a game can come from the context.

Further warning: the above is irrelevant if the mechanics are poor.

Generated or Created

Although academics and players writing about virtual worlds often use the terms *user-created content* (UCC) and *user-generated content* (UGC) interchangeably, there is actually a distinction between them.

User-created content is content explicitly created by users using (often in-world) content-creation tools. It's freeform, in that it doesn't have to have anything to do with the context. You can be in a fantasy world and user-create a red sports car if you like.

User-generated content is content implicitly created by the interaction between users and either each other or the virtual world. It's emergent. If I attack a monster and it summons its friends, and then I run away and I bump into you, suddenly you're faced with a train of monsters. Will you join me in fighting them or in running away? This is content, and it's content for you that wouldn't have existed without my actions; therefore it's user-generated. *All* multi-player games have UGC.

There is an intermediate stage that you can argue is both user-created and user-generated. Suppose, for example, that in a fantasy world you want to build a castle in a particular location. No other instantiation of the game world has a castle in this location, and castles are fairly durable; this would therefore be a simple example of user-created content. However, you may have to proceed by paying a non-player character architect to produce a plan, hiring a bunch of masons, carpenters, and general laborers to turn the plan into a building, then furnishing it with equipment and decorations and staffing it with servants and soldiers. This has all been undertaken in context, so you could argue that it's user-generated rather than user-created. Other examples include killing monsters, making cloaks, and locking doors. All are changes to the content of the MMO (although their persistence may vary), yet all make sense within the context of the virtual world.

It's therefore often more useful to refer to content formation as being *direct* or *emergent* and *freeform* or *contextual*.

Not that anyone *does* this, of course.

What Are the Rules?

When I was a teenager, I used to play games by post. I subscribed to a number of fanzines (which everyone called either zines or 'zines, depending on how conservative they felt about using leading apostrophes), mainly concerning the game *Diplomacy* but not always. Eventually, as I've mentioned, I went on to run my own zine, *Sauce of the Nile*. This explains why I'm a super-fast typist.

My favorite zine was Clive Booth's *Chimaera*. In one issue he started a new game, the description of which was: "You and I are playing a game. What are the rules?". You could send Clive yes/no questions about the rules, and he would answer them; the first person to get the right answer won.

After a few issues, the winner of the game correctly got the rules as: "I send you a question about the rules, to which you answer yes if it has an even number of syllables and no if it has an odd number of syllables". So, it was a variation on an old parlor game, then.

I played, but unfortunately my first question was: "Are there any rules?". The reply came back, "no," so I figured I'd won. I was a bit miffed to discover at the end that the answer was a lie. I was further annoyed because my second question, had the first been wrong, would have been: "Are the rules: 'We send you yes/no questions about the rules, and you answer them; the first person to get the right answer wins'?"

That's the trouble with games-about-their-own-rules: they're either complete but inconsistent, incomplete but consistent, or neither complete nor consistent.

Yes, as I said: I do know about Gödel's theorem.

Whatever

If an MMO designer wants a world with an economy, they can have one. If they want one without an economy, they can have one.

If you use your imagination, you can have whatever world you want.

Kinds of Rules

When someone says that games have rules, they're right, they do. However, ask them to *list* those rules and they won't actually be able to do so—not in their entirety.

What most people don't realize is that games have several *kinds* of rules. Some of them are stated explicitly in a rule set, for example that bishops move diagonally in *Chess*. These are what people normally mean by "the rules," and is indeed how I use the term myself.

But what about the rule that says *Chess* pieces can't go invisible during play? Ah, well that's a law of nature—it's physically impossible for *Chess* pieces to go invisible, so there's no point in having a rule against it. Except, it *is* a rule. You wouldn't necessarily want to play a game of *Chess* on a computer then all of a sudden your opponent's pieces disappeared—even though no written rules were being broken.

There are other rules that are also unstated but nevertheless present. No rule of *Chess* prevents my heating up a piece so you can't touch it to move it. You'd still probably complain if I did it, though. Besides, if the rules did prohibit it, they wouldn't prohibit me from paying someone else to do it; or if they did, then they wouldn't stop me blackmailing someone to put a beaker over the piece; or if they did, they wouldn't stop me from releasing someone from a favor they owed me if they slapped your hand when you reached for the piece; or if they did, they wouldn't stop me training a chicken to flap its wings in your face when I gave it a secret hand signal; or if they did—and so on *ad infinitum*.

Yes, there is indeed an *infinite* number of these rules, which is why no one can ever state them. Even catch-all rules fail to catch everything (which is why we need lawyers in real-world courts). For games, players "know" what is and isn't within the "spirit of the game," but that doesn't mean they all think the same way. I might believe it's fine to roll dice from my hands in *Monopoly*, but you might believe that this makes it too easy to influence the roll and insist I use a lipped cup. We agree in the main, but have differences in the margins.

Thus, when people play games, they each have a fairly solid idea of what the rules are, but they don't all have the *exact* same idea. You might think some piece of gamesmanship is okay and I might not, and we won't find out until you try it. Players have to take it on faith that the other players have a strongly compatible idea of the rules; conflict arises when the differences are exposed.

This faith that the other players are playing by rules acceptable to you is what gives a game its magic circle. Of course, that should really be *magic circles*, because each person's view of "the rules" is actually individual to them. It's something of a testament to the power of play that most of the time the overlap between these magic circles is so substantial that it's perfectly reasonable to conflate them all into one.

That's "most of the time".

Bubbles and Sandcastles

It's easy to break the magic circle. For example, if I wanted you to do something in an MMO, I could threaten you and your family in real life to get my way. That would do it.

Just because it's easy, though, that doesn't mean the mere possibility of it fatally undermines an MMO's claim to have a magic circle. If it did, then my threatening you in real life to vote a particular way in an election would undermine the entire electoral system.

In both cases, this is mere noise compared to the general robustness of the system. You're not pricking a bubble, you're pricking a sandcastle. Of course, if enough people prick a sandcastle then it collapses, which is why MMO operators and governments alike take sanctions against people they find abusing the system in this way.

(Or, in the case of some governments, insufficiently abusing the system in this way.)

Design and Prediction

Design involves predicting how something expensive-to-make will turn out without actually making it first.

An Important Distinction

Players treat play as separate from real life, but separation is not *itself* the magic circle.

Within the magic circle, players agree to abide by a set of rules in order to gain mutual benefit from doing so. They see their play as being distinct from real life—but there's nothing in the definition of the magic circle that says they can't at times conflate the two.

For some games, especially role-playing ones, players adopt a second conceit: that the imaginary world is non-imaginary. They temporarily override what they know to be true (they're not really a magic-using elf) in order to gain some benefit. As before, players are treating play as separate from real life; the difference is that in this second case the players will themselves to accept the presented world *as if it were real*.

The magic circle and the imaginary world conceit both rely on partitioning real life and play, but the two are not the same. They apply in tandem to MMOs, but they can be applied separately to non-MMOs, too.

For example, an actress on a stage inhabits a magic circle: by following a pre-scribed role, she gets permission to behave in ways that she could not behave in without the protection of that role and the consent of the others within the same magic circle. She may or may not also will herself *into* the role (method actors probably would; other actors probably wouldn't).

The audience for a play isn't in the magic circle. The audience accepts that actors on stage can do things that would otherwise be unacceptable (such as using racist language while playing a racist), but is not itself protected by that magic circle. However, the audience does apply the conceit that the action they are watching is real even though they know it's not. This is the whole reason why they're watching. They would be wasting their time if they took the attitude "that's not really Julius Caesar, he died centuries ago, and those guys haven't really just stabbed whoever it is".

In MMOs, the players are both actors *and* audience. The magic circle and the imaginary world conceit *both* apply to them.

Kinds of Rules and MMOs

So, rules for traditional games are of three kinds:

- Unwritten, but imposed by physics. You can't put all your pieces on one square in *Chess* because they don't fit.

- Written. Kings can move one square in any direction on the board unless they're blocked by one of their own pieces or the move would put them into check.

- Unwritten, but imposed by social norms. "Will you stop whistling?! I'm trying to think here!".

With computer games, the first two kinds of rules are often amalgamated. You can't put all your pieces in one square *or* move the king two squares, because the code won't let you. This leads players to think that if the game lets you do something, it's by definition allowed. Otherwise, it would stop you from doing it.

However, not all written rules *can* be coded—"no swearing," for example. This isn't a problem for single-player games, and it's manageable for multiplayer games, but it's a real headache for massively-multiplayer games.

The way that MMOs have evolved to enforce the written rules they can't implement is the End User License Agreement. Real-world contract law can be used when someone violates the EULA and breaks these written-but-uncoded rules.

What about *unwritten* rules, though?

Well, these have to be enforced by the players. If someone is not violating the EULA but is being a pain (e.g. by ninja looting—grabbing treasure that isn't rightfully theirs) then the other players will take action as a consequence. They may spread the word never to play with the ninja again, or they may follow them around and ninja their loot to see how they like it—there are many things they could do. In *MUD1*, they could kill the offending character dead.

If none of these work, though, and the offender keeps on refusing to abide by social norms, *then* you have a problem.

Egor

MUD1 was written so long ago that most of the people who played it to start with had never played a computer game of any kind before. I'd personally *written* more computer games than I'd played. Computer games just weren't all that available.

People had played board games, however. So it was that for its first few years, *MUD1* was played in the spirit of face-to-face games: in a word, "nicely".

Then, along came Egor.

In real life, Egor was Andrew Glaister; he later went on to design DirectX (he was technical director at Kinesoft). Back then, he was a precocious teenager who became *MUD*'s second external wizard (after his friend, Jez San, who himself was destined to be the first person awarded an OBE explicitly for services to the computer game industry).

Egor was different because before he played, no one deliberately broke any rules. They were told not to gank newbies, so they didn't. Egor also didn't break any rules, it's just that *his* rules were of the "what is coded in" variety rather than "what is coded in plus these extra, unwritten rules". If *MUD*'s code allowed you do it, he figured you could therefore legitimately do it (because otherwise it would have been coded out, surely?).

Recall that games have three types of rules:

- Ones determined by physical limits. I can't kick a ball that's five meters away from me as my legs aren't that long.

- Written ones. Fouls lead to free kicks.

- Unwritten ones. "Ungentlemanly conduct" catch-alls.

In non-computer games, the first of these is coded in and the other two work by social norms sustaining a magic circle. In massively-multiplayer games, the first two are coded in and the third is pretty well non-existent.

The problem is, there are many actions that are against the "rules" that you nevertheless *can't* actually code out. They don't even have to be gameplay-related—AOL's Scunthorpe problem, for example. Some of these against-the-rules actions are difficult to police (*MUD1* banned "looby-looing," meaning using a lower-level character to accumulate treasure for another, higher-level character to cash in for points). Some things are almost impossible to prove (*MUD1* also banned out-of-game inter-player communication while you were playing, believe it or not). Players of face-to-face games trust each other to stick to the rules, but beyond a critical mass this breaks down.

Egor was the first person to demonstrate this with *MUD1*.

Because Egor broke their perception of the rules, he was called a cheat by other players—"slaughtering newbies to get points is cheating!," that kind of thing. Nevertheless, Egor didn't have an "it's just a game," anything-goes kind of attitude. He did follow some rules that weren't coded-in, for example he didn't kill-steal. All players follow unwritten rules (although they don't always realize it).

Egor didn't believe he was cheating. Other players did, and told him to his face.

This raises an interesting question: Why is it that players of the same MMO can have different ideas as to what is cheating and what isn't?

Crossing a Line

Character A wants to exchange a Sword of This for a Sword of That. Character B wants to exchange a Sword of That for a Sword of This. They meet up. Character A gives Character B the Sword of This, then character B runs away laughing. Character A has been scammed.

If this is allowed within the context of the game (bearing in mind that few modern MMOs *would* allow it), then it's fine. If it were gold pieces rather than a Sword of This, it would still be fine. If it were dollars rather than gold pieces, well that would probably bring it into the real world (but still might not; it would depend on the game). So long as the *context* clearly remains that of the game, talk is just talk and promises are potentially worthless.

When the context is outside of the game, though, that's different. Even in *EVE Online*, which is the MMO that perhaps spills over into *Reality* the most, demanding that someone gives you all their ISKs or you'll tell their wife you're cheating on her isn't part of the game context, it's just blackmail pure and simple. At some point, a line has been crossed.

That line is the magic circle.

Context and Mechanics

There's a creativity relationship between context and mechanics. Context can come from mechanics, or mechanics can come from context, or they can both arise together. It's possible that the two are so intertwingled that you can't separate them. Almost always, though, you can.

So why would you want to?

- Because the context can get in the way when figuring out gameplay issues.

- Because if you understand the mechanics for one game, you can use them for another.

- Because no matter how flashy the dressing, no mechanics means no game.

So why would you not want to?

- Because a mismatch between mechanics and context can spoil the game experience.

In his book[1], Raph Koster gives a great example of a *Black Hole of Calcutta* game, in which you throw people into a pit and they pile up trying to get out. The mechanics of it are identical to that of *Tetris*, but the experience of playing is very different; I say "is" rather than "would be," because although it was only mentioned as a thought experiment, someone actually went ahead and *made* it (in Portuguese)[2]. In 2015, the idea was implemented as a "slave *Tetris* mini-game" in the educational *Playing History 2—Slave Trade*, only this time without any sense of irony. It did not meet with critical acclaim...

Context and mechanics are both employed by designers to say things to players.

Game design is an *art*.

---

[1]Raph Koster: A Theory of Fun for Game Design. Paraglyph Press: Scottsdale, Arizona. 2005.
[2]Calabouço Tétrico. Loodo, 2008.

World of Wiicraft

Yes, it would be great to have an MMO you could play using a Wii or Kinect interface, but three hours of that every evening would kill me within a fortnight.

The Magic Circle and MMOs

All games need a magic circle if they're to work. Few players or designers really think about it, though, because most of the time it's not under threat. It's like gravity: yes, it's important, but there's not much danger it's going to fail.

MMOs are different.

The rules for games only exist because the players agree that they do: this agreement constitutes the magic circle. Okay, so what happens if someone comes along who has a different idea of what the rules are?

There are four possible resolutions:

- One party brings the other party around to their way of thinking.

- Both parties live together in an uneasy peace.

- One party leaves and finds someone else to play with who shares their idea of what the rules are.

- One party is forcibly evicted.

With MMOs, the problem is that the third and fourth resolutions don't work. You can easily (albeit with gritted teeth) leave for another MMO, but the people who (in your view) have been "spoiling the game" can just as easily follow. Likewise, if you kick them out they can usually come back almost straight away.

So, MMOs have a particular kind of problem with regards to people who "break the rules," because the usual normative solutions—start your own game or kick out the miscreants—aren't available. This is why MMO players and designers find the subject of greater significance than do the players and designers of regular games, and why "protecting the magic circle" is the rallying cry of so many battles with the intrusions of the real world into the virtual world.

Plutarch

The difference between education and training was best summed up by Plutarch.

In training, the mind is viewed as a vessel to be filled:

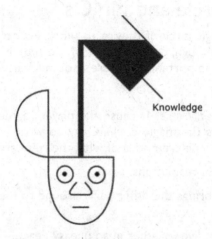

Knowledge

In this, knowledge is like water. You open up your student's head and pour it in. Hopefully, there's enough room for it.

Education views the mind as a fire to be kindled:

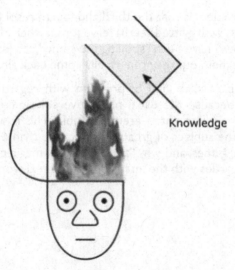

Knowledge

In this, knowledge is like oil. You open up your student's head and pour it in. Hopefully, there are flames in there that will ignite it, but if there's too much oil it could quench any flames instead.

What Plutarch actually said (translated) was: "For the mind requires not like an earthen vessel to be filled up; convenient fuel and aliment only will inflame it with a desire of knowledge and ardent love of truth."[3]

Let's not get picky, though.

Reskinning

If you take a game, strip away the context so you only have the mechanics, then you add a new context while keeping the mechanics intact, the new game is said to be a *reskinning* of the old one. The game *3-to-15* that I mentioned earlier was a reskinning of *Noughts and Crosses*. The *Black Hole of Calcutta* game was a reskinning of *Tetris*.

Sometimes, though, as a designer, you might build your game entirely around a mechanic without ever considering context. Your choice of what dressing to give it (if any) is entirely a marketing decision. There are many board games that are purely abstract in nature, but they've been cast as something more exciting so as to sell. Ancient Egypt, pirates, and historical cities are particularly popular. Sometimes it even works.

Computer games tend to go the other way around—start with the exciting marketing idea then try to build a game to fit it. Sometimes this even works, too.

---

[3]Plutarch: *On the Hearing of Lectures*. Trans. Thomas Hoy. Little, Brown & Co., 1878. http://www.bostonleadershipbuilders.com/plutarch/moralia/on_hearing.htm

Games Studies, Game Design

Some people study games as academic research: the field is known as *Games Studies* (or *Game Studies*). Yes, that is a dream job, but let's not get jealous. Instead, here's a question for you: should what these people say be useful to game designers?

In other academic disciplines, usefulness to practitioners can be seen as a bad thing. An anthropologist would be aghast if members of a tribe they were studying got hold of an ethnography then altered their behavior accordingly. Okay, so it's not quite that extreme with Games Studies, but the question does remain as to whether the people who design the games (and this includes MMOs) should find what's being said about them relevant. Should someone who studies games always bear in mind when presenting their work its usefulness to a designer?

I think they should, yes. Or, put another way, if their work isn't useful to designers then it isn't useful to Games Studies either.

Here's why.

If a bunch of academics are talking at a Games Studies conference, they share a connection that involves games. Games form the interaction space between researchers: all inter-disciplinary communication must pass through that domain. Otherwise, the researchers have no common ground, and the conference would be pointless.

The thing is, game designers *occupy* that common ground: it's their home territory. Game designers *study games*. Therefore, if people want to talk about that common ground, it's reasonable to expect that designers should be able to find something useful in what they say. If designers don't find your work useful, that means it probably didn't say enough for anyone else studying games to find it useful either—such as your fellow researchers. They may find it *interesting*, but that doesn't mean they'll find it *useful*.

The less that something can be said to be useful to designers, the more distant it is from Games Studies itself. People coming from related disciplines may still be able to engage in dialogue. For example, a sociologist studying games may gain valuable insights from an anthropologist studying games, even if the anthropologist's work has no utility for games designers. However, people studying games from a discipline that only intersects with the anthropologist's work through the domain of games (say, Artificial Intelligence) will not find an anthropologist's insights valuable to them.

I don't think Games Studies researchers should *have* to justify themselves to designers. As a designer, I find it more useful when they *do* justify themselves, because it means I don't have to go scouring the literature for relevant stuff—it's already flagged for me. Researchers shouldn't feel obliged to do that just for *me*, though, especially if it reduces the chance of their getting published in their "home" field. All they need to bear in mind is that if they can't explain to a game designer why their research is relevant, they're probably not studying games—they're studying something else.

Being able to justify your studies in terms of benefit to games designers anchors it, such that other Games Studies researchers coming from different angles can make use of it too. It's a form of relevancy check, not a piece of "you don't deserve to talk about this if you can't justify yourself to me" arrogance on the part of games designers.

That doesn't mean game designers *aren't* arrogant, of course, just that telling off "Games Studies" researchers for being irrelevant doesn't substantiate such an assertion.

PK

PK stands for "player killing". It's a verb, referring to the act of attacking the characters of other players. Those who PK are PKers.

The term PK has entered the general vocabulary of South Korea and China as meaning doing to someone something that's within the rules but in a kind of "ends justify the means" way, usually in order to beat them at something. Ordinary TV game shows can have a PK round, for example.

PK is actually a misnomer, as it suggests that players are being killed whereas in fact it's only their characters.

Ways to Think About Play

All game designers should read *The Ambiguity of Play*[4], by the New Zealand theorist Brian Sutton-Smith. It summarizes his observations from decades of studying play.

But hey, you're a busy person,; you have rep to grind and instances to run, so I'll give you a quick overview.

Basically, Sutton-Smith noticed over the years that different people had different ways of looking at play, each useful for a particular range of purposes. For example, a developmental psychologist may regard play as something that children do to advance and adapt, whereas a clinical psychologist may regard it as something self-destructive that gamblers do. You wouldn't want to mix those up.

In all, Sutton-Smith identified seven categories of describing play, which he called *rhetorics*:

- Play as progress
- Play as fate
- Play as power
- Play as identity
- Play as the imaginary
- Play as the self
- Play as the frivolous

Yeah, I know, rep to grind and instances to run. I'll spread out my explanations of what these mean so you don't have to eat them all at once.

Self-Belief

Can *you* be a revolutionary game designer? Can you see beyond the current paradigms to new ones that supersede them? Rather than tinkering with what's already there, can you add something completely new and original?

I believe you can, but my view is irrelevant. Do *you* believe you can?

If you don't, you won't.

---

[4]Brian Sutton-Smith: *The Ambiguity of Play*. Harvard University Press: Cambridge, Massachusetts. 1997.

Toweritis

I dread it when I come across a tower in a role-playing game, as I just *know* that 9 times out of 10 I'm going to encounter yet another example of *toweritis*. I've seen it in face-to-face RPGs, single-player RPGs, and MMOs. Oh, and books, too.

Here's what happens. The designer has this idea for a tower, with something big and bad at the top and lesser things underneath. Only, it's a *tower*, right, so it has to be *tall*, so there have to be *lots* of things underneath. *Lots* of them. Lots, lots, *lots*. Lots is *good*, right? It's *not* going to be a GRINDINGLY INSANE CRAWL that you endure just so you can eventually reach the boss you *actually* want to reach, the one right at the top? Oh, no, far from it! It's going to be fun fun funnity fun all the way.

Yeah, right.

Oh, and if in an MMO you *really* want to make it *really* fun, crock your looking-for-group mechanism and give your tower a hardcore attendance requirement. Then populate it with one-false-move-and-you-wipe minor bosses so you can have a break from the SENSELESS MONOTONOUS TRUDGE to the top while watching your guild SHATTER INTO TINY PIECES because people who have played for weeks to get attuned can't find a group to visit the place. Finally, call it Karazhan and claim it's been a big success.

Oh, wait, that's been done in *WoW*.

Well how about you make it the centerpiece of the final stage of your characters' narrative arc, and have people get to the top by going through three levels randomly-selected from 21, all of which have exactly the same linear layout with occasional breakouts such as a please-like-it *Pac Man* homage that if I did like it I'd be playing *Pac Man* not *The Secret World*.

Toweritis isn't hard for a designer to overcome; it just takes an awareness of the fact that there's a potential problem and a will of iron not to add in an extra two floors, four side towers so it looks like a hand, lava, a bunch of the LIVING DEAD, and a subterranean complex. And a cherry on top.

Lost Cities

There's a 1999 card game by Reiner Knizia called *Lost Cities*. I won't discuss the mechanics, except to say they're clear, clean, and classy, and the game is thoroughly absorbing. Instead, I'm going to home in on the context.

Here's a picture of one of the sets of cards in the game:

Lost Cities has 5 suits of 12 cards: nine have a rank (from 2 to 10); three cards are different from the rest; there are no aces. Nevertheless, its design roots in playing cards are pretty obvious. You could *almost* play it with a regular pack of cards, although having five suits instead of four does make for a better game so I wouldn't recommend it.

It's clear from this that the whole "lost cities" shtick is just dressing—a fiction to add appeal to an abstract game built around a mechanic. The game could be reskinned as interstellar exploration, or politics, or Greek myth, or any other of the myriad possibilities. The mechanics, and therefore the playing strategies, would be the same; only the context would change.

Lost Cities is an enjoyable and engaging two-player game. I mention it to demonstrate that it's entirely possible to design the mechanics of a game without reference to any context yet still end up with something eminently fun to play.

The Players' View

MMOs have a particular kind of problem with regard to people who "break the rules," because the primary normative solution—kick them out of the game—doesn't work. They just come back under a different name. This is why it's important for MMO designers and researchers to look at the magic circle. If we want to address the players' grievances, then we need to be able to characterize their view of play, and the magic circle embodies that view.

Players are offering a deal: I'll play by the rules if you do. This is the notion that the magic circle captures. Yes, each person's magic circle is different, because each person's view of "the rules" is different. They're not *actually* rules in a strict philosophical sense, either: they're willingly-adopted temporary limits on behavior. Nevertheless, the fact is that players have this notion of "rules," and that's the domain we're operating in if we're looking at people who don't play by them.

Reskinning and Perception

Imagine a 1,500-piece jigsaw puzzle of a country garden. It probably wouldn't be too hard to complete if you like jigsaw puzzles—it's a challenge, but not so much as to be tedious.

Now imagine the exact same 1,500 pieces cut the exact same way, but instead of a country garden the picture is of a box of assorted screws. That may or may not be as easy as the country garden, but you can bet that fewer copies of it would be sold. It's a different puzzle.

Similarly, although you can reskin a game so that its functionality and gameplay is the same and only the names have changed, that doesn't mean the *game* is the same. How it is *perceived* by the players is just as important as how it's implemented.

Studying Games Studies

A philosopher or linguist could write about the nature of a mathematical proof, but the proof itself would only be publishable in the right kind of mathematics journal.

What about people who study games? Is there a kind of research that could *only* appear in a specialist games studies journal?

In general, when it comes to an academic discipline, X, there are a number of views operating:

1. The study of X for its own sake.
2. The study of X as an application domain for Y.
3. The study of Y as an application domain for X.
4. The study of X as a subfield of Y.
5. The study of Y as a subfield of X.
6. The meta-study of any of points 1 to 6.

Examples:

1. "Here's a cool game mechanic."
2. "We can develop AI to play games."
3. "We can develop games to help people learn."
4. "Games are a form of play."
5. "Computer games are a form of game."
6. "COLLEGE GUNMAN IS VIDEO GAMER."

Which of these is or are Games Studies? All of them? Just the first one? Just the last one?

For me, it all comes down to game *design*.

Monolithic Worlds

If you tried really hard, you could implement *World of Warcraft* inside *Second Life*. However, if you'd written it for *Second Life* first, you'd be so bound by *SL*'s conventions that wouldn't have ever got anything like *WoW*.

Too much integration restricts experimentation. If all MMOs are made with the same tools and adhere to the same protocols, you don't end up with lots of worlds, you end up with one, monolithic world with lots of zones.

Fun

Games are fun!

Well, yes and no. Here are three games that anthropologist Thomas Malaby told me about, which he encountered while doing field work in Greece.

- **Drawing Lots.** Some Greek farms are very small. When the farmer dies, they wouldn't be viable if broken up into pieces and shared among the farmer's children. Therefore, the children draw lots. Whoever wins, gets the entire farm; the rest get nothing. Fun for the winner, not so much fun for the rest.

- **Determining Fate.** Some Greeks roll dice against each other with no skill or strategy involved whatsoever. If you win, it must be luck. So, that means fate is on your side, then! The games aren't fun, but you'll feel better going for a job interview if you know Someone Up There thinks well of you (or at least better of you than of the other player). And if you lost? Well, there's always tomorrow.

- **Aid to Philosophy.** Here, you use dice to help you make a decision. Should you buy a new car or a second-hand one? You roll the dice, and if they say yes then hmm, but where will I get the money? Should I take out a loan? Ask the dice again. Or if they said not to buy a new car, perhaps if you saw a really cheap one on special offer, that would work? You're using the dice to give your inner thoughts chance to emerge, which can be surprisingly effective. Not exactly fun, though.

So games *don't* have to be fun.

Even for ones that *are* fun, the fun is relative. There are different *degrees* of fun (and there are different degrees of unfun, too). Fun is also *subjective*. Not everyone will find the same thing fun in a game, nor will they find things fun for the same reason. Even *you* may find a game fun one day and not another, depending on your mood.

But what *is* fun? What does "this is fun" *mean*?

On Analyzing Gameplay

Gameplay simply isn't understood.

People approaching games from a Media Studies background tend to see the motifs and symbols of a game's setting, but not of the gameplay. That's in part because their home field doesn't have a vocabulary for gameplay, but mainly because it doesn't have a process-oriented view of the artifact being studied (the "text").

It reminds me of the arguments I used to hear in the early 1980s (when Computer Science departments still had computer scientists in them) regarding declarative *versus* procedural programming languages. Declarative languages say what you want done but not how to do it; procedural languages say what you want done in terms of how to do it. Computers are fundamentally procedural, but declarative languages are much more amenable to mathematical analysis (such as proving the correctness of a program). Their strength lies in the fact that they don't analyze process; however, that's a weakness if you actually *want* to analyze process. With games, gameplay is fundamentally procedural but if it's being analyzed using tools developed for declarative texts, well, they're not really going to be able to capture the essence of what's going on because they don't have any kind of a handle on process. It's akin to the declarative/procedural semantics distinction I mentioned earlier.

Interaction between players is procedural. That said, computer games are unusual in that most of those that have been written are single-player. Single-player games aren't *actually* games at all: they're puzzles. They only really qualify as games if they have computer-controlled opponents that players interpret as behaving intelligently, meaning that players feel they can "lose" to them. This suggests that a lot of the analysis of computer games is actually an analysis of a puzzle in the context of its symbolic dressing. The steps involved in solving the puzzle have a narrative connection that can be read declaratively; the core gameplay loop that gets you from one step in the puzzle to the next, however, *has* to be read procedurally, so tends to be ignored. It probably *can* be ignored most of the time, too, to be honest, as it rarely contributes to the narrative. Sometimes it does—for example in *Dragon Age* the narrative will unfold differently if you favor some party members over others for gameplay reasons—but this is uncommon.

Multi-player games are another thing entirely, especially if they involve competition as well as cooperation. Lit Crit style analyses of these are not going to get very far *at all*. What does the interplay between strategy and tactics in an RTS "mean" for a narrative? What do the abilities of a character in an RPG "mean" to its player? You can't evaluate, interpret, nor understand a game if you can't get a handle on its gameplay, and you can't get a handle on its gameplay unless you understand the *concept* of gameplay.

Gameplay is universal to games, whether they're computer games, board games, playground games, word games, or sports. The creation of gameplay is at the heart of what game design *is*. That's why it's of crucial importance to game design.

Yet, it simply isn't *understood*.

Content with Content Creation

Professed reason why MMO developers like the idea of user-created content: *we are empowering our players.*

Actual reason why MMO developers like the idea of user-created content: *they will make stuff for us for free!*

Okay, so this is a *little* unfair. There *are* some developers enlightened enough to recognize that MMOs are in a rut they see UCC as something worth experimenting with on the grounds that even if it comes to nothing they may at least identify some natural designers from it.

Of course, there are also developers who think they can make money by charging people to do UCC. Well, I guess if the vanity publishing market for books makes money, it's possible that this would work (if not entirely ethically).

Rhetoric: Play as Progress

Animals play. Young bears will fight each other, but nip rather than bite. Animals that do this have advantages over those that don't. They:

- Learn to adapt to new situations
- Train in skills to deal with expected situations
- Establish social hierarchies safely
- Discover new behaviors
- Bond
- Get an emotional boost

In this context, biologists see play as an activity that's evolutionarily useful to higher animals—which includes humans. By playing, animals will progress in their development. Animals experiencing play as fun will tend to play more than those that don't, so there's evolutionary pressure to find games fun, too.

Of course, it's rather hard to confirm any of this because we don't actually know *what* animals think.

We have only slightly more chance of knowing what human children think. It does seem that they develop more as individuals as their play increases in sophistication, and therefore play by children is often seen as a form of learning. This suggests that adults could intervene in children's play to help them learn.

Hmm. Would *you* have wanted adults to direct your play when you were a child?

The Play as Progress rhetoric has two major limitations. First, it implies that play stops when progress stops, i.e., at adulthood. It doesn't. Second, if play is evolutionarily useful then there should be a link between animals' brain sizes and the amount they play. There isn't.

So looking at play as a way to progress is useful under certain circumstances, but not all. Well, unless you're a serious games researcher whose funding is completely predicated on this rhetoric, obviously.

Oh, and also if you're an MMO designer. If you're wondering why, the question you should ask is: "*What* do people learn as they play?".

NPC

NPC stands for *Non-Player Character*. It's an old term from face-to-face role-playing games, used to distinguish computer-controlled characters from player-controlled characters (which were called PCs—*Player Characters*).

Nowadays, the term tends to refer more specifically to non-combat computer-controlled characters; they often have the same general appearance as player characters. Computer-controlled characters you fight are *mobs* (which is short for *mobiles*—a term I invented but didn't expect anyone to use, meaning "mobile objects"). Large, powerful mobs that have choreographed behavior and drop major treasure are called *bosses*; ones you have to kill on the way to the boss are *trash*.

In face-to-face role-playing games, the traditional vocabulary is slightly different. A combat-capable enemy can easily be an NPC, and is even likely so if it's also a boss; trash mobs are called *monsters* even when they include humans.

Thus, in *Dungeons & Dragons*, you might say you fought your way through monsters in a tower to confront the NPC wizard at the top, whereas in an MMO you might say you fought your way through trash mobs to confront the wizard boss.

Interactivity

The key to gameplay is *interactivity*.

In this context, interactivity means the *player's* interactivity: NPCs interacting with the environment do not qualify that environment as being "interactive".

Interactions change that with which they are interacting, so producing a new range of choices. With no interactivity, you have no changes, therefore no new choices, therefore no gameplay.

> *Gameplay is a series of interesting choices.*
>
> —Sid Meier

Are MMOs Games?

Well, duh, obviously! The G in MMORPG even stands for "game"!

Among people who study games, though, it's not so clear cut. In their landmark book[5], Katie Salen and Eric Zimmerman looked at eight earlier definitions of what the term "game" meant, extracting the essentials of all of them to come up with the following:

> *A game is a system in which players engage in an artificial conflict, defined by rules, that results in a quantifiable outcome.*

—Salen & Zimmerman

Okay, now this has a number of potential problems in areas such as cooperative games and single-player games, but the definition isn't intended to be black-and-white; its authors readily admit the possibility of borderline cases. MMOs fall into such a category, because they don't have a "quantifiable outcome". One of the leading lights of academic Games Studies, Jesper Juul, agrees: his six-feature definition of what makes something a game[6] states that they must have "variable, quantifiable outcomes".

As designer Greg Costikyan[7] (one of the people whose definitions Salen and Zimmerman looked at in composing theirs) points out, the problem for MMOs is the word "outcome". MMOs don't have clear winners and losers. Costikyan does believe the MMOs are games, though; indeed, even something like *Second Life* is a game in his view, as it's a form of structured play.

The situation is made murkier by the fact that some MMOs do have quantifiable outcomes—*MUD1* and *MUD2*, for example. So if I were to make a new version of *MUD2* that was identical to the first but with the single change that when you got enough points to "win" you just stayed there, this would mean that you could spend two years playing one and it would be a game, but two years playing the other and it wouldn't be a game—even if your experiences in each were indistinguishable.

---

[5]Katie Salen and Eric Zimmerman: *Rules of Play: Game Design Fundamentals*. MIT Press, Cambridge MA, 2004.

[6]Jesper Juul: *The Game, the Player, the World: Looking for a Heart of Gameness*. Proceedings of DiGRA conference *Level Up*, Utrecht, 2003. http://www.jesperjuul.net/text/gameplayerworld/

[7]Greg Costikyan: *MMGs are So! Games – and if Not, they'll Die*. November, 2003. http://www.costik.com/weblog/2003_11_01_blogchive.html

Personally, I don't think it makes an MMO less of a game if it doesn't promise players an end; neither do I think it's less of an MMO if it does. That said, there are good reasons (which I'll come to later) to believe that players will get more out of an MMO if it does have an end than if it doesn't.

Using this terminology, the best you can say in answer to the question "are MMOs games?" is "they're not *only* games".

Actually, though, I don't think they *are* games—but not for anything to do with the reasons Katie Salen, Eric Zimmerman, and Jesper Juul do, nor for why Greg Costikyan doesn't.

In my view, MMOs are *places*. They're no more games than a football stadium is a sport. People can go there *to play* games and to do a whole bunch of other things, but fundamentally they're places. Most of the people who visit these places engage in an activity that may or may not be considered to be a game (this is really what Katie, Eric, Jesper, and Greg are talking about); other people engage in no such an activity, though.

That said, a sense of "game" is what distinguishes MMOs from other virtual worlds such as *Second Life*. MMOs *are* places, but they have built-in gameplay and they're structured as if they were games, whereas social worlds have no such structure. Thus, throughout this book I refer to MMOs as "games" or "game worlds," even though strictly speaking I prefer the term "game-like worlds".

Most players (you included?) *do* consider MMOs to be games, though; so am I telling all those people they're wrong?

No, I'm not—and for a somewhat remarkable reason: for most players, MMOs are indeed games! The "quantifiable outcome" concerns their realization that—

Oh, I'd better stop for the moment, I'm getting ahead of myself here.

What's a Game?

Here's my definition:

1. Play is what happens when you freely and knowingly bound your behavior according to a set of rules in the hope of gaining some benefit.

2. Games are play at which you can lose.

Here's *why* it's my definition:

Freely, because play under duress or obligation is not play. If you feel you *have* to play, that makes it work.

Knowingly, because if you don't know you're playing, you're not. You may be a token in someone *else's* play, but that doesn't mean *you're* playing.

Bound, because you could otherwise do it. The reason I don't shoot laser beams from my eyes is I'm *incapable* of doing so; the reason I don't move a rook diagonally in *Chess* is I *choose* not to do so.

Rules, because play is considered. (The earlier *freely* implies that the rules are artificial). You don't need to know all the rules in advance, and they're not necessarily fixed.

Hope, because there's no guaranteed outcome.

Benefit, because play is purposeful. "To have fun" is a perfectly acceptable benefit. You don't necessarily need to know what the benefit will *be*, just so long as you hope there will indeed be one.

Lose, because games are goal-directed; not *win*, because games don't have to end.

Overall, statement 1 of the definition describes Huizinga's *magic circle* from an individual's point of view. *You're* playing when *you* do this—even if the other people with whom you *believe* you are playing are not, in fact, playing. Play is in the eye of the player.

Statement 2 implies you believe that the other players in your game have bought into the same rule set as you have in Statement 1, that is, you're playing the same game.

Playfulness

My *MUD2* arch-wiz arrives with a puff of thunder and disappears in a crash of smoke (as opposed to arriving with a crash of thunder and disappearing in a puff of smoke, which is the default).

You can do so much *more* with words.

Glory

There's a theory[8] that considers the driving motivations for MMO players to be the twin concepts of *glory* and *shame*. Players act how they act so as to gain glory and avoid shame.

Glory and shame are much stronger concepts in the Far East than in the West. In particular, *guilt* is more important in the West than shame is. Guilt arises because of how you perceive your own actions; shame arises because of how others perceive them.

Glory is also different, in that in the West it's less common to gain glory by association. Yes, you can benefit from reflected glory, but only if you've done something that contributed to it. In the Far East, merely knowing someone who has glory can boost your own glory level.

For glory to *be* glory, there has to be an observer who perceives it as being glory. If person A does something and person B is associated with person A, then for it to count there needs to be a person C to recognize person B's glory being reflected from person A. Without a person C, Person A isn't going to think person B is glorious, and neither is person B.

As always with theories, they're useful if they say something you can use and not so useful if they don't. Glory and shame may be useful if you're looking at *World of Tanks*, but not if you're looking at *Guild Wars 2*.

---

[8]Jonathan Baron: *Glory and Shame: Powerful Psychology in Multiplayer Online Games*. Proceedings of the *Game Developers Conference*, San Jose CA, 1999. http://www.gamasutra.com/view/feature/3395/glory_and_shame_powerful_.php

Tools for the Job

If I'm attacking a dryad then an axe is good, a rapier isn't so bad, but a mace is useless. If I'm attacking a skeleton then a mace is good, an axe isn't so bad, but a rapier is useless. If I'm attacking a yeti then a rapier is good, but both an axe and a mace are useless.

Different weapons do different kinds of damage in real life. Why wouldn't they in MMOs? In these examples, I've only used slashing, crushing, and stabbing damage; tabletop role-playing games have heat damage, corrosion damage, poison damage, electrical damage, ...and they have done for years. This isn't merely to give the imaginary world a greater sense of verisimilitude (although it does): it adds choice. Choice, unless it's arbitrary or meaningless, adds gameplay.

MMO players, unlike tabletop RPG players, don't see it quite that way.

They don't mind choosing between one configuration of armor/skills and another—in fact many of them rather enjoy creating different builds for different occasions. However, they do mind having to decide before they go somewhere which build to use. They want to be able to change to the most useful one instantly, rather than having to balance equipment decisions over the course of a series of fights.

For example, suppose there are ten people about to spend two hours in an instance in which one of the fights needs a fireproof tank. Do you have your tank wear fireproof armor the whole time, causing it to get beaten up unnecessarily when cheaper armor would do the job instead? Do you have a main tank in regular armor and a secondary tank in fireproof armor who can step up for that one fight? Do you try to find some other way to achieve fireproofing? Those are interesting strategic decisions.

Unfortunately, today's players are unlikely to think in those terms: they want the tank to be able to carry many sets of armor and to switch between them instantly.

Convenience costs so much.

Is it a Game?

There are some classic borderline cases that cause problems for definitions of games. Here's what my definition says about them:

- *Noughts and Crosses (Tic-Tac-Toe)*

This *is* a game, but only for people inexperienced enough to play it and occasionally lose. That generally means children. For most adults, it will always be a draw or a win and therefore not a game.

- Crossword Puzzles

These are games should you view them as a challenge set down by the compiler, with failure to complete them as being "defeat". I suspect that most people don't regard crossword puzzles as something you can lose at, however, and would therefore call them pastimes rather than games.

- *Dungeons & Dragons*

This is a game. You can't win, but you can occasionally lose. You can look on a *D&D* campaign as a setting for overlapping mini-games, each of which you can win or lose. The technical term for this kind of game is *game neverending* (which I believe is one of Greg Costikyan's coinings).

- *Snakes and Ladders (Chutes and Ladders)*

This is only a game if you gain some benefit from rolling dice mindlessly. For small children, and for the adults who want to keep them happy, it can indeed be a game. For everyone else, it's a chore and therefore not a game.

- Lotteries

Lotteries are games, just not particularly sophisticated ones.

- MMOs

MMOs are games until you realize they're not.

Accepting Bounds

If you want to call yourself a sculptor, you have to accept a 3D component to your work; if you want to call yourself a choreographer, you have to accept motion; if you want to call yourself an MMO designer, you have to accept fun.

Plutarch for Newbies

Plutarch's "vessel to be filled or fire to be kindled" dichotomy is usually applied to the difference between education and training.

New players of MMOs need to learn what to do and what the world is about. So, should newbies in MMOs be trained or educated?

The forces of commerce and (ironically) education press for the former. Newbies are empty pages upon which the designer can write what they like.

Designers themselves tend to side with the latter. Newbies are small acorns that, given content to help them grow, will eventually become mighty oaks.

Plutarch advocated the education approach.

I'm a designer. I'm with Plutarch.

Diverse Games

Having rules makes games more constrained than non-games, but only in some dimensions. In others, it's liberating.

The designer gets to decide where to constrain and where to liberate: what to disallow in order that it allows something else.

One of these days, I'll read a story about a Mulan-like man who dresses as a woman so he doesn't have to go to war and get killed, but can stay at home and look after his sick parents.

Will I ever be able to play an RPG in which that happens?

The more people who can make games, the more diverse those games will be.

Rhetoric: Play as Fate

This is perhaps the oldest of the seven rhetorics of play. It sees people as being at the mercy of fate/the gods/destiny/chance, and play as being a way of testing your luck (i.e., testing your future).

As I pointed out earlier when describing some of the games anthropologist Thomas Malaby encountered in Greece, this kind of game isn't necessarily fun. It can, however, be tremendously comforting.

Play as Fate is the foundation of many ancient religions and practices, some of them still quite prevalent today despite their being unqualified specious nonsense (e.g., astrology). It's strongly connected with the idea of superstition, which in turn links it to gambling. You only have to watch *Deal or No Deal* on TV to witness the amazing lengths that some people will go to in their attempts to impose predictively-useful structure on what is actually an exercise in blind chance.

Play as Fate is also closely linked with dreams. See, what this rhetoric does is to try to rationalize the chaotic by ascribing order to it (luck, magic, gods). Dreams are messages from the ordering body—visions of what your fate might be (but only *might* be—they could be wrong). Therefore, they're *connected*. This may even have a psychological basis, as dreams can indeed help people organize their understanding of the world—although it's not contingent on there being an ordering body.

The main limitation of this way of looking at play is that it doesn't work for all play. At its very center is the notion of chance—some aspect of play that is uncontrollable except by the ordering body. By testing yourself against this, you divine what the ordering body thinks of you. Except, not all games *have* this kind of chance—*Chess* doesn't, for example. It also has unsatisfying implications for the notion that play is voluntary, because if fate is inescapable then how can *anything* be voluntary?

Oh, later while you're reading this book, if you remember, look back on this rhetoric when you see the magic words *Atonement with the Father*. It *does* have something interesting to say about MMOs.

In Practice

When you get a board game out of its box and read the rules, you will usually play a few practice rounds to get the hang of them. Then, you'll start again and play the game properly. This used to happen with computer games in the distant past when players had to read manuals to play, but nowadays players tend to dive right in, maybe playing a tutorial if the game looks particularly daunting in its complexity. Tutorials are thus like practice games, just structured by the game designer rather than the players.

Are tutorials and practice games within the magic circle or outside of it?

This isn't an easy call. It's clear that a group of players who set up a board game and play through the rules are attempting to follow them, but it's also clear that they expect to make mistakes and to have to take back moves, and that they'll be debating what the rules actually mean. They do have a lusory attitude and a social contract, but they're not really playing a game, are they?

Well no, they're not. They are, however, playing. Play is what you get when you freely and knowingly agree to bound your behavior according to a set of rules in the hope of gaining some benefit. That's what's happening here: the benefit is that you'll be able to play the game. However, it's not itself a game, because you can't lose. You can only lose once you start to play the game "proper".

In other words, in this kind of situation you're not playing a game, you're playing *with* a game.

Opposites Reflect

Some things that are physical in virtual worlds are virtual in the physical world.

In the real world, for example, setting up a company is purely a legal affair; a company is not a physical object. In an MMO, setting up a guild is a physical affair, because it's implemented directly in the MMO's code.

Dimensions of Change

If you're designing a game, it can be useful to consider the *dimensions of change* involved.

Consider a pack of playing cards. Ask yourself what dimensions the cards can change along. Okay, so they vary in their colors, suits, ranks (numbers), and pictures. You can introduce others, such as whether they're face up or not, or their orientation on the table, but the suits and ranks are the main ones.

What we've identified here are the properties of one card that make it different from another card. Some are fixed (you can't change a card's suit) and some are variable (you can change its orientation). They're all examples of what you'd need to focus on if you were designing a card game.

Once you've identified the dimensions, you can look at those dimensions' own properties:

- Colors are basically a binary property and are tied to suits.

- Suits are small in number (4) containing a larger number (13) of elements, weakly ordered.

- Ranks are a larger number (13) of strongly-ordered values, of which there are a smaller number (4) of each.

- Picture is another binary property, tied to rank.

From here, you look at ways you can make the different dimensions interact with one another to present interesting choices. Suits look good for collecting sets, for example, and ranks look good for collecting sequences.

Can you think of something built around a more unusual property, though? Say, picture cards?

Try it.

Are Virtual Worlds Games?

No, I said: they're places. You can play games in them, and they may have physics that implement game elements, but they're no more games than is the Centre Court at Wimbledon.

Emergence

Content, behaviors, goals, or whatever are said to be *emergent* if they are not defined directly, but rather appear from the interaction of defined (or indeed emergent) systems.

For example, birds flying with other birds of the same species will obey three general rules:

- They'll try not to fly into each other.
- They'll try to align their direction with that of nearby birds.
- They'll also try to steer themselves toward the average relative position of nearby birds.

The result of following these rules means that birds flock. The behavior of a flock is hard to deduce from the basic rules, and is much more sophisticated than are the basic rules. Furthermore, the rules themselves are not obviously apparent merely from watching the behavior of a flock for a couple of minutes. The sum (the flock) is greater than the sum of its parts (the birds), but is entirely dependent on them. The behavior of a flock can therefore be said to *emerge* from the behavior of individual birds.

Emergence is important in computer games, including MMOs. It occurs at several levels, of which *emergent gameplay* is the most visible.

For example, in *MUD2* if humanoid characters slept outside in the rain then they could catch a cold. It didn't have a cure (no magic is that powerful!), and when you had a cold it would make you less able to fight. After a few minutes, though, you'd be over it and immune for a period. Every so often, anyone with a cold would cough and sneeze; anyone who was nearby them could thus catch it off them. Now sometimes, players would deliberately catch a cold then run off to the dwarfen citadel to infect a few dwarfs with the virus by sneezing on them. These would sneeze near other dwarfs, and the infection would then spread rapidly throughout the dwarf population. As soon as the player character got better, they'd attack the citadel and find that the miserable coughing and sneezing defenders put up much less of a fight. Some of them might even be asleep (to recover the stamina they'd lost from their battle with the cold virus), which made them particularly vulnerable. This was emergent gameplay, arising from interactions between the cold-passing mechanic, combat mechanic, and the game's geography.

Many academics seem to think that emergent gameplay isn't designed, and is some miraculous development due entirely to the ingenuity of the players. Sometimes, they're right, it is. Often, though, designers are perfectly well aware how their systems will interact and will adjust them so that a desired behavior will emerge. That's what I did with colds in *MUD2*, to the extent of play testing it in the dwarf citadel (where *MUD2*'s highest concentration of mobiles lived) in order to ensure I got the timing of the coughs and sneezes right to infect the dwarfs at a good, steady rate.

Just because behaviors emerge from interactions that players didn't plan for, doesn't mean the designer didn't plan for them.

That Question

As an MMO designer, a question I'm often asked by journalists and players is: "Where do you get your ideas from?".

Novelists, screenwriters, fashion designers, architects, landscape gardeners, painters, choreographers, etc. all get asked the same question.

Here's the answer.

What? Designers have *no need* for inspiration! They get ideas the *whole damned time!* They get more ideas than they know what to do with!

The question you *should* be asking is: "How do you decide which ideas to pursue?".

Conditions

When you're designing an MMO, you need a sense of what players will be doing in it (which is to say, what you'll be *allowing* them to do in it).

Interaction

The word *interaction* is used a lot in game design, indeed I've used it a lot already in this book. The player's interactivity is central to gameplay.

What does the word actually *mean*, though?

Well, it *can* mean a whole range of things. One way of looking at an interface is something through which a player "interacts" with a system, therefore in one sense all systems that have an interface are interactive. You "interact with" your TV when you change channels, for example. Likewise, a function in a program can "interact with" a database; a performer can "interact with" an audience.

To interact, you need at least two parties in the interaction. Interaction involves a cycle of events in which action by one party leads to a response by the other, which leads to further action by the first party (that is, a response to the response). A player might "interact with the environment" by planting a seed; the environment responds by (some time later) producing a plant; the player responds to that by picking the plant; the environment responds by removing the plant from its location model and transferring it to the player's inventory.

Now although game designers are alert to different senses of interaction, there's one particular use of it that is of key importance to them. This is the interaction between intelligent entities (which always includes players, but in MMO terms may also admit NPCs and mobs). This is what shifts gameplay from puzzle-solving to competition or cooperation.

Interaction between intelligent entities goes something like this:

- Step 1: Actor 1 performs an action of which actor 2 becomes aware.

- Step 2: Actor 2 considers a response to this action.

- Step 3: Go to Step 1, but with the actors reversed and the action performed being the one that Actor 2 decided to do in response.

As you can see, in this view of interaction both parties of the interaction are interchangeable. They react to one another's actions. Threads of responses will arise, pause, branch, overlap, die, and more. The game world is a context and a conduit for interaction between intelligent entities. From this, gameplay flows.

Interestingly, you can also argue that the players are interacting with the designer. The designer creates the system and embodies within it an indefinite number of canned responses to the player's actions: it's as if the designer is pre-responding the player's actions. Although this is a valid view, it's not really what designers tend to mean when they talk about "interaction," though. After all, you could say the same thing about a novel, which is a static entity rather than one with moving parts; the only "system" is the one the players construct in their heads.

So, when people say that "games are interactive but books/movies/painting/ music aren't," what they're really saying is that those who experience games can change the direction their experience goes by acting on the medium of the experience (the game), which will elicit a response from it that will cause them to think.

This isn't to say that other forms of art don't cause people to think; it is to say that they don't cause people to think *about what they're doing.*

Designed Parameters

If you were to give a group of children some red and some blue paint to play with, you'd have no idea what they might create with it. However, you *would* know that whatever they did create, it wouldn't involve any green or yellow, and therefore would have a certain mood to it.

When designers create MMOs, they don't know what the players *will* do, but they do construct the parameters that define what they *can* do.

Designers can and do design for what an observer might think is emergence.

Dimensions of Change Example

Picture cards: what can we do with picture cards?

Well the pictures are of royalty, so we could make a game about royalty:

- A war between medieval countries
- Intrigue between renaissance states
- Revolution and republic
- Don't rely on me, use your own imagination!

See how introducing context (royalty) has led to constraints, which have led to ideas?

Oh, I should say I'm making this game up as I write this, by the way.

Okay, so let's go with a theme that has sales potential: the Wars of the Roses. This suggests it's a two-player game. It also suggests we should split the cards, by suit or color.

I'm now thinking about what it is the players will do. Let's say they put cards from their hand face down at the same time—we'll call this a "battle". They reveal their cards at the same time, the loser taking casualties—getting rid of a card.

Hmm, how big a hand? How many cards to put down? How to decide the loser? What do our special picture cards do?

Well, let's experiment. Give one player all the hearts and the other all the spades. Throw out clubs and diamonds. Each player puts down two cards: on the reveal, you add up the card ranks and the player with the lower total loses the lower of the cards they played (aces are low).

Let's say that if one of your cards is a picture, this changes things. Don't allow people to play two picture cards at once, that'll over-complicate things.

If it's a jack, compare your other card to your opponent's lower card. The lower of the two wins. The other loses their higher card (which could be the jack). If it's a draw, nothing happens.

There are lots of ways I could tweak the rules for queens and kings:

- Add some randomness
- Target picture cards
- Some kind of nuclear win-but-lose option
- Look at the difference between card values

Notice that the *mechanics themselves* have now become new dimensions of change. We can adjust the order of play, the number of cards laid down, where the cards come from, where they go, and so on. The gameplay-driving interactions we seek can include these dimensions, too—and any new dimensions that they themselves introduce.

The key is to be *aware* of what you can change.

I kind a like the idea of giving you a single-shot win option, so let's say that if you play your queen, you always lose it *but* your opponent also loses their higher card. This means that the result of queen versus jack or queen would lead to the loss of both picture cards.

What about kings? Well, a king's bodyguard might be better than normal troops, so let's exploit that. If you play a king, compare your other card to your opponent's non-picture cards. If either of your opponent's cards is within one of your non-king card's rank, you lose your king ("peasant uprising"). Otherwise, your opponent loses both their cards (and you could still lose your king to a jack or queen).

At the end of the battle, you put any cards you didn't lose back into your hand and can use them in future battles. You win the game when your opponent can't fight a battle (either they have only pictures left, or only one card left). A draw is possible.

At this point, I'd probably want to play test the game. It feels as if it could be too short, and I have a suspicion that each battle would need a stake to give it relative importance (draw a random diamond/club to represent a "city" to be captured?).

What I've done just now shows an example of a design process in action. In general, the dimensions you identify provide a framework—the playground in which you design. You can do this with any design-to-a-context exercise—you could do it with a role-playing game if you wanted. It's a useful tool.

Oh, and if my mentioning RPGs just then gave you the fleeting thought that the game I just concocted could be made into one, that passive ability to flash an idea is probably more use to you as a designer than any of this could ever be.

Tokens, Rules, Features, and Gameplay

Game designers will regularly throw around what to them are actually technical terms, without any concern for what they mean.

So, here's what they mean. I should mention up front that this analysis isn't mine, it's that of Andrew Rollings and Dave Morris, distilled from their excellent book, *Game Architecture and Design: A New Edition*[9]. If you want a more in-depth discussion, that's where to look.

So, *tokens* are the objects that take part in the game. They have things done to or with them. There isn't really a standard term; I'll be using tokens, but I see them referred to as *entities, items, objects, pieces, nouns,* and more besides. They're the things that (in a computer game) you often have to make rather than program. If it has a texture or a sound or a mesh or any other asset, it's a token. Objects, buildings, NPCs, PCs, and the environment are examples of tokens.

Rules are the definitions of what you can and can't do to and with tokens. Often, they'll state explicitly what the tokens represent. You need both rules and tokens for a game (and in some games, such as *Nomic*, the rules themselves can be tokens).

Features are ways of organizing tokens under the rules, and are emergent from interactions between rules. Example:

- Rule 1: Artillery kills infantry with no cover.
- Rule 2: When artillery kills infantry, it makes craters.
- Rule 3: Craters provide cover for infantry.

Emergent feature: terrain needs to be managed.

Note that just because features are emergent, that doesn't mean they aren't designed.

Features+rules+tokens-context=mechanics.

---

[9]Andrew Rollings & David Morris: *Game Architecture and Design: A New Edition*. New Riders, Indianapolis, IN, 2003.

Less formally (and therefore confusingly), features are also what makes this game different from other games. There are three types:

- *Integral features*, which are vital to the working of the game. The quest system in an RPG is an integral feature.

- *Chrome*, which enhances look and feel but doesn't affect gameplay. Character portrait creation is an example of chrome.

- *Gameplay substitutes*, which offer uninteresting choices. Having 23 near-identical kinds of longsword would be a gameplay substitute. This kind of feature is a *bad* idea, by the way.

Gameplay is emergent from feature interactions in the same way that features are emergent from rule interactions. Gameplay is what players do to have fun. There are subjective degrees of gameplay—*Bridge* has "more gameplay" than *Happy Families*.

Let's consider an example.

"It's a Wild West game, with cowboys and cattle and fields and bandits!"

- These are tokens. What's the gameplay?

"Cowboys consume coffee and beans. Cattle live in fields. Cattle are sold in towns. Coffee, beans, and ammunition are bought in towns. Bandits rustle cattle. Cowboys with ammunition can shoot bandits."

- These are rules. What's the gameplay?

"Herd sizes must be balanced. Cowboy numbers must be watched. Expansion must be planned. Supply requirements must be predicted."

- These are features. What's the gameplay?

"You supply your cowboys in the field with coffee and beans; they raise your cattle which you take to market and sell so you can buy more land, more coffee and beans, and more ammunition to fend off the bandits."

- *That's* the gameplay. It's what you *do*.

The Sad Truth About UCC

User-created content sounds great in theory, but in practice it's unpolished, garbled, inconsistent, incoherent, derivative, unimaginative, incomplete, or (quite possibly and) mutually-incompatible. That's except for the 1% that isn't.

Unfortunately, all those users who create user-created content think theirs is in the 1%.

They're not designers.

For designers, it's more like 5%.

Emerging from the Dark

MMOs are great places for emergence, because they're social. A lot of emergence comes from interactions between players.

So, if you're a designer, should you create gameplay that encourages people to group together, right? More grouping means more emergence; emergence is good, therefore more grouping is good.

Well, often emergence *is* good. However, there's emergence you design for and there's emergence you don't design for because it genuinely *does* emerge without having been anticipated. The latter is often wildly good, but you can't assume it *will* be good.

For example, in the heyday of *EverQuest* it was believed that locking players into small groups that played together gave them social cohesion and kept them wanting to play; this was true, it did—except for those who were unable to commit to playing the game every day at a certain time. These players couldn't get groups, so they left. Their voices were never heard. If you'd asked the players of *EverQuest* if they liked the group system, most of them would have said yes, they did; that's because the ones who didn't like it had left.

When *World of Warcraft* came along, it allowed players to progress reasonably well playing solo, with social cohesion coming through less gameplay-oriented systems (such as guilds). *WoW* picked up swathes of ex-*EQ* players who liked the concept of MMOs but not *EQ*'s particular take on it.

Of course, Blizzard's designers were later to repeat the *EQ* mistake in their *Burning Crusade* expansion, when they strong-armed everyone in the end game to go through a dungeon (Karazhan) with punishing raiding requirements. People who could only play casually were unable to access the content, but they couldn't play beyond it; it was a guild-breaker. Those who could play through Karazhan really liked it, and it was perceived by Blizzard as a success. It wasn't.

Although a lot of the emergence in MMOs comes from players, it's not always goodness-for-free.

Besikovitch's Game

Here's a card game with one of my favorite mechanics. It was invented by Abram Samilovitch Besikovitch, a Russian mathematician, in the 1950s.

- The two players take one suit each from a standard pack of cards.

- A third suit is shuffled and turned face up.

- The players simultaneously bid one card from their hand for the uppermost card of the third suit (the prize card).

- The player of the higher of the two bid cards adds the prize card to their trophy pile (if it's a draw, neither gets it); both players lose their bid cards; the new uppermost card in the third suit becomes the next prize card.

- At the end of the 13 rounds, players total the points in their trophy pile (ace=1 to king=13). Highest wins.

Besikovitch's Game has perfect information and symmetrical starting positions. It's essentially a game of bluff. I love it!

Organic Design

Early computer game design was more experimental than it tends to be today. You had an idea, you sat down and wrote some code, you played with it, you tried out new ideas, you tested them, you modified them, you threw out the bad ones, you extended the good ones, and eventually you had a game.

This is called *organic design*. The design of the game is affected by its implementation, and vice versa. You can get some highly innovative and original games this way.

We don't see a lot of it these days.

Spotting a Designer

All game designers have stacks of game designs lying around, each in various states of completion. Some are just vague outlines, and others are polished and playable.

That's *all* game designers. Older game designers will have accumulated the most, but even young designers will have some. If you think you're a game designer but you don't have any, well, you're not—sorry! Well, you're not *yet*.

I used to write my designs on paper, but nowadays I do most of them on my PC. That way, I have a fighting chance of being able to read them should I return to them later. I only started to keep my designs (rather than throw them out) when I was in my teens, beginning with a game I've mentioned before called *Wizards and Heroes*.

Actually, it was initially called *Wizzards and Heros*. I still had to learn to spell a few words.

Anyway, just to give you a flavor of what kind of volume I'm talking, here's a picture of my design notebooks for the period 1992–1997:

Remember: that's *all* game designers.

Speedboats and Cruise Ships

Multi-player is like a speedboat; massively multi-player is like a cruise ship. People who are used to creating speedboats should ensure, when they switch to making a cruise ship, that they *do* end up with a cruise ship—and not a speedboat with hundreds of extra seats.

Predicting the Unpredictable

Just because individual players are unpredictable, that doesn't mean the body of players as a whole is unpredictable.

An MMO's design may deliberately be formulated such that interesting things are seeded to happen. The actual interesting things themselves may not necessarily be predictable, nor do they even *have* to happen; nevertheless, because the *space* of potential interesting things is shaped by the designer, designers can and do frame their designs to promote or demote particular interactions.

As a very rough analogy, it's as if the players are a thunderstorm and the designer sets up the terrain beneath the clouds. It's predictable that lightning *will* strike, but *where* it will strike is unpredictable; nevertheless some places (such as trees and tall buildings) are more likely targets than others.

The designer creates the system, but has no control over it beyond that. Nevertheless, that creation is in itself a very powerful form of control.

Four out of every five people killed by lightning bolts are men.

Inorganic Design

Back in the Dark Ages, people built houses organically. They had an idea what they wanted, but no actual plans. They used local materials and constructed a building that both shaped and was shaped by the landscape. It worked just fine, and the houses that arose were bespoke and eminently habitable.

However, when they tried building castles and cathedrals that way, they fell down. It turned out that bigger and more complex structures had a better chance of not collapsing in an expensive mess if people planned what they were going to do in advance.

This is why most of today's large-scale computer games are not created organically. Maybe their prototypes are, but the games themselves aren't.

The Sleeper

On November 17th 2003, around 180 members of the top three guilds on the Rallos Zek *EverQuest* server killed Kerafyrm, also known as the Sleeper[10]. It took about three hours, which, given that the Sleeper had 10,000,000,000 hit points, means that the average DPS must have been around 5,100.

---

[10]Andrew Phelps: *I Saw God and I Killed it. Got Game? The Future of Play*, November 2003.

The opinion was that "10,000,000,000 hit points" was designer code for "unkillable"—a view reinforced by the fact that the first attempt made by the guilds on the Sleeper ended when a games master stopped the encounter with the Sleeper at 27%. The next time, the powers that be relented and the guilds killed a supposedly unkillable boss. Not only was there rejoicing across *EQ* for this phenomenal feat, but players in other MMOs that heard about it were thrilled, too. The players had beaten the designers! To this day, the death of the Sleeper is held up as an example of how direct action by players can achieve undesigned-for ends.

In this particular case, yes, it does. It doesn't *always*, though.

In *MUD1*, I had a dragon. The dragon was the most powerful creature in The Land. If you went up against it in a fight, you lost. If ten of you went up against it, you all lost. If every player in the game went up against it, they all lost. No matter what level you were, it killed you first hit and never missed.

However, I made it so it *was* killable. I purposefully gave it a large number of hit points rather than give it a "nokill" flag, in the hope that players might find a way to kill it. Maybe they *would* do so, maybe they wouldn't, but the point was that it was a design intent that once players figured out they *could* slightly dent the dragon's hide they'd work together to figure out how to dent it some more. In other words, the possibility of direct action was purposefully encouraged by the design—a "design feature" of the kind that looks exactly like the undesigned feature in *EQ*.

Did the players ever kill the dragon? Yes, they did: they set up a teleport bridge between where they entered the MMO and where the dragon was in combat. When their character was killed, they came straight back in with a level 1 newbie, used the teleport bridge to get to the dragon, and waded back into the fray. So long as at least one player was fighting the dragon at all times, it couldn't escape. Eventually, after a long and epic battle, they brought it down.

Okay, so there weren't 180 players (more like 20) and it didn't take them three hours (more like one), and their DPS was in the region of 0.014 (because level 1 characters got one very bad chance to hit it while it incinerated them). Nevertheless, they felt just as glorious and empowered as did the victors over The Sleeper, only they did it 15 years earlier.

I mention this as a cautionary tale for those who believe emergent behavior can't be designed-for. It can. Just because a designer designs something to be "practically unkillable," that doesn't mean that they don't *want* it to be killed, nor that they would be unhappy if it were. One of the biggest thrills for a designer is when players use the options available to them in the context of the world to do something special that the designer hadn't anticipated, but *had* foretold.

I know this is like the third time I've mentioned that emergence can be designed-for, but the number of academic writings on the subject that assume it can't really does annoy me.

Why Detail Matters

I remember reading a comment thread in which *WoW* players were expressing their delight at seeing a wolf kill a rabbit in the forest. What wonderful attention to detail!

Well yes it is fairly nice, but what would *actually* be wonderful would be if the players could think, "Could I maybe buy a cat from the crazy cat lady, release it near this big wolf that's in my way, then run past it while it eats the cat?". *WoW* isn't that detailed. Some of the better text MUDs are, but modern MMOs aren't.

Detail matters, because it allows players to be creative.

Maybe that's why modern MMOs don't want it?

Idea Ideas

I said earlier that designers get ideas the whole time, which is true. They rarely get to implement them, though, because most of the time they have to design what their employer tells them to design.

This involves taking an idea and developing it. In thinking about how this happens, it's useful to look at two approaches at opposite ends of the scale, between which designers typically switch as fancy takes them. These are known as *top down* and *bottom up*. In top-down design, you begin with the overall structure and expand it into more and more detail. In bottom-up design, you begin with the details and build up an overall structure from that.

Example: Design a game called *Macho Women with Guns*.

Top-down design: Okay, so clearly the title defines a faction, so that means there must be an opposing faction—some non-macho women without guns. If there are guns, then there are probably other weapons, which makes this a combat game. This further suggests tactical play, rather than something at a strategic or role-playing level, etc.

Bottom-up design: Wow, so they can have like special SAS skills in kick-ass weapons, and we could make them nuns and have them ride motorbikes, and they can fight using their macho rating and out-macho each other, and we can add like strength and dexterity and looks and health, so this is maybe some kind of tactical combat game, and then oh, we can use dice, etc.

Designers rarely stick with one of these techniques—they'll switch between them seamlessly (and without having to think about doing so, too). It depends on the design and the designer. Top-down gives good structure but risks having details that don't gel; bottom-up gives good content but risks having it make no overall sense.

Try both as an exercise, say for a game called "Moon Gods Rising".

Ripping Off Game Ideas

When I described the rules of *Besikovitch's Game* earlier, you may have had the vague feeling that I'd mentioned it before.

Well yes, I had—kind of. The *Wars of the Roses* game I made up on the fly had a mechanic that is suspiciously similar. It wasn't a complete reskinning of the *Besikovitch's Game* (it used two cards at a time instead of one), but nevertheless it took its core mechanic from *Besikovitch's Game*.

So what gives here?! Don't I feel in the least bit *guilty* about ripping off game mechanics from a mathematician who fled the aftermath of the Russian revolution in fear of his life?

Well no, I don't feel guilty. The reason I don't feel guilty is because Besikovitch himself ripped off the mechanic from an old Russian card game called *Svoi Kozyri*.

There's a difference between a *reskinning*, an *adaptation,* and an *original*. I'll describe these here in terms of designer intention, but I dare say that patent lawyers wouldn't see things *quite* the same way.

- If game A is a reskinning of game B, game B's mechanics were left substantially untouched in game A, but its context was significantly changed.

- If game A is an adaptation of game B, most of game B's important mechanics were used but there are significant differences; whether the contexts of A and B are the same is immaterial.

- If A is an original, its mechanics are its own and it is not informed nor inspired by those of any game B.

Generally, designers only reskin their own games. They will readily adapt the games of others, but probably with a change of context. If they come up with an original mechanic, they'll be very pleased with themselves.

This is why I celebrate, rather than fume over, the evolution of MMOs. Well, I *do* fume, but only because such evolution isn't happening quickly enough.

At heart, I'm a game designer. I just want better games.

From Tokens to Gameplay

Here's an example of how you can derive gameplay from tokens and rules via features. It's for the classic game *Rogue*, but you don't need to have played that to understand what's going on.

What follows isn't exhaustive, it's just enough to demonstrate the process.

Tokens:

- The rogue, monsters, hit points, coins, magical weapons, squares, rooms, passages, doors, secret doors, and steps

Rules:

- [R1] When the rogue and a monster attempt to share a square, they reduce the hit points of each other.

- [R2] When the rogue or a monster reaches zero hit points, it dies.

- [R3] Hit points recover slowly.

- [R4] Magical weapons do more damage than normal.

- [R5] Only coins count toward the final score.

- [R6] Lower floors have more coins.

- [R7] Lower floors have more magical weapons.

- [R8] The deeper the level, the more hit points the monsters there have.

- [R9] The rogue and monsters move.

- [R10] Treasure doesn't move.

Features:

- [F1] Players must manage the need to obtain coins with the danger of confronting monsters [R5 v R1].

- [F2] Players must balance the risk of going to a lower level with the rewards of greater treasure [R6, R7 v R8].

- [F3] Players must consider the chance of finding treasure against the chance of being cut off by monsters [R9 v R10].

Gameplay:

- Players try to find the steps to the next level as soon as possible so they have an escape route [F2 v F3], then attempt to clear as much of the level as they can while avoiding the toughest monsters [F1 v F3], in order to gear-up to increase their survivability so they can obtain more treasure [F1 v F2].

Analyzing game mechanics in this way is useful when you have a game design that isn't showing much gameplay. It helps identify where the problem lies. I find it particularly useful when people who aren't game designers present me with a design that contains no gameplay but which they insist does.

Oh, you'll notice that I didn't use rules R2 to R4. See if you can combine them with other rules to create a feature, then use that feature to add more detail to the gameplay.

No, I'm not going to give you a solution later in this book, but feel free to look ahead fruitlessly anyway.

The Solo Dungeon

This is the front cover of my first professionally-published game:

It's a choose-your-own adventure from early 1978 (although I'd self-published it before then).

It differed from other CYOAs of the period because it was open-ended rather than run-on rails. In other words, it was sandbox rather than theme park.

Freedom, freedom, freedom.

Changes to Games

Sometimes, designers take things for granted that aren't actually well-known. I once gave a talk in Barcelona that mentioned how games and genres of games evolve over time, and afterward was congratulated for pointing this out. This surprised me, as I thought everyone knew they evolved anyway.

Anyway, since apparently everyone doesn't know, this basically gives me permission to ramble on a bit about the subject. Designers can ignore this; there's nothing new for you here.

Okay, so I may be stating the obvious, but there are actually four kinds of changes that happen to games.

First, there are incremental version changes made within a single game. In the old days of video games, this meant patches based on user feedback (or bugfixes); nowadays, it means changes informed by A/B testing and other metrics-driven approaches that gradually shine and polish a game, buffing out the dents and making it more attractive to its current users. This is a hill-climbing exercise, though, which will find a local maximum of experience but not necessarily a global one. It also assumes that all players have similar tastes and reasons for playing. While it's useful a tool, it's not something a designer should follow slavishly; it's input into the design process, but it's not instruction.

Second, there are larger incremental changes made between iterations of a game within a series. *Civilization V* is different from *Civilization IV*, but in some sense they remain the same game; the latter is an evolution of the former (and so of its predecessors in the series). The changes made for these games usually involve an adjustment to gameplay based on player or designer ideas, but they can also include updates to the presentation (better graphics) or a new marketing opportunity (*Patrician III* was more of a patch to *Patrician II* than a true "next game in the series," but I bought it anyway). In design terms, they serve to shake things up a bit so that a new hill-climbing exercise can begin that will find a different, hopefully higher, hill.

Third, there are incremental changes so large that they lead to new, separate games. These take ideas from another game (or perhaps several games) and put them together to make a new game. Often, there's only one major gameplay change, such as the switch to swoop patterns in *Galaxian* (which I was good at) from the relentless linear advance of *Space Invaders* (which I sucked at). This is what we normally mean by "game evolution": the creation of new games from ideas established in older games. As it happens, game designers are as likely to take an idea from somewhere else entirely ("ant nests!"— although that particular example is more a programmer thing than a designer thing). However, they do know a good mechanic when they see one, and they're not afraid to repurpose it. Better, you can't patent game mechanics so there's no barrier to reusing them.

Finally, there are changes so radical that they're revolutionary, not evolutionary. These don't come from other games, they come from the designer's imagination. There were no god games before *Populous*; there were no real-time strategy games before *Dune II*; there were no first-person shooters before *Wolfenstein 3D*. Well, there may have been, but they fell by the wayside and had little or no effect on the future development of the genre.

Roy Trubshaw's and my *MUD* falls into this type four category: we did have influences from other games—the interface is straight out of *Colossal Cave* (*ADVENT* to us), for example—but the "virtual worldliness" was original and new. "Original" is only relative, though: I've said many times, other people also invented virtual worlds independently of Roy and me; it's just luck that ours was the one that took off.

Anyway, following a revolution you'll then get a series of evolutions as in the third point (above), which allows for a family tree to be constructed. Such family trees can only tell you what descended from what, though, not how or why a child differs from its parent(s).

In parallel to all this, you can also change a game's skin but not its mechanics. It can have a different emotional or intellectual effect if you do that, but it's not really an evolution/revolution thing, it's more of a relabeling.

Games themselves *evolve*. They always have and they always will.

Dead-End Evolution

In a 2008 interview, I was asked: "are you planning on playing games like *Age of Conan* and *Warhammer* when they come out?" My reply began: "I've already played *Warhammer*: it was called *World of Warcraft*."

The other 3,726 words in the interview did not attract the same degree of publicity.

Disappointingly, I actually made the remark to defend *Warhammer: Age of Reckoning*, not to attack it: *Warcraft*'s IP is derivative of *Warhammer*'s. Mark Jacobs, who was *W: AR*'s lead designer, is one of the very few MMO designers who doesn't come from a *DikuMUD* tradition; he wasn't ripping off *WoW*, he was evolving his own ideas.

This is all incidental, though. The point is, almost all the post-*WoW* MMOs are basically only *WoW* with at most evolutionary changes. Even dropping the idea of levels, like *The Secret World* did, is only an evolutionary change.

Where are the *revolutionary* changes?

Massively Small

So, I materialized in my local game store with the express purpose of reading the back of the box for the (at the time) upcoming *The Lord of the Rings Online: Shadows of Angmar*. There, it stated that the virtual world featured "50 million square meters" of Middle Earth.

Hmm. 1 million square meters is a square kilometer, so that's 50 square kilometers. Or, to make that easier to visualize, it's just over 7km by 7km square. For those of you who don't work in metric, try 4 miles 693 yards instead.

Put another way, *The Lord of the Rings Online* compresses all of Eriador into an area smaller than that of San Marino. Then, they boast about it on the box.

Scale is another one of those things *Reality* does better than virtuality.

Licenses

Many games are based on famous books or films, or other intellectual properties: *The Simpsons*, 007, Tony Hawk, *Yu-Gi-Oh*, and so on.

Why? Aren't these kind a restrictive? J. K. Rowling famously keeps a tight leash on anything to do with ~~miserable whiner~~ chirpy schoolboy Harry Potter. Don't designers have enough imagination to think of ideas of their own? Why do they so often work with the ideas of other people?

Well yes, designers *do* have enough imagination—many times over. The decision to use licenses is not a creative one, it's a business one. Here's what you get when you pay for a license:

- Market awareness—People already know the name.
- Existing fan base—People are itching to buy anything with the right logo on it.
- Tie-ins—If the movie has a huge promotions budget, you get to ride on the back of that.
- Reduced time on concept design—The concept is already designed.
- Validated company credentials—It shows that your organization is the kind of big player that can afford a major license.

Here's why you might have second thoughts:

- It's expensive—Not only the initial outlay, but also the royalties.

- Intellectual property—If your game's content is original, it could be the movie-makers and book publishers paying *you* instead of the other way around.

- Mismatched properties—You want to license the Hercule Poirot *universe*, not every single damned book.

- You may be sold a lemon—Even high-profile movies fail at the box office.

There isn't a problem with lack of ideas. *Every single person* working for a game developer has ideas for games. Rather, it's to do with sales and marketing.

That said, I for one would buy a game in which Harry Potter died and stayed dead.

Toy Games

Sometimes, designers deliberately design games not to be *played* but to be *played with*. They're usually made for testing purposes—mechanics, balance, funness, whatever—in which case they would be called a *prototype*.

Sometimes, though, they're made for other, external reasons. Say, for example, you want to show off some Artificial Intelligence technique you've developed. You might write a game that demonstrates it. People will use the game as a vehicle for interacting with the AI. This doesn't make the game a prototype—it's a finished, fully-fledged game—but it does mean that people aren't really playing it in the spirit of a game. Winning or losing isn't the point.

Games that are played *with*, rather than played, are called *toy games*. This is one of those strange terms that most game designers seem to have come up with themselves while designing games when they started out, so they all know what it means even though they thought it up individually from first principles. People play games, but they play *with* toys; they're playing *with* this game, therefore it's a toy game, not a game game.

Yes, I'm pretty sure most of them have made up the term "game game" independently, too.

A Wise Designer

A wise designer listens to their players. An unwise designer either doesn't listen, or listens but doesn't edit what they hear.

Many of the holes the industry finds itself in at the moment are as a result of knee-jerk reactions by non-designers (e.g., marketing departments or customer service sections) leading to ill-conceived design changes to address public relations failures.

60 Seconds of Gameplay

When people start describing to me their MMOs, they'll tell me the backstory, the systems, the Really Cool Bits, the advances they've made over other MMOs—they'll go into enormous detail. That's fine, I need to know these details. However, I need to know something else before hearing any of this: what do the players *do*?

In other words, what's the gameplay?

It's surprising how few designers actually give this much thought. They'll say that the players will kill stuff to get stuff so they can kill bigger stuff to get better stuff; they'll say there's crafting, and instances, and housing, and you can train your mount to do tricks, and they'll pull out a notepad and start drawing diagrams if you let them.

What they won't say is exactly what the players *do*. If you were to stand behind a player and watch, what would that player be *doing*?

A technique for eliciting this is *60 Seconds of Gameplay*, which I first came across in a book by designer Erik Bethke[11]. It's pleasingly simple: you write down every thought that goes through the player's head for 60 seconds mid-game. Okay, so MMOs aren't really games, but you can do the same thing for them.

In doing so, you get right down to the bare bones. It's here that you find out whether the backstory, the systems, the Really Cool Bits, the advances, and everything else, are just so much hot air or if they actually deliver gameplay.

It's all very well having grandiose schemes, but designers should never lose sight of the fact that *people* will be playing their MMO, and those people are going to want to *do* something. 60 seconds of gameplay forces you to think about *what*.

---

[11]Erik Bethke: *Game Development and Production*. Wordware Publishing: Plano, Texas. 2003.

Macho Women with Guns

Lest my earlier example of a game called *Macho Women with Guns* offended your sensibilities, yeah, that was supposed to happen. It was supposed to happen because (for those of you who didn't know), *Macho Women with Guns*, is a real, published game by Greg Porter. It was followed up by *Batwinged Bimbos from Hell* and *Renegade Nuns on Wheels*.

It's a parody. It's riffing off the social mores of the 1980s (it was published in 1988), consciously placing over-masculine stereotypes in an over-feminine context to create a statement about both. It's also a gem of a tactical combat game.

So yes, I chose it as a mild provocation, because that's what its designer intended. It was always supposed to give you cause to sit up and listen. When you find out what it's saying, though, you may have to reappraise what you thought you were hearing.

As with books, games can be read.

Here's the cover of my (signed inside) third edition. How could that *not* be a parody?

Rhetoric: Play as Power

For adults, play often takes the form of sports, contests, and festivals. Victory shows the superiority of one group over another, or of an individual over the environment. The winners bring glory, and even the losers can bond with them—those boxers who hug each other after trying to damage one another's brains for 12 rounds are not doing it out of mere politeness.

In the Play as Power rhetoric, play is seen as a microcosm of life: good at play, good at everything. It brings prestige. It's used to explain why national anthems are played at the Olympic Games, why the owners of teams are more important than the players, and (in tandem with other arguments that I thankfully don't have to justify here) why most major sports are played mainly by men.

Furthermore, playful contests give people aspirations and a sense of success that comes with *order*. This view that "order is good" then contributes to the notion that civilization itself is good, and thus play aids in civilizations' rise and development.

(Well, that's what Johan Huizinga said; personally, I think he was overstating the case somewhat.)

Play as Power is a useful way of looking at games if you're a sociologist or an Olympian. It only really makes sense for games of order, though, not for games of disorder (such as gambling). It therefore sits uneasily alongside the rhetoric of Play as Fate. Also, loud though it is on the subject of competitive play, it's somewhat silent regarding cooperative play.

In MMOs, this rhetoric often appears in the elder game, in which the wearing of epic items often translates to "look where I've been and what I've done, preen preen". This is why "look what I've paid $$$ for but am pretending I haven't" doesn't always go down well in such communities.

Balance

What do designers mean when they say a game is *balanced*?

Well, they mean one of three things.

- *Player/player* balance is when each player has the same chance of winning from the start. This means the game is *fair*. It's the default meaning of "balance".

- *Player/gameplay* balance is when the game is neither too easy nor too hard for the player. It ensures that the game is *fun*.

- *Gameplay/gameplay* balance is when the cost of using an option is appropriate for its pay-off. It means all game options will be worth using at least sometimes (and therefore weren't a waste of time implementing).

It's very difficult to guarantee balance in a game, but designers do have some tricks they can use to achieve the next-best thing—*equilibrium*. What they particularly don't want to happen is for success to breed success, because then whoever gets ahead first can become unassailable. Thus, they will often arrange matters so that the further you are in the lead, the harder it is for you to maintain that lead. For example, the more you expand your territory, the thinner your defenses become, so the easier it is for your opponents to recapture what they've lost.

The way I visualize equilibrium is as a sword fencing match in which the competitors have lengths of bungee rope attached to their waists. I've never tried fencing, but even against an experienced opponent I'd reach a point where I could mount a successful defense if they had a bungee rope on them. This is because the more that they drove me back, the harder it would become to drive me back further. Eventually, they'd have to spend so much effort resisting the rope that even I could keep them at bay.

Sadly, neither balance nor equilibrium scale up well. I once consulted on a trading game which was perfectly balanced for four different commodities, following extensive use of a simulation that perturbed the market in multiple, complex ways. This was very impressive, except that the final product was going to need more like 40 different commodities, not four. The developers weren't entirely gleeful when I told them this, which wasn't surprising given that they'd been running the simulation non-stop, day and night, for eight weeks.

Ralph Vaughan Williams

Here's a paraphrasing of an anecdote I once heard on the radio.

The English composer, Ralph Vaughan Williams, collected and orchestrated many folk songs. In one of these, he included some harp music which the harpist in the orchestra found impossible to play. Frustrated, she asked Vaughan Williams how he expected anyone to play it. Vaughan Williams sat down at the harp and said, "Well, I thought like this". He went through it note by note, very slowly, showing the fingering he had envisaged in his mind. The harpist followed what he was doing, then suddenly understood. She took back her seat and played the piece through from start to finish flawlessly.

The thing is, Vaughan Williams *couldn't play the harp*. However, he *did* know what *could* be played on it.

MMO designers don't need to be able to program, draw, animate, or anything else, but they do need to know that what they've asked for *can* be delivered.

If *you're* designing an MMO and someone wonders how in the world they're supposed to do something impossible that you've demanded of them, then *you* need to be able to say, "Well, I thought like this".

Fixed Values

To an MMO designer who doesn't think too deeply, fixing the prices in shops is no different from fixing the points values of mobs.

Actually, the designer who doesn't think too deeply is right: there is no difference. Both are bad ideas.

60 Seconds of *Spunky Princess*

Here's an example of 60 seconds of gameplay as applied to an actual game. Rather than make you log into an MMO, which is rather hassle some, this is a simple web game I wrote at the turn of the century called *Spunky Princess*[12]. Go play it, then come back here.

So, you played the game! Maybe I should have mentioned it looked antique even when I wrote it? I rather like it myself, but then I'm 100% biased.

Anyway, the point of this is to show you what a 60-seconds-of-gameplay transcript looks like. Here's mine for *Spunky Princess*:

- I'm standing in the top left-hand corner of the map on level 10.
- I can see a path to the bottom-right corner where the steps are, right through the middle.
- There's only one square I can move to, to the right, so I'll go there.
- Okay, two more spaces open up, both empty.
- I'll take the lower one.
- Still all clear, I'll move to the right.
- Damn! A tiger blocks my way.
- I can see another route, though, if I go up, right then down.
- I go up, but to go right I have to pass a flunky.
- Flunkies cost 2 spunkiness or 3 stealth to get past without risk, and tigers are 4 spunkiness.
- I'll take the flunky route and pay in stealth, because stealth is hard to get rid of otherwise.
- Blast! There's another flunky below this one! I'll stealth my way past him, too.
- Okay, the route is clear to the steps now, four moves and I'm there.
- Down to level 9.

---

[12]Richard A. Bartle: *Spunky Princess*. 2001. http://www.youhaventlived.com/spunkyprincess/

- Charm and spunkiness are still on 10, stealth is on 5 now.

- There's a lot of open space in the middle, which is good, but I have a servant to the right and those devils can *move*.

- I pay 2 charm to get past the servant, because I want to keep my spunkiness in case I meet tigers on lower levels.

- She moved to the right, but I can go down and get around her.

- Gaah! Guard to the south and flunky to the right!

- Guards are no-brainer 2 charm to get past, but I'm gonna spend more stealth and take the flunky route, as there are two possible exits from there (as opposed to one from the guard's square).

- Stealth is down to 2, both squares after the flunky are clear, it doesn't matter which I take.

- Etc...

Yes, these things *are* that detailed. Even if you couldn't be bothered to go and actually try *Spunky Princess*, you can at least see from this exercise that it has gameplay (regardless of whether it makes a whole lot of sense).

The point is, though, that as author of the game, *I* can see it has gameplay. That's why I ask designers to do it when I'm being paid to look over their work—so *they* can see whether their MMO has gameplay.

Try doing it for your MMO of choice. You might be surprised!

Anti-Design

Some people don't like the idea of planning everything out in advance when creating an MMO. They feel that up-front design has issues that organic design doesn't:

- It constraints freedom of expression.

- It means interesting new avenues revealed during development can't be explored.

- It sets the design in stone, meaning flaws can't easily be corrected even when they become apparent.

These people are *correct*. All these alleged failings of inorganic design are indeed failings!

However, for all but the smallest of teams and the longest of deadlines, development is just too costly to do otherwise.

Classifying MMOs

Suppose a new MMO was coming out, and you wanted to describe it to a friend. Apart from its name (obviously!), how would you go about it?

Well, the chances are you'd state (or imply) its genre, make some comment about the graphics, and then launch into an explanation of its features and gameplay.

Now suppose that it's been running awhile and another friend of yours asks what it's like. Would you add anything else to your description? Well, if you'd played it then you'd probably go into more detail, but you'd also mention something you wouldn't have mentioned regarding a brand new MMO: the players. You'd probably say how long it had been running, too, to show whether it has staying power (or, if you're a pessimist, that it's out of date).

There are other quirks you could bring up, such as its revenue model and its fiction. There's quite a range of things you might relate, in fact.

Resulting from this sort of exercise is a way to classify MMOs. MMOs that have the same particular feature or attitude or atmosphere can be lumped together for easier comparison. If you don't like "elves in tights" worlds, or you prefer cartoon-style graphics, or you like your MMOs gritty and uncompromising, then you're appealing to an informal classification system that gets its credibility from the fact that enough other people have also hit on the same categorizations to produce a common vocabulary.

In the era of textual worlds we had much the same categories, but naturally there were differences. We didn't say how good the graphics were, but we did say how good the writing was (or, more commonly, wasn't). More interestingly, because we had a wider range of MMOs (or MUDs, as they were called back then), we had additional ways to classify them. Some of these are still important for designers today.

Well, two in particular are: *degree of persistence* and *player impact*.

Busy-Body Bosses

When a professional game designer is given a job, the starting point will be a number of business constraints: this much money, this genre, this platform, this demographic, by this deadline. The designer's job is to come up with a game that meets these criteria, expressed as a design document.

Some newbies designers go into too much detail. They tell the programmers how to programmers, the artists how to draw, the animators how to animate, the marketers how to market. This isn't a good thing: designers should trust the people who turn their designs into product—after all, doing so is *their* job, and *they* know what to do much better than *you* do.

Likewise, some company high-ups will tell designers how to design. They'll include design fragments in the business specification that are unrelated to it, and they'll try to use selective marketing data as ammunition to shoot down counter-arguments. This is particularly a problem with MMOs.

Everyone wants to be a designer…

Okay, so sometimes—surprisingly often, in fact—these unwelcome intrusions are fine and as a designer you can live with them or even riff off them. If they're not fine, though, what do you do? Well, you have five options:

1. Grit your teeth and do what they ask. You'll end up with a poor game.

2. Try to negotiate. Surprisingly, some suits are perfectly reasonable people who don't view changing their mind as a sign of weakness.

3. Tell them you're going to do it your way, whether they like it or not. Expect speedy unemployment.

4. Offer your resignation. Ditto.

5. *Say* you'll do as they ask but then *ignore* what they said. Ha! They'll *never* find out in time!

Despite the obvious attractions of 2 followed (in the event of failure) by 1, some designers go straight for 5. This is because 2 would tip the boss off to be wary.

No, I'm not joking.

Reading Up

When a designer begins to work on an MMO, there's always some background research to do. This research could be on any subject, and the designer doesn't have to find it interesting or even likeable. So long as there are no moral issues that the designer finds uncomfortable, the genre shouldn't matter. Good designers should be able to design for any genre, much as good authors should be able to write for any setting.

The point of reading up on a subject is to understand it. Designers have more ideas than they know what to do with, and researching a subject is a way of narrowing these down. The more you understand about the topic you're designing for, the better you'll be able to draw on ideas that are appropriate for it.

Here's a list of the kind of things designers pick up when they research a new topic (some of which I touched on earlier when discussing designing to context):

- A sense of what it's *about*
- A feel for what aspects of it prospective players would like
- Must-have tropes that define the genre
- Anything that sparks gameplay ideas
- Ways to pull it all together in a clean, coherent fashion

Note that this isn't a checklist—designers don't think, "Hmm, what are the must-have tropes here?". All this just *happens* if you're a designer.

Research itself requires source material. The most important ones are the same sources that prospective players will have encountered—popular fiction, movies, TV series, and so on. However, designers must also read factual material that most of the players haven't encountered, because this is what the more populist sources will themselves ultimately have been based on. You can watch a movie about pirates and come away with no idea that there was ever a slave trade in the Caribbean; you can play a game about pirates and get the same impression. However, both the screenwriter and the game designer *must* know about the slavery, because they need to make a decision as to how to address it. Ignorance is *not* an option.

The best resources when you come at a subject new are, perhaps not surprisingly, other games. Role-playing games are particularly good here. For example, if you want to know how much the effect of firing a 3lb cannonball from a 4'6", 1,000lb cannon diminishes with range, a quick look at the Cannon Information Table from the RPG *Roll Out the Guns* will tell you.

The *GURPS* system is particularly good for this kind of thing, because it uses a generic rules system. This means that the various supplements it provides for different genres aren't cluttered with the basic how-to-play rules—they're focused on the subject matter alone.

In general, MMO designers don't need to know *everything* about the world they are designing. However, they do need to know one level of detail more than does the typical player. If they can achieve that, it's usually good enough to meet the players' expectations of the fiction. If they can't, though, players will see the machinery through your too-thin fabric and their sense of immersion will suffer irreparably.

Caps

What's the level cap in your MMO? What's the skill cap?

Why have caps?

$1 + \frac{1}{2} + \frac{1}{4} + \frac{1}{8} + \frac{1}{16} + \ldots$ is an infinite sum that is capped at 2 but you can never quite reach it.

$1 + \frac{1}{2} + \frac{1}{3} + \frac{1}{4} + \frac{1}{5} + \frac{1}{6} +$ is an infinite sum that has no cap, in that the total tends toward infinity.

Both of these may have effective earlier caps, beyond which people just can't face taking the next step, but usually there will someone willing to try so long as it's theoretically possible that they'll succeed.

If having a fishing skill of $n+1$ means you catch one extra fish a day than having a fishing skill of n, why not let those who really, really want to catch an extra fish go for it?

And Another Thing

Earlier, I said that user-created content was "unpolished, garbled, inconsistent, incoherent, derivative, unimaginative, incomplete, or (quite possibly and) mutually-incompatible".

I was being kind.

It's:

- **Inconsistent and self-contradictory:** Sometimes water-based spells beat fire-based spells and sometimes fire-based spells beat water-based spells.

- **Incoherent:** Spank the right kitten and flowers will grow from the face of the innkeeper.

- **Selectively deep:** There is a subtle distinction between glaives that have four prongs and glaives that only have three, however all wall paintings are just "paintings".

- **The wrong mood:** It's light when it's supposed to be epic, or epic when it's supposed to be light. All attempts at humor fall into this category.

- **Muddled:** Functionality is there, but it's attached to the wrong object or is carried through unnecessarily. Why would my Bleeding Wound ability work on a golem or an air elemental or a ghost? They don't bleed.

- **Derivative, clichéd, and unimaginative:** In *MUD1* I didn't implement dogs because I hate dogs for their mindless loyalty and sharp teeth. As a result, I noticed that among the first ideas people would always propose I add to the game was "a dog". They said this as if no one else had ever thought of it.

- **Unfinished and unpolished:** People dabble but get bored, or they start to test but get bored, or they have some other, better idea and start afresh.

- **Poorly written:** I remember the day someone in *MUD2* made 99 red baloons. No, not balloons, baloons.

- **Strangely specific:** You don't get drunk if you drink alcohol, unless it's this particular brew made by this particular dwarf.

- **The wrong style:** If you want American spelling and I give you British spelling, you will be cross. Likewise punctuation, grammar, irritating sports analogies...

- **Incompatible:** I love your rescue-the-dragon-from-the-princess quest, but this is a Cyberpunk universe.

Fortunately, most creators of UCC have no critical faculties so they'll think I'm only insulting everyone else, not them.

Oh, and *every* designer started out creating work just like this, so it isn't really an insult anyway. Indeed, the more you *think* your own work is like this, the *less* like this it probably is.

Purge World

Suppose that a new, large-scale MMO were launched which announced that every three months its character database would be wiped clean and everyone would have to start from scratch again. Would people play it?

I'm guessing some would. If the shards were phased so there was always a freshly-purged one available (to ensure that newbies would not be dumped into a "lame duck" instantiation), a fixed time limit could be attractive in several ways:

- You only have to commit for a known period, not indefinitely.

- There's greater narrative scope for the designers.

- As most of the characters will be of the same "level" anyway, the concept of levels can be replaced by some less grindy means of measuring success.

- You're free to reinvent yourself periodically, instead of having to wear a character that might have been appropriate for you two years ago but who just isn't "you" any more.

- Content can be arranged so that players will want to be in similar geographic areas at similar times. You won't need as many players per shard to get that "village" feel.

- It would discourage real-money trading (RMT), because investments won't be seen as sufficiently long-term.

- Lots more.

Yeah, I know, *you* wouldn't play because you don't want to lose your stuff.

Well in your current MMO, no, you wouldn't, but if you knew when you started that it was going to happen?

Degree of Persistence

When an MMO reboots, what survives the reboot?

Well, at the very least, the player characters must do so. Otherwise, you may as well be playing *Counter-Strike*.

Early MUDs (from *MUD1* to *AberMUD*) would keep the character, the world map, the initial configuration of the objects, and that was about it. Everything else—including the contents of your inventory—was reset.

The next step up, as exemplified by DikuMUDs, was to protect certain objects that the player characters owned. By the time of *EverQuest*, this also included certain classes (in a programming sense) of unowned objects.

Taking it further, objects could be saved by location: if an object was left in a bank, say, then it would still be there after a reboot. *Asheron's Call* did this kind of persistence.

Of course, if you want to have a full, living, breathing world, you don't want anything to reset at all! You want it to start up after the reboot being exactly how it was immediately prior to that reboot. This is what *Ultima Online* did— very successfully, I might add. If you built a house and put 10,000 shirts in it, the shirts would still be there after a reboot.

You can even take it a stage further than this. Some worlds, such as the MOOs and MUSHes (or, if you want a more contemporary example, *Second Life*), allow players to create content directly—including the code that is run when that content is used. Players would be cross if all new such functionality was lost in a reboot, so these worlds save that, too.

Thus, it can be seen that although all virtual worlds have persistence (unsurprisingly, as it's inherent in the definition of what a virtual world *is*), there are different *degrees* of persistence[13].

There's actually a subtle design reason for this.

---

[13]Raph Koster: *The Tiers of Data Storage.* http://www.raphkoster.com/gaming/book/6a.shtml

Indian Lottery

There's a certain type of lottery that runs in parts of India which has a most beautiful mechanic.

In slums and shanties the world over, people develop informal (and usually illegal) lotteries. The best-known example is the "numbers game" that used to be run by 1920s gangsters. The way this worked is that you paid a small stake and picked a number between 0 and 999. One number from the thousand possibilities would win, picked basically at random but in a public manner so that everyone could see there was no cheating. The final three digits of the daily published balance of the U.S. Treasury was a popular such random-number generator. If your number came up, you'd win around 600 times your stake (depending on the racketeers' cut).

What they do in India is just a little bit different, but in a quite delicious way. There, you pick your number as before, but you receive *1,000 times* your stake if you win. That sounds *much* fairer! But how do the people who operate it make a profit?

Ah, well the thing is, *they* pick the number that wins. In other words, for your number to come up, you simply have to choose the same number as the fewest other people. The winning number is published, the successful gamblers get their stake times 1,000 back, and the system repeats. There's no "draw," just a count.

I don't know what the average take is of the organizers of these Indian gambling rings; I don't even know what this kind of gamble (if that's what it is) is called. I love the way it works, though.

One of these days, I'm going to find a use for it in an MMO's design.

Levels of Functionality

There are four levels of functionality in the architecture of MMOs (and of virtual worlds in general)[14]. From closest-to-hardware to furthest-from-hardware, these are:

- Driver
- MUDlib
- World Definition
- Instantiation

Collectively, these comprise the *codebase*—a stand-alone suite of programs and data that make up the software of an MMO.

The *driver* is the most basic part, and consists of interfaces to the operating system (input/output, packet-handling, time-outs, etc.) and of low-level interpreter components (memory management, command interface, primitive data structures, etc.). The driver makes two foundation concepts available to the higher levels: entities from which the MMO can be constructed (*objects*) and the association of I/O channels to certain of these objects (*player characters*).

MUDlibs are so called (when they're called anything at all, which nowadays they usually aren't) for obscure historical reasons. They handle the *physics* of the MMO (timers, mass/weight, movement, containment, communication, etc.). A MUDlib will also handle some higher concepts such as the magic, combat, and economic systems (which, in an MMO, are *de facto* part of the physics).

The *World Definition* (also known as the *world model* or *static database*) completes the software needed to run the MMO. In conjunction with the driver and MUDlib, it's fully descriptive of the virtual world: if it were a board game, it would be the board, pieces, and rules. It defines new objects and object interactions consequent on the physics—but it doesn't define new physics.

The world definition acts as a template for creating new *instantiations* of the MMO. It implicitly describes all possible states that can occur, but still allows for a wide range of differences between them (in board game terms, Mrs. White did it in the Billiard Room with the lead piping *this time*). The data values that uniquely describe any particular such instantiation make up the final level of the software: it's how it can be that on one shard the dragon is rampaging through the fields of frightened peasants and on another shard, it's dead.

---

[14]Raph Koster: *Overall MUD Architecture.* http://www.raphkoster.com/gaming/book/6b.shtml

The instantiation is the only component of the MMO that changes in real-time, moment-to-moment, and so it's also known as the *run-time database*.

To summarize:

Driver:

- Everything is made from *this stuff*.

MUDlib:

- *This* kind of stuff interacts with *this* stuff like *this*.
- This stuff is for weapons, this stuff is for containers.

World Definition:

- The stuff we're going to *use* looks like *this*.
- We have swords and crossbows and purses and boxes.

Instantiation:

- On *this* shard, right now, stuff has its variable properties configured like *this*.
- Sword2521 is in box834.

Biennial Wipe

So let's say that instead of purging the character database every three months, a developer creates a large-scale MMO with a wipe every two-years. After the purge, everything is reinitialized.

Suppose that everyone is told from the start that this will happen. Newbies are accommodated by having new shards with a two-year lifespan starting up in a staggered fashion.

Would everyone quit when their server's database reset?

Would anyone even play it, knowing that this was going to happen?

What if it were five years instead? Or ten years? Or one year?

Think about your answer. What's important here?

Player Impact

The fact that I mentioned it earlier may have tipped you off that there's been a lot of talk in recent years about *player-generated content*. There are different sorts of this, but in brief it means that players are creating content that it would cost the developers a fortune to create themselves (and the players may well be paying for the privilege of doing so, too).

Now you might not know it from today's MMOs, but in the MUD days there was actually a hierarchy of who got to create content. It went something like this:

- Only the coders. This is how it was in early MUDs such as *Shades*.

- Plus trained administrators (AberMUDs, DikuMUDs).

- Plus trusted players (*EverQuest, Ultima Online*).

- Plus experienced players (LPMUDs, MUCKs).

- Plus non-newbies (TinyMUDs).

- Oh, just let everyone create stuff (*LambdaMOO, Second Life*).

This hierarchy reflects what is known as *player impact* (a term coined by Raph Koster). High player impact means that individual players can make tangible changes to the world; low player impact means that few people other than the developers can change the content.

Okay, so there are potential problems to do with intellectual property laws when you look at who can modify the content of an MMO, but leaving that aside for the moment, it's clear that the degree of player impact that an MMO has is basically determined by the philosophy of the designer. Do you want any of your players to create any non-emergent content for your world? If so, which players? Is it in-context or out-of-context?

Some designers like having total control (and some players like their having it). Others prefer a more sandbox kind of world (and other players like this best, too). Indeed, some designers want merely to create the framework for players to become designers themselves—Philip Rosedale was like this with *Second Life*.

Naturally, there are technical issues here. Interestingly, they are strongly tied to the notion of persistence.

Humor in MMOs

Designers have to be *very* careful about humor in MMOs. I don't mean that they should worry about being offensive (although that *is* an issue); I mean that they should worry about how they handle the *concept* of humor. It's very easy to do it very wrong.

The most basic mistake is to put in humor explicitly *as* humor, so everyone can see you're deliberately trying to make them laugh. Even if they agree with you that something is hilarious, they will feel quite the opposite after their 20th encounter with it. If "funny" is only there to check some design box, your MMO is doomed.

The solution is to *engender* funny rather than try to be "about" funny. You could use comical-looking artwork to attract players, for example, but once the "humor" of this wears thin your players can nevertheless still become immersed; indeed, losing the humorousness may be the first step to immersion. The key is that the humor is part of the MMO's *personality*, not some kind of self-conscious, awkward addition.

The main way that a designer can introduce humor, then, is to set up the conditions for the players to be able to do humorous things *themselves*. A whimsical world puts players into a different frame of mind than does a gritty world; monsters that die slapstick deaths give a different overall impression than when they die in splats of visceral blood. Gnomes are funnier than elves. If a designer wants players to build a culture in which humor plays a part, this can be encouraged through design; if they don't, it can be discouraged. The MMO's own character is reflected in players' characters.

That said, direct humor can work and is not immersion-busting if players have to seek it out themselves. Even in the most intense MMO, humorous Easter eggs are often fine. It's also generally okay to use humor in response to players' attempts to do humorous things.

Oh, one last thing: if an MMO *boasts* about its sense of humor, *don't play it*. It's going to be among the most embarrassingly unfunny experiences you've ever had.

Levels of Data Definition

Driver, MUDlib, world definition (static database), and instantiation (run-time database) are the main levels of functionality in an MMO codebase. Another important hierarchy concerns levels of *data definition*. These map onto the functional levels, but vary more widely[15].

Normally, when people think of "data" they think of facts and figures. This is fine; these do constitute data, but only one kind—*non-executable* data. It's information that is used by programs, but isn't itself program.

There's also *executable* data. Programs are data in a particular form that is meaningful to computer hardware—you can run them.

This seems a simple enough distinction, but there's a gray area in between. Sometimes, data can be meaningful as code to a program. Such programs-as-data are usually called *scripts*; they're said to be *soft-coded*, or *interpreted* programs, as opposed to *hard-coded* or *compiled* ones. A scripting language such as LUA is usually interpreted, whereas a systems language such as C++ is almost invariably compiled. There is some hand-waving over general-purpose languages that compile to a virtual machine (such as Java), but in what follows I'll treat these as if they were compiled.

When it comes to an MMO, some of it must be compiled, because ultimately the code has to run on hardware. If some of this code acts as an interpreter for a scripting language, then some or all of the remainder of the MMO could be interpreted. Both the interpreted and compiled code will also need some non-executable data to hand, too.

So, we have three levels of data definition:

- Hard-coded
- Soft-coded
- Explicit data

How does an MMO decide which to use for each of its levels of functionality? We have three levels of data definition (hard-coded, soft-coded, and explicit data) and four levels of functionality (driver, MUDlib, world definition, and instantiation), so they can't map onto each other one-to-one.

---

[15]Raph Koster: *Overall MUD Architecture.* http://www.raphkoster.com/gaming/book/6b.shtml

Well, there are two rules we have to obey here. The first is that the driver must *always* be hard-coded, and the second is that once you go up a level of data definition, you can't go down a level for higher levels of functionality (so if your MUDlib is soft-coded, then your world definition must be soft-coded or explicit data, it can't be hard-coded).

The part of a codebase that is hard-coded is known as the *game engine*. The more that a game engine encompasses, the greater its *extent*. Different code-bases have game engines with different extents:

- MUSHes and MOOs: just the driver

- LPMUDs: driver plus MUDlib

- DikuMUDs: driver, MUDlib, and world definition

Most commercial MMOs use the *DikuMUD* model, but social worlds (such as *Second Life*) that feature user-created content use the *LPMUD* model. Web 2.0-style MMO development systems such as the now defunct *Metaplace* go with the MUSHes and MOOs approach.

Advantages of wide extent:

- Runs pretty well out of the box

- Run-time efficient

- Fewer bugs

Advantages of narrow extent:

- Flexibility

- Expressiveness

- Variety

The trade-off is between how much creative capability you want your users (or designers) to have, and how much you want to have a system that is fast and robust.

Beyond the Holodeck

Remember the holodeck in *Star Trek: the Next Generation*?

We can do a lot more in a holodeck than we can in a screen-based world, but we're still limited by real-world physical concepts. You can carry a shrunken me in an MMO, but not in a holodeck. I can stand inside a TARDIS that's inside itself in a text MUD, but not in a holodeck. A holodeck is not the end point of what's possible here.

Conceptual *versus* Euclidian

MMOs don't have to be 3D spaces. They could be 4D or 5D if we wanted them to be. Some textual worlds did have multi-dimensional components like this (although primarily only to show that they *could* have them).

The reason we tend to stick with 3D is that if you want to mess with the way that humans internally model the world they're in, you need a very good reason to do so. People are used to their sense of location in the world's being updated automatically for them using cognitive faculties delivered through millennia of evolution; if you disrupt that, they'll notice and they'll expect an explanation.

There are nevertheless several ways to implement 3D in MMOs. The two main ones are *Euclidian* and *conceptual*. A Euclidian space implements the world in terms of geometry—straight lines, planes, trigonometry, and so on. A conceptual space implements the world in terms of abstract connections between the objects in that space. Graphical worlds are all Euclidian; textual worlds are almost all conceptual. The "almost all" there is because although you can't do conceptual in Euclidian, you can do Euclidian in conceptual.

A conceptual framework allows places to be defined by their significance, rather than their physical size. A mountain can be less important than a corridor; a desert that's 12-rooms side to side can feel wide without taking forever to cross. However, if you exclusively use Euclidian, you can more easily exploit some properties of the domain to your advantage (e.g., distance vision). For graphics, a conceptual representation isn't even an option, you *have* to use Euclidian.

In their heads, though, people don't model the world in Euclidian space. Think of the layout of your desk. Think of the vastness of the ocean. They both have their cognitive boundaries and fit neatly in your mind's eye, but they're at greatly differing scales. In a Euclidian world, you have to give the players the picture from which to build up their internal model; in a conceptual world, you can give them something far closer to what that internal model will be—and you have a much stronger ability to shape it.

Inheritance

MMOs will usually deal with *classes* of *objects*. Traditionally, these are:

- Player characters
- Rooms
- Mobiles
- Containers
- Objects

Yes, there are two uses of the word "objects" there. The one on the first line is a technical term used in object-oriented programming; the one on the last line is a regular English word with its regular English meaning. In MMO design, programming objects are often identified with objects in the game world, which is a major mistake in my opinion (they should be identified with commands), but hey, what do I know?

Anyway, objects are arranged in a *hierarchy*. Player characters are creatures are containers are objects. This means that objects can inherit characteristics from their ancestors. If you have defined all the functionality of a "container," then anything that's a child of "container" will inherit all this functionality automatically, as will its own children, and so on. Items lower down in the hierarchy can override this higher-up functionality if desired, and they can introduce new functionality of their own.

Inheritance is a powerful tool, as it means you don't have to recode the same behavior many times over. As I showed you earlier, in *MUD1* (which had only limited inheritance), every time I added a new edible object, I had to say that any object of class nanny (it was a nanny goat) could be fed that object. It would have been much, much easier if I'd only had to say once, "any goat can eat any edible object".

Apart from being a labor-saving device for coding, inheritance has other benefits. It means several programmers can work on a program at the same time without interfering with one another; it promotes efficient use of data storage; it guarantees consistent behavior (if something works for one object, it will work the same way for a similar object).

This all sounds wonderful, and indeed it is. There's just one thing, though: what if you want an object to inherit from more than one parent object?

Agents

Anything capable of independent action in an environment is called an *agent*. In MMOs, agents fall into four categories:

- Environmental agents
- Mobiles
- Bots
- Players

Environmental agents are inanimate but animate-appearing items such as the sun. If you're an ancient civilization with no knowledge of astronomy, then the sun appears to be an object capable of independent action. Okay, so we know today that it acts in accordance with physical laws, but of course the same applies to human beings—it's just that we don't know how we work yet.

Mobiles, or now more commonly *mobs*, are objects with some degree of artificial intelligence that are controlled by the MMO server. NPCs are a type of mobile, but today are usually humanoid, non-attackable quest providers or participants.

Bots also have some degree of artificial intelligence, but they interact with the MMO through the same interface as players. They're programs that play MMOs, in other words. The vast majority of them these days do so to farm resources in the MMO which can then be sold to players; there are some less contentious academic uses for them too, though.

Players are people, sitting at computers (or, I guess, standing). They have more intelligence than anything else in the MMO, but they don't always show it.

Cooler

The water cooler at a studio I visited for a consultancy gig had two taps on it. The red one was for room-temperature water; the blue one was for cooled water. So far, so normal, except…

…except the red one was marked "Hit Points" and the blue one was marked "Mana".

Gotta love game developers.

Production

The glamorous side of computer game development—the one that all those undergraduates on computer game degrees want to get into—is called *development*. This is where you actually make the games.

The less glamorous side, where you pitch ideas to publishers, manage resources, buy in middleware, organize motion capture, audition the voice actors, negotiate with distributors, deal with mad customers, schmooze at conferences, bargain with magazine editors, sit in on endless meetings with accountants, and suck up to senior company management, is called *production*.

As a designer, I find production dull. The *concept* is fine, it's just the *doing* it I can't abide. I do accept that production is needed, though, and that plenty of other people find design every bit as boring as I find production. Also, just because I find something dull, that doesn't mean it's not important (which is why I studied for my finals).

Not all developers think like me, though. Some can regard those on the production side as having made a pact with the devil—they're gamers who have abandoned their principles and thrown their lot in with the suits. Those who play games often tend to this same viewpoint, hence production's somewhat negative overall image.

Yet production accounts for around half the individuals employed by the game industry. Those "boring," managerial things it does are essential if developers are to do their "exciting," creative things. All businesses need suits, and the game industry is no exception.

As for how production people view development people, it's akin to how adults view children: they're noisy, they're hard to control, they keep wanting new toys, and they spend too much time playing instead of working. However, they represent our best hope for the future.

Production isn't a necessary evil, it's a necessary good.

It's still dull, though.

Stealth

Today's MMOs still have problems in many of the same areas that olde worlde MMOs used to have—player behavior, for example, or grinding. However, they also have problems in areas that olde worlde MMOs didn't find problematical. One of these is stealth.

Stealth is when one character can't detect another character because this other character is hidden from them by the world's physics. This means that the stealthier character can attack at unexpected times, to devastating effect. Because stealth is a binary concept (you're either stealthed or you're not), there is no way to debuff it. If you can see them, they're not stealthed; if you can't, they are.

We had stealth in both *MUD1* and *MUD2*: it was implemented as invisibility. If I can make it work in an MMO with permadeath, you can perhaps imagine why I have little sympathy for people who can't make it work in an MMO with a hit-with-a-feather-duster concept of death.

There were three components to how I implemented it:

- Anyone with enough magic to go invisible could go invisible. We didn't have "classes" to "balance"—the spell was available to all.

- Anyone with just a small amount of magic could cast a visibility spell to make nearby invisible players/mobiles visible.

- It cost actual stamina/health points to go invisible. In a modern setting with healers, you'd make it that invisibility could be sustained only if the invisible character remained below some stamina threshold.

That's all I did, and it worked.

If it's a gameplay-dependent decision as to whether stealth is going to help or hinder, that makes it more interesting. If, however, it amounts to simple permission for one group of players (e.g., rogues) to tax random other players, it's not only uninteresting—it's undesirable.

Text and Nodes

MMOs can represent space in different ways, each of which is better for a particular display format.

Nodes (that is, points on a graph) are used only by textual worlds; they implement *conceptual space*. In these, a node represents an atomic location (a room), which can't be smaller than the space into which a player character can fit but can be much larger. Nodes are connected to one another by compass-point directions, plus perhaps some contextual directions such as "out". You type a direction to move: east will transfer you go to the room pointed at by the exit corresponding to east in the travel table for your current room. A map for a textual world therefore consists of a number of nodes connected to nodes using arrows labeled with directions.

Nodal representations can implement any other representation, but have some features that the other representations don't have:

- Arrows need not be bidirectional. East from room X may lead to room Y, but west from room Y may lead to room Z.

- Arrows need not connect to different rooms. East from room X could lead back to room X.

- Rooms are objects like anything else, so can be picked up, carried around, and placed inside other objects (or indeed inside themselves).

- Arrows can be changed dynamically to point at different rooms at different times. If it's raining, east takes you to room X; otherwise, it takes you to room Y.

If you make your rooms all the same size and the same distance apart, then arrange them in a 2D or 3D array, you get a grid—the *Euclidean* space I mentioned earlier. Grids actually make for pretty boring room collections in text worlds and are used only for featureless areas such as deserts (if they're used at all). They restrict what you can do without any obvious payback.

That's in text worlds. If you want a graphical world, that's where grids can really take off.

Boring Production

Okay, so I find production boring. As Stephen Reid (at the time Creative Concepts manager at NCSOFT Europe) once told me, though, on the production side you can meet famous actors, give TV interviews, attend movie premieres, and choose which of 200 scantily-clad models best suits your marketing needs.

Hmm. Well I suppose every job has *some* highlights, but for me the core mechanic is still boring.

Art and Education

Game design is a form of expression, so as a designer you're communicating with your audience. You therefore have to ask yourself:

- What voice do I want to use?

- What words does this audience understand?

- What do I want to say to this audience?

If a game's payload is an educational one, then you need to align the gameplay with the educational message. If it doesn't align, you're doing the equivalent of writing an instruction manual on how to swim. The message may be important, but it doesn't fit the medium and gets in the way of what it's trying to help you do.

If the message does align with the gameplay, then you need to stop short of telling the users what to do. This is because telling them what to do is boring, and not being boring is why you wanted to do this using a game in the first place, right? The aim is for the students to be playing a game that has systems underpinning its gameplay from which they can divine what it is you're trying to teach them. However, most such games end up having an alignment at the fiction level but not at the gameplay level. This is precisely the wrong way around. The fiction does have to match the gameplay, but it's actually better if it *doesn't* match the formal educational context.

Oh well, for an educational game few students would be allowed more than 15 minutes or so of play anyway, which means a fun fiction attached to dissonant gameplay may well be just about enough to sustain their interest before they're told to stop playing.

How Some People Are

During a UK general election campaign, I listened to piece on TV featuring a group of trainee teachers deciding how they would vote. One said she wouldn't vote Liberal Democrat because their policy on funding local councils through having local income tax would cost her more than the current method of charging a flat tax based on property occupancy. She shared a building with other people as she was in student accommodation; therefore, she would pay more if there was a local income tax.

Well yes, she would—for about a year. Then, when she wasn't a trainee teacher sharing a house, she'd spend less for pretty well the rest of her life. She didn't think of it that way, though.

So it is with many players. Often, they look at how things affect them *right now* and don't look to the future at all.

I'm not being critical; as the trainee teacher example showed, it's just how some people are. Designers—especially of live MMOs—need to be *aware* of it, but they can't do anything *about* it.

Chain Mail Bikini

Here's *WoW*'s loose chain vest:

That's on a female character. On male characters, it looks like a loose chain vest.

Area Map

This is what a room map of an MMO looks like:

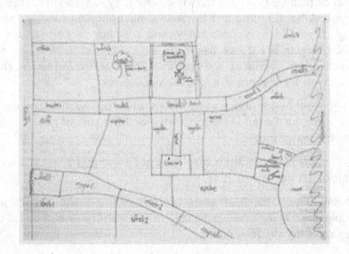

That's a scan of the Narrow Road area from Roy Trubshaw's original design for *MUD1*.

Normally, for a textual world, you wouldn't bother making a nodal map; you'd simply write the travel table direct from the room map.

Not So Massively Multiplayer

Instanced content: it's as if everyone got aboard the cruise ship, hooked up with a few other people they met there, then spent most of the cruise going on speedboat rides. The virtual world is merely a glorified lobby for meeting potential playmates.

While there's nothing wrong with this *per se*, it does mean that the very special and particular experience that can only come from a massively-multiplayer world is regularly cast aside in favor of a multi-player experience that you can easily and better get from regular games specifically written to be multi-player (rather than massively-multiplayer).

World and Content

In the text world days, the game world and its content were created together. You'd create the rooms a few at a time, populating them with content as you went. In graphical worlds, it's not so easy.

A problem graphical worlds have is that it's hard to create them piecemeal. You can do it for a small area such as a ship, but you can't do it for a town—there's just too much space you have to fill. Although techniques do exist for creating such spaces relatively rapidly, the point that they're still large doesn't go away. You have to create the content to go with the geography: the players have to be able to do things there. If the density of quests is low, the area will feel thin and boring; if you pad it with mobs, it will feel thin and grindy.

The problem is particularly felt in worlds set in a modern or futuristic setting, which tend to have large office buildings (barely any of which you can enter) surrounding wide, empty, multi-lane highways (with no real reason to have content of their own). The result is like a desert. Open space everywhere but nothing in it.

This is why my heart sank when I saw the Tokyo expansion of *The Secret World*: like the planet Corellia in *Star Wars: the Old Republic*, the bulk of the effort went into making the world that was to host the content, leaving little time left to create sufficient content to make it remotely worth a visit.

Why yes, they did sell the content later separately.

Levels of Responsibility

Suppose that if you go up a level you gain responsibility. Perhaps you acquire some land, with workers. You have to organize them, decide what crops to grow, and deal with their needs, otherwise they won't produce as much money for you. If you go up more levels, you can delegate this to lords of the manor, but then you have to deal with their bad decisions, politicking and attempts to defraud you.

Would you get to a stage where you think, "you know what, maybe I don't *want* to go up levels any more"?

Single Inheritance

Single inheritance is the situation in which an object has only one parent (but parents can have multiple children). This means it can be drawn as a tree:

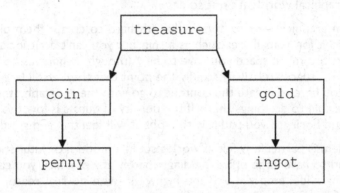

Here, we have two kinds of treasure: coins and gold bullion. We have one kind of coin (pennies) and one kind of gold bullion (ingots). If we define the value of treasure to be 100, then all coins and all gold bullion will also have a value of 100—we have no need to restate it, as it is inherited from their common ancestor. If we decide that gold bullion is worth more than the default, we could set its value to 200, say. Now, all ingots would be worth 200, but all pennies are still worth 100.

In a textual world, the commands GET COIN and GET PENNY would pick up any pennies in the room; GET TREASURE would pick up any pennies and any ingots in the room.

This is *single inheritance*. It runs fast and is fairly expressive. It's what most object-oriented programming languages use.

There are occasions, though, where you want to say things that single inheritance can't say. In those cases, you want *multiple inheritance*.

In my view, MMOs are such a case.

The *Morgan Bible*

Louis IX was 12 years old when he was crowned King of France in 1226. Back then, France was only a third of its present size* and was militarily and economically weak; by the time Louis died in 1270, it had grown to become the largest and wealthiest country in Europe, with the biggest army.

By all accounts, Louis was a likeable and highly pious individual. He went on two crusades, and in 1238 spent half his yearly budget buying the Crown of Thorns from Emperor Baldwin II of Constantinople. He was loved across Europe for his kindness and hailed as the archetypal Christian prince; 27 years after his death, he became the only French monarch to be canonized (the city of Saint Louis, Missouri, is named after him).

Sometime during his reign, Louis commissioned what is now known as the *Morgan Bible*—a book containing around a hundred 270mm by 230mm (10.5 by 9 inches) paintings and no words. The paintings are in gorgeous colors, including a dazzling gold. It's regarded as a masterpiece of gothic art.

Why are there no words? Okay, so words *were* added by later owners, but there were none there originally. Why not?

The pictures are typically arranged in panels, cartoon-style. They are laden with visual cues and symbolism. Without words, the reader has to interpret the pictures to construct the narrative; in so doing, their imagination draws them into the work. A highly-motivated individual with sufficient mental prowess could *will* themselves into the action—envisioning their actually *being present* in the scriptures.

Louis IX was such an individual. He had the *Morgan Bible* made so he could *feel* what the scriptures were saying, in order that he could tell when his actions in the real word reflected their message—they *felt* the same[16].

*In Europe, that is: modern France includes territories overseas that add greatly to its notional surface area.

---

[16]*Sense in communication.* Douglas A. Galbi, 2003. http://www.galbithink.org/sense1.pdf

Games and Education: a Rant

There is a problem with computer game education in the UK, namely that it doesn't exist. The reason it doesn't exist is simple: computer games aren't academically respectable.

Here's how things stand at the moment. There are basically two types of computer game programs in UK universities: vocation-oriented and research-oriented. The vocation-oriented courses are, in the main, put on by universities that weren't universities until 1992; they do a good job in churning out large numbers of competent programmers, artists, musicians, and "designers". They're at undergraduate level. Research-oriented programs occur at the "traditional" universities. These degrees tend to be at the postgraduate level, but increasing numbers of undergraduate programs are now cranking up mainly for opportunistic reasons.

So, if you're a smart wannabe-designer/developer, where do you go? You don't want mere *training* in computer games development, you want an *education* in the subject. So, that would mean you'd try to pick a research-oriented university. The thing is, though, that computer game research at UK universities *doesn't research computer games*. It researches Education or Artificial Intelligence or Psychology or Sociology or Grief Management—it researches a whole bunch of things, *none of which are actually core to computer games*.

People who go on Film Studies courses may simply want to develop the technical skills necessary to work in the movie industry (training), or they may want to understand film-making so they can make films (education). That's their choice. Imagine if Film Studies courses worked the same way that UK Games Studies courses work, though. You'd get the technical skills, but all the research would be into documentaries or acting or viewing patterns—you wouldn't see any research into making better movies. It would be all slipstream stuff.

Yes, we do need to look at how computer games can be used in teaching. Yes, we do need to know how female players are disenfranchised by dysmorphic body images. Yes, we do need to know what intellectual property rights players should hold in creations held in shared virtual spaces. However, above *all* of this, we need to know how to make *better games*. Without that knowledge, the rest is moot. Yet nowhere is anyone looking at this. Why?

Ultimately, it's because the subject is not taken seriously enough; this means there's no funding for it.

If I want to get a grant to analyze gameplay, where can I go to get it? There's no body that awards funds for research into games *as games*. If I want to get a grant to pursue automatic quest-generation systems, okay, well I might be able to get some funds from an AI source, but then I'd have to couch my work in terms of its benefits to AI, not in terms of its benefit to games. Games are treated much as politicians treat poor people: engaging with them for a while does wonders for your street cred, but you wouldn't want to have to live among them.

Game design touches all manner of subjects. I've read textbooks on economics, anthropology, screenwriting, physics, ancient and medieval history, management, mythology, and programming—those being just some of the ones on the bookshelf behind me as I type this. You need to know a little about an awful lot to design games. If, to research design, you have to make applications to fund-awarding bodies, though, where do you go? The economics, anthropology, screenwriting, and so on, isn't ground-breaking stuff. What's new and important and in need of research is the means of *combining* all this knowledge to *make games*. That's just on the applied side; where you would get funds to do fundamental, *pure* research in games is anyone's guess—maybe mathematics or philosophy sources could be persuaded, if you spoke fluent Mathematics or Philosophy.

Bah!

Fault Lines

If I walk up to a painting in an art gallery and throw ink at it, I can't hope to get away with it by saying "well the artist should have put it behind glass if they didn't want people to throw ink at it".

Likewise, just because people can break the rules of an MMO, that doesn't make it the designer's fault.

This is the same kind of thinking that says the wearing of revealing clothing is an invitation to sexual assault.

Basic Model of Production

Computer game development is a form of software engineering. In general, a computer game is just a database with a pretty interface, whereas an MMO is just an operating system with a pretty interface.

So, that means computer games and MMOs are developed in much the same way as databases and operating systems, then?

No. Here's the basic model:

- Find four or five programmers with a range of specializations.

- One of these programmers will be a genius. Make this the lead programmer.

- Provide some artists for the programmers to boss around.

- Give the team a design that will take two years to implement.

- Lock everyone in a room for 12 to 18 months and supply them with pizza and Red Bull.

Voila! One computer game!

Okay, so that description *may* be a little cynical, but game development nevertheless *is* markedly different from regular software development. In part, this is because of the history of the genre, which grew out of the bedrooms and garages of 1980s whiz-kids. Back then, it was possible to for one person to design and code a game in under two months. Only when computers got more powerful, so games (or at least their graphics) could become more sophisticated, did the need for additional programmers—and therefore project management—arise.

The main reason games are not programmed using the same practices as other pieces of software is, however, because of the type of programmer it attracts. Games programmers are the latest incarnation of the hackers of yore (not the "we broke into your system ha ha" kind of hacker, the "computers are fun" kind). They are innovative, experimental, and they push at the boundaries of what's possible. Games development is one of the few areas where they feel liberated from "process," which is why—despite their talent—they will work long hours for a game developer when they could be being paid much more in a 9-to-5 job programming container port management software.

Game development allows programmers to write *new* code. Elsewhere in software development, it all too often means maintaining or stitching together someone else's code. With game development, you actually get to write *programs*.

The fact that the people who like writing programs are also the kind who like games is probably fully explained in some Psychology textbook somewhere.

Something Going Around

Back in September 2005, a story of how a "virtual virus" in *World of Warcraft* caused mayhem and destruction gained international attention. It was suggested that virtual worlds could be used to study how people react to real-world epidemics (indeed, it still is; I regularly read academic papers that mention it to justify an assertion that game worlds can be used for serious purposes).

Amusingly, *WoW*'s "deadly bug outbreak" really *was* caused by a bug: a contagious debuff that was supposed to be contained within a 10-person instance could be exported to the rest of the game world by means of hunters' pets if they were dismissed while infected and then resummoned outside the instance.

What I personally found interesting about this was that this "plague" was widely reported as being the first example of a contagious disease in a virtual world. It wasn't. Sure, it may have been the first in an MMO with (at the time) four million players, but we'd long had them; indeed, we'd even coded them in deliberately.

Earlier, when I was talking about emergence, I mentioned that 10 years earlier in *MUD2* players would deliberately catch their characters a cold so as to spread it among the population of dwarfs. I'm sure *MUD2* can't have been the only textual world in which things like this could and did happen.

New ideas are rarely new, they're just new to *you*.

Multiple Inheritance

Multiple inheritance is when an object can have more than one parent. This means it can be drawn as an acyclic (i.e., no loops) directed graph:

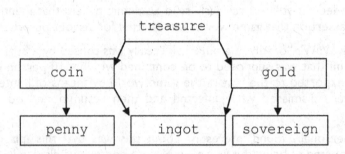

Here, we have an object—a sovereign—which is both a coin *and* gold bullion. In a textual world, you'd want GET COIN to pick up pennies and sovereigns, and you'd want GET GOLD to pick up sovereigns and ingots.

Inheritance in such a system gets more complicated. If the value of treasure is 100 and the value of gold bullion is 200, then what's the value of sovereigns?

Well, what *should* it be?

What it *should* be is 200. This is because gold overrides a value that sovereign would inherit via coin from the same source (treasure). So the value of the sovereign is 200. Easy!

What if we also override the value of coins, though? Suppose we made coins be worth 150: *now* what should the value of the sovereign be?

Here's where it gets tricky: the value of the sovereign is genuinely undetermined. We *don't know* what it inherits! To be useful to a programmer, though, it *doesn't matter* what it inherits—just so long as it always inherits the same thing, consistently. So, let's just pick one at random and stick with it.

Multiple inheritance is not as fast as single inheritance. However, it *is* more expressive. You can go a long, long way with single inheritance, but eventually you either have to fake multiple inheritance some way or you end up doing the same kind of unnecessary repetition I did with what the goat ate in *MUD1*—just at a more tiresomely sophisticated level.

Bad Chef Analogy

Chefs take ingredients, they mix them together, and they produce something for people to consume.

The best chefs don't just know how to cook, they know how to combine ingredients in a recipe. The don't put an ingredient in merely because people like it: they put it in because in doing so, people will like the overall dish more.

The chef knows why each ingredient is there, what the effect each ingredient has, and the quantity in which it needs to be present. The chef *has* to know this, because the chef created the recipe. If the chef's understanding only extends to using an ingredient because it's present in other folks' recipes, this reduces the chance of creating something people will want to eat.

You can replace "chef" with "designer" in this description.

Designers aren't perfect, but they do have an understanding (intuitively at least) as to how their designs fit together.

Players, on the other hand, just see that the recipe contains mushrooms and complain about it because they don't like mushrooms. That's fair enough, but it doesn't mean the *recipe* is bad, it's just that the player isn't one of the people for whom the dish was prepared.

What Players Want

"What players want" comes in three varieties:

- What they *say* they want
- What designers believe they *actually* want
- What no one knows they want until they see it

Giving the players what they want is therefore tricky. They may not think they want what they do want, or they may think they want what they don't want, or they may not know what they want (but want it anyway).

Area Map

I realize that describing textual world maps in terms of nodes and arrows would benefit from an example, but we didn't often used to draw them that way. Nevertheless, occasionally we would do so, and I did manage to keep one example from all those years ago.

Here, then, I present a scan of my original nodal map of *MUD1*'s Dwarf Realm area:

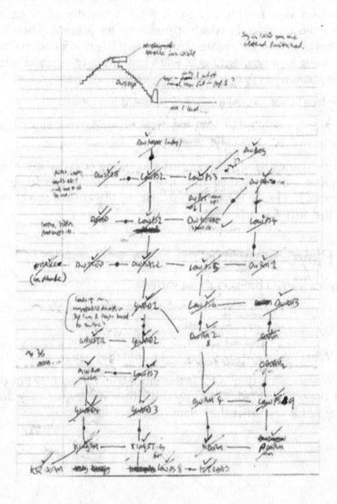

As you can see, Roy Trubshaw's handwriting is rather better than mine.

Persistent Irritation

There were several proto-MMOs around before *MUD1* came along. It wouldn't surprise me if there were half a dozen *actual* MMOs out there, too, predating *MUD1* and awaiting discovery by computational archaeologists.

What constitutes a virtual world is not always apparent, though. One of the joys of being an historian is that you can choose what you want to be the answer to your question and then make a case for it. What seemed important at the time doesn't have to seem important to a future interpretation of that time.

For example, as I've mentioned earlier, the first PLATO program that would absolutely definitely qualify as a virtual world was *Avatar*, which was based on a game called *Oubliette*. In my opinion, one of the reasons *Oubliette* itself falls short is that it wasn't fully persistent (i.e., if all the players quit, the game didn't hang around); its sucky level of inter-player interaction doesn't help its case, either.

However, I have to say that although *MUD1* was suitably excellent at interaction, it wasn't all that great at persistence either. The little program we wrote to ensure it remained in memory the whole time was banned within a week by the DEC-10's operators; thus, were everyone to stop playing, it was merely the whims of the operating system that determined whether the ongoing instantiation would persist. It generally did (at least until the mainframe crashed or was taken down for maintenance), but it could have disappeared within seconds of the last player's exit if the timesharing system was under heavy load. Also, even though it did persist, without our prodding program, it was frozen in time—the mobiles wouldn't move, for example. That said, character data survived reboots, which is all that's formally required to count as "persistent" in an MMO.

Therefore, depending on how hard-line you are in your definition of "persistent," either *MUD1* qualifies as a virtual world but *Oubliette* doesn't, or they both do, or they're both mere honorable mentions.

So it is that history can be less cut-and-dried than people might imagine.

Impact *versus* Persistence

The more you hard-code your game engine, the harder it becomes to allow a wide range of people to change that code. So: more hard code and less data means lower player impact.

On the other hand, the more information that is stored in data files, the more can survive across a reboot. So: more data and less hard code means higher persistence.

It looks as if there may be a relationship here. We have three possibilities:

1. Increased persistence leads to increased player impact.

2. Increased player impact leads to increased persistence.

3. Player impact and persistence are independent.

We can't test these hypotheses very well using only today's MMOs, because they're so derivative that the sample set is too small. However, if we include textual worlds' codebases, we do see something interesting:

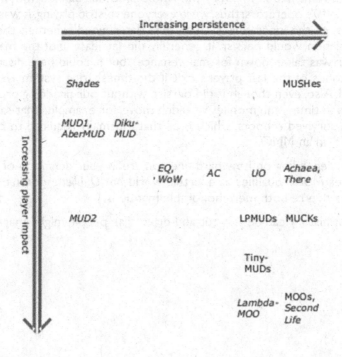

It looks as if you can have high persistence but low impact (e.g., MUSHes), but if you want high impact then you have to have high persistence. This means hypothesis 2 is correct: if you want a virtual world in which players have great control over the creation of content (i.e., high impact) then you need to make sure you can save that content (i.e., high persistence).

This has serious implications for the architecture of virtual worlds. In particular, it determines the extent of the codebase (i.e., how much is hard-coded). A low-impact MMO can hard-code much more than can a high-impact one; it loses the flexibility of scripting, but it gains in speed and efficiency. The fact that DikuMUDs weren't resource hogs contributed to their domination of the textual worlds scene in the 1990s.

I must give credit where credit's due here: we owe awareness of this relationship entirely to Raph Koster and Rich Vogel, who formulated it while working on *Ultima Online*.

Interesting NPC Activities

NPCs are typically used for things such as: guarding; quest-dispensing/rewarding; buying/selling; training; help/tutorials; interface to other functionality (transport, banking, etc.); and atmosphere.

Some of those are tasks that people might want to do. Should they get to do so? It's unlikely that they would want to do them all the time, but they might want to dabble. Also, what happens when several people want to be the local ferry operator? What happens when none do?

NPCs offer a permanent, uncomplaining, full-time solution for undertaking mindless tasks.

This means they could probably be programmed to do raids, too.

Graphics and Grids

Grids are used mainly by graphical worlds. You can think of them as an array of squares, with each square being a fixed-size node adjacent to other nodes in a prescribed manner. Sometimes, as with *Minecraft*, they may be cubes; usually they're squares, though. I'll talk about them as if they're squares, here, because that makes it easier.

Grids are useful only because they enable a space to be displayed graphically. As we've seen, *Island of Kesmai* used text to display a square, *Kingdom of Drakkar* used bitmaps, *Ultima Online* used bitmaps with an isometric viewpoint, and *Meridian 59* used a first-person point of view and a height map to give 2½D visuals. All of these, despite looking very different, have the same basic underlying representation.

I should point out that despite this similarity, *UO* and *M59* didn't descend from *IOK*. They took their graphical cues from what was going on in single-player games, rather than the *IOK* line (which eventually died out).

Although you get immediate-impact graphics with a grid-based system, tessellating the nodes introduces some design restrictions:

- Constant scale means you can't finesse distance. 20 rooms of textual wilderness could have to be 2,000 squares of isometric wilderness.

- Because distance changes, so does velocity. You need some means of fast travel (ships, hot air balloons, teleportation portals, —whatever fits the fiction) so people can get from one side of the world to the other in reasonable real time.

- The world is only 2D. Buildings are restricted to one story; caves and bridges are impossible. (Note: This doesn't apply if the world uses a *Minecraft*-style 3D grid.)

The last of these was the most problematical for grid-based worlds, and was addressed by introducing a degree of nodality back into the system. Some squares were flagged as being *coincident*: if you stand on one square (illustrated to look like a staircase, say), then you are teleported to another (that is part of the "upstairs" grid); reverse to do "downstairs".

The granularity of a grid representation is normally quite fine—one square typically represents a square yard/meter. This is better than in a straight nodal system, but it's not perfect. In particular, anything too large to fit in one square is awkward to move, and curves on large features (such as rivers, buildings, and paths) are blocky-looking. Creatures tend to move using comical, right-angled turns.

In short, a world made of squares tends to look and feel as if it it's made of squares.

A Crocodile, a Tiger, and an Elephant

Suppose you went into a room and found a crocodile, a tiger, and an elephant there.

If you were a dragon, you might decide to kill the tiger and the elephant, but leave your cold-blooded relative the crocodile unharmed. You'd want to KILL MAMMAL.

If you were a minotaur, you might want to leave your fellow herbivore, the elephant, unharmed. You'd want to KILL CARNIVORE.

You can do this in a multiple inheritance system, because you can define crocodiles to be both reptiles *and* carnivores, tigers to be both mammals *and* carnivores, and elephants to be both mammals *and* herbivores. In a single inheritance system, you have to hack it somehow.

Is the jack of spades a jack, a spade, or both? Is a pitchfork a tool, a weapon, or both? Is music a sound, a form of entertainment, or both?

Multiple inheritance is just *so* much more expressive than single inheritance.

A Little About a Lot

Another thing that game designers have in common with each other, which I've alluded to earlier in this book, is that they know a little about an awful lot of things. For MMO designers, it's pretty well part of the job description.

There are a number of reasons why this is so.

First, designers have played a lot of games. Games include facts, and designers remember those facts. My knowledge of the Chinese warlord Cao Cao doesn't come because I've studied Chinese history—I haven't studied it. I know about him because I've played games based on the *Romance of the Three Kingdoms*, an historical novel from the 14th Century which is one of the most famous and enduring pieces of literature in China. No, I haven't read the book itself.

Second, designers read up on subject areas when they create games. I know who Anne Bonny and Mary Read were because in my late teens I designed a pirates board game, and then a few years later read up on the history of pirates with a view to making a computer game on the subject (*MUD1* took off, so I never got around to it).

Third, designers sometimes find some things inexplicably interesting and dive into them to the exclusion of all else. I've no idea why this *is* the case (er, otherwise it would be explicable), but it is. It's as if they sense that something will somehow help their understanding of a system—terrain, elves, griefing, alchemy, whatever—and it fires them to investigate it.

Obviously, if you're designing an MMO—which requires a very broad range of knowledge—then you do need to know a little about a lot of things. Whether it's a desire to design MMOs that causes people to widen their knowledge, or whether widening their knowledge causes a desire to design MMOs, I don't know. However, I do know that I can look at my bookshelf behind me and see volumes on economics, anthropology, the *1,001 Nights*, Queen Victoria, antique art, Medieval cities, and screenwriting, and that if I look at the bookshelves (or Kindles) of other MMO designers, I'll see a similarly eclectic mix.

MMOs and Education

Normally, when people use the words "education" and "MMOs" in the same breath, they mean using MMOs as a teaching tool. A question that is less rarely asked is what should we teach *about* MMOs?

So, you're a university lecturer who's just been told you have to teach a module on MMOs, on the grounds that you used to play one so it stands to reason you're qualified. This is like asking someone who takes aspirin to give a series of lectures on pharmaceuticals, but hey, it happens. What are you going to teach?

Well, the easy thing to do is to ask people who are working in the MMO industry what kind of skills they want from recruits. Then, all you have to do is teach what they tell you. Okay, so this amounts to training rather than education, but education does have to include *some* foundation material.

To this end, I asked three senior MMO developers (two North American, one European) what they felt should be on an undergraduate MMO curriculum. They all gave the same response: they felt that they were unable to come up with anything even remotely concrete. Even vague opinion had to be wrung from them drop by drop.

Conclusion: The MMO industry *doesn't know* what it wants. It just knows when it doesn't get it.

Content Discontent

When you reach the end of an MMO, you should be told so and it should be game over.

People don't read a book and then complain that all the time and effort they invested in reading it is wasted because they've now finished. No, if they feel they've got something out of it they go on and try *other* books by the same author.

Why should MMOs be any different?

The Image of the City

I once had a conversation with an academic who was considering writing a paper about how the layout of *MUD2* exhibited features used in urban planning. He'd noticed that it had paths, edges, districts, nodes, and landmarks, as described in the seminal book on the subject, Kevin Lynch's *The Image of the City*[17]. He thought it fascinating that a haphazard world put together by a game designer/programmer could nevertheless match the theory very well.

I explained to him that I had read *The Image of the City*, which I came across while researching my PhD. I was therefore familiar with Lynch's theories when I wrote *MUD2*. We already had the makings of most of his elements in *MUD1*, but only by happenstance. The exception was districts ("areas" in *MUD1*), which we had deliberately created to be consistent collections of rooms sharing a collective atmosphere; I didn't have to do anything different with those for *MUD2* from I'd been doing anyway.

For the new areas of *MUD2*, I planned the major paths and nodes so they hung together in a less haphazard fashion. Edges were far less common than in a living city, but apart from the borders that stop you falling off the world, I did deliberately insert a major edge (a river), and then later (during expansion phases) added other edges. This gave me something (along with paths) to use to separate the districts, plus some pinch-points (nodes) where they were crossed.

In some ways, landmarks are harder to do in text than graphics, but in others they're easier. You can't simply see them and judge for yourself whether they're memorable, but then even in graphical worlds you can't do that at a great distance as it fogs out. At least in text you can reference a landmark from as far away as you like (although if people don't read the long descriptions of rooms, they're not going to pick up on it).

Time and time again, academics looking at MMOs will spot that some theory applies to them and then write it up as a paper, pleased that they've noticed a formal pattern emerging from the mass of undirected creativity. Time and time again, they are oblivious to the fact that the reason the pattern applies is because the designer was actually aware of it and used it purposefully. That was the case with Lynch's theories applied to *MUD2*, for example, but it happens all the time.

---

[17]Kevin Lynch: *The Image of the City*. MIT Press, Cambridge MA, 1960.

I'm on the editorial board of several games journals and have in the past rejected papers I've reviewed for publication on the basis that they presented an observation as new when it was created to be observed. It's not a major revelation that an NPC exhibits all the classic symptoms of psychosis if you know that the designer has read up on psychosis and consciously made that NPC behave in accordance with them. It's like saying that the stained-glass window in a famous church looks like a saint: *of course* it does! It was *made* to do so!

Just because academics don't know a great deal about game design, that doesn't mean game designers in turn are clueless about all academic work.

Another Coincidence

It's not just grid-based worlds that have coincident points. Here's a screenshot from *The Secret World*, on an occasion when I fell through the architecture while doing its "Nightmare in the Dream Palace" quest:

Those large, tunnel-like sections are all part of the same space: you get to the end of one and it teleports you seamlessly to another. From this, we can divine that the zones in *The Secret World* are basically square, so if you want a long, long tunnel then it's more efficient to divide it into sections and lay them alongside each other, making the end points coincident.

That works if all the end points *are* coincident, of course, and some annoying player doesn't go deliberately looking for a hole through them because of a knowledge of how these things work.

Graphics and Polygons

Polygons are now the dominant display method for MMOs. There are so many good 3D graphical engines available out there that really there's no excuse not to use them.

Typically, the base for a modern graphical MMO retains the 2½D structure of yore; this is because the tools for creating worlds are *so* much easier to use when they're 2D. Polygons are used to override the 2D structure when necessary.

In a tile-based world, there's a one-to-one mapping between the data structure representing the space (i.e., an array) and the space itself as displayed (i.e., textured tiles or blocks).

In a fully-3D system, this relationship between data structure and display is no longer present. Instead, polygons represent *surfaces*—of the ground, of buildings, of mobs, and of other objects. Open space is any apparent volume that does not have a surface in it. Thus, instead of creating a set of nodes or squares corresponding to a particular location, a "location" is but a mere *point* in the 3D coordinate system. Most of the world is therefore empty, so does not need to be represented explicitly in a data structure; lists of objects within visual range are held instead, and are rendered in terms of the polygons that make up their surfaces.

The reason developers prefer 3D over the other alternatives is that it's the more *persuasive*: it *looks* more like it's real than do grid-based worlds or textual worlds. That doesn't mean such 3D worlds are perfect, of course—that impressive, glistening ocean usually meets the sandy shore in straight lines, for example, and the wheels of carts are inefficiently octagonal (or even hexagonal).

Straight lines are still better than straight-lines-at-90-degree-angles, though, or requiring that players have an imagination.

Mobs and Bots

Mobs are "mobile objects" in MMOs. I can say this with certainty because, as I continually boast to people, I invented the term. I needed a word to describe monsters, NPCs, and other mobile objects in *MUD1*, so I called them *mobiles*, with a vague nod in the direction of those ornaments that people hang from ceilings which move around in constrained but not easily predictable patterns. Over time, the term was shortened to *mob*. Newer players will often think that a "mob" is a collection of trash mobiles, rather than an individual one, which is closer to how the word "mob" is used in everyday speech. They can therefore get confused when asked to "CC the nearest mob" or something, because in their mind they can only crowd-control individuals, not groups of them.

Mobs are computer-controlled by the MMO server. They therefore have access to the MMO database and can in theory cheat by using knowledge they shouldn't have (such as your exact character and weapon stats) or by manipulating the figures (so the blow that would have killed them doesn't *quite* do so). This is considered very bad form, however, and the players *will* notice.

Bots are also computer-controlled, but they are external to the MMO. They play as if they were players, using the same remote connection to the MMO (although not necessarily the same client—they could have a bespoke client embedded in them). Bots are typically used to perform tasks that are either mindless (farming resources while you're asleep in bed) or that benefit from faster reactions or accuracy than players have (never-missing head shots when sniping).

Although mobs and bots can have very powerful AI controlling them, typically they're just mechanistic. AI is computationally expensive, so it makes little sense for a designer to use it to control the movement of a guard who is going to walk the length of a city wall in perpetuity. For this reason, mobs and bots usually exhibit mechanistic behavior until something odd comes along (they're attacked, their path is blocked, their bags get full); *then* they'll switch to the full AI system.

Except, this won't be all that smart either: players don't like being beaten.

Methods

Almost all MMOs these days are programmed using an object-oriented programming language such as C++ or conceivably Java. These languages tie functionality to objects using an established programming mechanism called *methods*. Basically, the behavior associated with an object is kept with and governed by that object, rather than being described independently of it.

Object-oriented programming is the technique of choice for large-scale systems. It produces code that's portable, maintainable, and that can be worked on by several programmers at the same time.

However, crucial to all this is the correct identification of objects. MMO programmers routinely associate programming objects with in-world objects—weapons, clothes, doors, whatever.

I am of the opinion that this is a mistake: tying a method to an object is fine for single-parameter commands, but it gets into a mess for multi-parameter commands.

Here's an example of its working fine: let's say you want to drop an axe. You look at the drop method for axes, find that it inherits from some general portablething object, and you execute the method that you find there. The result is that the axe falls to the floor.

Now suppose that you want to drop an axe into a bag. You have to decide whether the drop method is associated with the axe or with the bag. Is it a property of objects that if you insert them into bags, *this* happens, or is it is a property of bags that if you insert objects into them, *this* happens?

Okay, well that decision is perhaps a *little* arbitrary, but so long as you're consistent you're okay. You'll probably have drop tied to the axe, but have that query the bag to make sure it doesn't have any ideas of its own as to whether the object can go in there or not. It's doable.

Here's something altogether different. Suppose you touch a candle to a match: what happens? Well, if neither is lit, nothing happens. Otherwise, they both end up alight. So, is it a property of candles that if you touch them to a match and either the match or the candle is lit, then they both end up lit? Or is it a property of matches that if you touch them to a candle and either the candle or the match is lit, then they both end up lit? And what if, instead of touching the candle to the match, you touched the match to the candle? Or a match to a match? Or a candle to a candle?

Well, the thing to do would be to associate the touch method with a general combustiblething object. It's a property of combustible things that if you touch them to other combustible things and one of them is lit, then they both get lit.

That would work, but it's missing the point.

What's *really* going on here is that the behavior isn't associated with candles, matches, or indeed a generic combustiblething object. It's associated with the *command*. It's a property of [touch combustible1 combustible2] that the lit properties of combustible1 and combustible2 are ORed together. The functionality lies in the action of making contact, not in the objects that are being put in contact.

Okay, so this is essentially a philosophical point. It makes the description of what's going on easier from a designer's perspective, but not from a programmer's. Taking a pragmatic, programming point of view, it doesn't matter where the functionality lies so long as it can be found. A programmer doesn't care whether you tie verbs to nouns or nouns to verbs if you can hack it either way.

There are, however, programming reasons why you would not want to use game world objects as programming objects.

Oh, did I leave one of those hanging implications around again, in a weak attempt to build tension by suggesting that later on I'll explain?

Load Balancing

When you have an MMO with hundreds of thousands of players, you have two options: put all of them in the same world (like *EVE Online* does) or run multiple instantiations (shards) of the world. In either event, these days you will still probably have more players in your world than you can handle on a single computer (unless it's a supercomputer, but those are expensive). The "server" is actually a cluster of computers (sub-servers) that together implement the MMO.

To get the most efficient use out of the computers that make up your server, you need to spread the work they do equitably. By far, the greatest amount of work that a server must perform is associated with player activity. For every command every player issues, a server has to:

- Lock all the database records it may need
- Test that the command is (still) valid
- Update the database to reflect the consequences of the command
- Unlock the records it locked

This means heavy overheads, and introduces *server lag* while commands are queued up waiting to be processed. It doesn't matter how much parallel processing you have: if two commands want to access the same database records, one has to wait.

Idea! Most commands by usage are movement-related, so partition by virtual geography. You don't have to lock records if you own them. This is the logic behind most load balancing in MMOs.

There are two approaches to handling this kind of load balancing: fixed and dynamic.

Fixed load balancing has each sub-server handling a given area or set of such areas. This is easy to implement, and the world can be designed in such a way as to help it out.

Dynamic load balancing has each sub-server handing several smaller areas, but those areas can change. If a server gets too busy because several of its areas are experiencing too much load, it can pass control of an area to an under-used server, thereby balancing the load. It can also subdivide areas into smaller parcels, although of course there is an "atomic" area size beyond which further division is impossible.

Modern MMOs take dynamic load balancing further by using a cloud-based system that balances load across several (potentially all) of the MMO's shards. It's possible for them to share player presence, so if there's a particularly under-used zone then the players from several different shards could be placed there together and interact with one another. It's even possible for them to group in the shared zone and to exit it to a more heavily-loaded zone without being ungrouped and spread across several sub-servers.

Fixed load balancing has fewer overheads than dynamic load balancing, and is the slightly better option 90% of the time. However, few large-scale MMOs use it anymore because for the remaining 10% of the time it's significantly worse. It has major flash-crowd problems: if half the players log into the same zone at once, say for a one-off or seasonal event, it's going to suffer big time.

The design of the MMO can to some extent mitigate the effect of flash crowds. For example, *Dark Age of Camelot* was the first mainstream MMO to feature three separate realms plus borderlands, such that characters of one realm couldn't enter the other two realms. This meant that a sub-server could handle a mix of zones from each of the realms, secure in the knowledge that there couldn't be more than a third of the players in any one of them (assuming a linear distribution of players to realms). Making sure that no sub-server handles geographically adjacent zones also helps.

Nevertheless, the ability of a dynamic system to respond very quickly to unexpected demand, and for the cloud-based version to commission and decommission sub-servers from a central pool on the fly, mean fixed load balancing has probably now had its day.

That's for large-scale MMOs, though. There's no reason why a small-scale MMO, with only a few hundred players, couldn't run on its own dedicated single-computer server just fine.

The Palestine Liberation Organization

One of my students once dropped into my office at a moment critical for the completion of his final-year project. He was supposed to spending every waking moment finishing it in time for the deadline, but instead he'd invested six crucial hours indulging a sudden fascination with the inner workings of the Palestine Liberation Organization in the 1970s. He was frustrated and angry that he'd allowed himself to do this, because how was he ever going to become a designer if he could so easily be distracted at a time when he should have been directing all his energy toward his project? As a Greek, he didn't have any connection with the Middle East and had no idea why he'd suddenly felt compelled to learn about the PLO's management structure of decades earlier.

I told him that, quite to the contrary, it meant he was *absolutely* designer material. When I myself was an undergraduate and was supposed to be studying for a programming examination, I spent two (it might even have been three) days reading about pagodas in the library.

Most people don't do that kind of thing, but designers, well, we just can't help ourselves.

Cognitive Maps

People don't conceive of environments as collections of 3D polygons or coordinates. As *The Image of the City* showed, they conceive of them as agglomerations of paths, districts, edges, boundaries, and landmarks in a *cognitive map* that they build up inside their heads. They can build those images up whether the input is from visual information or symbolic (that is, textual) information.

Amazingly, they can also do it without either (as exemplified by blind people).

Novelists and Programmers

Suppose a novelist spent a week writing a difficult chapter, but at the end of it, realized that it could have been done better. What would the novelist do?

Well, the chances are that the novelist would write more to fix it, in order not to have to throw away what so much emotional effort had invested in creating. The pain of doing this is so common that it even has a name, "killing your darlings" (or, occasionally, "killing your babies"), variously attributed to Mark Twain, William Faulkner, F. Scott Fitzgerald, Dorothy L. Sayers, George Orwell, Stephen King, and Sir Arthur Quiller-Couch.

Suppose a programmer spent a week writing a difficult routine, but at the end of it realized that it could have been done better. What would the programmer do?

Well, the chances are that the programmer would throw it away and write the better version.

To authors, bad writing is only bad because there isn't the context to explain it, so they add more context. They end up with bloated novels that, although self-consistent, are flabby and meandering.

To programmers, bad code is just outright bad code, and they'd feel rather pleased to figure out a better way of doing something. Who wants to write rubbish code?!

MMO designers: be like programmers, not like novelists. If it doesn't fit, then no matter how good an idea it is, drop it.

Just Not Me

My *Second Life* character has my own name. I gave a talk there early on and they set it up for me.

My avatar, on the other hand, is the default white-T-shirt-and-jeans dude you get when you sign up. I was offered a customization so he would look like me, but I declined it.

This way, he's more like text.

World Wide Web of Worlds

What if you had your own, personal MMO? You have your own social network pages, so why not your own MMO? You could link to other MMOs if you wanted to, but you probably wouldn't wish to integrate them permanently.

This is how the World Wide Web works. There are thousands of millions of web pages (of varying quality), hyperlinked together. At any one moment, you can be browsing several web sites in different windows, or different panels of the same window. Other people can be browsing your web site.

We can have the same thing for MMOs, except that MMOs are real-time interactive, shared spaces, whereas the WWW in general isn't.

Your MMO would run on your own PC, or on some kind of cloud-based hosting service. You'd start it up when you wanted to receive visitors. People on your friends list could get in without asking. Whether other people could get in would depend on whether you wanted to accept spammy unsolicited entrants or not. Yes, if they're a friend of a friend? Yes, if they send you $1 via PayPal first? Yes, if they're a member of some organization you trust?

Your personal MMO could handle several instantiations of itself at once. You could hold a party in one instantiation while speaking to the loser friend you don't want spoiling it in another. You could have several separate MMOs running simultaneously. Doors could connect them to each other and to other MMOs or web pages.

You could also visit other people's MMOs. Crank up your client, type in their World Wide Web of Worlds address, and if you're on their pass list, you're in! If you're on their block list, you're out. Otherwise, you wait until they either admit you or bounce you.

You may or may not be able to come as your own avatar: it would depend on its model (e.g., number of polygons) and on the MMO (role-playing fantasy means no wookies). *You* can always display your avatar how you like, it's just how other people see it that would be at issue. The same kind of scheme would apply to objects you wanted to bring in with you, with a system of digital certificates guaranteeing that such objects conform to standards and have no suspect functionality.

You could be visiting several worlds at the same time in different windows. It wouldn't matter if your avatar were damaged or destroyed in one of these worlds, because they just use copies. If it suffers permadeath in one MMO, it's only permanently dead in that one MMO. Whether you can take an item into or out of an MMO would be up to the MMO's owner, but you're only taking a copy anyway—it's not as if it would no longer be available in the world where it originated.

Ahh. This is what I want to see. In the text days we could have had it, but we didn't as there was no incentive to develop it. Today it would be even worse: there would be problems finding art assets; the ratio of people who prefer creating content to those who prefer consuming it is out of whack; it would end up as a network of deserted *Second Life* style social worlds rather than MMOs.

It's a shame, but progress sometimes comes in the wrong order.

Antiquated Laws

Some of these old laws that have been on the statute book for hundreds of years really ought to be repealed.

Every year, one such piece of ancient legislation prevents me from undertaking the quite reasonable action of meting out physical violence to the 50% of my students who are unable to spell the word "lose" correctly. Given that I teach on a games course and "lose" is one of those special technical terms we academics use (it refers to the opposite of "win"), I don't think I should be prohibited from delivering blows from a cricket bat to the person of anyone spelling it "loose". But no, we have to adhere to these arbitrary decrees that are throwbacks to the Middle Ages, when spelling wasn't even an issue because most of the population was illiterate.

Surely there's some kind of exception clause that would at least allow me to place in the stocks students who say "a dice" instead of "a die"?

Open and Closed

MMOs can be described along a number of dimensions. Persistence and impact are two, but one of the oldest is whether it's *open* or *closed*.

An open world leaves players to do pretty well whatever they like within context. *MUD1* was like this. A closed world isn't completely closed (because then players couldn't do anything at all), but it's less open. Many of *MUD1*'s immediate descendants were like this. Open worlds are also known as *sandbox* worlds; closed worlds are also known as *structured* worlds or *theme park* worlds. Openness therefore means the relative freedom to walk your own path as a player. There's an ongoing dialectic between designers as to which of sandbox or theme park worlds carries the higher payload of potential fun, but (you'll doubtless be pleased to know) I'm not going to address that here.

Now, although this is how *designers* use the term "open," players sometimes use it to mean whether or not they (as players) can modify or add to the world. In this respect, it's like the term "open source" in software development. For MMOs, following the work of Koster and Vogel that I mentioned earlier, designers call this kind of openness *impact*. They measure it on more of a sliding scale than the straight is-or-isn't binary view that players tend to adopt.

If players *can* add new content to a world, the question that then arises is whether they can do this in a freeform or merely a contextual manner. Contextual changes fit the fiction; freeform changes *can* fit the fiction, but they don't have to do so. Designers themselves have the ability to make freeform changes, but they do it all contextually; indeed, it's what defines the context.

Giving players the ability to make freeform changes increases the chance that such new content will not be contextual, thereby breaking the fiction. This is why most of the virtual worlds that allow freeform content creation are social worlds rather than game worlds: they don't have a fiction to break, so are free to allow players to give their imaginations full rein. They often make a big play of the fact they're letting players create, as opposed to imposing a creation on the players in the manner of an MMO.

All designers of virtual worlds have to decide whether to make the world they create be freeform sandbox (as in *Second Life*), contextual sandbox (as in *EVE Online*), or contextual theme park (as in *World of Warcraft*). Freeform theme parks don't exist except with very small groups of players (as with *D&D*, but that's not an MMO).

Interestingly, when a designer chooses to make a freeform sandbox world, then those who create in this world have the same what-kind-of-world-to-build decision as the designer did, only one level down. If, in *SL*, you create a sub-world, *you* have to decide whether it's freeform sandbox, contextual sandbox, or theme park. Again, if you choose the former, then anyone who creates a world within your world within *SL* has to face the same decision, and so on indefinitely until someone chooses to make a contextual sub-world.

From this perspective, it becomes apparent that even in social worlds with no context, at some point they do have designers who are creating contextual worlds. This is important, because freeform sandbox worlds are frequently praised by their players and by non-playing commentators for their liberating nature. MMOs, being contextual, are chastised for oppressively denying their players the ability to create freeform content. Such an argument is rather blinkered, though, because it's basically accusing all those who create contextual content within a *SL*-like freeform sandbox of being whatever it is that the MMO developers are accused of being.

We thus have a chain of design. I design for you, you design for her, she designs for him, he uses. At some point, someone *has* to make something that someone else can just use, otherwise it's never-ending. The chain may be long or short, but it's what's at the end that's important: that's the point at which players just get to *play*.

Whether your world is sandbox or theme park, freeform or contextual, eventually someone has to have fun just from playing.

The person who creates the content that is being played can claim to be that most wondrous of things: its *designer*.

Classes of Actions

Let's say we want to implement a command to hit things. If you HIT a creature, a message is generated, an animation is run, and combat starts. So, in object-oriented programming terms, that's the creature as the object and hit as the method: creature.hit().

Now suppose we want to add some similar commands that do the same sort of thing but with a different message or animation. Okay, well that's easy enough: we can create creature.punch(), which calls some generic creature.strike(PunchString, StrikeAnimation) function. Fair enough.

Of course, you can hit, punch, thump, and whatever-else-the-thesaurus-says more than just creatures. You can hit hard objects, such as paving stones, which may hurt you; you can hit soft objects, such as pies, and hurt them. If you hit a door, you might want to cause a noise to be heard in the room on the other side; if you hit a bag, it could give you some idea of what's inside. Each version of hit here is different.

Okay, well we can handle those, too. We can write hardobject.hit(), softobject.hit(), door.hit(), bag.hit()—we can write a version for any type of hit we like.

Hmm, but we also have to write hardobject.punch(), hardobject.thump(), hardobject.smite(), hardobject.slap(), hardobject.whack(), and so on. We have to do the same thing for softobject, door and bag, too.

This is starting to look somewhat repetitive.

It was this kind of problem that the object-oriented programming philosophy was developed to address. Unfortunately, though, it only works on objects, not methods. You can't have a hierarchy of methods, only of objects; if you need a hierarchy of methods, it means that what you have as methods shouldn't be methods, they should be objects.

This is why programmers should be looking at making commands be programming objects, rather than using in-world "objects".

Listening to Players

MMO players often don't know what they want, or they think they know what they want but they don't want it. They'll say they want a PvP world then not play it. They'll say they want photorealism then play the cartoony world. Some will say they want to be able to pay for game advantages with real money and some will say they don't; people from both groups will then do the opposite of what they publicly advocate.

Designers would be foolish not to listen to players. However, they would be even more foolish to listen to them uncritically.

MMO Database Use

Large-scale commercial MMOs make a lot of use of databases server-side. These are the main ones:

- **The login database:** This stores account details and other player-specific information (e.g., which servers you have characters on).

- **The template database:** This is used by MMOs that hard-code the world definition, and is where the term "static database" originates.

- **Instantiation data:** This stores whatever data makes this shard different from the next shard, and is where we get the term "run-time database". It defines what can persist across a server reboot.

- **The scripting database:** Here is where user-created code is stored; it's primarily a social-world thing, but it doesn't have to be (role-play MUSHes implement all but the driver as scripts, but they also have low player impact).

- **The assets database:** This is used for artwork and sounds uploaded by the players. Again, it's more for social worlds in which user-created content is a big deal—game worlds will keep assets client-side.

Areas, Regions, and Zones

The three ways of representing space in MMOs (nodes, grids, and polygons) follow a path to increasing detail: room to square to point. In a 3D world, you are located at a point but feel as if you occupy a space that's bordered by planes, giving you the impression of a room.

There's also a path of *decreasing* detail. Adjacent rooms are grouped into conceptual collections of related content called *areas*. Although these originated with textual worlds, they remained useful in graphical worlds and are still in evidence today. When you fly around in *WoW*, say, and a message appears saying where you are, that indicates a change of area.

Groups of areas are called *regions*. Areas concern content; regions concern geography. A group of areas that comprised a desert would make a region, as would a group that comprised a city or a sea.

A *zone* is a collection of one or more regions; sometimes, a zone *is* a region. Originally, zones were primarily an implementation concept used for load balancing and for preloading textures (so you didn't have snow textures in memory for a zone made up of tropical areas). Nowadays, though, zones are mainly content-related, grouping regions by level, atmosphere, and quest narrative.

The maps that designers draw for areas and regions (and therefore zones) are pretty much the same today as they were in the old text MUD days. The way MMOs are displayed and the way they implement the world in their underlying data structures may have changed, but the fact that they are *worlds* remains constant.

Freeform Creation

Is Lego a game? No, it's a toy. You can't "win" or "lose" at Lego. You can, however, use it to *make* a game—or to make more toys.

With *Minecraft*, the game aspect (such as it is) *can* be won or lost, but the puzzle-creation and playspace-creation is done in sandbox mode. It's orthogonal to the game. It's like doing machinima in *Half-Life*; the game is set aside for the emergent art form to shine through.

People will always create in games, regardless of whether you as a designer want them to do so. The important question is how much said creativity is part of the game. Some forms of creativity—for example, the formulation of solutions to strategic problems in a war game—are fully part of the game. Others—for example, the way you choose to dress your character in *The Secret World*—are not (although perhaps at times they should be).

Freeform creativity allows players to create objects with whatever functionality they choose. It's the mainstay of social worlds such as *Second Life*, but is it appropriate for game worlds?

The key point is whether the creativity in question has any impact on the gameplay without itself being a deliberate part of the game. If it doesn't, all you risk breaking is the fiction. If it does, the players will screw each other over to the point of meaninglessness.

This is because anything that has impact on the gameplay *is* part of the game.

Victorians

Oh, the misfortunes of being a game designer.

I've got lots of work I should be doing right now, but I spent a whole day looking up and downloading photographs of Victorians. I've no idea what I'm going to use them for, just that they're going to come in handy some time for some game or other. Maybe.

Oh well, at least it wasn't like with pagodas that time in pre-WWW days, when this kind of thing took three times as long.

Socialist Quiz

Back when I was at school, in those happy days when no national curriculum prescribed every single minute of every single educational day by government diktat, we would occasionally have events such as school quizzes. The last one of these during my time (I'd just turned 18), was a house-based competition for teams consisting of one boy and one girl in the sixth form.

[Translation for non-British readers: *Houses* are in-school teams that you get allocated to when you join the school and are kept with all the way through it, to give artificial groups that can be used for competitive events such as sports and quizzes. The *sixth form*—a term still in use despite its being out of date even in my day—is made up of pupils who are either taking age-18 exams or retaking age-16 exams.]

So, the quiz.

Well, the teacher who ran it, Dr. Dorney, had a PhD in Chemistry but actually taught Mathematics and (a miracle in 1978!) Computer Science. He was head of the sixth form, and one of those people who cared passionately about the downtrodden. Dr. Dorney was a genuinely nice guy, and well-liked by all the sixth-formers, including me.

So the quiz began. Dr. Dorney had all the questions written down on cards. When it was your team's turn, you were asked a question. If you got it right, you got a point. If you got it wrong, oh well, no point for you (and no chance for the other teams to get a point as we didn't have buzzers). So, it was all very simple. Except, it wasn't *quite* like that. You see, this wasn't an ordinary quiz: this was what might be called a *socialist* quiz.

I noticed after a few rounds that one of the teams was getting exceedingly easy questions. This was the team with the weakest members—they'd been selected on the basis that they were the two heads of house, which meant they were good at sports but not necessarily (or, in their case, remotely) good academically. So while I and my partner were being asked questions such as "what do the letters in the acronym MASER stand for?," they were getting "What is the capital city of England?". It wasn't just me who noticed, either. People on the other two teams were giving us and each other odd looks, too.

It was then I spotted what Dr. Dorney was doing. When it was the turn of the weaker team (representing St. Mary's house), he was reading the question to himself, and if he thought it was too hard then he put it to the back of the pile and went on to the next question. *Uh?* He did this for several rounds as I and my partner watched in astonishment.

Then, he did something worse. By this time, our team was in the lead. He looked at the question we were going to be asked, deemed it too easy, and put it, too, to the back of the pile.

I couldn't believe it. "Did you just put our question to the back of the pile?" I asked.

He was entirely up front about it. Yes, he had done. What was the point of asking me a question that he knew I'd know the answer to?

"But St. Mary's have been getting really easy questions! You went through the cards looking for ones you knew they could answer!"

He replied that no, he hadn't. He'd just *not* asked the ones he knew they *couldn't* answer.

But ... but ... it was a quiz! The whole *point* of a quiz is to find out who has the best general knowledge! It's not to find out whose general knowledge the quizmaster has most underestimated!

The fact that the St. Mary's team was so poor that they still got questions wrong was no justification for his actions. The mention that he just happened to be in St. Mary's himself, he took as an assault on his integrity. "Are you accusing me of cheating?" he asked.

Yes I was, and I said so. I didn't know what his motivation was, but he certainly was *not* playing by the rules. I was absolutely livid!

I'll continue this later, I'm getting angry again just writing about it.

UCC Issues

There are several well-known issues with user-created content, apart from the fact that most of it is garbage (except to its creator and their friends). Fortunately, there are often well-known solutions.

For example, it's trivially easy to use UCC to grief people. It's also trivially easy to snuff this out—ban perpetrators with vigor.

If you let your players create functionality for their objects—that is, write scripts to give them behaviors—then that's basically letting them program. Programs can crash and they can hang. You can trap the former and time out the latter, but it's better if it doesn't happen at all. You can do this by crippling the scripting language: no loops, no recursion; access only to pre-existing classes and methods. I did this in *MUD2* and it worked just fine; sure, it meant there was less the players could do in theory, but in practice there were plenty of workarounds.

Disposal of poor content is a problem, although not as bad as it used to be. Content of any kind accrues swiftly and clogs up databases: you don't want abandoned or rarely-accessed content sitting around wasting space or, more worryingly, slowing down access to more frequently-used content. You can discourage it by using a pay-to-exceed-quota system, but this can be counter-productive as it then discourages creativity among those players who have a gift for design (and yes, these people *do* exist). You can't despawn added content dynamically, because different components may have different time-stamps—you really want to get rid of it all at once. The solution is therefore to swap out untouched content when you do your weekly maintenance run, reloading it dynamically should anyone actually wish to access it.

There are some legal issues to do with UCC, mainly the twin intellectual property horrors of players ripping one another off or "paying tribute to" some real-world IP. Lawyers seem to have this covered, judging by the dearth of lawsuits in the area. Deluded or devious players will eventually claim that *you* ripped off *their* ideas, by the way, but if you document what you do you should be able to defend yourself (unless you *did* actually rip them off, which would rather suggest you're in the wrong business).

What's perhaps more interesting is what you do if your UCC endeavors actually strike gold and you find someone who has created great content that you want to make available to everyone else. Well, you'll have to pay them. "Congratulations, you won the competition" isn't going to fool anyone and will alienate all your other creative players. Be fair and properly remunerate them, then everyone will be happy. Oh, and also be aware that in most countries (the United States being the most notable exception), creators have "moral rights" to their creations, allowing them to do things such as insist on being identified as creators of their own objects. They can also demand you remove their work if it's being used in a way that impugns their reputation. If you're worried, look at joint copyright as a solution.

Le dernier problèmeestla localisation. You knew that, though, right ?

Bad Luck?

One MMO developer I was consulting for had a scheme to track down rogue servers. Very, very infrequently—once every two months, say—the server would send a packet to the developers to check in. If the developer didn't reply, the game obliterated itself. The infrequency of the check-in meant that packet-sniffers were unlikely to spot it during tests, so when it did fire up it wasn't stopped.

So far, so what?

Well, this MMO had a similar scheme for client software. If a client detected that it had been compromised in some way, it didn't self-destruct (as nuking a player's computer would probably fall foul of some obscure EU health and safety law). Instead, the server flagged the player's account as being "unlucky". Thenceforth, the game would become some 20% more difficult for client-hackers, because of all the bad rolls they were getting from the random-number generator.

What do you think?

Sadly, the developer lost their funding when the dot-com bubble burst, so the MMO in question was never made. They were confident that the technique would work, though, because *they already did it in all their single-player games*.

Instantiations, Servers, Shards

All the zones of an MMO collected together are not the limit of geographical abstraction that an MMO can have. They do comprise the full world model, but there can be more than one copy of them. These are known variously as *instantiations* (an old term now rarely used), *incarnations* (ditto), *shards* (from *Ultima Online*, still used by some designers), or *servers* (the predominant term).

Technically, the term "server" is incorrect, as it's hardware-based: an MMO instantiation will usually be running on a cluster of several computers that act as servers for particular zones. There will also be a login server and a bunch of instance and PvP servers, too.

Call them what you will (I'll go with "instantiations," just to be old-fashioned), they are running examples of the virtual world, built using the same world model but with changes resulting from player activity and the behavior of random-number generators. In one instantiation, there may be a dragon rampaging through the city; in another, the players killed the dragon and they're all off fighting a zombie invasion.

Instances are instantiations not of the world model in its entirety but of zones. They're small, pocket universes of content meant for size-limited groups of players. Four of us walk through the door and wind up in the same instance; the next four people walk through the same door in the same instantiation of the world, but wind up in a new instance. Instances use a sudden-reset approach, which allows for them to have more sophisticated content. However, the fact that they are instances means they have no impact on the world except in terms of the gear and experience or reputation points the players take out of them.

It's possible for an MMO to overlay instances, a system known as *phasing*. Here, although players are ostensibly in the same zone, actually they're getting data from different instances of the zone. This means that I might see a mountain but you might see an erupting volcano, because you have followed a quest line in which that volcano erupts but I haven't got that far yet. This kind of thing can be very confusing for players travelling in groups, some of whom are in one phase and some of whom are in another, so it tends to be used only scarcely.

MMOs don't *have* to have multiple instantiations, by the way: they can also be *single-shard*, as with *EVE Online*. Such worlds tend to have load balance issues if players clump up together too much, but could be considered well worth a bit of lag as they allow for a much greater volume of emergent content and player impact. If there aren't dozens of near-identical instantiations of the same world to synchronize, big changes can be made. For example, the developers could allow the players blow up a random star system if they wanted and it wouldn't compromise future patches in the same way that it would on a multi-shard system where the star system would still be present in most instantiations.

Server merges occur when player numbers start to drop, leaving instantiations under-populated. It's generally taken as a sign that the MMO is failing, but given that all MMOs suffer a dip in usage a few months after launch (once people have reached the end-game), this isn't necessarily the case; it could easily be just a readjustment to a stable norm. Server merges are actually just a transfer of players and their stuff from one instantiation's database to that of another instantiation; it doesn't involve actually merging the virtual spaces together, although the way some players talk you might be forgiven for believing it was this cataclysmic.

Instantiation to zone to region to area to room to square to point: this is how space is represented in MMOs.

Yeah, I know, you don't care: you just want to know where to go to kill stuff.

Clone World

One MMO I consulted on, which was developed in the west for the Korean market, included a fully-fledged, make-your-own-face system that they had to remove after adverse reaction from Korean focus groups. The reason given by prospective players was that they didn't like creating characters that turned out not to be as good-looking as characters created by other people with better face-sculpting skills. In other words, they'd rather all look the same but beautiful than different but plain.

You never know when real-world cultural differences are suddenly and unexpectedly going to kick in.

Creature Feep

A common problem in software engineering in general and computer game development in particular is *feature creep*. It can happen at any point during production at which there is the opportunity for someone to be creative and insightful, which for games is to say pretty well anywhere.

Here's how it works:

1. While working on an existing feature, you have a cool new idea.
2. This cool new idea can be incorporated into the existing framework "almost for free".
3. Go back to Step 1, with your cool new idea as the existing feature.

Here's why it's a bad thing:

- It may take very little time to implement your change, but it *still takes time*. This gradually adds up.

- The cool new idea will not appear in the existing documentation, and will therefore be a devil to maintain.

- "Almost for free" doesn't mean "consistent with the vision". The more you add, the more you risk changing the project's soul.

For further discussion, see the definition in *The Jargon File*[18] (which, despite some recent revisionist changes, remains a wonderful document that all programmers should read at some stage in their career).

Never think about what you could *add* to your game to improve it unless you've first thought what you could *remove* from your game to improve it.

Rhetoric: Play as Identity

I don't particularly like this rhetoric of play, for two reasons.

First, to me the name has connotations of individuality, whereas actually it's all about the loss of individuality. It's a vision of play as a mechanism by which people bond and build community—parades, celebrations, mass spectacles, and so on.

Second, it's very close in aspect to Play as Power. The purpose of an expression of power is to assert the superiority of your culture, community, and traditions; the purpose of an expression of identity is to expand and share your culture, community, and traditions. Yet why would you do the latter if not for the reasons of the former?

I suppose that one advantage of Play as Identity is that it can help promote your values even if you lose. The British Empire managed to operate for decades on a principle of "it's not the winning, it's the taking part"—good news for the peoples whose armies they had just crushed, because that at least meant they knew they were appreciated.

Specializing in a small number of games—particularly sports—can make a community stronger. New Zealand, South Africa, and Wales go with *Rugby*, at which they can beat the teams of countries that are much more powerful in absolute terms but where *Rugby* is less popular. India, Australia, Pakistan, and the West Indies are *Cricket* strongholds. In South America, the biggest expressions of national identity lie with *Football* (or, for American readers, *Football*—your game is called *American Football*).

Play as Identity is a way to organize play to a community's ends; it helps establish the hegemony of the community's dominant group. Sadly, while this can be a fruitful way of looking at play for anthropologists and political scientists, it's rather a stretch to say it applies to all games. People who play *Cluedo* are not doing so in order to further their own cultural identity.

In MMOs: guilds.

---

[18]Raphael Finkel, Guy Steele, Eric S. Raymond *et al*: *The Jargon File*. http://www.catb.org/~esr/jargon/html/

Localization

When *MUD* was launched on CompuServe, the name was changed to *British Legends*. A name change was needed anyway, as "MUD" didn't impress CompuServe's marketing department (not that they ever did a great deal of marketing). Why change it to *British Legends*, though? Ah, because that way they didn't have to wait for me to go through all the text changing the spellings to American English.

Localization is the name given to the process of adapting a game for a specific territory that has its own requirements. People have different tastes in music, beauty, decency, and even interface layout, so these need to be taken into account.

Sometimes localization issues have a legal basis (no blood splats in first-person shooters in Germany); sometimes they're cultural (8 is a lucky number in China); sometimes they're practical (speech bubbles in German need to hold 40% more characters than in English and 80% more than in Chinese); sometimes they're insurmountable (don't expect your *Ice Hockey* management sim to sell as well in the United Kingdom as it does in the United States).

Sometimes, localization only needs a change in graphics (change the flag's swastika to SS, change the pile of skulls to be a pile of dirt); other times it needs code changes (which side of the road cars drive on, which direction words read). Sometimes, it needs editing (pad out or pare down the voice actor's script so it hits the beat of the accompanying action); sometimes, it needs replacing entirely (showing a picture of a duck to tell you to duck makes sense in English but not in Spanish).

As for any text used by your game, today that's usually done by translating everything in advance and putting it into language-specific tables. The programmer codes to print message 153; you get to see whatever text your language table has in that slot. Unfortunately, for reasons to do with such concepts as word order and gender, sentences can't be built up dynamically very easily this way.

Few textual worlds were translated into different languages. Interestingly, this made them great tools for … language-learning!

UGC Issues

User-created content isn't alone in having issues: user-generated content has some, too.

The main problem is that if you allow users to create content in the context of your game in such a way that it has an impact on the game (for example they build a castle), that means your servers can get out of line. This shard has a marauding pack of wolves; that shard doesn't because it was wiped out by a group of players.

This divergence means you can't:

- Merge servers
- Phase across servers
- Do WoW: *Cataclysm* style whole-world reboots

It also has advantages:

- UGC is more immersive than UCC, as you don't have to leave context to do it.
- It's also more immersive than standard content-by-respawn MMOs, as players actually have impact.

If you reduce the number of players per server, then these advantages are amplified. Based on how it worked out with textual worlds, something like 250-500 active users per server is probably the sweet spot; beyond that, it's your guild that has impact, not you.

Whenever anyone wants to add UCC to an MMO, it always comes down to UGC. Perhaps that's *why* so many people tend to use the terms interchangeably?

Programming Language Choice

In practice, pretty well all programming languages have the expressive power of a Universal Turing Machine: They can, in theory, be used to write anything that can possibly be programmed. When it comes to selecting a programming language in which to write an MMO, the issues are therefore:

- How easy is it to say in the language what you want to say?

- How efficiently does the language execute what you tell it to execute?

- How many existing resources are available to this language?

Modern programming languages, which for MMOs usually means C++ or some other C derivative, are acceptable for the first point and tremendous at the other points. That first point hides a problem, though.

The easier it is to say something in a language, the less time it takes to write a program in that language and the easier it is to maintain. Those are good things. If the way the language achieves this is by structuring the code well, that means many programmers can work on it at the same time, which is also a good thing. The problem comes when the language encourages you to say particular things in a particular way. That particular way could limit what you're *able* to say.

In George Orwell's book *1984*, people spoke an artificial language called Newspeak. This language was stripped of words that could express ideas of rebellion and freedom, the result being that no one who used the language could even *think* about such concepts, let alone talk about them.

Programming languages can also work this way. For example, the language Pascal was deliberately designed with a rigid data type system (integer, real, Boolean, char) in order to force programmers to take proper account of types. The idea was that programmers who grew up with Pascal wouldn't have bad programming practices in their vocabulary, so therefore couldn't make type errors. This was all very noble when Pascal was used as a teaching language, but got in the way when it was used for serious projects. This was because by then, competent programmers knew exactly what typing was and didn't like being straitjacketed into following an inflexible system that wouldn't let them break its rules even when they knew what they were doing.

Programming languages can also influence programmers in the opposite direction, though, which is more insidious. If a language contains many words and phrases to express particular concepts, this means that those concepts are naturally seen as important (I call this the "fifty words for *snow*" approach). If you use a programming concept regularly, you're going to think of that concept first when it comes to cracking a new problem. This is generally a sensible thing to do, but it falls down when the tried-and-trusted words you're using don't actually reflect what you're trying to say.

For example, C++ and its peers are object-oriented (OO) programming languages. For a system the size of an MMO, this is pretty well essential. However, it's critical that when you're programming in an OO language you get your objects right. As I mentioned earlier, MMOs have "objects" such as weapons and armor in them, so because of the way that C++ is all about objects, a C++ programmer is naturally going to create classes to represent these objects. The language almost leads them by the hand in this direction.

Unfortunately, C++ is a language that has only single inheritance. You can't have objects inherit properties and functionality from multiple parents with interwoven inheritance trees. This makes some otherwise expressible concepts inexpressible without a design change.

The language you use affects not only what you can say, but how you choose to say it.

Dupe Bugs

A *dupe bug* is one in which some object or transferable property in an MMO can be duplicated with next to no effort. They're most often associated with the creation of in-game currency, but anything of value that can be replicated at will with no cost and then sold to an NPC vendor will do.

Dupe bugs happened in text MUDs, but because you don't think that's relevant any more, I'll give an example of how an early one worked in *Ultima Online*.

So, *UO* had such a large map that territory had to be divided into several zones, each of which was handled by one cluster of computers. If you crossed a zone boundary, you would have to wait while the new zone loaded (as indeed is still the case to varying degrees in most MMOs). What players discovered was that if they dropped items on the ground then crossed a zone boundary, they could shut down their client software before the zone was loaded. This would leave their character in a kind of limbo between zones. When they logged back on, *UO* wouldn't be able to find their character so would restore its data from the last backup. The character would have all the stuff they had on them at the time of that backup—much of which they had just dropped. They or an accomplice could pick up the dropped items and vendor them. The exercise could then be repeated indefinitely.

This bug remained in *UO* for months before it was discovered by the developers and fixed. A later dupe bug allowed currency to be duplicated directly and was even worse, leading to massive inflation as word of it got around.

When a dupe bug hits hard, in-game currency can become worthless overnight. Players who wish to trade with one another have to find some alternative they can use instead. In *Meridian 59*, they used dark angel feathers; in *Asheron's Call*, they used keys and shards; in *EverQuest*, they used peridots. Anything portable, stackable, tradable, and desirable will do.

Dupe bugs have affected and continue to affect MMOs. To name but a few, *Star Wars Galaxies*, *RuneScape*, *EverQuest 2*, *EVE Online*, and *The Elder Scrolls Online* have all fallen prey to them. Interestingly, though, although dupe bugs trash the game's economy, players still continue playing and in general still have fun[19]. That said, dupe bugs have serious long-term effects if not removed, so

[19]Zachary Booth Simpson: *The In-Game Economics of Ultima Online*. Game Developers Conference, 2000. http://www.mine-control.com/zack/uoecon/uoecon.html

developers tend to react strongly. They'll even revert to an earlier save of the character database to undo the effects of one, taking the reputational damage that comes with telling players that everything they've done the past week or whatever has been lost.

Note that if in-game currency can be sold for real money (legitimately or not), dupe bugs become a far, far more serious matter. So it is that while you may find MMO developers selling in-game money for real money, they are reluctant to attempt the reverse.

Easy Target

So, in a sword fight, which part of the body is most likely to be struck?

The number of times I see female armor where the shoulders are impregnable and the vital organs exposed, it makes me wonder what artists know that I don't (or vice versa).

Rewarding Risk

Let's say that there is a part of the game world where you get ten times the loot you would get elsewhere, but you have a six times greater chance of being "killed" than you would elsewhere.

Now this looks like a good deal: on the whole, individuals would gain far more than they would lose, because the rewards significantly outweigh the risks.

That's not how most players would see it at all, though. They wouldn't yield an inch on their chances of being "killed". No matter what the reward, they would call this area a death trap. Furthermore, they would insist on equal loot for the safer parts of the game, on the grounds that such loot is clearly available and therefore they must be entitled to it. Once the precedent of "10 times loot" is set, the players will know that the designer has no objections in principle to that kind of drop; they're just holding out by not implementing it as a game-wide concept.

Personally, I think this kind of pandering to players is a bad thing in the long term. Players can't have both excitement and low risk; if they insist on low risk, they'll pay for it in excitement.

While designers (or, more accurately, marketing people) continue to be willing to give/sell the players what the marketers think they want, the games that result are always going to end up boring after a while.

MMO Data Flow

Here's the data flow for a typical MMO:

1. A player issues a command. Maybe they typed something or clicked on something, or one of their macros was triggered.

2. The client cleans up the user command and complains about obvious errors.

3. The client packages the command and sends it over the Internet to the server.

4. The server receives packets asynchronously from multiple players. It puts these in an input queue.

5. The server takes the packets one at a time from the input queue to process.

6. The server performs a sanity check, in case a hacked client sent an impossible command.

7. The server parses the packaged input to derive a command. This is easier for mouse clicks than for the full sentences we had in the text world era.

8. One input can lead to multiple commands (e.g., emptying a bag). All individual commands are queued for execution.

9. The command is executed. Commands are complex database operations, which usually entail a change to the runtime database (although sometimes they just query it). All commands generate a response.

10. The server places the response in the despatch queue for each client that needs to know about it.

11. The output is packaged and sent to the client. This is in the form of instructions for the client to execute, not full-motion video.

12. The client receives the packet from the server. Packets can be either *solicited* (as a result of a command transmitted by the client) or *unsolicited* (as a result of a different client's commands on an in-world event such as the sun rising).

13. The client stores the input from the server in an input queue.

14. The client pops its instructions from the input queue and uses them to update its own world model.

15. The client updates the player's screen in the context of its new world model (if this has any effect).

16. The player decides what to do in the light of this. Back to Step 1.

Design Failure

Suppose I design a game and say, as part of the rules, that some activity X isn't allowed. If it then it turns out that people do X anyway and it adversely affects gameplay, is that a failure in the design?

No, it's not—it may be a failure in some players, but it's *not* a failure in the design.

Suppose I design a second game and say, as part of the rules, that activity X is, this time, allowed. If people thereupon do X and it adversely affects gameplay, okay, well that would indeed be a failure in the design.

People breaking the rules and thereby spoiling the game is not a design failure; a design failure is when people follow the rules and do something that spoils the game.

A Player's Understanding

Modern MMOs often feature a weekly or monthly Dev Diary, in which developers talk about various aspects of the MMO they're making. Generally, these are pleasantly revealing. Before launch, they help sustain the buzz around the game; after launch, they're a way of keeping players interested and informed. They're a Good Thing.

There's a lot they don't cover, though. For example, if a designer says they're considering putting X into the MMO, then for some players this will be read as a guarantee that they *will* put X into the MMO, and said players will react accordingly (depending on whether they like the idea or not). Developers are therefore cagey about stating what *may* be in the game, only saying anything concrete if they're sure they *will* be putting it in the game.

As for explaining anything deep behind the philosophy of the game, well woe betide any designer who does that! The problem is, designers have both a designer's and a player's understanding of what an MMO is about, but players only have a player's understanding. In a player's understanding of what MMOs are about, the up-front elements of a design as it's directly experienced are all that's important about it. Abstract notions of the cleanliness or sweetness of a design are irrelevant. As an analogy, it's like saying "I like atoms to come in Hydrogen and Oxygen, and all this worrying about whether you give me water or Hydrogen peroxide to drink is just mushy thinking".

Designers look at the structure and the range of experience and design for different types of players, not just one. They also like their designs not to be fatal.

Rhetoric: Play as the Imaginary

This is generally lighter than the other rhetorics of play. It sees play as a means to enable the transformation of ideas and is associated with creativity, romanticism, and (this is the big one for MMOs) mythology. Play is not an intellectual contest or a competition or a parade so much as a way to *think* about things (in this sense, it's conflated with art). It's the sort of play you might be indulging in if you were "playing with words"; it's a kind of dabbling that may or may not free an idea.

Play as the Imaginary tends to be favored by creative people. The word "play" is basically metaphorical: it's a mechanism for allowing the subconscious to articulate itself—to create patterns that the conscious mind can recognize and take further. Sometimes the play is free, sometimes it's directed; sometimes it's top-down, sometimes it's bottom-up; sometimes it's play *within* play, sometimes it's playing *with* play. It's whatever and wherever fancy dictates.

Although the release of the imagination is a powerful concept, Play as the Imaginary has problems with its own meaning. It has so many relationships to metaphor and deconstruction that it's hard to tell when play itself starts and ends. It's a very useful rhetoric for people who want to explore ideas, but it's not much use to explain anything beyond that.

Design Decision

The choice of which programming language to use is a *design* decision.

An interesting question here is the extent to which this design decision (which is made by the lead programmer) should impact an MMO's design. A programmer shouldn't be able to say, "you can't have full-blown multiple inheritance because C++ doesn't have full-blown multiple inheritance," but should be able to say, "you can't have a mind-reading device because the program has no access to people's minds" or "you can have the degree of AI you want, but it will cost this much and run this slowly".

Socialist Quiz Continued

The quiz continued. Now you might have supposed that having been exposed as a cheat, Dr. Dorney would have stopped doing what he was doing—but not a bit of it! In order to demonstrate that there was nothing untoward in his actions, he continued with them. At one point, he ignored a question, asked me the next one, and I told him he should skip that one too because I knew the answer. It was a total farce, and yet he insisted he was doing nothing wrong. He was just "leveling the playing field".

What? It was a *quiz*. It wasn't a quiz with 11-year-olds versus 18-year-olds, we were peers—we should have been asked the questions as they came. If he felt some of us needed handicapping, he could have given the weaker team a head start in points. Ah, but then we'd have *known* what he was doing. He was trying to conceal it, at least until I challenged him. Then, he tried to brazen it out. "So if we answer a series of questions wrong, will you start asking us easy ones so we can catch up?" I asked. No, he wouldn't: we should have got those questions right.

What? *What?*

I have to say, at this point I was the angriest I have ever been in my entire life.

He skipped another question. Before he could ask the one after it, I insisted he went with the one he skipped. He refused. I said I wanted that one, not the new one. He said he wouldn't ask it, because I knew the answer. I said there was no point in my being there if he knew how I'd answer every time—he could just give me the marks or not, without my having to say anything. If he didn't ask the question he'd skipped, I was quitting.

He asked the question, but said I wasn't allowed to answer it, only my partner. She was bright, too (hi Mel!) and got it right.

Dr. Dorney finished the round and brought the competition to a premature end. I think we came second to the team on our left, with the other two in joint third.

The discussion among sixth-formers that followed grew close to rebellion. Everyone in the audience had been entirely on our side and were both stunned and appalled by what Dr. Dorney had been doing; he was universally condemned as a cheat, and opinion of him dropped from very positive to alarmingly negative. He may have been trying to save the poor, down-trodden St. Mary's from an embarrassing defeat, but they were expecting to be thrashed anyway against six star pupils from the other houses. They were more embarrassed by his patronizing attitude than they would have been by losing, and opined that they would have been just as riled as I was had he obliged them to play football with 20kg of weights on their back to make it "fairer" to the rest of us who weren't as good as they.

I was still red-faced with rage 10 minutes later when lessons started. Guess what I had? That's right—mathematics. Mathematics, taught by Dr. Dorney.

There, he patiently explained his philosophy and told me I was a sore loser.

There, I tore into him with an unrestrained, no-holds-barred demolition of his philosophy *as applied to games* that shocked him to the core. I can still see his face now.

The thing was, at the center of his argument was a contradiction. On the one hand, he felt he was allowed to bend the rules because it was "only a game"; yet on the other, he felt the need to bend the rules because it *wasn't* "only a game". If it really were "only a game," there would have been no problem with St. Mary's expected dismal performance. Because he felt the need to intervene, that meant he *did* think there was a problem, so dismissing it as "only a game" was untenable. I was hitting him with logic, which is the deadliest weapon of all against a mathematician. He was visibly shaken not by my explosion of emotion, not by the ferocity of its delivery, but by its content. He suddenly realized he *had* been in the wrong.

That's what happens when you apply general social and economic theories to games. Games are *different*.

The other (three) pupils arrived, the math lesson continued as normal, and we never spoke of it again.

Rhetoric: Play as the Self

This is the youngest of the seven rhetorics of play, and the most powerful. It derives from the modern notion of individualism and asserts that play has its basis in the psychology of the player. All other forms of play are emergent consequences of this: you're playing only because—for whatever reasons—*you want to play*.

As for what those reasons are, well they could be anything: compulsion, compensation, wish-fulfillment, mastery of anxiety, tension release, reality-testing, stimulus seeking, neurological arousal, and so on. You are playing in the hope (which may be subconscious) of gaining some benefit. The meaning of play in this rhetoric is found in the quality of the player's experience: the more fun it is, the better it is.

Yes, this is indeed the rhetoric of play that I personally favor.

Play as the Self is most closely related to Play as the Imaginary. Both regard play as a form of freedom, and both are individualistic rather than communal. The difference is that in Play as the Imaginary, people play to *create* and the *creating* is fun; in Play as the Self, people play to *be* and the *being* is fun. In other words, in the former you play for a purpose, and in the latter your purpose is play.

So powerful is this rhetoric that advocates of other rhetorics of play will, when asked to explain why any individual player plays, usually give an explanation that's couched in terms of Play as the Self.

The rhetoric has a flaw, though. It's hard to say who this "self" is that's playing. All those reasons I gave earlier involve some transformative change to the individual, but if "you" change then who is this "you" who's playing? "You" are a different person at the start of play than at the end! Identity is seen by many philosophers as an ever-fluid construction; describing play in terms of changes to the self is like trying to nail down water.

Personally, I don't worry about it. Whoever you are at that moment, *that's* the you who is changing.

Hey, it works for differential calculus.

Retreads

One of the questions MMO designers ask themselves is why would anyone play their new game instead of, say *World of Warcraft*?

The problem is that if you can attract people away from the current big shiny by being the next big shiny, that means you end up with a user base of people who are attracted to big shinies. When the next-but-one big shiny comes along, they'll show you exactly the same amount of loyalty that they showed the current big shiny, and leave.

To get non-transient players, you have to target either MMO newbies (of which there will be fewer in coming years, thanks to all the kiddie worlds out there) or MMO oldbies who have tired of old-style gameplay.

The only major ways left to acquire substantial numbers of MMO newbies are:

- Locating a vast untapped source (India?)
- Using a wildly popular IP (are there any left?)
- Diving in big time on an emerging platform (3D goggles?)
- Offering something that changes the paradigm (because if the newbies liked what was already on offer, they'd be playing it)

For oldbies, you have to give them the "familiar but the different": they don't want to play what they already play, but they don't want what they play instead to be *wildly* dissimilar. One big idea might just be enough to get them.

There is sometimes a third option: pick up stalled newbies who were attracted to one MMO but after playing it for a while grew disillusioned and left. They didn't leave for a new MMO, they just left, waiting for something to appear that would give them the same kind of experience but without whatever it was that put them off. *WoW* garnered a lot of ex-*EQ* players this way.

All these solutions rely on creating something genuinely new, though, rather than merely retreading what has gone before.

Yes, like *that's* ever going to happen.

Consider This

Most modern MMOs have a *con system*. Although this sounds as if it means the mechanism by which they execute confidence tricks on people, actually it means those details about a mob freely given to players so they can decide whether or not to attack it. "Con" is short for "consider".

The reason we need a con system in a modern MMO is fundamentally because all the mobs look the same. If you come across a wolf, it could be level 1, it could be level 40, it could be level 80, or it could be level 100. The higher-level ones look bigger and meaner and have red eyes and spikes or whatever, but after a few rampings up like this it's hard to tell how killable the wolf you're looking at actually is for someone of your level. This is where a con system comes in. The mob's name or health bar will be color-coded to say how powerful the mob is relative to you (as an individual), which usually comes with implications regarding what kind of reward you'll get for killing it. There may also be an indication as to whether the mob will attack or leave you alone if you stray too close.

Con systems actually *predate* graphical MMOs, though. So why did we have them back in the old days when we were able to have as many varied and different monsters as we wanted because we only had to type a line of text to create their look? Well, the system was a little more asymmetric than what we see today.

Take *MUD2*, as I happen to know that one best. From the player's point of view, all you know is what the mob's name is, how healthy it looks (from "full of life" to "close to death"—yeah, it's different for undead), and what it's carrying (because if it's carrying a weapon, it will usually wield it). To tell if one mob is tougher than another, you use your common sense: an eagle is more dangerous than a raven, a vampire is more dangerous than a zombie, a giant is more dangerous than a goblin. The old man probably won't attack you, but if you attack him then expect a hard time of it—you don't get to wander around a land infested with monsters and live to be an old man unless you can defend yourself.

As for whether mobs will attack other mobs, well because they can't make sense of textual descriptions they use their *own* con system. When a mob encounters another creature (mob or player—in *MUD2*, mobs couldn't tell the difference), they first consider whether their potential target is something they can actually attack at all; water snakes can't attack people in boats, for example. If they can attack, they decide whether the creature is something they like or not; birds don't like rodents. If they don't like their possible target, or if they have a vendetta against it (perhaps because it attacked them earlier), then they'll decide if they think they'll win or not; a firefly isn't going to stand much of a chance against a dragon. If they think they have a chance, they'll attack.

It's the last step of the con system where things get interesting. To figure out whether it can win the fight or not, the mob calculates how many rounds it will take to kill its opponent and *vice versa*. If it will finish first then it goes for it. It does this by looking at the defender's health (modified for regeneration, etc.) and dividing it by the mean damage per round (a round being two seconds long in *MUD2*) that its attacker will do against it (modified for weapons, etc.).

The result is pretty accurate—or at least it would be if mobs used it properly. Some do, but most have an inaccurate sense of their own abilities and will multiply the true figure by another number. Mobs that are over-optimistic, such as the goat, will attack stupidly often; mobs that are under-optimistic, such as the ox, will rarely attack at all. This rating, which *MUD2* calls *pacificity*, is used for attacks; another rating, *cowardice*, is used for fleeing. This means that you can get mobs that attack often in acts of bravado but then flee as soon as the going gets tough (such as the mad March hare), or that rarely attack but when they do they're relentless (Santa, a Christmas mob, is like this).

The result of this con system is that *MUD2*'s mobs each have their own personalities. Some you get to like, especially if they rescue you when you're in trouble; some you get to respect; some you get to despise, or to fear, or to hunt. The reason for this is because the *mobs* have their own con system, not because the *players* do. For players, the con system can be summarized as: "if it looks dangerous, well, then it probably is".

Ah, history.

I in 10

It's my experience that only maybe 1 in 10 students on undergraduate computer games courses in the UK have an actual future working on/in/with computer games. The rest can forget it. Some universities have a higher proportion, and some have a lower proportion, but 1 in 10 is fairly representative.

But hey, if you're a prospective computer games undergraduate, you're not fazed by this at all: you think *you're* that 1 person in 10 who cuts it.

You could well be right, too! After all, you were enthusiastic enough to read (and if I'm lucky, buy) this book. However, bear in mind that by "have a future" I mean "*could* work in the game industry"; I don't mean "*will* work in the game industry," because there are fewer jobs than there are good students.

All I'm saying is: have a back-up plan.

Socialist Quiz—Coda

It isn't because of the Socialist Quiz incident that I'm against people doing things in games that they know are against the rules but that they don't think matter. However, it does illustrate the anger I feel at them for doing it.

When you're playing one, *no* game is "only a game".

I did apologize to Dr. Dorney for any misunderstanding that may have arisen as to his motives for cheating (i.e., helping his own house), but I didn't apologize for calling him a cheat—nor did he ask me to.

To Be an Elf

There were four abortive attempts to make an MMO based on *The Lord of the Rings* before Turbine were able to succeed. I did some design work on the second one.

One of the problems the first attempt encountered was that everyone wanted to be an elf. Whenever they asked Tolkien groups what character race they wanted to play, the vast majority said they wanted to be elves. It's hard to create a *Lord of the Rings* MMO if everyone wants to be an elf, yet that's what the data said.

We now know that no, everyone did not want to be an elf. People who were such fans of Tolkien that they were active in online Tolkien communities wanted to be elves, but as for people who had merely read the book (or these days, seen the movies), well, some of them quite liked the idea of being dwarves or humans or hobbits, actually.

The designers of *Star Wars: Galaxies* identified a similar problem: everyone wanted to be a Jedi. The rich, crafting-oriented systems the designers envisaged were intended to attract a particular kind of gamer, though, rather than *Star Wars* fans. The fiction of the *Star Wars* universe couldn't handle many Jedi, so the solution adopted was to aim for people who didn't want to be a Jedi anyway. The designers made no one be a Jedi to start with; you could get to be one only if you became a master in a bunch of non-Jedi professions, so it was an elder-game only thing.

Unfortunately, this time the data told the truth and everyone *did* want to be a Jedi. This is one reason why in *Star Wars: the Old Republic*, they set the game in a period of *Star Wars* history when everyone *could* legitimately be a Jedi (or a Sith, which by then had been popularized by a new set of movies).

Market research is always advisable when you're designing a product you hope to sell, but you need to make sure that you identify the right market to research.

Mind and Senses

Text worlds and graphical worlds are both fundamentally worlds. They both try to reproduce themselves in the imaginations of the players, but they use different methods: text talks to the mind through the language of the mind (i.e., words); graphics talk to the mind through the language of the senses (i.e., pictures).

Reading allows the author to connect with the *mind* of the reader, thereby plugging in directly to the imagination; images allow the author to connect with the *senses* of the reader, which must then be interpreted before they can reach the imagination. The imagination is where all the action is. Because the human mind is wired up to process visual patterns very easily, it can be less work to understand a scene from a picture than from a description; however, because images must nevertheless be interpreted, they can't touch the mind as strongly as words can.

If you want a simple world lacking in emotional content for people who don't want their imaginations exercised (that is, a world for the majority of the population), then the superior interface is graphical. If you want a simple or complex world with emotional depth or shallowness for people who do want their imagination fired, then the superior interface is textual.

It's just an interface issue, though. Text or graphics doesn't make the worlds different, any more than being real-world deaf makes the real world different; it only affects your *experience* of the world, not the world itself.

Art and Computer Games

One of the frustrations I have regarding "art and computer games" is that whereas artists are all-too-ready to consider art created *within* computer games as art (e.g., Machinima), they are often reluctant to call computer game design itself art. It doesn't help that many people who work in the game industry themselves don't regard it as art.

How could it *not* be art?!

Virtual Architecture

Should MMOs employ real-life architects to design their biggest, most important buildings?

Architects have a theoretical basis to their work, but this has a strong grounding in physical reality. If the physical rules are different, which they are in MMOs, then were architects to create virtual structures in an MMO their governing theories would need to be picked apart to ensure that the rationale behind them is still appropriate.

For example, architects have theories concerning natural light, but in a world where one light is no more natural than another, is this an issue? Is the fact that natural light means a view of the outside what's *really* important? If so, they can adopt that part from their theories of light, but leave behind the component about feeling more comfortable in natural light. They could use some of the relationship of light and space, but as players can (and do) switch off shadows they don't need to use it all.

So there are (or at least there should be) architectural theories that apply to virtual spaces. A house would still have walls, not because it needs load-bearing structures to keep the roof on, but because it delineates private space from public space. Some new theories will doubtless apply only to virtual spaces. For example, houses shouldn't have to adopt features of real-life houses that are redundant in a virtual world—no rain, no need for a sloping roof. However, looking like real houses adds to the persuasiveness of an environment, so it's generally a good thing to have some mimicry. The degree to which these structures should match, though, is not yet formally considered.

Given the lack of interaction between architects and game designers in the past (we still see medieval-style castles in worlds where there are multiple creatures that can fly or burrow, which in voxel-based worlds includes player-characters), it's not surprising that designers are having to learn the principles of architecture anew, nor that architects will criticize them for their naïveté (or would, if they ever to get around to paying MMOs any attention).

Latency and Lag

It takes time to transmit data. The speed of light through glass is such that if you had a direct fiber-optic cable from Sydney to San Diego, it would take 0.06 seconds for the signal to get from one end to the other.

Of course, you *don't* have a direct connection, so the distance is actually longer. Each router adds several hundredths of a second more, and security or snooping software can add further delays. If you still have an analogue modem, add another third of a second.

The minimum time it takes for data to get from your computer to a host computer is called *latency*. It's a general term for relatively uniform delays in data transmission. As an illustration, consider someone in the Houses of Parliament listening to the chimes of Big Ben both directly and over an FM radio. They would hear the radio version slightly ahead of the direct version because it's quicker to send a microphone pick-up to a transmitter, then to a satellite, then to a receiver, then to a radio mast, then to a radio set than it is for sound to travel a hundred meters through air. The two methods have different latencies.

Lag (or *jitter*) is when data is delayed above and beyond latency. There are three main ways it can happen:

- *Server lag* is caused by the time it takes to execute a command.

- *Traffic lag* is caused by more data being sent along a connection than the connection can carry.

- *Client lag* is caused by the time it takes a client to execute a command.

Suppose in *Second Life* you went to a party and the place was crowded with people all showing off their wonderful animations and full-flowing hair. The server has so much work to do that if you issue a command, it will have to wait in line to be processed—server lag.

Suppose you were playing *World of Warcraft* over your super-fast cable line, when one of your neighbors starts to download vast quantities of pornography. Data from your *WoW* server would take longer to reach you because of the bandwidth being used by your over-excited neighbor—traffic lag.

Suppose you entered an instance in *WildStar*. Most of the data that's required to draw what's inside it is sitting on your hard drive, but it has to be loaded into the client before it can be displayed. This takes time, because although normally such data can be loaded as a background task while you're playing, this time it has to be done all at once—client lag.

Okay, so in MMOs most of the lag you experience will be server lag arising when you get switched around between the computers of the server cluster. If there's a lot of UCC then it will mainly be traffic lag: when players create their own content, it can't be pre-cached on your hard drive and therefore must be downloaded when it's encountered anew (which explains the alarming amount of time it takes for a scene to resolve in *SL*). Client lag, fortunately, isn't all that much of an issue most of the time except when entering a new and fussy instance.

Informally, for a data packet's return trip, latency+lag=ping.

Latency is containable as a problem in client/server architectures because it's predictable. If you design your virtual world figuring of a maximum latency of half a second, the players probably won't notice if they have a slow connection. Also, if one person is having trouble then that doesn't slow everyone else down (which it would in a peer-to-peer architecture).

Lag is the main issue, as it's unpredictable—traffic lag in particular can last for seconds. Predictive algorithms are used to remove the *perception* of lag (e.g., keep someone moving in a straight line), but sometimes they can be wrong. When they are, corrections will either be made instantly (e.g., teleporting the image of the character to where it should be—*warping*) or gradually (e.g., moving it to where it should be—*fading*). This leads to the worrisome fact that players can't always trust what they see on the screen to be a true reflection of the virtual world.

If you're grumpy because your play experience is being interrupted by minor jerkiness, or how everyone else seems to get their fireballs off ahead of yours, just be thankful you didn't play in the 1980s and that I no longer have to explain the concept of *line noise* to you.

Rhetoric: Play as the Frivolous

Work consists of whatever a body is obliged to do. Play consists of whatever a body is not obliged to do.

—Mark Twain

This rhetoric of play is ancient indeed, but how it was viewed in the past is in stark contrast with how it is viewed now.

Play as the Frivolous sees play as nonsense and inversion. It's done entirely for amusement, although further meaning can occasionally be derived from it (court jesters jested, but from their jests could be read truths and ideas). At its core, though, this rhetoric says that play is worthwhile for its own sake and needs no justification beyond that. In times when the opportunities for entertainment were rather more limited than they are today, this kind of play was to be cherished.

Unfortunately, the arrival of the Protestant work ethic changed things. Play for its own sake was decried as a waste of time. If you play, it must be for some productive reason, be that learning, prestige, socialization, or any of the others used by earlier rhetorics. Play is separate from work and inferior to it. This is why, if you're a games researcher, you can get grants for applying games to teaching or AI or even accountancy, but you can't get them for studying games as games. Games are understood to have no *intrinsic* value whatsoever; they're mere indulgence.

I loathe and despise this interpretation. It's a false dichotomy: if you enjoy your work, is it play? If you're paid to play, is it work? If you're neither working nor playing (nor asleep), *then* what are you doing?

I like the way that Play as the Frivolous can be used to characterize all the other rhetorics. Look objectively at what people are doing in the Olympic 1,500m, and basically it's ridiculous—they're trying to cover an arbitrary distance as quickly as they can when they could do it on a quad bike in half the time. When it comes down to it, *all* play is frivolous to some degree, because it all relies on the consensual adherence to constraints (rules) that are ultimately whimsy. Okay, so regarding play as frivolous isn't always helpful, but regarding its frivolity as negative *is* always *unhelpful*—except when it's downright damaging.

Play is freedom. Freedom is *good*.

On Fun

Immersion

What is immersion?

Simply put, immersion is the feeling that *you* are *in* a virtual world.

Don't Mind if I Do

In some religions of the Indian subcontinent, most notably Hinduism and Sikhism, an *avatar* is an Earthly incarnation of a deity or other supreme being.

Okay, so it's not hard to notice that the idea of a supreme being deliberately descending into a created reality bears some similarity with the way that players in the real world descend into an MMO as a character in that world. It isn't surprising, then, that the word "avatar" has been associated with MMOs several times independently. For example, Randy Farmer and Chip Morningstar used it in their early graphical world, *Habitat*; Richard Garriott used it in *Ultima IV*, a non-MMO ancestor of *Ultima Online*; Neal Stephenson used it in his influential cyberpunk novel *Snow Crash*; and *Avatar* was the actual title of the 1979 world written by Bruce Maggs, Andrew Shapira and David Sides. "Avatar" was also used as a term in face-to-face role-playing games and as a name for the root user on some Unix systems.

The way the term got into today's MMO vocabulary is somewhat debatable. Textual worlds had always referred to the characters played by players as, well, "characters." When graphical worlds came along, a need arose to have a way to refer to the graphical appearance of a character, rather than to the character itself. The word "avatar" came into use, although it's not clear from where. It could have been imported from Sanskrit yet again, or from any of the sources mentioned above. An extensive 2001 discussion[1] on the subject among MMO designers and developers was unable to reach a conclusion, the result being that *Snow Crash* is usually credited because that's what the researchers for the *Oxford English Dictionary* supposed.

This use of "avatar" in a technical sense to mean a graphical representation of a character persisted among designers, but new players and then the media came to believe it meant the character itself rather than how it looked on the screen. *Second Life* popularized this new definition, with the result that it became the dominant one. People would refer to their character as their avatar.

---

[1]Raph Koster: *First Use of "Avatar"?* MUD-DEV. 11 Dec 2001. http://www.disinterest. org/resource/MUD-Dev/2001q4/021577.html

Today, the preference for "avatar" over "character" in MMOs is fading. Players seem to have expanded the meaning of "character" to include what it looks like on screen, and "avatar" always sounded suspiciously pretentious. "Avatar" is still a staple of social worlds and some forum software (where it retains its "pictorial representation" meaning), but MMOs have moved on.

As for why there was a pushback in MMOs that favored "character" over "avatar"—well, it may be something to do with the original meaning of the word. An avatar is an *incarnation* of a deity, but it *isn't* the deity. When players play MMOs they don't want to be *incarnated* in the virtual world, they want to *be* in the virtual world. This is a theme I'll come back to again and again in this section: why people play.

Avatar? Don't mind if I do.

Newbie

Although *n00b* is a pejorative term, *newbie* isn't. It simply means someone who is new to an MMO (or, nowadays, to anything else). *Absolute newbies* are new to all MMOs; *relative newbies* are new to this MMO but not to MMOs in general.

The term was invented in *MUD1*, although I later discovered that it had also been invented in British public schools many years earlier (where it was a diminutive of "new boy"). The reason it's in use across the Internet at large is because *MUD1* used it, and it spread from there.

No, I don't expect Wikipedia to reflect this state of affairs.

"Public schools" in Britain are "private schools" in the USA, a rare transatlantic example of the exact opposite words being used to describe the exact same concept. Either way, they're only a good thing for those able to attend them.

Hacker Culture

Back in the early days of computing, a hacker culture developed in computer labs across the globe (described in Steven Levy's book, *Hackers*[2]). This was before the word "hacker" was stolen by the media to mean "a nerd who does bad things to computers"; original hackers were people who played with computers just for the sheer *joy* of it.

I was such a hacker.

Note: you only got to *be* a hacker if another hacker called you a hacker—you couldn't declare *yourself* to be one. It's a bit like the word "cool" at present: anyone who says they're cool is, by definition, uncool. *The New Hacker's Dictionary*[3] describes *MUD* (a program I co-wrote) as a hack, which is why I don't feel bad about saying I was a hacker (but I would have felt bad without giving an explanation).

Levy identified the *hacker ethic* as follows:

- Access to computers should be unlimited and total.
- Always yield to the hands-on imperative,
- All information should be free.
- Mistrust authority, promote decentralization.
- Hackers should be judged by their hacking.
- You can create art and beauty on a computer.
- Computers can change your life for the better.

So where did the hacker ethic come from?

Well, the hackers brought it with them. When I arrived at Essex University in 1978, there was an existing hacker culture already in place; I didn't *adopt* it, though—I already had it. The hacker ethic was just plain obvious—it was *my* ethic as far as I was concerned, and everyone else just happened to share it. The same was true of all the other hackers there.

Back then, programming was not as it is today. There were few tools, few libraries, few resources, few teams—we wrote compilers from scratch as our final-year projects. You couldn't succeed as a programmer unless you *loved* programming—unless you regarded it as *fun*. Only people with an innate hacker's ethic were in the position to *find* it fun.

---

[2]Steven Levy: *Hackers: Heroes of the Computer Revolution*. Anchor Press, 1984.
[3]Eric Raymond (ed.): *The New Hacker's Dictionary*. MIT Press, Cambridge MA, 1991. http://catb.org/~esr/jargon/

In other words, in the 1970s programming *selected* for hackers.

That was then. Now is not then.

In *Dungeons & Dragons* alignment terms, hackers were chaotic good: they made their own rules, because they knew best! They acted for the benefit of humanity.

Programmers of the next generation were lawful good: they treated programming as a puzzle-solving exercise, but were still idealistic.

These days, programmers have to be lawful neutral to get a job. They do what the suits say, whatever they say. It's not a world for hackers.

So where have all the hackers gone?

Pseudonymity

When people who don't play MMOs think about them, one of the first things they hit upon is the notion of anonymity. You don't know who the other players are—they're anonymous!

Actually, they're not anonymous, but *pseudonymous*: you don't need to know who is behind a representation, just that it's the *same* person who was behind it last time you saw it. With anonymity, there's no guarantee of any persistent bond between a representation and the person behind it. For MMOs, there is this guarantee.

Whether the representation itself is an avatar, a handle, a signature tune, or a particular shade of green doesn't particularly matter. So long as I can easily tell it from someone else's representation, and no-one else I'm likely to come into contact with has the same one, it's fine.

With anonymity, you can have no reputation. With pseudonymity, you can.

What is Fun?

"Fun" is a wide-ranging term. Here are some things that are fun:

- Making toddlers fall over.
- Hiding your mother's purse.
- Riding a rollercoaster.

Yes, there are plenty more...

These kinds of fun do apply to some games; in such cases, the game exists merely as a structure for having fun doing something else.

What kind of fun do you get from the act of purely *playing* a game, though? I mean games in general here, not some particular draw-moustaches-on-monkeys game for which the visceral attraction of seeing comical simians is the whole point. What is it about playing games *itself* that's fun?

What kind of fun does *gameplay* deliver?

Portable Characters

One of the regularly proposed ideas that designers and developers of MMOs hear is that of portable characters.

The argument goes that it's a real pain to work my way up to the top in one MMO and then have to do it again if I want to play a different one. Why can't I just take everything with me from the first MMO to the second?

Hmm, let's see.

So if I play in world *X* and become a huge success, I can go to world *Y* and take with me all the trappings of this success, neatly translated so all my world *X* objects become their world *Y* equivalents?

Instantiate world *X* as *World of Warcraft* and world *Y* as *Reality* and you have your answer as to why this is a poor idea.

Game for a Survey

Ask drivers what they want most in a used vehicle, and the top answers will concern upholstery, sound system, air conditioning, satellite navigation, four-wheel drive, and the like. Some people *may* mention engine size, but their reasons for doing so will vary (van drivers for power, teenagers for speed, travelling sales staff for fuel efficiency).

Few people are going to say brakes, though, even though brakes are really, really important for vehicles—second-hand or not.

So it is with games. People will play different games for the same reasons and the same games for different reasons. They'll say they want superficial features they don't, and then moan when you deliver them—not even considering critical features such as gameplay. The classic example is that players will forcefully state that they want new, original games—only to spend half their money on games with numbers at the end of their titles instead.

Be cautious and skeptical when presented with the results of any survey about games. Unless the designer of the survey knows a lot about surveys and a lot about games, you need to be very wary regarding its conclusions.

As for media reporting of survey results, raise that wariness to the power of 2.

Games as Story

Games—MMOs included—can *have* story, but are games *themselves* story?

This is an important question. Story, in its multiple forms, has been studied for hundreds of years; techniques have been developed for understanding and improving stories. If games are just another form of story, that means we can draw on this existing body of knowledge to improve games. If they're not, we can't.

What's *your* opinion?

Mysterious but Unmistakably Powerful

In an MMO, you get to be someone you're not. So why do so many people choose to be the same someone else as someone else?

I can perhaps best explain what I mean by referring to the process used in many textual worlds. There, not bound by the limitations of the character creation system's graphics, people could give themselves any description they wanted. There were no limits—they could literally describe their character in exactly the way they wanted it to be seen.

There was indeed a wide variety of extremely imaginative individual descriptions. However, some people seemed to have rather similar imaginations—so much so that their characters were almost clones of one another.

Two of these were particularly prevalent across a wide range of textual worlds:

- Mysterious but unmistakably powerful men.
- Green-eyed women with red hair that tumbles down to their waist who move with the grace of a dancer.

This wasn't just in game worlds—it was in social worlds. Indeed, the phenomenon was first identified by *LambdaMOO* author Pavel Curtis[4].

Why would so many people share the same aspirational identities that they became clichéd? And why those particular clichés?

Look around at your fellow avatars. Are they all wildly different, or are there certain stereotypes for which you just *know* what kind of person is behind them?

Are *you* such a stereotype?

What isn't Fun

Fun in a game is dependent on the mechanics. It can fail in two distinct ways.

Too *few* constraints can make a game *no fun*.

Too *many* constraints can make a game *unfun*.

---

[4]Pavel Curtis: *Mudding: Social Phenomena in Text-Based Virtual Realities*. Proceedings of *Conference on Directions and Implications of Advanced Computing*, Berkeley, 1992. http://w2.eff.org/Net_culture/MOO_MUD_IRC/curtis_mudding.article

Training Skills

In real life, professional soccer players spend all week training so they can spend 90 minutes playing at the weekend.

Real-world fire crews spend most of their time training rather than fighting fires. Real-world military units spend most of their time training rather than in combat. Real-world astronauts spend most of their time training rather than being in space.

Virtual-world characters spend most of their time applying the skills that were trained in the moment it took to click a button.

You really need to work on the fiction explaining that, people.

Recipient

I'm allowed to use this logo:

Did I mention I'm an award-winning author?

Okay, so I didn't win the award for *being* an author, but that's just splitting hairs.

Book Review: *A Theory of Fun for Game Design*

Anyone wanting to understand why people play games should get hold of Raph Koster's book, *A Theory of Fun for Game Design*[5]. It only takes about three hours to read cover-to-cover, helped mainly by the fact that almost every right-hand page is an illustration rather than text. You are going to prefer either the text side or the illustrations side over the other—it's pretty well guaranteed. What's more, in reading the book you'll get an inkling of why; it operates at many more levels than its cheerful veneer would suggest.

This is an extraordinarily accessible book from one of the few game designers who not only thinks deeply about the design process but is able to articulate it in a form that both enlightens and humbles the reader. The basic premise is that games are important. They're important because the brain is a highly efficient machine for recognizing patterns, delivering pleasure when you learn new patterns. Games provide a context for recognizing patterns with no external pressure to do so; this is what people call "fun."

The argument develops that games are also an art form. If people are learning things from playing games, then those who create games in some way determine what will be learned. However, although many game designers do have an implicit understanding of what they're designing, few (if any) have an explicit enough understanding to reason about the design process itself. To be able to discuss what is in effect an internalized process, they need a theory of game design; that is what Raph's book aims to deliver.

It actually does reasonably well in this regard, and I'll be reiterating many of its points here myself. The test of a theory is its ability to be used predictively, and although *A Theory of Fun* does not come up with a bounded set of rules that can be applied to determine whether any given game will be fun, it does have a non-exhaustive set that can be applied to determine if a game *isn't* fun. Fail even one of these rules, and your game is looking bad.

The scholarship behind the formulation of these rules, by the way, is considerable; it's one of the glories of *A Theory of Fun* that its results seem to be effortlessly derived. I put this down to its being a book by a game-designer; the crafting of its structure is just so elegant. All is there that needs to be there, yet with imaginative doors that open wider when you push them with thought. Whatever your game-design experience, it will appear just right for you; that's the skill of a first-class game designer at work. Knowing this, at times it's breath-taking.

---

[5]Raph Koster: *A Theory of Fun for Game Design*. 2nd edition, O'Reilly: Sebastopol, California. 2013.

Of course, if fun *is* learning, this may explain why people *play* games—but that alone doesn't explain why people *choose* to play games rather than learn some other way. Is it only some people who like to learn from games? Or are games only good for learning certain things?

I guess I should fess up that, despite all this praise I'm lavishing on *A Theory of Fun for Game Design*, I don't actually buy the Play as Progress rhetoric it espouses. Fun *is* often learning, but it can be other things, too; what's more, it can be these in games. Contact sports, for example, are mainly fun because they allow for a controlled outlet of physical exuberance, not because the players enjoy learning through play. Trivia games are about what *has been* learned, not about learning; the fun comes from feeling superior from knowing more than your fellow players. There are also ways to look at fun in games as a composite of the various different emotional responses that they elicit in players (e.g., Nicole Lazzaro's "four keys to fun" approach[6]).

All this is by the bye. If you put what Raph recommends in this book into practice, you *will* have a fun game. That doesn't mean it's easy, but it does mean it's easier than if you don't take what Raph says on board.

Overall, *A Theory of Fun for Game Design* is a fun book, with a fun message. If you're an aspiring game designer, you should buy it immediately if you haven't already. Yes, that is a gold-plated recommendation.

Personally, I could have done without the illustrations, but they make great slides for me to pinch for my presentations, so I'm not about to advocate their removal.

---

[6]Nicole Lazzaro: *Four Keys to Fun*. XEODesign, 2005. http://xeodesign.com/4k2f/4k2f.jpg

Laughing Heartily

Type /bow in *World of Warcraft* and you get the response, You bow down graciously.

But that's not how I was bowing! I was bowing obsequiously, or slowly, or sarcastically, or flippantly, or rudely, or…

Here's what's supposed to happen, from the olde texte worlde days.

If I type nod, then I just get Richard nods.

If I want to nod emphatically, I type nod emphatically. If I want to nod with a wry smile and a wink, I type nod with a wry smile and a wink.

How hard is that?

Here are some more examples of simple emotes that are strangely lacking from some modern MMOs:

> ;feels a sneeze coming on. This produces Richard feels a sneeze coming on.
>
> :) or :-). This produces Richard smiles.
>
> "hello? This produces Richard asks, "hello?"
>
> "hello! This produces Richard exclaims, "hello!"
>
> say hello! This produces Richard says, "hello!"

These aren't hard to implement. They give players much more expressive capability, they don't jar, and they don't make your character behave in a way you didn't ask for it to behave (thereby breaking your immersion).

Why add the unnecessary and intrusive adjectives? Let players create their own.

Immersion Terminology

What gamers mean by "immersion" isn't what psychologists mean by it.

Psychologists use a definition that is all about swamping the senses in order to trick the mind into believing that something is more real than it is; MMO players use a definition that's more to do with how much they feel they are *in* the virtual world.

Thus, an experienced player in a textual world could feel far more immersed than a new player in a graphical one, but a psychologist wouldn't see it that way at all.

Toon Time

The word *toon* is short for "cartoon."

Originally, it meant what your character looks like on the screen, but shifted to mean the character itself. The word was coined because the word *avatar*, which originally meant what your character looks like on the screen, shifted to mean the character itself.

Every new wave of players brings with it its new misconceptions.

Ludology

Game designers like to think that games are different from stories. Although games and stories can contain similar elements, there are some things that games can do but stories can't. This viewpoint is known as *Ludology* (from the Latin for game, *ludus*).

In the past, though, creators of other new media—theatre, film, television—have also thought this, only to be proven wrong. So are game designers wrong? Or is there something about games that is *fundamentally* unobtainable from stories?

No-Win Situation

As an MMO designer, I don't find them the same kind of "fun" as pretty well everyone else does. I find them designer-fun, not player-fun, and I can get designer-fun from an hour of watching someone else play and maybe reading the help pages. Because I know MMO design so well, I don't actually have to play them to understand them.

When I say this, people often get cross. It's true, though: I don't need to play them. Nevertheless, the cross people will tell me either that I'm out of touch or no good at playing; that's when they don't tell me I'm both. Tired of having to defend myself from such accusations, I therefore resolved to address it at its source and actually play an MMO right the way through to the top level three times over. The one I chose was *World of Warcraft* because that's what all the cool kids were playing at the time (okay, so I was given a free copy of it, which helped me make up my mind). I took a paladin, a mage and a warlock all the way up to the level cap, 60. I also got the epic mounts for the paladin and the warlock, plus the dungeon set 2 for the mage (excluding the head-gear because, although I had all the necessary components to summon Lord Valthalak, I couldn't get one last group for Upper Blackrock Spire before the *Burning Crusade* expansion came out).

I played these characters up to level 60 to acquire credentials: I did it *only* so I could say I'd done it. I knew pretty well exactly what I was in for by level 6, but I persevered nonetheless. I was half-hoping that the cross people who suggested that I don't know what I'm talking about might shut up when I got my first 60, but of course they didn't. Too many of them seemed to need to qualify their own achievements by establishing my place as lower down in the pecking order; I was told several times that, of course, *World of Warcraft* only really *begins* when you reach level 60.

Yes, I *know* that. I *knew* it by level 6. For me, I only need to experience the *design*, not the play; the play is just going through the motions—it's the design I find interesting. Having seen enough, I can extrapolate the rest; I don't have to sit down and play my way through it. Indeed, it's quite painful for me to do so.

To keep my qualifications intact, I took my characters up to 70 with the *Burning Crusade*. I was fairly pleased with this, but then I was accused of being a *WoW* fanboi. In response, I took up a character to (the then level cap of) 50 in *The Lord of the Rings Online*, whereupon I took a screenshot and deleted my account. I later did the same thing in *Rift*, pausing only to give all my stuff to the one person who had spoken more than one sentence to me the entire time I'd played.

I did still have a problem answering the "ah, but the real game is raiding!" point because I'd played *WoW* on a US server (the free copy I was given was for a US server). This meant I couldn't make normal raiding times because of the time difference. Therefore, when *Star Wars: the Old Republic* came out, I zipped a healer up to the max level and joined a raiding guild. Over the course of 137 days of real time, I racked up 33 days of playing time, or about 25% of my life. That gave me the final qualification I needed in order to have a riposte to accusations that I know squat about raiding elder games.

Nevertheless, I'm sure that there are those among you right now thinking up reasons why this does not, in fact, give me any right to talk about MMO elder games. Perhaps I lack playing skills? Well, when I quit *The Secret World*, I was ranked one of the top 50 players in the entire game across all servers. Just because I don't have player-fun, that doesn't mean I'm not actually fairly good at playing.

Back in *WoW*, I'd continued to 80 with the *Wrath of the Lich King*, then 85 with *Cataclysm*. Fortunately, by the time the *Mists of Pandaria* expansion appeared, a few of the more prominent bloggers were now having I-don't-need-to-play-it-I-can-see-what-it'll-be-like moments of their own, so I was spared having to dance with pandas.

So, at last I can say YES I AM IN TOUCH and YES I CAN PLAY AN MMO and YES IT WAS UTTERLY POINTLESS DOING IT BUT I DID IT ANYWAY JUST FOR YOU. In the case of *WoW*, I did it for an accumulated 225 days of /played time before I cancelled my account.

Ah, but "today's MMOs are so different that your old experience is worth nothing!"

Great. In order to demonstrate that I don't need to play MMOs, I need to play them.

I just can't win.

May Day

Christmas, Halloween, New Year, assorted other festivals, and national days: every once in a while, the real world changes and becomes something other than what it normally is.

Should MMOs also change at these times?

When the real world temporarily wears a different mantle, it presents a problem for MMO designers: should they embrace the change by putting, for example, Christmassy stuff in, or should they remain apart and offer no support whatsoever?

If they don't go with the flow, many players will do so anyway and will be put out that their home-from-home isn't joining in. On the other hand, if they do take major real-world cultural events on, this will annoy those players who feel it somewhat breaks the fiction (and no, your attempts to cover it with lore or backstory won't help—you're not fooling anybody).

Most MMOs seem to go with the acknowledge-*Reality* approach, and have done so for decades (even *MUD1* did, despite being far more conscientious about separating the real from the virtual than today's MMOs). They still have a problem, though: which events do they put in and which do they leave out?

Unfortunately, different parts of the real world have different festivals. July 4th is big in the USA, but passes without comment everywhere else. Likewise, Chinese New Year, Saint Patrick's Day, Bonfire Night, Eid al-Fitr, Diwali, and Easter are important to some people in some places but not to others elsewhere—and some of them move around the calendar, so can cause collisions.

Which religion or country do you want to insult by not putting its favorite festival in your MMO? Which players do you want to annoy by holding some inexplicable seasonal event that disrupts their fun?

Is May Day a friend or foe of immersion?

Go Grok Yourself

Human beings are amazing pattern-matchers. Msot Egilnsh sepkaers culod raed this snetecne. It doesn't matter whether the pattern is exhibited in the senses, through action, or in the mind: we can spot it.

The more a pattern is encountered, the easier it becomes to recognize. People come to learn the pattern—and then they recognize it automatically. If I were to show you a picture of Einstein that you'd never seen before, you'd know it was of him—even though he died in 1955.

Learning a pattern means you can instantly recognize it, but things don't just stop there: if you encounter a process enough, you can *internalize* it. By this, I mean you can understand it to such an extent that it becomes a unitary concept for you. Complex systems that were once difficult become such that you don't even have to think about them unless something interrupts you—as with driving a car, for example. You may have started lessons by thinking in terms of steering and accelerating and braking, but after a while you just think in terms of *driving*.

Thanks to author Robert A. Heinlein, we have a word to describe this concept of internalized knowing: *grok*. If you grok something, you have an implicit understanding of it to the extent that you just *know* all there is to know about it without having to think.

Grokking raises its head in two ways when it comes to understanding MMOs, both to do with fun. One of them is a red herring, and the other is everything.

Engrossed *vs.* Immersed

It's harder to get people engrossed in a textual world than in a graphical world. However, once a player becomes engrossed, it's easier for them to become immersed in a textual world than in a graphical world.

Presence

Psychologists have a concept they call *presence*. There are actually several kinds of presence, but the general theme is that it's what you get when a mediated experience appears, perceptually, not to be mediated[7].

Here's an example: suppose you are waiting in your car at a set of traffic lights and someone coming up behind doesn't quite stop in time. There's no damage done, but you're not happy. When you meet up with your friends later, you say, "some idiot ran into the back of me this morning." You don't say, "some idiot ran their car into the back of my car this morning," even though that's actually what happened. You might say something like that as a passenger, but not as a driver. This is because, when you're driving, you regard the car as an extension to your body.

The same sort of thing applies to chopsticks, computer mice, puppets, mechanical digger scoops, MMO characters, ...

When you control your character in an MMO, there's actually a lot of hardware between you and that character—and the character isn't even a physical entity. Nevertheless, once you've been playing awhile you can control it effortlessly. You're effectively treating your character as if it were part of your own body. That's presence (or *telepresence*, if you want to differentiate this particular subdivision of presence from other subdivisions).

The concept of presence is strongly linked by psychologists to that of immersion. This is indeed the case—for the definition of "immersion" that psychologists use. Unfortunately, this definition is not in line with what *players* mean when they say "immersion."

Players mean something altogether more special.

---

[7]Richard N. Held and Nathanial I. Durloch: *Telepresence. Presence: Teleoperators and Virtual Environments* 1, pp 109-112, 1992.

On your Second Read

If you remember by the time you get to the end of this book, look at the title and subtitle of Levy's work in the light of all I've said by then. They're … apt.

Olton Hall

The role of the Hogwarts Express steam engine in the *Harry Potter* films was played by Olton Hall, a Great Western Railway "Hall" Class 4-6-0, number 5972. It was built in Swindon in 1937[8].

---

[8]Rail UK: *BR/GWR Collett 4-6-0 Class 4900 Hall No. 5972 at Woodham Brothers Scrapyard 1966* http://www.railuk.info/gallery/album_search.php?offset=22&first_id=1&last_id=59&item=&album=2

Inter-World Trust

If a number of virtual worlds *completely trusted* each other, they could implement a protocol for the transference of characters and property between those worlds. What you'd have as a result would effectively be a single virtual world with a bunch of different "countries," not multiple virtual worlds. It can work, though.

I know it can work because I actually implemented this with *MUD1*. The restrictions on how much memory a program could use on the mainframe during prime time changed, and *MUD1* became too big. I therefore created another world, *Valley*, that sat next to it geographically but was small enough to be played during the day. Out of prime time, when *Valley* and *MUD1* could both be run, it was possible for people to walk from one to the other and back. Thus, it wasn't so much that players were transferring between *different* virtual worlds, as that they were transferring between different parts of the *same* world.

This exercise was only possible because *MUD1* could trust what *Valley* told it, and *vice versa*. For a more general system, though, this issue of trust is a big problem. One rogue world would completely compromise the whole system. If my MMO is easier than your MMO but characters can transfer between them, you can guarantee that players will come to my MMO, level up (or skill up or kit up or whatever), and then return to your MMO to brag about how great their character is. This is not something that other people in your MMO will necessarily appreciate.

Social worlds are more likely to buy into the ideal of each being part of some same, glorious meta-world because they're not competitive in the same way as game worlds. Even they face problems of trust, though: if everyone in *Catworld* is a cat, what happens when you try to enter it from *Carworld*, where everyone is a car? Does *Catworld* trust *Carworld* not to send it any visitors? Or does *Catworld* have to act as its own gatekeeper, converting any non-cat visitors (such as cars) into cats? It might even have problems accepting visitors from *Felineworld* if they have the same names as existing players of *Catworld*.

So the upshot is that you *can* have inter-world travel, but unless the worlds 100 percent trust each other, the recipient world has to be able to decide how much of you, if any, to admit.

Narratology

Looking at games from the point of view of film, literature and theatre, games are texts to be read. Like drama, they are a medium that allows individuals to assume a different role and act out different scenes. In that respect, games are just another form of story—a viewpoint known as *Narratology*.

Yet games are very non-linear, whereas even the most *avant garde* theatre is still heavily linear by comparison. When you try to fit games into existing theories of literature and drama, it's very, very hard—you have to reduce the definition of what constitutes a "story" to a point where it's almost vacuous.

You *can* do it, though.

That said, why is it we're only noticing this now, with computer games, when games as a concept *predate* narrative? Animals play games, but they don't tell stories. If games were just another aspect of narrative, why hasn't this been spotted before? Perhaps games *are* something different?

You're Only Supposed to …

In the 1969 caper movie, *The Italian Job*, a group of British criminals steal a shipment of Chinese gold headed for a bank in Turin. They then make their escape in three minis, taking a splendidly bizarre route to avoid the gridlock caused by their earlier modifications to the traffic control computer's files.

I guess I should have given a spoiler alert, but if you haven't already seen *The Italian Job*, you must be purposefully avoiding it. Well, either that or you could be something other than British, in which case it won't be a movie you're likely to see anyway…

Floyd

The 1983 text adventure, *Planetfall*, designed by Steve Meretzky, is legendary among game designers.

The premise of the game is that following some explosions aboard the spaceship you work on, you escape in a pod and crash-land on a nearby planet. There are signs of civilization, but not of people. While trying to figure out a way to get back home, a series of clues gradually reveal what has happened, what the implications of this are, and that you don't have a lot of time to find a solution.

Early on, you encounter a very endearing robot called Floyd, who seems to be the planet's only remaining inhabitant. He not only helps advance the plot, but he's a great source of comic relief. When you save the game, for example, he says "Oh boy! Are we going to try something dangerous?" During the course of the game, players came to grow very fond of Floyd and his engaging, childlike ways.

Warning: spoiler ahead.

Thus, they were very shaken when Floyd sacrificed himself so they could win. "Floyd a good friend, huh?"

Vicariousness

You don't get to change the protagonist's nature in a novel; the author does. You're experiencing the narrative second-hand: you identify to a greater or lesser degree with the protagonist, and absorb his or her experiences, but you can't influence how the character's character changes because books aren't interactive.

This is how narrative has been for time immemorial. You don't get to be a hero from reading a book—the protagonist gets to be the hero. All you can do is try to put yourself in the protagonist's shoes and look for resonance between the character's situation and your own.

Improving Players

Imagine if novels started off as an easy read but got progressively hard to follow. Why would you continue to read a novel if it just got harder and harder as you read it?

Imagine watching a movie that was clear at the beginning but became impenetrable by the end. Why would you continue to watch a movie if it just got harder and harder as you watched it?

Imagine playing a game that was easy to start with but became more difficult as you played it. Why would you continue to play a game if it just got harder and harder as you played it?

Well, games *do* do that.

No-one can be good or bad at a book or a movie, but they *can* be good or bad at a game.

Players *improve* as they play.

Real Life API—Educate

CPopulation::Educate

int Educate(CKnowledge *rcKnow*)

- *rcKnow* Specifies the knowledge to be understood.

Remarks

Improves the population's knowledge of *rcKnow*. The nature of the improvement is dependent on, and defined within, *rcKnow*.

- Knowledge of a factual nature is transmitted very well.

- Knowledge of a procedural nature is not transmitted well.

- Knowledge about thinking is transmitted very well.

- Other SDKs may offer complementary or superior equivalents to **CPopulation::Educate**.

Return

0 on success, otherwise:

- **E_PDE**—population denies education to some of its members.

Games & Learning

When people play games for fun, they're trying to grok them. This means they actively *want* to learn something.

Idea! Why not use games to teach people things? Games are fun, education is unfun; therefore, combining the two will lead to fun education!

Well, as I said before, it's because it generally leads to unfun games.

The trouble is, educationalists who want to teach something via a game will too often try to make the thing they are trying to teach be the central plank of the game. Classically, if they want to teach people how to add up, then they make the game have addition as its core mechanic. It's possible that this can work (although easier to do in puzzles than in games), but it's missing the point. This is somewhat ironic because *missing the point* is the best way to learn in games.

I can name all the countries in Europe. I can do so not because I ever sat down and learned them, but because I've played so many games featuring a map of Europe that I just picked them up through osmosis. None of the games I played which taught me this geography were *trying* to teach me it, it just came as a side-effect.

All games that contain facts teach you those facts. Facts are the easiest things to get across in games. Anything you need to learn by rote can be taught in a game, simply by making it be involved in the gameplay. My kids can find every capital city in Europe because we play a travel game I designed which involves moving between capital cities in Europe. Okay, so maybe they don't know what Ljubljiana is capital *of*, but they know it's a capital and its whereabouts on the map. The game isn't *about* capitals, though, it's about travel; capitals are just what you happen to travel between. The game would be just as much fun if I'd made up the map and the city names; my kids would still have learned the locations, but this way what they learned has some real-world relevance.

Skills are *not* easy to teach through games. I don't know offhand what 123*123 is, but I do know that I can work it out in my head, and I also know that I wouldn't like playing a game where I was required to do that. Unfortunately, this is exactly the kind of game that educationalists aim at because skills are precisely what they want to teach people. This is why many of their efforts are so miserable. The thing is, you *can* teach skills in a game, you just don't make it that those skills are *required*. Rather than building the gameplay about mathematics, so that the person with the best mathematical skills always wins, you build it about something fun and make the mathematical skills merely *incidental* to the gameplay.

The best kind of skills that games teach you (and *all* games that aren't pure chance do this) are high-order problem-solving skills. People can really benefit from these, and games are probably *the* best way to learn them. However, these in-demand skills are by their very nature non-specific. This is rarely acceptable in the classroom because educators don't just want to use games to teach, they want to use them to teach *particular things*.

Okay, that's fine, games can be pressed into doing that—just so long as you don't make those particular things comprise the game mechanic. If you really want to get the most out of games *and* be specific, concentrate on facts: games are *good* at facts.

In Tanzania, there's a crater with a floor area of 260km^2 and walls 610m deep. It's the world's largest unbroken volcanic caldera. The chances are you've never heard of it before; however, when I tell you its name, some of you will immediately recognize it and you'll remember it for ever more. Okay, maybe not the exact spelling, but probably the basic sound, and certainly the fact that it exists. It's called Ngorongoro. *World of Warcraft* players who thought that the name Un'Goro was made up: now you know it wasn't. Furthermore, in 20 years' time, when you're on *Who Wants to be a Millionaire* and they ask you which of these four national parks in Africa contains a large crater, you'll be able to answer.

Don't try fireballing tigers, though. I'm guessing that doesn't transfer so well from *WoW* to RL.

Flow

In evolutionary terms, if you didn't learn, then you got **eaten by bears**. Therefore, those organisms that evolved mechanisms to encourage learning did better than those that didn't. As a result, it should come as no surprise to discover that people (being very good at learning) are hard-wired to find it an enjoyable experience.

Put another way, the process of grokking something is pleasurable.

Of course, once you grok enough similar games, you grok the whole concept they embody. If all Fantasy RPGs seem the same to you, that's either because you have too little understanding of them or too much.

Okay, so when you're playing a game for fun, you're trying to grok it. Once you've mastered it, though, it stops being fun—it's "no fun." If you haven't mastered it and are making no substantial progress, it also stops being fun—it's "unfun."

So what about in between?

Unfun games are too hard. You get frustrated and eventually stop. *No fun* games are too easy. You get bored and eventually stop. Yet some games stay fun for extended periods. What's going on here?

Psychologists have a concept called *flow*, which was proposed by in 1975 by Mihály Chicks-sent-me-high (pronounced "Csíkszentmihályi"). Flow is a Zen-like state that people can get into when they're doing a task that is neither too easy nor too hard for them. They don't *have* to get into it, but they can.

There are eight components of flow:

- *Clear Goals.* Expectations and rules are easy to grasp.

- *Concentrating and Focusing.* You limit your attention field and dive deeply into it.

- *Loss of Self-Consciousness.* Action merges with awareness.

- *Distorted Sense of Time.* "Was I really doing it for that long?!"

- *Direct and Immediate Feedback.* Success and failure can be easily recognized.

- *Balance between Ability and Challenge.* It's never too hard and never too easy.

- *Sense of Personal Control.* You feel that the activity is dancing to your tune.

- *Intrinsically Rewarding.* The effortlessness of your actions itself feels worthwhile.

Hmm, does this sound familiar to you? Like, maybe when you're playing a game?

Well, this is the argument made by Raph Koster in his book, *A Theory of Fun for Game Design*[9]—and he's right, there *is* a connection between flow and fun:

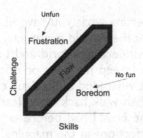

If you experience flow in games, it will indeed be fun. However, you can experience fun *without* flow. In particular, you can be having fun already and *then* go into a state of flow. Flow is sufficient for fun, but it's not necessary.

So flow is not a psychologist's synonym for fun, even in regular games. For MMOs, it's even less so.

Personally, I think flow is a red herring. MMOs *are* about grokking, but they're not about flow. It's *what* you grok that makes MMOs compelling, not merely the fact that right now you are grokking it swimmingly *well*.

Seamlessness

Earlier, when I was talking about portable characters, I mentioned that one of the "new" ideas that come up every so often is that of being able to move between MMOs seamlessly. You're playing in one world, you pass through a door, cross a river, walk out of a forest, whatever, and you're now seamlessly in another world without having broken your immersion. Wouldn't that be great?

Hmm. So even if the worlds trusted one another completely, this is still an idea with a number of issues.

- **Design**: it'll be as if you're reading chapters of an enormous book that have all been written by different people. Unless there's a system in place to ensure they all conform to the same style, you'll spot the difference whether the designers would like you to or not.

---

[9]Raph Koster: *A Theory of Fun for Game Design.* Paraglyph Press: Scottsdale, Arizona. 2005.

- **Experiential**: as I'll be explaining over the coming pages, people play MMOs to become themselves by being others. They have to feel at some point that they have "finished." That's not going to happen for a world that's made up of many worlds, because there's effectively no end to it.

- **Technical**: converting what you have in one world into an analogue in another world is not easy. If I have a bow and arrow in Neanderthal World and I walk into Wild West World, do I keep my bow or does the software have to work out what kind of handgun cognate I should be packing? If I then walk back into Neanderthal World, do I get the same bow I had before or a different one because of imperfections in the mapping? Or do I get to take with me the rifle I found in Wild West World?

- **Legal**: as I've mentioned, back in the early days you could walk from *MUD1* to its sister world, *Valley*, seamlessly. Nevertheless, this idea has been patented several times since then, so if you want this kind of seamless transaction today, you'll have to speak to the people who will sue you if you don't.

- **Security**: if I can create my own MMO, why wouldn't I award myself god-like powers and then walk into someone else's world to exercise those powers there? I could give myself the best equipment, a glowing reputation, the ability to move faster than the speed of light—anything I want. You may have trusted my world when we first connected, but since then I've become egomaniacal.

If all of these issues were addressed, it *would* be great, though, wouldn't it?

No, sorry, it wouldn't be great. Designers simply wouldn't accept players coming to their MMO bringing with them the reputation, gear and power they've acquired in another MMO, for the exact same reason that the real world wouldn't accept it: what players tend to want to transfer between worlds tends to be fundamentally non-transferrable.

Two Definitions of Immersion

Psychologists have two ways of looking at immersion[10]:

- *System immersion* concerns how persuasive an environment is. An environment in which light casts shadows is more immersive than one in which it doesn't.

- *Immersive response* concerns how persuaded users of an environment are by it. An environment in which people feel they are present is more immersive than one in which they don't.

Presence is the wire that connects these together. If the environment resists presence (i.e., the system immersion is poor), then the player will struggle to experience it (i.e., the immersive response will also be poor). Likewise, if an environment is not persuasive, players will struggle to feel immersed in it.

Neither system immersion nor immersive response captures what *players* mean by the term "immersion," though. Both can be factors, but neither *is* immersion.

---

[10]Mel Slater: *Measuring Presence: A Response to the Witmer and Singer Presence Questionnaire. Presence* 8(5), pp 560-565, 2003. http://www.cs.ucl.ac.uk/staff/m.slater/Papers/pq.pdf

Elementary

Rift is an MMO in which rifts open from elemental planes, and elementals pour through. There are six elements: water, fire, earth, air, life, and death. Fair enough.

So, I'm playing *Rift*, and my character is some kind of fighting priest who can heal, but who can also do a bit of damage. I have spells with names like Dehydrate, Spirit Rupture, and Drown (which "fills the lungs of the target with sea water").

So, if I'm attacking something that's made of water, I might expect Dehydrate to do considerable damage. Against a fire elemental, though, well there's no water to remove, so it should be pretty ineffectual. Likewise, filling with water the lungs of a creature that lives under water shouldn't really do much—only mammals have lungs anyway. Similarly, casting Spirit Rupture on an inanimate object (such as a wardstone) shouldn't do it a great deal of damage as it has no spirit to rupture.

None of this happens. The damage that a spell does is pretty well independent of the elemental nature of the target. I don't have to select my spells carefully, adapting for different opponents: I just use the same ones every time. I do have *some* decisions to make (don't use Crushing Wave if it might blast your opponent into some enemies and so set those on you too, that kind of thing), but the whole six elements thing just isn't a factor. Given that this is a game about elements, this seems rather unsatisfying.

This is almost always how it is with MMOs that have elements in them. I've no idea why.

Too Immersive?

MMOs are immersive experiences. They're more immersive than books, movies, TV, and coloring-in pictures of flowers. Surely this level of immersion is dangerous and must be banned?

Well, no. The real world is even more immersive than MMOs; if you want to ban MMOs on the basis that they're too immersive, you're going to have to ban *Reality*, too.

Griefing

It used to be that the term *griefer* had a very specific meaning in MMOs: it meant someone who deliberately did something for the pleasure in knowing it caused others pain.

To old-timers like me, that's what it still means. What does it mean to modern MMO players, though?

Well, nowadays, griefing can mean a range of things:

- Deliberately causing others pain for the pleasure of knowing this (e.g., attacking someone not because you like it, but because you know they won't like it).

- Deliberately doing something pleasurable which you know will cause others pain (e.g., ganking newbies).

- Deliberately doing something pleasurable which indirectly causes others pain (e.g., exploiting a bug to get more money).

- Deliberately causing others pain but not feeling there's anything wrong in it (e.g., scamming them).

- Deliberately causing others pain but believing they Okayed it (e.g., winning at PvP).

- Unthinkingly causing others pain through selfishness (e.g., ninja looting).

- Accidentally causing others pain through error or incompetence (e.g., Leeeeroy).

- Unknowingly doing something someone else doesn't like (e.g., outbidding them in an auction).

Lots more—player vernacular changes all the time. So much has the term *griefer* lost its potency that people will now talk instead about specific kinds of griefing, such as *training* or *kill stealing*. However, the reason the word *griefer* got used in the first place is because it's *really handy*. If we can't use it any more for what it used to mean, we need a replacement.

So the next time you complain that someone "griefed" you by picking the flower that you were going to pick after you picked the one after the one you're currently picking, see if you can think of a new word that would describe someone who deliberately caused your raid group to wipe on its final attempt after four hours of trying, just because they knew it would spoil everyone's evening.

Dynamic Difficulty Adjustment

Flow is about achieving a balance between challenge and skill. If something is too hard, it's unfun; if it's easy, it's no fun. The aim of designers should therefore be to keep players in the zone where challenge matches ability: where there is flow, in other words.

W-w-what?!

There's a theory of game design which suggests that if the aim of the gameplay is to keep people in the flow-state zone, then the game itself should adjust its difficulty levels dynamically to ensure that this is the case. If the monsters are giving you too hard a time, then artificial intelligence techniques can be used to monitor this and make the monsters easier. Likewise, if you're breezing your way through content, you must clearly be finding it too easy to be fun. If it were made a bit harder, you'd enjoy it more.

This concept actually has a fairly long tradition in computer game design. Racing games have long used *rubber banding*—a technique that makes sure you don't get too far ahead of or behind everyone else, so the race remains exciting.

I *loathe* dynamic difficulty adjustment (DDA).

Players are *all different*. The proposition that they all like a balance between challenge and ability is reasonable, but that doesn't mean the balance point is the *same for everyone*. If you and I have the same skill level for a game, one of us could still think it's too easy, while the other thinks it's too hard. The notion of "challenge" isn't absolute, it's *relative to individuals*.

It's also easy to game. I never bother much with technology research in *Civilization V*, because I know that the technology output of AI opponents is buffed/debuffed to match my own. In a race game, if I know that no matter how fast I go the cars behind me will speed up to remain in contention, the smart thing for me to do is to drive slowly so as to trick the AI into thinking my skills are poor. It will then slow down the cars it controls, to keep me in the flow zone. Thus, when at the start of the last lap I zoom off like a rocket, the AI is caught completely off guard. The rubber-banding mechanism itself becomes part of the game mechanic, to be exploited accordingly. It's a component of the very system it's trying to regulate.

This leads me to what *really* annoys me: the way that the concept of "challenge" in a DDA game feeds into itself. If I know that whatever decision I make will lead to gameplay appropriate for my abilities, then this isn't a tuned level of challenge—it's *no challenge at all*. I can't do anything wrong! I can't do anything right! Whatever I do, no matter how well or how badly, the outcome will be the same. Augh!

Sometimes, I *want* to try pushing myself: if the game tones down its opposition, how can I do that? Sometimes I *want* an easy ride: if the game beefs up its opposition, how can I do that? Do I set some difficulty level? Plenty of games have that feature *anyway*, we don't need DDA for it!

This almost killed *The Elder Scrolls IV: Oblivion* for me. *I'll* decide what I think is and isn't fun, thank you very much.

So what has this to do with MMOs?

Well, would *you* go into an instance for which the difficulty and loot levels were automatically adjusted to match the gear levels of the party you were in?

You *would*?

What kind of player *are* you?

Spider Lore

In *MUD1*, there was a silken thread lying on the ground. If you picked it up, you discovered it was a spider's web and you were stuck in place. A few seconds later, a giant spider appeared and automatically killed you. You could, however, escape the web by setting it on fire before the spider arrived.

Now the thing is, spider webs aren't actually all that easy to set on fire—indeed, you could legitimately call them fire-resistant. I didn't know that at the time and neither did most players, but enough did know that every few years I'd get a complaint about it telling me that cobwebs shouldn't burn.

That's fair enough. The interesting question, though, is why people would complain that I had cobwebs that burned but *not* complain that I had a spider the size of a sheep.

Playing for Kicks

So, I was playing *World of Warcraft* back in the early *Cataclysm* days, and I queued my warlock up to run a random heroic instance. The queue was 46 minutes long. When I finally got to the front, I found myself a new member of a party that was standing in front of one of the optional bosses at the end of the Halls of Origination. The other party members were all in the same guild as each other.

They said "hi" and I said "hi."

They said "r?" and I said "yes."

Then, they kicked me out of the group.

I couldn't have been there for more than 30 seconds. I thought I'd be returned to the front of the queue, but no, I wasn't. I had to rejoin it, whereupon I discovered I'd have to wait 51 minutes for another group.

If I played MMOs for fun, I can see how this might have been a tad annoying.

Achievers

People who treat MMOs as if they were games are called *achievers*. They give themselves game-oriented goals and set out to achieve them. Such goals include:

- Going up levels
- Obtaining treasure
- Downing raid bosses

Achievers say things such as:

- busy
- Only two bars to go
- LFG 25 VoA
- Ding 105 :)

Achievers do not like their achievements being undermined. If someone paid real money to buy the same high-status object that the achiever got through dedicated play, that would do it.

System Immersion

Here's the standard theory of how increased perceptual realism leads to a greater sense of presence.

When you can control your character in a virtual world without having to think about the interface, this is presence. You feel that you are "present" in that other environment.

In general, the more the target environment gives the appearance of being real, the easier it becomes to establish presence:

- Black and white silent movie.
- Black and white talkie.
- Color movie.
- Color movie with stereo.
- I-MAX cinema.
- Disneyland *Star Wars* rides.

However, if it's not quite right, then this can stop presence dead:

- 1950s 3D movies.

The reason for this is that evolution (or, if you're one of those people who don't believe in it, then your imaginary friend) has created a human brain which is hard-wired to be able to process real-world visual scenes very quickly and efficiently—we have a whole cortex devoted to it. People don't usually have to think consciously about interpreting what they can see, they just *do* it. What's more, they can't *help* doing it.

You're predisposed to believe whatever your visual cortex tells you. Therefore, if you look at a representation of an environment and it *seems* real, you'll be more inclined to believe it *is* real.

System immersion concerns the creation of stimuli that together persuade the brain that you're somewhere other than where you really are. In this view, presence is therefore an emergent consequence of system immersion.

That's the standard theory.

Anyone who thinks it explains presence in MMOs is sadly mistaken, though...

Ludology *versus* Narratology

Ludology and Narratology are in direct opposition: they can't both be right. Here's how the battle between them panned out.

The narratologists were the first to stake their claim on computer games, the charge being led by Janet Murray in her influential book, *Hamlet on the Holodeck*[11]. Murray argued that MMOs (well, MUDs as they were known back in 1997) opened up new opportunities for storytelling, but couched this in terms that made it clear she felt that games were, nevertheless, only a *form* of storytelling.

Around the same time, Espen Aarseth took on the challenge of actually applying traditional models of literature to computer games (including, specifically, MMOs—Aarseth had played *MUD1*). He concluded that existing tools were not originally designed for games and weren't up to the job; to make them work, they would have to be extended. To this end, he developed a powerful new theoretical framework that he called *ergodic literature*[12]—literature that requires non-trivial effort to get through. Aarseth's formulation was highly insightful; it became (and remains) a central pillar for New Media Studies.

Aarseth criticized Murray's work for its inability to account for the non-linearity of games. Although his own theories extended existing theories of literature to bridge this divide, it was apparent to him that the difference between them was so great as to amount to a separation. Games do benefit from story, but story is incidental: what's important is *gameplay*. Aarseth can therefore be regarded as fundamentally a ludologist.

The narratologists nevertheless took enough substance from Aarseth's work to assert that their position was still basically sound: games are an *exotic* form of literature, but they remain, when all is said and done, a form of literature. This line was held fairly successfully until the ludologists counter-attacked.

A famous paper written by Gonzalo Frasca in 1999[13] disputed that Narratology was a helpful way to look at games. He argued that games are games first, stories second (if at all). If you want to understand a game, you should study it *as a game*, not as a narrative (a position echoing Aarseth's). When people describe a game, they do so in terms of rules and play, not text and reading.

---

[11]Janet H. Murray: *Hamlet on the Holodeck: The Future of Narrative in Cyberspace*. The Free Press, 1997.

[12]Espen J. Aarseth: *Cybertext: Perspectives on Ergodic Literature*. The Johns Hopkins University Press, 1997.

[13]Gonzalo Frasca: *Ludology meets Narratology: Similitude and Differences between (Video) games and Narrative*. Parnasso v3, Helsinki, 1999. http://www.ludology.org/articles/ludology.htm

After much discourse over the course of several years, eventually the narratologists retreated. It was Janet Murray herself[14] who explained the conclusion:

- Games are not subsets of stories.
- Objects exist that have qualities of both games and stories.

She also suggested that the Narratology position was itself an invention of the ludologists—she had never been as hard-line as ludologists had made out, and was far more open to having a variety of tools in her toolbox than ludologists had given her credit for.

Nevertheless, the ludologists had made their point. Games are worth studying first and foremost *because they are games*.

Pepper

MMO developers will consciously tolerate a certain amount of aberrant behavior, as it adds drama to the game—it gives people something to talk about. A small number of griefers will add to the sustainability of the community.

This is something we've known for years. Only when an objectionable play style starts being taken up by so many people that it seriously disrupts overall play will developers change the MMO's rules to prevent said objectionable play style.

A little pepper will spice up an otherwise dull meal. What you don't want is for someone to empty a whole pot of pepper onto your plate.

---

[14]Janet H. Murray: *The Last Word on Ludology v Narratology in Game Studies.* Proc. DiGRA 2005, Vancouver. http://inventingthemedium.com/2013/06/28/the-last-word-on-ludology-v-narratology-2005/

Portable Characters Again

One of the reasons usually offered for having portable characters that can move from one MMO to another with impunity is that the players want it. Okay, so *seamless* travel may not be an option, but transferring characters from one MMO to another must surely be possible in one form or another?

Hmm.

So, go out and grab hold of some *World of Warcraft* players. Tell them that players who reached the end game of *EverQuest* in 2002 are going to transfer to their server and have all their *EQ* gear translated into equivalent *WoW* gear. Tell them that they'll be joined by end-game players from *Runescape*, as well as by people from *Ultima Online* who have bought their gear using real money. Oh, and there'll be players from *Second Life* who created their own world and gave themselves insanely high-quality gear because hey, they could.

Warning: wear body armor when you tell them this.

Some players might indeed want to be able to move from one game to another *themselves*, but could they all stomach it when they saw *other* people doing it too?

A Narrative Experience

When asked, many players say they kinda like the idea of having a narrative experience in their MMOs. So adding a narrative experience to an MMO is a good idea, then?

Hmm ... what makes such a narrative experience "good"? What makes it *so* good that you'll spend two to four hours a night, every night for a year, to experience it?

The problem with narrative in MMOs is that there is no fun in it. There can be fun in it when it's *your story* that's unfolding as you play, but then it isn't really a narrative any more—it's a game.

The Game Allows it

Remember Egor? When people play games on computers, they often assume that if the computer lets them do it, they can do it. Only if it doesn't let them do it is it against the rules.

This is fine for single-player games played against the computer, as it's only you who's affected. If you play a save/lose/reload strategy to beat AI opponents, for example, you're doing something "the game" allows, but it's not itself part of the game. Should you therefore use it relentlessly? Well some people might, but others might refrain from using it so their eventual victory feels more earned. The former would complain if the random number seed was saved (so that reloading didn't help); the latter would complain if the game design forced you to use trial and error (e.g., there's no way of knowing in advance which is the one door that isn't booby-trapped).

When you play a single-player game, it's up to you how much you push at the rules. When you play a multi-player game, it's not this simple. Some people might be playing the game where you don't train guards on people (because use of a dominant strategy spoils the game for everyone), and some might be playing the game where you do do it (because "the game lets me"). If two people are playing the same MMO but different "games," it's unsurprising that conflict can arise.

This gray area is one beloved of griefers. They can do things that annoy the hell out of other players (thus bringing enjoyment to themselves), but claim that they're doing nothing wrong because "the game allows it."

Presence in Context

Without feeling some degree of presence, people couldn't play MMOs. It's a hugely important factor.

However, without computers people couldn't play, either. A computer is not the reason people have fun in MMOs, although it is an important enabler. The same applies to presence.

Persuasion

Standing someone in a room in which every sensory stimulus is presented so as to give the impression that the individual is in a different physical location may mean that this person is *immersed in the virtual environment,* but it doesn't mean they're *immersed.*

Making a virtual world seem real is *persuasive* of that virtual world, but despite what presence theorists would have us believe, it's *not* what makes it immersive. The most powerfully immersive virtual worlds discovered to date are *textual,* not graphical—they have barely any presence-enhancing, sense-tricking properties at all. Yet how can that be?

Graphics are very good at persuading players new to MMOs that they are in a virtual world. Text is hopeless at this, which is why so few new textual worlds are being played any more. Text has a real problem with system immersion, whereas graphics revels in it.

However, once the players of textual worlds have stuck with it awhile, their imagination kicks in. At this point, text's immersive power rapidly surpasses that of graphics. This is because players' imaginations automatically adapt to give a best-fit match to the world. Do objects cast shadows in a textual world? Yes, they do—if they need to. If such things are important to a player, they will be supplied by their imagination; if they're unimportant, the player will not even notice their omission.

In other words, system immersion and immersive response are *the same thing* when the imagination is doing the rendering.

This isn't intended to be a pro-text rant (I know you won't try a text MUD whatever I say). I'm just using the example of textual worlds to show that immersion is not reliant on the persuasiveness of the environment. You can be immersed where there is no direct sensory stimulation at all.

Come to that, presence isn't quite what it seems, either.

Unfanboied

So, I was given a free collector's edition of *The Lord of the Rings Online: Shadows of Angmar*. Okay, well, I'm given a lot of such freebies, it's no big deal.

Except this time round I was given two copies of the client. Also this time round, my elder daughter was looking to try out an MMO and our week of failed attempts to install *Age of Conan*'s launch patch meant she had to cast her net elsewhere. *LotRO* was convenient, so she went with that.

I decided to play, too. It meant I could more easily defend myself against accusations that I was a *WoW* fanboi.

My daughter made it to level 37 (out of 50, which was the cap at the time) before it finally got too much for her that every level was pretty much the same as the previous level. I, however, soldiered on, and duly reached the top. I thought the name of the quest I did it with was mildly appropriate:

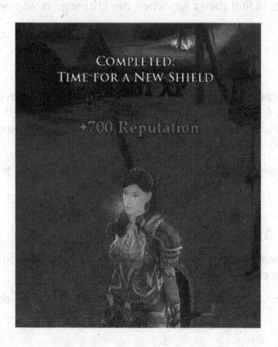

Yes, it's another female paladin captain, but this is what happens when I let my younger daughter create my MMO characters for me.

Unfun?

Patch 3.2 of the *Wrath of the Lich King* expansion to *World of Warcraft* introduced a new boss, Emalon the Stormwatcher, to the Vault of Archavon instance.

What a pain! For a start, you can only get into VoA when your side holds Wintergrasp, and the way the instance locking works you basically only get two shots at it per week (one 10-man regular raid plus one 25-man heroic raid—the latter is where the achiever quote "LFG 25 VoA" came from). The fight itself is a beast. The first five PUGs I tried it with all wiped before they got anywhere, despite multiple attempts.

The sixth, though, was different. We wiped, yes, but in so doing we sensed something: we were good enough to *win* this. We tried again, and again, and on the tenth attempt we took that sucker and his stupid exploding alts *down*. We were elated! Ohhh *yes!* Finally, he was *owned*. **In your face, Emalon!**

Sometimes, people find things fun when the challenge is way, way *above* their ability level.

No Fun?

Prior to the release of its *The Burning Crusade* expansion, the level cap in *World of Warcraft* was 60. The first thing I did when I hit it was to go kill Hogger in Elwynn Forest. He gave me so much grief when I was level 9, he *deserved* it. Ho boy, did it feel good! Muahahaha! **Eat that, Hogger!**

Sometimes, people find things fun when the challenge is way, way *below* their ability level.

Reductio ad Absurdum

Nowadays, it seems, you get to qualify as a griefer simply by doing something more than once that someone else doesn't like.

By that definition, I grief my students by setting them examinations.

Too Real

In the same way that everything on the stage in a theatre is there because someone consciously put it there, every action carried out on the stage is undertaken because someone consciously undertook it. Anything that happens by chance immediately reminds the audience that they're watching a play.

This isn't all there is to it, though. In his famous philosophical study of theater[15], Bert O. States points out that actions carried out on the stage by inanimate objects—clocks, fire, running water—can also snap the audience out of their immersion. This is because the audience members perceive what they see as being (literally!) staged; and as such, it has an aesthetic quality. Working clocks, fire, and water are *too real* to have this feeling of being staged.

Children are also too real. When you see one on stage, you always think how well or badly they act "for a child." You switch from the frame of the play to the frame of the performance. Animals are even worse: no matter how well-trained they are, they don't *know* they're in a play any more than running water does. This, incidentally, is why actors say "never work with children or animals": it's not the fact that they're uncontrollable or scene-stealers, it's that they're illusion-breakers.

MMOs have no problem showing fire or running water; they have no problems showing animals; the only problems they have with children are to do with the range of sizes they can have, which entails a lot of expensive animation work. They do tend to have a problem with clocks, as game time rarely matches real time. Most clocks in today's MMOs are non-functional textures.

Players of MMOs are frequently reminded that they're in MMOs, as *Reality* often intrudes. However, could anything in the *staging* of MMOs ever be considered "too real"?

Personally, I'd like to get to the point where the way MMOs are staged is actually a thing.

---

[15]Bert O. States: *Great Reckonings in Little Rooms: On the Phenomenology of Theater.* University of California Press, 1992.

Two Sides of the Same Coin

In the same way that procedural and declarative semantics are two sides of the same coin, so are Narratology and Ludology.

Narratology looks at games as story, which is to say as statements rather than processes. However, in order to make sense of this, it has to construct a reading—itself a process.

Ludology looks at games as a process—you play them. However, in playing them, you accrue a personal narrative (I've called it a "history" in this book), which is entirely story.

So, you can look at games both in terms of story structure and as the creation of story through action. Which one you choose depends on the reason why you're looking. Narratology can't say a lot about gameplay, but it can still say useful things about what the player experiences. Ludology can speak volumes on gameplay, but is it really the best way to describe look and feel?

That's how the debate finally ended, and it brings us to the present *status quo* (well, the present as I write this—I can't speak for when you read it).

It's not *entirely* over, though. See, if it's useful to describe games in terms of story, might it not be equally useful to describe novels in terms of gameplay? In other words, if you can beneficially use "reading" to describe "play," why not use "play" to describe "reading." We have, indeed, already seen the beginnings of this in Ian Bogost's book, *Unit Operations*[16].

Perhaps Ludologists have as much to offer story as Narratologists have to offer games.

---

[16]Ian Bogost: *Unit Operations: An Approach to Videogame Criticism*. MIT Press, Cambridge MA, 2006.

Third Places

There's a concept in Sociology (first identified by Ray Oldenburg) of *third places*. These are informal gathering spaces such as bars, coffee shops, post offices, and bookstores—places where people go to get away from their first two places (home and work). Third places are public, but neutral ground; people can escape their everyday concerns there, simply enjoying the company and conversation.

One of the perennial questions that people ask about virtual worlds is why they're so compelling. One of the answers that are perennially supplied is that it's because they're third places.

Well yes, they are. That's not why people play them so much though. It can't be: there are plenty of convenient real-world third spaces around that people could use instead of virtual worlds, and many people do indeed prefer them; why don't the ones who play virtual worlds go there? Also, although people do have a need for third places, they don't have that need for several hours a night, every night, for months or years on end.

Besides, it's more complex than that. Sometimes there are third places *within* virtual worlds, such as banks, auction houses, and cantinas. Players go there when they're not questing or grinding or whatever it is they do "normally." Designers have for years deliberately engineered such spaces, giving players a non-compelling reason to visit them, but one that will allow them to dally long enough for social interaction to occur by serendipity.

I guess a sociologist could argue that what starts off as a third place over time becomes a first or second place, which then requires a third place of its own.

Yet people don't play virtual worlds *because* they're a third place—they're just one possible third place among the many available. People play them because of what they can *do* in them.

Reasons to Design

Here are some possible reasons that MMO designers design MMOs. One of them is valid, the rest aren't:

- Purely by accident.
- They wanted a new challenge.
- They get to create what they play.
- They're only obeying orders.
- It's part of their grand scheme for world domination.
- It's fun.
- For the money.

Which do you think is the key one?

Anniversary Achievers

July, 2013: *The Secret World*'s one-year anniversary. It's celebrated by a week-long event across all servers. The event does not go entirely to plan.

Okay, so in *TSW* you progress by getting what they call AP (Ability Points). If you do quests at the time of this event, you can normally rack up about 10 AP an hour. In the celebration event, though, you get 10 AP for participating in the killing of any one of the eight bosses that are roaming the world, or 20 AP if you drank the potion Funcom gave you to double AP gain temporarily. These bosses have 15,000,000 health points and it takes an army of several dozen characters to kill them. Each one only spawns once every few hours; if you miss it, you have to wait. You are not expected to down many. The fights are all about co-operation and organization. They'll bring players together.

So, quite a good event, then?

Hmm.

If you have a friend on your *TSW* friends list, you can issue them a "meetup" request. This takes you to your friend's server. You may have missed the boss on *your* server, but it could still be alive on your friend's. It's also possible to set up a communications channel that players can read from every server.

More hmm...

This is what happened: a cross-server channel ("anniversity") was set up. Spotters were posted on every server. As soon as one of them saw an event boss spawn, they informed the channel and anyone who wanted to kill that boss made the spotter a friend. These (temporary) friends then issued meetup requests, which the spotter accepted. Seconds later, a hundred players had descended on the boss; ten minutes later, it was dead. You could kill five to seven bosses in an hour this way, racking up 50 to 70 AP. There was a two-hour cooldown on the reward for downing each individual boss, so after you'd killed all eight, you either took a turn as a spotter or you switched to an alt and repeated the process. There were regularly 800 people on the anniversity channel. AP were raining on them from the skies.

It wasn't just AP, either. The bosses dropped other stuff, some of which was useless (fireworks, pets) but some of which was not. In particular, they dropped rare signets (which are end-game equipment enhancements) and black bullion (which at the time was *TSW*'s currency for endgame items). My alt wasn't yet qualified for the endgame, but garnered enough black bullion to buy some handy, over-powered gear with it.

It got worse (for Funcom). A ninth boss had been positioned in the middle of one of the PvP zones ("Fusang Projects"). If you wanted what it dropped, you needed to go into the PvP zone for it. PvP was never tremendously popular in *TSW*, so there weren't many PvP servers set up. Suddenly, more people wanted to get into Fusang than it was geared to accept. You could find yourself queuing for six hours to enter Fusang and still have to give up because the queue was more than six hours long.

To fix this queuing issue, Funcom needed a patch. The patch couldn't be implemented until the next Tuesday (patch day)—which was supposed to have marked the end of the anniversary event. Patching in a Fusang fix meant that Funcom had to extend the anniversary event for another week in order to assuage the anger of all the players who still wanted the pet that the ninth boss dropped. As a result, AP continued to rack up in abundance, thereby helping people max out their characters and shortening the length of the elder game.

Ah, achievers.

Paradoxically, the event proved so popular that Funcom now repeats the format several times a year, and doesn't insist you're friends with someone to meet up with them.

Look on it as emergence in action.

Design Flaw

All games have the same design flaw: they can't stop people from not playing by the rules. It's intrinsic to what a "game" is.

As a player, all you can do is stop playing with those people who break the rules.

How do you do that in an MMO, though?

Double Presence

The concept of presence is Boolean: either you're sensing it or you're not. You may have to put in more or less effort to sustain it, but you can't be in a state of "near presence." Either it clicks or it doesn't. A phrase such as "some degree of presence" means you can hold it intermittently, not that you're 75% there.

Similarly, if you're already experiencing presence, you can't experience nested presence. If you're drawing with a pencil, you can feel that the pencil is part of your body; if you're controlling a robot arm, you can feel that the robot arm is part of your body; if you're good enough to use a robot arm to draw with a pencil, then you can feel that the pencil is part of your body, but you can't feel that the robot arm is—it's just part of the mediation process now.

If you go for a walk and have a daydream, can you have a daydream within that daydream? And when the second daydream ends, come back to the first one? No, you can't: you can have a chain of daydreams, but when one ends you don't automatically snap back to where you were in the one that invoked it.

So, imagine you're in an MMO and you come across a place where, several months ago, the lower-level version of yourself had a hard time beating some mob (yes, Hogger, I *do* mean you). You might drift off into a wistful daydream, reminiscing about how you used to wander around here, how everything was fresh and exciting and new, how there was that time you spent ages trying to catch fish but couldn't work out how to do it. Ah, happy days.

Then, you snap out of it. Where are you? Sitting in a chair looking at a computer screen? *No*—you're in a virtual forest on a horse. You had the daydream while in the virtual world—which *you never left*.

If presence alone were necessary to explain immersion, this should be impossible. You shouldn't be able to experience presence while already experiencing presence. Yet in MMOs, you seemingly can. Why are MMOs different?

The answer is that the "you" in "you never left" really is *you*.

Double Flow

On the face of it, flow and immersion look very similar; might it be that they're two ways of looking at the same thing—that what players call "immersion," psychologists call "flow"?

So you're sitting around waiting for the healer to mana up. Are you immersed? Yes. Is this a flow state? No, there's no ability or challenge, you're just waiting.

So you're arguing with your guild mates about last night's wipe. You say the first problem was that the hunter's pet pulled the pat, and the second problem was that the tank engaged the boss before everyone had healed up after the first problem. Are you immersed? Yes. Are you in a flow state? No—you're angry!

So you're moving through a zone and spot a useful herb. You go to pick it, and then spot another, so you go pick that, and you get into a rhythm of finding the herb, killing whatever's guarding it, then looking for another. Only when your bags are full do you notice that you've spent an hour gathering herbs. Were you immersed? Yes. Were you in a flow state? Yes. Are you still immersed? Yes. Are you still in a flow state? No. You just came out of a flow state; flow states don't nest, so how can you still be in one?

You can experience fun without flow; you can experience flow while having fun. Flow is *not the same thing* as fun.

You can experience immersion without flow; you can experience flow while immersed. Flow is *not the same thing* as immersion.

Can you experience immersion without fun? Can you experience fun without immersion? In general, yes: immersion and fun are *not the same thing*, either.

However, in MMOs at least, what you find fun depends on the degree to which you are immersed, and the degree to which you are immersed depends on what you find fun. They're in a symbiotic relationship.

People play MMOs to become immersed, not to experience flow. If you want to experience flow, do a 1,500-piece jigsaw puzzle.

Story

There are three kinds of story in computer games:

- History
- Backstory
- Narrative.

That's what I call them, anyway. The player creates the first one, and the designer the other two.

Norms as Rules

There are plenty of things which, if everyone did it, would ruin an MMO.

If everyone were a loot ninja, people wouldn't group because of the unfairness; if everyone were a gold farmer, there'd be no-one to sell gold to; if everyone used exploits in a battleground, the battlegrounds would only contain people who thought one-shotting and being one-shotted was fun.

If there's a dominant strategy, then either everyone uses it or everyone agrees not to use it. If it's no fun when everyone uses it, then social norms develop not to use it. If one person breaks ranks, then everyone has to break ranks—which means less fun for everyone except conceivably the one who broke ranks.

If *you're* the one who broke ranks, expect to be called a griefer. Saying "the game let me do it" will not save you.

Core Belief

Personally, I believe that there's a core sense of identity that holds a personality together; I don't see the human mind as being an onion that you can peel the layers off until there's nothing left. Sooner or later you hit something irreducible.

People can easily believe their own lies; MMOs allow them to believe their own truths.

Levels of Immersion

People who play MMOs over time gain progressively deeper levels of immersion.

We have two entities involved: a player (human being) and a character (in-world object). How the former regards the latter is a measure of immersion.

The lowest level is *unimmersed*. An unimmersed person regards the virtual object associated with them as just that: an object. It's like a data file or a word processor document—something you manipulate in order to achieve some end, nothing more.

Next up is *avatar*-level immersion. Here, the player regards the virtual object as a distinct personality—the player's *representative* in the MMO. The player will refer to the avatar in the third person ("he was attacked by an orc"), almost as if it were capable of independent thought. This maintains a distance between player and object; it's as if the player accepts there is a connection between the two, but doesn't want to admit to anything beyond that.

Sooner or later, the player acknowledges that the in-world object they control is, in some sense, a reflection of their own self: this is *character*-level immersion. A character is the player's *representation* in the MMO—a personality that the player wears. It can be referred to in either the third person or the first person ("I was attacked by an orc").

Finally, we have *persona*-level immersion. This is the player *in* the MMO. There's no distinction between player and virtual object, they're one and the same. You're not role-playing a being, you *are* that being; you're not projecting a self, you *are* that self. There's no indirection, no filtering: *you* are *there*.

Persona-level is as deep as it gets; it's sometimes called "full immersion." Players will always use the first person when fully immersed, except when referring to a particular alt. After all, if that really *is* them in the virtual world, it would be weird not to.

Advergaming

Oh gawd, please no.

At first when people wanted to make money from web site content, they did it by charging a subscription. That didn't work because who wants to pay a subscription for every single web site they ever visit? These days, unless the content is very good or very specialized or very pornographic, web sites get income from advertising instead. Hey, if it works for Google.

What about MMOs? Who wants to pay a subscription for every single one of those they ever play? Well, several million *WoW* players, obviously, but who else? Surely the thing to do is to make your MMO free and support it with commercials?

No no no no no!

Okay, so if the ad is *in context*, it can work. It can even promote immersion. You're playing in an MMO set in 1920s New England, you walk into a grocery store and see a prominent sign for Del Monte canned peaches: that's fine, it makes sense. What do you care if Del Monte paid for the sign in real life? If the shop sold a range of virtual objects with a gameplay purpose to them, you may not even notice it was an ad at all. They had Del Monte canned peaches in 1920s New England.

However, if it's a sign for a Nissan QASHQAI all mode 4x4® then you're not in a 1920s world any more, you're in the real world and you're not happy. *Out-of-context* ads are A Bad Thing.

Many MMOs have ads in them naturally. Players sell things to each other in-world, and they shout out ads for those in-world products. This is fine, it's what you'd expect. If the ads are for out-of-world products, though, that's when the problems start. It's not an issue for those social worlds that are integrated into *Reality* anyway, but in game worlds (MMOs) it can be immersion-busting. You really don't want to see an ad for the latest Brad Pitt movie when you're in the mood to slaughter orcs, whether it appears discreetly to one side of your interface, is posted politely on a nearby wall, or shows as an interstitial while you're switching between servers or characters. You just want to kill orcs, dammit! And no, not orcs with Brad Pitt's face!

Even if the ads are witty, intelligent, and amusing, they'll still annoy. They'll annoy so much that players will consider paying *not* to see them. At that point, the operators will set up ad-free servers that people pay a different way to access. This then leads to the ludicrous situation in which advertisers pay for their product to be shown to people in order to make those people pay to avoid seeing them.

Oh, and they hate the advertiser for spoiling their fun, too.

In-context ads are fine. How do you know Del Monte didn't pay me to use their name as an example, back there? I could have chosen Kellogg's cornflakes or Campbell's soup. It was in context, so you didn't notice it. *That's* how ads should work in virtual worlds.

Except, maybe if you saw the *same* damned logo *everywhere*, or ads on *every* available surface… In-context can become out-of-context if overdone.

Still, I trust our advertisers to be restrained.

Yes, that was sarcasm.

Believe it or not, in the olde days *developers* used to have to pay *advertisers* to use their brands. If you wanted an in-game sports ground to feature realistic marketing boards, you had to hand over cash to have those boards show real-life brand names.

How Times Change.

Preference

It's small wonder that people prefer the stories they get from playing games to the stories they get from reading books or watching movies.

In a game, through play, you make your own story, personal to you, with a meaning personal to you.

With books and movies, you're trying to divine scraps of relevance to your own existence through subjective identification or objective analysis.

Unrealistic Worlds

Here are just some of the things that a time-travelling player of an early text MUD would find laughable about (to take an example) *Lord of the Rings Online*: .

- If I kill some orc and it was carrying a sword, why was it hitting me with a stick?

- The only way to be a Scholar is if I'm also a Farmer and a Metalworker? Uh?

- Why do all the NPCs wear the same clothes when it rains as they do when it's sunny?

- These troublesome animals you want me to kill don't actually seem all that threatening...

- How come I suffer morale damage when I fall off Weathertop? Did I somehow "flee in fear" before I hit the ground?

- I can walk through people? And horses? But I don't fall through my own horse when I sit on it?

- Didn't I see you depart with the Fellowship from Rivendell not ten minutes ago, Legolas? Why are you back here issuing mundane quests?

- You can dye metal armor? But you can't paint it? But you can paint the walls of your house? But not walls in general?

- Why do I merely suffer morale failure but the bad guys suffer death?

- In the middle of a fight, time stopped and these combo buttons appeared—just the same as what happens in real life fights...

- Flowers appear to be every bit as open at night as they are in daylight.

- Why, when I salute, does it say I salute smartly? I wanted to salute bitterly.

- What's with this "make it look as if I'm wearing these clothes when I'm actually wearing *these* clothes" system? Either you're wearing plate mail or you're not!

- How come those bad guys aren't running to stop me killing their buddies? I can see them—why can't they see me? And does this sword come with a silencer, so they can't hear it striking armor?

- So... you let people wander around called Arraggorrnn?

Okay, so I am such a time-traveler, which is why I've mentioned some of these already. Don't pretend you don't have something similar in your own MMO of choice, though. The question is, why don't you actually *care* about such discrepancies?

Story as History

History is the (re)telling of an inter-related sequence of episodes. In games, these episodes encapsulate how the interactions between player and game unfolded. Players perceive history at a personal level, both within a single playing of the game and across several playings of it. It's the best kind of story for players because it means interesting and important things happened to them.

If a player has no history, that means nothing interesting happened in the game (and therefore that it was useless). Designers, of course, want interesting things to happen because then interesting choices have to be made. They want games that players, having played them, can recount to each other. They therefore try to arrange for events to occur in a compelling sequence, so as to enhance the player's experience. As for what that compelling sequence *is*, well that's another, er, story...

All good games enable history. *Tetris* enables history. Yes, it's an abstract, single-player game you always ultimately lose; nevertheless, if you'd just played a game you could excitedly tell someone else how you got a string of T-shapes and S-shapes one after the other and you built like this tower thing and they just kept on coming but you'd managed to keep space for a single straight piece and you were hoping one was going to show but it was all T-shapes and S-shapes and then finally, just as you were almost at the top, you saw one in the queue, flipped it in the split-second after it as it came out, then shunted it to the edge, dropped it into its slot and took our four rows at once.

That's a history. A game design embodies an indefinitely large set of possible events, a player threads their own path through them, and that path—that *history*—is their tale.

Pulling Up the Ladder

Many people who organize pick-up groups that result in a recorded achievement will only accept people into their group who already have that achievement.

Achievers apparently don't do irony.

Player IDs

Even though players can't look forward to being able to move their characters freely between game worlds any time soon, that doesn't mean that *some* data can't be transferred. They may not like it, though.

Suppose that all the major MMO developers hated one another to distraction. Is there anything about which they may nevertheless still feel able to co-operate? Well, yes there is—actually, there are several things. One of them, though, is preparing and sharing lists of problem players.

The main requirement for this would be some formal industry body (which we need anyway) that could act as honest broker to provide yes/no answers to "has this credit card been banned by another member of the scheme before?" The organization would need to have the right to withhold information from developers, though, because, well, developers are gamers, and some might be tempted to exploit the situation (say, by listing their most profitable players as problems so that other MMOs won't take them if they try to leave).

I'm sure there are hideously complex data protection laws in the EU that would make this kind of system a nightmare, but the USA seems somewhat less worried about such matters as far as I can tell.

If we have credit reference agencies, why not player reference agencies?

Everyone loves a blacklist!

Intention in Griefing

Intention is important in griefing. If someone ninja-loots because they need what they looted, that's just plain theft. If someone ninja-loots something useless to them because they know *you* desperately want it, they know how mad you'll be that they took it, and they get a kick out of knowing they've made you mad—*that's* griefing.

Not Present, Not Correct

Psychologists have looked into MMOs as exemplifying a kind of what they call *presence*, but (like so much theorizing about computer games) have usually done it to support their general theories, rather than to develop theories specific to MMOs from the actual evidence.

We're never going to understand what's going on while this kind of attitude prevails, but until psychologists find what happens in MMOs interesting enough to study for its own sake, things aren't going to change.

Interference

Back in the olde days of ye *MUD*, wizzes could drop mobiles anywhere they liked. Sometimes, where they liked was on top of or close to player characters.

This is something that works well *if* the players involved are up for it. Sometimes they're not. If they're not, they tend to regard it as interference in their play.

Wizzes could also attach to a mobile and control its movements (i.e., play as the mobile). They could therefore make it behave differently from usual—more cleverly or unpredictably, say. Again, this is something that works well *if* the players involved are up for it. If not, they regard it as a form of cheating.

Of course, if players who don't like interference aren't aware that it *is* interference, they can't complain. If the mobile concerned could conceivably have done everything on its own, it looks more like bad luck than a wiz's attempt to brighten up a dull period of play.

Unfortunately, what to some players is a dull period is to other players a nice relaxing flow experience. Generally, therefore, it's not a good idea to allow privileged players or admins to interfere surreptitiously with the way an MMO works automatically unless the player being interfered with explicitly requests it.

Unrealistic

The less work the brain has to do to sustain the illusion that a virtual environment is real, the easier it becomes to do so, and therefore the more persuasive that environment is.

This is why graphical worlds beat textual worlds. You look at a picture, and the processing power of your visual cortex effortlessly converts it into a scene inside your head. You don't have to think about it because your in-head hardware can just *do* it.

This doesn't mean you see everything uncritically, of course. If something looks wrong, it will jar; jarring breaks immersion. Having been jarred, you have to decide whether you wish to override the jarring and accept what you saw as fiction, or to find some way to switch it off, or to stop playing because it's really *too* irritating to dismiss.

Most of the time, people will choose to ignore it when they see something that doesn't make sense. However, this puts an extra load on them: they have to filter out the things that don't make sense before these reach the conscious mind and jar it.

For example, many MMOs have lax collision detection. You put on a sword, and it cuts through your cloak as you run; you make a potion, and your staff goes right through your head as you do so; you rear up your horse, and your feet stick out from its belly. The first time you saw it, you were surprised; now, you just ignore it.

These are differences at the level of visual processing. They can, however, lead to differences at the cognitive level. For example, you can ride through creatures so big that you can see their (hollow) insides, but you get caught on a tiny branch of a tree—that can't be right, can it? You can swim across a river and emerge looking exactly the same as you did before you got wet. You can stop running part-way down a flight of stairs and notice you're floating slightly above them.

These differences are more problematical because they rub up against logic. You can jump higher than a person's head but not over this waist-high wall— why is that? Well obviously it's because the designer doesn't want you to jump over the wall, but why in fiction terms is it impossible? It makes no sense. You have to will yourself not to notice if you're to continue playing.

There are similar issues entirely at the cognitive level. Where are all the doors? Surely, if you had the slightest idea of security whatsoever, you'd have doors in your building so you could, you know, **lock people out**. You might also notice that 25 meters away down the corridor, right where they can **see and hear** the massive fight you're having with their friends, is a bunch of orcs just standing and watching. Perhaps they're making sure that their pet worg has a **pair of plate mail boots** hidden about its person, so that when it dies you'll have something to loot? Naturally, these boots will be a perfect fit for the first humanoid to wear them, whether male or female, tall or short, human or **cloven-hoofed cow person**.

All these anomalies gradually chip away at the persuasiveness of an MMO's environment. You have to accept each one as it is, even though your mind is telling you, "eek, that's not what I'm used to!"

Back in the textual world's days, having a degree of verisimilitude was regarded as a selling point. If you swam across a river, not only did you get wet, but **all your biscuits turned to mush**. The word used to describe things that didn't make sense was *unrealistic*. People would say things such as, "dragons shouldn't be able to use bows, it's unrealistic."

Now given that dragons themselves are (spoiler alert!) imaginary creatures, it would perhaps seem rather moot to decry their archery skills as "unrealistic." However, it's not. Given a world in which dragons do exist, their anatomy is such that taking aim with a bow would be next to impossible.

In the real world, everything conforms to the same set of physics. This is so ingrained in your understanding of the world that you don't have to think about it. Let go of an egg, and it's going to fall and go splat. You have a working model of real-world physics that you can use predictively without a passing thought.

If an MMO conforms to this physics, you can use the same model: this helps persuade you that the MMO is a real place—it reflects the physics. If it doesn't, and it jars, then that impedes immersion. *This* is what players meant by "unrealistic."

Morbid Griefing

There's an argument that, if you take an emotive word and you apply it to things which are not quite at the intensity it describes, then that will cause those other things to be regarded with the same strength of alarm as the primary case and people will treat that equally emotively. Society will therefore be the better for it.

For example, in MMOs the strict, formal definition of *griefing* is very strong. People do *not* want to be accused of being a griefer! By widening the term to apply to less intense but still socially undesirable activities, it could be argued that people will realize that these are unacceptable, too. As a result, they'll stop acting like jerks and MMOs will be much more pleasant environments.

Unfortunately, this has the effect of diluting the original meaning of the word. In real life, the definition of *obese* was extended to include people who were merely overweight, so as to shock them into exercising in preference to being labeled "obese." This did not last long, though: after a while, people began to regard "obese" to mean the same thing as "overweight," rather than the other way round. Nowadays, doctors and dieticians have to talk about *morbidly obese* to capture the meaning *obese* once had.

If you have a powerful word and over-apply it, it loses its power.

Maybe we'll have to talk about *morbid griefing* before people will understand what we once meant by the term.

A Bit of a Gamble

In MMOs, you kill things and they drop stuff. Most of the time what they drop is rubbish, but sometimes you get something unexpectedly valuable. Usually, the harder the mobs are to kill, the greater the chance you'll get something good from them, but it's still a bit of a gamble as to whether you'll get anything good or not.

Is it an *actual* gamble, though? There are lots of laws about gambling. The USA pretty well bans it over the Internet, for example. Should MMOs such as WoW be subject to anti-gambling laws because they use this kind of game mechanic?

What about the case of the Chinese MMO *ZT Online*? In that game, there are chests that, when you open them, sometimes have something really good in them and sometimes don't. You can *buy* those chests for real money, one at a time. Indeed, you can buy the chest and open it in a single click. It's like pulling the handle on a slot machine.

To me, the above looks a lot more like gambling than does WoW's system of loot tables. In WoW's end-game, you're killing bosses in the hope that they'll drop the item you want, but the time taken to do it and the fact that you may not succeed in even getting to the boss is enough to make sure players don't get into a gambling flow. In the leveling game, players will rarely (if ever) kill monsters repeatedly in the hope of getting a rare drop—they just want the XP so they can move to the next quest. You can definitely get into a flow state with the *ZT Online* example, but whether anti-gambling laws take such things into account is another matter.

I'm sure there's a definition of "gambling" somewhere that could cover just about any transaction.

Explorers

Players who try to find out as much as they can about an MMO are called *explorers*. They usually begin with the topology (*breadth*) of the world, then gradually move on to its physics (*depth*).

Explorers say things such as:

- Hmm...
- How come this basilisk dropped two spines?
- Well, yes—why wouldn't you be able to do that?
- Try pulling the fire elemental through the waterfall.

Explorers know more about an MMO than any other kind of player. They probably know more than the designer, come to that...

Story Structure

Stories are not merely ordered sets of sentences: stories have structure. The earliest recorded recognition of this is courtesy of Aristotle, who proposed that stories have three acts: a beginning, a middle, and an end. He took more words to say it than that, but the full, lumbering quote is rarely given so as to spare the reader. I shall follow this convention; you can thank me later.

Aristotle also identified the difference between events as they *occurred* and events as they are *reported*, which is a little less obvious. It's a particularly useful observation in understanding game narratives because, although players *experience* a sequence of events, they don't list every last one when recounting their experiences to other people—they only mention the interesting ones, plus those relevant to explaining the interesting ones. This is what makes player stories histories, rather than transcripts.

A couple of thousand years after Aristotle, modern literature's take on this began with English novelist E. M. Forster in 1927. He drew a distinction between *story* and *plot*. A story, he suggested, was a chronological sequence of events ("the king died and then the queen died"); a plot is the causal structure that connects events ("the king died and then the queen died of grief"). In a classic narrative, you read the story and discern the plot.

Games are not like this. In a game, you play the plot and discern the story.

A student of literature could regard the playing of a computer game as the unfolding of a story through play. This is perfectly valid: the story in question is that of the player, their *history*. However, this unfolding is not achieved through the following of a narrative, it's achieved through the following of a plot. Actions have consequences: they cause events. Players undertake actions, therefore they cause events to occur; in so doing, they create multiple fragments of plot; they favor those that advance the narrative.

Is this narrative predetermined? In some sense, it must be at least partly so because the game's design limits what can occur. Is the *plot* predetermined, though?

Okay, well at this point we run into some minor problems because game designers tend to mix up their vocabulary (and yes, as a fully paid-up game designer, I'm guilty of this myself, too). When designers talk of a "plot," they invariably mean one of two things: a goal ("rescue the monarch's child") or a *fixed* plot ("kill the ogre to get the sword to defeat the dragon to rescue the monarch's child"). The former isn't a plot *per se*, but it implies that players will have to create a plot through their actions in order to achieve it. The latter is a predetermined plot because it's in some sense already written.

Games only really *need* the first of these, but the second can help give direction. In the general case, a game's plot doesn't have to be fixed as it will be created on the fly by the player through their actions. When this occurs—as it must in every game—gameplay provides the challenges, conflicts, and decisions that the player drives through as plot, and which in the retelling becomes story (history). The "plot" here is created organically through the chaining together of the player's decisions.

A fixed plot (a game may have a small set of these) lies on top of this stratum. It can be there to add context, or to provide goals, or for its revealing of the narrative to be the goal. Whether a game *has* such a plot is for the designer to decide. Something like *Tetris* does not have—nor need—a fixed plot: it's all at the level of "here's my goal, let's see what I can do to achieve it." On the other hand, a game like *Pillars of Eternity* has a strong fixed plot: it's at the level of "if I do this and I do that then I'll find out what to do next."

Much of the conflict between ludologists and narratologists arises because they misinterpret each other's terms.

My opinion: games *are* different from literature, but that doesn't mean literature's tools can't be repurposed to help in the understanding of games.

What are the Odds?

Some MMOs have lockboxes as a money-making system. These are either normal drops that you need a paid-for-using-real-currency key to open, or they're boxes you need to pay to obtain in the first place. They may have something very valuable in them, but then again they may not.

This looks like gambling. Normally, though, gambling regulations require the house to state your odds of winning. MMOs tend to say *what* you can win, but not the actual chance you actually *will* win. Is that... right?

Collusion in Banality

The majority of attempts to make MMOs interesting are not recognized as such by most players. What most players want is for their MMO to be exactly the same as the first MMO they got into, only better. The more deviation an MMO exhibits from the first one that they got into, as it was when they got into it, the less likely they are to accept it.

There are two tragedies associated with this:

- Most players are doomed never to find the MMO they want because they aren't willing to accept the changes that would make it the world they want it to be.

- Most new MMOs are doomed to be evolutionary rather than revolutionary.

I worry that some of the improvements that are being touted as solutions to boredom are only going to make things worse. I have no doubt that procedurally-generated content will be fun—hey, I enjoyed playing *Rogue* myself—but it seriously dulls what MMOs are about. Likewise, trained puppet-masters performing for the benefit of rapt crowds will be fun—hey, I enjoyed *D&D* myself—but this merely papers over the cracks.

The best—and in the end, the *only*—solution is to make the MMO itself such an interesting and richly interactive place that the reason you'd want to repeat the consumption of a piece of content was that you liked it so much you want to try it again. Hey, I enjoy chocolate myself!

3 Acts

Screenwriter Robert McKee's summarized Aristotle's three-act structure as follows:

- Act 1. Get your hero up a tree.
- Act 2. Throw rocks at him.
- Act 3. Bring him down.

Okay, so as plans go this works but it's fairly simple.

What do you suppose: are there story structures with a bit more detail than this?

MMOs from the Inside Out

Non-MMO Immersion

If you read a good novel or watch a good movie, you can find yourself strongly identifying with the protagonist. If the feeling is strong enough, you can project yourself into the fictional world as if you were watching events unfold before your own eyes. You may, if you try hard, even imagine you *are* the protagonist for a short while.

However, it's only fleeting. The protagonist may be a cipher for you, but it's clearly *not* you: you have no control over what happens next, except insofar that if you don't turn the page, then it won't happen. If you do imagine yourself to be Cathy out of *Wuthering Heights*, then you're her only while the text is paused. When the text moves on, you can feel what she feels, but you can't *be* her.

In MMOs, the fully-immersed player *is* their character: your persona is both you and your character as one—*identity*, not identification.

Academics who have never played an MMO enough to experience full immersion, yet who nevertheless feel qualified to write on the subject, invariably seem to stop at character-level immersion. They don't understand that there's a level *beyond* this. As a result, we get all kinds of pontificating that's based on a false premise.

Immersion isn't about fooling the mind into believing the body is some place it's not: it's about the *mind* being somewhere it's not—somewhere it can be *itself*.

Another World

Imagine a pointillist MMO, in which all objects were made of equally-sized spheres that interacted with one another using gravity-like forces.

How long would you be able to play in such a world before you went back to an MMO with a more standard appearance?

Why?

Story as Narrative

Narrative is a predefined storyline that players follow—it's what most people mean when they say "story" in reference to games. It often comes with a back-story, and its primary use is as fictional cover to link (or separate) thematic parts of gameplay—providing new goals that follow the resolution of old ones. Its secondary use, which is the one that players notice more, is to keep them immersed and engaged.

Games don't have to have just one narrative; they can have multiple, overlapping narratives—plots and subplots, soap-opera style. There will nevertheless usually only be one main plot, though, which determines the overall pace.

Also, narratives don't have to be linear, they can branch—leading to multiple endings, depending on what the player does. That said, if they do branch, it can rapidly become very difficult for the designer to keep each branch under control as their number increases exponentially. For this reason, branches tend to collect towards the end of an "episode," as each loose end is tied up until only one (that of the main narrative thread) remains. These comings-together are known as *plot points*, and they can best be observed in quest-based RPGs. Typically, in between plot points players have a good deal of freedom to act as they see fit, but if they want to progress, then eventually they'll have to pass through the next plot point. This is sometimes marked with a formal change of "chapter" or a cut scene, as in the *Baldur's Gate* RPGs (which I mention often because I happen to adore them). Such an arrangement is sometimes described as a *string of pearls*, with the pearls representing areas of narrative freedom and the points where they touch representing the plot points on the (narrative) thread.

Branching narratives add to a game's *replay value* because, if you miss content in one playing, then you can encounter it on a subsequent occasion. They also allow multiple solutions to a problem, so if a player gets stuck with one approach, they can try another. Furthermore, players can individually choose to experience the particular kind of content that they themselves prefer— perhaps deciding to try a diplomatic approach to a crisis instead of a violent one. This means they'll have more fun because they choose what to do precisely for the reason that it *is* fun (for them).

Content is expensive to create, however, so designers don't like to over-produce it. Besides, even from a gameplay-only point of view, it can be a bad thing. If there is too much content, (or at least too much that the player sees at once), this can lead to a condition known as *quest fatigue* in which players go from branch to successive branch with no end in sight and manage to get both bored and frustrated at the same time (thereby demonstrating that a game can simultaneously be no fun at the level of individual quests and unfun at the level of the quest chain—and causing major problems for people who explain fun in terms of uniplanar flow).

Letter from the Future

With *60 seconds of gameplay*, you find out what the players are spending their time doing. With *letter from the future*, you find out whether it's fun.

Here's the conceit: you imagine that development of your MMO is complete and it's been running for six months; your future self sends your present self a letter explaining what you (as a player) did in the MMO last night. Your aim is to identify what you did that was memorable and fun, and why.

Letters from the future are pretty good for the way they can help a designer to think through their planned MMO's atmosphere. Their main purpose, though, is as a check that the MMO's gameplay is sufficient to sustain it. If you can't think of anything that you'd want to enthuse about, well, the chances are there *is* nothing. If you have to try persuade yourself that something not all that interesting is interesting, again, you're just clutching at straws.

What a letter from the future is asking is: what's the player's story? Or, to be more precise: what's their *history*? Histories are built of interesting events; if a history is sparse, what does that say about how much the player enjoyed playing?

NPCs with Personality

If you go back to text MUDs, players had much more emotional engagement with some NPCs (and even some non-humanoid mobiles). You don't need human controllers or well-designed quests to do it—we had it in *MUD1*, where certain mobiles (such as, yes, the goat) were able to cause apoplexy in even the calmest individuals by their behavior.

In *WoW*, the only NPC that came remotely close to this was Hogger, but of course *WoW* doesn't have permanent death, so the effects of being ganked are merely tedious rather than gut-wrenching.

Nevertheless, as I *may* have mentioned with great enthusiasm before, the first thing I did when I made the then level cap of 60 was to go back and kill Hogger.

Realistic Worlds

Earlier, I pointed at some of the things that *LotRO* does and declared that players of old text MUDs would have considered them a joke. The reason for this is that the things I listed (and I could have listed many more) would have been regarded as being *unrealistic*.

Text MUDs prided themselves on their *realisticness* (note: this isn't the same as *realism*—and yeah, I expect I will explain the difference later). MUDs that let you fight two opponents at once would mock ones in which you could only fight one-on-one; ones that allowed bags within bags within bags would mock ones that had no bags at all; ones that doused the flames of your torch when you swam across a river would mock ones that kept it burning brightly. Realisticness kept up an evolutionary pressure on design (or at the very least a reason to maintain standards). In comparison to yesterday's MUDs, today's MMO are not very realistic at all.

I chose *LotRO* as my example because in some aspects it goes out of its way to be realistic. Its landscapes are rendered to look like real landscapes, it doesn't have cartoon-style avatars, its geography is consistent, and it uses a covering fiction for concepts such as fast travel and death. Why does it not carry this through, though?

Socializers

Players who treat an MMO as a context for interaction with other players are called *socializers*. The virtual world's goings-on give them something to talk about.

Communication is very important to socializers. They say things such as:

- Have you heard? Nilrem's left the guild!
- Gratz!!!
- He's not mad at you, he just wants some time to himself.
- /dance

Socializers are the most obvious in-world expression of an MMO's *community*.

Cognitive Dissonance

The social psychologist Leon Festinger introduced the concept of *cognitive dissonance* in 1956[17].

Cognitive dissonance is what happens when individuals hold two or more contradictory views at the same time. Festinger formulated the notion when studying a group of individuals who profoundly believed that the world would end before dawn on December 21st, 1954. Come daybreak, the cultists couldn't reconcile their unshakeable faith that it *would* end with the undeniable evidence that it *hadn't* ended.

Most cognitive dissonance is not quite at this level of disparity. However, it happens all the time in real life. People who eat too much know that overeating is bad for their health, but they keep on over-eating anyway; they try to reduce the dissonance either by underplaying the health risks or by underplaying the degree to which they over-eat—a process known as *rationalization*.

Killers

Players who enjoy imposing themselves on other players are called *killers*. This is because most of them get their kicks from griefing, but there are some (e.g., many guild leaders) who impose through kindness rather than unkindness.

Killers (of the griefer persuasion) say things such as:

- HA!
- Die!
- n00b
- pwned!!1!

They are often people of few words.

---

[17]Leon Festinger: *When Prophecy Fails.* University of Minnesota Press, 1956.

In Defense of Psychologists

It may seem that I'm giving psychologists a bad time here, griping about their lack of understanding about immersion in MMOs. They haven't done anything actually wrong, though.

Psychologists study many phenomena, not just MMOs. I know, I know, it's their loss, but that's how things are. Their tools are therefore adapted to handle a wide range of topics. Their concept of "immersion" has to work for many situations—books, cultures, work—as well as for (the relative latecomers) MMOs. They need a universal theory, not one that only applies to a particular kind of computer game.

If you look at it like this, a generic definition is a perfectly reasonable and rational idea.

What's not reasonable is when such a generic definition is conflated with the more particular definition that players use, and false assertions are made as a result. This does sometimes happen when a rogue, non-gamer psychologist sees the opportunity for a quick publication. It's unfair to slag off psychologists in general for this, though! They do tend to know their stuff.

Oh, except when it comes to games and violence. Most of the ones who study that are laboring under a monumental misapprehension.

Floyd, RIP

Yes, I know the above heading reveals what previously I only mentioned behind a spoiler alert, but is there really anyone who doesn't read on after a spoiler alert anyway?

One reason why Floyd was such a memorable character in *Planetfall* was that he was so well written.

Another reason is that he did something he knew would kill him, in order that the player might live.

What makes him *really* stick, though, is that the player was helpless to stop him. No matter what the player did, if they wanted to win, then Floyd had to die. Floyd's death was a plot point. It was a *narrative* conceit, not a *gameplay* decision.

Now it *could* have been a gameplay decision. The way the story was set up, the entire population of the planet was held in cryogenic suspension awaiting the day that their computers found a cure for the plague which would have killed them all if they hadn't taken this radical action. You *could* have been asked to decide between taking Floyd with you or sending him to his death in order to save the lives of the millions of people who would otherwise perish when the planet blew up (oh yeah, I should have said: the planet was close to blowing up).

However, you never got the choice. Floyd took it upon *himself* to end his life that others might live. It was the sheer inability of the player to act, at the one point (in a game that was otherwise all about action) where you *really wanted* to act, that gave Floyd's self-martyrdom the incredible power it had.

This isn't about what you can do with narrative, nor even about what you can do with game. This is about what you can do with *design*, and *that's* what makes *Planetfall*'s climax so breathtaking for designers.

Adaptive AI

One of the more popular ideas for the use of artificial intelligence in computer games concerns *adaptive AI*. This is the suggestion that the game adjusts its gameplay to ensure that it's always commensurate with players' abilities; I described one aspect of this, *dynamic difficulty adjustment*, earlier. I mentioned that I loathe it.

I hate it for single-player computer games, whether it's rubber-banding for racing cars or having itinerant bandits armored like dreadnaughts in RPGs. I particularly despise the idea for MMOs, though.

Here's why: basically, players get no real sense of progression if, no matter how skilled or unskilled they are, the bad guys *always feel the same*. A super-powerful character can't go killing low-level monsters for the sheer joy of watching them go down with a single hit because the AI will "learn" that they are having too easy a time of it and boost the monster's stats to make it more of a fight. The character didn't *want* a fight, though—they wanted to let off some steam. Similarly, a low-level character going up against a boss is basically training the AI to lower the boss's stats until the fight is at the right difficulty level.

What players need is for monsters to be reasonably *static* in their degree of difficulty. This doesn't mean mobs have to be stupid, or that they all have to have the same AI. What it does mean is that they should behave consistently. If they don't behave consistently, players can't tell whether they (the players) are improving or not. Being level X is meaningless if you only ever see opponents of level X +/- 2. *Mobs* can learn and adapt to how you're fighting them, sure—they can even level up from their victims' deaths—but only until they get killed; then, they should respawn reinitialized, and need to learn all over again. Adaptive AI isn't really about mobs, though: it's about the virtual world *itself* as an intelligent entity.

I don't care whether this is for individuals or for instances: such tinkering is equivalent to making the MMO adapt to the player, rather than the other way round. AI gets genuinely exciting when it's used for controlling discrete NPCs, but that's not what's happening here; it's like having an intelligent universe. "Oh dear, poor Johnny wandered into the swamp and can't move very fast, I'll just reduce the viscosity of the mire in his location so he can speed up a bit." It's the same kind of thing. Johnny shouldn't have wandered into the swamp in the first place, but by helping him out, he doesn't know that.

As for the effects when several players try to interact with the same object, dynamic difficulty is really going to make things look weird to some of them.

While doing some consultancy for a major MMO in about 2001, I was asked whether I thought this was a good idea. I said at the time that it was a very bad idea, and I stick by that. If your skill level doesn't count for anything, why bother learning?

For educational worlds, okay, adjusting the content to match ability could be a hit. For fun, though? I think *I* know what I'll find fun right now better than your AI does.

Innovate!

Humans are great at pattern-matching, in games as much as anything else. It can happen at any level:

- **System**. "This new, genre-based battle system for the Android is like *Top Trumps* all over again."

- **Gameplay**. "Hey, this combat system is basically the same as the one in *Top Trumps*."

- **Mechanics**. "This bartering system works the same way as *Top Trumps* except there are more properties and they have a linear distribution over a smaller number of values."

- **Skin**. "This *Twilight* edition of *Top Trumps* is just like the *Buffy* edition, except it sets feminism back two decades instead of forward one."

Believe it or not, this means that if you use the same ideas over and over again in games, people will grok them and grow tired of them.

Innovate!

Story as Backstory

Backstory is what is supposed to have happened before the start of a game. It's not absolutely essential, but most computer games do have one.

There's often confusion between backstory and history. Backstory is actually *prehistory*—it describes events that occurred prior to the start of play, giving the game its explanatory context.

There are two main reasons for backstory: the official reason and the unofficial reason (also known as the "real reason").

The official reason for backstory is that it adds richness and depth. It can establish the overall goal of the player and can aid in making a game (or game world) more *immersive*.

The unofficial reason is to make illogical features of the game seem logical:

> **Player**: Why can't I see any citizens or peasants?
>
> **Backstory**: Because the gods make them invisible.
>
> **Player**: So why can't I see their shadows?
>
> **Backstory**: Those are invisible, too.
>
> **Player**: Then why don't I hear or smell them?
>
> **Backstory**: Because they're inaudible and, er, inscentible.
>
> **Player**: Why don't I bump into them when I move?
>
> **Backstory**: They keep out of your way.
>
> **Player**: Why can't I see them pick stuff up?
>
> **Backstory**: Look, do you want to play this game or not?

Ideally, if you're going to have backstory, then that backstory should come first; it should not merely patch awkward programming or gameplay problems.

Not all backstory is about describing past events; some simply decrees how the world works. This kind is referred to as the *fiction*. Why can't I cast fireballs while wearing plate mail? Well the fiction is that iron interferes with arcane magic. The fact, however, is that if you could, then everyone would be a battlemage and all sense of class balance would be out the window…

Wood, Trees, Trees, Wood

There is a debate current among Game Study theorists concerning the difference between research undertaken by personally playing games compared to that undertaken by observing people playing games. In the former, the danger is that you can't see the wood for the trees; in the latter, the danger is that can't see the trees for the wood.

I personally have a foot in both camps: I criticize most of those who don't play for not having a full appreciation of the details, yet I also criticize most of those who do play for not having a full appreciation of the abstract. This is because, as a designer, I have to understand *both* the details *and* the abstract if I'm to create a coherent whole.

The way it goes, though, if you study games enough, then eventually you don't need to play them to make sense of them—you just need to have played enough of something similar that you can grok it.

The Charging Moose

In 2007, a 12-year-old Norwegian boy called Hans Jørgen Olsen was out walking in a forest with his 10-year-old sister when she was charged by a moose. Using what he had learned from *World of Warcraft*, he taunted the moose off her, and then, after it butted him in the backpack, he played dead. The moose wandered off, leaving both children unhurt.

Earlier, I mentioned two examples of things you can learn from *WoW*:

- The name of the real world's largest unbroken volcanic caldera is Ngorongoro.
- Sabre-toothed tigers don't like being fireballed.

The charging moose is one of those happy occasions where the game world experience was close enough to real life to be actually useful.

It's lucky that taunt and play dead don't share a cooldown, though.

Seal of Evil

I once bought a game called *Seal of Evil*. It's a *Baldur's Gate* lookalike, set in ancient China at the end of the Warring States period. It was on special offer at GAME, so I thought I'd give it a go.

I played it for two days, but no more.

I can stand bad voice acting. I can stand bad *Scooby Doo*-style ground-moves-at-different-speed-to-characters animation. I can stand having to download a walkthrough just so I can find the main character's bedroom in the tutorial. I can just about stand the absence from the quest log of most of the quests. What I can't stand, however—what I *really can't stand*—is making me *play* through cut scenes. Never, ever again.

I do mean playing through cuts scenes. It goes to "15 years ago," and you have to click a character to start the conversation. They tell you to go somewhere as fast as you can, and when you eventually find it, there's someone else there for you to click to make talk. Then you go to the combat, which it's impossible to lose because the bad guys don't do any damage to you.

All you can do is invoke a conversation, move about and fight unlosable battles. There's no other interaction, it's just one step to the next.

Games with a narrative have a game part and a narrative part. There's a reason for this: the game is the fun part, the narrative adds context to the game part. It is *not fun* to have to click your way through a flashback. A flashback is not a game, it's a narrative; if you treat it as a game, you get the most boring kind of game imaginable—one in which you have *no* ability to change the outcome *whatsoever*. When it takes maybe 15 minutes to "play" it, that's it, that's enough. I thought *Seal of Evil* referred to the story, not the product.

Never again.

Anniversary Killers

As I mentioned, one of the bosses for *The Secret World*'s anniversary event was in Fusang Projects, a PvP zone.

When the boss respawned (the wait between respawnings being several hours), most of the people in Fusang were there solely to kill it. They didn't care about PvP, they just wanted to down the boss and claim their fancy pet reward. Most of those who were there for PvP also participated; after all, there's no fun in attacking people who aren't geared for PvP and can't defend themselves.

Well, no fun for *most* people.

A handful of individuals ignored the boss and just slaughtered everyone they saw from the opposing factions, knowing that almost none of them were able to respond in kind because they were equipped to kill the boss, not player characters.

Others didn't ignore the boss, but used it for their own ends. They taunted it off whoever was tanking it and led it away from the bulk of players, sometimes into stupid places such as underground. Collision detection not being Funcom's strong point, this meant that you could see the boss's head and the occasional limb bob up through the concrete at ground level, but then it would disappear.

Another trick some players did was take over the bases of the opposing teams, so that when they were assassinated, they resurrected far away and had a lengthy run back to the action. Oh, I should also mention that the death of every character in the PvP zone during the fight *healed* the boss.

All this meant that a boss that should have taken 150 cooperating people 10 minutes to down took 140 cooperating people plus 10 uncooperating people 45 minutes.

Ah, killers.

The Meaning of *Realistic*

If a world has dragons and vampires, how can we ever say it's "realistic"? Well, we certainly can't say it has high *realism* if it contains dragons and vampires because realism concerns authenticity. Realisticness, however, concerns *believability*, not authenticity. We can, therefore, call a world that has dragons and vampires "realistic" if it's consistent with whatever fiction you have to buy into to play the world. So, "realistic" means "having realism, relative to the fiction."

Because people rarely notice when things are realistic but do notice when they're not, we usually talk about a world as being *unrealistic* rather than its being realistic. An unrealistic world has one or more features inconsistent with its fiction.

It's a little more subtle than that, actually. Fiction defers to *Reality*, in that if the fiction says nothing about how some aspect of the world works, people assume that it works the same as in real life; *Reality* therefore becomes the default fiction.

There are thus two ways a world can be unrealistic: it can be inconsistent with the stated fiction, or it can be inconsistent with that part of *Reality* to which the unstated fiction defers. The latter is a bit like realism, but it's not: it *is* part of the fiction, it's just a part that works the same way as *Reality*.

Cover as Code

Problem: if a player's character is full of arrows, then they really should be dead, but you don't want them to be dead because That Would Be Bad.

Solution: implement the laws of chivalry as physical laws. If an arrow would kill the character, then the archer is forbidden from firing it.

Fictional cover has turned into code, but it makes more sense than having people wandering around looking like porcupines (which itself makes more sense than having arrows in flight evaporate upon contact with a solid object).

Gaming AI

Games with adaptive AI to them don't ultimately work. Players just end up gaming the AI.

I was playing a trains/transportation game once and noticed that whenever I was looking somewhere and planning to build a route, my computer opponent would start building in the same place. If I looked elsewhere, it didn't build in the first place, but built in the elsewhere.

I therefore adopted a strategy of looking at locations for half-decent routes, tempting the AI into building there, then zooming off to the good location and building in that location myself before the AI could get enough money together to compete. It worked, but it was annoying: I wasn't playing a build-a-railway game anymore, I was playing a deceive-the-AI game.

So it is with all adaptive AI because the AI is contained within a game-world box that the player is outside. The player doesn't get into a flow state by competing against the AI, they get into one by tricking it.

It doesn't matter what the game is, players will always make their *own* fun.

Narrative Art

Many commentators see narrative as an example of *real art* in computer games—it's literature!

Okay, so narrative *is* part of the designer's art, but it's not the main part. This is probably just as well because narratives for computer games are universally weak—a result of the foreshortening that occurs when trying to fit a linear convention into a non-linear form.

Backstory is also weak because it has to paper over so many cracks. History is immensely strong, but only at the personal level—what's highly meaningful to you is just so much bad fan fiction to someone else.

For MMOs, large-scale narratives are utterly pointless, but don't even get me *started* on that...

Too Much Magic

Here's part of a screenshot from *World of Warcraft*:

Here's another from *The Secret World*:

What happened to physics? In the days of text, when MMOs only used imagination to render them, we could manage to make snow melt when it was put somewhere warm and water evaporate when put somewhere hot.

I guess this must be either "magic snow" or "magic fire" or both...

Ask Dr Psycho

From this week's *Practical Serial Killer:*

Dear Dr Psycho

Can you recommend a good computer game for me to play? I want to learn how to kill people better. I have heard World of Warcraft is good, but its subscription looks a little pricey.

—Abe

Dear Abe

Don't play WoW. I played for two years, and all I learned was that if you want to kill murlocs then frost magic is a safe method.

I recommend instead that you go to the library and rent out DVDs of old Columbo TV shows. Find one that has a method of killing people that you'd really like to try out, then simply repeat it yourself!

Important: at some point in the show, the hero will make a mistake that Columbo notices. In your reconstruction, don't make that same mistake.

—Dr Psycho

Feelings

MMOs engender feelings in their players. Stories can package up feelings and deliver them with pinpoint accuracy. Should MMO designers therefore add more story to their world, to give the players a more emotional experience?

Personally, I'd caution against it. I don't place a lot of emphasis on feelings *per se*, so long as there are few constraints on them. Offering up parcels of pre-packaged feelings for the players to choose between is too fettered; I want players to be able to find their *own* feelings, and therefore their own selves.

Undermining Achievement

MMO players tend to want to measure their performance relative to that of other players. "I'm level 40, you're level 30, therefore I am a better player than you." This is how achievers think.

However, such a view is completely undermined if anyone can spend a few dollars and raise themselves up. "Ha! Now I'm level 50 so I'M a better player than YOU!"

Suppose you're at college and you take a set of examinations at the end of your first year that will contribute to your final mark. It may be that you don't do as well as you hoped you would. Should you be able to buy some of the score of someone who did better? Well personally, I don't think you should: the whole point of the examination system is to rate individuals' expertise relative to one another, and buying marks that other students don't need corrupts that system.

Many gamers see progress in MMOs like that. They are proud of their achievements and furious when these are undermined by someone who has money rather than (what achievers see as) ability. They view the virtual world as a meritocracy and *don't* like being disabused of this idea. It's not as if higher-level characters are more fun to play than lower-level ones, given that an MMO's gameplay is pretty much the same whatever level your character is; to an achiever, the important thing is that they've got where they are, not what happens once they get there.

I'm not saying that selling achievement markers or the means to obtain them makes for an unfun MMO. All I'm saying is that it would be a different kind of fun, for a different kind of game, played by a different kind of player.

Jaina Proudmoore, Giantess

Here's a picture of my mage standing next to Lady Jaina Proudmoore, a lore character in *World of Warcraft*:

She's fairly tall, isn't she? I barely come up to her shoulder.

That was her in Theramore, where she's the ruler. Five minutes later, I took this second picture of her in the Halls of Reflection in Northrend:

Now, I barely come up to her waist.

Gawd knows what she ate in the five minutes it took to get from Theramore to the Halls of Reflection, but if she has any more of it she's going to start banging her head when she goes through doorways.

Other Story

The story that describes what a player did is that player's history. In virtual worlds, however, players are not alone: every player has their own history, and these histories overlap. A guild can have a history; a shard can have a history; an MMO as a whole can have a history, played out through the actions of many players in many guilds on many shards. These are collective histories that emerge from the interactions between the histories of individuals.

In movies, every major character has a story arc. Player characters of computer games also have story arcs of the player's own making within a narrative structure determined by the game's design. What about non-player characters, though? Can they have story arcs? If so, should they?

Yes, they can have story arcs. There are good reasons to give them such arcs, too, in certain kinds of games. It's not always the case, obviously: you don't care that the reason this kobold is trying to kill you is that it was mistreated as a cub by cruel miners and it blames all humanity for the recurring nightmares that plague its sleep; all you care is that if you don't kill it, it'll try to kill you. You don't especially want to get involved with that kind of NPC.

Some NPCs, you do want get involved with, though. Designers put in the mechanisms for such involvement because it gives you an emotional investment in the NPC's future. This allows the designer to add context and atmosphere, and the ability to *say* things to you as a player. You can reply through your choices; it's a form of prewritten but unpredictable, unfolding dialogue. It can be very powerful, if done right. Remember Floyd?

As part of a game's general context (i.e., that which, if you changed it, would be a reskinning), all major characters should have backstories wherever possible. Hey, even Mario is a plumber! Players don't always need to know any of this, but the more rounded a character in its design, the more able a designer is to give it rounded actions. The character's name, age, family background, plans, what happened immediately before the game started—all this is useful material.

Okay, so actually I *am* lying a little here, in that designers don't always have to think about this kind of thing explicitly—they've thought about character enough in the past that they can pluck fully-functioning, consistent, interesting personalities from thin air. However, they do write them down because that means they can explain them to other people who need to know such things (e.g., animators, voice artists, themselves 18 months later, ...).

When player character narratives intertwine with those of non-player characters, the results can be very compelling. It can add tremendous emotional impact to a game.

Yet all this is *as nothing* compared to the impact another *player character* can have.

Way to go, MMO!

Always a Pawn

Every role-playing game plot is like this.

Act I:

Something happens that gives you a definite enemy. You track down the enemy and defeat it.

Act II:

Oh no! The enemy is merely a pawn! You have to spend ages collecting the necessary plot tokens to discover who and where the real enemy is.

Act III:

You track down and defeat the real enemy in a grand showdown. You may need to kill the enemy several times, but eventually one of the battles will be the "real" final one. The world is safe again.

Or is it? We might want a sequel.

The first boss is always a pawn.

Narrative Arcs

Maintaining a single story arc for an entire MMO is not usually a great idea.

Stories end, and unless you're prepared to end your MMO when this happens, you're cheating your players. Sometimes the MMO *does* end, as happens most notably with *A Tale in the Desert*, but it takes a brave developer to do that. Most arcs either peter out forgotten, or end and leave themselves in a narrative limbo, or never end unless the MMO is closed down.

Stories also begin. If you join a story-driven MMO after a couple of years, this means you've missed its beginning. Everyone else is into the story, but you're not. Okay, so just as you can watch a TV movie that you walked in on half-way through, you can pick up the story for an MMO. However, which would you prefer: watching the second half of a movie, or watching all of one?

Story arcs are also non-interactive. If you make your narrative arc a big selling point, as *Asheron's Call* did, then yes, you can attract players through that story. However, when they realize that they have no influence on it, they can and will cheerfully follow it on the Internet without having to pay to watch it unfold.

What's that? You can have interactive story arcs?

Well yes, you can. *A Tale in the Desert*'s is interactive. *ATITD* is a relatively small, bespoke MMO, though. It only has one shard. Large-scale worlds with multiple shards have problems if they try to make story arcs dependent on what players do because people on one shard might do different things to what they do on another, and then it's hard to add further patches to advance the arc.

This, in fact, happened with *Asheron's Call*. For a year, the narrative built up to the freeing by player characters of the entity Bael'Zharon from his crystalline prison. With the destruction of the sixth soul stone, he would be released to wreak death and devastation across the world. This indeed happened on every server—except one. On Thistledown, a group of players decided that it would be a bad thing to let loose this evil, so they defended the soul stone against all-comers on a round-the-clock watch.

They were successful, too. This meant that the next planned storyline update wouldn't work on Thistledown—but it *had* to work! Otherwise, Thistledown would have needed its own development team to support its branch of the storyline while the main team worked on updates for the rest of the servers.

Eventually, the developers (Turbine) took matters into their own hands and released Bael'Zharon anyway. At this point, the players realized that they were impotent when it came to changing the storyline—they may as well have just sat back and watched it unfold, they couldn't *do* anything about it.

Grand, narrative arcs may work as a fiction to introduce new content, but they're not interactive. Only very rarely does a player base get to change what's happening in them.

They're not the only kind of arc, though.

Place as Serendipity

If socializers like chatting to other players, why don't they simply use *Internet Relay Chat*? What does a sense of place give socializers that *IRC* doesn't?

Well, what it gives is the possibility of meeting people by accident—"bumping into" them. Crucially, these people might not be actively seeking interaction. With *IRC*, you can check different channels, but you never get to talk to someone who wasn't also planning on talking to someone. With MMOs, you do.

MMOs as Virtual Worlds

You don't have to treat a world as a game for it to be a world. Formally, MMOs only have a game component to give people a plausible *explanation* of why they want to play; the *reasons* people play MMOs are to do with the worlds and the players—the game just gives a context (or excuse).

You think that's not true? Ah, well you're an achiever, then (or a designer who noticed that achievers wouldn't see it that way).

Cognitive Dissonance in MMOs

The reason I mentioned cognitive dissonance is that it helps explain what happens in MMOs at the point where the virtual environment's persuasiveness fails and affects immersion.

So, your brain is used to dealing with the real world, and the more that the virtual world operates like the real world, the more your brain is predisposed to find it real (i.e., to be persuaded by it); however, if something happens that is clearly at odds with the prevailing evidence that the virtual world is real, there's cognitive dissonance. On the one hand, you think it's just like *Reality*; on the other, you think it's not like *Reality*. Something has to give.

Such dissonance is traditionally reduced by fictive explanation. Why are there dragons here? Well, it's a Fantasy world, so it has dragons. How come the dragons can fly when they're too big to do so? Well, dragons are magical entities so use magical help.

This is fine so long as it is consistent. If the fiction is *inconsistent*, it can make matters worse. Why can't dragons swim under water? Because water interferes with their magic. So … why can they fly when it's raining?

There has to be *some* dissonance in MMOs because otherwise they wouldn't be worth playing—they'd be just like real life. Typically, the differences between virtual world and real world exist for one of the following reasons:

- **Implementation.** It's too hard/expensive to let dragons swim under water.

- **Gameplay.** No-one would use a dolphin mount if dragons could swim under water.

- **Fiction.** If dragons could swim underwater, their fireballs would make no sense.

Such dissonance is fine *if* the fiction explains it. If it doesn't, players will have to ignore how things *should* be in order to work with how they *are*. This lessens the persuasiveness of the virtual environment.

Here's the thing, though: play an MMO enough and this constantly willed suspension of disbelief can *itself* become a learned activity. The MMO is not persuasive of *Reality*—but it *is* persuasive of being an MMO.

This explains how come so many modern MMOs have 24-hour shopkeepers and waveless seas, yet no-one bats an eyelid except for absolute newbies.

Verisimilitude

The word *verisimilitude* means the property of resembling *Reality*, of having likeness to the truth.

I want a word that means the property of resembling *a* reality, of having likeness to the *fiction*.

Suppose that when a dragon breathes fire it can set houses ablaze. I can't comment on the verisimilitude of this situation because in *Reality*, fire-breathing dragons don't exist (our primitive ancestors must have eaten them all). However, I can say that *if* dragons did exist, *then* the fact that their breath could set buildings ablaze would, in that context, make sense. You'd be disappointed if dragon breath *didn't* burn down houses and make their poor occupants homeless.

Okay, so there probably *is* an English word that means what I want, but I've no idea what it is. When I started reading the dictionary for it, I only got half way through the first chapter ("A") before boredom overcame me.

The word "verisimilitude" comes from the Latin *veri similitudo*. Veri is the genitive singular of *verus*, meaning "real"; *similitudo* means "likeness." Likeness to falsehood is therefore easy to construct: it would be "falsisimilitude" in English. I don't want likeness to falsehood, though; I want likeness to the fiction.

The word "fiction" itself has Latin roots, ultimately deriving from *fingere*, meaning "to make by shaping, to feign, to concoct a story." This isn't really helpful, then, as the English meaning of the word is too remote from the Latin.

The key is to note that, whereas realism is about authenticity, realisticness is about belief. The Latin for "belief" is *fides*, as in "fidelity," which has the genitive singular of *fidei*. This would make the English word meaning "likeness to that which is believed" *fideisimilitude*.

Hmm. I can't say it's likely to catch on.

Story Machines #1

Games are machines for generating stories.

Earlier, I mentioned E. M. Forster's take on the relationship between story and plot. In his celebrated book on the craft of storytelling, *Aspects of the Novel*, he defines a story as a "narrative of events arranged in their time sequence." In other words, events happen; some of these events are selected and described in the order that they will be read (if not necessarily the order they occurred); the way they are told is a narrative; the result is a story.

A plot is not the same as a story because it is predefined and includes causality. One event happens because another situation, event, or series of events preceded it. For example, consider the following story, which consists of two events: "I ate a bar of chocolate. I was sick." You don't know whether eating the bar of chocolate made me sick, or whether I ate the bar of chocolate because I was sick. You don't know that the story isn't going to continue: "I stroked an armadillo. That's three things off my bucket list."

Much of the enjoyment from reading a story comes from reconstructing the plot that underpins it: figuring out the causal links that connect key events. It doesn't have to be *all* about this, of course—I love Chekhov's short stories because of their characters, not because of any discernible plot. However, the reconstruction of the plot from the events presented in the story—recognizing what caused what or anticipating what will cause what—is at the heart of why stories are compelling.

A narrative is the telling of the story (although you could also regard it as the conveying of the plot through the device of the story). The term tends to be used to mean the telling of the story as a whole; if you mean it at the nuts-and-bolts, words-on-the-page level, it would be a *discourse* rather than a narrative.

Backstory is the retelling of events that preceded the events of the story. Although fragments of backstories can be directly present in a story, more often their effects are felt only indirectly. For example, in designing a character who is a charity worker, an author may have constructed for them a backstory in which they spent six months of their youth in prison for credit card fraud; this would be felt in the story by their need for atonement for their past indiscretion, but it would not necessarily have to be mentioned at any point.

A history is the retelling of a related series of events or episodes that have previously taken place. When the events are not presented as causally connected, what you have is merely a set of records; when they are, it's history. For real events (as opposed to fictional ones), there is no overall plot created by a god-like author; nevertheless, there could be plots authored by historical individuals or groups (as in the Gunpowder Plot). The job of the historian involves looking at the records and providing explanations and interpretations as to why certain things turned out the way they did. Although the resulting set of causal connections may look like a plot, it isn't one unless those connections were authored. For example, the historian may realize that the crops failed because the smoke from a volcano in a distant land obscured the sun: this is a causal connection, but it's not a plot because it wasn't predefined—it was unauthored, as far as the resulting narrative is concerned. A chain of events doesn't have to be plotted to be causally connected.

So, what happens when we apply these terms to games?

Unpredictable Interactions

A player hits a door. The door opens.

Why is that? It's just as easy in programming terms to make hitting a door cause flowers to grow from the sails of a windmill.

Well, unless there were some heavy hints somewhere that this was No Ordinary Door and there was some connection to No Ordinary Windmill, such an unpredictable interaction would confuse players.

The default, therefore, is for things to work as players expect them to work. This means that they accord to real-world experience or to well-known fictional tropes such as magic.

Or, of course, to "that's just how it works in games."

Anatomy of a *Rift* Quest

Round 1

- NPC1: I want you to go kill a bunch of these bad guys.
- NPC2: While you're there, kill a bunch of these bad guys too!
- NPC3: And these particular bad guys there are only a few of!
- NPC4: I don't want you to kill bad guys. I want you to collect a bunch of these *things*. They're guarded by bad guys.

Round 2

- NPC1: I want you to go back there and kill a bunch of these other bad guys you could have killed while killing the first set of bad guys.
- NPC2: While you're there, kill a bunch of these other bad guys you could have killed before, too!

- NPC3: And these particular, *named* bad guys you could also have killed before!

- NPC4: I don't want you to kill bad guys. I want you to collect a bunch of these *things*. They're carried by bad guys you could have killed before.

Round 3

- NPC1: I want you to go *through* the previous bunch of bad guys and kill a bunch of these new bad guys.

- NPC2: While you're there, kill a bunch of these new bad guys too!

- NPC3: And N of these particular bad guys that there are only N-1 of!

- NPC4: I don't want you to kill bad guys. I want you to activate these machine *things*. They're guarded by two bad guys each.

Round 4

- NPC1: I want you to go through both sets of the previous bad guys I asked you to kill and kill this one *really* bad guy.

- NPC2: While you're there, kill a bunch of these slightly different but still bad guys nearby too!

- NPC3: Hey! Don't I do the named bad guys? What gives here?!

- NPC4: I don't want you to kill bad guys. I want you to collect a bunch of these *things*. They're parts of the bad guys' bodies.

Round 5

- NPC1: I want you to go down the road and speak to my replacement NPC1 there. Have fun!

Why Realistic?

For board games with a simulation component to them, "realistic" is in opposition to "playable"[18]. The more complexity you add, the more realistic the game is, but the harder it becomes to play. For computer games, in which the administrative burden of complexity is taken off the player's shoulders, it's much easier to make games which are both realistic *and* playable.

Text MUDs took advantage of this and increasingly strove to be realistic. They did this for two main reasons: *persuasiveness* and *emergence*.

Persuasiveness helps with immersion, as it gives the player less to have to ignore. If you can trust the world to behave as you'd expect, you don't constantly have to work out whether it will let you do something or not—you just *know*. Believing in it becomes easier, so believing that you yourself are in the virtual world becomes easier. Because players already have a decent understanding of how the real world works, any game world that behaves similarly creates less friction of belief. Thus, the more realistic a game world is, the more immersive it will be.

Emergence is the process by which interactions between a system's subcomponents create new systems. It's desirable for MMOs because it creates content. The more detailed an MMO's world, the greater the opportunity for interesting interactions between components, leading to more for the players to do. *EVE Online* is the primary example of an MMO which has almost entirely emergent content. When a world is unrealistic, players can't so easily reason about how subsystems "should" interact, which dampens down the amount of emergent behavior.

These two reasons—persuasiveness and immersion—apply as much to today's MMOs as they did to their forebears. That being so, the worlds of today should be just as keen to be realistic as were the worlds of the past. Why, then, are they more unrealistic?

---

[18]Steve Jackson: *Realism versus Playability in Simulation Game Design*. Proceedings of Joks i Tecnojocs Conference, Barcelona. June, 1991. http://textfiles.com/rpg/realplay.txt

False Choices

If you're presented with a choice and no matter what option you choose the eventual outcome of the game doesn't change, is that choice worth anything?

Games often have such false choices—especially in their narratives. You may side with the spoiled brat prince or with the pompous politician, but either way you'll still end up with their country's army on your side for the final showdown. If a choice doesn't affect the outcome of the game, why have it?

Well, games are about making choices (it's what makes them games), but they're not *just* about that. They can be about thrills, or nostalgia, or suspense—they can be about many things. If a false choice changes the meaning of a game's ending, then there may be no *material* gameplay difference resulting from it, but there could be an *emotional* one.

False choices annoy many gamers because gameplay is an exercise in decision-making; having a choice that is no such thing therefore means there's less game and your choice was meaningless. That may be unfortunate, but it's nevertheless often legitimate if the choice *is* meaningful, only at a non-gameplay level. If it changes the feel of the game, then the experience of the game can change even if the gameplay doesn't.

Why Unrealistic?

There are some valid reasons for deliberately making an MMO less realistic than it could be.

- To make an artistic point. If you're parodying the real world, you don't want to simulate it exactly.

- Realisticness can be opposed to fun. This is why your character never has to use the lavatory.

- Realisticness can be opposed to balance. This is why you can use a sword to kill a giant even though you can't reach above its ankle.

- It's expensive to implement realistic effects in a graphical world. Some animator has to model that wet hair.

- New players can mistake realisticness for complexity. This scares away all those casual players you want.

So there are logical reasons for wanting your MMO to be unrealistic to some degree. None are show-stoppers, though, and all can be mitigated. Parodies only need to mismatch in their one, key area; people don't use lavatories often enough in the real world to notice they never have to in a virtual world; swords can do systemic magical, electrical, or toxic damage; the effects of wet hair can be implemented without having to be shown visually; new players don't have to experience the full glory of the world's level of detail until they've mastered the controls.

So why *are* so many modern MMOs unrealistic?

Here's the interesting part. Recall that there are two main components to a world's fiction: the stated fiction and the unstated fiction (which defers to *Reality*). This means there are two ways a world can be unrealistic: it can be at odds with the game's explicit fiction or with its implicit fiction. The thing is, modern MMOs tend to be every bit as realistic with the former as were the MMOs of yore, but comparatively unrealistic with the latter. They support the stated fiction very strongly, but may take a few liberties with the unstated fiction behind it.

Fantasy MMOs over the years have introduced increasingly baroque-looking swords. Nevertheless, *Star Wars: the Old Republic*'s lightsabers ten years from now will look pretty much the same as they do today. In *The Lord of the Rings Online*, Tom Bombadil isn't going to show up in Rivendell. You're never going to see jeeps in *Everquest* or bazookas in *The Elder Scrolls Online* or Queen Victoria in *WildStar*.

MMOs regard it as important to be tight to their fiction. *The Secret World* is consistent in its handling of the Filth because, if it weren't, then it would lose persuasiveness; its skill wheel is a brilliant exercise in priming emergence, giving its gameplay wonderful depth. Its designers do not, however, regard tightness to the non-lore part of their fiction as equally important. For example, the game has an "exsanguinate" spell that allows you to damage an opponent by sucking its blood out; this would be fine, but it works on crates, robots, plants, rocks, and even the occasional creature that actually has blood.

What's going on, here?

Story Machines #2

For games, the story is the linear sequence of events experienced by the player. It doesn't have to be the same for each player nor for the same player over each (re)playing of the game.

The plot of a game is a not-necessarily-linear series of events predetermined by the design team. It will account for some of the more significant events that occur to the player, but only a minority of the overall number of events. Most of the events that the player experiences will take place as a result of interactions between the player and the game system. Although these are also predefined by the design team in the sense that the game's design implicitly embodies the totality of all events that can possibly occur within the game, they are not predefined *as events*. They are predefined as a system for *generating* events.

When game designers talk of narrative, they usually mean the way that the explicitly predefined (that is, plotted) events unfold for the player. They don't usually mean the way that events contingent on the predefined game system unfold. Designers do have authorial control over that, but they call it gameplay, not narrative.

The events that took place prior to the player's beginning to play a game are its backstory. Often, the story will pick up as an ongoing continuation of the backstory; in this case, the backstory is authored, fixed, and will be the same for each playing of the game. However, this does not always have to be the case. For example, a new player joining *EVE Online* will discover a web of relationships between players and corporations built up over the several years of the game's existence. From the new player's perspective, this is backstory: it's a series of events that took place before they started to play that predicate and provide the contextual springboard for many of the future events that will affect the player. It's immaterial to the new player that these events weren't conceived by a designer, they're backstory either way.

From the perspective of a long-term player of *EVE Online*, the events of the past are not backstory, though: they're history. They're the part of that player's ongoing story that has already been read. Importantly, though, they only become part of the player's history in the retelling: as events, they merely constitute an ordered set of records. When players selectively choose which of all the events that have occurred to them to relate (either to themselves or to someone else), the resulting interpreted story is a history.

These stories—these histories—are the ones that matter for games. If you can't tell another, attentive player what interesting things happened to you, that means *no interesting things happened to you*. If no events worth speaking of occurred, why were you playing the game? You had no decisions to make, you had no unexpected situations to deal with, you had no obstacles to overcome, you had no heart-stopping moments: nothing of interest to you happened.

When you read a novel, you are presented through the narrative with a series of plotted events arranged as a story. When you play a game, you may also be presented through the narrative with a series of plotted events; however, you will also be presented by the gameplay with a series of unplotted events. In design terminology, games (particularly MMOs) that are heavy on plot-driven events are *theme parks*; ones heavy on gameplay-driven events are *sandboxes*.

It's clear, therefore, that games and stories are related, but what *is* that relationship?

The Hamzanama

> Umar asked the Amir for permission to cut off the perpetrator's head, but the Amir wouldn't grant it. So Umar held the point of his dagger over his own heart, and said, "if you don't give me permission, I'll kill myself." The Amir gave in, and Umar left.

When a storyteller was relating this tale, he (it probably would have been a he) could emphasize the Amir's reluctance to have the perpetrator hunted down, or he could dramatize Umar's resolve to commit suicide if his wish was not granted. The flat text allows for both these interpretations to be made, depending on the audience[19].

---

[19]*Sense in communication*. Douglas A. Galbi, 2003. http://www.galbithink.org/sense1.pdf

Personal Arcs

As I've mentioned, a narrative arc for the whole of an MMO is either an ultimately unsatisfactory device for providing the fiction for new content, or it means the MMO is going to end.

Overlapping arcs aren't *so* bad—smaller storylines that play out as others unfold, as in soap operas—but they lack the grandness of a full-blown arc. If you want a full arc, then, you're going to have problems, yes?

Actually, no. You can have *personal arcs*.

A personal arc is a storyline *just for you*. In practice, everyone gets their own copy of the same arc(s), but it's an arc in which they are they hero. Bioware—a developer renowned for its storytelling—has taken this furthest with individual personal story arcs created on a class-by-class basis for its MMO, *Star Wars: the Old Republic*. Its designers have honed *every quest* in it so that each character class gets a narrative entirely different to the narratives of the other classes. This is a ton of work, but it's awe-inspiring in its scope.

Another MMO that has personal storylines is *The Lord of the Rings Online*. This has ordinary quests, some of which are chained together in mini-narratives, plus "epic storyline" quests broken up into books and chapters. Some of these epic storyline chapters aren't themselves particularly epic—it's hard to believe that the fate of Middle Earth rests on your bringing Radagast the Brown moss from bog crawler nests—but the storyline itself is fairly strong and interweaves well with Tolkien's novel.

This would work fine, but in *LotRO* you can do the quests out of order. This can be a boon because it means you don't get stuck when one of the quests demands a group of six people and you can't find anyone to join you. However, it can introduce continuity errors if (as happened to me) you get to wave goodbye to the Fellowship of the Ring, with everyone from Frodo to Bill the Pony heading off into the distance; and then the *very next quest you pick up* has Legolas, who's still hanging around in Rivendell, coming with you and your group to kill a bunch of wood trolls.

Hmm, a little sequencing problem there, methinks...

Artemis & Actaeon

Boston Museum of Fine Arts contains a type of bowl[20] (a *bell krater*) from Ancient Greece, used for mixing wine and water. It was made in Athens about 470 BC and is ceramic with red figures. The figures were created by an artist known today as the Pan Painter.

One side of the vase shows Artemis shooting Actaeon.

Okay, so Actaeon was a famous hunter, and one day he was out hunting with his dogs. He saw a stag run into a small copse and raced ahead to shoot it with his bow. However, among the trees he stumbled across a pool, in which was bathing Artemis—goddess of the hunt. She was completely naked and stunningly beautiful.

What Actaeon *should* have done was say, "Excuse me, have you seen a stag come this way?" What he *did* do was gawp.

Somewhat annoyed by this, Artemis transformed Actaeon into a stag, whereupon his dogs arrived and tore him to pieces.

Strangely, the image on the mixing bowl shows Artemis fully clothed. I say "strangely" because Actaeon is naked but for a cloak over his left shoulder. Even more strangely, on the other side of the vase is the signature picture that gave the Pan Painter their (modern) name; this depicts a, hmm, let's say "highly aroused" Pan chasing a shepherd boy.

Maybe the Pan Painter didn't want to irk Artemis by showing her in her full glory?

Unrealistic Reality

It's important for an MMO to be tight to its fiction. This isn't just the case for ones that are based on a well-known intellectual property (*LotRO*, *SW:TOR*, or even *WoW*): if players are signing up to spend time in an imaginary world, they don't want that world to be inconsistent with either itself or with what they already know about it. In short, players want it to be *believable*. An MMO's fiction is one of its greatest selling points. If it's unrealistic—machine guns in Middle Earth, for example—then prospective players won't accept it.

So why, then, if it's so important for immersion for an MMO to be tight to its fiction, is it not important for it to be tight to the deferred-to reality that supports that fiction?

---

[20]Museum of Fine Arts, Boston Accession number 10.185 http://www.mfa.org/collections/object/mixing-bowl-bell-krater-153654

The answer is that MMOs *are* tight to that reality—it's just that this "reality" isn't *Reality*. Rather, it's the players' *expectation* of what physical reality is.

Players think that as soon as you take your finger off the W key, you stop moving. There's no deceleration, it's instantaneous, TWANG!, like in the Road Runner cartoons. They don't think this way when they drive their car to work in the morning, but they *do* think this way in games because they've played so many that this is how they expect it to be. If you were to correct it, then, perversely, the very disrupting-immersion effect you're trying to avoid would kick in. Therefore, you defer not to *Reality* but to the player's *expectation* of what "reality" means for this world. In the absence of fiction, MMOs today default not to how the real world works, but to how MMOs work.

So while the reasons that 1980s textual worlds strove to be realistic have not gone away, they have evolved. Nowadays, players have so many preconceptions (from having played so many games and MMOs before) that it's these that are the basis of what's "real" for an MMO. Immersion is better served by defaulting to "game physics" rather than to real-world physics.

Immersion is only half the story, though. The other half, emergence, suffers greatly from this. Game physics is simpler than real-world physics, primarily because when it was being developed it had to be—the computers couldn't handle anything too complicated. Unfortunately, simplicity does not give much opportunity for systems to interact in either seen or unforeseen ways and for new content to emerge. As a result, except for a few honorable exceptions (*EVE Online* springs to mind), today's MMOs are shallow. Content has to be created at great expense by designers, rather than arising from the interactions of conditions that designers have set up.

Eventually, the increasing weakness of the paradigm will become so apparent that MMOs will have to reboot. Someone will develop an MMO that defaults more to *Reality* than to a naïve approximation to it; after all, players can learn, and if they're learning something they already know, then it shouldn't take long. They merely have to get over the initial shock of finding that, if they make a noise, distant monsters will hear them, and that they won't be able to run away as fast wearing a full suit of armor as can someone wearing a calf-length robe.

It's another one of those, "I hope this happens while I'm still alive but I don't suppose it will" things.

Multiple Narratives

There is a difference between multiple narratives and one narrative with multiple threads through it.

MMOs, being games, are driven by player actions. Narrative removes meaning from action. Offering three, four, or five different endings *still* removes meaning. Your gameplay experience is running on rails that are all going in the same direction, and switching tracks doesn't change that.

MMOs should be richly-featured enough that they don't *need* imposed narrative; events can unfold as a result of player action and interaction, taking individual players' personal experiences into uncharted waters. Players shouldn't merely get the chance to *redirect* the narrative, they should get the chance to *define* it.

Story Machines #3

Games don't actually need to have plots. Abstract games have no plot by definition because they have no fiction to give foundation to their chains of causality. They nevertheless do create story because the causality is implicit in their rules and mechanics. If you've ever told anyone what an amazing game of *Minesweeper* you just had, how you couldn't believe your luck, how there was no way to know which of two squares was a bomb and you had this gut feeling it would the one on the left, and you were correct, and then the whole of the rest of the game just opened up before you in a glorious sequence of unfolding success, each click revealing which square to click next in a just-in-time fashion, putting you on a roll until you were looking at an empty field and a new personal best high score; if you've ever related that kind of experience, you've told a story—a history—of an abstract game. Yet *Minesweeper* has no plot whatsoever. All it has is gameplay and some fiction to explain that that some of the tokens will lose you the game if you click them.

If games don't need to have predefined plots, why is it that so many bother with them? Is plot simply a way of adding dressing to make a world more believable and so more immersive? I had a long conversation about this several years ago with screenwriter-now-game designer, Lee Sheldon, and one of the points he made struck home: some people are just *better* at creating stories than others. Left to their own devices, players will always do things that initiate events, but these events may not necessarily be the stuff of which great stories are made. If you encourage someone proficient in crafting stories to create a plot that directs events such that they are more emotionally loaded, more intellectually significant and lead to a more satisfactory and meaningful conclusion, then this will enhance the player's overall experience.

This is a view I do accept. However, following it through to its logical conclusion raises the question: why bother with games? Why play a game when you can watch a movie or read a novel, with a plot constructed by someone so much better at creating plots than you are?

The answer is that people are individuals. Some things are incredibly important to *them*, but not to anyone else (or at least not to many other people). In playing a game, a player can cause events to occur that might not even impinge on the consciousness of the majority, but which are a major experience to that one person. They don't even have to be a *major* experience, they can be a minor experience that the player is using as a building block to construct a more meaningful story in their mind. That story may well be garbage to anyone else, but it's not to the player concerned. They did what they did in the game because it generated (or is working towards precipitating) an event that is a continuation of the unique causal chain the player is assembling, extrapolating, appropriating, honing, and personalizing.

Games, as systems, allow players to experiment with events, picking from them the ones that make the best story *for them*, which will lead to the further stories that are best *for them*. An overall, plot-driven series of events can also do this, but by necessity it's offering a general rather than a specific story. Games allow people to weave these plots into their *own* story—the one that is arising from the gameplay they are manipulating.

Games can, of course, be played automatically by bots to create a random series of events that make causal sense; that doesn't make the results stories, however. When players play, the events they create *aren't* arbitrary—they're purposeful. Why that one series of events, out of all the possible series, rather than another? It can only be because of the choices the player made, which ultimately can only have been made because at some level they were somehow significant or important to that player. There may be some randomness involved, there may be some plot involved, but there will *always* be gameplay involved.

Games are machines for creating stories. Play them, and your imagination will construct ones that work for you.

Everyone likes stories, but they like their *own* stories most of all.

Don't Mix Them Up

People who have never played MMOs aren't going to be able to understand a new one merely by watching other people play it.

People who have played MMOs for thousands of hours are.

Don't mix them up.

Player Types

Achievers, explorers, socializers, and killers are collectively called *player types*. These types are not just some arbitrary list like the "10 different kinds of teenagers" enumerations found in newspapers—they're actually related.

Here's a graph:

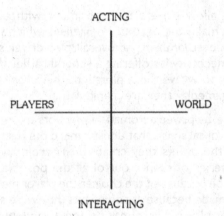

The x-axis goes from an emphasis on the *players* of the virtual world to an emphasis on the *world* itself. The y-axis goes from *acting* on (the world or players) to *interacting* with (the world or players).

Each of the quadrants of the graph describes a player type. Achievers act on the world, explorers interact with it, socializers interact with players, and killers act on players:

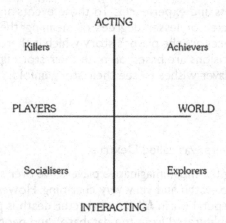

This basic four-type model is used in most MMO design today.

Unrealistic Physics

At some level, all MMO physics is only approximate. Even so, any virtual world will have to consider how to deal with concepts such as object compositionality and the propagation of actions' effects through time, whether or not it tries to match real-world physics.

The real world has the whole of *Reality* as its hardware. It can do anything instantly, without computation—it just *works*. MMOs have to run on computers embedded within the real world, so can never hope to match its speed and accuracy. We might eventually be able to create worlds that are able to fool people into treating them as real most of the time, but we won't create worlds that model *Reality* at the speed *Reality* runs.

Thus, even if you want your MMOs to be realistic, at best they're only going to be so at some level of abstraction. They're inherently *unrealistic*.

However, "unrealistic" to players means "not working conformant to the fiction" (where the default "fiction" is "real life"). A Newtonian model of physics would probably be "realistic" enough not to jar for most people.

The key point in determining the persuasiveness of a virtual environment is not how well it models *Reality*, but how well it models players' *view* of *Reality*.

Story Summary

A game is a system for generating stories. The designer defines the domain of possible stories for the game; the player, through decisions made during play, generates events and experiences. To these events and experiences, the player attaches greater or lesser degrees of meaning; the retelling of these events and experiences are the player's story, which is therefore a history. The player's evolving decisions are based on both their story up to that point and the ways that the player wishes to see their story unfold.

Dextrus

One of MUD2's players was called Dextrus.

Dextrus was among the most imaginative players I've ever seen—very innovative, very exciting to watch and very, very charming. However, she had something of a bad girl reputation: in MUD2, character death is permanent (if your character dies, it's obliterated from the database), and people got exceedingly cross when Dextrus appeared out of nowhere, beat them to a bloody pulp and took their stuff. It was made worse by the fact that she was invariably at a lower level than her victims when she did this.

One day, Dextrus decided to renounce her killing ways. Tired of being shunned, she announced that she would thenceforth fight no other player characters except in self-defense. Sure enough, that's precisely what she did. In the weeks that followed, she redeemed her previous indiscretions by helping out other people unstintingly; she rushed to their aid when monsters caught them unawares, she gave them her own equipment to use, and she led thrilling expeditions to the more far-flung and dangerous parts of The Land. Because she was so charismatic and kept true to her word, in a short space of time she became hugely popular.

So it was that some three months later she volunteered to accompany another player, a mage, on his "wiz run." In MUD2, once a character has sufficient experience points, they are promoted to the level of wizard/witch (wiz for short); this is the point at which the regular game is over for them—they achieve immortality as (basically) an administrator. A wiz run is when you're trying to get those final few points you need, with everyone else either cheering or chasing you. It's often a player's most exhilarating and enjoyable time, a climax long to be remembered and relived. Dextrus had generously offered to be the mage's bodyguard as he endeavored to rack up those last, remaining, immensely-important experience points.

The pair descended deep underground to the Dwarfen Realm. The risks were high—there were a lot of dwarfs—but the rewards were enticing. The mage and Dextrus fought their way side-by-side through several heavily guarded rooms until they finally stood on the threshold of the treasure chamber. The contents of this trove would be enough to push the mage over the finishing line and into wizardhood.

Suddenly, disaster struck! Dextrus went off to the Royal Bedroom to deal with the dwarfen queen, but the king appeared before the mage could follow and immediately attacked him!

The fight went right to the wire. The mage was still injured from earlier fights, and despite trying every trick known to him, he seemed certain lose. Then, right in the nick of time, Dextrus, having finished off the queen, raced back and downed the king.

And before the mage could even say thanks, Dextrus downed him, too.

She'd been tracking the king, knew where he was, knew when he was about to appear, and had *deliberately* left to kill the much-easier queen *knowing* that the king would attack the mage a split-second later. Having dispatched the queen in a timely manner, Dextrus patiently waited until the mage was close to death before returning heroically to save the day.

Then, in one perfect, exquisite moment, she killed a mage who was 30 seconds short of making wizard. It was exactly 100 days since she'd last killed another player character, *right down to the hour*.

Seconds of stunned silence passed. Then, a zero-points novice bearing the same name as the deceased mage entered the game. He shouted a single, agonized word: "WHY?"

The reply was simple: "Because I'm Dextrus."

Are MMOs

Are MMOs:

- Games? Like *Chess, Soccer, D&D*?
- Pastimes? Like reading, gardening, cooking?
- Sports? Like huntin', shootin', fishin'?
- Entertainments? Like nightclubs, TV, concerts?

Rail Games

Why do people like stories?

Well, one of the reasons is that they can have experiences that would be dangerous or expensive or even impossible in the real world. "Experience" here is indirect, though. Stories only allow readers to have these experiences vicariously: they get them second-hand, from accounts of people who did have them (or, if fictional, can be believed to have had them). If I were to read a story about a Roman legionary, that wouldn't mean that I experience what the legionary experienced; rather, it means I can *imagine* what the legionary experienced. There's a difference between imagining an experience and experiencing it.

Games allow you to experience a story directly, though, because they're interactive. This explains why there is a market for games that have a strong story element. There's a balance that has to be struck, however, between the story that the designer wants to tell and the story that the player wants to experience. If the player can't alter the story in any substantial way, what results is a game that runs on rails—a *rail game*. MMO stories, particularly quests, tend to be mini-rail games.

Now you could argue that this is no bad thing. Rail games allow people to choose whether or not to experience optional sub-stories, so individuals are able to tailor their experience to their desires. However, they can only do this if they know what kind of experience the sub-story promises; in rail games, the only way to find that out is actually to embark on the sub-story. Then, if you don't like it, you backtrack. Unfortunately, this is usually counter-immersive—as is reading/watching someone else's account of it.

Playing through a story you can't affect is not generally fun. Playing through a game with a story fragment as a reward (a cut scene, say) is better. Establishing the context of a story (again, through a cut scene) can add meaning. Creating your own story through your own actions is best of all.

So why do we still see so many rail games in MMOs?

It's because one player's rail game is another player's sandbox. Imagination matters.

Level Design

Narrative is often broken down into self-contained chunks—"missions," "quests," and "levels," for example. Creating them is called *level design*.

Level design involves:

- Exploring different aspects of gameplay.
- Matching the degree of challenge to the player's experience.
- Resolving the previous narrative obstacle.
- Setting up an obstacle for the next level.
- Conveying a sense of progress along the narrative path.

The same thing applies for areas and zones in virtual worlds.

Even if designers deny that there is narrative in their MMOs, there is. The only point of interest is whether it's implicit in the challenge level or explicit as an arc.

(The answer should always be that it's implicit in the challenge level, by the way).

Achiever, Explorer, Socializer, Killer

I ought perhaps to mention that sometimes these player types are called *Bartle types*. That's because the theory that introduced them is my theory[21].

I'd feel embarrassed about foisting this on you if it weren't for the fact that this theory enjoys widespread use. Actually, that doesn't help: I still feel embarrassed. Oh well, given that I wrote this book, you were kinda expecting me to tell you my ideas, right?

Besides, I *have* to mention Player Types theory because ultimately it leads to an answer to the single most important question in MMO design: "Why do people play MMOs?"

That's *ultimately*.

---

[21]Richard A. Bartle: *Hearts, Clubs, Diamonds, Spades: Players who Suit MUDs. Journal of MUD Research* 1(1), 1996. http://www.mud.uk/richard/hcds.htm

Elsinor

Elsinor is one of those esoteric games that has a mechanic (if you can call it that) which can act as a catalyst for discussing game-design theory—or it would, if only game-design theorists knew about it.

The rules for *Elsinor* were published in a British play-by-mail magazine (a *zine*) called *Son of Bellicus*, back in 1974. *Son of Bellicus* was a spin-off from *Bellicus* that merged back into the main zine a year later.

Here is a summary of the rules from *Bellicus* 19:

> *Elsinor is a fantasy game in which anyone can write as much as they please, provided it is consistent with what has gone before, and it makes interesting reading. Anyone may play, and for as long as they wish: all they need to do is submit sagas for their characters or nations when they feel like it. When players' sagas conflict with each other, the better written will generally prevail. The GM retains the right to alter factual and numerical information as he sees fit, though in practice he hopes such rights gain little exercise.*

There were some maps in *Bellicus* 19 to bring readers and potential new players up to speed.

Okay, so this is a game in which what players say becomes true by fiat. The role of the gamesmaster (the editor of *Bellicus*, Will Haven, hence the use of "he") is supposedly to stop random griefers from exploding the planet and destroying everything, but in practice it was merely to exist: the presence of such a role meant that no-one ever did send in such contributions, at least not as far as I know (*Bellicus* didn't have many 12-year-old readers).

Like *Mornington Crescent*, *Elsinor* is the Magic Circle incarnate. It's entirely free-form. Players can literally (and, since they're writing, I guess that's *literally* literally) make anything they want to happen, happen. That they don't is because they know that if they did, the game would end. They don't want the game to end, therefore they don't do it. They continue playing only because they enjoy the world they are collectively constructing, the story they are collectively writing, and the drama they are collectively enacting through their competitiveness.

It's like a modern wiki story. However, it isn't one: it's a game. Players are trying to improve their character or country at the expense of other players (the maps suggest that there are limited resources over which to compete). Their goals are personal, not shared; they share the context as a precondition to playing, but they have no reason to desire that *Elsinor* has, say, a beginning, middle, and end. Overall story structure is irrelevant. They decide what they want to achieve, then set out to achieve it. This is in the knowledge that they *could* achieve it in one sentence if they wanted to, but where's the fun in that?

The players of *Elsinor* dropped in and dropped out, but the world and its story-now-history lived on. I believe it was eventually removed from *Bellicus* because too many new subscribers hadn't been following it and objected to paying for 2 or 3 pages of partial story they didn't understand each issue. I don't know what became of the game after that.

A story-telling game that's held together only by the imaginations of the players, though: what a concept!

MMOs Are

Are MMOs:

- Games? Like *Chess, Soccer, D&D*?

  Yes—to achievers.

- Pastimes? Like reading, gardening, cooking?

  Yes—to explorers.

- Sports? Like huntin', shootin', fishin'?

  Yes—to killers.

- Entertainments? Like nightclubs, TV, concerts?

  Yes—to socializers.

Complete

The Player Types model is *complete*, in that there are no players who play MMOs for fun yet fit none of the types.

That doesn't mean they're necessarily a *good* fit, though.

Plot Creation

Suppose that you want your game to have a predetermined plot. This isn't an unreasonable suggestion: you may well be able to give players a better experience by explicitly directing their play than they would get simply by stumbling around in the dark.

So, what tried-and-trusted methods are there for creating plots that people will find appealing?

Ah. Well if there are any, they've yet to be discovered. Nevertheless, although we have no guaranteed formula for creating perfect plots, we *do* have formulae that describe the *shape* of such plots. What's more, these are eminently transportable into games.

The medium perhaps closest to computer games in its outlook is film, and it will perhaps come as no surprise to you to learn (if you didn't know already) that most movie scripts follow a fairly rigid blueprint. Around the time that Roy Trubshaw and I were programming *MUD1*, a book was written that has come to dominate how Hollywood movies are scripted. This is *Screenplay*[22] by Syd Field.

Syd Field's job was reading spec screenplays and recommending whether or not they should be made into movies. He read *thousands* of them, and noticed that the best ones all seemed to share the same pattern. He called this the *paradigm*.

Very briefly, Field noticed that the top screenplays all had a traditional, three-act structure with the parts broken down into roughly-similar page lengths (one page of screenplay converts to approximately one minute on the screen):

- Beginning. The first 15-25 pages establish the situation.
- Middle. The next 50-60 pages describe conflict leading to crisis.
- End. The final 10-20 pages resolve the conflict.

Furthermore, what happened *within* the acts also had a lot in common:

- Act one contains a *catalyst* within the first 10 pages, in which things are knocked out of whack. **Buzz Lightyear arrives**.
- Act one ends with a *big event*—a major change leading to a new, challenging situation. **Buzz falls out of the window**.

---

[22]Syd Field: Screenplay: the Foundations of Screenwriting. Dell Books: New York. 1979.

- Act two begins with the protagonist forced to address the issues of the big event. It's a series of *rising conflicts* with some successes but mainly failures.

- In the middle of act two comes the *pinch point.* Something awful happens, and the protagonist hits rock bottom. The only way out is for them to commit to their cause. **Buzz realizes he's a toy**.

- Following the pinch point, the conflict intensifies and the pace quickens as the protagonist fights back.

- Act two ends with the *crisis.* The worst thing possible happens, all seems lost, and the protagonist faces a crucial decision. **Buzz believes Andy doesn't want him back**.

- Act three begins with the *climax.* The protagonist defeats the antagonist and wins the day. This is what the whole movie has been building up to. **The toys gang up on Sid**.

- Act three ends with the final *resolution.* Loose ends are tied up, and the protagonist's life returns to some sort of balance. **Buzz and Woody are reunited with Andy**.

Next time you watch a regular modern movie, look out for a moment of total despair half-way through: this paradigm is used *very* extensively to structure screenplays... What's more, it can be and has been applied to games, most notably in Michael Bhatty's 2004 RPG, *Sacred*, in which he specifically and successfully retooled it for the games medium.

There are two points I'd like to make for those designers planning on using Syd Field's paradigm to structure their game's narrative.

First, remember that unlike the case with movies, you *aren't* creating the story—you're creating the *plot* that the players will *interpret* as the story (narrative).

Second, there *are* other paradigms.

Penguins

The above is a scan of the title page of my copy of Raph Koster's book, *A Theory of Fun for Game Design*. As you can see, someone has drawn on it.

I had a copy of the book anyway, but at a Game Developers' Conference party the publisher gave me another one. I was going to ask Raph to sign it, but weirdly it was *already signed*. As the book is 50% pictures, I asked Raph to draw a picture in it instead.

He did more than that: he drew four pictures. The pictures are of penguins illustrating the four player types, each bearing a suit motif. This was special for me, not just because I was up for the First Penguin award the next day (did I mention I won it?), but also because penguins are a running theme in Raph's book. I was very pleased with the result, and grateful to Raph for taking time out to do the drawing (he had to go to three other parties that night). That book was destined for pride of place on my bookshelf.

When I got home, there was a note in my luggage from Covenant Aviation Security, LLC, the company entrusted with inspecting every piece of luggage to leave San Francisco International airport. The note explained that they had opened my luggage. It did not explain that they had taken my First Penguin award to pieces then reassembled it so badly that it came apart in my suitcase and the metal base scrunched up the cover of the book, damaging it irreparably.

Kishōtenketsu Question

This is a question I asked my second-year students in an examination in 2013. It was worth 20% of a 2-hour paper.

Question 3

(a) [3%]

Briefly explain the relationship between *story* and *plot*.

(b) [3%]

Explain why it is important that players should be able to construct a story about what happened in a game they have just finished playing.

(c) [8%]

Write 60 Seconds of Gameplay for the game *Rogue*.

(d) [6%]

An oriental story-telling form called *Kishōtenketsu* does not use a three-act structure and contains no conflict. Instead, it has four acts. In the first act, something normal happens; in the second act, a twist is added; in the third act, something seemingly unrelated happens; in the fourth act, a contrast is drawn between the first two acts and the third act.

For example:

- Act 1: A girl goes to a drinks machine for a bottle of cola.

- Act 2: The bottle won't come out. She has to hit the machine to free it.

- Act 3: A boy sits alone on a park bench.

- Act 4: The girl arrives and surprises the boy by giving him the cola.

Assess the suitability of *Kishōtenketsu* for use in computer game plots.

Not Getting Player Types

In 2011, I did three MMO consultancy gigs in the space of two weeks. All three of the in-development MMOs I saw used the Player Types model as a character class system.

No no no!

Ask yourself this: if someone is an explorer, and they look at four character classes corresponding roughly to achiever, explorer, socializer, and killer, which character class will they choose? The answer is: all four of them. They'll try out each and every one of those character classes. They're explorers: they explore game systems. What did you *think* they explored?

What would achievers pick? Well, they'd look at the rewards on offer for each of the classes. They'd pick the one that gave them the best rewards. They wouldn't care which one it was, they'd take it. None of the other player types would even regard the "rewards" associated with classes as a factor. Why would they? They're not achievers!

What would killers pick? They'd pick the class that gave them the best opportunity to be annoying. It could be any of them. Consensual player-versus-player has its moments, but life as a killer is so much sweeter when people can't meaningfully fight back.

What would socializers pick? Actually, in all three of the cases I saw, they probably *would* pick the socializer-targeted class—but only because from their perspective it's the least bad. It's the only one in which you get to socialize properly, but in all likelihood only with other socializers.

The Player Types model applies to the *whole MMO*, not merely to some neatly defined system-within-the-world.

Breadth and Depth

Breadth and depth are two very old concepts of MMO design, dating back to the early MUD days.

Breadth means the size, number, and variety of things to see and do in an MMO.

Depth means the effects, complexity, and interactions of things to see and do in an MMO.

Breadth is about form, depth is about function; breadth is about player choice, depth is about player understanding; breadth is about scope, depth is about detail.

Breadth is range, depth is extent.

Despite what today's players might believe, most modern MMOs aren't actually all that deep. There are some exceptions—*EVE Online*, for example—but even something like *World of Warcraft* pales in depth alongside, say, *LegendMUD*.

Where modern MMOs leave MUDs for dead is in breadth. They have a lot of space, and they pack it with content goodies. There's always plenty to do in them. Newbies in particular love breadth.

Yet after a while, when they've done the same kill-10-rats quest *yet again*, players begin to sense the superficiality of it all. It's all just the same thing, being said in different words. Where is there some content you can actually get your teeth into?

Newbies may love breadth, but oldbies *love* depth.

Two Questions, One Answer

Why are MMOs so important to you that you'll spend many hours of your time playing them?

Why are MMOs so important to their designers that they'll spend their one and only life* making them?

* Mileage for your religion may vary.

Balance and Overbalance

If you take the standard four-type player graph for an established virtual world, the player types will be in equilibrium. This doesn't mean you have equal numbers of them, it means that you have them in balance. One killer might have the weight of 50 socializers, for example.

If you, as a designer, want to promote or demote players of particular types, you can do this by making changes that will encourage the balancing point to shift.

Most designers do this by tackling the types head-on. This can work, but it's often misunderstood as a technique. For example, suppose you want more explorers. The right way to do it is to present something mouth-watering and just leave it at that (the long-inaccessible airfield next to Ironforge in WoW, for example, tantalized explorers). The wrong way to do it is to give them experience points for entering a new zone: XP is an achiever reward, not an explorer reward.

Perhaps a better way to do it is not to think in terms of players but in terms of the axes of the player types graph. If you add more world, you will benefit both explorers and achievers; if you add more interaction (basically, more things to do), then that will benefit both explorers and socializers. In this approach, design is a bit like one of those ball-bearings-in-a-maze games, where you tilt the plane of the maze to move the balls so they end up in the right indentations. With MMOs, you tilt the plane of the player interest graph to try get more people into the segment you want them in (hopefully without making the ones already in the right place pop out).

This is how MMOs can be made to balance. However, it's possible to tilt too much and cause all the players to rush to one edge of the plane. This leads to overbalancing. When a virtual world overbalances, it ceases to be a virtual world:

- Too much emphasis on players at the expense of world leads to a mere communication channel, like a chatroom.
- Too much emphasis on world rather than players makes for an effectively single-player game.
- Too much emphasis on interaction rather than action makes the player reliant on the actions of others or of the game world—they may as well be watching TV.
- Too much emphasis on action makes play monotonous and grindy.

Virtual worlds (yes, this *is* a theory that applies to the likes of *Second Life*, as well as to MMOs) occupy a sweet spot in the middle, where everything comes together. It's what makes MMOs special.

Well, it's what *allows* MMOs to be special. What *makes* them special is something else…

In or On?

Do you log *in* to your MMO of choice, or log *on* to it?

Back in the olde days when we used to use mainframes, some people would "log on" and some would "log in." The former always felt more passive than the latter and was mainly the preserve of casual users; experts would usually "log in," but if they weren't busy they might say "log on." Thus, a conversation might go like this:

> A: Are you logged in?
>
> B: Not at the moment, why?
>
> A: Can you log on to CompSoc 1? I want to see if you show up in my snoop program.

There was a similar, but not identical, distinction for "log off" and "log out": the former would mean you hadn't really finished what you were doing, but the latter was more final. You'd usually say "I've got to log off" rather than "I've got to log out."

In the same way that on/in usage for mainframe sign-ups seem to indicate a depth of understanding of the machine as an environment, perhaps for MMOs it's a measure of your degree of immersion?

So do *you* log in or do you log on?

Mirror Neurons

Game designers draw on many aspects of Psychology and have done so for ages. Flow, presence, and common theories of fun all began life as theories from Psychology. Another theory that game designers use is that of *mirror neurons*.

It turns out that neurons in the brain aren't activated solely by doing things; they can also be acted by seeing things being done. This is fairly obvious (if neurons didn't activate when you saw something, your brain couldn't interpret your vision); what makes mirror neurons special is that they activate both when you're doing something *and* when you see someone else doing the same thing.

The way mirror neurons were discovered (in Italy in the 1980s) is rather gruesome, but it does show the system's basic principles at work. Essentially, monkeys that had been wired up with electrodes in their brains were being monitored to detect which individual neurons fired when a monkey reached for an object (a banana). The experimenters found that the very neurons that fired when a monkey went for a banana itself also fired when it saw someone else grasping a banana. The researchers called these "mirror neurons."

Neuroscientists are still debating the effect of mirror neurons on the brain's abilities, and it's not even entirely clear whether mirror neurons are different to regular brain cells or whether their behavior is due to their connectivity. Psychologists use the term as shorthand to mean the way in which people copy or model other people (or, in the case of characters in books and computer games, pretend-other-people). It's particularly popular for explaining emotional responses.

The way it seems to work is that you observe someone doing something, your mirror neurons recognize the pattern, and then they fire as if you'd done it yourself. This ripples out to the rest of your brain, which reacts as if you had indeed done the action yourself, as the stimulation received is the same. For example, seeing facial expressions that trigger emotions can (via mirror neurons) cause those emotions to trigger in you, too. Hence, empathy.

For MMO designers, this is most important in characterization. If the body language of an NPC or your avatar is carrying an emotional payload, mirror neurons help you feel for that character. Although primarily an animation thing (your lead animator is the real expert here), nevertheless the characters' behavior has to match. You don't want a character looking apprehensive in a situation in which there is no perceived threat, for example: that would work against identification with the character, and serve to detract from the persuasiveness of the virtual world rather than enhance it.

Categorization

Some people don't like categorization. They feel that everyone and everything is different, and to categorize is to treat distinct entities as if they were the same. It ensnares thinking, and obscures important subtleties that differentiate between cases.

What these people *particularly* don't like is when *they* are categorized, as it runs up against their sense of individuality.

Well, if you *are* against categorization as a concept, this means you can't in all conscience tell anyone about it. Words are categorizations for concepts, so applying them to argue against categorization is to argue against yourself.

What you *can* argue against is *bad* categorization or *useless* categorization. If a theory of player types were to split people into groups depending on what letters their real-life names began with, that would be a useless categorization (at least in game design terms; psychologists might make something of it). If a theory were to split people by the absolute level of their main character, that would be a bad categorization because different MMOs have different advancement structures (although it could be okay if it referred to a single virtual world).

Categorization enables us to talk about related concepts in a cogent and well understood way. Sure, some people without a great deal of intelligence might be unable to think outside these categories, but I feel that in general members of the human race are somewhat brighter than that.

Tank Types

I usually play MMOs as a healer because that way people like me and, if I don't like them, I can passive-aggressively kill them. This means I spend many playing hours watching tanks being pounded.

I've seen hundreds of tanks in my time, and as a result have noticed some similarities in behavior among them, standard across MMOs. Here are a few of my observations, for the benefit of those who may be thinking of becoming a healer or those who already are and wish to vent their frustration by recognizing their favorite stereotype. Note that this is an incomplete categorization, not a model:

- Tanks who position themselves in set-piece boss battles like no other tank *ever*, yet insist that "everyone does it this way."

- Tanks who have so much health that you just know they have no damage mitigation whatsoever and they're as likely to survive as a house of cards being hit by a bowling ball.

- Tanks who are alts of people who normally DPS, who know the fights backwards as DPS, but are utterly clueless as tanks.

- Tanks who are undergeared and over-apologetic. Yes, I know you're wearing armor made of tissue paper, you don't have to keep saying you're sorry every time I have to scrape you up off the floor.

- Tanks so single-minded that they are oblivious to the presence of the rest of the group. Was someone explaining the fight in chat? Too bad.

- Tanks who are last to be ready for every fight, then start it without warning and complain that no-one else was ready.

- Tanks with less health than me. These are usually among the testiest when they get smashed to pieces, as clearly it's the healer's fault they can be one-shotted.

- Tanks who wear pumpkins or other comedy head furniture. We can tell you're in your early teens by your vocabulary, you don't have to wear the uniform, too.

- Tanks who say they're going in, then don't. They will, of course, complain heartily if anyone took them at their word and stepped into aggro range because "pulling is the tank's job."

- Tanks who tell the healer how to heal. This is like being rescued following a road traffic accident and telling the paramedics that you want blue bandages. No, not that way up, the other way up. Oh, and put them on using a paint roller.

- Tanks who never say anything, ever, for any reason.

- Tanks who complain that everything is bugged. "It's that bug where the boss resets aggro." No, it's that moment where the boss always resets aggro, and you were all out of taunts.

- Tanks who stand in the fire, then complain that you can't heal them through it. "I thought you were better geared!" Yes, and I thought you were better-brained. *Don't stand in the fire!*

- Tanks who are brittle and unforgiving. The slightest mistake by anyone (tank excepted) and they're screeching about how they hate PUGs and why don't people learn the fights. They threaten bitterly to quit the group if people don't shape up. Everyone is immensely relieved when they make good on this promise.

- Tanks who use weapons meant for DPS, which they justify by appealing to some obscure, under-reported feature that they claim helps tanking, even though you know the real reason is that they don't *have* any other weapons.

- Tanks who are certain of falsehoods. No amount of argument will persuade them that there is a simple way to beat this boss that doesn't involve the healer's having to stand in the fire.

- Tanks who are easily confused. If the fight goes how it went in the YouTube video they watched, they're fine. Any slight deviation, though, and they spam every one of their abilities not on cooldown. If they survive, they'll usually compliment your healing, which is sweet of them, given how much they just made you panic.

Ah, I feel much better for having written that!

Effect and Affect

Immersion is often regarded as a key reason why people play MMOs (by people who don't play them all that much—or by people who have played them a very great deal).

Actually, it's a key *expression* of why people play MMOs.

Where Have All the Hackers Gone?

So where have all the hackers gone today?

Well, they haven't turned into crazed computer vandals—that's a misappropriation of the term "hacker." Yet can they really have simply disappeared?

The answer is that they've not so much disappeared as *migrated*.

Let's see: is there anywhere today that an idealistic, maverick, creative genius with a love of playing with systems can go?

Yes, that's right—they go into MMO development.

Hmm, I sense raised eyebrows.

Okay, so they *do* go elsewhere, where there are frontiers. Academia has a fair few of them and so does regular computer-game development. There's a *very* high concentration in MMO development, though. It's not a coincidence, either.

I'm going to talk about designers here, but a similar argument applies to programmers, too. So: how did most designers get into the industry? In the main, it's because they *played the games*. By playing the games, they absorbed the systems—systems put there by hackers and only really fully appreciated by hackers.

MUD1 was written to embody hacker ethics. Some got in by mere osmosis, but some were placed there on purpose. For example, Roy and I put freedom of identity at the core *deliberately*. This is something that MMOs still value highly.

Why? Because their *designers* still value it highly.

Designers have played one or more MMOs all the way through. They've grokked them. In so grokking them, they've had to absorb the hacker ethics embodied in them, and therefore to have had hacker ethics themselves for it all to make sense.

By the time they've reached the elder game, they know what virtues MMOs deliver—freedom, tolerance, individuality, imagination, art, rebellion, understanding—and they want *others* to experience these, too. They want to be *designers*. So they design.

The basic ideals that they instill in their MMOs through their designs will affect their players—for some, their *millions* of players. Many of these players will themselves become designers and pass those same ideals on to *their* players, and so on, *ad infinitum*. You thought my casual early reference to our "grand scheme for world domination" was a joke? Eventually, *everyone* will be able to create MMOs, their ideas shaped by those creating them now—by those who have art-and-beauty, life-changing, freedom-loving hacker ethics.

Designers create MMOs because they can put a piece of their *soul* into them. Their MMOs are an expression of themselves—of their beliefs, hopes, fears, demons... Through developing MMOs, they develop *themselves*. This puts them in a rare and privileged position: that of *artist*.

Designers create MMOs because that's the latter-day hacker's medium for self-expression, and they *are* such latter-day hackers.

And the reason they're such latter-day hackers? It's because MMO design *selects* for hackers.

Killer or Achiever?

Many people confuse killers and achievers. For example, Players who attack other players in a consensual PvP environment are usually achievers, rather than killers: they want to achieve within the context of PvP. Killers may also engage in PvP, but they'll be the ones camping the spawn points to catch lone players running back to their groups.

Killers measure themselves against other people. Achievers measure themselves against absolute standards. A killer wouldn't particularly care that they had 1,000 kills to their name, except that it shows the game supports their actions; likewise, an achiever doesn't care how other players are doing, except insofar as it validates their own status.

Elitism

Many achievers not only like to achieve, they like others to know they've achieved. It helps them affirm their belief that their achievements matter.

One of the outcomes of this is a tendency towards elitism. If you think you're good, then you want to play with the big kids; you don't want to play with the little kids. That way, you feel more like a big kid yourself because the big kids accept you.

This has led to situations in which players who want a pick-up member for a group they're in will openly and publicly ask for players who have a high gear score or possess some item you can only get from having completed content they deem sufficiently exclusive. As a result, players who don't meet the criteria rarely get a chance *to* meet it: if the only way to get the gear is to run the instances and the only way to get into an instance group is to have the gear, well, you can see the problem.

There is, surprisingly, a solution to this: start your own pick-up groups. If you demand that would-be members of the group "be geared and experienced," applicants will tend to assume that you yourself are both. They very rarely check. So long as you know what to do, you stand a good chance of getting away with it. You can increase your odds even more by playing as a tank or healer, so your embarrassingly low damage-per-second doesn't ring any alarm bells.

It's simple and it usually works. It rarely occurs to people who want to be accepted as elite that the person who is asking them to prove they're elite isn't in turn elite.

Of course, the smart designer has less competitive ways of allowing players to authenticate their elite status, so that players can still feel good about themselves without having to make others feel bad about themselves as a consequence.

Tank Types (Better)

Not all tanks are vainglorious psychopaths. Here are some of the more positive types you see:

- Tanks who never give up. The DPS is clearly incompetent and there's no way we'll defeat the boss before the server is taken down for maintenance next week, but the tank just gets up without complaint, goes straight back in and gets beaten into goo time and time again. You have to admire their perseverance. Maybe one of the DPSs is a relative or something.

- Tanks who are an order of magnitude better than everyone else. Did the rest of the group get killed by that earthquake? No problem! The tank will just solo the boss.

- Helpful tanks. Ones who actually teach people useful stuff without mocking them for not having boned up for the fight as if it were an exam.

- Good, adaptive tanks. Ones who go where they're supposed to go, are hit by what they're supposed to be hit by, interrupt what killer moves they're supposed to interrupt, who self-heal when they spot the DPSs are standing in fire and the healer has to fix them. These are a joy to heal.

Fortunately all tanks think they're one of those listed above, so no-one is going to take my earlier remarks personally. This is just as well: tanks are good at taunting.

Hmm, I really should think about categorizing these; there's probably a Master's dissertation in it at the very least.

Player—that's *Player*—Types

Player Types theory only applies to people who play virtual worlds for fun. It doesn't apply to people who play but not for fun, such as journalists, researchers, or designers.

If you want to break the theory, "it doesn't account for gold farmers!" is not going to do the trick. It's not *intended* to account for them.

Partitions

The Player Types theory way of partitioning players isn't the only one possible, of course. Here's another (let's call it New Partition #1):

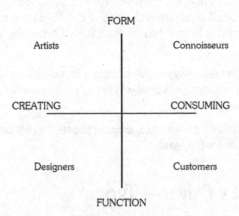

Here's yet another (New Partition #2):

Both of these are complete (they have no gaps between their types) and reasonably correct.

New Partition #1 tells you nothing you didn't already know. It's not useful for MMO design, unless your MMO has physical implications involving wombs (or lack thereof) and age. New Partition #2 has more interesting things to say. You could vaguely use it to identify who plays what games (*Minecraft* for artists, *Mass Effect* for connoisseurs, *Angry Birds* for customers, *The Sims* for designers)—or maybe not.

These graphs are easy to construct:

You were deciding which one you are, admit it. As it happens, this one is actually useful for MMOs: solo *versus* group play; sandbox *versus* theme park.

There are plenty of existing psychometric profiling systems that you can use to make these graphs. It's not hard to take one, give it cool labels and describe it as "player types." This one is a slice of Myers-Briggs[23]:

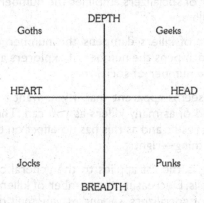

That's thinking *versus* feeling, extraversion *versus* introversion.

Given this, why use the Player Types model?

Well, other typologies look at personalities or activity or world view. Player Types theory looks at *fun*.

[23]Myers & Briggs Foundation: *My MBTI Personality Type*. http://www.myersbriggs.org/my-mbti-personality-type/

Player Type Dynamics

Players of different types don't exist in isolation from one another in MMOs—their paths continually cross. How they deal with this depends on the types of the players involved.

For example, achievers tend to regard most explorers as nerds and losers, although highly-skilled ones will be accepted as eccentrics. Nevertheless, achievers depend to some extent on explorers for puzzle-solving. Those web sites where you go to look up quest solutions, raid fight tactics, and how best to level your long-neglected cooking skills don't get written on their own. As a result, the number of explorers in an MMO has a slightly amplifying effect on the number of achievers. The reverse is not true, though: a rise in the number of achievers will have almost no effect on the number of explorers.

If we examine all permutations of player type pairings, we find:

- The number of achievers amplifies the number of killers and slightly dampens the number of socializers.

- The number of explorers slightly amplifies the number of explorers and achievers, and slightly dampens the number of killers.

- The number of socializers amplifies the number of socializers and killers.

- The number of killers dampens the number of achievers, slightly dampens the number of explorers and greatly dampens the number of socializers.

Looking at this list, it seems apparent that if you want more players overall, then you should get rid of as many killers as you can. The number of socializers will shoot up as a result, and as this has no effect on explorers or achievers, it must be a good thing—right?

Well, *almost*. The thing is, the list applies to the general case, but if you push things too far, then it fails. Decreasing the number of killers will indeed greatly increase the number of socializers, *so long as you don't decrease it too much*. Socializers need something to talk about, and killers provide a vast amount of drama (and hence material) for them. If you eliminate too many killers, then the number of socializers will *also* start to drop; furthermore, because the number of socializers has a feedback effect on socializers themselves, this could lead to a mass exodus.

If we take these edge conditions into account and run the dynamics as a system, we find there are only four stable states that a virtual world can have:

1. A balance, with all four types having a parity of influence.

2. Killers and achievers in equilibrium, with socializers few and far between, but a healthy dash of explorers.

3. Socializers heavily dominant, with killers all but disappeared and explorers and achievers not staying for long.

4. An empty world. The killers drove everyone away, then left themselves.

The first case, where the player types are in balance, is the hardest to set up, and it doesn't scale well. However, it is the most stable—you need fewer incoming newbies to keep it going. It was the default approach for the first decade or so of virtual worlds' existence, until the Great Schism that separated game and social worlds. Game worlds (case two) and social worlds (case three) are also stable configurations, which is why this separation remains the *status quo*.

It doesn't *have* to be this way, of course...

Programmers' Self-Image

Games programmers see themselves as different to programmers working in the wider software industry. They [warning: wild generalization incoming!] see themselves as:

- Individualistic.
- Creative.
- Talented.
- Better than their peers.

This means they dislike working in teams, doing so only perhaps with grudging acceptance if they're the leader of such a team.

The thing is, on the whole their self-image is actually *right*...

VoIP

VoIP means "voice over IP," where the IP in turn means "Internet Protocol" rather than "intellectual property."

VoIP covers a number of technologies for communicating over the Internet using voice. Sometimes, MMOs have a built-in VoIP facility, so they can tie speech to the names and pictures of the avatars engaging in it, but most don't bother. Instead, players use third-party solutions such as TeamSpeak, Ventrilo, Mumble, and even Skype.

Not everyone uses VoIP in MMOs, although it's usually a requirement for end-game activities such as raids and team-based PvP. Note that *speaking* isn't always a requirement, but being able to hear some leader's instructions is. This is just as well because many players don't actually like the idea of speaking to other players. Sometimes it's because they don't want to give away some detail about their real-world self (age, gender, nationality, stammer); sometimes it's because they share a house and speaking annoys everyone else there; sometimes it's because they know that if they do speak, they'll end up being roped into running raids themselves.

The universally-accepted excuse for not participating in VoIP as a speaker is "I don't have a mic." Sometimes, it's actually true, too.

Beyond MMOs

Player Types theory doesn't apply to people who play things that aren't virtual worlds for fun. As great as it is to see its being used successfully for web site design, the theory itself makes no claims in that area.

Because of this, if you try to use it for railway-passenger management and it fails, that doesn't invalidate the theory.

What Determines a Player's Type?

It's easy to look at what a player does and decide that player's type on the basis of this—"She kills a lot of player characters, she must be a killer," or, "She talks a lot, she must be a socializer."

It's easy, but it's a mistake.

Sure, there's a correlation between actions and words, but the important thing in determining a player's type is not to know *what* they did, but to know *why* they did what they did.

Sometimes, critics of the theory will say something like, "I like crafting, but you don't have a category for crafting! Your theory sucks!" They're right in that the theory doesn't have a category for crafting, but they're wrong in that this doesn't mean the theory sucks. They should ask *why* they like crafting:

- Is it because they want to upgrade their gear? Then they're an achiever.

- Is it because they want to give the stuff they make to their friends? Then they're a socializer.

- Is it because they want to find out what kind of advanced things can be made? Then they're an explorer.

- Is it because they want to undercut someone else's prices for the pleasure of bankrupting them? Then they're a killer.

Yes, I know there are other reasons ("I want to sell what I make at a profit"), but they all map onto a player type ("well you're an achiever then"). It's the *why* that's important, not the *what*.

Despite having spent 100 days passing every field test for being a socializer, Dextrus was a killer.

It's the *why*.

The Proteus Effect

What is symbolized by the color black? Yes, so actually it's a shade, not a color, but as I'll be talking colors here, it's too finicky to say "color or shade" the whole time.

Okay, so although black is often used in a context of formality, elegance, and sophistication, it's mainly associated with death, evil, and depression (at least in the Western world). That's just symbolism, though: no-one would treat you as if you were malevolent if you dressed in black.

Well, yes they would. A 1988 study of American football and hockey teams[24] found that the ones playing in black had more penalties awarded against them than teams playing in other colors. The experimenters also staged choreographed plays with 50/50 decisions in them, with one team wearing red and the other wearing black or white: when they showed these to referees, the referees penalized the team wearing black more often than the team wearing white, even though the events were pretty well identical.

What this means is that people treat you based on how you look, whether you like it or not. That's bad enough, but it actually gets worse. The same study found that not only did teams playing in black get more fouls awarded against them, but they committed more fouls in the first place when wearing black kit. In other words, players' *self-perception* also changed depending on the color of their strip (well, uniform, as this was in America).

What has this to do with MMOs? Well, if something as simple as the color of the clothes you're wearing can affect how you behave, what about the appearance of your avatar?

Experimenters at Stanford University[25] had women using female avatars interact with male avatars for a while. The women's avatars were dressed in a range of outfits from gender-neutral (jacket, jumper, jeans) to rather more suggestive (crop top, miniskirt, fishnets, knee-high boots). The researchers found that the women who were given the less conservatively-dressed avatars were afterwards more likely than the other women to agree with statements such as "In the majority of rapes, the victim is promiscuous or has a bad reputation." In other words, their real-world opinions had been influenced by their avatar's clothing.

This means the traffic between player and avatar is two-way. Not only do players affect how avatars behave, but avatars also affect how players behave. This is called the *Proteus Effect*, after the shape-changing Greek sea god of that name.

In the same way that through mirror neurons we can observe other people, we can observe our own internal selves. If you regard your avatar as yourself, you get to do both: observe yourself externally and internally at the same time. You can change your self-perception as a result—or not change it, if you don't like what you see.

On average, tall people earn more salary than short people.

---

[24]Mark G. Frank and Thomas Gilovich: *The Dark Side of Self- and Social Perception: Black Uniforms and Aggression in Professional Sports. Journal of Personality and Social Psychology* 54(1), 74-85, 1988.
[25]Jesse Fox, Jeremy N. Bailenson and Liz Tricase: *The Embodiment of Sexualized Virtual Selves: The Proteus Effect and Experiences of Self-Objectification via Avatars. Computers in Human Behavior* 29, 930-938, 2013.

What Programmers Want

Games programmers want the following from their employers:

- Free pinball tables, pool tables, and bar football on site.

- The ultra-latest hardware.

- Free games, toys, T-shirts, and trips to major overseas conferences.

- A pizza delivery firm within a five-minute radius of the building.

- Top-quality coffee and a fridge full of fizzy, sugary drinks. Oh, and Mars Bars.

As these wishes are shared by everyone on the development side of the game industry, plus a sizeable chunk of the production side, it perhaps comes as no surprise to learn that the programmers often actually get what they want.

Kishōtenketsu Answer

This is the mark scheme for the examination question I showed you earlier.

Question 3

(a) [3%]

   Briefly explain the relationship between *story* and *plot*.

   ```
   Stories consist of an ordered series of
   events.                          [1]
   Plots are ordered series of causally-
   related events.                  [1]
   Fiction involves reassembling the plot
   by reading the story.            [1]
   [For extended ramblings about story/
   history/backstory, award up to 2. They
   need to cover plots to get all 3.]
   ```

(b) [3%]

   Explain why it is important that players should be able to construct a story about what happened in a game they have just finished playing.

   ```
   Such stories are constructed from the
   retelling of significant events.  [1]
   If there are no significant events,
   that means the game had no interesting
   choices.                          [1]
   Therefore it lacked gameplay (i.e., a
   series of interesting choices).   [1]
   ```

(c) [8%]

   Write 60 Seconds of Gameplay for the game *Rogue*.

   ```
   [Note to examiners: the candidates have played Rogue for a class
   discussion.]
   ```

   ```
   For describing about a minute's worth
   of play.                          [1]
   For mentioning key features of Rogue
   (your character, movement, combat,
   treasure, darkness, levels, etc.) [2]
   For conveying a sense of the gameplay.
                                     [2]
   ```

> For describing the player's available
> choices.   [1]
> For describing the player's reasons for
> making particular decisions.   [2]

(d) [6%]

An oriental story-telling form called *Kishōtenketsu* does not use a three-act structure and contains no conflict. Instead, it has four acts. In the first act, something normal happens; in the second act, a twist is added; in the third act, something seemingly unrelated happens; in the fourth act, a contrast is drawn between the first two acts and the third act.

For example:

- Act 1: A girl goes to a drinks machine for a bottle of cola.

- Act 2: The bottle won't come out. She has to hit the machine to free it.

- Act 3: A boy sits alone on a park bench.

- Act 4: The girl arrives and surprises the boy by giving him the cola.

Assess the suitability of *Kishōtenketsu* for use in computer game plots.

> [This is open-ended, so marks can be awarded for other approaches. However,
> it is expected that candidates will propose that Kishōtenketsu is suitable
> for computer games because it allows for interesting choices to be presented
> from which a personal narrative for the player can be constructed. Economic
> arguments as to the sales potential of such games should be afforded fewer
> marks. Note that if the candidate points out that this exam question follows
> the Kishōtenketsu structure, they'll get full marks—they have a definite
> future in game design.]

None of the 25 or so students who took the exam got the 20 marks for spotting that the question followed the *Kishōtenketsu* structure. However, some did go on to get jobs in game design.

As tests for potential game designers go, I'd therefore rate it sufficient but not necessary.

Fishing

One of the common ways to attack Player Types theory is by using the counter-example-that-isn't. People will say: "I like fishing, but that isn't one of the types!"

Well, that's right, it isn't one of the types. It would be some crazy-detailed theory that had a category to explain why people like fishing. However, remember what I wrote earlier: the rationale with player types is not *what* people do but *why* they do it.

Why do you like fishing?

- You like increasing your fishing skill? You're an achiever.

- You want to share health-giving meals made from fish with your friends? You're a socializer.

- You want to see what kinds of fish you can catch with what probabilities? You're an explorer.

- You hope to lure someone else into joining you so you can suddenly assault them while they're armed only with a fishing rod? You're a killer.

It might alternatively be that you just like the fishing mini-game, in which case the theory doesn't even apply to you: you're not playing the MMO because it's fun in and of itself, you're playing it simply so you can play the fishing mini-game for fun.

If you want to break Player Types theory, a fishing (or building or crafting) example isn't going to do it.

The Soul of a Game

In the same way that you can look at people as either sets of behavioral traits or as some central core of being that manifests itself through behavioral traits, you can regard "game structure" as either sets of reactions to actions or a central core of design that manifests itself through reactions to actions.

In people, we call that central core of being a "soul."

We do the same in games, too.

The Uncanny Valley

Mirror neurons have a better chance of firing if what they're exposed to is close to what they're usually exposed to. Yes, you can read the emotion of a cartoon face, and yes, you can tell how someone in a book feels by how they are described. However, neither works as well as a real face, thanks to millions of years of evolution designed to optimize the task. Or, if you're a creationist, thanks to the millions of years of evolution that gave your deity universe-creating powers.

I'm guessing that you've heard of *the uncanny valley* already, as it's fairly well-known. It was discovered in Japan in 1970, in the context of human-looking robots. People warmed more to robots as they became more human-looking, until suddenly they were repulsed by them. The robots did look more human than before, but in a way that creeped people out. They were nearly-but-not-quite human-looking. This switch from positive to negative opinions is followed by a switch back to positive opinions when the robot starts looking and behaving so human that it's hard to tell the difference.

In computer games, the uncanny valley began to make its appearance as graphics became more photorealistic. You'd be looking at a character that seemed human and behaved human, then it smiled and AIII! What the hell is THAT?! However, the reason I mention it isn't so that you can dredge up your own chucklesome memory of unsettling characters; rather, it's to point something out that's nothing really to do with animation at all.

See, you can experience the uncanny valley not only through watching odd-looking, disturbing movements. You can also experience it from watching not-quite-right behaviors. Animators rule animations, but designers rule behaviors. If you see a character eating a chicken, then whether or not it creeps you out depends only on your level of vegetarianism. If you see a character eating a chicken with the feathers on, that's something different. Likewise, adult characters being overly-friendly to child characters could also feel creepy. You'd draw negative conclusions about such characters, even if the only reason they were acting that way was because of emergence in their AI.

Any human-like behavior of characters can lead to the uncanny valley. Just be aware...

The King's Opinion

Imagine an MMO in which a powerful NPC, a king, will only help you if he holds you in high esteem. Players would have to work to get him to respect them. Then, they'd have to maintain his respect or his opinion would change.

Wouldn't that be something special?

Well no, not really.

The King's opinion is just a number. All I have to do to ingratiate myself with the king is find out what particular buttons I need to press and then press them. You want me to kill 2,000 orcs? Okay, I'll kill them. You want me to kill a particular boss? Okay, that boss is going down. You want me to collect dragon eggs that spawn infrequently in odd places? It's boring, but hey, I'll do it. Want me to visit a bunch of obscure locations, or make some particular robe, or provoke some noble? They're just quests like any other.

Where it could get interesting is if the king's opinion of you is not independent of his opinion of other people. However, for that to work you'd need an MMO with far fewer players per shard than we have at present.

The other way to do it would be to have the king's opinion be a structure, not a number.

Kings with artificial intelligence: now that *would* be something special.

Design by Referendum

Why try figure out what the players want when you can just ask them to vote on ideas? It introduces democracy to design. Democracy is good!

Who decides what players get to vote on? What happens when votes are passed to implement incompatible things? What happens when organized groups of griefers manage to pass a vote that mandates a change to the vote-counting code?

Where's the artistic *vision* that imbues the MMO with a soul?

Why Achiever-Only MMOs Don't Work

I'm sick of telling people this, so I thought I'd write it down. Next time, I can innocently ask whether they've read this book and sell them a copy if they haven't.

So: achievers like to achieve. They like to think they are a cut above other players. Their collection of rewards is their yardstick. They look at their own rewards, look at the rewards of others, and feel like they've achieved something if their own are better. It doesn't matter how these rewards are manifest—levels, points, gear, money, army size, achievements, special items of clothing—so long as an achiever can use them to tell that they're better than someone else.

This means you need a "someone else" for the achiever to be better than. Socializers have miserable sets of rewards. In an MMO that has a reasonable contingent of socializers, almost all achievers can therefore feel superior to almost all of them. The socializers, not being achievers, have no incentive to achieve anything; they plod along entirely happily, mainly to be with their friends. Progress-indicator achiever rewards mean nothing to them.

Now what if there are no socializers? What if your MMO is pitched so strongly at achievers that the socializers stay away?

Most of the achievers will look down and see someone below them. However, some achievers will be near the bottom where the socializers were. They don't like being near the bottom. They want to be better than other players, but they get no sense of that because everyone else is better than they are. After struggling and failing to improve their status (because they really *aren't* as good as everyone else), they quit.

Now, someone *else* is at the bottom. They weren't at the bottom before, but they are now. The same reasoning applies, so they fall away, too. The process continues, until eventually you end up with a game full of either equally expert, high-skill players or masochists. You lost all the other achievers as they gradually fell away from the bottom.

If you have socializers, they act like a hem that stops the cloth above them from fraying. Therefore, if you want to maintain a lot of achievers, you need to keep a viable number of socializers around.

Point of View

First-person shooters offer, as you may suspect, a first-person viewpoint. You see the game world through the eyes of your avatar. Indeed, at least while you're engaged in combat, this is the only point of view you're likely to get.

At first, 3D graphical MMOs also offered the first-person perspective as default. Then, they began to allow other camera positions, such as over-the-shoulder. Nowadays, you can choose from a range of settings for your default.

In theory, how you choose to view your character—first-person, second-person, or third-person—*should* say something about how immersed you are in an MMO. A first-person point of view (PoV) should be more persuasive than a third-person PoV. Failing that, at the very least it ought to say something about how much you identify with your character.

I say "in theory" there, but unfortunately there *isn't* actually any formal theory that links point of view to sense of immersion in MMOs. There is some work that says women prefer first-person and men prefer third-person (by a ratio of around 2:1 in both cases)[26], which is interesting but, again, doesn't come with an explanation.

What perspective do you use? Have you tried others? Is it for purely practical purposes, or does it just "feel" right?

Non-ebook readers: scribble your answer in the box below.

Good, that should make people buying this book second-hand wish they had a new one. More royalties for me!

[26]Nick Yee: *It's a Matter of Perspective. The Daedalus Project*, July 2004. http://www.nickyee.com/daedalus/archives/000816.php

Feedback Loop

If an MMO designer designs for four player types, then when we analyze who actually plays their MMO it shouldn't come as a surprise if we discover it's packed with examples of those four player types. If the model is complete and correct, then this is a good thing; if it's overlooking some players or mischaracterizing them, then it's less useful.

When I first described player types, back in Internet prehistory, we were seeing MMOs created for only *one* type—that of the designer. Vast swathes of potential players were being put off because they didn't share the designer's idea of what fun was. We were getting into a feedback loop: design for an achiever, attract achievers; then, when some of those achievers themselves become designers, they'll also design for achievers, only even more so.

My aim with player types was to raise the possibility in designers' minds that there were other types of player *at all*; if that's the only enduring legacy of the theory, I'll therefore consider it a job done.

The Designer's Lot

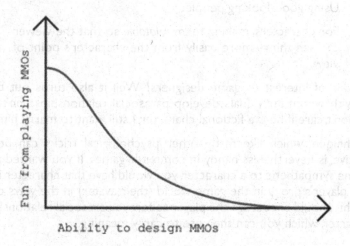

Parasocial Relationships

A *parasocial relationship* is one that a person has with someone who doesn't know them.

This may seem strange, but it happens all the time. It was first studied in the 1950s with regards to actors, TV show hosts, news anchors, and other people whom their audiences felt they "met" regularly. People are very good at building models of other people in their heads—it's how they can tell how other people will act. They can form opinions of these people, which is fair enough; they can also form one-way relationships with them, though, which is rather more interesting.

It was discovered that people who do develop parasocial relationships with TV personalities are more likely to engage with their shows. TV producers therefore set about trying to engender such relationships. The methods they used included:

- Addressing the viewer directly. "See you next week!"

- Using nonverbal communication such as eye contact. Teleprompters help here.

- Using good-looking people.

- For characters, making them *relatable* so that the viewer can see things more easily from the character's point of view.

Why is this of interest to game designers? Well it also turns out that the people with whom individuals develop parasocial relationships *don't have to exist!* "I don't care if he *is* a fictional character, I still want to marry him."

This technique, which like many other psychological tricks can be mildly exploitative, is nevertheless handy in computer games. If you wanted a player to become sympathetic to a character, you would have that character interact with the player's proxy in the game world (their avatar) in the ways outlined above. This should encourage the player to form a parasocial relationship with the character, which you can then use to carry meaning.

This wouldn't really be worth mentioning in an MMO context but for one further point: in MMOs, people can develop parasocial relationships *with their own avatars*, which is to say with themselves. This takes the whole concept into uncharted territory. Nevertheless, it does happen: people will treat some of their characters differently to others, as if they were separate and distinct individuals in their own right.

I'd be moderately upbeat about this if I hadn't seen one-too-many movies in which the ventriloquist's complex bond with their dummy takes a slightly murderous turn.

More Why

Suppose you want to identify your MMO's socializers. How would you do that?

Well, socializers communicate. Therefore, if you check through your log files and find out who talks the most, those people will be your socializers, right?

No.

Some socializers are enthusiastic listeners but unenthusiastic speakers—"socializer" does not mean "extrovert." Yes, some socializers *do* like to talk a lot, but two explorers could hold a three-hour long conversation exchanging notes. Sustained banter in guild chat could easily be driven by friendly and open socializers, but it could also occur because achievers are getting bored grinding; and if you don't give them something fun to do *real soon*, they're going to be so fed up they'll leave.

Besides, socializers could be chatting on a VoIP channel or playing alongside friends in the same room.

As I keep saying: it's not what people *do* in an MMO that defines their player type, it's *why they do it*.

I should mention that testing a theory when you can only observe what people do and not why they do it is very difficult. Perhaps this explains some of Player Types theory's resilience to attacks.

Faults in the Player Types model

The Player Types model—achievers, explorers, socializers, killers—has been used successfully in MMO design almost since the day the theory was published (*Ultima Online*, which was launched one year later, used it). It's still relied on in MMO design today (*WildStar* used it). As theories go, it remains the best one out there—in part because it's pretty well the *only* one out there…

This doesn't mean it's perfect, though. It has been rightly criticized for falling short in a number of areas, primarily:

- It doesn't explain how or why players move between types, which is known to happen.

- It has two very different subtypes of killer for no apparent reason.

- It doesn't account for the concept of *immersion*.

- The theory doesn't connect to any established theories outside of MMO design, so isn't fully grounded.

Thus, although the theory has practical uses, it's incomplete and therefore troubling to theorists.

It's also troubling to MMO designers: given that the theory works, it would be constructive to know *why* it works.

Different Views

How would you like the ability to present your avatar so it looked different to different people? You might want to look old and fat to one set of characters but young and slim to another. You might want to be female to some players and male to others. You might want to look like your real self to your real friends, but not to others. How would you like that ability?

How would you like it if you could change the way that others looked to you? So all gnomes were human-sized, or you didn't see their clothes, or they had huge noses?

How would you like it if people could change the way *you* appeared to *them*, without your knowing?

Losing

The problem with losing in MMOs is that (except in very few examples) ultimately *everyone* loses; or at least, they don't win. How do you "win" *Guild Wars 2* or *WoW* or *LotRO*? You don't. You win battles, but you can never win the war.

How about if MMOs *did* let you win?

Let's say that there are 50 levels, and when you get to level 51 you are given the option of retiring or going back down to level 50. If you retire, congratulations, you've won, your character sails off into the sunset and disappears from the database except as a proud entry in the Hall of Fame and maybe a 3D-printed figurine. If you don't retire, you'll be asked again next time you reach level 51.

What would happen?

What would happen if you didn't get asked at level 51 whether you wanted to retire—you just retired automatically?

What if retiring were the *aim* of the game? If stopping playing was *how* you won?

Don't think of it in terms of the MMO you currently play, think of it in terms of an MMO designed for this kind of play. If it were the escape-from-a-prisoner-of-war-camp idea I mentioned earlier, you'd know from the start that when you escaped, it would be game over. Would *that* make a difference?

You're thinking, right?

Drift

It's long been known that players change their playing style over time—indeed, the observation *precedes* that of player types by over a decade! The term we always used to describe it back then was *drift*.

Here's what we (well, I) noticed happening when a room full of newbies was introduced to *MUD1*:

- They started by killing each other.

- After losing one-too-many times, they abandoned killing and went exploring.

- In the course of exploring, they would gain points and go up levels, and would slowly switch to this as their primary playing style.

- Finally, those who kept playing for weeks and months would become grizzled old-timers who spent all their time talking to each other.

Some of this, in particular the switch away from killing, was intentionally designed-in. I didn't really consider the rest explicitly—I just knew that I had enough checks and balances that it would all work out.

Anyway, using the Player Types model now available to us, we can lay out the track that players follow as they drift: killer to explorer to achiever to socializer. Because most players by far progress this way, it's called the *main sequence* of player development. Here's what it looks like on the player types graph:

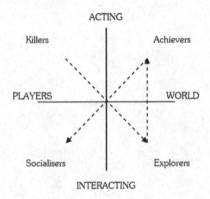

Although this is the main sequence, that doesn't mean it's the *only* sequence. There are other sequences, too, which seem to oscillate. Some players, for example did this:

- Dived right in and tried to score points.

- After realizing that the game was more sophisticated, they decided to be more scientific about their approach and began exploring.

- After gaining enough knowledge to continue, they went back to racking up points.

- They ended their playing days months later as experts who knew the inner workings of the game implicitly.

This goes achiever to explorer to achiever to explorer—the *achiever sequence* (if you can call it a sequence).

Here's another thing some people did:

- Begin by killing each other or shouting abuse.

- Give up on the antisocial behavior and start making friends and asking for help.

- When they had many contacts, they would begin leading groups of players.

- Finally, they'd pass the baton on to someone else and wind up as grizzled old-timers.

This goes killer to socializer to (a different kind of) killer to socializer—the *socializer sequence*.

There were other strange progressions, too. All this shows that, although the Player Types model allows us to label the various stages of the main sequence of player development, it's fairly obvious that it isn't up to describing the other sequences. In other words, it's limited.

Well, in its *present* state it is, yes.

Mechanical

Games have mechanics, but games are not their mechanics. You don't get gameplay from a set of do-this, do-that components. You need the components, yes, but they're a means to an end.

Game design also has mechanics, but game design is not its mechanics. You don't get art from a set of do-this, do-that components. You need the components, yes, but they're a means to an end.

Designers and players alike can recognize mechanistic games when they see them.

Designers and players alike can recognize mechanistic game design when they see it.

Noble Content

In the old days of CompuServe, there was the concept of "noble content." This was the feature set that subscribers used to justify paying for their CompuServe account: "to follow stock prices"; "to educate my children"; "to read book reviews"; "to send electronic mails." Good, wholesome, acceptable-to-society stuff.

However, people *actually* used CompuServe mainly for other things: chat rooms and games. With no noble content, people wouldn't have signed up; with no ignoble content, they wouldn't have stayed.

The world has changed since the 1980s. With MMOs, "this is a game" is now the noble content. People sign up because they want to Play A Game. Once they're there, they come across the ignoble content—the socializing, the exploring, the killing—and it's *that* which keeps them. Well, many of them.

If the ignoble content weren't there, they wouldn't stay; if the noble content weren't there, they wouldn't come.

"This is a game" is the noble content for MMOs, at least at present. "This is not a game" may be true for non-achievers, but it won't be noble content until it can be used as a gateway to ignoble content of its own.

SkySaga

These are 3D printouts of characters from *SkySaga*:

They're eight inches tall, full color, and cost several hundred pounds each; but if they were two inches tall, they'd be much less expensive. Remember them when you read the word "boon" later in this book.

Texts

A text is a (normally sequentially-ordered) collection of symbols from which meaning can be extracted. Yes, normally that means writing, but that's not all it means. If someone can convey meaning through a dance, then that dance is a text.

Texts are either fixed or fluid.

Stories are primarily fixed texts. In reading a story, you do have some freedom to interpret the words as they best suit you, but your ability to affect the plot is zero. The same applies to all fixed texts, whether movies, TV shows, or photography.

Not all texts are fixed, however. Stage actors have some room to change their performance in response to the audience's reaction. If someone tells you a story, then they can alter that story on-the-fly to suit how you're engaging with it. The tale of Umar from the Hamzanama can be told multiple ways. Stories can be adapted by the storyteller in the telling, for the benefit of those listening.

With non-fixed texts, you can gain wider insights. However, you are dependent on the storyteller to hone the telling so it's right for you. If the storyteller is not up to it, you'll miss out.

The best stories are flexible, but you have to be told them by a good story-teller—who even then is not as good as you yourself would be, because you understand yourself better than anyone else does. The best storyteller for you is therefore, well, you! However, it's hard for you to tell yourself anything other than fixed stories—you don't get much chance to change them.

If you could tell yourself unbounded stories, in which you have control over both the way the story is told and the way it is interpreted, then how wondrous that would be! There would be no need for any level of metaphor: you'd be saying what you needed to hear, how you needed to hear it.

This is life, or at least it would be if life were fiction.

The best stories aren't told; the best stories are *lived*.

Alter Ego

Back in 2004, I visited an exhibition of photographs in London called *Alter Ego*. It was by photojournalist Robbie Cooper, and it consisted of more than 100 large panels (20 inches by 24 inches) showing pairs of pictures. On the left of each pair was a real person; on the right was their virtual world avatar. Some were from game worlds (MMOs), some were from social worlds; all were striking.

See? Striking.

Some of the people featured looked just like their avatar. Others resembled them in more of a "have you noticed how dogs often look like their owners?" kind of way. Some looked radically different.

Robbie spent considerable time seeking out more people to photograph in this manner and eventually put together a collection in book form[27]. I was one of those he photographed, which is why I get to call him Robbie and you don't.

For historical reasons, my image comes first in the book. The photograph alongside that of me is a screen shot of my "avatar" from *MUD2*:

Richard the arch-wizard is here.

The book has short interviews with the people pictured, telling their stories. Some of these are themselves utterly compelling.

Why do you suppose that the real images are on the left and the corresponding avatars are on the right?

---

[27]Robbie Cooper: *Alter Ego: Avatars and their Creators*. Chris Boot, 2007.

Right Rewards

When I first went to school, any written work we did that was particularly good was given a star. A similar system exists to this day in most schools, so I expect you know what I mean.

We had three levels of stars: gold were the best, then silver, then stars in block colors (red, yellow, blue, green). The latter were much more common than the golds and the silvers, which I suspect was mainly to do with the fact that every packet of stars had one sheet of each of the six possibilities, so there were always going to be four block-color stars for every gold and silver star.

Many children aspired to win the coveted gold stars, but interestingly there were others who only wanted them if their friends got them. They complained if they got a gold or silver and their friend got a green. As a general rule, they wanted their own stars to be the same colors as those of their friends. They appreciated that you had to do something special to get any kind of star at all, but thought gold stars were often "the wrong color."

Okay, so gold stars are achiever rewards. You give them to achievers. People who want them are achievers, so that's good, it gives them an incentive (at least until a few years later when they realize that such stars are actually worthless). Those who want stars the same color as their friends' are socializers. If you give them stars of any kind, you're giving them achiever rewards. Why would they be interested in those? They're socializers! Give them socializer rewards!

The solution to the above is to give people *either* a gold star *or* three block-color stars. Silvers are two block-color stars. You can even give a silver and a block-color to make a gold if you want to teach the beginnings of arithmetic. This way, children who are smart socializers can be flagged as smart to the achievers, but can also have the same color as their Best Friend Forever. It uses up a few more stars overall, but you're probably going to have a lot of spares anyway with a 4/1/1 distribution.

Schoolwork isn't an MMO, but the same principle applies: make the reward fit the type!

In the Bag

I gave a talk at the Gamification Summit in San Francisco in June, 2012. Such events usually give attendees goody bags with initial stuff in them plus room for any more stuff they might pick up during the course of the day. The Gamification Summit was no different in this regard, except it printed four versions of its goody bags:

Clockwise from top left: killer, achiever, explorer, and socializer.

I was rather chuffed.

Baby Learns to Walk

Baby thrashes around, finding how to move arms, legs, fingers.

Baby combines sequences of actions to kick, to balance, to sit.

Baby uses these sequences to achieve goals, thinking about what to do, toddling.

Baby repeats until the sequence is automatic and can be used as a single, compound action: walking.

Evil Characters

Have you ever played an evil character in a modern MMO?

The chance that you have is exceptionally remote. You may have played characters that are *labeled* as evil, but you almost certainly won't have played any that actually *are* evil.

An orc in *LotRO*? An undead warlock in *WoW*? A dark elf, arasai, iksar, ogre, sarnak, ratonga, or troll in *EQ2*? The worst they are is "naughty."

(They're all "races", too, but that's a different rant).

Evil people are as likely to attack each other as anyone else: it's rule by fear. In an evil world, you do what your guild leader says not because you agree with it or because you don't want guild drama, but because if you *don't* obey orders, they'll **halve your score**.

If evil characters really *were* evil, only evil, stupid, or curious people would actually play them. Everyone else would play good—or play some other game. "Evil" is just a role-play sticker. How can you be evil if you can't actually *do* anything to anyone?

Likewise, "good" is only a label. Self-sacrifice is so cheap in today's MMOs (a couple of minutes of corpse running plus a few further tiresome seconds reacquiring your buffs) that even evil people will do it. You may be hailed as being good for saving your buddies, but "nice" would usually be the more accurate word.

People who play "good" characters and think they're play-acting good would be horribly shamed if exposed to *actual* goodness. People who play "evil" characters and think they're play-acting evil would have an even worse time of it if exposed to *actual* evilness. Today's MMOs rarely have the interactions necessary to support either concept in any depth. If they did, how many people would play them?

Good and evil in MMOs are labels. As with all labels, choosing one (when you create your character) says something about you, but *believing* what it says is a completely different matter.

In-World IP

An idea that crops up from time to time is that of having secret recipes in MMOs. The idea is to reward explorers who are more interested in crafting than killing.

Leaving aside the fact that explorers are interested in neither (they're interested in exploring), this nevertheless sounds reasonably attractive on the face of it. If you find the secret recipe, then your swords will be better than those of other people, so you can charge more money for them.

You can take this further, by giving the first person to discover the recipe code-supported intellectual property rights in it. This means that if other people discover it later, they have to pay the first person a royalty to use it. The real world works like this, so why not do it in virtual worlds?

Well, let's see what would happen.

People who start playing six months after the MMO launched would find themselves having to pay royalties for something they were quite capable of "discovering" themselves. They would not like this. They would complain. They would look for some other MMO to play, where this kind of reward-the-early-birds system was not in operation.

It's a shame we can't do that for real-world patent-the-obvious ideas, too.

Still, backtracking away from the suggestion of enforcing in-world IP, this discovery idea can *almost* work. Blacksmith Bill adds a ton of stuff to his magic sword mix and creates swords that last longer or do more damage than the swords made by Blacksmith Brenda. If Bill told Brenda his secret, or if she experimented and found out herself, she could produce the same swords and not have to pay Blacksmith Bill anything. Blacksmith Bob, without the requisite knowledge, would be stuffed, though.

I say "almost work" because those explorers who were first to find a recipe would simply put it on a web site. Groups of them may even cooperate to find the best combinations. Every other player would know them if they had access to, oh, let's say a **search engine**.

The usual response to this is to say that recipes should be randomized for individuals, so that your recipe for the perfect sword is different to mine. This would mean that only people who spent a lot of time doing trial-and-error experiments or were incredibly lucky would find "their" recipe.

Sadly, this approach is so much at odds with how things work in real life that it bears no relation to how players feel crafting "should" function. It means that recipes can't be sold or traded, and spells hours of frustration for anyone who hopes to have a playing career in crafting.

Gameplay doesn't *have* to have any fiction to cover it, but it makes an MMO less persuasive if it doesn't.

Oh, and if you think I'm making this idea up only so I can knock it down, *Asheron's Call* did something very like it for spell research. Just because an idea is bad, that doesn't mean it won't be implemented. Indeed, in some cases you may not know it's bad *until* it's implemented.

Rocks

Suppose you are standing on a rocky hillside. You pick up a rock and throw it as far as you can. What will the rock do?

Well, it might bounce down the hillside as far as it can: in that case, it's an *achiever* rock. Or it could skitter off some other rocks and bounce away in some unexpected, wild direction: this would make it an *explorer* rock. Perhaps it will land among a group of other rocks and nestle there, meaning it's a *socializer* rock. Or maybe it will strike another, weaker rock and shatter it to bits—clearly a *killer* rock, if ever there was one.

But ... we're talking about rocks here. Rocks have no motivation whatsoever. You can't figure out anything about their intentions when they're thrown down a hill because they *have* no intentions.

Over-eager people can sometimes over-extend a theory. For the Player Types model, I make no claims beyond the domain of people who play virtual worlds for fun. If the theory does apply elsewhere, to rocks or anything smarter, well that's great; personally, though, I've no idea why it should.

Alternate Character Models

EverQuest 2 has three character models. There's the original, then there's a set created by a company called SOGA to bring EQ2 to the Far Eastern market, and then there's the bobbleheads you get in /cutemode.

So, you may see yourself as a gaunt stranger, your face half-hidden by hair, but the people you're playing with may see you as a fresh-faced, slightly concerned individual—or as a bobblehead.

There's nothing in the technology that would prevent an MMO from allowing players to use the character-creation system to build models of other people's characters to be displayed locally instead of the official version. I could decide to see you as a bat-faced crone when everyone else sees you as a suave movie star.

It's not hard to implement this, so why don't MMO developers implement it?

In a word: identity.

Inappropriate Armor

From my Dungeons & Dragons first edition Men & Magic, fourth printing, November 1975:

AMAZON

D&D didn't even have Amazons.

Deathtraps and Giveaways

With user-created content, if the content the users create has any effect on the game as a whole, you only ever get two kinds created: deathtraps and giveaways.

Deathtraps are designed to maim, kill, frustrate, taunt, and otherwise cause grief to those experiencing it.

Giveaways are trivially easy. You walk through the portal and there's the treasure, or there's the glass-jaw boss, or there's the mass of critters you need to raise your reputation all standing in the fireball-friendly pit.

Why is this?

Well consider why anyone would want to create content, then think about what content they would create:

- Killers would create deathtraps because these press two of their buttons: death and traps.

- Explorers would create complex, esoteric, elaborate experiments that are perceived by everyone else to be deathtraps.

- Achievers either wouldn't create anything or they'd create giveaways as a cheaper alternative to pay-to-win.

- Socializers would create giveaways so people will like them.

Everything, therefore, is either a deathtrap or a giveaway.

Exception: if you have a player who is transitioning to becoming a designer, they *might* create something else.

Features from Mechanics

There's a trend in MMOs to have hard-to-reach objects dotted around for players to find. The idea originated in *Meridian 59*, which had puzzle-guarded objects that permanently increased a character's mana pool. The idea was imported into *Star Wars: the Old Republic* as "datacrons" (by Damion Schubert, who designed *M59*'s system), but they crop up as "vistas" in *Guild Wars 2*, "datacubes" in *WildStar*, "lore objects" in *The Secret World*, and so on.

The purpose of these objects is to encourage and reward exploration. Getting to one will usually net a minor prize (a few points, a stat increase, a cinematic, some backstory), which justifies their existence to achievers; they're mainly *aimed* at explorers, though.

In general, they work, too: explorers like thinking, "I wonder if that ship container floating out there in the ether might have some lore in it?"— and then going to find out. They might even like thinking, "I can see the lore in that ship container floating out there in the ether, and I'm going to figure out how to get to it."

What explorers don't like, however, is this: "I can see the lore in that ship container floating out there in the ether, and I know how to get to it, but I can't make the stupid platformer-style sequence of jumps I'm required to make in order to get to it." Why on earth *would* they like that? I remember a particularly awkward datacron in *SW:TOR* that it took a team of people to get.

I'm actually pretty good at MMO character control, so I managed to get to the ship container floating out there in the ether (which was in *TSW*) on my first attempt. Then again, it took me about 20 attempts before I managed to jump from a car onto a narrow wall in Seoul, so I'm not *that* great.

If you're designing a feature for a particular type of player, design the mechanics that support that feature for that particular type of player, too. Otherwise, you lose what you were hoping to gain.

Go, GoPets!

GoPets was an MMO for children, with a revenue model based on selling virtual objects for (ultimately) real money—the default approach in Korea, where it was based.

GoPets was designed as a social world and (in the words of the designer, Erik Bethke) it "carpet bombed" the socializer segment of the player types graph. It integrated all manner of socializer-friendly things into its environment, including powerful yet very usable social networking tools. It did reasonably well.

One day, when Erik was looking at the results of a data-mining exercise to find out what virtual goods were selling best, he discovered something peculiar. A fruit tree which produced one fruit every hour (if you stood next to it for that entire hour) was being bought by players who were, once the numbers were run, some *44 times* more likely to be profitable than the average *GoPets* player. This fruit tree was one of the very few achiever-friendly elements in the otherwise heavily socializer-oriented world.

Looking at the statistics for the "content-creator" feature—one of the only explorer-friendly features provided—yielded even more dramatic results. Explorers were *64 times* more likely to be profitable than the average (i.e., socializer) player.

As a result of this, Erik added some more very simple achiever and explorer elements. Seven days later, *GoPets'* revenue had *doubled*. *GoPets* was still heavily socializer-oriented, but now much more profitable than it was.

Virtual worlds—whether social or game in orientation—need players of *all* types. If you only design for one, you may come to rue your decision.

Historical note: Zynga bought *GoPets* in 2009. It was swiftly closed, coinciding with Zynga's launch of *Petville*.

Really Evil Characters

In early MMOs such as *MUD1*, players *could* perform major acts of substance to other players' characters. These were days when permadeath was the norm, after all. There weren't other MMOs you could flee to if you didn't like it, so people *could* bully and harass and impose themselves on others. There *were* evil characters.

However, the way that these early worlds were designed, playing an evil character was not a viable strategy: good players could easily gang up on you, and you would be attacked on sight.

Wouldn't other evil characters help you out, though? Well no, they wouldn't: evil is a state of mind, not a philosophy. Other evil characters would *also* attack you (and if they didn't, well ha!—some evil *they* were…).

You can still just about get "good" in today's MMOs, but they don't make kindness and self-sacrifice easy. You can't really get evil except in a social context, where players do still have the chance to land a blow that hurts.

In MMO terms, evil=naughty, good=nice.

Let's just hope people don't take those impressions back with them when they return to the real world.

Adult Learns to Drive

Adult presses pedals, moves wheel, shifts gear, adjusts mirror, finding out what does what.

Adult combines sequences of actions to move forward, in reverse, to turn.

Adult uses these sequences to achieve goals, thinking about what to do. Stay wide of the parked cars, then pull over in front of them, put on handbrake, put into neutral, switch off engine.

Adult repeats until the sequence is automatic and can be used as a single, compound action: driving.

A New Dimension

Two of the problems with the Player Types model are related:

- There are two subtypes of killer in the player types graph.

- The socializer and explorer sequences of player development oscillate between only two types.

Both of these seem to suggest the same solution: the theory is missing a dimension. In other words, instead of being a 2D graph, it's a 3D graph.

So, what dimension is missing?

Well the differences between politician-style killers and griefer-style killers suggest several possibilities:

- Politicians believe they're helping people, whereas griefers know they're hindering them;

- Politicians feel superior to other players, whereas griefers feel inferior;

- Politicians work through subtle influences, whereas griefers are very in-your-face.

Of these, it's the latter that is the biggest clue to what's going on (and in the end explains the other two, as well). Basically, politicians tend to act on other players in a calculating way, whereas griefers behave in a more impromptu fashion. This doesn't mean that politicians can't grief (Dextrus was a kind of "criminal mastermind" politician), nor that griefers have to cause pain and anguish (Robin Hood players steal from pompous players to give to random strangers). It's a good, general distinction though.

Formally, then: some people think about what they're doing and others don't. The technical terms for this situation are *explicit* (able to explain your actions openly) and *implicit* (unable to do so—you just do what you do). Politicians act on other players explicitly; griefers act on other players implicitly.

What about the other three types? How do they split up?

Splitting Killers

Adding a new dimension splits the killer type, giving us two new types:

Griefers—implicit killers

- Attack, attack, attack!
- Very in-your-face and attention-seeking.
- Unable to explain why they act as they do.
- Vague aim is to get a big, bad reputation.

Politicians—explicit killers

- Act with foresight and forethought.
- Manipulate people subtly.
- Explain themselves in terms of the benefits they bring the MMO.
- Secret aim is to get a big, good reputation.

Splitting Socializers

Adding a new dimension splits the socializer type, giving us two new types:

Networkers—explicit socializers

- Find people with whom to interact.
- Get to know their fellow players.
- Learn who and what these people know.
- Find out who's worth hanging out with.

Friends—implicit socializers

- Interact with people they already know well.
- Have deep, intuitive understanding of them.
- Enjoy their company.
- Accept their little foibles...

Splitting Achievers

Adding a new dimension splits the achiever type, giving us two new types:

Opportunists—implicit achievers

- See a chance and take it.
- Look around for things to do.
- If there's an obstacle, do something else.
- Flit about from place to place, from objective to objective.

Planners—explicit achievers

- Set a goal and aim to achieve it.
- Perform actions as part of a larger scheme.
- If there's an obstacle, overcome it or work round it.
- Pursue the same objective doggedly.

Splitting Explorers

Adding a new dimension splits the explorer type, giving us two new types:

Scientists—explicit explorers

- Experiment to form a theory.
- Use theories predictively to test them.
- Acquire knowledge methodically.
- Seek to explain phenomena.

Hackers—implicit explorers

- Experiment to reveal meaning.
- Have a tacit understanding of the virtual world—they have no need to test.
- Go where fancy takes them.
- Seek to discover new phenomena.

The term "hacker" here is in the traditional sense of "computer guru," rather than the "some bastard who breaks into your computer" sense that arose from the media's complete inability to understand jargon.

Player Types Revisited

By adding an extra dimension to the player types graph, we go from this:

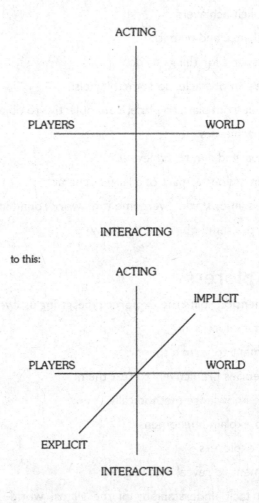

Instead of four squares, we now have eight cubes, each corresponding to a player type. Because of this, the new model is referred to as the *8-type model*, as opposed to the original *4-type model*.

This 8-type model explains why we have two kinds of killer, also bringing attention to other dichotomies that were bubbling under the surface. For example, we can see why some explorers prefer looking at the breadth of the world and others prefer looking at the depth: the former are scientists, the latter hackers.

What? You want me to *draw* the 8-type's cubes?!

Not Seeing Yourself as Others See You

As I mentioned earlier, *EverQuest 2* has special character models that differ in style to the original but are included in its client so that anyone can use them. Some people do use them. You can't tell that they are using them, which means you could think your character looks like *this*, but to someone else it looks like *that*.

This could easily be extended to any cosmetic difference between characters. Your character could consistently look a different age, race, or gender to the one you chose, but you wouldn't *know* unless someone pointed it out. You'd think everyone saw you as a gorgeous, blue-skinned elf babe, but everyone else could be seeing you as a hideous, bearded barbarian.

When players play characters different to themselves, this can influence both their real self and their character. Much of playing an MMO involves making tiny adjustments to your perception of yourself and to your perception of your character until eventually the two align. It's as if there's a dialogue between them, the resolving of which affirms (or reaffirms) the player's sense of identity.

The main worry I have about having people look different depending on who's doing the looking is that it means players are operating under a false premise. I don't particularly care that, say, overall attitudes to men and women could gradually be affected by the build-up of impressions gained from untrue presentations because that could actually go some way to stamping out stereotypes. However, I do care if an individual is screwed up by such an accumulation.

For example, a player might think they're being treated nicely because "it's my great sense of humor" whereas actually it's because "you look hot!" When they find out, it could have a deleterious effect on them: the edifice of the personality they were building would have been constructed on bad foundations.

A person's gender (or lack thereof) is often an important part of their identity. How would *you* feel if you discovered that everyone else saw *your* character oppositely-gendered to how you saw it?

8 Player Types

Rather than spend four hours in a CAD program creating a fancy cube-based rendition of the 8-type version of the Player Types model, I spent half an hour digging out the old Duplo™ box:

So, as with the 4-type model, the left/right axis is player/world and the up/down axis is acting/interacting. We add a front/back axis for explicit/implicit. This gives us a cube, represented by the 8 figures in the photo. I'll describe them in a clockwise fashion, nearest-plane first:

- **Dog = planner** (acting, world, explicit)

  Planners are classic achievers. They pursue their goals doggedly.

- **Pig = scientist** (interacting, world, explicit)

  Scientists are explorers, trying to make sense of the world. The pig is the Chinese zodiac sign for such hard-working, thoughtful, intelligent people.

- **Panda = networker** (interacting, players, explicit)

  Pandas are socializers who are actively looking for friends, as opposed to those who already have them. Hey, everyone loves a panda!

- **Hen = politician** (acting, players, explicit)

  Hens are those killers for whom the word didn't really work. They're often guild leaders, acting like mother hens for their brood.

- **Bear = opportunist** (acting, world, implicit)

  Bears are early-stage achievers who do whatever is easiest, about which they don't have to think too much.

- **Cat = hacker** (interacting, world, implicit)

  Cats are explorers who own the world. Nothing bothers them, and they can't be made to do anything they don't want to. They go where they will.

- **Old Man = friend** (interacting, players, implicit)

  Old men (and old women—I chose which figure to use at the toss of a coin) are socializers who stay with their close-knit friends whom they've known forever (at least in MMO terms).

- **Tiger = griefer** (acting, players, implicit)

  Tigers are the killers that gave the 4-type version its name. They eat people.

The figures I chose here were kinda forced on me by what was in the Duplo™ box; but believe me, it's better than the mass of lines that would have been the illustration…

Oh, and yes, my Chinese sign of the zodiac is indeed pig, since you ask.

Automatic Justice Systems

If you want to make the MMO itself punish players who misbehave, you have an *automatic justice system*.

Automatic justice systems usually fail and do so for one of two reasons:

- Because the justice system itself is griefable. 40 griefers acting in concert can wreck a system used by 1,000 non-griefers acting independently.

- Because the game can't know whether an act it detects as being "evil" is actually being committed with evil *intent*.

Sort those out and you're on to something.

Drift Revealed

Our shiny, new, 8-type model obviously fixes one of the problems we had with the 4-type model— "two very different subtypes of killer for no apparent reason." Less obviously, though, it can help with "how or why players move between types."

The main sequence for player development, translated into the 8-type model, goes griefer to scientist to planner to friend. We could see this in the 4-type model because it has one representative of each of the original four types in it. The main explorer sequence, though, goes opportunist to scientist to planner to hacker: we couldn't see that because it only involved explorers and achievers.

This kind of progression is obscured if we look at the 8-type cube from the front. However, if we remove the player/world axis instead of the implicit/explicit one, then looking at it from the side we'd see this:

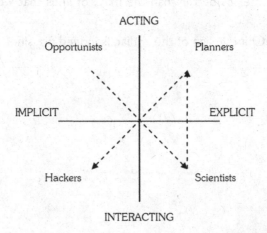

It's the same, reverse-alpha shape (that would have been an alpha if I'd thought of all this when I was writing the original Player Types paper... sigh...).

Likewise, we couldn't fully see the main socializer sequence because we were looking at that end-on, too. Whereas the main explorer sequence occupies the four subcubes to the right of the 3D model (bear, pig, dog, cat), the main socializer sequence occupies the four to the left (tiger, panda, hen, old person). Removing the player/world axis again (to make it easier to draw), we get the following:

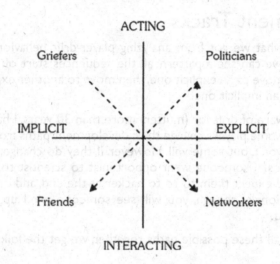

This has helped clear things up a little, in that at least we can see what's going on, now. In 3D, we can also follow other development paths, in particular the minor sequence (which is seen quite a lot in today's MMOs): opportunist to networker to planner to friend.

As it stands, we do have some new information from this exercise that's useful to designers. We can see, for example, that someone who is drifting from scientist to planner has no use for opportunist content, so in zones where such transformations are intended to occur it's going to be better to emphasize quest chains over one-off, take-it-or-leave-it quests. Most designers will know to this anyway, though—it's not a new observation.

So although knowing *where* people drift can be useful, what designers *really* want to know is *how* and *why* people drift. So far, this new-fangled 8-type model doesn't really help in that regard.

So far.

How Myth Works

When you read a story that resonates with your personal feelings and experience, you gain an insight—perhaps ever so slight—into your own condition. You experience it vicariously, through the eyes of the protagonist, but you experience it nonetheless.

Thus, slowly, you learn if not who you are, then how to *find out* who you are.

Development Tracks

If we look at what we got from analyzing player-drift behavior through the 8-type model, we can see a pattern: all the sequences start off in an implicit subcube, then move to an explicit one, then move to another explicit one, and then return to an implicit one.

Having been aware of drift for (mutter) more than 30 years, I have to note at this point that some players change their development paths from what you'd expect. Most won't, but some will. However, if they do change, it's usually at the intersections. If someone went opportunist to scientist to planner, then ordinarily you'd expect them to go to hacker at the end, and ordinarily you'd be right; occasionally, though, you will see someone wind up at the friend subcube instead.

If we combine all these possible paths together, we get the following *development tracks*:

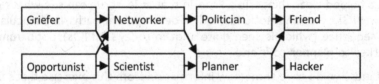

What this means is that if you're a planner, say, then you were either a networker or scientist before, and you'll become a friend or a hacker next.

The case for politicians is unusual, in that politicians were only ever networkers immediately before and will only ever become friends next—their path is relatively fixed. I've no idea why this is, it's just that I've never seen those other transitions take place. However, rather than lying about it so as to make the development tracks diagram look complete, I thought it best to fess up. ~~That way, I can lie about other things and you'll think I'm being sincere.~~

Looking at the development tracks diagram, it's now possible to describe the general nature of the changes in type that players undergo as they play:

- They start by determining the boundaries of the world into which they have arrived. For some, this means primarily social boundaries ("can I swear?" "can I steal your kills?") and for others it means primarily physical boundaries ("can I pick up rocks?" "can I swim?").

- Having found the limits on the actions available to them, they begin stringing together sequences of such actions in meaningful ways. They'll do this either through experimentation or by asking people who already know what to do.

- Once they have established a repertoire of actions or a circle of friends, they use these to advance their goals. They may become guild officers or try race through levels, getting the best loot.

- Finally, having been there, done that, they retire in the company of their closest friends or potter around trying out weird and wonderful things for their own, private amusement.

Put succinctly, this sequence is: locate, discover, apply, internalize. Find out what your limits are, find what you can do within those limits, apply yourself to achieve success, and then it'll all become second nature.

It's how babies learn to walk, how adults learn to drive.

So now we have a model of *how* players progress through types, if not *why*. However, it's a bit, "So what?" So what if we *do* know this, what actual *use* is it?

Well, it's the key we need to unlock the secrets of why people play MMOs.

Using a Player Types Model

What use is positioning players into types defined by two, three, or however many axes?

Well, it depends on who you are and what the labels on the axes say. To a social scientist, it may be more useful to have axes labeled old/young and male/female; to a player, it may be more useful to go with pirate/ninja and elf/dwarf[28]. To a journalist or teacher, it may not be useful to make any of these kinds of distinctions at all.

Just because a model exists and is useful to *someone*, that doesn't mean it's useful to *you*.

---

[28]Tom Coates: *From Pirate Dwarves to Ninja Elves...* . March 2004. http://www.plasticbag.org/archives/2004/03/from_pirate_dwarves_to_ninja_elves/

Myth

All human cultures have myths. That's *all* human cultures.

Early myths were stories that developed in preliterate civilizations, the outward purpose of which was to explain important aspects of the world—natural, supernatural, and societal. Because these stories were not written down (you saw that word *preliterate*, there?), each generation of storytellers was free to interpret the story in their own way. Old parts that didn't work would be discarded or replaced; parts that did work would be embellished—sometimes so much so that a previously minor character gained sufficient importance that they merited their own spin-off series (as with TV today).

Because the stories were oral, the storyteller could adapt them for each audience. Telling a group of young men about the arrival of Odysseus back at his home in Ithaca after 20 years away might focus on how he killed the 100-plus rowdy youths he found living it up in his house and attempting to seduce his wife, Penelope. The same event to an older audience might emphasize Penelope's loyalty and fidelity, and gently chide Odysseus for ever doubting her. *He* may have changed while he was away, but *she* didn't.

These stories were told and retold time and time again. Each retelling allowed storytellers to make changes, honing the tale over—well, over *centuries*.

In the same way that a rough stone worn down in a running stream will become a smooth pebble, so a rough story worn down through countless retellings will become a smooth story; and in the same way that all pebbles in a stream, though each is individual, eventually attain the same basic shape, so all stories, continually retold, also come to have the same basic shape.

These stories have the same shape because people have the same needs. They want to know what their place is in the world—the physical world, the spiritual world, and the society in which they live. They want to know *who they are*.

I'm going to use a theory of myth to explain, at last, *why* people play MMOs.

Griefers *versus* Grievers

In March, 2006, a funeral was taking place in *World of Warcraft*. One of the game's players had died of a stroke in real life and her in-game friends decided to hold a ceremony to mark her passing. They advertised it on message boards, including (as this was on a PvP server) a request not to mess things up because they were making a video to show her family.

Needless to say, things were well and truly messed up. Slaughter and mayhem ensued when a guild attacked the assembled, largely unarmored throng.

Virtual worlds are virtual places. If you take any of the real world into them, then you are inevitably going to get a clash between those who want their fantasy to remain a fantasy and those who want their fantasy to extend to their reality.

In the case of the raid on the virtual funeral, it was all about *Reality*. The mourners were acting out-of-context (characters in *WoW* don't suffer permanent death; players in real life do), so an in-context attack on them could be excused (because on a PvP server, gameplay centers on opposing sides attacking each other). However, in this particular case, the attack was *also* out-of-context because the attackers knew the mourners were holding an in-game commemoration of a real-world death, which meant that they were fully aware of the real-world consequences of attacking them. On a role-play server, neither side should have done what it did; but as this wasn't a role-play server, both sides acted within the bounds of what is permitted.

It's also permitted to point to this event as an illustration of what happens when 50 assholes get organized.

Sound and Vision

When you speak in MMOs using your VoIP system of choice, people hear your real voice.

Communication isn't *just* about voice, though. People who study computer-mediated communication often lament the lack of visual cues in online communications. Where's the body language? Where's the twinkle in the speaker's eye?

So: what if someone were to produce a piece of software that could super-impose a live, webcam image of your face over that of your MMO character? I don't mean that it would motion-capture your facial movements and map them onto your character's face; I mean that your in-game character would have your real-world face streamed through it. Now when you say something, we can see you rolling your eyes, or smiling, or wrinkling your nose; we can tell you look intense, or frightened, or cautious. Adding an extra channel helps refines meaning further. If voice is a good thing, surely voice+face must be a better thing?

Would *you* play an MMO in which your avatar's face was your own?

If you play an MMO in which your avatar's *voice* is your own, why not?

Nondescript

Most textual worlds allow players to give their characters descriptions. Other players can therefore tell that you're a mysterious but unmistakably powerful green-eyed redhead who moves with the grace of a dancer.

MUD1's characters didn't have descriptions. We could easily have given them descriptions, but I didn't want them.

With no descriptions, characters can change. As soon as you have a description, you can't change, you're locked into it. I wanted characters to change as their players changed.

Besides, as I mentioned a while back, in *MUD1* there was a sex-change spell. That would have messed up character descriptions no end.

Will I Go to Hell for playing an Orc?

No, you won't.

Okay, so I'm the wrong person to ask here as I'm an atheist, and therefore don't believe there's a Hell, Heaven, Nirvana, or Elysian Fields, anyway. However, for those of you with a religious disposition, the question is a serious one: if I play a supposedly evil character in an MMO, will I increase my chances of being condemned to an eternity of damnation as a result?

The answer is still no, you won't.

There are many reasons why people might want to play an "evil" character. Very few such people actually *do* do evil things while playing them, though; it's as if they're exploring the boundaries of their own behavior, but pulling back from going as far as they *could* because they find that they don't *want* to go that far—even though it's permitted within the MMO's magic circle. Through playing, they have thus discovered something worthwhile about themselves that they didn't know before; what's more, they've done it in a game context, which meant they didn't have to hurt real people in any significant way to be able to draw their conclusions.

Now why would a real-life deity be unhappy with that? Surely any self-respecting omnipotent being would easily recognize what you were doing. This being would know that sometimes you have to go down from the top a hillock to climb up a mountain, and that because it's all couched in terms of a protected "just a game" framework, you specifically *meant* for it all to be make-believe the whole time. You were playing "evil" to gain a better sense of what it means to be *good*.

Hmm, come to think of it, a more accurate answer to the question "will I go to Hell for playing an orc?" is that it depends.

See, if the god(s) you worship are *themselves* evil, they may send you to Hades on a whim anyway. Let's hope they're not. Still, if it's any consolation, I'm probably up for an even worse fate than that, as at least you haven't had the temerity to deny their very existence in print, unlike me.

The Hero with a Thousand Faces

All narratives of a mythical nature, worn smooth by retelling after retelling, adhere to a common template known as *the hero's journey*, or *monomyth*. Both terms were introduced in *The Hero with a Thousand Faces*[29], a famous book written by the American academic, Joseph Campbell.

Campbell was a scholar of myths, and he looked at a *lot* of them, from the ancient civilizations of Nigeria, North America, Australia, Phrygia, China, Iceland, Bali, Persia, Mexico, Finland, Cambodia, Peru, and many others. He also looked at specific myth cycles, such as the epics of Gilgamesh, Arthur, Vishnu, Osiris, Moses, Cuchulainn, Buddha, Jason, and Mohammed.

Oh, yes, I should mention: many stories involving major religious figures follow this same pattern. Please filter out and ignore from the above any that you happen to consider are true accounts rather than myth—it's not my intention here to give you grief over your beliefs. Just because a history follows the pattern of a myth, that doesn't mean it *is* a myth.

Campbell's monomyth also works for many classic novels and fairy stories, such as Dante's *Inferno*, the *Sleeping Beauty*, Tolstoy's *Anna Karenina, Faust*, and the *Frog Prince*. It even applies to more modern works, created after Campbell wrote his book. Sometimes this is done intentionally (the original *Star Wars* movie follows the hero's journey because George Lucas had studied Campbell's ideas) and sometimes it's not (as with the first *Harry Potter* book, for example). The reason its pattern is so often repeated and reinvented is because it is in tune with a deep need: it shows the way for an individual to understand *who they are*.

So, the hero's journey consists of three phases, each composed of a number of steps that are taken in the same order (although there is some leeway for reversals and omissions). There are 17 steps in all, which I shall delve into later. Should a person follow those steps, then they will emerge a hero.

Indeed, that's what the term "hero" originally meant. When you say "that guy who dived into the freezing lake to save that little boy is a hero," what you're *really* saying is that he was acting heroically—as in, how a hero would act. It's a metaphor which today has largely shed its metaphorical connotations. In the past, the only heroes were those in the myths, and they became heroes only because they had completed their hero's journey. Today, we use "hero" more generally to refer to people who show exceptional courage or meet certain predefined criteria (e.g., winning an Olympic medal). The term's origins remain important, though.

---

[29]Joseph Campbell: *The Hero with a Thousand Faces. Bollingen Series 17*, Princeton University Press, 1949.

Now some people really *are* heroes even under the old understanding of the word, having undergone an actual, personal hero's journey. This isn't something most people would wish to attempt, though, because it generally involves something like being shot at in a war. For ordinary individuals, a hero's journey can't be experienced directly, only vicariously. When you listen to a tale of myth and identify with the hero, some small resonance between you and he (yes, it's always a *he*; I'll explain why later) will speak to your own experiences—or at least that's the hope. It's not a *great* hope, but unless you want to leave your home and go somewhere strange and dangerous for 18 months, it's the *only* hope most people have of coming to understand who they truly are.

Well, the only hope until now.

I once blogged that the prospective students I interview should, when asked if they've any questions of their own, have a response ready. I remarked that when *I* was in their position, I would ask the interviewer: "What's the most important book your shelves?"

Sure enough, my having mentioned this, next day a student in a lecture asked me to name the most important book on *my* shelves. Also sure enough, I had anticipated this and had my reply to hand.

It's *The Hero with a Thousand Faces*. Despite the fact that in terms of "I know every word in this sentence but I don't know what the sentence means," it's only beaten by the feminist literature I read when that field's attention temporarily turned to MUDs, I nevertheless have no hesitation in rating *The Hero with a Thousand Faces* the most important book on my shelves. The second half is eminently skippable, but as for the first: if you are at all interested in MMO design and haven't read it, do so. Order it right now. It's something you *need* to know.

Hero's Journey Phases

The way the hero's journey works, there are three *phases*.

The first phase is set in the mundane world where the hero-to-be lives: this is the *Departure* phase. It's where Odysseus' ship is blown off course, where Eliza Doolittle encounters Professor Henry Higgins, where Arthur pulls the sword from the stone.

In the second phase, the hero arrives in a new world of excitement and adventure, which is similar to—but in important ways very different from—the mundane world. This *Initiation* phase is where the bulk of the action takes place. It's where Perseus slays Medusa, where John McClane runs over broken glass, where Neo meets Trinity.

The final, *Return* phase, describes the hero's return to the mundane world. It's where Indiana Jones brings back the Ark of the Covenant, where Thumbelina escapes on the back of a swallow, where Jesus resurrects.

The three phases always appear in this order, but they don't always all appear. Crocodile Dundee leaves Australia and goes to America, but he doesn't go back to Australia again (well, not until the second movie, anyway). Stories will often focus on a particular phase—or even an individual step—of the hero's journey, and they will sometimes show what happens when a would-be hero fails to make the grade (Lot's wife being a classic example). There's great scope for storytelling here: the hero's journey is not a narrow, prescriptive formula.

That said, the general premise is something like this: the hero has the goal of retrieving some object that is needed to benefit his community—a golden fleece, a holy grail, Private Ryan. To get it, he has to venture to a strange but exhilarating new world, where old certainties are no longer true, and where his every move is challenged by a far more powerful opponent. He finally wins over the opponent and returns back to his original world with the object he originally went to get. However, in the process of undertaking this journey, he has become transformed: he is no longer the unsure, self-doubting person he once was. He is a hero.

Voice = Bad

I'm not a fan of having players speaking to one another using voice in MMOs. There are two reasons for this, one practical and one theoretical.

The practical reason is one I mentioned earlier: speech makes a noise. If you're in a house with other people and you're shouting into a microphone while they're trying to watch TV, they get upset. Anyone in such a situation is effectively rendered dumb by this inability to participate in conversations. Sure, you can type something and hope it gets noticed, but it's hard to win an argument when the other person has a microphone and you don't.

The theoretical reason is to do with immersion. MMOs are *virtual* worlds: people play them to get away from *Reality*. In an MMO, you can be someone else; by being someone else, you can become a better you. Why do people play the same game for hour after hour, night after night, week after week, month after month? It's not because they like the *game*; it's because they like *being who they are*.

If you introduce too much of the real world into an MMO, it's no longer a virtual world: it's just an adjunct to *Reality*. It ceases to be a place, and reverts to being a medium. Immersion is enhanced by closeness to *Reality*, but thwarted by isomorphism with it: the act of will required to suspend disbelief is what sustains a player's efforts to *be*, but it disappears when there is no disbelief required.

Bringing *Reality* into a virtual world robs it of what makes it compelling. It takes away the most important distinction between virtual worlds and the real world: the fact that they are *not* the real world. Yet voice *is* the real world.

Ah, but what if it's not *your* voice? What if it's transformed through the miracles of modern technology? Well then instead of sounding like I do in real life, I can sound like what someone in real life does after they've had their voice put through a processor. Besides, even if the pitch and modulation changes were good enough to make men sound like women and *vice versa*, it wouldn't alter accents. "Hey, this elf babe is from England!" Hello *Reality*.

Voice in MMOs is not good. Except...

Voice = Good

Voice isn't in itself any more disruptive of the MMO experience than are photo-realistic graphics. It's fine to fool the senses, to make MMOs appear to be real, so long as that final step—their actually *being* real—is not taken.

Suppose you had a piece of software that converted speech to text, and another piece that converted text to speech. In theory, I could say something in my male, English voice, it could be converted into text, transmitted as text over the ol' Internet, and then replayed to listeners in a female, New English voice. It would be real-time voice communication, but no more "me" than my graphical avatar: just clothing for an alternative identity.

It would work because it *sounds* real, but we know it *isn't* real (hence we have disbelief to suspend). It would work because it permits us to role-play—to help us become the someone that we want to become. It would just *work*.

At the moment, though, this is mere whimsy. Current speech-from-text generation software is actually pretty good, but it doesn't convey emotion very well. Text-from-speech is also pretty good (or they wouldn't install it on phones), but not if you have a strong accent or are screaming for help because a dragon is eating you.

Give it a few years, though, and who knows? This could add a whole new dimension to virtual worlds! Not only do you *look* like a marsh troll, but you *sound* like one, too. How groovy is that?

It's very groovy! Unfortunately, what we have now is ungroovy: a few people dominating the voice chat that today's learn-the-dance raiding systems apparently require, with the rest just having to listen.

Real-time voice communication in virtual worlds does promise great things—it's just that we haven't got them quite yet.

MMOs and Religion

Religions are not virtual worlds because religions are not places. However, there is a lot of overlap between the two because at some level they address the same needs.

The formulator of the hero's journey, Joseph Campbell, used many examples from religions in his book, *The Hero with a Thousand Faces*. As we shall see, the link between MMOs and the hero's journey is very strong, so it's not surprising to find that there's a connection.

This isn't to say that MMOs need share the same basic philosophies as religions; it's merely to point out that they are sometimes driven by similar forces. This shouldn't be too surprising because religions don't always share the same basic philosophies as each other.

For example, most religions have a "golden rule" about how to treat your fellow human beings. In some, such as Confucianism, it can be paraphrased as "Do not do unto others what you do not want done unto yourself"; in others, such as Christianity, it's "Do unto others as you would have them do unto you." These are not the same thing: in the former, if I don't want pity, I shouldn't pity others (even if they do want it); in the latter, if I want pity I should pity others (even if they don't want it).

In MMOs, the equivalent is more like, "Do unto others what will get you XP."

Departure

The first phase of the hero's journey is *Departure*. It has the fewest number of steps of the three phases, but usually takes longer to tell than the third phase.

Here's what goes on. For those of you who are interested in psychological mumbo-jumbo, some explanation of what the steps signify is given; for the rest of you, don't worry, I give a complete, step-by-step example of the hero's journey in action a little later. Then, you can worry.

So, the five steps of the Departure phase are:

- **The Call to Adventure**

  The protagonist—the would-be hero—receives an indication of things to come. This is symbolic and tells the protagonist that his destiny is awakening.

- **Refusal of the Call**

  Although the protagonist is required to act, he doesn't. He has failed to recognize what the Call to Adventure symbolizes.

- **Supernatural Aid**

  A guide appears to help the protagonist. By having his strengths pointed out to him, the protagonist realizes that he (the protagonist) is more than the person he first thought he was. The protagonist gains the formal goal to obtain some mystical object (the *boon*—symbolizing his transformed self) that's in a hard-to-get-to world of danger and adventure.

- **The Crossing of the First Threshold**

  The protagonist leaves the world he has always known and enters the unknown world of adventure. Although the way seems blocked, the protagonist's faith in his destiny allows him to pass through. You didn't think I mentioned the Hogwarts Express for no good reason, did you? Platform 9¾.

- **The Belly of the Whale**

  This is the protagonist's final separation from his old self: he's now a new person in a new world. This step got its name because so many myths involve the protagonist's being swallowed by a large creature. There are definite womb-like connotations in this step—the protagonist is metaphorically (and sometimes literally) being born anew. Caves and wells are also popular venues for the same, like-a-womb reason.

The next step is in the next phase, *Initiation*.

Heaven and Hell

Religions aren't virtual worlds because they're not places, but what about the places they talk about? Are Heaven and Hell virtual worlds? This is a question which does occasionally get asked, so it's worth considering what the answer might be.

Well if they are virtual worlds, that would mean they must be imaginary, right? They're not real because otherwise you wouldn't need that "virtual" adjective. Now although I personally have no problem with characterizing religions as imaginary constructs used by people to ask their imaginary friends to alter *Reality* for them, that's because I'm an atheist. People who are not atheists may not be so keen on having their faith presented in this light. They may indeed be offended by it (especially when disparaging, jokey language is used, as above). To them, Heaven and Hell are very real places, but they're *separate from Reality*.

So, the answer is that Heaven and Hell are *not* virtual worlds. If you believe in them, they're not virtual; if you don't believe in them, they're not worlds.

So Female

Ask a female player of male characters why she does it, and she'll tell you something along the lines of, "I get hassled so much for being female, I have to play as male to escape the attention." In other words, *I'm so female that I have to play male characters!*

So Male

Ask a male player of female characters why he does it, and he'll tell you something along the lines of, "I'd rather spend my playing time looking at a female character's butt than a male character's butt." In other words, *I'm so male that I have to play female characters!*

Reputation Systems

Some people are prats. Some of these prats play MMOs. Non-prats would prefer not to play with prats, but have no way of identifying them; this is because whenever systems are implemented to identify the prats, the prats use them to make non-prats seem like *they're* the prats.

In other words, there isn't a reputation system yet invented that griefers can't use as an instrument of griefing.

So, indulge me here.

Assumption: your MMO has a reasonably good pseudonymity regime. This means that you can't just change your character's name or server to escape being identified as a prat, and that you're unwilling to abandon a character (because, say, it took you weeks to get it to its current level).

Okay, so the simplest way to tell who is and who isn't a prat is to keep notes. You play with someone for a couple of hours, you draw a conclusion, you write it down. When two weeks later you see them again, you look at your list, see "prat," "angel," "judgment reserved," or whatever, and then either group with them or politely decline. You build up a usable personal-reputation system this way, but you have to play with everyone at least once in order to rate them. But what about people you *haven't* met before? How do you know whether *they're* worth playing with or not?

Here's the idea.

First, instead of taking notes on a notepad, take notes in-world. Click the character, click the "rate this character" option, check whatever checkbox is most appropriate, and there you are. Next time you see the character, your opinion of them will be visible to you (name in a different color/size/font, heart/skull-and-crossbones over their head—however it's done).

Now suppose every player is doing this. Wouldn't it be great if you could look at the list of a like-minded person and see what *they* thought of someone you hadn't yet met? You wouldn't want to see the opinions of prats, just those of people who happen to share your opinion.

Insight: *you can find those like-minded people by comparing lists.*

The server can record every list of player opinions and intersect yours with those of everyone else. When it finds one with which you're in broad (or even total) agreement, it can use this to augment your list. It doesn't matter who made this list (that would be kept secret); what's important is that their opinions are in line with yours. You like A, they like A; you dislike B, they dislike B; you haven't met C, they like C, so C is probably someone you'd like. The greater the intersection between your list and mine, the greater the chance that we'll have similar views.

The fatal flaw in most reputation systems is that they can be gamed, especially by griefers. What can griefers do here, though? They can call you a prat when you're not one, but what do you care? All it means is that other griefers will think you're a prat, which is fine because you don't want to play with them anyway. Sounds a good deal!

Lists would have to be kept separate, to avoid error propagation: the server can't allow people to initialize or update their list from someone else's, as a single slip of the mouse could mean everyone in a guild thinks you're a prat when you're not. The date-stamping or status-stamping of opinions could help (you may have been hell to play with at level 10, but have grown up by level 40). It might also be advisable to have second opinions, so that you don't just get the views of the nearest match to yours, you get two or three others, too ("Hmm, the person I have a 93% match with reserves judgment on this guy, but the ones at 92% and 90% like him; okay, I'll give him the benefit of the doubt").

The main drawback of this is that it requires a lot of computational oomph. 10,000 players with 10,000 opinions might be tiresome to cross-index even using a strictly binary like/dislike system. It depends to some extent how much information is involved (I suspect that the opinion array will be fairly sparse), but it looks as if the algorithm would have to do rather a lot of work.

Still, if it means I can avoid prats, it gets *my* vote.

Initiation

The second phase of the hero's journey is *Initiation*. It's where the most fun-filled, dramatic, and exciting events take place.

Careful, there's a lot of symbolism here:

- **The Road of Trials**

  The protagonist is presented with a series of obstacles, usually three. The protagonist may suffer setbacks, but his failure is not fatal. It's during this step that the protagonist discovers the nature of the world of adventure and his place within it.

- **The Meeting with the Goddess**

  The goddess here is a mother-figure; the protagonist regards her uncritically as the embodiment of perfection. As such, she represents the totality of knowledge; it is here that, for the first time, the protagonist fully understands what lies ahead of him. If he can cope with this knowledge, he continues armed with a new sense of purpose. If he can't cope, well, that's why I mentioned Artemis and Actaeon.

- **Woman as Temptress**

  Having full knowledge of his destiny, the protagonist may believe that this is enough. Why bother to go through with the rest of the journey when he's not going to learn anything from it? The mundane world, often symbolized by a love interest, needs him back *right now*, not after some self-indulgent further prolongation. Basically, this step asks whether he's in it for the long term or not.

- **Atonement with the Father**

  All the time, the protagonist has been aware that a supreme, unknowable power—often a father-figure—has been exerting control to thwart him. If he is to succeed, the protagonist must defeat this father. However, the father is defined to be unbeatable: the protagonist can only defeat him if the father *consents* to being defeated. The father will only do *that* if he believes in the protagonist. So, does he? Well the protagonist doesn't know—as I said, the father is unknowable. The protagonist can only go by the belief he has in *himself*. This is, in fact, the whole point: the father represents the protagonist as he *was* in the mundane world; here, this old self finally accepts that it has become the new, reborn self. The protagonist's old and new identities are aligned, and revealed to be the same. The protagonist *is* the father, and the father *is* the protagonist; he has become the person he *always was*.

- **Apotheosis**

  "Apotheosis" means "to have attained godlike stature." Having been accepted rather than obliterated, the protagonist enjoys a period of bliss, peace, and rest, fêted and celebrated by the people of the world of adventure in which he has made his mark.

- **The Ultimate Boon**

  In this step, the protagonist formally receives the object he went to the world of adventure to acquire, which betokens his renewed sense of self.

Of all the steps in the hero's journey, the keystone is that of Atonement with the Father. All the steps before it are leading up to it; all the steps after it are leading back down.

The next step is in the final phase, *Return*.

Split Screen

I was watching a film on TV with my dad once when I was a young lad, and suddenly the screen split in two. One piece of action occurred on the left side and another piece occurred on the right side. I asked my dad which one I should watch.

Split screens are part of the language of film. The first time I saw the "word" of the split screen, I didn't know what it meant. I *guessed* that the movie had split in two, with two different plots, one in each half; I wanted my dad to tell me which one he thought I'd enjoy watching the most. I was annoyed, though, because I wanted to watch both.

My dad told me that a split screen meant that the two events were going on at the same time. I should try to follow both, but not to worry as it wouldn't last long. Sure enough, 20 seconds or so later the split screen disappeared in a cut to show a single screen where some other character on the phone turned to a colleague and said, "They've done it."

This didn't bother me at all. I already knew what cuts meant.

Return

The third and final phase of the hero's journey is *Return*. It's the shortest (in terms of duration) and can contain some light-hearted moments.

These are its steps:

- **Refusal of the Return**

  The protagonist has respect, honor, power, peace—why would he want to leave the world of adventure? Well, the thing is, he has the boon. Other people in the world of adventure also want it. He can't both stay *and* have the boon.

- **The Magic flight**

  Hotly pursued by people who want the boon, the protagonist makes a run for it. This is often played for laughs, although it can also be thrilling (as it is in *The Italian Job*).

- **Rescue from Without**

  The protagonist receives help from people in the mundane world, enabling him to make good his escape. The old world needs him back, but he also needs to be back in the old world.

- **Crossing the Return Threshold**

  The protagonist returns to the world of the mundane. He must now reconcile the old with the new.

- **Master of the Two Worlds**

  The protagonist uses the boon to fix the real-world problem he went to get the boon to for in the first place. As a result, he has a sense of balance. The world of adventure has lost its mystical significance; it is a place, just as the mundane world is a place.

- **Freedom to Live**

  The protagonist has the freedom to be the person he has discovered he always was—himself. He is a *hero*.

I guess you want a concrete example of all 17 steps of the hero's journey in action, huh?

All the same if you don't, you're going to get one.

Back End of a Horse

The "so male I play female" and "so female I play male" responses given by players to explain why they play characters of the opposite gender are now used so routinely that they've become accepted as the truth.

Unfortunately, they're both false.

We know they're false because, if you look at the figures, you find that roughly 40% of male players will be playing a female character at any moment and 10% of female players will be playing a male character[30]. These percentages are *unchanged* from the days of text MUDs[31].

In textual worlds, you can't claim you're directing your gaze at your character's gorgeous butt the whole time, because your character's butt isn't being displayed. You can't complain that people are hitting on you because you're so desirable because your desirability is not visually apparent.

We used to get a wide variety of superficial explanations as to why people played cross-gender in text worlds, none of which were very persuasive. The one that least impugned the masculine self-image was, "I play as a female character so losers will give me stuff and help me." Amusingly, the one that least impugned the feminine self-image was the same but inverted:"I play as a male character, so losers won't give me stuff and help me."

Next time someone asks you why you play characters of the opposite gender, assuming that you do, try not to come up with the usual stock answer. Instead, see if you can figure out the *real* reason you do it.

Oh, and when I tried that "I prefer to look at a female character's butt" line on one of my daughters, she made a simple observation that completely undermined it:"But Daddy, you spend most of your time looking at the back end of a horse."

[30]Nick Yee: *The Norathian Scrolls: A Study of* EverQuest. 2001. http://www.nickyee.com/report.pdf

[31]Lynne D. Roberts and Malcolm R. Parks: *The Social Geography of Gender-Switching in Virtual Environments on the Internet.* In Eileen Green and Alison Adam: *Virtual Gender: Terminology, Consumption and Identity.* New York, Routledge, 2001.

Abstracting Evil

As I mentioned earlier, many MMO players seem to enjoy playing "evil" characters. They like the idea of being able to torment non-player characters or, better yet, player characters; they like being able to take things that belong to other characters and claim them as their own; they *especially* like being able to kill other player characters.

Now this is fair enough. If you're playing a role-playing game, then the whole rationale is predicated on trying on other personalities in order to understand your real self better. Modulo the designer's morals, there's nothing intrinsically problematic in allowing players to play as evil characters.

Well, except they don't. As I explained earlier, players generally don't play evil characters: they play naughty characters. Evil works through fear: people do what you say because they're afraid of what you'll do to them if they don't. It's not that they obey you simply because they agree with what you're doing—that would merely mean they have a warped philosophy. Warped philosophies can (and often do) go hand in hand with evil, but not necessarily: the Nazi party attracted many evil people, but the Flat Earth Society didn't.

Back in the early days of text MUDs, when player-killing and permadeath were standard, we had player characters who were (from the point of view of other players) *bona fide* evil. They ruled by fear. If one was around, then you played far more cautiously, always watching your back, always trying to track where they were so they wouldn't catch you unawares. This meant that if they did attack, you were prepared, and the combat was exciting even if you lost. You were frightened of them, but they added something to the game.

In small-scale virtual worlds—those with player numbers measured in the hundreds—this sort of set-up is possible without being game-breaking. This is because it's self-correcting to some degree: what happens is that when the evil characters start to assert themselves, the other players gang up on them—or at least call in help when they're attacked. The evil characters can bully *some* players into doing what they want (such as handing over their stuff—i.e., being mugged) but they're outnumbered. It transpires that numerically there are many more good people than there are either evil ones or good ones role-playing evil ones.

With larger-population worlds, though, this doesn't scale. What happens is that once there's a critical mass of players who want to hurt other players, they'll group together themselves. With strength in numbers, they can then proceed to gank the spirit out of innocents with complete impunity. They defend themselves from complaints by saying that they're only *role-playing* being evil, and point out that the game mechanics do allow them to behave that way.

Except, as we know, they're not entirely role-playing being evil. If they were, then they would rapidly turn on each other. One person in the group would be ruling by fear and the rest would be obeying either because they hoped to usurp the leader or because they were afraid of what would happen to them or their loved ones if they didn't comply with the leader's orders. Evil people use fear and manipulation to get other people to do unpalatable things; these other people go along with it only because they're scared of what would happen if they didn't.

Roaming gangs of bandits in MMOs are made up of players who know that what they're doing is transgressive and annoys others (it's why they're doing it), but having a mob mentality doesn't make them evil. Evilness is a property of individuals, not of actions or groups: the collective effect of a lot of naughtiness may be to imbue in the players who are being abused a sense that the *group* is evil, but it's a phenomenon that emerges from the actions of 40 *individuals* being naughty together. The members of the group most likely *aren't* evil—they're just naughty.

Allowing players to "act evil" individually can add some zip to an MMO, but allowing them to do so collectively can empty a game. Is it possible to code a solution in an open PvP world that discourages the latter without discouraging the former?

There *is* a way. See if you can think of it.

Frodo's Journey

As an example of the hero's journey in action, I'm going to go through how it works for *The Fellowship of the Ring*. There's no spoiler warning because, if you haven't read *The Lord of the Rings*, you must stop RIGHT NOW and go read it. Yes, RIGHT NOW. I warned you about your messed-up priorities earlier.

Things to note before I do this:

- *The Fellowship of the Ring* is only the first book (well, strictly speaking, two books) of *The Lord of the Rings*.

- It's not unusual for minor steps to be missed out, swapped around or repeated.

- The above two points work in concert. If a narrative is part of a larger arc, this can lead to repetitions and step swaps and omissions in places where the local and global arcs touch.

So, here goes:

- **The Call to Adventure**

  Elven writing appears on the ring.

- **Refusal of the Call**

  Frodo offers Gandalf the ring *and* (later) Frodo offers the Council of Elrond the ring.

- **Supernatural Aid**

  Gandalf tells Frodo to leave the Shire *and* (later) Bilbo gives Frodo his dagger and armor.

- **The Crossing of the First Threshold**

  Frodo leave the Shire *and* (later) Frodo leaves Rivendell.

- **The Belly of the Whale**

  The group is attacked on Weathertop. Frodo puts on the ring and is stabbed; the experience deeply changes him.

- **The Road of Trials**

  There are several of these, of which the most severe is the Balrog encounter.

- **The Meeting with the Goddess**

  Galadriel explains all to Frodo—including what the ring will ultimately do to him.

- **Woman as Temptress**

  The mirror of Galadriel shows atrocities going on in the Shire, which Frodo could prevent if he went back now and used the ring.

- **Atonement with the Father**

  Boromir attempts to take the ring. All this time, Frodo has been dominated by the powers of good—the elves, dwarves, and men. Following this incident, he answers only to himself; he *is* the destiny of the free world.

- **Apotheosis**

  Frodo understands that the ring will destroy him, and so gains a kind of peace.

- **The Ultimate Boon**

  Frodo takes the ring with him, now fully knowing what it will do to him.

- **Refusal of the Return**

  This step is missing!

- **The Magic flight**

  Frodo flees from the orcs.

- **Rescue from Without**

  The rest of the fellowship arrives and takes down the orcs.

- **Crossing the Return Threshold**

  Frodo crosses the Anduin.

- **Master of the Two Worlds**

  Sam is the old world, Gollum the new.

- **Freedom to Live**

  This step is missing, because the book segues into the greater story arc. However, as Gandalf says: "All we have to decide is what to do with the time that is given to us."

Tolkien knew nothing of Campbell's work when he wrote *The Lord of the Rings*. However, he did know a great deal about myth; therefore, it should not be altogether surprising that Frodo follows the hero's journey.

So what has any of this to do with virtual worlds in general and MMOs in particular?

Well, it finally allows us to explain *why* people play them.

One Question

At the Games Developers' Conference in 2005, I attended the talk at which Will Wright described his (then) new game, *Spore*. It was the first occasion he'd gone into any detail about it, and he's a highly entertaining speaker, so the room was packed. I arrived 15 minutes early myself and still had to stand—there must have been 800 people there, all computer-game professionals.

Will began his description of *Spore* with the words, "You start off at the microscopic level."

I had only one design question after I heard him say that. Any idea what it was?

Evil as Evil

Earlier, I asked how you might stop people role-playing as being "evil" from banding together and slaughtering innocents in an open PvP world.

This didn't happen in small-scale worlds, so it caught designers on the hop when MMOs scaled up. When they first observed roving groups of people whose aim was to attack other players, the immediate response (in *Ultima Online*) was to flag them as evil then have town guards attack them. Unfortunately, this meant that, when confronted by a group of charging enemies, offense-is-the-best-defense often led to the evil-flagging of non-evil characters. Eventually, designers were forced to retreat, abandoning first the concept of looting and then non-consensual PvP itself. The best we have nowadays is "evil" as an alignment in MMOs such as *Star Wars: the Old Republic*; it's a nice idea, but gives very little sense of what being evil actually *means*. Clicking the option that increases your dark side rating without even bothering to read it is an act borne of impatience, not profound immorality.

Overall, this soft-play padding has led to a diminishment of the experience of playing MMOs. There's an edge that has gone. It makes sense, though: people who are playing solo can't really be expected to stay for long if they're being attacked by gangs the whole time in combat so one-sided that they stand no chance. Okay, so there are plenty of individuals who don't want to be attacked by other players *ever* for *any* reason, but they're unlikely to be playing on a PvP server, anyway. I'm more concerned here with the fate of players who are hankering after an anarchic, old style of play, but can't get it because they're eaten alive by packs of griefers. The people who liked that early-*UO* frisson in their worlds have nowhere to go any more (well, except some ancient text MUDs, but they're never going to try those).

It's actually not all that hard to give them this experience in a large-scale world, as it happens.

First, you have a threshold-based flagging system. If you attack a non-evil opponent, your evilness rating increases. If they attack you, your evilness rating isn't affected. NPCs will treat you according to your evilness rating, which will decay over time if you don't attack non-evil people. Once it rises above the threshold, you're flagged as being formally evil. That's harder to shake off than merely playing on an alt for a few days while it wears off: perhaps you have to kill evil player characters to remove it.

Now as it stands, this system won't work. Evil-flagged players will wear their flag as a badge of honor and continue to gang up in order to beat the life out of unflagged players, just as they did in *UO*. We can, however, stop them—and fairly easily, as it happens.

So: instead of calling them evil when they're naughty, we abstract the *quality* of evil and apply to them the effects that someone who really *was* evil would attract. Basically, we debuff them if they're within shooting distance of another evil character. The explanation is that they're so busy watching their backs that they can't direct as much attention towards other targets. Furthermore, we make it cumulative.

If 40 evil-flagged characters only perform with the same collective effectiveness as four equivalent non-evil characters, suddenly it's not so much fun wandering around in groups attacking innocents who could very easily survive and leave you XPless and lootless. A pair of over-strength NPC caravan guards could massacre a party of ten bandits. Also, if you managed to trick a victim into attacking a "good" character secreted in your midst, it would be counter-productive: your effectiveness would reduce further as there'd be an additional evil person in range. The good-flagged-as-evil character will still be able to play with their buddies later, as they'd be the only evil character in the group so wouldn't be debuffed—except when an evil character attacks, which would also debuff this attacker. There are actual gameplay possibilities here.

In summary: the main problem with PvP in a PvE world is roaming gangs of PKers. The main problem with a flagging solution is that you still get roaming gangs of PKers. The answer is therefore to stop them from ganging up by debuffing them punitively when they do. You'll still get PKers, but they'll be lone wolves—enough to add spice, but not enough to overpower the recipe.

Needless to say, given the ever-more casual way that today's MMOs are heading, I don't expect we'll see this any time soon. Maybe come the MMO reboot…

The Hero's Journey in MMOs

MMO designers have known about the hero's journey for, well, longer than the term "MMO" has been around. Back in the heyday of textual worlds, when experimentation was so much quicker and easier to do, several designers looked at different narrative structures with a view to improving their quest lines. That's how I first came across the concept myself.

As a result, some virtual worlds were indeed designed with monomyth-formula quest chains. However, this didn't seem to make a lot of difference to their appeal. Why would that be?

Well, the hero in these particular journeys is the *character*, not the player—the player is still one level of indirection away from the actuality of a hero's journey. *You* don't get to be a hero watching *Star Wars*—Luke Skywalker does. *You* don't get to be a hero playing an MMO—Jimbo the orc does. You're one step away from the experience.

Except, you *do* get to be a hero. Playing an MMO is *itself* a hero's journey—starring *you*.

New Arrivals

Here's why MMOs have been going down the pan in design terms for the past decade or more.

Even for the most compelling of MMOs, players *will* eventually leave. For the MMO not to decline, new players have to arrive at the same rate or better than old players leave.

- **Point 1:** MMOs live or die by their attractiveness to newbies.

  New players come to MMOs with a set of preconceptions that they got from other MMOs, or from regular computer games, or from what the world around them has told them. They won't play MMOs that confront these expectations when there are other MMOs around that don't. If you want your MMO to attract new players, you therefore shouldn't include features that will offend them. This includes features that long-standing players love.

- **Point 2:** Newbies won't play an MMO that has a major feature they don't like the idea of.

  Players spend much less time playing their second and subsequent MMOs than they do their first. The first MMO you get into is a magical, enchanting, awesome, never-to-be-repeated experience; later ones are pale reflections. It's to do with the fact that they don't have an *Atonement with the Father* step, if you must know.

- **Point 3:** Players judge all MMOs against the first one they got into.

  When MMOs change (as they must), players only ever judge the merits of the change based on its short-term effects. A long-term benefit will not impress them if there's a short-term loss. This means developers can't add something that's long-term good but short-term bad, nor remove something short-term good but long-term bad.

- **Point 4:** Short-term good, long-term bad design choices cause players to leave.

From these four points, we can construct an induction.

Point 4 says that players leave any MMO built on the results of their own short-term views. **Point 3** means they won't recognize that what caused them to leave was indeed the cause. **Point 2** says they won't play an MMO that lacks that feature (the very one that drove them to leave). **Point 1** says that those that do lack the feature—that is, *those with the better design*—will fail from lack of newbies. Any absolute newbie for whom this is their first MMO will be educated to think that this is how things should be. The whole process thereupon repeats itself.

Normally, the way game evolution works is that each generation takes the good design genes from the previous generation and propagates them. We do see that with MMOs, but they propagate poor design genes more readily. The best MMOs don't pass their genes around because they have high retention (why quit for another MMO when this one suits your needs just fine?). Poor design makes players leave sooner, so the features they like (which ultimately led to their leaving) are the ones that become must-haves in the next generation.

In other words, for a new MMO to succeed, it has to have all the features that caused its ancestors to fail.

The MMO Player's Journey

The hero's journey involves:

- Leaving the world of the mundane.

- Becoming reborn in an "other world" of adventure and the unknown.

- Returning to the world of the mundane with a renewed sense of self.

So: *Reality* is the "mundane world." The virtual world you play is the "other world":

- **The Call to Adventure**

  The player hears about MMOs, perhaps through an advertisement, an article on a web page, or a display in a shop.

- **Refusal of the Call**

  Fears of inadequacy, the existence of a healthy real-world social life, the expense, or the time requirements.

- **Supernatural Aid**

  A friend who already plays, an endorsement from a celebrity, your favorite IP.

- **The Crossing of the First Threshold**

  Installing the client software.

- **The Belly of the Whale**

  The character creation system.

- **The Road of Trials**

  The player finds their feet. What can they do in this world?

- **The Meeting with the Goddess**

  The player seeks knowledge. What are their goals, and what tools are available to accomplish them?

- **Woman as Temptress**

  The transition from learning to doing. The player now knows what to do to get to the level cap—but are they prepared to do it?

- **Atonement with the Father**

  The player tries to succeed on the MMO's own terms—
  to "win" it. The MMO's lead designer is the "father" here.

- **Apotheosis**

  The player understands the virtual world and its people.
  They bask in their new-found status.

- **The Ultimate Boon**

  Oh-oh! Virtual worlds are virtual; how can you take anything out of them?

- **Refusal of the Return**

  The player has power, respect, and friends—why leave?

- **Rescue from Without**

  All the time you've been playing, your parents, significant
  other, and real-world friends have been saying, "Why do
  you spend so much time playing that computer game?"
  Now, you actually pay attention to them.

- **The Magic flight**

  Oh, those expansion sets—just when you're about to
  quit, they bring out another one!

- **Crossing the Return Threshold**

  You stop playing because you don't *need* to play anymore.

- **Master of the Two Worlds**

  Your virtual self and your real self are one. The virtual
  world is a place just like any other—it's lost its mystical
  significance. Okay, so it's a fun place to visit, and you have
  lots of friends there whom you like to hook up with, but
  it's not *special* any more.

- **Freedom to Live**

  Having *become* themselves, players can finally *be*
  themselves.

Note: the order of Rescue from Without and The Magic Flight has been
reversed here. This is because the magic flight isn't so much breaking out as
declining to break back in. Recall that missing, reversed, and repeated minor
steps are not uncommon in the hero's journey.

Ah, yes, missing steps: what's with The Ultimate Boon? How can you take *anything* from a virtual world? To do so, wouldn't it have to be real—and therefore not virtual? Well, yes, it would—and it is: it's *you*. The boon is symbolic of your sense of self anyway; taking yourself out of the virtual world merely collapses a redundant metaphor.

So, we can now see how the hero's journey can be applied to virtual worlds. There's a difference between "can be applied" and "applies," though. After all, you *can* apply the hero's journey to all manner of transformative journeys, some of which have no basis whatsoever (try composing "my breakfast's journey"—it hits almost every step, with "rescue from without" being particularly entertaining if you're aged 12).

This is not just some happy match between a player's MMO experience and the hero's journey, though. If it were, it would be a curiosity but little else. There's something about it that gives it *substance*.

Look back at the player types stuff I described a while ago.

Master of the Two Worlds

Some of *MUD2*'s players have been playing it since the 1980s.

Sure, they "won" long ago.

Violent Changes

By default, people who play MMOs for fun will follow whichever development track best suits them. However, very, *very* infrequently someone will flip their lid and effectively derail. Where they'll finally end up is anyone's guess, but most often they just stick where they are, unable to make progress and becoming increasingly frustrated. In such a case, they're called *broken*, as in *broken planner* or *broken networker*[32].

It usually takes great psychological trauma or an external, real-life event to cause such a violent change of direction to happen, so you won't see it very often. This is probably just as well, given that the results aren't usually desirable. The most alarming case I've experienced is that of a hacker who became a griefer after getting his carefully-constructed research disrupted by a regular griefer once too often. This turned him into maniacal super-griefer, leading to much hilarity for him and much weeping and wailing for his victims.

---

[32]This term originated with one of my *MUD2* players, who called herself Lexley Vaughan but *no way* was that her real name: Lexley Vaughan: *Player Killers Exposed. Imaginary Realities* Vol. 2 (10), October 1999. http://www.paxlair.com/library_files/1_in_progress/player_killers_exposed/player_killers_exposed.htm

Speak Like an Academic

> *The way I see it, the diegetic evil enables a player to resolve a dialectic between the extra-diegetic "good" of their real-life existence (as imposed by society) and the extra-diegetic "evil" that is their potential future if they were to rebel.*

Become an academic, and you, too, can speak like this.

What I'm saying is that the "evil" that exists within the context of the MMO world is useful as a tool to help people work through issues of conformity with social norms in the real world.

Here's another way of putting it.

> *Day 1: "What makes me think I'm not evil?"*
>
> *Day 60: "Even when I role-play evil, I still wind up acting good. Evil isn't as cool as it's made out to be."*
>
> *The temptation to be evil hasn't been overcome here, it's been rejected. Evil is for losers.*

Become an academic, and you can speak like this, too.

In the first example, I was in research mode; in the second example, I was in teaching mode.

Most of this book is written in teaching mode. It has very few references and no non-reference footnotes. Criticisms are often "straw man" in nature because, although I can name names when I begin with "some people think…"—I really don't want the grief and lawsuits that would follow if I did so.

I tell you this so that if you're enthused or outraged enough by what I've been saying to delve deeper into any of the topics I've raised, expect walls of text like the "diegetic evil" one to greet you.

I now return you to your regularly scheduled program.

The World of Adventure

Here's how we know that the fit between a player's experience of an MMO and the hero's journey is not merely coincidence.

Look at the steps of the hero's journey that take place within the world of adventure, and compare them to the development tracks for player types (in order):

- **The Road of Trials**

  This corresponds to the opportunist/griefer step of player development. The player is trying to find out what the limits are of the MMO's physics and cultural norms.

- **The Meeting with the Goddess**

  This corresponds to the networker/scientist step. The player is trying to find out what the task ahead will involve.

- **Woman as Temptress**

  This corresponds to the transition from networker/ scientist to planner/politician. The player is level 20, say, and can see that the next (cap-20) levels will be pretty much more of the same. Will they play those levels through, or restart, or stop playing?

- **Atonement with the Father**

  This corresponds to the planner/politician step. The player attempts to satisfy the goals that the MMO itself states through its design. This is where most MMO players spend the bulk of their time, typically leveling up or collecting endgame gear sets.

- **Apotheosis**

  This corresponds with the Friend/Hacker step. The player understands the world, its people, and their place within it.

This is such a strong match with what we *know* happens as players develop in virtual worlds that it *can't* be a coincidence. People who play virtual worlds for fun *must* be engaged in their own, personal, hero's journey.

If you think about it, why *else* would they invest two to four hours every night for 18 month playing the same computer game? They're doing it because *they get to be themselves.*

That's all that people anywhere throughout history have ever wanted to be.

One Answer

The one design question I had after I heard Will Wright say, "You start off at the microscopic level" was this: "Does the universe turn out to be microscopic to another universe?"

It was obvious to me from that first line that he was going to start small, then get gradually bigger until eventually he had an entire universe. I wanted to know whether this universe would be the starting spore of a new, start-again universe, or whether universes didn't wrap around like that.

I therefore watched in growing amazement as the crowd whooped with delight each time Will pulled out the viewpoint. Microscopic to naked eye—whoop!—to local—whoop!—to global—whoop!—to stellar—whoop!—to universal—whoop! whoop!

These people *hadn't seen it coming*. I was in a room with the cream of the computer game development community, and 90 percent of them didn't seem to know what Will was going to tell them next. Couldn't they see? It was *obvious!*

Well, obvious to *me*: I'm a designer. It was also obvious to those other designers present that I spoke with afterwards. Most members of the audience, however, were not designers. You may have design ideas, and those ideas may be good ones, but that doesn't make you a designer.

You're a designer because… you're a designer.

Oh, and the answer is no: the universe doesn't wrap around. Probably a good call: it would have been aesthetically more pleasing as a design if it had wrapped round, but players would have had less of a sense of having *built* something.

Why People Play MMOs

We can at last say why people play MMOs.

It's a quest for identity.

By being someone virtual, people find out who they are for real.

Whatever they are doing at any one moment to pursue that aim, they regard as fun.

That's why they play so much.

That's why virtual worlds are here to stay.

HiPiHi—Words and Meaning

At a conference in 2007, I went to a talk given by the Infocomm Development Authority of Singapore. I got there early, mainly because my alarm had failed to go off the day before, and I'd missed a keynote, so I was feeling guilty. While waiting, I spoke with some of the other attendees. One of them was Hui Xu, founder and CEO of *HiPiHi*, who was present with his translator, Zafka Zhang. I knew that *HiPiHi* was starting out as a well-funded Chinese virtual world along the lines of *Second Life*, so there were many interesting and penetrative questions I could have asked.

Of these many interesting and penetrative questions I could have asked, I nevertheless chose to go with the one that anyone who had read about *HiPiHi* really wanted to know: how do you pronounce its name?

Zafka was visibly excited that I'd asked this, because there had been some serious thought involved in choosing the name. He explained that the fact that there are three Is in *HiPiHi* is auspicious in China because three is a "good number" (the word for "three", *sān*, sounds vaguely like the word for "living, growing," *shēng*). Taken as three parallel lines, they are associated with creation; I guess that would be because three unbroken parallel lines in the *I Ching* have that meaning. He also said that the three Is looked like the Chinese character for "society," but I don't know where that comes from—it looks more like the one for river to me (川).

As for the letters in between, they're tied to the Is. The pair *pihi* has connotations of an innocent or perfect child (sadly, too informal for my Anglo-Chinese dictionary). The *hipi* pair sounds a bit like the English word "happy" to Chinese ears.

Okay, so that's all very interesting, but #1 on the FAQ is not, "What does the name mean?" It's, "How do you pronounce it?"

Zafka's reply was, "Oh, some people say *hypie-high*, some people say *hippy-high*, some say *high-pie-high*. Say it how you like."

Sure enough, over the course of the conference, both he and Hui Xu pronounced it all three ways with merry abandon, as did everyone else. *High-pee-high* was another popular rendition.

I thought it a bit strange that they'd go into so much depth regarding the symbolism of the word, but not at all care how it's pronounced. I suppose if you're aiming for world domination, the key point is that it's pronounceable at all in other languages, not so much the exact way the locals choose to say it.

I myself decided to go with *hippy-high*, because hippies get high. That way, Chinese and American cultural values could fight over its connotations and leave me in peace.

HiPiHi ceased to exist in 2012. The name must not have been quite as auspicious as it was believed to be.

Atonement with the Father

Today's MMOs don't do the Atonement with the Father step very well *at all*.

The step requires the MMO to accept that a player has "won" and effectively say, GAME OVER. Marketing people don't like this idea because, well, if you tell players that they've won, surely they'll stop playing?

Bad news, marketing people: *all* players will stop playing eventually. The best you get to do is delay the inevitable.

If you don't tell players they have won, then they don't complete the Atonement with the Father step of their journey. Either they'll grow increasingly frustrated and irritated ("what do I have to *do*?!") or they'll self-actualize anyway without you ("you know, I've nothing left to prove here"). Either way, you're building up resentment. If you were just to *tell* them when they've finished the game aspect of play, they could move on.

We did this in the early days. You reached the level cap—congratulations! You're now a wizard/witch (delete as appropriate). It would be a brave MMO developer who let a designer try this in a $50 million title, though.

Still, with the right scenario.

Remember: that's the *1980s* for some *MUD2* players.

Designeritis

Suppose you go to see a movie and find yourself sitting next to Stephen Spielberg (unless you are Stephen Spielberg, in which case this whole conceit breaks down). Two hours later, when the movie has finished, what could you possibly say to him about it? His knowledge of movie-making is so much deeper than yours that he'll have seen things you haven't seen, picked up on nuances that passed you by, understood symbols you didn't even know *were* symbols: it's almost as if you've watched two different movies.

Yet *you* may have had the better experience. For you, the magic of the movies is still real.

As with movie directors, designers of MMOs know so much about their subject that they don't see them in quite the same way as players. When they enjoy an MMO, they enjoy it for the beauty of its design, not of its artwork; for the imagination of its gameplay, not of its guilds; for its expression of ideas, not of its action.

I can't play an MMO as a regular player for fun. I *do* have fun, but not the same *kind* of fun that non-designer players have. I've seen and experienced that kind of fun every which way for well over 30 years, and its enchantment has long since worn off—if it was ever there to begin with. My fun comes from creating and from experiencing the creations of other people (although some of this can be painful—not all design is beautiful).

In other words, I've grokked games, but not game design.

I'm not alone in not being able to play as a player. Although the condition doesn't affect all designers, it's nevertheless so common that it has a name, "designeritis" (coined by Raph Koster).

Players are deeply wary of this. It's not only a pompous attitude to take ("my understanding is far in advance of yours"), it sounds like a bad thing. After all, if *you* don't have fun playing your own MMO, how can you expect your *players* to have fun doing so?

Pomposity aside (because okay, it *is* pompous), this would be a valid criticism were it not for the fact that players *don't all have the same idea of what's fun in an MMO*. If I were, say, an achiever, I'd certainly create an MMO that achievers would find fun, but what about explorers? What about socializers? Given, then, that I *have* to design for playing styles not my own, wouldn't it therefore be better if I was agnostic about them, rather than believing in just one? That way, I'm not going to be biased in favor of my own style over the others.

You don't have to experience something at an emotional level to understand those who do; indeed, if you *do* experience it, it can get in the way.

This is known as the "most gynecologists are men" defense.

Gome and Gomen

One Monday in 2012, when I was supposed to be doing some miserable, pointless administration that I just wanted to GET OUT OF THE WAY, I instead spent several hours reading up on *Sir Gawain and the Green Knight*.

Don't you loathe it when you're watching a TV detective series and the detective looks at a scene, "knowing something is wrong" without being able to put their finger on it? It's basically an invitation for the viewer to see if they can spot the clue. Real detectives never get that kind of I-can-see-something-is-out-of-place-but-I-don't-know-what moments. That kind of consciously inaccessible observation just doesn't make sense.

Okay, so I was looking for a short tale that follows the formula of the hero's journey in order to get my students to analyze it. The previous year's cohort had done *The First Voyage of Sindbad the Sailor*, but that was a little short and we'd finished early, so this time I thought I'd try find something longer. *Sir Gawain and the Green Knight* is too long in its original form, but I could probably use an abridged version as it was the plot that I wanted, not so much the alliterative poetry. The reason I was keen to use it was because it has a "beheading game" in it, and I was teaching it as part of a games module. Ultimately, Gawain breaks the rules of the game and feels shame because of this, which is rather interesting.

Then, I had a TV detective moment. There was something I knew about games and something I knew about Middle English that suddenly connected them. But what?

Fortunately, my ability to query my own insights far exceeds that of TV detectives and I knew the answer less than a second later. The word *bridegroom* used to be *bridegome*, with *gome* being a Middle English word for *man* (the Spanish surname *Gomez* has the same root). The Middle English for game is (er, I guess that's was) *gomen*. That's a pretty cool similarity: I wondered if the Middle English version of *Sir Gawain and the Green Knight* uses those words?

Well, yes it does.

It uses *gomen* several times in several ways (some of which are more akin to meaning "play" than "game") and it uses *gome* even more often in even more ways. It turns out that there's a school of thought which asserts that this is no coincidence and that one of the central themes of the poem is that men treat life as a game. There's even an argument that the poem is *itself* a game to be played by the teller with the audience.

So this is why I spent an afternoon reading papers about a classic of medieval literature when I should have been reading a wad of project reports I was meant to be externally examining. Damn!

Oh well, that's game designers for you.

;shrugs

People typically play MMOs for two to four hours most nights. If they don't quit within six months, they'll continue for between 18 months and two years before easing off.

Even the most dedicated player of a Facebook game is not going to be able to do that while remaining sane. The only reason they can do it in an MMO is because they're undertaking a hero's journey.

The hero's journey underpins Player Types theory. Why then, would you use Player Types theory for Facebook games? Or for mobile phone games? Or for any other kind of game except MMOs?

Yet some people do.

;shrugs.

Oeuvres

Game designers have *oeuvres*. If you're told a game is by Will Wright, you know what to expect.

The same applies to (among others) Sid Meier, Peter Molyneux, Raph Koster, Reiner Knizia, and Mark Jacobs.

Game design is an *art*.

Azax

The point at which I knew for certain that Campbell's monomyth applied to MMOs was when I read about the Atonement with the Father step.

I'd seen it happen, before my (virtual) eyes.

It was in *MUD1*. One of our players, Averazix, was a classic explorer type. He tried out anything and everything. Some of these things were legitimate; some were borderline; some were illegitimate. I busted him down to 0 points several times, but he just bounced back. He had a major line in whinging to try to get to see things that people didn't normally get to see, and he really annoyed some of the players in authority—the wizzes.

As I explained earlier, in *MUD1* when you obtained enough points, you became a wiz (wizard for male characters, witch for female characters). Wizzes had tremendous powers—they could do anything from eradicating other characters to raising them to wiz level, too.

After being reduced back to 0 points yet again (for exploiting the kiss command—no, really!), Averazix decided to play it straight. He changed his name to Azax and determined to play *MUD1* as intended so as to reach wiz in such a squeaky-clean manner that he was beyond reproach. Then, the instant he had access to his wizly powers, he would use them to kill anyone and everyone, thereby wrecking the game and punishing the wizzes for having punished him.

What he didn't know was that I, as an arch-wizard, had seen him discussing his plans with a friend while I was invisible, so was waiting, ready, when he began his final wiz run. If he *did* run amok, I would have been able to stop him. Wizzes were powerful, but not as powerful as arch-wizzes.

Sure enough, he steadily accumulated the final points he needed, cautiously and scrupulously, the moment of his revenge drawing ever closer, until finally he crossed the line and—

—and in the space of about four seconds, he was hit by the realization that what he wanted to become so he could defeat it, *he already was*. He suddenly *understood* what being a wiz *meant*. It was amazing to behold. He *transformed*.

From being a whinging, whiny, yet smart kid, Azax became *MUD1*'s 44th wiz, a position he held until I made him an arch-wiz a couple of years later.

I talked to Azax afterwards about this, and he confirmed it as accurate. He had intended to wreak death right up until the moment the message appeared, "Your level of experience is now wizard." Then, when he saw it, he knew he had never needed to do so.

I often mentioned this in conversation about *MUD1*'s wizzes, but it wasn't until some 18 years later that I read *The Hero with a Thousand Faces* and saw it described in words.

There are plenty of skeptics who doubt that the hero's journey applies to MMOs, but for me it answered a question that had been bugging me since 1984: what *happened*, there?

Real Life API—SelfActualize

CPlayer::SelfActualize

void SelfActualize()

Remarks

Causes the player to be and become who he or she really is. Depending on properties defined within **CPlayer**, effects can include:

- A willingness to embrace truth rather than deny or ignore it.

- An interest in solving problems.

- Spontaneity.

- Self-acceptance and an acceptance of others.

- A lack of prejudice.

It is recommended that this method only be employed on players with a **plPlayed** value in excess of 1,600 hours (game worlds) or 3,200 hours (social worlds).

Failure of Atonement

Although their lack of Atonement with the Father is a problem for MMOs, there are other ways to screw up this step that MMO designers (or those who pay their salaries) are all too eager to attempt.

Undeserved Atonement. For Atonement with the Father to mean anything, it must *only* be available to those who have passed the tests. If the Father can be fooled into granting atonement to those who haven't passed the tests, this makes it worthless.

This explains why so many players dislike anything that undermines their own sense of achievement. They regard any way to side-step the MMO's progression system as cheating. The buying of any in-world advantage using real-world money is anathema to them. It eats at the trust that is necessary for this part of the journey to work.

Premature Atonement. An MMO that is too easy can enable Atonement with the Father to be obtained before the player is ready for it. First-time players normally take 18-24 months at normal rates of play to reach the necessary level of immersion. If Atonement comes too soon (in the scientist/networker phase, for example), then it will feel all wrong.

This implies that MMOs need a critical mass of content if they are to be valid as the "other world" of a hero's journey. With insufficient content, or content of an insufficient level, Atonement will be granted before the player can draw any benefit from it.

It also implies that there is such a thing as too much content, which players will interpret as grind. Nevertheless, too much is better than too little: so long as *some* end is realistically attainable after the player has passed the scientist/networker step but before they've reached the hacker/friend one, Atonement will feel acceptable and merited.

Lack of Journey. Social worlds have a major problem in that they offer no metric by which players can measure their relative success. Game worlds also suffer to some extent, albeit almost exclusively to those players who follow the main socializer sequence. Often in such situations, players will come up with their own pecking order instead of a game-prescribed one (for example, "leading a guild").

In other words, if a virtual world is sufficiently separated from real life to qualify in players' minds as an "other world," they will make up their own "game" to drive their activities. Unfortunately, because the virtual world itself doesn't recognize the terms of this "game," it will rarely be implemented as an Atonement mechanism.

Meaningless Atonement. This is perhaps the most challenging problem facing those designers who wish to give their players the complete hero's journey experience. For Atonement with the Father to mean anything, it must only be given to those who have passed through the previous stages of the journey. The sad fact is, however, that not every player is *able* to do so: not everyone can be a hero.

Sooner or later, it occurs to players even of MMOs boasting a winning condition that failure was never an option. All it takes to keep going is time. Tests and trials may get harder, but they're never so hard that you can't pass them. Anyone with half a brain can plod, plod, plod to "the end," wherever that is. What, then, is the point of trying? The only way you're not going to finish the journey is if it becomes so boring that you lose interest. Atonement with the Father is guaranteed for all, it's just a matter of stamina.

There are two known solutions to this, neither of which is ideal.

The first is permadeath. Players who fail a step must create a new character, start again, and attempt to recover their lost self (creating in the process a stronger, new self).

The second is a failure penalty. Players don't lose their character when they mess up, but they do lose something that materially puts them back—experience points, for example. In the process of recovering what they lost, they could well lose again, until they reach an equilibrium in which their gains are balanced with their losses. They run but stay in the same place, so don't ever reach the winning post.

My advice to MMO designers is this: give players a meaningful, deserved "win" condition that arrives at the right time, is triggered by a valid measure of mastery and is plod-proof; in return, they'll give you your virtual world.

It's okay, don't feel bad: I know you're not going to act on it.

So Little Time

Interested observers always make a big thing of the amount of time that players spend in an MMO. Server logs for *EverQuest 2* show[33][34] that the average is around 29 hours per week for women and 25 for men. It's clear that people can spend a lot of time in virtual worlds.

Is there, however, a minimum amount of time they can spend, below which they simply don't get the full benefit of an MMO? Might it be, for example, that if you can only play a random 5-10 hours a week you aren't going to form enough of a social relationship with other players to get that virtual world "feel"? Or perhaps you won't get that growing sense that you and your character are one and the same, which so marks out MMOs from regular computer games?

If this is indeed the case, and there is a minimum time commitment to get the best out of an MMO, then any game designed to appeal to "casual" players faces a dilemma. It may have the form of a virtual world, but if the players don't inhabit it as traditional players do, then it won't have the effect of one. Therefore, should it even have the form of one? It might be a better casual game if it didn't.

Yeah, yeah, you don't really care, just so long as the non-casual MMOs don't go the same way.

Þe Gome of þe Grene

Sir Gawain and the Green Knight follows the hero's journey. Gawain fails the last step on the Road of Trials by accepting a gift that he doesn't mention to his host, thereby breaking the rules of the game they are playing. He pays for it with a nick to the neck during his Atonement with the Father.

All stories, continually retold, come to have the same shape. All existence is a game.

---

[33]Dmitri Williams, Nick Yee and Scott E. Caplan: *Who Plays, How Much, and Why? Debunking the Stereotypical Gamer Profile. Journal of Computer-Mediated Communication* v 13 pp 993-1018, 2008. http://dmitriwilliams.com/Whoplaysfinal.pdf
[34]Erwin S. Andreasen and Brandon A. Downey: *Measuring Bartle-Quotient*, 1996-present.

Evidence

So, people who play MMOs for fun are undergoing a hero's journey—a narrative path to self-understanding. As they progress, what they find fun in the MMO changes, reflecting their current position on the path. This is immensely compelling because, for the first time in human history, ordinary individuals can go on their own hero's journey instead of having to identify with those of the characters in other people's stories.

Yes, this all hangs together very nicely. However, is there any *evidence* for it? Just because it *looks* neat, that doesn't mean it's *right*. It's conceivable that even *I* could be, be, be, be *wrong*!

Anecdotal evidence suggests that players buy into the player types, if not the theory itself (players of RPGs are notorious for not liking the idea that theories of any kind apply to them). The *Bartle Test of Gamer Psychology*, which is based on my work (no, I didn't give it that name) has had more than 850,000 respondents since it started in 1996. Surely this would not be the case if there weren't at least *something* in it.

Does it stand up to *academic* scrutiny, though?

Over to Nick Yee.

Newbie Induction Examples

Here are two examples of short-term/long-term good/bad ideas in MMOs. I chose these particular ones because, well, you'll see why.

Permanent death is short-term bad, long-term good. It's *really* bad, when it happens to you. However, properly done, it doesn't happen all that often, and it has huge benefits.

- It prevents early-adopters filling all the positions of power.

- It reuses content efficiently because you can see the same content from different angles.

- It's the default fiction for real life.

- It promotes identity exploration because you're not stuck as one character.

- It validates achievement because a high-level character implies a high-level player.

Many designers and experienced players would like to see a form of permadeath in their MMO, but it's not going to happen. Newbies wouldn't play such a game; therefore, eventually neither would anyone else.

Permadeath is short-term bad, long-term good: rejected.

Instancing is short-term good, long-term bad. Groups of friends (or, increasingly, groups of random strangers you'll never meet again) can play together in their own walled garden of peace and tranquility.

Where's the player impact, though? How can you have any effect on the world if all you're doing is repeating a story capsule inside a pocket universe that disappears as soon as you leave it? Where's the sense of *being* somebody?

Players don't see it that way, though. It's familiar and fun, so they like it. Only in the long term do they discover the downside—it's grindy, repetitive, predictable, and creatively moribund. So what do they do? They wait for new instances to appear or go play some other MMO that has instances. What they *don't* do is go play an MMO that doesn't have instances—they still only see the short-term good, not the long-term bad.

Instancing is short-term good, long-term bad: accepted.

I chose two examples because the chances are that most of the readers of this book will make my point for me. You probably would not play an MMO with permadeath on principle. You probably would not play an MMO without instancing on principle. That's why we have the latter and don't have the former, even though in pure design terms it would be better to have the former and not have the latter.

It's not just permadeath and instancing. There are many things now in the paradigm that could make for better MMOs if they weren't there, including teleporting, banks, soulbound objects, and weightless money. Players have come to these expect things:

> **Player**: Why won't this shopkeeper buy my broken wand?
>
> **Designer**: It's a cheese shop. You need a magic shop.
>
> **Player**: So I have to spend 45 seconds walking to the magic shop to sell my broken wand? That sucks!
>
> **Designer**: On the way, you might see other shops, pick up quests, bump into friends—
>
> **Player**: Are you NUTS? I have a raid in like 20 minutes! I want to sell this crap RIGHT NOW!
>
> **Designer**: But how will you ever discover anything new if you don't explore?
>
> **Player**: Are you listening? RIGHT NOW!
>
> **Designer**: *Mutter. Grumble.*

It's not as if *any* shop, let alone a cheese shop, would ever buy a broken wand anyway. Try selling a broken clock to the proprietor of an actual clock shop in real life and see how far you get.

MMOs build a pressure on designers to create worlds that, while not outright bad, are long-term bad. Each succeeding generation adds more not-quite-good-enough features to the paradigm, which leads to a downward spiral. It's not so much evolution as erosion.

There are some wonderfully original, joyous MMOs out there. They're gracefully balanced, rich in depth, astonishing in breadth, alive with subtleties, and packed with fun, interesting people in an atmosphere of mystique and marvel without compare. You would love these worlds, but you're not going to play them. You're not going to play them because they're text.

Text is an example of short-term bad, decades of long-term good: rejected.

Nick Yee's "Motivations"

The first person to do a major study looking at the Player Types model was Nick Yee of Stanford University[35]. He surveyed 6,700 players of *EverQuest* (82%), *Dark Age of Camelot* (15%), and a smattering of other MMOs, asking a number of questions designed to find out what motivated players to play.

From the data, Nick found five such motivations. Here they are, each paired with the player type that matches it:

Grief	Killer (griefer)
Leadership	Killer (politician)
Achievement	Achiever
Relationship	Socializers
Immersion	Er..?

As you can see, Nick found no evidence for explorers, but did find evidence for something entirely absent from the Player Types model—immersion.

More recently, Nick analyzed[36] a massive dataset for *EverQuest 2* (massive as in 60 terabytes of data cataloguing the activities of 400,000 players—*that* kind of massive). He was able to go into much more depth with this and tease out more subtle relationships; in all, he discovered ten motivations which factored neatly into three groups:

- **Achievement**

  Advancement, analyzing mechanics, competition.

- **Social**

  Chatting, developing relationships, teamwork.

- **Immersion**

  Geographical exploration, role-playing, avatar customization, escapism.

---

[35]Nicholas Yee: *Facets: Five Motivation Factors for Why People Play MMORPGs*, 2002. http://www.nickyee.com/facets/home.html
[36]Nicholas Yee: *Motivations of Play in Online Games. CyberPsychology and Behaviour* 9, pp 772-775, 2006. http://www.nickyee.com/pubs/Yee%20-%20Motivations%20(2007).pdf

Compare these motivations with the 8-types model:

Advancement	Achiever (planner)
Analyzing Mechanics	Explorer (hacker)
Competition	Killer (griefer)
Chatting	Socializer (networker)
Developing Relationships	Socializer (friend)
Teamwork	Killer (politician)
Discovery	Explorer (scientist)
Role-Playing	Er..?
Avatar Customization	Er..?
Escapism	Er..?

This doesn't look *too* shoehorned a fit. There's nothing that matches achiever (opportunist) directly, but that could be because it's superficially close enough to explorer (scientist) to be caught in the same net.

The interesting parts are the extra three motivations that Nick identified, which do not correspond with anything in the 8-types model. They're all examples of what Nick classifies as "immersion."

So, from both the early and later work that Nick has done here, we can see that a notable proportion of players consistently rate immersion as a reason why they play. This poses something of a problem for the Player Types model because it doesn't have a fit for it. Furthermore, because the Player Types model is supposed to be exhaustive, it *can't* have a fit for it without major reconstructive surgery.

A hint at the solution comes from the observation that immersion isn't orthogonal to the other factors. You can't be both exploring and griefing at the same time, but you *can* be both exploring and immersed at the same time. This suggests that immersion could be emergent (don't you love it when the English language clashes like that?).

As a hint as to what's going on here, I'll perhaps point out that it's no coincidence Nick Yee called his 2014 book *The Proteus Paradox*[37].

---

[37]Nicholas Yee: *The Proteus Paradox: How Online Games and Virtual Worlds Change us – and how they don't*. Yale University Press, 2014.

The Player Life-Cycle

Aside from the work on player types, how does the rest of my grand MMO theory stand up to close investigation?

Well, there hasn't actually been a lot of work in this area, although what there has been has come from—you guessed, yet again—Nick Yee[38]. He tracked the stages that players went through as they played, and discovered that over their entire playing career they followed a pattern:

- Entry
- Practice
- Mastery
- Burnout
- Recovery

Because you're so observant, you will have noticed that this is an abstraction of the hero's journey. Entry is the Road of Trials; practice is The Meeting with the Goddess; mastery is Atonement with the Father; burnout is Apotheosis; recovery is Master of the Two Worlds.

The burnout stage is slightly problematical, in that the name suggests that it's a negative experience. This is generally supported by the data, too: players tire of grinding, raiding, and starting new characters, and feel there is nothing left for them to do. Apotheosis is not supposed to be like this, though: the hero's journey expects them to feel relaxed and at ease. So what's gone wrong?

Well, it's a consequence of the botched Atonement with the Father step. If the players had been told at the peak of their mastery that they had beaten the game, then that would indeed have led them to a positive Apotheosis. However, because they weren't told this, they had to figure it out for themselves.

Thus, players grow weary of doing the same old things for no discernible gain, and eventually begin to question the point of it all. Sometimes they'll set themselves another futile goal, but eventually they'll either leave in frustration or come to realize that there's no pressure on them any more—they've *won*. They move into the stage Nick calls "recovery" and are free to have fun again.

---

[38]Nicholas Yee: *Player Life-Cycle*, 2009. http://www.nickyee.com/daedalus/archives/001588.php

Immersion and Identity

If you think about it, it's fairly obvious what immersion is in MMO terms. If immersion means the feeling that *you* are *in* a virtual world, and there exists an entity in that virtual world which you control, then it follows that *you* must *be* that entity.

It's an identity thing. The more you feel that your character is you, the more immersed you are. When the two finally become one, the result is a persona—*you, in* the MMO.

That's immersion.

Induction in Action

When the AOL MMO *NeverWinter Nights* shut down in 1997, the players flooded to *Meridian 59*[39]. There, they demanded the inclusion of every single feature of *NWN* that *M59* didn't already have. This included those very features that had caused *NWN*'s decline.

Players judge all subsequent MMOs against their idealized view of the one they first got into. If you're an MMO player, that *includes* you.

Not Actually Famous

None of the players in any of the MMO guilds I've been in have recognized my name when I've told them. Even if they've done the "Bartle Test," they don't remember my name. Among MMO players, I'm not actually famous. I'm not even relatively famous.

This is probably how it should be.

Beyond the "Hero" Label

With MMOs, for the first time pretty well ever ordinary people can *themselves* experience a hero's journey. You can never be Neo from *The Matrix*, but you don't *want* to be Neo—you want to be *you*.

Instead of having to gain occasional glimpses of facets of your self through a patchy, second-person alignment with a fictional character, with MMOs you can experience it *directly*. You *can* become a hero. What you *can't* become is a stereotype, which is the vision of what it is to be "a hero" that many players (and yes, sadly, designers) have today.

---

[39]Damion Schubert: *The Single Most Fun Thing you can do with Hundreds of Other People without Wearing Anything Made of Latex*. 31st December, 1999. http://www.gilcon.net/meridian/faqs-get.asp?ID=89

On Missing Types

"Where is the player type for people who just want to help others?"

Often, people ask me where some player type they feel exists or wish to believe exists would fit into the Player Types model. As I've explained several times already, the answer is always the same: look at what they find fun. It may be that no fun is involved, in which case Player Types theory wouldn't even apply.

People who help others are doing it for their own reasons, whether those are moral, religious, genetic, or ulterior. If I go out and help people because it gives me a warm fuzzy glow to do so, sure, people will benefit, but I'm basically doing it for myself. If I hate helping people but nevertheless go out of my way to help them, it'll also be for some personal reason—maybe to assuage some guilt, or because I've decided it's the "right thing" to do and don't want to contradict myself by acting otherwise.

Only if people help other people out for fun (i.e., the warm, fuzzy glow) would the Player Types model apply, though. So, that's probably friends-style socializers or politician-style killers, then.

Of course, if you're helping someone because in so doing it will lead to a different kind of fun, then the player type associated with that different kind of fun would cover it.

Attunement

It's rare that MMO designers consider themselves to be artists, even though they are. It's even rarer that players see MMOs as works of art.

Some players do, though. This presents them with a potential difficulty. The thing is, if players are attuned to the "art" of an MMO's design, they must as a consequence be aware of their own place in that art, which means that they can no longer act as regular players. Instead of living the virtual world, they are now one step removed—they see it objectively, not subjectively. This should take a lot of the fun out of the game for them.

Well, yes, this does happen. However, a growing critical awareness by players that they are participants in the art they are critiquing doesn't actually hurt them as much fun-wise as you might think. After all, all players *know* that virtual worlds are not real, they *know* that everything they see is a construction, they *know* that they are only pretending to be mages or warriors or priests.

However, they really, *really* want all these falsehoods to be true, to the extent that they put all the truths to the back of their mind: in the traditional way, they *will* themselves to believe that what they *want* to be true *is* true. Thus, if knowing that they are components contributing to what makes an MMO art gets in the way of their play, then they will simply ignore it while playing. They may well think about it at other times, but not really while they're playing.

The difference between designers and players is that players get their fun from playing, which is why they are prepared and able to switch off troublesome critical faculties for a while if they cause them not to have fun. Designers get their fun from designing, not from playing, so they are not going to have that same powerful desire to throw themselves into the role to the exclusion of all else that players have. There are some designers who say they can do this, but I'm not one of them.

This is why designers get designeritis, but even highly critically attuned players don't.

Perverse Evolution

With regular computer games (and board games, for that matter), the market is driven by hard core players. They buy more games than casual players and they consume them faster. They understand game design implications better, and they won't buy games that they can tell at a glance have poor design. Good games are rewarded with higher sales, so the evolutionary pressure is to create better games.

Go, Darwin, go!

In MMOs, the hard core either wanders from one MMO to the next, trying to get the Atonement with the Father they were denied in their first MMO; either that, or they have yet to leave that first MMO. They spend no more money than casual players; indeed, in a free-to-play revenue model, they may even pay less. MMO developers are therefore not rewarded by appealing to the players who can distinguish between good and bad design, and could well be punished for it instead. The evolutionary pressure is directed at attracting newbies, who by definition have a simpler idea of what makes an MMO experience attractive than do oldbies.

No, Darwin, no!

Temporary Visitors

The Atonement with the Father step of the hero's journey basically says that players want to "win" an MMO. If it doesn't acknowledge they've won, though, they'll leave in frustration and try to win elsewhere. At some point, this elsewhere either fails to match the experience of the original MMO, or it matches it all too well. In either case, the player will either return to the original MMO to seek atonement there once more or move on to the next ersatz version of it, looking for an end that is never going to come.

Either way, any game that lures them away from their first love has a big problem in keeping them.

Say What You See

The UK magazine *games™* has an occasional feature in which it ridicules people in the game industry for the things they say. Here's something it picked up from the mouth of Shigeru Miyamoto, designer of everything Nintendo:

> *The only time I play is maybe the 20 minutes I spend testing rivals' new machines. I don't play videogames in my free time.*

This is what it said in response:

> *No… say it isn't so. Please. When the last bastion of innovation in gaming can't be bothered to play games, what hope is left? Maybe he's just losing his skills.*

Sorry, *games™*, it *is* so. The reason that Shigeru Miyamoto doesn't play games is precisely because he *isn't* losing his skills.

Everyone thinks they're a game designer, and journalists for *games™* are no exception.

Dead Mages

One day, I came across this while visiting Stormwind in *World of Warcraft*:

That URL for a gold-selling site is spelled out in the bodies of dead level 1 mages.

Love them or loathe them, you have to admire the inventiveness of these companies.

The Future of Old Ideas

MMO designers are usually forward-thinking people. However, they also have to be backward-thinking if they're to have a full handle on what they're doing.

Designers need to be aware of old ideas.

Now I don't mind people disregarding old ideas if they know about them and have reasons for dumping them; I *do* mind when people are looking for solutions to problems that only exist because someone in the past threw out something they didn't like without realizing it would lead to said problem.

Here's an example. If you have a world with levels and experience points and stuff, and your character loses a fight, should that character also lose some experience points? The designer who asks the question will weigh up notions of speed of advancement, class balance, sense of achievement, player expectations, consequences for the elder game, and so on. They will basically have to decide whether they want players to value the leveling game or the elder (usually raiding) game most, and whether it will put players off playing in the first place. That's their call. Blizzard thought about this with *World of Warcraft*, and went with the no-XP penalty approach. Anyone with enough time to reach the highest level will indeed reach that level. If they'd penalized character death with XP loss in addition to a corpse-run time penalty and repair costs, then it would have been possible for players to reach a plateau, in which they gained XP at roughly the same rate that they lost it—something that occasionally happened in *EverQuest* (*WoW*'s inspiration).

Now suppose that years later some new designer comes along who grew up playing *WoW*, but who dislikes its double-gameplay model and wishes to remove the raiding game for their new, purer *WoW++*. What's going to happen is that, after a few months, the characters will be bunched up at the highest level. What's the new designer going to do? Well if they knew why the characters were bunching up in the first place (no XP penalty for fight losses), then they'd know reinstating it was a possible solution; they might not want to run with it, but they'd know it was *available*. If they knew of even earlier solutions, such as remorting from the old text MUD days, they'd have more weapons in their armory to solve the problem.

If they went so far as to look at the underlying theories as to why people play virtual worlds, they may even decide that it's not a problem, so much as an inevitable and desirable consequence, and celebrate the end of every player's time in the game rather than attempt to extend it indefinitely—or maybe they wouldn't.

The point is, the more the designer understands why it is their MMO is in the position is it in now, the better able they are to decide how to address any issues. They can disregard all the accumulated wisdom if they like (how else is new wisdom ever arrived at?), but the more they know about what they're designing, the better their decisions are going to be.

If you know there's a wheel, at least you have the choice as to whether to use it or to reinvent it.

Text and Voice

Suppose that voice had all the major features of text—storability, searchability, scanability and so on—except that it still didn't have editability. When I type something, I can backspace and retype it before anyone gets to hear it; when I say something, I can't do that.

So, let's further suppose that an MMO forum switched from text to voice, so that all the posts had to be spoken rather than typed. Would that be a great boon to communication, or would it be a hindrance? Would you be more encouraged to post there or less encouraged to post there?

Does the fact that people can edit what they say in an MMO before they say it add to or detract from play?

It depends on the MMO.

Theory of Immersion

This all fits together.

The aim of the hero's journey is for the would-be hero to become their true self—the hero. They accomplish this by shedding their old self and being reborn in a world of adventure and excitement. Eventually, with the Atonement with the Father step, the new self and the old self are aligned and reconciled.

This is what's happening with immersion. When you start an MMO, your character is like a new you. As you play, though, you gradually identify more and more with your character, until eventually you *become* your character (or, if the thought of that spooks you, your character becomes *you*—the you who you really are).

In MMO terms, the practical result of the hero's journey is for the player and their character to become one persona. Immersion can thus be seen as the outward manifestation of this: **the further along the hero's journey you are, the more immersed you will be**.

This can be bad news if it's not done right. MMOs with insufficient content (such as *Mist*, which used the *MUD1* engine) will have players finishing without having become immersed; these players will achieve Atonement with the Father prematurely and will consequently feel unfulfilled.

Similarly, MMOs with too much content (such as *EverQuest* and most of the AAA MMOs that followed it) will have players becoming immersed without finishing; these players will have yet to reach the Atonement with the Father step, and will consequently feel frustrated.

Designers should strive to make the two events—Atonement with the Father and a sense of full immersion—coincide.

Yeah, like *that's* ever going to happen.

The Touchstone

MUD1 had no character classes. You got to use more magic as your character went up levels, but there was no obligation to do so. Even the most spell-happy player would still use a non-magic solution most of the time.

MUD2 also had (well, has, but it's so old I'll talk about it in the past tense for now) no character classes. However, it did have a distinction between those characters who could use magic and those who could not. Everyone started off unable to use magic; to gain access to it, you had to touch a mystical object called the *touchstone*. If you did so, then either your character gained the ability to use magic or it died (and that's "died" as in "permadeath"). The higher your level was, the greater was your chance of success. Even at the highest level, though, there was still a meaningful chance of failure. As you had to have magic to become a wiz, at some point you *would* have to touch it to be able to "finish" the game.

I put the touchstone in as a rite of passage. There's a blurring as to when people decide to subject themselves to it, which means that we got level 7 champions/championnes (with no magic) alongside level 7 sorcerers/sorceresses (with magic), but those weren't separate character classes; magic-users were the same as fighters in almost every way except that they could cast magic whereas fighters couldn't. There was really only *one* character class, in the same way that a caterpillar and a butterfly are only one insect.

The touchstone marked a conscious acceptance by a player that they were no longer a newbie. It forced them to think about who they were in the virtual world and bound them to their chosen character. In Hero's Journey terms, it equates with the "Meeting with the Goddess" stage. This is actually fairly interesting from my own perspective because I created the touchstone many years before I read *The Hero with a Thousand Faces*. I'm particularly impressed that my reasons for putting the touchstone in a "cave of stars" make very good sense in this (at the time unknown to me) context.

I wonder how many designers today could put in an object which characters had to interact with at some point in their career that would obliterate roughly 30 percent of them?

Immersion and Player Types

Nick Yee's identification of immersion as one of the reasons people find MMOs fun is troublesome for Player Types theory as it has nowhere to put the concept. Immersion as an important driver is clearly present—Nick's research is *very* solid—and therefore if Player Types theory can't account for it, the model is pretty well holed below the waterline.

Having looked at immersion in detail, though, we can now see that the theory *can* account for it—not as a player type, but as a measure of progression *through* player types. An increasing depth of immersion is a symptom of how far along the player development tracks you are.

This explains why you can be immersed and a socializer at the same time, whereas you can't be a socializer and an achiever at the same time: it's a separate concept.

That said, degrees of immersion *are* linked loosely to player types because types occupy fixed places along the development tracks. If you're a fully immersed explorer, that means you're going to be the hacker subtype; if you're less immersed, you'll be the scientist subtype.

People who say that they enjoy MMOs because they like the immersion are perceptive of the reason why ultimately everyone who plays MMOs for fun enjoys them. If you're fully immersed, then you're *you*.

The Clue is in the Title

Everyone playing an MMO for fun is a role-player, except those who have played their character for sufficiently long that it has become them and they have become it.

MMO is just an abbreviation of the acronym MMORPG. That RPG part is *important*.

On Heroes

A hero is someone who has completed their hero's journey. As I explained earlier, when we talk of people being "heroes" or acting "heroically," what we mean is that they are acting in the way that a hero *would* act; we don't mean that they themselves *are* heroes. Acting like a hero doesn't make you a hero, any more than acting like an elf makes you an elf.

Acts such as self-sacrifice, bravery, the defending of the weak, and so on are frequent characteristics exhibited by heroes, and examples of such deeds may often play a large part in an individual's personal journey. On the other hand, for a different person, they may play no part at all.

Not only *can* heroism occur in MMOs, it's the *very reason people play*. The undertaking of a hero's journey is driven by a completely intrinsic motivation. You do it because you *want* to do it; you want to do it because you *need* to know who you are.

Everyone can indeed be a hero. However, they're not heroes until they've finished playing (and started living). Giving them gameplay choices that make them *feel* as if they're heroes does not *make* them heroes, though; *they* decide when they're heroes, all by themselves.

Missing Types

The thing about the Player Types model is that it's a *model*. It's not a list—you can't just add a new type when you think of one—it's a *system*. There are eight types (or four types in the earlier version) for a reason: the structure of the model requires it because of the number of axes the graph has.

If you identify a new type, then this either means the model is wrong, or that it's too abstract, or that the type is orthogonal to the model, or that the model doesn't apply to the type.

One of the types people most frequently notice is "missing" from Player Types theory is that of *builders*: people who explicitly create content. They're most obviously present in social worlds, but you could probably count MMO crafters as builders too if you wanted.

So, where do builders fit in?

Well, if they do indeed fit in, it would depend on why they're building. If they're building in order to make money (if that's how the MMO measures success) or to complete their model of King's Landing and get kudos, that might be an achiever-like motivation; if they're doing it to see what kinds of things can be built and to push the building system to its limits, they are probably explorers; if they're doing it to enhance their world and make it more attractive or salubrious for others, they could be doing it for socializer reasons; if they just want to crash the server or spread a plague, that's killer/griefer behavior.

This sort of analysis covers most builders, *but not all*. Some people build because they want to design. They still get some fun from playing, but they're transitioning from wanting to play to wanting to design.

Okay, well this couldn't be an additional type in the Player Types model as it simply doesn't fit. It's not part of a splitting of an existing type (as griefers/politicians from killers is); it's not emergent from movement through types (as immersion is). However, it's enough about fun and play that it *ought* to link in somewhere. Some players really *do* like creating for reasons that are entirely to do with creating and not to do with playing for regular fun. This makes them *designers*, rather than (just) players.

We can posit that there are designer types as well as player types, and that designers follow their own hero's journey; they use their designs to articulate aspects of themselves that they couldn't communicate in any other manner. In the same way that there's a "main sequence" of player progression, there's one for designer progression: they start off as players (experiencing content), then become level designers (implementing form), then progress to being fully fledged designers (implementing experience), and then graduate to creative director (experiencing form). At this last stage, they can read the designs of other designers very well; this is why many top designers don't play games all the way through, or even play them at all: they can get all they need from them by playing only part-way through—or sometimes by simply reading the manual, if it's good enough.

More pretentiously, this doesn't just apply to MMO design—it can apply to any art form. I remember being struck by how similar Scott McCloud's description of the various stages of comic artist development fit in with this, for example[40].

From this perspective, the builder "type" concerns the point where the player begins the switch from being a player to being a designer. I'd expect it to happen primarily to high-end explorers (*hackers* in the 8-type model) and socializers (*friends*), but it could happen to anyone sufficiently inspired. They start to move away from playing for regular fun and towards playing for designer-fun. The more they move in that direction, the less they'll need to play and the more they'll need to design—which for some may be giving up too much, but for others may be opening up parts of their self that have been bursting to break free for ages.

I genuinely love it when that happens.

---

[40]Scott McCloud: *Understanding Comics: the Invisible Art*. Tundra Publishing, Northampton MA, 1993.

Unsung

You'll have come across them: players who long ago stopped playing your MMO as a *game*, but who still log in and hang out with their guildies.

They do this as a result of their having finished their hero's journey. Those players are heroes. They're not what people might think of as *stereotypical* heroes, but heroes are what they are, each and every one of them.

Did they save the world? Did they defeat the big bad? Did they risk self-sacrifice to save others? Probably not, but they didn't *have* to: those are just examples that second-person retellings of the hero's journey use in their larger-than-life ways to illustrate the fact that heroes face obstacles, but in overcoming them learn more about themselves.

It's not a very great selling point to newbies, "Become a hero! Chat with your friends on the porch!" Yet that's what, in the end, heroes tend to do.

Wanting Immersion

Players *want* to be immersed. They want to be immersed *so much* that they'll ignore all kinds of inconsistencies, distractions, and suspect gameplay to *become* immersed. Like Louis IX and the *Morgan Bible*, they'll *will* themselves into immersion, if that's what it takes.

A non-gamer watching a character swim across a lake and not get wet will wonder why the player doesn't notice. Well, the player *does* notice. In some MMOs, the character may indeed get wet and the cake they had in their bag will be all turned to sludge; that would mean the physics of the world was more persuasive, so the player will have one less thing to worry about. However, if the conflict with how things "should" work isn't too annoying, the player will just blank the discrepancy and get on with playing.

Players really, *really* want to be immersed.

Hard and Soft Role-Play

The role-playing advocated for RP servers is "hard" role-play: you learn from the character, but the character doesn't learn from you. On non-RP servers, it's "soft" role-play: you and your character both learn from each other. Eventually, over time, you and your character become the same person—the "real you."

Soft role-playing isn't even recognized as role-playing by most of its exponents in MMOs, but it is. They don't throw themselves into their character and try to "be" elves or whatever. Rather, what's happening is that their choice of (in this example) which humanoid race to use implicitly sets some parameters on their behavior within which they will act. The same person playing a dwarf behaves at least marginally differently when playing an elf or a gnome. The same person playing a character of their own gender behaves at least marginally differently when playing the opposite gender. Other players see the characters as flags indicative of personality and adjust their behavior towards one another accordingly. Even if you resolutely play your pink-haired female gnome mage with exactly the same personality you play your butt-ugly male tauren warrior, other people *will* treat you differently. You can't help but play a different role for each one, whether you like it or not, because all roles have a socially-determined component to them.

This is what I mean when I say everyone role-plays. The only people who don't role-play are those who have already been there, done that, or those who have no sense of immersion at all.

Signifying and Signified

A novelist can write a novel about heroism, but the reader never gets to be a hero. An artist can paint a picture of heroism, but the viewer doesn't get to be a hero. A composer can compose a symphony about heroism, but the listener doesn't get to be a hero.

MMOs are different. An MMO designer can create an MMO about heroism, and the player *does* get to be a hero.

A picture of an apple doesn't make the apple real. An MMO does make its heroes real.

Hard to Mean Soft

Back in *MUD I*, we looked at people who pretended to be alack-a-day elves as kinda weird. This kind of explicit role-playing of the kind that actors do wasn't something that happened a lot.

What we did have was the ability to be *not-you*, which paradoxically enabled you actually to *become* you. The freedom to be someone else is the gift to become yourself.

That's the *soft* kind of role-playing that goes on in MMOs; the "my parents were killed by murderous orcs and now, emotionally scarred, I'm out to avenge them" *hard* kind is much rarer.

Because hard role-playing is the variety that most people associate with the term "role-playing," it's difficult to talk about soft role-playing as a phenomenon unless you explain it all patiently beforehand.

Yes, I know, that's why I just did it, except without the "beforehand" bit.

If Dolphins…

If dolphins could pass stories from one generation to the next, perhaps they, too, would have a monomyth—but one which need not necessarily bear much relationship to ours.

About Face

If voice is good for communication, then face must also be good for communication because face adds more to communication than does voice alone.

People who use VoIP in MMOs tend to argue that they don't care about its real-life intrusiveness. That being so, why should they care if other players see their real face instead of some computer-generated face? If they don't consider that they're role-playing, they won't worry that their face is not the face of a troll shaman any more than they worry that their voice is not the voice of a troll shaman.

Yet people *aren't* as happy to let their faces be seen as they are to let their voices be heard. Do their reasons for not liking it equally well apply to voice? If so, why don't they apply them? If not, why can't they apply them?

Voice is only used in MMOs when it's necessary for organizational purposes or when the people communicating know each other in real life anyway. Face doesn't help in either of these situations. Both voice and face get in the way of soft role-playing, but in one case the benefits of using it occasionally outweigh the inherent disadvantages (in the players' eyes, anyway); in the other, the disadvantages are emphasized.

CRASH

MUD I had a CRASH command available to its wizzes (admin-level players).

The thing was, wizzes could do so many things that would cause the virtual world to crash that I pre-empted their experimentation by providing a command that would immediately crash it. Thus, when someone told me that if they picked up the rain and dropped it in a room that already contained it, they could cause a crash, the answer was: big deal, you can do that anyway with the CRASH command.

People did occasionally use the command, too, which was a nice incentive to mortals ("Blimey, wizzes have powers to crash the game! Gimme!"). It's not something that necessarily scales well, though...

Immersion Strategies

There are two main approaches to creating characters in MMOs, which each result in a separate strategy for becoming immersed.

The first approach is to create a character diametrically opposite to how you see yourself (overweight male trucker plays svelte female elf). The second approach is to create a character that is an aspirational version of how you see yourself (mother-of-three plays svelte female elf). Most people will be somewhere in between—comparable in some areas, different in others.

Now although players will create characters with a range of similarity/dissimilarity to their current self-image, they nevertheless tend to fall into two distinct camps insofar as immersion strategies go. Basically, if you want to become your true self you can either create a character more extreme than you are and come at it from both directions, or you can create a character a little closer to who you are and follow along just behind it as it moves towards the sweet spot.

Imagine a line showing a spectrum of identity. Yes, I realize this is a tall order, but bear with me. Put a box on the left of this marked P, which shows the player's sense of self when they start. Put another box on the right marked C, which shows the character the player has created. A third box in between, marked H, indicates the hero—the renewed sense of self the player gets from having played the MMO and completed their hero's journey.

Oh wow, this is something so easy to draw that even I can do it!

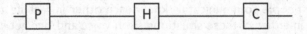

Here, the player has created an exaggerated character, so their ideal self is between their current self-image and the character they created. Through play, the player gradually changes their self-image and the image of the character, inching them together until they collide and lock (at the box marked H). Here's the same player, approaching immersion:

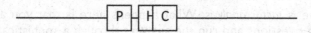

This is a *bidirectional* search strategy. The other way of doing it is a *unidirectional* search. In this case, the player creates a character just ahead of their perceived self-image, and then moves the character towards their true self with the current self following and gradually catching up. Pictorially, it starts off something like this:

The current self finally catches the character self up at the hero point, whereupon they lock, as in the bidirectional example.

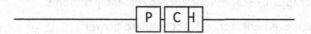

As a *very* general rule, players following the main socializers sequence tend towards the unidirectional strategy, with the others following the bi-directional strategy. I've no explanation for why this is the case, however. It's just something I've observed.

Oh, I should point out that all this talk of "players becoming their characters" is purely in terms of sense of self. The trucker never *actually* gets to be a female elf (which is probably just as well); the elf is a complex set of symbols and metaphors that means something at an intuitive or emotional level to the trucker. Through play, the trucker adjusts his understanding of what those symbols mean, and how facets of his own personality reflect them in ways previously obscure to him. Gradually, he becomes more aware of his own identity (the P box moves right) and of how the package of identity signifiers embodied by the elf apply to him (the C box moves left) until the two coincide (at the H box). At this point, he has Atonement with the Father, full immersion, and a bunch of guildmates in awe of his l33t healz skillz.

Incidentally, by tradition the truckers in examples such as these are always from Milwaukee. I've no idea why.

Factor Analysis

The Player Types model is based on observations made concerning players of text MUDs. It wasn't done all that scientifically, but nevertheless it's what social scientists call "grounded"—it comes from direct experience. There are many ways to obtain data of a higher quality, though.

One of these is *factor analysis*. What happens here is that you ask a set of wide-ranging questions and run the answers through a sophisticated statistical program to find patterns. This is the technique used by MMO researcher Nick Yee to obtain the *motivations* I mentioned earlier. In general, it produces excellent results.

Obtaining clusters is not, however, an entirely simple matter. For example, there are several different techniques you can use for analyzing factors from a data set, and they don't always find the same factors. Nick's original work, if you recall, found five factors; when he changed his approach and reanalyzed his data, he uncovered a sixth (equating to explorers). Here's his modified list:

- Relationship: make friends; offer and give support.
- Grief: scam; taunt; annoy; dominate.
- Immersion: story-telling; role-play.
- Escapism: escape; vent; forget real-life problems.
- Achievement: achieve; accumulate power.
- Analyze: rules; mechanics; mapping

Now as Nick was quick to point out, a factor analysis is only as good as the questions it asks. If you don't ask about immersion, it won't be picked up in the answers. This means that the factors detected are not *exhaustive*—there may be other ones that it would take more subtle questioning to reveal (indeed, as I mentioned earlier, Nick found another four factors himself when he did his very polished analysis of the enormous *EverQuest 2* data set).

Another problem with factor analysis is that the factors get to be labeled by the analyst. These labels are not always good ones (my own use of "killers" is a case in point). Nick identified "immersion" as a factor, but someone with a Narratology axe to grind could have called it "story" instead.

A third issue is that of categories. Suppose you were to ask people what kind of things-that-grow-on-trees they like to eat: you might get back answers such as "apple," "orange," and "fruit." These would be picked up in the factor analysis. The fact that apples and oranges are themselves fruit would not be picked up unless the analyst made the effort (which, given that apples aren't technically fruit, could present its own problems).

This means, for example, that it could be possible for every MMO player to be a role-player at heart, only some are more aware of it than others. These people might well say that they like MMOs because of the role-playing. Pressing them further as to *why* they role-played, however, might give an answer related to achievement or relationship, say, which wouldn't show up in the original data.

Now a good researcher (Nick Yee in this example) *does* tell you all this. If you want to make use of Nick's results, you should read his caveats first. Unfortunately, though, many people who just want a quick-fix solution will look at summaries of results without bothering to understand what they *mean*. Then, they'll blame the researcher for being wrong, in a "you should have told me sunscreen isn't good for plants!" kind of way.

Factor analysis is a very useful research tool. It can point out potential problems with a theory ("where are the explorers?") and potential blind spots ("where is immersion covered?"). It can be used to inform the construction of a new theory; however, it isn't *itself* a theory any more than statistics about church-goers are a religion.

The Player Types model *is* a theory. The player types are situated in a graph that asserts they are separate and orthogonal, and therefore exhaustive; you can't add more types except by refining the existing ones through the addition of a new axis. The types are related in ways that can be used predictively: *if* you are a networker, *then* you will become either a planner or a politician.

This leads to an important point: although both a theory and a data analysis can be *improved*, only the theory can be *disproved*—and data analysis can be the weapon of its destruction. However, in destroying it, the means for constructing a new, *better* theory can often be determined.

Such is science.

Mood Systems

Players shouldn't have emotional control over their characters. They shouldn't be able to issue a command that says, "I'm angry now."

Players *are* their characters. If they're angry, then they want to *express* their anger, not merely flip their character's "angry" switch. They want to be able to glare, snarl, stomp, turn up their nose, and froth at the mouth.

That said, some textual worlds had a *mood* system, which would alter your character's body language appropriate to your stated mood. For example, if you set your mood to "happy," it would modify your description so it said you were smiling. I don't know of any MUDs that read your mood directly from the emotes you issued, but I don't doubt some may have existed.

I'm ambivalent about mood systems (at least the explicit, /mood variety), but I prefer them to systems that set emotional states. Mood systems are like long-term pre-packaged emotes. With a mood, you're saying "this is how I feel"; with an emotion-state system, you're saying "this is how my character feels." The latter may be preferable in hard role-playing situations, but the former works best for soft role-playing—the kind where you don't really think you're role-playing.

It's all about *immersion*.

The Intangibility of Role-Play

Role-playing is part of the *fun* in a role-playing game, but it's rarely part of the *game*. You won't see many games that tie role-playing into their mechanics. Role-playing doesn't make me hit harder or resist magic better or sell my horse for a higher price. It takes *people* to recognize role-playing, not rule-based systems.

If you do try to integrate role-playing into a game's mechanics, people start to view the role-playing not as role-playing but as something to be gamed. The meaning is diminished—it's just a number to be lowered or raised.

Mechanics can be conducive to role-play, but role-play is like a quantum wave: the moment the mechanics touch it is the moment its space of possibilities collapses.

Non-Hero Heroes

The hero's journey is a journey to self-understanding. It's called a hero's journey because, having completed it, you become a hero. That's the definition of "hero" in this context: someone who has completed their hero's journey. If you talk about "hero" in the modern sense, as in "he saved the little boy from the mad dog—he's a hero!"— you're using the term in what was originally a metaphorical way. The person who saved the little boy is not a hero (he hasn't completed his hero's journey), but he's exhibiting the qualities of someone who *has* done so.

Words change meanings. If someone brings you a coffee you wanted but didn't have time to go get it yourself, you might say "what a hero!" as thanks. You don't mean they *are* a hero, just that they've done something selfless for you. It's like that with the "hero" who rescues the little boy, but a step up; he's taken a risk, doing something selfless for someone else, just as a hero might.

He's not a hero in the traditional sense, though.

No matter how many times I repeat this, I have the feeling that it's making no difference at all.

Fazed by Phases

At this point in the history of MMOs, many players have been playing for years. It's a maturing market: attracting newbies is hard, so instead new MMOs have to attract oldbies who are looking for more intelligent content.

Having played for years, a large proportion of these established players have friends they like to play with; this is only to be expected, as it's one of the two end states of the 8-type player model. When a new MMO comes out that a group likes the sound of, it decamps to it so its members can level up and have fun together.

Phasing! Don't you love it? Well, I don't, but plenty of people do. It's when the server creates a special instance integrated into the world that's particular to you. You go to a place where the big bad is causing havoc, you have a mighty battle, as a result of which the big bad is defeated and the world changes. Thenceforth, when you subsequently visit that location, the big bad is no longer there, a bunch of new NPCs are ready to dole out quests, and reconstruction work is ongoing to repair the damage the big bad did (or that you did in defeating the big bad).

The aim of phases is to give players the illusion that their actions actually have world-changing effects. Before you complete the quest, the server routes you to one phase; once you've completed it, it routes you to a different phase. Your actions haven't *actually* changed the world, of course; all that's changed is which subcopy you go to. Nonetheless, it's better than nothing, and it helps with quest storylines.

Back to friends. When you're leveling up with people you know, you want your quests to be in step. If there are two of us in a group and we both have the same quest, then the quest should work at the group level. If I kill four rats and you kill six, that's the kill-10-rats quest done for both of us—we shouldn't have to kill ten rats each. Likewise, only one of us should need to interact with the quest object to advance the quest for both of us; otherwise, we'd need to press the button that summons the boss twice in succession. That would be rather annoying.

Some MMOs *are* rather annoying, though. We both have to press the boss-summoning button if we both want to advance our (shared) quest. Now imagine how much worse this already irritating situation is with phases. We go into an area and there's a boss to kill. I go first, and press the button to summon the boss.

Okay, so together we beat the boss. Great! My quest advances and I'm now in the post-boss phase: the world has changed as a result of my actions. Well, it's changed for *me*: you're still in the pre-boss phase. I can't see you, you can't see me. We're effectively in different bubbles of space. When you summon the boss to advance your own quest, I won't even be able to see the boss, let alone help you.

If your players are mainly playing solo, none of this matters. However, as I said at the start, increasing numbers of players want to play in groups with the people they've played with for years. They really wouldn't like it if you didn't lock group quests together and gave them a deluge of phases.

Would they, *The Elder Scrolls Online?*

Missing What's Missing

What I dislike about using your real voice in an MMO is that it detracts from the soft role-playing that makes MMOs special.

Old-timers see nothing wrong with voice because they've already established their MMO identity as being one and the same as their real-world identity, so they're comfortable with it. New-timers don't know what they're missing, so won't complain that they don't have it.

Both will miss what having it destroys, but neither will know why.

The Heroine's Journey

The hero's journey concerns just that—a hero. This isn't some modern-day "when I say *actor* I also mean *actresses*" attempt to dignify the contribution of women: the hero's journey really *is* about men, not women. So, where do women stand, then?

Joseph Campbell's position was this:

> In the whole mythological tradition the woman is there. All she has to do is to realize that she's the place that people are trying to get to. [1]

Thus, for a woman, myth serves to enlighten her as to how wonderful her nature is; she doesn't have to pretend to be male to do this.

Campbell was talking about myth, however, and while his view may (or may not) apply to that particular domain, it doesn't mean there isn't some kind of "heroine's journey" that myth doesn't pick up.

This was the opinion of Maureen Murdock, who, ignited by Campbell's remarks (which didn't seem to match her experience at all), worked out her own, female-focused version[41]. Unsurprisingly, it has little to do with myth and much to do with women's view of themselves in western culture.

Personally, I find Murdock's analysis a little too subjective, with some over-enthusiastic interpretations of the evidence and occasional selective ignorance of context. Nevertheless, what she produced does seem to resonate with many women. That being the case, it makes sense to consider whether it could be used as an alternative to the hero's journey to create a female-friendly framework for story arcs in games (and, perhaps, player-development tracks in MMOs).

Well, it *could* be used, yes, but the chances are that the result would not be a success. The reason is simple, but devastating: *it's not fun*. It involves diving into the depths of despair and having a thoroughly bad time of things before emerging content (if not exactly happy) at the end. Here's a brief overview of how it goes:

- **Separation from the feminine.**

  In order to succeed, the woman feels she has to act like a man.

---

[41]Maureen Murdock: *The Heroine's Journey: Woman's Quest for Wholeness.* Shambhala Publications, 1990.

- **Identification with the masculine and gathering of allies.**

  The woman begins the traditional hero's journey and looks for role models who can help her on the way.

- **Road of trials: meeting ogres and dragons.**

  The woman determines her strengths.

- **Finding the illusory boon of success.**

  The woman achieves the success she sought, but realizes that it's not what she actually wanted. This is where things start to go downhill.

- **Awakening to feelings of spiritual aridity: death.**

  The woman feels as if she's somehow betrayed some of her potential by playing the man's game. There's a lot of resentment here.

- **Initiation and descent to the goddess.**

  This is a major period of depression. Murdock says it's "filled with confusion and grief, alienation and disillusion, rage and despair." Not something you would necessarily look forward to experiencing when you log in to your MMO every evening, then.

- **Urgent yearning to reconnect with the feminine.**

  The woman realizes that she has separated her mind from her body: what she *wants* to be from what she *is*.

- **Healing the mother/daughter split.**

  This is the recognition in a woman that she must trust her emotions and intuition rather than rely entirely on the logical skills she picked up earlier. Murdock herself found this the most painful part of the journey.

- **Healing the wounded masculine.**

  Only when the woman understands why she is conflicted can she reconcile her remaining turmoil.

- **Integration of masculine and feminine.**

  The woman rejects the male/female dualism that caused her to set off on the hero's journey in the first place. She is who she is.

As you can see, this isn't a whole bundle of laughs.

The *hero's* journey sends you off to an other world of danger and excitement where you learn that you are the hero you've always been. The *heroine's* journey sends you off to the same place, but it suddenly turns into a pitiless hell, out from which you can only drag your flayed soul if you have formidable strength of character, whereupon you realize (exactly as Campbell stated) that you didn't have to go in the first place.

Famous Last Words

In July, 2007, round about the same time that Blizzard announced *World of Warcraft* had reached nine million subscribers, I received a bunch of questions by email from *The Guardian* for their games blog. There were ten questions in all, although some were multiple and I split them up into pieces. The last one was: "If you could take over control of one major MMORPG—which would you choose and what would you do with it?"

Okay, so it was basically a throwaway question at the end of a lengthy interview just to make up a round 10, but hey, it was asked. Given that there is zero (0) chance of my actually taking over control of a major MMORPG I could have answered, "I'd cure disease, eliminate war, and give all the world's children a teddy bear" for all it mattered. I decided, though, that in the spirit of the interview, I should perhaps keep my answer on-topic.

The problem is, I wouldn't actually *want* to take control of anyone else's MMO, major or minor: I'm a designer, I want to *design* worlds, not tinker with the designs of other people. I considered repeating my view that an MMO should give players an honorable end, to allow them to feel they've "won" (maybe print off a 3D model of their character as a token/boon), but that would have entailed a long, boring diversion explaining why I believed this.

The question used the word "major." So, what major MMOs were there? Well, there was *WoW*, and, er, some in Korea? Whereas five years earlier we'd had several major MMOs (*UO, EQ, AC, DAOC,* and *AO*), now they were all minor compared to *WoW*. *WoW* did a fantastic job of engaging with players, giving them a great experience, and educating them in the ways of MMOs. Indeed, if it weren't for *WoW*...

Hmm. Actually, given that *WoW* has done all that, if it were to disappear overnight, then it would be a huge boost to the rest of the industry. Okay, so that gave me an easy answer: if I were given control of a major MMORPG of my choice, I'd choose *WoW*, and I'd close it down. It wouldn't take long before the majority of its players agreed on some next-new-shiny place to nest, but enough would stick in the smaller, up-coming worlds to give those a chance to shine, too.

Of course, actually doing this *would* be guaranteed to make nine million people very upset (including my at-the-time level 30 druid daughter), so it would be stupid actually to *do* it. It's not as if I'm ever going to be *given* control of *WoW*, though.

The headline of the blog was:

> **"I'd close World of Warcraft!" MUD creator Richard Bartle on the state of virtual worlds.**

;sighs

Voice Fonts

I've got no objections in principle to using voice in MMOs. My objections are when that voice has to be your own voice.

I would have no problems if your real-world voice went through an intermediate representation that matched your character before being transmitted to the other players. You say "good morning"; the client converts this to a sequence of abstract symbols (*phonemes*) corresponding to the sounds (*phones*) you used; the clients entitled to hear your words are told these phonemes, plus the fact you're a male night elf; from this, these clients generate the appropriate phones to match those words; the other players hear "good morning" spoken by a male night elf.

Okay, so there are tweaks that can be done here. Emphasis and tonal changes from the speaker can be picked up and passed on in the encoding:

- "GOOD morning!"
- "good MORNING!"
- "good MORNING?"

A character-specific base tone and timber can be mixed in, so that although you sound like a male night elf, you don't sound like every other male night elf. Input can be accepted in text but replayed as speech, for people who can't talk while they play because it will wake up their sleeping children.

It's by no means perfect, of course. You're still going to know I'm English because I resolutely refuse to split infinitives. You won't be able to tell I'm a man with an East Yorkshire accent, though.

On Art

A Rape in Cyberspace

One of the most important articles ever written about virtual worlds is Julian Dibbell's, *A Rape in Cyberspace*[1]. The title alone is sufficiently provocative that 18 years after its publication, one of the administrators at Essex University (where I teach) made a formal complaint about me when picking up an order of class handouts I'd had printed of it. This was more than a little ironic, as its content is above all about *context*.

The article concerns an event that took place in *LambdaMOO*. *LambdaMOO* is not a game world and it's textual in nature, but what happened there nevertheless has important consequences for MMOs.

So, in *LambdaMOO* it was possible to perform freeform emotes. Unusually, with the use of a device called a *voodoo doll*, you could also do them for other characters—not just your own—without their permission. A character by the name of Mr. Bungle proceeded to do so in such a way as to make it appear that some of the other characters were sexually servicing him. His efforts became increasingly violent, and he couldn't be stopped until a player character called Zippy was summoned to shoot a supergun at Mr. Bungle that put him into stasis.

So, classic griefer behavior from Mr. Bungle, there. What makes this article important isn't the reporting of an activity that was well-known even in 1993; rather, it's the discussion of what happened in the aftermath. The players explored ideas of power, the right to wield power, the relationship between players and characters, the notion of when the virtual was real—all foundational concepts for how virtual worlds (including MMOs) are governed and the competing philosophies that determine the right to govern. Julian Dibbell's style is borderline Cyberpunk in this article, too, making it a cracking good read.

I'm not going to explain here what was discussed. However, I shall shortly give you some points you can think about after you've read it yourself.

Best go read it, then…

---

[1] Julian Dibbell: *A Rape in Cyberspace*. *The Village Voice*, 23rd December, 1993.
http://www.juliandibbell.com/texts/bungle_vv.html

Just Like Game Design

"Managing a network involves satisfying multiple constraints in a scientific fashion, just like game design."

"Configuring a database involves satisfying multiple constraints in a scientific fashion, just like game design."

"Customer service involves satisfying multiple constraints in a scientific fashion, just like game design."

"Marketing involves satisfying multiple constraints in a scientific fashion, just like game design."

"Programming involves satisfying multiple constraints in a scientific fashion, just like game design."

If you have the skills and are good at employing them, why would you become a game designer when there are so many other things you could do with them?

"Game design involves game design." That's why.

Needed Skills

Designers have design skills. Game development companies need people with those skills.

While someone needs your skill, *you* need that someone. Ultimately, you want to get to a place where the someone who needs your skills is you yourself, although if someone else gives you free rein to create, then that also works.

Once you're there, you are creating *because that's what you do*—it's who you are. You create for reasons you can only explicate by doing the creating, rather than because someone else *needs* you to do the creating.

At that point, design has changed from craft to art.

The Wisdom of Crowds

Take a large bottle full of M&Ms or Smarties or whatever they call them where you live, and ask people to guess how many there are in there. (Originally, this was the weight of an ox, not the number of Smarties in a bottle.)

Of course, you'll get wildly different estimates. However, if you take the average of these estimates, the result will be very close to the answer. This phenomenon, identified by James Surowiecki in 2004[2], is known as *the wisdom of crowds*.

Imagine a computer game where the player shoots at odd-looking space amoeba. Actually, those are not space amoeba! Those are human tissue cells. Actually, that's not just odd-looking! That's cancerous.

In 2006, Stanford University professor Byron Reeves did exactly this using a *Star Wars: Galaxies* medical screen showing real-world imagery. Individual gamers were generally around 60% as accurate as a trained pathologist in identifying suspect cells; average the decisions of 30 of them playing this shoot-the-amoeba mini-game, though, and you'll get a response of equivalent quality to that of the professional (albeit not with the same degree of reassurance to patients). 30 gamers equal one pathologist.

So, if the wisdom of crowds works for life-or-death decisions, why not for something more mundane? Specifically, why employ a designer for your MMO when all you need to do is average the suggestions from 5,000 forum postings to find out what people *really* want?

My World, Your World

The designer creates the world and sets up the conditions for it to prosper in whatever directions they see fit. However, the moment it goes live, the world no longer belongs to the designer; it belongs to the players.

---

[2]*James Surowiecki: The Wisdom of Crowds: Why the Many Are Smarter Than the Few and How Collective Wisdom Shapes Business, Economies, Societies and Nations. Doubleday, 2004.*

The Art of Persuasion

Back in November 2008, I was playing through the (at the time) shiny new *Wrath of the Lich King* expansion to *WoW* when I came across a quest called "The Art of Persuasion." It's one link of an eight-link chain of quests. Earlier quests in the series have informed you that mages are being kidnapped at random and that Lady Evanor is among them. Lady Evanor is an archmage of the Kirin Tor—a "good" faction of NPCs opposed to the Lich King. Their city, Dalaran, was almost destroyed when an earlier archmage was turned evil, so the Kirin Tor want Lady Evanor to be rescued before the bad people can break her will and turn her evil, too. To help save her, you have captured one of her kidnappers, a Beryl Sorcerer. All that remains is for someone to persuade the Beryl Sorcerer to reveal where Lady Evanor is being held captive.

This is the point where the Art of Persuasion quest comes in. Here's how it's presented by the Kirin Tor quest-giver:

> *It is fortunate you're here, <race>. You see, the Kirin Tor code of conduct frowns upon our taking certain 'extreme' measures—even in desperate times such as these. You, however, as an outsider, are not bound by such restrictions and could take any steps necessary in the retrieval of information. Do what you must. We need to know where Lady Evanor is being held at once!*
>
> *I'll just busy myself organizing these shelves here. Oh, and here, perhaps you'll find this old thing useful…*

At this point, you receive a device called a Neural Needler. The quest summary states:

> *Librarian Normantis on Amber Ledge wants you to use the Neural Needler on the Imprisoned Beryl Sorcerer until he reveals the location of Lady Evanor.*

So, all you have to do is zap the Beryl Sorcerer with the pain stick a few times, and you're on to the next quest, right?

Sadly, yes: that *is* right. ."

Unconference

I once went to a games "unconference" in London organized by *The Guardian* newspaper. At an unconference, attendees choose what they want to talk about (if anything), put a sticker on a noticeboard for a slot, then at the appropriate time anyone who's interested shows up and the person whose slot it is leads a discussion. This particular unconference was attended by many professionals working in games and social media.

One of the talks I went to was on game design. Its content was—well, I was a little shocked, to be honest. It was presented by a guy whose company creates games of all types as advertising vehicles, so sometimes they may be PC games, sometimes viral web games, sometimes mobile phone games, whatever the brief asks. The company starts the process by trying to get to grips with the business constraints, so the requirements can be stated; this is fair enough—designers need to understand what it is they're supposed to be designing.

It was the next part of the process that I found alarming, though: how they brainstorm ideas. It doesn't matter so much how they did it; what matters is that they had to do it *at all*. The problem for game designers isn't thinking up ideas—ideas come for free all the time. The problem is deciding which of the many ideas they have is the one to go with. They shouldn't *need* to brainstorm ideas.

I hassled the session speaker about it afterwards, and it turned out that there were other reasons to do things this way. For example, it increases the investment that the brainstormers (which include representatives of all parts of the development team, including the receptionist) have in the final product.

In other words, it *was* a session on how to design games, but only for *non-designers*.

On the Origin of Species

Here's what *City of Heroes* designer Jack Emmert said during his keynote speech on designing MMO behaviors at the 2006 Serious Games Summit:

> *Game design is actually a new phenomenon in video games as a whole. It really came about around 10 years ago. ... Originally, you'd have a programmer and an artist, maybe. There were games that were done by just a programmer. As the graphics ability got better, they hired artists. Now, as stories and content are more central to the game than they were a dozen years ago, you've got to have somebody who thinks just about the game, hence, game designers.*

No no no! What you had originally was a *designer*. One person *did* do the programming and perhaps the artwork, but that wasn't because they were a programmer—it was because they were a designer. If they were a programmer, they wrote a theater-booking database or their own input/output libraries; only game designers wrote games. They wanted to create games *so much* that they were driven to implement their ideas themselves.

In time, successful designers could offload programming to programmers and artwork to artists, freeing themselves to concentrate on design. Design is what they *always* wanted to do, though. Otherwise, why do it?

It's wrong to say that early computer games were designed by programmers. Early computer games were programmed by designers.

Corn Dollies

If I go into a farmer's field and start making hundreds of corn dollies for sale at craft fairs, do I own them because they're the fruits of my labor? Or does the farmer own them because I used the farmer's corn to make the dollies?

If I sell characters I worked up in an MMO?

Assaulting the Citadel

It's hard getting a job as a game designer these days because so many people have computer game design degrees that it's difficult to get noticed.

Idea! Why bother with a game design degree at all? Why not go for something different and parlay that into a game job? Being different, you'll stand out!

For example, a Masters in Business Administration (MBA) gives you skills in dealing with economic systems. Systems are systems: if you can balance an economic system, you can balance a game system. Designers should be interested in employing someone with an MBA, shouldn't they? Let's send out that CV!

Well, whether designers *should* be interested or not is irrelevant. The response to the suggestion that someone with an MBA can do game design will be different depending on the designer you approach, but the result will be the same in every case:

- The self-confident game designer will simply laugh. It's as if they are a skilled movie director with years of experience and you're a novelist coming along to tell them they don't understand story. To them, you're from a different medium that's only tangentially relevant.

- The open-minded game designer will shake their head. Maybe if you were a mathematician with experience in stochastic processes, they would be prepared to listen. However, you're a jack of all trades and a master of none. Scientific methods *can* be applied to aspects of game design, but they can be applied by people with more apposite backgrounds than an MBA.

- The thoughtful game designer will sympathize, but point out that they already have tried-and-trusted systems for balancing, and that often there are other design-critical reasons why things Have To Be The Way They Are. So although you have skills that *could* be useful, unfortunately they are skills the designer already has; what's more, the designer has other skills you don't have that allow for the wider context. In short, they know about gameplay, but you don't.

- The jaded game designer is going to say you have tremendous impertinence suggesting that an MBA somehow gives you an edge that hasn't been possessed by generations of designers before you. They'll then launch into some interminable anecdote they once heard about how some PhD fresh from college ignored advice to use a billhook and tried to chop a branch from an old tree using an axe, nearly breaking his arm in the process. Just because he had a PhD, that didn't mean he knew better than 3,000-years-worth of farmers. Just because you have an MBA, that doesn't mean you know better than 30-years-worth of game designers.

- The newly employed game designer is going to consider whether their game design degree would get them a well-paid job as a finance director. Concluding that it wouldn't, they would see no reason that the converse shouldn't also apply.

The thing is, though, having an MBA *may* be enough to get you to a long list of candidates. Once there, *then* you can show off your design chops the same as everyone else being considered. If the MBA does indeed help you design systems better than if you didn't have one, then your game designs could actually stand out from the crowd. Then again, they could disappoint.

The advantage of any qualification isn't that it *is* a qualification; the advantage is what you learned while getting it.

What Makes a Designer Design?

MMO designers, along with most people, can do many things. So why do they design MMOs? Why don't they do one of the following, say:

- Program MMOs?
- Write novels?
- Drive trucks?
- Authenticate nuclear power station software?
- Practice law?
- Feed the poor?

They could do *plenty* of other things. Why do they design MMOs?

Design Philosophy

MUD1 was all about freedom. The goal was the freedom to be and become yourself, which was mirrored by the freedom of the game design. It was very open-ended, with no character classes or formal quests—and it was that way deliberately. Roy and I wanted people to be able to free people from the constraints of their real-life situation so they had the space to become who they really were. It would have made no sense whatsoever to put unnecessary artificial constraints in the game world: we'd just have been replacing one rigid framework with another had we done so.

Was this ideological? Well yes, of course it was! Back then, the people who were attracted to and could succeed at programming all had a particular world view that gave rise to hacker culture. Programming offered freedom and creativity, and if you had neither yourself, then you wouldn't make it as a programmer. I didn't *sign up* to the hacker culture, it was how I thought (and still think) anyway: freedom to do leads to freedom to be. In *MUD1*, I strove to give people the chance to do this in a place where those who chose to abuse this freedom couldn't do a great deal of damage.

Today's MMOs are no different. Sure, there are the paint-by-numbers MMOs that feel mechanical and soulless, but even they are rippling the views of earlier designers onward. The MMOs that do have a strong vision behind them are more clearly expressing what their designers wanted to say.

Example 1: suppose you didn't know where *Second Life* was developed. If you had to choose one city on the whole planet that was most closely aligned with its politics, where would you pick? Or, put another way, it's not just a happy coincidence that it came out of San Francisco. Likewise, it's not entirely chance that Austin has become the primary MMO development center of the USA.

Example 2: *Warhammer: Age of Reckoning* has two factions competing in a perpetual struggle that neither can ever win. So has *World of Warcraft*, but *W:AR* isn't ripping off *WoW* here despite launching four years later. Before working on *W:AR*, Mark Jacobs designed *Dark Age of Camelot*, which introduced the realm *vs.* realm (RvR) concept to MMOs; RvR is an established part of his *oeuvre*. It captures something he wants to say in his design. Two sides, locked in an eternal struggle, with transient gains and losses, but an underlying futility to their warring: neither side will ever win and ultimately things don't change. Now irrespective of what you read into that, ultimately it's there because Mark Jacobs *wanted* it there. The artist creates; others interpret.

People have personal beliefs and philosophies. The virtual worlds they create are shaped by these. MMO design is art.

Torture

"The Art of Persuasion" quest in *WoW* is basically a torture quest. Some people who are forbidden by their own rules to commit torture (the Kirin Tor) ask you to do their dirty work for them. When you do, you complete the quest, you get the next link in the chain, and off you go to save Lady Evanor and possibly the world.

I don't have any problem with torture quests in computer games. They can appear for any number of legitimate reasons, just as torture scenes in books and films can be there for good effect. Where I do have a problem, though, is when a torture quest comes without warning in a game that has previously given me no indication that I would be required to do anything like it.

Up until that point, the players of the Alliance faction (yeah, sorry Hordies, I wanted a human character) have only been asked to do things that fall within the approximate boundaries of the Geneva Conventions. The Alliance is supposed to be "good" (leastwise its members look on themselves as being good). Suddenly, though, they're asked to torture someone. Isn't that something that only evil people do? Indeed, isn't that one of the ways storytellers emphasize *just how evil* an evil character is?

So, why wasn't the quest flagged?

Kindred Spirits

The session on game design at the *Guardian*'s unconference included an "inspiration" exercise.

In this, we were given the same general topic and had to draw a game-related idea for it. There were about 20 of us in the audience. We all showed our ideas at once, then went around explaining them. I didn't need to hear what anyone was saying, though—there was clearly only one rendition I could see that had any originality or imagination to it whatsoever. I looked at the person who had done it, but he was already looking at me having reached the same conclusion about my own idea.

We caught up with each other afterwards to affirm our kindred spiritness. It turned out he was a game designer from Derby, teaching on the university course there.

This is always how it is with game designers. There were 20 people there, but only two actual designers. The other 18 couldn't tell who the designers were, but we designers could because our stuff was of a different order to what everyone else was creating.

It's like this all the way up with game design: the very-best designers can tell the very-best designers from the second-very-best designers, but the second-very-best designers can't tell the very-best designers from second-very-best designers.

Note that if a game you design makes a lot of money, that does *not* prove that you're a great game designer. You might well be, but games that sell don't have to be *good*, they just have to be *not awful*.

We Are Who We Are

If Roy Trubshaw and I had written *MUD* at Oxford or Cambridge, I'm sure people would have taken the concept more seriously. However, if we'd had the kind of backgrounds necessary to get ourselves into Oxford or Cambridge, we probably wouldn't have written *MUD* in the first place.

Games You Should Have Played #1

A game developer friend, Adam Martin, once asked me to list "ten games you should have played" as part of a response to a useless list of that title he had encountered on the Internet. Modulo all the usual complaints about lists of ten and what the word "should" means, I obliged.

I didn't have any rules *per se*, but I assumed that the list was for people who play games or design games or who want to know more about games.

Oh, you may notice that this is not a list of games by name, except #10. That's game designers for you...

So, here's the first one:

A game you have bought but haven't played yet.

You should always have a game ready to play. I don't care what it is, but unless there *is* one, you're never going to expand your gaming horizons.

As I type this, there are two unplayed games and four partly-played games waiting patiently on my PC (or in the case of the two I bought as DVDs, next to it). These are non-casual in nature and I expect to invest many hours playing each one. Of the unplayed games, one has been installed and I've read its manual, the other (a historical one) hasn't been installed yet. When I'm done with the game I'm currently playing (an MMO that snuck in at the front of the queue because it sounded interesting and I can count it as work), I'll switch to one of these two games, or perhaps return to the one I was playing before the MMO came out. All the while, I'll be looking for another game to play when the two new ones are completed—hopefully, one that's not another damned sequel.

I Like Living in Houses, Me

Suppose you are a lecturer in Architecture at a university, interviewing 17-year-olds who have applied to come and study your subject. The first question you ask them is: "Why do you want to study Architecture?" The prospective student answers, "From an early age, I have always enjoyed living in houses, so I want to become an architect."

Hmm. Isn't that rather shaky ground upon which to build a career?

How about this: you're a lecturer in Brewing and Distilling (yes, there are degree courses in this at respectable universities), interviewing 17-year-olds who have applied to come and study your subject. The first question you ask is: "Why do you want to study Brewing and Distilling?" The prospective student answers, "From an early age, I have always enjoyed drinking alcohol, so I want to become a brewer."

Yes. Mayyyyybe you need to think that through a bit more?

"From an early age, I have always enjoyed cutting up mammals, so I want to become a veterinary surgeon."

"From an early age, I have always enjoyed watching TV, so I want to become an actor."

"From an early age, I have always enjoyed spending money, so I want to become a shop manager."

"From an early age, I have always enjoyed laughing, so I want to become a clown."

The reason I mention this is, of course, because: "From an early age, I have always enjoyed playing computer games, so I want to become a games programmer." Of every three prospective students I interview on a Wednesday afternoon, the chances are that two of them will give some variant of that reply.

Look, if you like programming—if *programming* is what you find fun—then you don't *care* what you program so long as it doesn't offend your morals. For a programmer, there's no reason why programming a game would be any more fun than programming a dishwasher, except you don't get paid as much working on the game.

Ah, but "I want to work on something I'm interested in." Of *course* you do. You really, really want to write the calls to the middleware that the tool you're working on with three other people will use, so it can be passed to a level designer who will use it to script the behavior of a group of monsters which will delay the player for all of 45 seconds *en route* to the next boss in what starts off as a Fantasy RPG, but suddenly morphs into one about koalas when some new product manager takes over at the publisher's office.

What you *actually* want to do is *design* games. You may not realize it—you may well deny it—but that's what's driving you. The only question is whether you want to design games that *you* want to play, or that *people* will want to play.

Kasparov *vs.* the Rest of the World

In 1999, Garry Kasparov took on the rest of the world at *Chess.*

The event was sponsored by MSN Gaming Zone, and anyone with Internet access could vote for the rest of the world's next move. There were discussion boards to mull over strategy, explore the consequences of particular moves, and other *Chess* champions were aboard to issue advice.

Four months and 62 moves later, Kasparov won.

Grandmasters always win these games. The wisdom of crowds doesn't help.

6 Days, 22 Hours, 40 Minutes

When I play MMOs these days, I take notes. Here's the 56th page from the ones I made for *SW:TOR*:

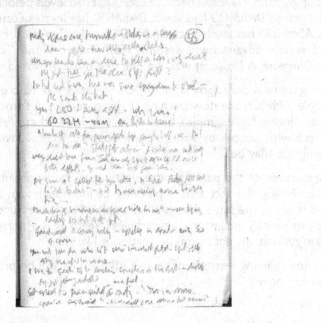

Yes, I can read, er, a lot of that.

Unlike most of the other MMOs I play to the top level, with *SW:TOR* I didn't immediately stop and close my account. I had a reason for this.

I got up to page 93 before I stopped playing.

Paradigms

Why does *World of Warcraft* have levels?

World of Warcraft has levels because *EverQuest* had levels before it. *EverQuest* has levels because *DikuMUD* had levels. *DikuMUD* has levels because *AberMUD* had levels. *AberMUD* has levels because *MUD1* had levels. *MUD1* has levels because, of the several advancement systems Roy Trubshaw and I considered, levels (from *Dungeons & Dragons*) was the one that most delivered what we wanted.

MUD1 gave us a paradigm; later MMOs updated this to create today's paradigm. New MMOs are now pushing at this paradigm in some areas (they may not have levels, for example), but reinforcing it in others (you can still communicate with people by name at any distance, irrespective of how fiction-breaking this may be).

Some features of the paradigm are defining, in that without them you don't have an MMO: the fact that a plurality of individuals can access the same shared space at the same time is an example of such a feature. Other features, while not strictly necessary, nevertheless seem to be perpetuated without much argument: distance communication is like this.

What non-defining features of today's MMOs will still be present in them 20 years from now?

The Artist

Lots of people have creative input into an MMO. They can all call themselves "artists." I don't mean "artist" as in "someone who makes pretty pictures"; I mean it as in "someone who creates a work of art."

MMOs are works of art. So who is "the artist" for an MMO?

Because so many people contribute artistically to the creation of a modern MMO, it's tempting to suggest that there is no "the artist." It used to be this way in Film Theory, too, until the 1950s when it was finally understood that movies do have an individual with overall artistic responsibility: the director. Sure, the screenwriter is an artist, the cinematographer is an artist, the actors are artists, the costume designer is an artist: they're all artists, but the director is *the* artist. The other artists were chosen because their work was of a kind that fit the director's vision.

In MMOs, the (lead) designer is *the* artist.

Letting Creatives Create

When a prestige construction project is proposed, its design is put out for tender. Architects bid for it by submitting plans, and whoever is funding it selects which one best suits them. They may ask for a few modifications, and the architect may or may not go along with them. However, once the paymaster has chosen which plan to go for, they're in the architect's hands. This is the only way it can be if a project is creatively-driven.

Next time a publisher wants to break into the MMO industry, they might consider asking for design documents to be submitted for appraisal. If they want an MMO that has levels and no crafting but features talking shoes, well OK, they'll choose a design that has that. If none have it, it's their own fault for not saying it; if they did say it and got no decent designs, it's their fault for asking for something no one wants to make or that can't be made given the time and budget constraints.

Once they've chosen it, though, they have to sit on their hands and let the developers do their jobs. Suits telling designers how to design is like designers telling programmers how to program: specify the problem, and answer any questions about it they may have, but otherwise stay out of it. *They're* the experts, not you.

Research Audience

Computer game research speaks to a number of constituencies:

The game industry: This traditionally views universities as training establishments. They want academics to train their future employees. They see no reason why they should contribute towards this in any way: it's their inalienable right. They tell academics exactly what they want, then complain bitterly when they are given it. Oh, and academics are out of touch, so their work isn't worth a jot anyway.

Government: A lot of games research is prompted by government concerns, which is to say tabloid newspaper concerns. This tends to about, addiction, violence, children, and, er, well that's about it. Lack of understanding of games is regarded as no impediment to doing research on the subject—indeed, it ensures the researcher's impartiality. If a researcher produces the wrong answer, they're told to go away and come back again when they've produced the right answer.

Academia: Games are cool and hip and trendy. All other academic disciplines, without exception, are mind-numbing stodge. So, why not combine games with Education or Artificial Intelligence or Psychology or Economics? Well, because if you do, you get cool and hip and trendy mind-numbing stodge, that's why not.

Personal interest: Many academics who study games do so because they like them. Yes, they have a dozen explanations as to why this is a mistaken view, but they're lying. They do like games; in fact, they love them. However, games are fun and therefore not serious. Even serious games are not serious. People who study games because they like them have to be very careful, so they say that's not why they're studying them. Otherwise, it would be the same as people who study criminology professing to like taking part in crimes.

Am I coming across as too cynical here?

Flagging

To *flag* a quest is to inform a player that the quest is abnormal. If you have an abnormal quest and you don't flag it, the players think it's normal. This can have consequences on the fiction and on the players' appreciation of the game.

There are any number of ways that the Art of Persuasion quest from *WoW* could have been flagged. Here are some examples:

- There could have been a way to refuse to do the torturing, which might enhance your standing with the Kirin Tor ("You have passed our test").

- There could be a way to reason with the Beryl Sorcerer so you don't have to needle his neurons, perhaps involving a short side quest.

- There could be bad consequences for torturing the Beryl Sorcerer, such as his giving you the location of a trap instead of Lady Evanor.

There are lots of ways to flag this quest to say, "This is not a normal quest." However, none are present: the quest is *not* flagged.

So what's going on here?

Symbolism

At a fundamental level, whatever the kind of MMO a designer is creating, that MMO must:

- **Have value**: Players must be able to act to accomplish goals.

- **Have meaning**: The players' actions and goals must involve changing or querying their context.

- **Make sense**: The connection between actions, goals, and context must be rational.

When the **connection** between actions, goals, and context is two-fold (text and subtext), that's *symbolism*.

Bear With Me on This

Designers, through their designs, say things to their players.

Most of these things are said to help enhance or direct the player experience. A long, dark passageway with a turn at the end says, "Be careful"; a dead tree in the middle of an open field says, "Come here"; a beautiful view that is revealed when a boss dies says, "Well done."

Occasionally, the designer will instead choose to say something external to the MMO—about philosophy, or the human condition, or the real world. For example, there could be a group of NPCs that is trying to bring down an oppressive regime; the designer could demonstrate the justice of the campaign, involve the players in the fight for freedom, and have every guard call them "terrorists."

Not all that designers say is overt like this. Sometimes, their message is implicit rather than explicit. Most MMOs with a guild system only allow a player to be in one guild at a time; there's no gameplay reason for this, though, so at the very least the designer is expressing a view about loyalty. Is the designer necessarily aware of this? No—but that doesn't mean they're not saying it!

Lost Value

Because they offer people a chance to undertake a hero's journey, MMOs provide a service that ordinary people can't get anywhere else. Watering them down to attract a wider audience reduces the effectiveness of this service to barely noticeable levels.

The service is of exceptional value to those who want or need it. So, either MMOs will be made that provide it, leaving those that don't in a (probably much larger) subgroup, or they'll effectively disappear until the concept is rediscovered.

We had something no one else had, and now we're throwing it away to get something that everyone else has had forever.

Nature *vs*. Nurture

MMO design isn't the authoring of plots and quests and activities, it's the authoring of structures and spaces and frameworks, both social and worldly. Within these, players have the freedom to play. The designer creates the playground, the players create the play—all the while confined by the designer's design.

This doesn't mean that designers can claim authorship of play, any more than a novelist can claim authorship of reading; authoring the context is not the same as authoring what goes on within that context. It's a nurture/nature thing. For an MMO, a designer provides the nature and the players provide the nurture. The designer can claim authorship of the nature, and can legitimately say that through said authorship they influence the players' authorship of the nurture. Nevertheless, designers themselves can't claim to author the nurture.

Well, they can *claim* it, but it wouldn't be an MMO if that claim were well-founded.

Why Ask?

So, I asked what non-defining features of today's MMOs will still be present in them 20 years from now.

In so asking, I wasn't so much trying to prompt you to think about what the necessary features of the paradigm *are*, as to alert you to the possibility that some of them are unnecessary. Unnecessary features that are faithfully implemented in MMO after MMO do no one any favors.

I want to *free* designers from those constraining legacies of the past that they don't need; I want them to *know* what they can change; even if they don't want to change it, I want them to *understand* why they don't want to change it, rather than simply take it as part of the basic "what MMOs are" formula.

What aspects of an MMO's design can and should its designers think about? It's not so much, "How many levels should we have?" Rather, it's more, "Should we have levels at all?"

Motivation for Designing

There are many means by which individuals fall into MMO design, but only one reason why they stay there: *because it's fun.*

It's fun for *them*, that is. The "fun" they experience is not necessarily going to be appreciated as such by non-designers, but it *is* fun for designers.

For programmers, the fun is in the programming. They'll happily program games they won't play. This is just as well, or there wouldn't be any games for 5-year-olds.

For designers, the fun is in the designing. They'll happily design MMOs they won't play. Again, this is good news for Barbie MMO fans.

For players, the fun is in the playing. If they program a game or design a game, it's because they want to play the result. Why else would they do it?!

Players of MMOs are primarily interested in *experiencing* them. Designers of MMOs are primarily interested in creating *that which can be experienced.* Player-designed MMOs never consider the big picture, and they never consider other types of player experience. If you're an achiever-type player, you're going to create an MMO that favors achievers, whether you mean to or not.

Designers see the system as a whole. Visualizing how the components go together to have the effects they're supposed to have is what they find fun. They don't actually want to *play* the result except perhaps to validate that it works. If you're a designer, where would be the fun in that?

Off Trade-Offs

In real life, individuals can be strong *and* clever *and* fast *and* skillful *and* good-looking *and* have any other positive quality you want. Positive qualities are not mutually exclusive.

The only reason there "has" to be trade-offs in an MMO is because your design hits a wall if there isn't.

Semiotics

Semiotics is the study of the association of meanings to signs. A split screen in a movie "means" that multiple events are occurring at the same time.

In any system of meaning, the aim is for universality within a context. This explains why you might try to kill a monster in an MMO but you won't try to kill a speech bubble or a quest marker—you know that these, while appearing in the world, are not physical parts of the world. Yet why *would* you know that? Well, you've read comics and newspaper cartoons; MMOs have appropriated symbols and meanings you already know.

Likewise, when you come across some NPC and click it, it will be highlighted in what color if it's on your side? And what color if it's an enemy? Green and red, right? Neutrals will be either blue or yellow (yellow is now dominating, though—thanks, traffic lights).

There are deeper symbols, too. That avatar on the screen is just a collection of pixels, but it carries profound meaning as a vehicle for your sense of identity in the MMO. Yet why should you invest any emotion in it at all? You wouldn't if it were presented as a bundle of stats from a database. It's because for *this* kind of symbol, you assign *this* kind of meaning. The interesting point for MMO designers is that this the-character-is-you symbol didn't really come from any-where else—it's intrinsic to role-playing games.

Symbols have two purposes in an MMO:

- To make statements about the virtual world.
- To make statements about the real world.

The examples I gave earlier are all of *internal* symbols—they say things about the world (e.g., "this is speech" or "this thing will try to kill you"). Such sym-bols can be far more subtle than this, of course: a series of dark rooms is warning you of danger, for example.

External symbols say things about the real world. For instance, a rigid charac-ter class system is speaking about order and conformity—basically, making a political point. Sure, it might make for good gameplay, but that's not the issue: there are plenty of ways to implement good gameplay, but the designer chose *this* one. That choice is *saying* something.

What's more, it's something that couldn't be said *any other way.*

Why Designers Design

Game designers design games because designing games is fun. Their aim is to create a game that some particular player demographic will enjoy.

Players design games because playing games is fun. Their aim is to create a game that they, personally, will enjoy.

Designers don't care about playing games themselves. They do play, but their fun is in the designing, not the playing.

It's art.

Players in their Place

Sometimes, whether for political or personal reasons, players or researchers will insist that designers are wrongly placed above players in terms of MMO creation. In this view, players are co-creators and innovators, and designers are merely facilitators for these co-creators.

No.

Designers have to design the MMO in order for the players to become co-creators and innovators. Furthermore, how they co-create and innovate is shaped by the designer's design. An MMO intended to encourage players to become co-creators, but which was badly designed, would stop them from creating much no matter how creative they were.

Co-creation doesn't just happen; it happens because some designer *designed* for it to happen.

I may make my world yours by opening it for play, but its *design* is still mine.

Levels

Why did I put levels into *MUD I*?

Here's a partial answer. It's the one I used to give when I was asked why I put levels into *MUD I*. It's true, but it's not the *whole* truth.

So, Roy's original vision of *MUD* was a freeform world in which you could do anything the physics allowed. It would support you in your endeavors neutrally. If you wanted to play it as a game, then you could do that; if you wanted to explore or chat, you could do that, too—whatever took your fancy.

I realized, though, that if we wanted anyone to play it, then it had to be a game: not a playground, but a *game*. They could use it as a playground if they wanted, but the default would have to be that it was a particular game, its rules supported by the code. Other games could be compatible with the code (e.g., playing tag), but the software itself only recognized one game.

As for the kind of game, well we still wanted it to be freeform, so that meant giving players rewards for doing things that we felt they might expect rewards for doing (if we could identify what they'd done in code). That meant finding treasure, working things out, killing monsters, and killing each other. We settled on a points system because that gave us some relativity (if a task was easy, you got fewer points than a task that was risky or difficult). This was simple and pretty much what other early games had done, so it would be familiar to our prospective players.

We only *needed* points. However, I also wanted a way that players could tell how many points someone else had, so they could judge relative worth. Rather than having the command LOOK <player> stamp a number on their forehead, I gave them a title: Bill the hero was not as good as Bill the sorcerer, who was not as good as Bill the legend. Players had incentive and some kudos for getting a title because a title showed their worth. They could also judge how skilled and powerful someone else was from their title.

To get titles, I had to introduce bands of points, which meant levels (as in *D&D*—that's explicitly where I took the idea from). Thus, levels were born in *MUD*. I increased stats when you went up a level, and added other powers (e.g., spells) once the stats maxed out. The difference between level X and level X+1 was mainly in the skill of the player, but there were some minor tangible differences as well to back this up.

So that's why I put levels in *MUD I*. If it had been a graphical game in which some visual feature could have determined how experienced your character was, I might have gone with that instead. I did look at some other ways of rewarding players, but levels was the only approach that made the labeling clean. It was essentially a technology-driven decision.

As I said: true, but not the whole truth.

Games You Should Have Played #2

An abstract game.

Games can be many things, but unless they have gameplay, they're not games. An abstract game *only* has gameplay. To understand games, whether to design, play, or study them, you need to understand gameplay; an abstract game shows you the game mechanics with everything else stripped away. They're like naked games.

In my case, I guess the abstract game I played most would be *Chess*. I captained my primary school Chess Club, but my interest in the game waned when I realized that the openings were always the same and that people who were less good at the fun, thinking part could win by doing the boring, memorize-the-openings part. That came straight from an appraisal of the clear-for-all-to-see mechanics.

That said, the abstract game I like the most is the altogether more obscure *Besikovitch's Game* that I mentioned with enthusiasm earlier. Now *that's* a mechanic with potential.

Possible Explanation #1

One explanation for why there's the Art of Persuasion torture quest in *WoW's Wrath of the Lich King* expansion is that it's an artistic statement.

As part of the expansion's wider fiction, the Lich King is a dual entity, formed from the merger of the original Lich King and Arthas Menethil, a human prince who became so consumed in his attempts to defeat evil that he himself became evil. He kept pushing his moral boundaries further and further back in an end-justifies-the-means way, each small incremental change being another step on his path towards wickedness.

By asking the player to do a "small" wrong (torture) in order to do a "greater" right (save a life), the designer could be giving the player an insight into Arthas' descent. The quest provides players a short glimpse into his thinking and allows them to understand how a man who starts out good can gradually become the opposite.

Now this is actually a pretty solid reason to have such a quest, but it should have been flagged. If you want to point out that someone has crossed a moral line, you do actually have to *point it out*. If you don't, people either won't notice (so your message is lost) or they will notice but think you don't believe any line was crossed (that is, that you're a jerk).

Woman as Temptress

The transition from networker/scientist to planner/politician has its own hero's journey step—Woman as Temptress—but none of the other transitions do.

I don't actually know for sure why this is. I suspect it's because both sides of the transition involved "explicit" player types, and therefore the demarcation line between them is less strong. However, that's really nothing more than a guess.

If you want to attack the theory, this would therefore seem a good place to start.

What Games Say

So, there's an orc. What do you do to orcs?

Well, typically you kill them. Orcs are the sword fodder of RPGs.

Hmm, but what's going in here? What's the designer saying? That sentient creatures can be evil just because of their culture or how they look? Is any given orc evil because of what it does or simply because it's an orc?

Tolkien's orcs were definitely evil, but then Tolkien was a Roman Catholic who believed in original sin. He had a whole theological statement going on there. Evil can't create, only imitate; orcs are the corrupted version of elves, and they're manufactured whole—there are no baby orcs.

Do most designers know that? Do they care?

Well, they ought to. See, if you say it's fine to kill orcs purely on the basis that they're orcs, how can you argue with anyone who wants to kill Arabs, Afghans, or Americans purely on the basis that they're Arabs, Afghans, or Americans?

Promoting Understanding

Many of the people who are designing MMOs today cut their teeth playing *WoW*. Their MMO design is informed by that of *WoW*, much as *WoW*'s design is informed by that of *EQ* and *EQ*'s is informed by that of *DikuMUD*.

Now this kind of evolutionary approach is good, but only if the designers using it understand what they're designing. If they incorporate a feature from *WoW*, then they should know **why** it was in *WoW* and **why** they want it in their MMO; they shouldn't take the basic *WoW* paradigm and tweak it because, unless they understand how the whole design hangs together, they may discover that their tweaks undermine some other part of the design that they've just taken aboard without thinking.

I want people to understand the paradigm, not so it can be *perpetuated*, but so it can be *superseded*.

Related Aesthetics

How do we know that MMOs are a different art form to other art forms?

Over the years, plenty of existing artistic traditions have shown an interest in MMOs. Literature, Theatre Studies, Film Studies, RPG Theory—all these and more have applied their aesthetics to MMOs and come away thinking "job done."

Some of these see MMOs as a direct subset of their field, including "MMOs as performance," "MMOs as oral folk-stories," and "MMOs as community." Some are even right to do so (as with Espen Aarseth's *ergodic literature*[3] from Games Studies, for example).

Although these different traditions can situate MMOs within the boundaries of their own aesthetics, none of them can establish MMOs to be mere examples of them. MMOs are not just another form of literature, or theatre, or film, or even RPG. They're *different*.

How do we know they're different? Because their *symbolism* is different.

---

[3]Espen J. Aarseth: *Cybertext: Perspectives on Ergodic Literature*. The John Hopkins University Press, 1997.

Hill-Climbing

Playing an MMO—or a virtual world in general—is a hill-climbing exercise through identity space. The hero's journey is a good algorithm for finding a local maximum. Through playing, you get to affirm who you are.

Or, put another way, you are a multi-faceted diamond. Playing an MMO means you get to see more facets of yourself than you would in ordinary life.

Damn, but you look good!

Winning by Changing

Suppose your character is out exploring the wilderness. You spot a huge bear trying to scoop fish from a river. It's hungry: if it sees you, it might attack. However, you only have four arrows left. Are you going to shoot it while it's unaware of your presence, thereby wasting ammunition even if you one-shot it? Or are you going to sneak round and hope it doesn't notice?

Well, you're just going to shoot at it until it's dead. Having only four arrows left is not a factor.

Today's MMOs are tiny. Even if you are miles from civilization, there's always a way to teleport there and back, or to access your bank while staying where you are (not that real banks let you keep arrows in their vaults, let alone spider intestines or live birds). Besides, you probably have an infinite supply of arrows, so you'll never run out anyway.

All gameplay presents a challenge at some level. If it didn't, it wouldn't be fun. How do you decide which challenges to keep and which to sidestep?

If players think your challenges are boring, they will want them removed. Unfortunately, different players think different challenges are boring. Also, whatever the most boring challenge is, if you take it out purely on the basis that it *is* the most boring, then whatever was second-most boring will now become most boring instead. Eventually, you take away all your challenges.

Listen to what players say because sometimes what they say is important. Ultimately, though, it's your design. If some players don't like your design, let them play something else. Don't change your message only because some people don't like what they hear.

If You Don't Like it

If you don't like it, don't play.

Don't continue to play, especially if you do so in a way that makes everyone who liked it before stop liking it.

Top Five

The Guardian once asked me in an interview: "Apart from yourself, who do you think have been, say, the five most important people in virtual environment/MMO history? Why?"

This isn't the question they *reported* they asked me, which would have elicited a different reply, but that's newspapers[4].

It took me maybe an hour to answer the question. At first, I thought I'd have to cut it down somehow, perhaps by restricting myself only to designers. That would have meant leaving out Jess Mulligan, though, and she deserves to be on any such list *twice*.

So how about if I ignored designers and focused on producers and non-industry figures? Oh, but that would mean omitting Jake Song, which would be unconscionable given the seismic changes he brought about in Korean society (changes that are still being felt elsewhere in the Far East).

My next tactic was to construct a long list of every person I could leave out but really, really didn't want to leave out. That tactic didn't work either because I realized that every name I added meant I had to add others, too—it rippled out unceasingly. MMOs are what they are today because of so many people that it's impossible to draw the line. I had to have Ted Castronova, who finally made MMO research respectable. So should I have put in Pavel Curtis, whose *LambdaMOO* brought virtual worlds to academic attention in the 1990s and laid the foundations of their study in so many disciplines? But people only heard about *LambdaMOO* because of Julian Dibbell's *A Rape in Cyberspace* article, so Julian should be in the list. Only, does that mean I should also include Mr. Bungle, the virtual rapist his article concerns, because without him the article would never have been written?

There were some names that made me feel particularly bad about omitting because I don't believe they get the recognition they deserve for what they did. Without Alan Cox, for example, MUDs would not have got to the USA when they did. It was a critical point in virtual world history, but Alan rarely

---

[4]Keith Stuart: *The Five Most Important People in the Virtual World* http://www.guardian.co.uk/technology/gamesblog/2007/jul/17/thefivemosti

gets a mention for his contribution. So should I have perhaps limited myself to relatively unsung individuals? In the end, I decided against it: nobody wants to be on a list for reasons that look like pity, even if it's not meant that way.

So in the end, I decided to bite the bullet and just list who I thought were indeed the five most important people in virtual world history. Having spent so long thinking about it, I already knew I wanted Roy and Jess, and Jake Song, Raph, and Ted.

Oh! List full!

- Roy Trubshaw
- Jessica Mulligan
- Jake Song
- Raph Koster
- Ted Castronova

So that's what I answered.

The "apart from yourself" bit in the original question was unnecessary, as I wouldn't have included myself in the list, anyway.

Possible Explanation #2

A second explanation for the Art of Persuasion torture quest is that it could be a political statement.

The US government is forbidden by the US constitution to torture prisoners, but, having prisoners it wished to torture, is alleged to have outsourced it using a process known as "extraordinary rendition." The quest could have been drawing parallels between the Kirin Tor's desire for you to do their torturing for them and the US government's extraordinary rendition program.

Again, this is fair enough. It has to be flagged if it's to work, however. If the prisoner were to give you false information, or if other factions turned against you (or the Kirin Tor) because of your actions, then you would have some pause for thought.

It's not flagged, though. People will therefore either fail to notice, or (if they're into politics) suspect that the designer put in the quest without comment in order to show tacit support for extraordinary rendition (that is, that they're a jerk).

Level Down

Levels in MMOs are no longer doing their job. Here are some of the complaints I have about them:

- There are so many that going up a level isn't particularly special. They don't deliver the goal-oriented payload they did originally.

- No one goes down levels these days. They don't even lose experience points. Your level isn't a measure of your skill, it's a measure of how many hours you've played.

- The power ratio between high and low levels is ridiculous. A million level 1 characters couldn't hurt a highest-level character.

- What you learn as you go up levels is of no use when you get to the highest level, which becomes all about gear and group play.

- If a player wants to play with a friend of a different level, either the friend's character has to be boosted to the level of the player's character, or the player's character has to be handicapped down to the level of the friend's character. This never makes any sense in the game's fiction.

- There's mad inflation in the numbers. Every time a new expansion comes out, the relative power between player characters and mobs is the same as it ever was, but the way this is reflected in absolute numbers is laughable. Kill a minor trash mob at level 90 and you'll get as much experience in one go as you needed to rise from level 1 to level 20.

- There's no fictional cover for why trash mobs at the highest level are as tough as they are. People in starter areas are worried about the wolves wandering around? Shouldn't they be worrying about that one moth the size of a cow that could flutter by and kill them all if someone brought it back as a pupa and let it hatch? It could flatten a city!

It's not difficult to get rid of levels altogether.

Example: suppose you have some kind of secret agent game. Player characters have gone through training in their back story and are now ready for the field: they are all as skilled as each other. You don't have to have completed a thousand quests to be able to figure out how to use some over-powered sniper rifle: it's the same as any other sniper rifle, you just aim and pull the trigger. You don't get to use the heat-seeking drone bomb only when you've killed a hundred enemy agents, you can use it straight away if you can get hold of one. The only difference between your character fresh out of training and that of an experienced player is that you're not yet trusted by your agency, yet your colleague is. Your colleague has completed five hundred missions in places like Oslo, Vienna, Rome, and Algiers, and is now reliable enough to go to Moscow, Warsaw, Prague, and Shanghai. If *you* want to go there, you have to do the missions in the "easy" cities or persuade someone who has already done them (i.e., a friend) to take you as part of their team. When you get there, your character is every bit as good as their character in terms of skill. You may need some equipment that you don't have, but you can use it if you find it. You can take it back and use it elsewhere if you like, although it might be better to save it for the more dangerous places.

In this example, experience points equate to trust. Do more missions, build up your status, and get access to new content. Or, if you prefer, don't: just repeat the content you know and love. You'll still gain experience points, you'll still increase your level of trust, and you'll still be able to go to the harder-content areas if you so desire.

I thought up that example off the top of my head as I typed. It's not hard to do this kind of thing: the hard parts (for a designer) are first realizing that you *can* do it, and then persuading the non-designers who hold the company's purse strings that it's worth trying.

I find it incredibly frustrating that, after well over three decades of virtual worlds, we're still not seeing anywhere near enough innovation. It's as if we've sailed off in the fifteenth century and discovered a whole new world of virgin territory, but we're only ever building in the same colony. There's so much more out there to explore!

Sigh. Another attack of despair.

The Need for Games Research

Games are not the same as other art forms because game designers are not the same as other creative artists. In Literature, academics read novels and interpret what the novelist is saying; in Games Studies, academics read games and interpret what the designer is saying, *then* the designer reads what the academics have said and assimilates it. This is not a dynamic you see much in other creative industries.

Despite my cynicism, it's true that industry does need games research—and not just on the technical side. Designers want research on games *as games* because then it allows them to speak about what they do.

Likewise, government needs games research. It's one thing to harp on about addiction, violence, and children; but when there are inter-governmental conferences taking place trying to negotiate the regulation of game IP, virtual currency tax, and freedom of speech, they're not going to get very far if all your research is directed at the psychological aspects of games. Game developers can't advise on this kind of regulatory framework matter, but academics can (and do—I've been to Council of Europe and OECD conferences about games myself). If no one is researching this area, a government could easily find itself wrong-footed.

If I want to teach using a picture and I can't draw, I should get an artist. If I want to teach using a game and I can't design, I should get a designer. For educational games, you need people who understand both education and games. Educators would laugh if a game designer created a learning system using a ridiculously naïve pedagogy, yet educators themselves are affronted when game designers laugh at the games *they* create. Any academic wanting to study how to use games to teach—or to do anything else with them—needs to understand game design. Someone therefore has to research game design.

As for academics who study games because they themselves like them, should they feel perhaps a little guilty about it? Is it OK?

HA! It's more than OK—it's absolutely terrific! Playing games is one of the most important things human beings do. Far from being some new, Johnny-come-lately cultural fad, games *predate* culture. **Bears play games**, but they don't write books. Eat that, Literature!

Only with the advent of computers has the significance of games gradually become recognized, primarily because they make so much money that the cultural elite grudgingly has to pay them some lip service. This means that there *is* a truly vast, unexplored territory out there! Who wouldn't want to be a pioneer, exploring that land, opening it up, and being the first to behold its wonders? Even better, because designers listen, you get to decide where people settle, too!

Now is a marvelous time to be studying computer games, for whatever reason. The old walls are crumbling and the glorious vistas they hide are waiting to be revealed. Those academics lucky enough to be able to call themselves scholars of Games Studies will be the ones to reveal them, the first to understand them, and the people who get the blindingly-obvious-in-hindsight theories named after them.

Most importantly, though, they'll also get to play the better games that result.

Damn, but I hope I live long enough to see some of the fruits of this.

Games You Should Have Played #3

A tabletop role-playing game.

Everyone thinks they know why *they* want to play games, but they also need to know why everyone *else* plays games. They're not going to get that unless they understand what it means to be part of the game. In a tabletop role-playing environment, with the other players right there next to you, there's no escape: you have to participate, you have to involve yourself, you have to become part of the game, part of the narrative. In short, you have to *live* the game. Unless you've lived a game, how can you ever hope to understand what's gamingly possible?

For me, the hours I spent playing *D&D* with my friends in my late teens were some of the best gaming experiences I've ever had. I wish I'd been able to get a *Call of Cthulhu* group going, but it came out too late for me. I read through the rules and six expansion modules, so I did get rather a lot out of it; I'd have liked to have experienced how it played, though.

No Consequences

In *MUD2*, we had a special event over one Christmas (I think) in which, for no good reason other than it might be fun, we took a snapshot of the entire player database and had a day of "no consequences." It was announced well in advance, and there were other announcements upon entry lest anyone be left under any illusions.

Things went pretty much as you might expect, with everyone attacking everyone else, giving one another outrageous gifts, cheating, lying, and tricking each other. There was also some "real" play, in which people risked their characters exploring areas that they would generally have regarded as being too dangerous.

The players universally enjoyed it as a one-off, but it wasn't the kind of thing that they would have been keen to see happening very often. Most of them seemed to conclude that anarchic freedom is fun in small doses, but they wouldn't want to play in an MMO that was like that the whole time.

Why don't we ever see experiments like this in today's MMOs?

Symbolism through Breadth

Breadth is global to an MMO, therefore its symbolism must pertain in global systems.

Example: suppose an MMO has 50 ways to combine ingredients for baking cakes and five ways to combine components for making armor. This is *saying* something to the players. If it were the other way round, it would be saying something different. You already know which version you'd prefer to play because you could *read* the symbolism without having to think about it.

Breadth is revealed through general systems, so its symbolism is useful for making general points. *MUD1* said "be free" using general systems, not a number of highly-focused ones.

Symbolism Through Depth

Depth can be localized in an MMO, therefore its symbolism can pertain in local systems.

Example: suppose the orcs in an MMO are usually anonymous grunts, but the ones you've come across in this glade have names and live in family groups. That's flagging that there's something different about them. Will you treat them the same way as other orcs?

Because depth is revealed through local systems, its symbolism is useful for making local points. *MUD1* said "other players are people, too" by using a number of highly-focused systems, not general ones.

Possible Explanation #3

A third legitimate reason for having a torture quest a short way into *WoW's* *Wrath of the Lich King* expansion would be to change its direction. When *WotLK* came out, *WoW* was four years old. Adding more mature content would be one way to reflect its growing maturity.

Again, though, this is only OK *if* you let the players know what's happening. This isn't something that can be flagged within the game context: you have to tell the players outside of it. Nevertheless, you *do* have to tell them that you're shifting the game's direction, so they can decide whether or not to continue playing. This is what the developers of *Star Wars: Galaxies* did when they introduced its New Game Enhancements: they warned the players in advance so they could unsubscribe if they didn't like it (and many did indeed do just that). *SW:G* could have just implemented the NGE patch and sprung it on the players, but it played fair and told them.

If *WoW's* developers wanted to turn the game from a cartoon-violence MMO into a grittier, more rugged MMO, they would have been well within their rights to do so. All it would have taken was an announcement or two to let anyone buying the expansion know what to expect—or at least not be surprised when asked to use a Neural Needler on an NPC tied up in a chair.

There was no announcement, though. The quest wasn't flagged externally, either.

Art Within Art

When academics who study art consider computer games in an artistic context, they all too often regard them as venues for art, not as works of art in their own right.

You *can* have art within MMOs—of course, you can! Play is a creative process and players are incredibly creative, so artistic behavior emerges *all the time*. It can even take forms that a disdainful art museum curator might recognize as avant garde: sculpture in *A Tale in the Desert*, piano making in *Ultima Online*, anti-McDonalds draw-rude-things-using-cola-cans protests in *The Sims Online*, machinima in pretty well everything—these are all examples of art within MMOs.

They're not the art *of* MMOs, though.

We know they're not because their *symbolism* is different.

Journey's End

I don't have exact figures, but I'd guess that of *MUD1*'s players who stayed beyond a week, only between five and 20 percent reached the end. Of the ones that didn't make it, some grew disenchanted, some were driven off, some found better virtual worlds, some lost access; but most simply didn't *need* to finish.

Breadth and Depth Limitations

Although it's possible for designers to communicate ideas through breadth and depth, in practice what can be done is fairly limited. This is because players are not, on the whole, sufficiently attuned to MMO design principles to realize that changes to breadth or depth may be deliberate—they all-too-readily regard them as bugs. If you try to hint that an apparent inconsistency may have been put there purposefully, they'll think you're stupid. If they don't think it's fun, they'll think you're arrogantly jerking them around for self-indulgent reasons (and they may indeed be right!).

Also, the bandwidth of breadth and depth is such that there aren't many things you can say through them anyway. You can set a broad tone, or make a pointed comment, but you're only going to be able to do that half a dozen times with any fidelity before you've exhausted the possibilities. If you push it further, things start to fall apart.

Breadth and depth are powerful voices, but they can't be called upon often: designers therefore tend to use them primarily to articulate their most important points. This means that, if you're looking to find out what a new MMO is "about," you can usually pick up the gist of it from a swift look at its feature set.

If breadth and depth were the only means available to speak to players, design would be a frustrating business. It would be the same as having a novelist who was only able to communicate through plot—not character, dialogue, turn of phrase, or any of the other myriad of tools in the authorial toolbox.

So how *do* designers talk to the players through their design?

Designers vs. Developers

Here's a handy way to tell the views of MMO designers from the views of their employers:

- Designers say, "It's the socializing, stupid."
- Developers say, "It's the stupid, socializing."

A Rape in Cyberspace or Not?

So, I'm assuming you've gone away and read *A Rape in Cyberspace* (if you hadn't read it already). Here are some questions you can ask yourself about it. Warning: these will make little sense if you *haven't* read it...

LambdaMOO's problems of March 1993 centered on the use of a *voodoo doll*:

- Why would a virtual world ever allow ordinary players to make something with this kind of power?
- Why would a virtual world ever *not* allow ordinary players to make something with this kind of power?

Zippy stopped Mr. Bungle's virtual assault by firing his supergun at him:

- Was Zippy right to do this?
- By what authority did Zippy do this, or did he need any?

The players of *LambdaMOO* routinely referred to Mr. Bungle's actions as "rape":

- Was it rape?
- Should real-life law consider in-world actions like this to be rape?
- Who should be regarded as perpetrating the alleged rape? Mr. Bungle or the player behind Mr. Bungle?
- Is a "crime against the mind" less of a crime than a crime against the body?

HerkieCosmo hypothesized: "perhaps it's better to release ... violent tendencies in a virtual environment rather than in real life":

- If Mr. Bungle had got away with what he did in *LambdaMOO*, would that have had any effect on the likelihood that he would have abused a woman in real life?
- Could the fact that Mr. Bungle was thwarted in *LambdaMOO* have caused him to abuse a woman in real life? If so, would those who thwarted him have been in any way culpable?

Acting alone, JoeFeedback @toaded Mr. Bungle:

- Was JoeFeedback right to do this?
- Mr. Bungle could have argued that if what he did was rape, then what JoeFeedback did was murder. Is this a reasonable position?

- Was Mr. Bungle's punishment severe, or was it no punishment at all?

Haakon wanted to be a servant of his players, but had to wield his godly powers to enforce changes to the New Direction:

- Can developers ever be mere servants, or is the fact they're gods inescapable?

- What would Haakon have done if the players of *LambdaMOO* had voted within his rules to ban all real-world female players? (Aside: a top-rated *WoW* guild did exactly that because "they cause too much drama").

Mr. Bungle said he'd engaged in "thought polarization":

- Is it OK for players to experiment on other players (without their permission) in an MMO, whether for fun or for some other reason?

- Is it OK for developers to experiment on their players (without their permission) within the context of their MMO?

The players of *LambdaMOO* wanted to keep the punishment within *LambdaMOO* because that's where the crime was committed:

- Was the crime indeed committed in *LambdaMOO* or somewhere else?

- Should the player behind Mr. Bungle have been reported to New York University, given that this would in all likelihood have resulted in his being kicked off his course for misuse of computing resources?

Evangeline said she was "a survivor of both virtual rape ... and real-life sexual assault":

- Does this make Mr. Bungle's actions a greater transgression than they were already?

- Does your answer to the above change depending on whether Mr. Bungle knew or didn't know about evangeline's past experiences?

This essay addresses the boundaries between the real and the virtual:

- Are MMOs all just words and pixels?

- Does the "it's just a game" defense always hold true or never hold true?

- Are there boundaries between the real and the virtual, or are they the same thing?

Atmosphere

"Atmosphere" is a catch-all term referring to the means by which designers influence players' moods. This sounds manipulative, but it's not as bad as it seems: players are willing participants.

There are many ways to suggest atmosphere. Obvious ones include music, sound, and artwork—the kind of things that you might in real life say contributed to the atmosphere of a place. The people present are very important for atmosphere too, of course, but the nature of a locale is part of the reason they're there.

Here are some other ideas for suggesting atmosphere:

- **Open vs. closed form:** Cramped areas restrict choice, wide ones open it up.

- **Lightness vs. darkness:** The less you know, the easier you're spooked.

- **Vistas vs. corners:** The less you know, the more you want to learn; the more you know, the more you want explore your knowledge.

- **Familiarity vs. alienness:** A time to be confident or a time to be uneasy.

- **Ease vs. difficulty:** Harder quests imply a harder environment.

- **Large vs. small:** Bigger is more powerful (all cats know this!).

- **Beauty vs. ugliness:** Goodness, safety, aspiration, success—or not.

There are plenty more of these techniques—screen tints, changes over time, ambient creatures, hot vs. cold, wood vs. metal, water vs. sand, and so on. All say something that the players are able to pick up on without even thinking about it.

In other words, atmosphere is suggested by *symbols* that players *read*. Designers *say* things to players through atmosphere.

Peers

The population of the UK is about 200 times the population of Iceland, but both countries are equal in terms of international law.

World of Warcraft has about, oh, let's be conservative and say 20 times the population of Iceland.

Making Associations

In *MUD1*, I used a metaphor of anachronism for danger. The more removed (into the past) from the present a location or object was, the more powerful and deadly it was.

Is this an example of the use of atmosphere? Well, only vaguely: age *vs.* youth does carry meaning, and could be utilized in a specific situation to engender a particular mood. That wasn't what I was doing here, though: I was taking a concept (age) and building a relationship between this and another concept (danger). I was associating the two things together, in order to give myself a means by which I could inform players how challenging an area or an object was.

Initially, I wasn't actually aware of this. It was only after maybe a year or two that I realized I'd done it. I formalized it for *MUD2*, but for *MUD1* it "just happened."

Was it luck that it happened? Well, clearly not—the odds against its arising through chance are enormous. No, I was articulating some deep-down sense of rage against the past for the problems of the present—rage I hadn't really been able to express before. Through my design, it just came out. Only in reflecting on the design did I notice it and realize where it came from. It still says what I feel about the long reach of the past better than I could say in words.

Enjoy, psychologists. Me, I see this kind of thing as art.

Aesthetics and Meaning

Game design is not an art in the same way that programming and mathematics are art—only able to be appreciated by a practitioner. Players of games can and do read what the game designer is saying to them through the game.

Game designs give rise to an aesthetic appreciation, but they *also* carry wider meaning.

The Whole Truth

So why did I *really* put levels into *MUD1*?

Well the formal reason I did so was in order to give players goals and allow them see how well they were doing in comparison with other players—what I called at the time an *achievement system*. This formal reason is correct: it is indeed why I did it—but it's not the *only* reason I did it.

The thing is, at the time I considered several alternative achievement systems. Levels weren't the only show in town; I also looked at the following:

- Equipment. This is how the elder game in modern MMOs works.

- Skills. This is how many pen-and-paper RPGs work, but some MMOs use skills in place of levels (notably, *The Secret World*).

- Experience points without levels.

- Quests linked in a choose-your-own-adventure style.

- Achievements (which I called *tasks* when I finally added them to *MUD2* a decade or more later).

- Some more *outré* ones such as democracy.

I settled on levels because they gave intermediate goals, were easy to understand, did not preclude rewards for varied activities, and they gave players an immediate sense of their current place in the social order.

The key word there is *current*. Other options from the list could have met all the same objectives as levels, but for that final one.

Brace yourself.

Roy Trubshaw and I were both working class. I came from East Yorkshire, so to the predominantly middle-class students who went to university at that time I sounded like a farm laborer. Roy came from Wolverhampton and sounded like a factory worker. Along with most of our fellow computer scientists, we were really only tolerated at university because the country needed people who could program: Computer Science was not regarded as a proper object of study. People who wanted to get on in the world studied Law or History or English Literature—or even an actual science.

That wasn't the case for us, though. The British class system had labeled us and packaged us and allowed us a glimpse of the level above us only because Computer Science was necessary but unfashionable, and we were clever.

We raged against this! People should *not* be trapped by society through the accident of their birth—it's unjust!

Levels in *MUD1* were our response.

MUD1 had ten levels (you don't need dozens when you have permadeath). Each had its own personality; players spent enough time at each one to form an opinion of what being a "warrior" or a "champion" or a "legend" *meant*. Crucially, all that stopped you from rising levels was your own ability and strength of character (or lack thereof).

Yes: the reason I chose levels over the other possibilities was to make a political statement.

Now I knew this, and Roy knew this, but the people who wrote the MUDs and MMOs that followed didn't know this. They employed a system that made sense in one context without appreciating either why it was there or why it worked. They reduced the character death penalty, so leveling became merely a matter of time, not skill; they then liberally added more levels to compensate, until finally they had to employ other achievement systems when the levels inevitably ran out.

Did they have any idea what they were doing? Those different achievement systems all have different meanings! They're not just mechanics, they're *symbols*. The gear-based approach adopted by most MMOs for their elder game is waxing positively about consumerism: do the designers who put it in *realize* that? Fair enough if they do—but then why do they have the leveling game? Is the leveling game like school and the elder game like work? What are they trying to *say*?

Whether or not the designers or players like it, every MMO makes statements. If these statements are at odds with one another, then the designer is either working through some internal dialectic, working under heavy external pressure, or clueless.

MUD1 was all about freedom. MUDs—and thence MMOs—have *always* been about freedom.

Uses of Atmosphere

If atmosphere can be used by designers to say things to players, what kind of messages can be conveyed?

Here are some of the things atmosphere was used for in *MUD1*:

- To hint at what's to come.
- To promote social interaction.
- To signal the start or end of an action sequence.
- To throw players off guard, prior to surprising them.
- To warn or encourage players.
- To reward or punish players.
- To signal a break or breathing space.
- To make an ethical or philosophical point.

You saw that last one?

Although the Narrow Road Between Lands was *MUD1*'s starting location when we opened the doors to external players, it wasn't actually the *original* starting location. That, which was written by Roy Trubshaw, was the Road Opposite Cottage. Here's a reminder of its description:

```
Road opposite cottage.
You are standing on a badly paved road with a cemetery to the north and the
home of a grave-digger to the south. An inscription on the cemetery gates
reads, "RESTING PLACE OF LOST SOULS".
```

This establishes the opening atmosphere of the game world; it's incredibly important because it sets the baseline for all of what follows. So what did Roy say with it? He said you'd just come from a *graveyard*. He equated *Reality* with a cemetery. You were dead there, but you're *alive* now. He's bridling against it: where you are now is a *better* place! Here, you can *find your soul*.

To those who chose to look, this was a rejection of moribund 1970s English society. To those who didn't, it was just atmosphere—a hint at a lifted gloom and an enticement to, well, that was up to you!

I moved the start two rooms to the east so I could link *MUD* more easily to the smaller MMO I wrote called *Valley*. I've regretted doing so ever since.

Possible Explanation #4

The fourth obvious reading of the Art of Persuasion quest in *WoW* is the default one: the quest is not flagged because its designer didn't feel it fell outside the boundaries of the game. Because it offended no expectations, it didn't need to be treated any differently to any other quest.

Well, the designer was wrong. Sufficient numbers of players did notice it, did consider it problematic, and did think it was definitely an issue. So either the designer didn't know where players drew their moral lines, didn't care, didn't think the quest crossed those lines, or (and this is what I believe is the most likely explanation) didn't think about it beyond the level of its mechanics. If you're scratching your head wondering how to use the limited number of quest components available to you to make each quest seem different, well looking at the list of available tools and seeing how you can repurpose one is perfectly natural.

That said, although there were plenty of players who did notice the moral dubiousness of the Art of Persuasion quest, there were many, many more who didn't notice it at all.

Why would that be, then?

The Hunter or the Hunted

In MMOs that allow players to do things to other players non-consensually, players have different views. Some think, "I can do this to other players? Cool!"; some think, "I can have this done to me by other players? Uncool!"; and some think, "Players can do this to each other? Cool/uncool" (depending on their preconceptions).

Players aren't necessarily *against* unfettered PvP in principle, they're just against PvThemPersonally. Whether that's too important for them to ignore is contingent on whether they see themselves primarily as the hunter or the hunted.

Game-Design Mistakes Every Designer Makes #1

Every game designer makes game-design mistakes. I'm going to list some of these. Oh, and as I'll remind you after each one, they're mistakes that everyone makes—not just designers; however, if I restrict my criticism to designers, there'll be fewer people camped outside my door demanding that I let them hit me.

The first mistake designers make is falling for the hype. They judge games by their success in the market, not by their gameplay. Games can succeed for many reasons, of which good design is but one:

- **Marketing**: *Black & White* sold two million copies.

- **Naïve audience**: *Monopoly* and *Farmville* are among the favorites of people who don't know there are much better games out there.

- **Right place, right time**: *MUD I* was like this.

Games can also appear to be successful while not actually being so. Everyone thought *EverQuest* was a huge success until *World of Warcraft* came along.

Designers, too, tend to judge their fellow designers by the commercial success of their creations, rather than by the quality of their designs. Here's a game-industry secret for you: most big-name designers are *not all that great at game design*. Before you get too smug, though, most of the rest are even worse and are still in a different league to most players. The basic problem is that a mediocre designer can't tell a good designer from a world-class one: they all look like mediocre designers. A good one can tell a mediocre one from a good one, but can't tell a world-class one from a good one. A world-class one *can* tell the difference, but will tend to overlook brilliant unknowns (because there are so many non-brilliant unknowns that it's hard to encounter them). World-class designers may also not be commercially successful; just like any artist from any medium, a designer could die unrecognized and in poverty, only becoming successful posthumously—if even then.

Ideally, designers should be objective. As a designer, you should *of course* look at best-selling games from famous names because they *could* be great. If you can't see anything great about them, look again: the beauty of the design may be too subtle for the eye to spot straight away, attuned or otherwise. If you still think the gameplay sucks, though, trust yourself—it does. Don't fall for the hype!

Ok, so falling for the hype is indeed a mistake made by every game designer, but then so is dressing badly. Is it a *game-design* mistake, though?

Well yes: it's imperative that game designers *understand* game designs. Knowing that a game *is* good isn't enough; a designer needs to know *why* it's good. Otherwise, how are you ever going to make games that are in any sense better?

Note that believing the hype is also a mistake every non-designer makes.

Speaking Through Atmosphere

Atmosphere isn't the only way designers can speak to players. As I've mentioned already, they can do it through depth, breadth, association (anachronism for danger), command availability (change-sex spells), and many, many other ways.

However, atmosphere is the only way I need to have detailed if I'm to *show* that designers can speak to players. I need to do *that* because, well, you'll see shortly.

What's that? You didn't think I was rambling on pretentiously about symbols and meaning without good *reason*, did you? The very suggestion!

Imposition

Designers impose an ethical framework on players whether they (the designers or the players) like it or not.

The only questions are: whose ethical framework are they imposing, and why?

Meaning in Games

Games don't generate meaning. Players and designers generate meaning. Games are the objects or tools from and through which meaning is generated, but it's the people who generate the meaning.

Games are a great way for someone to encapsulate meaning, but they themselves aren't responsible for it. If I choose to interpret a game of pure chance as evidence that the gods love me, or that I'm cleverer than those I beat, that's my doing, not the game's. You might instead view the same game as a means of collectively helping one player obtain a material reward.

The meaning in games is *interpretative*.

Knowing When

MMO design is in essence an art; and like any art, there are different degrees of capacity to create that art between different individuals. Some people paint, some sculpt, some dance, some take photographs, some compose music, some write plays—and some write MMOs. Some are good at it, some are bad at it; all are passionate about it.

MMO players who come to understand what it is they're playing, why things are the way they are, and why some designers do things differently to others—those are the players who can become designers. When they have designed, have realized they have choices, have agonized over which way to take their designs, and have understood that their decisions are in some way an expression of their thoughts and emotions; when they know that MMOs are, for them, a means of articulating something they can't say any other way, *that* is when they *are* a designer.

Having a job as a designer doesn't mean you're a designer. *Being* a designer means you're a designer.

A Critical Aesthetic

I've stated on several occasions in this book that MMO design is an art and that MMOs are an art form. I'm now in a position to prove it.

Artists use art for expression—to convey some meaning. It's not a requirement of art that people need know what a work means; it *is* a requirement (indeed, it's the only requirement) that they know how its meaning is conveyed. A system of ascribing meaning to individual examples of an art form is called a *critical aesthetic*. Therefore, to be recognized as art, MMOs need their own critical aesthetic, distinct from that of any other work of art.

A critical aesthetic has four components, which can be stated as a set of questions:

- How is the value of the art form determined?

- What must people understand in order to appreciate this art form?

- What rules apply to all examples of this art form?

- What symbolism exists within this art form and within the way the art form is presented?

Let's answer these for MMOs:

- **How is the value of the art form determined?** Players come to know more about themselves, through undertaking a hero's journey.

- **What must people understand in order to appreciate this art form?** In MMO terms, appreciation equates to having fun. This is explained by the Player Type model.

- **What rules apply to all examples of this art form?** Those imposed by the MMO paradigm: it's a virtual world with gameplay.

- **What symbolism exists within this art form, and within the way it is presented?** Atmosphere. It's not the *only* symbolism, but I don't have to be exhaustive here; one example is sufficient.

Check, check, check, check. MMOs have a critical aesthetic; therefore, their design can be recognized as an art form; and therefore, their designers are artists. *Voila.*

Now that You Mention it

The most obvious reason that people might not have cared that there was torture going on in *WoW's* Art (doesn't that word seem out of place now?) of Persuasion quest is that they saw nothing wrong with it. Torture seems to be effective in TV shows such as *24*, which is (fortunately) the closest most players will get to seeing it in action. Actually, it's not very effective in real life: when people will tell you anything to make you stop, they will indeed tell you anything—true or otherwise. That's not necessarily how most players will understand it, though. Besides, worse things than torture go on in *WoW*—for example rogues routinely garrote people, blind them, backstab them, and so on. If players think torture is no worse than some of the things that they knew they'd encounter when they signed up to play, why *would* they care about it?

Although I have no doubt that the above does apply to many players, it's not the full story. When the torture quest was brought to the attention of players who hadn't cared about it when they did it, the reasons they gave for its being OK were often along the lines of, "It's just a game." This suggests that, now you mention it, there *is* something a bit odd about it; but hey, no real Beryl Sorcerers were harmed, so it's fine. The magic circle doesn't legitimize torture, but it does allow it to be dismissed. That said, if you saw nothing wrong with torture, you wouldn't feel the need to come up with a reason to dismiss it when pressed; therefore, those who do dismiss it did feel a little uneasy when they reflected on what was going on in it.

My own view is that most people didn't care about the nature of the Art of Persuasion because they were so caught up in the headlong flight to level 80 that they lost all sense of narrative. They decoupled the inducements to act from the acts themselves. In other words, it's a mirror of how the quest got in in the first place: people looked only at the syntax ("do this") and not at the semantics ("torture this NPC"). When the semantics were brought up, shrug, it's just a game.

The *WotLK* expansion had some other quests that were out of line, too. "Tormenting the Softknuckles" involved hurting baby gorillas until their mother was enraged enough to come out of hiding, whereupon you could kill her. "Surrender…Not!" was a comedy quest in which you dressed up in a wacky murloc suit and got to the enemy leader under the cover of a white flag, so you could kill him. I mention these two quests because, apart from "The Art of Persuasion," they were the only morally abnormal ones I came across in *WoW* that were unflagged. Given that *WoW* had 7,650 quests in total as of the release of the *WotLK* expansion, that's pretty good going.

I'm not, therefore, having a go at *WoW* here because of a weak quest. I'm talking about it to make a point.

As for what that point *is*, I guess I'll reach it eventually.

How to Read an MMO

It's all very well, my patiently and elitistly arguing that MMO design is an art and that MMOs are an art form, but if it's possible to "read" an MMO, OK, so how do you do that?

Well, you think about everything you notice and ask *why* it's there. From this, you can construct what it *means*.

Find the tokens and consider what they're saying; then, consider what they're *really* saying.

By Any Other Name

What does a rose smell like in an MMO? Nothing! How do you even know it *has* a smell?

Visible vapor surrounding an object is the MMO cipher for its having a smell. You have to deprettify the image of the rose by adding a "smell" graphic to it. When you (somehow) smell it, what happens? Basically, you're told in text that it smells of rose.

What if this isn't a graphical world, but a textual one?

Well, the rose will be described as being heavily scented. If you smell it, you'll still be told that it smells of rose. However, the medium through which the message is delivered is the same one through which you experienced the rose. Overwriting a graphical image with text detracts from both the image and the text; accompanying a textual description with text enhances both.

Continuing *SW:TOR*

My grand theory of why people find MMOs fun draws on Campbell's *Hero's Journey*. It comes down to this: self-actualization occurs when *you* accept that the *MMO* accepts that you've won. In most modern MMOs, the game never admits that you've "won" because the developers believe that, if it did, you would stop playing and go off to some other MMO, instead. Their preference is to keep players around for long enough that an expansion can be built to move the finishing line further away. Players do one of three things: self-actualize through their own strength of will; become increasingly bored or frustrated and drift away; or become trapped at an earlier stage (typically that of planner/achiever) and keep going until they burn out.

Now this belief that players shouldn't get to "win" because then they'll quit sounds pretty logical. However, the evidence from the old text MUDs that *did* let them win points to the contrary: players kept playing for years (in some cases, decades and counting) after they won. This is in keeping with Campbell's theory: once you can treat the virtual world as a place like any other, you return because you like it there, not because you have a purpose there.

For years I argued that someone should make a major MMO with an end-point, and I was beginning to wonder if the concept of what an MMO "should" have as an elder game was going to become so ingrained that even if one of them *did* allow players to win, by the time it happened too many of said players would be too set in their ways for them to accept it. This was until *SW:TOR* went ahead and did it: it told players at the end of their class quest line that their story was over. There are other stories, but your main one has come to an end. Congratulations, you've won.

This raised the question: what would players do next? Would someone who has worked their way through an epic (albeit corny) story "graduate" to a raiding elder-game? Or would they start up a new character or two and repeat the process for different stories? More to the point, what did Bioware *want* them to do?

Traditionally, MMO developers will try to keep players occupied until the next expansion is ready; they'll do this by teaching them to dance through interminable raids that feature gameplay bearing little resemblance to the gameplay the players experienced to get to that point. When the new content is eventually added, it almost all goes at the high end; developers may even inflate rewards at the lower levels, so that players can skip through it faster to get to the "real" game.

Bioware could have taken a radically different approach, though. They were in a position where they could keep the level cap at 50 indefinitely and add new content for the leveling game. If their rock-solid belief is that the core of engagement lies in each player's personal story, then the natural way to expand would be to add more story—creating more content for the *player*, not for the *character*. In this view, if you get to level 50 and want to start all over again with a new character at level 1, you're the kind of person they want. After all, if you liked raiding, you'd be playing *WoW* anyway.

So would Bioware take the traditional route and add content for an ever-aging elder game? Or would it do something entirely different and create new storylines for the leveling game?

That's what I wanted to find out, and that's why I didn't immediately cancel my subscription upon reaching the *SW:TOR* level cap.

From Zero to One

From *The Guardian*, 9ᵗʰ October, 2009:

> Online game addiction rising, counsellors warn
>
> Obsessed players may forget to eat or sleep
>
> Patient, 23, treated with 12-step abstinence course
>
> *Addiction to online games is becoming more widespread among vulnerable young people, according to a treatment centre that has begun running abstinence courses in Britain.*

Fortunately, "a treatment centre that has begun running abstinence courses" isn't going to be entirely unbiased in its opinions here, so I feel free not to listen to a word it says.

Unfortunately, the anxious parents who pack their kids off to such places aren't going to think quite the same way as me.

The Writer's Journey

The Hero with a Thousand Faces is a dense and difficult work. Coincidentally, many full-time writers are also dense and difficult. They want to follow the formula of the hero's journey, but without the bother of having to understand why it works.

Encountering this problem, screenwriter Christopher Vogler summarized the hero's journey in a short studio memo while working at Disney (and as a result the movie associated with it, *The Lion King*, is pretty well textbook monomyth). Following this, he realized that there was a demand for a user-friendly interpretation of the hero's journey, so he wrote *The Writer's Journey*[5] to meet it.

The writer's journey has fewer steps (12 rather than 17) than the hero's journey, and is easier to reconcile with Syd Field's paradigm. It's helped a lot of people create powerful storylines. However, stories are short-term affairs; the identity growth that the writer's journey ultimately derives from takes much longer than a story to appreciate—it has to be lived, not told.

---

[5]Christopher Vogler: *The Writer's Journey: Mythic Structures for Writers*, Michael Wiese Productions, 3ʳᵈ Edition 2007. http://www.thewritersjourney.com/

The writer's journey is an example of an *abstraction layer*. Each such layer simplifies the one before it:

- Base level: actual human experience.
- Shared and multiple retellings of this experience emerging as myths.
- Campbell's interpretation of mythic structure.
- Vogler's interpretation of Campbell.
- Later simplifications of Vogler, for people who like paint-by-numbers plotting.

Vogler can help us understand Campbell; Campbell can help us understand myth; myth can help us understand human experience. Neither Vogler, Campbell, nor myth is *prescriptive*, however: they're *descriptive* of something that goes on at a deep, fundamental level for all of us.

Trying to write an MMO to follow the hero's journey would be to miss the point; players *already* follow the hero's journey when they play. The hero's journey merely describes what's going on, *anyway*. The reason that designers need to be aware of it is only so that they don't do anything that gets in its way.

Art as Fun

I've explained that what MMO designers do is art, but why is it fun? I don't mean fun to *play*, I mean fun to *design?*

Let's recapitulate what's happening here. MMO designers design MMOs as a means of personal expression. They're artists, and MMO creation is their medium. Their MMOs are their way of articulating parts of their selves that they can't express any other way. In common with other artists, their art enables designers to *discover* themselves, if they want to do so.

Hmm, *discover* themselves. Now where have I heard *that* before?

Here's another graph:

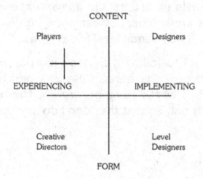

Players experience content; level designers implement form; designers implement content; creative directors (or lead designers) experience form.

Player to level designer to designer to creative director.

Designers are on their *own* kind of hero's journey, right from the moment they begin as a player. It's not as heavily signposted, and it takes much longer, but it's there.

Designers design for the same reasons players play: because it gives them the freedom to be and become themselves.

Everyone *wants* to be a designer because, in some sense, they already *are* designers.

The Carpenters

The Carpenters were a brother-and-sister duo who were the best-selling American musical act of the 1970s. Their records still get airplay today—*Close to You, We've Only Just Begun, Rainy Days and Mondays, Yesterday Once More, Calling Occupants, Please Mr. Postman*, and many more.

The big attraction of the Carpenters was Karen's voice. Richard was the keyboard player. In 1979, when Richard had to take a year out to recover from accidentally getting addicted to sleeping pills, Karen went solo. After all, keyboard players are ten a penny, right?

Karen's resulting album was so bad that music industry executives refused to release it. When it finally appeared in 1996, you could understand their point. Sure, Karen could sing superbly, but she had *poor critical faculties*. She couldn't tell which songs were appropriate for her voice and which ones weren't.

Few members of the general public knew it at the time, but Richard was the real genius of the act. His musical instincts, coupled with his world-class skills in arrangement, meant that he, not Karen, was actually responsible for most of the duo's success. Karen's voice alone was insufficient to sell albums, and it only worked with particular melodies—melodies selected and arranged by Richard specifically to showcase her voice.

Lesson for game designers: no matter how good you (think you) are, *always* get a second opinion. You don't have to conform to it, but always get it.

Eating Your Own Food

When a chef sits down and eats their own meal, they're not eating the same meal that everyone else in the restaurant is eating. They understand the meal at a different level to everyone else. They can't stop being a chef and become a diner; they're always going to be a chef.

It's the same when MMO designers play their own MMO.

Games You Should Have Played #4

A spectator sport.

If a game of any kind is interesting enough that people will pay to watch it played, you should make some effort to understand what it's like to play it. This gives you an insight into the theatrical aspects of games that you wouldn't easily get from merely observing the performance. You don't actually have to be any *good* at the game, and the game itself doesn't have to be all that good either (in my case, *Snooker* fits both these categories); the important thing to understand is what gives a game charisma. I don't care whether this aspect is high skill, clever strategy, visceralness, or physicality—if you don't play, you won't entirely appreciate it.

In my own case, at school I played *Association Football*—colloquially, soccer (attacking midfielder, if you must know); I was good, but we were never taught any ball skills, and most games descended into kicking matches. This was nevertheless enough for me to come to understand what makes it "the beautiful game." I watch it to this day.

The Wisdom of Game Designers

In the same way that the wisdom of crowds doesn't stop Garry Kasparov from beating the rest of the world at *Chess*, it doesn't help any one design a better MMO. A first-rate designer genuinely *could* and almost certainly *would* design a better game than any number of players. The designer:

- Can see further than the mean distance.
- Keeps ideas consistent and coherent.
- Can explore new, original avenues.
- Has a piece of their *soul* in the game—the "vision."

Individual players don't like being told that a world-class designer knows what they want as a group better than they do, but unfortunately for them, that's how it is.

Nesingwary's Mastery Quests

The Nesingwary "mastery" quests are in Stranglethorn Vale in *World of Warcraft*. STV is a problematic zone for a number of reasons to do with the consequences of earlier design decisions. In particular, it is the first zone in which Alliance and Horde characters come into regular contact with each other—which on a PvP server inevitably involves serial ganking.

Here's how I first read the Nesingwary quests, taken from the Alliance point of view. This was pre-*Cataclysm*, so much of this has now changed.

So, STV has a jungle setting (which, given the ganking, should come as no surprise). The place is teeming with wildlife—tigers, gorillas, panthers, raptors, basilisks, and more. Those characters with the skinning craft (often hunters) will want to kill scores of these beasts because pickings were slim in the previous, undead-dominated zone. Other character classes are also given a motive to kill the critters: big cats will annoyingly attack them when they follow the road. If they try to kill these cats *before* they're attacked, they'll aggro a bunch more of them and end up having to run for it.

Players are being clearly set up to want to kill "big game" here; why, then, are there no early quests to do just that?

Well, the answer is that when you finally *do* come across such quests, you're *more* up for them than you would be if they were there as soon as you entered STV. Even if you don't like them, the chances are you would have disliked them even more without this groundwork.

The mastery quests are handed out at a point where an east/west valley meets a north/south river. If you were looking at a place to put an important quest hub, this would be it. Players are *meant* to find it. So what is it they do find?

The quests come in three sets of four: kill the young, regular, and elder versions of panthers, tigers, and raptors, plus a boss for each. There's a final, kill the boss-of-bosses quest, as a pay-off. So basically we have the same kill-10-rats quest nine times, plus four boss encounters. It's just routine, then?

Well no, because these quests are *stepped*: the levels appropriate for the tiger mastery steps are 31, 33, 35, and 37; for the panther mastery steps, they're 31, 33, 38, and 40; for the raptor mastery steps, they're 34, 36, 41, and 43. This interleaving allows for variety, and it dispatches the players off to various different parts of STV where the target creatures congregate, thereby causing happy interactions with other quests relating to areas they pass through.

However, even though this is very well done, as it stands it's basically just highly-capable craftsmanship. What we *also* have here, though, is some actual *art*.

The stepped nature of these hunting quests mean that whatever level you first encounter the Nesingwary camp in STV, there's going to be a quest of an appropriate challenge for you. You *will* encounter them, too, because there are several east/west valleys that, if you fall into them, it's much easier to follow them than it is to get out. They lead either to the camp itself or to the river—and thence the camp. It's like a net, spread wide to catch players.

You saw that? A *net*, spread wide to *catch* players?

The Nesingwary camp is a content trap, and the players fall right into it. They may *believe* that they're in the driver's seat, hunting down the wildlife that Nesingwary and his colleagues have listed, but it's the players *themselves* who are prey. This quest hub is saying: as you do unto others, so shall others do unto you. It's saying this in the zone where PvP first happens on an industrial scale. That's simply *stunning!* I was *awed* when I first saw it.

There's much, much more to these quests than I've described here[6]. There's the way the zone is shaped like a funnel, the pressure for players to spark down the road, the turning point of Booty Bay, and the whole hunter-and-hunted motif that brings it all together.

I've described this to you so that I could show a glimpse of something which only a few people would normally even care to notice: the ability of MMOs to *tell* players things. The example I chose, the Nesingwary mastery knot of quests, uses internal symbolism to help players transition from PvE to PvP. It even has some weak external symbolism ("Hemet Nesingwary" is a somewhat forced anagram of "Ernest Hemingway"). It's art.

It's *art*.

---

[6]Richard Bartle: The Hunter and the Hunted. QBlog, May 2009.
http://www.youhaventlived.com/qblog/2009/QBlog170509A.html

Fire in their Bellies

When Roy Trubshaw and I worked on *MUD1*, we saw it as a means of giving people freedom. For players, freedom to do and to be; for us, freedom to make our imaginations real (well, OK, virtual). Most of the early UK MMOs that followed had that same sense of idealism.

Yet I look at today's big hitters and I wonder: what happened?

Players still have freedoms, but they're overly-restricted. The designers don't let you be who you *want* to be, just who from a number of class/race combinations you *think* you want to be when you start out. They don't let you do what you *need* to do because then you might upset random people inconvenienced by it in some small way. The limitations are much stronger than they were before: even the designers themselves have less freedom, being increasingly wrapped in creative paradigms from which they can't escape.

Why is this? Well, today's graphical worlds have many more players than the old textual ones, and this makes it harder to monitor abuses of freedom. Is it therefore merely a question of scale?

I don't think so: these constraints began to creep in well before graphical worlds appeared in number. Also, some of the restrictions (such as character classes) aren't linked to abuse in the same way that, say, PvP is.

No, it's something deeper than this. Designers make these kinds of decisions primarily because they have an artistic vision of what their MMO should be like. Their design articulates some inner conviction or conflict of a kind that other people might express through writing, painting, or composing. MMOs are therefore manifestations of their designers' core philosophy.

Philosophy that affects others isn't philosophy, though: it's politics. *MUD1* and its peers were highly liberal by today's standards, and nowhere near as paternalistic. Through their code, people gained freedom—and learned that responsibility went with such freedom. Basically, *MUD1* reflected the hacker ethic that Roy and I entertained when we wrote it (and still do today).

Although it may be convenient to say that the hacker ethic in today's MMOs has been crushed by commerce, I don't believe that's an issue here, either. Designers still have plenty of scope to create worlds that reflect all kinds of views of How Things Should Be. It's just that most of them are happy with How Things Are, so they don't. MMOs select for hackers, but that doesn't mean the hackers understand the *power* they have.

Wistful though I am for the kind of virtual world I wanted more than 30 years ago, I'm not proposing we now turn back the clock. I'd kinda like to know why it is the clock doesn't seem to be ticking, though, and why there aren't different time zones.

Where are the designers with *fire* in their bellies?

Characters' Character

Decades of playing virtual worlds means I can now become immersed at the flick of a switch. I've created so many characters in the past and played them through that it's now easy for me to don any character I've created, effortlessly.

This has applications outside MMOs. For example, if I'm writing fiction, then I don't have to think about how a particular character would act: I simply have to explain the situation to them, and they'll tell me how they would act. Then I can immediately switch to another character and see how they respond.

It's rather fun, to be honest, although it works better for screenplays than novels.

The more that people play MMOs, the more that they will come to understand other people. Swapping characters in and out is a mere party trick; empathizing with other people is a life skill.

Crown Film Unit

During the Second World War, the Crown Film Unit in Britain churned out more than 300 films. All of them were documentaries—generally pretty good ones, too!

The thing is, though, they *were* documentaries. Although some were entertaining, entertainment wasn't their purpose: their purpose was conveying information. Although Britain had been a pioneer of movie-making in the 1930s, the government of the day only funded serious films; entertainment was regarded as too low-brow to merit public funding.

So where is the British film industry today as a result of this? Well, our documentaries are often superb; but in terms of entertainment, Hollywood ate our lunch. Nowadays, we have to subsidize our film industry to keep it alive.

Games today, like films in the early 1940s, need to be "serious" to attract government funding. I think that's probably all I need to say for you to see where I'm going with this.

Funding bodies and university research departments are not interested in games-as-games. It will be 20 years before today's game-playing students become tomorrow's game-playing professors, by which time it could be too late. I suppose, just *maybe*, the reality of the economic power of games could outweigh institutional distaste for popular forms of entertainment sooner. Judging by the experience of Film in this regard, however, I won't be placing any bets on it.

Demeaning

Doesn't it demean players to call the world they are a part of a "work of art"?

If so, that can't be helped. MMOs *are* works of art, whether we like it or not.

Game Design Mistakes Every Designer Makes #2

Designers don't fully understand the power they have.

Games can and do transform people's lives, and I don't mean by turning quiet school kids into cold-blooded killers (that's the job of opera…). I mean they liberate the imagination, free the soul, and allow people to *be*. MMOs are especially good in this regard.

Designers are hesitant to believe this.

One reason for their hesitancy is, as I've just explained, that games are regarded as low-brow, populist culture, much as movies were in the 1930s and 1940s. "How presumptuous that a base form of entertainment aspires to compete with millennia-old established art forms such as literature, theatre, poetry, blah blahblah…" Remember: games *predate* all these! They are one of the most ancient forms of expression around. Hold your head up high, games!

You can do *amazing* things with games that you simply can't do with *anything else*. Games have **power**. Good Designers suspect this, but they figure they must be wrong (because if they were right, why wouldn't games be ubiquitous?). Consequently, they hold their fire. Not-so-good designers don't even realize they have fire to hold.

Game designers need to wise up to the fact they have freedom to design. They can do anything with games! Anything! The only shackles you wear are the ones you put on yourself. Don't leave game design to non-designers: that way leads to Skinner Box World. You *have* the power, so *use* it!

So why is not understanding the power you have a game design mistake? Well, it's because it confines design. If you limit your horizons, you never reach those horizons: you work within artificial boundaries that you should be far beyond. How can you ever say something if you forbid yourself from using the very words that say it?

Note that not realizing the power of games is also a mistake every non-designer makes.

Magazine Reviews

Much game criticism today takes the form of online and print magazine reviews.

How these work:

- Game publisher gives editor/journalist blogger/podcaster a review copy of the latest beta a month before launch (three months for print magazines because of the slower turnaround).

- Reviewer plays the beta for a few hours (if playable) and takes some screenshots (if not provided) and videos.

- Reviewer writes/records a review.

- Magazine/blog/podcast releases review at an agreed date, usually before the launch date.

What if the review is upbeat?

- Game publisher is happy.

What if the review isn't upbeat?

- Game publisher is reticent to send betas to this reviewer in future.

- Magazine/blog/podcast loses readers/viewers (because others get the scoops).

- Game publisher takes out fewer ads on the review site.

- Game publisher is reluctant to pay the reviewer (or the reviewer's agent) to look at future releases.

- Review site loses money.

Hmm. Is that the best environment for reading honest, unbiased opinion?

Well no, it's not—and it's incredibly annoying that the argument was hijacked by #gamergate, as a result of which we're not going to see much change to the situation any time soon.

Society Speaks

Society doesn't build MMOs. Those who do build them can therefore use them to say things about society that they couldn't say if they were speaking on behalf of society.

Why does no one want to take this power to shape society and *do* something with it?

There are different ways of looking at MMOs in terms of the politics they embody. My lament is that these days they mainly have the *same* politics, and it's largely uninspired. Why are designers wandering meekly across the political landscape like sheep when they could be charging at it like bulls? You can say things through MMO design that *can't be said* in other ways. I want designers to realize that, and if possible, to *act* on it. Society affects MMOs, but MMOs can *also* affect society. If real life society is so perfect, why do people play MMOs? And if real life society is imperfect, why can't MMOs work to change it through their players?

MMO designers have beliefs, opinions, anger, and dreams, but they don't make much of them in their designs. Why not?

We're getting these homogenous world views because designers *don't follow their own passions*. It's not that they can't, or they won't: it's that they *don't realize* they *can*.

I repeat: where are the designers with *fire* in their bellies?

A Somewhat Limited Audience

How many designers in the whole world have put enough of their soul into one or more MMOs *and reflected upon it* that they can appreciate the way other designers have done their thing? It should be that *every* serious designer can do this—and that most long-term players should have their own views of what a world's designer is saying through their design, too. Yet how many actually *can*?

Back in 2004, I said there were maybe 20 such designers, world-wide. The remark passed without comment.

I said the same thing again five years later and was flamed for it from two directions simultaneously that can be summarized as follows:

- There are no designers who can do this.
- Every designer and most players can do this.

So, that "20" should be "between 0 and 20,000,000," then. My mistake.

The Price of Man and Woman

In his 2003 study[7] of *EverQuest* characters offered for (black market) sale on playerauctions.com, economist Ted Castronova discovered that the average price was $333. However, female avatars cost $40–$55 less than their equivalent male avatars. There are no differences in capabilities between genders in the game itself, so why don't they cost the same at auction?

Well, two answers were speculated in the original paper:

- Female characters are assumed to be played by less effective players. This would be because of discriminatory beliefs imported from the real world.

- More men play *EverQuest* than women, and in general they prefer to play using male avatars.

The second of these is a supply-and-demand, market-size thing. The first says that MMORPG PLAYERS ARE SEXIST SHOCK HORROR! Well, it does if you're a journalist looking for a men-value-women-less-than-they-value-men story. Actually, players of whatever gender value a character's *level* far ahead of anything else.

OK, so MMO players may well *be* sexist, but there are other, less contentious ways of explaining the price discrepancy. Here are some examples (most of which, like the study itself, draw on the well-known positive correlation between player gender and character gender):

- The biggest determinant of avatar price by a long way is its level. Perhaps fewer women are into the power-gaming thing, so they have no desire to buy avatars, so the demand for female avatars is lower?

- Women in the real world are paid less than men, so perhaps they can't afford to pay as much as men for avatars?

- Perhaps the people who manufacture characters for sale on the market as a business distort the market by their own avatar gender preferences?

- To find out the price of avatars, the winning bids in auctions were used. Actually, most characters were bought using a "buy it now" option. Perhaps more women prefer this option, so fewer of them will bid for female avatars in auctions, so the demand was lower and the price was consequently less?

---

[7]Ted Castronova: *The Price of 'Man' and 'Woman': A Hedonic Pricing Model of Avatar Attributes in a Synthetic World.* 2003. http://papers.ssrn.com/sol3/papers.cfm?abstract_id=415043

- According to the study, 18.3% of all players have a female main character, yet 20.1% of avatars in the auction are female. Perhaps the price is lower because more people (of whatever gender) who are in possession of female characters want to sell them?

- Avatars aren't spread evenly for sale by gender. Female characters are skewed towards lower levels (where there is an over-supply) and male characters are skewed towards higher levels (where supply is limited). Perhaps this supply-and-demand imbalance is important?

- Perhaps female players are more particular about what their avatars look like, so they won't bid on ones with which they don't identify, therefore most sell for a lower price as there's less demand?

- Perhaps the order in which characters were presented for sale at playerauctions.com influenced how much people bid for them?

- Equipment is linked to level, but it's not the same for all characters of equal level. It could be that male players want different equipment to what female players want. Perhaps the equipment for female avatars is therefore less desirable to male players (who outnumber female players) than that for male avatars?

- The Terms of Service for *EverQuest* banned the trade in avatars. Perhaps female players are more law-abiding than male players?

I don't actually agree with all of these, but then I don't agree with the speculation that female characters are undesirable to the tune of $40 each merely because some male players think that female players can't play. I think it's far more likely that men who devalue female avatars do so because, for social and psychological reasons, they don't want to play a character that is a gender other than their own. The same could also be said of female players devaluing male characters (in fact more so, as more men play cross-gender than women do). As there were more male than female players of *EverQuest* in 2003, female avatars were therefore harder to sell, so the price for them dropped to compensate.

What the study definitely shows is that men have to pay more than women to buy an avatar that matches their real-world gender. As sexism arguments go, for women this is definitely a cloud with a silver lining.

May the Force be Without Me

On May 4th, 2012, I cancelled my *Star Wars: the Old Republic* account. I would have done it earlier, but I held out because I wanted to see if anything special happened because of the date (it didn't).

By this time, *SW:TOR* was shedding players. I believe that the fundamental reason for this was the too-large dissonance between the leveling game and the elder game. The leveling game is all about story and solo play; the elder game is all about group play and grinding through dailies. There's too much of a disconnect, especially for players new to MMOs (which *SW:TOR* was very good at attracting). If new content had been added to the *leveling* game in patch 1.2, things could have been different. However, the new content added was at the *elder game*; indeed, the developers' view seemed to be that players would want to skip through the leveling game quicker on their alts, judging by the introduction of shared buffs across all your characters and legacy items you could use to over-gear them. *SW:TOR* was sold on the strength of its story elements; *of course* encouraging players to scoot through the story to get to a generic endgame was going to cost it players.

Which has the better story, *SW:TOR* or *WoW*? Well, *SW:TOR*. Which has the better elder game? Well, *WoW*. Why did it make sense, then, for *SW:TOR* to be all about the elder game? Bioware had the chance to put its story-based philosophy on the line and give us something different, but when decision time came, it passed. Oh well. So *SW:TOR* became just another MMO, then.

The game does have its strengths. The companion system adds to the gameplay (once you get the right companion, which for my smuggler was tiresomely late). The storylines also work well, even if they are a bit predictable (I foresaw what my Jedi knight would be doing at the end well in advance—oh, but I *hated* the end of Chapter 2: you *do not* wrest control of a character from the player in an MMO). I think the combat system was well-designed, well-balanced, and allowed good players to outshine worse players with better gear; other MMOs could learn from it. I also liked the space combat mini-game, but that may have been because I was unexpectedly superb at it–probably from playing so much *Starfire* in the arcade where I worked in my teens.

The game's weaknesses were mainly to do with either its over-copying of *WoW*'s mechanics or its integration of single-player story into a multiplayer environment. If my character has just inherited a vast spacefleet from putting down a rebellion, why am I going into this same cave to rescue the same prisoners I rescued yesterday to help out the same officer who's standing in the same place with the same sob story about his own incompetence? Also, if the story is of primary importance, then so must be the fiction that supports the story: that being the case, how come my gunslinger can call my spaceship to fly by and do area-of-effect damage that works underground and in Rakata mind traps?

Unusually, though, for *SW:TOR* there was an actual, identifying point of design that finally persuaded me that the wrong people were winning the designer arguments.

Yes, I'll tell you what it was—whether you want me to or not.

Player Type Misuses #1

Some designers apply Player Type theory to get results. They don't care *why* it works, just that it *does* work—it's like a magic formula, a means to an end.

Such designers will write their game to fit the theory, then afterwards, when they test it, they will find that it has worked: lo and behold, analysis shows that all of the player types are present in their game and no others. The theory works! Job done!

Except, *of course* the player types are all present: you wrote your game to fit the theory! You herded players into the four types. There could have been a dozen other different player types that dropped out because the game was only aiming to attract those four.

If your design filters for four types, you're only going to get those four types. It's self-fulfilling design.

"Saving Silverlake"

Just so that the WoW players among you don't think it's only WoW that has oh-dear-oh-dear morally doubtful quests, here's one from *Vanguard: Saga of Heroes* to cheer you up:

- A Zar cult has taken over some farmers near a town called Silverlake by possessing them with Zar souls.

- A group called the United Races of Thestra (the URT) wants to ingratiate itself with the inhabitants of Silverlake, so it decides to free the farmers.

- A group of bandits has stolen the URT's "soul render" device, which can suck the Zar souls out of the farmers. You have to go get it from them.

- Once you have killed sufficient bandits to obtain the soul render, you use it to suck the Zar souls out of ten farmers. The souls attack you, but the farmers don't because they're left in a daze.

- The URT learns that the soul render not only sucked out the Zar souls, it sucked the farmers' own souls out, too. They're not in a daze, they're basically zombies. If this is noticed, the locals won't like it.

- Zombie farmers are attracted by the dust of gargoyle-like creatures called Netherbeasts. You need to kill a bunch of them to collect 25 piles of dust.

- You use the dust to lure three zombie farmers, one at a time, to Silverlake's nearby mill. There, you kill each one and put their bodies into the meat grinder to dispose of the evidence.

- Finally, you conceal the pieces of ground-up farmer meat in a food barrel, and you're done. The reward is a nice piece of leg armor.

Vanguard flagged the quest as being played for laughs from the beginning because the URT were already established as a well-meaning but incompetent outfit. Nevertheless, say what you like about WoW, you're unlikely to be asked to make burgers out of farmers in it.

I Could Be Wrong

That reading of the Nesingwary mastery quests I gave could be utter hogwash. Blizzard might have used trained chimps to do the design, and I've been seeing patterns where there are none.

Well, I don't care. The reason I don't care is because, however those quests got there, for whatever reasons—conscious or subconscious—they made me *think*. I came away from them knowing a little bit more about quest design than I did before I went in.

I'm a designer, though. Players don't care about artistic content, so long as what they're playing is fun.

Should they care, though?

Welcoming Newbies

Today's MMOs are more welcoming to newbies than were the old, textual worlds. Their built-in tutorials ease the players into the game and set them on their way gently.

Today's MMOs are less welcoming to newbies than were the old, textual worlds. Their players rarely say anything to one another, except to spam general chat with questions because they can't be bothered to look up the answers that beta-testers have put on the Internet.

What player types are you trying to welcome?

Is being welcoming a good thing or a bad thing anyway?

If you don't wrap newbies in brushed cotton and feed them sweet marshmallows on silver spoons, then sure, your MMO won't be as welcoming for some players. However, it might be more immediately fun for others.

Everyone's a Critic

Suppose you were a restaurant critic (or, if you are one, don't assume it).

As a restaurant critic, what can you legitimately comment on in a restaurant review?

Here are some suggestions:

- The location and type of restaurant.
- The ambience of the restaurant.
- The service (wait staff, waiting time).
- The price.
- The reputation of the chef.
- The quality of the food served to you.
- The quantity of food served to you.
- The preparation of the food.
- How well the menu dishes go together.

Suppose you were a computer game critic. Actually, scratch that: when it comes to computer games, everyone's a critic.

What are the computer game equivalents of what a restaurant critic can comment on in a review?

- The platform and genre of game.
- The look-and-feel of the game.
- The service (customer service, patches).
- The price.
- The reputation of the developer/designer.
- The quality of gameplay you encountered.
- The quantity of gameplay you encountered.
- The polish of the game.
- How well the various aspects of gameplay go together.

Restaurants are mainly about the food, so restaurant reviews will focus on that. Computer games are mainly about the gameplay, so game reviews will focus on that.

Game reviews tend to feature a lot of eye candy, though, especially if the beta the critic was playing is too thin or non-functional to give them much to write about. Pictures make great padding.

Themselves

MMO players aren't trying to create an identity they didn't have before; rather, they're trying to find which of the many possible identities they could wear fits their true self best.

Games You Should Have Played #5

A game in which you can lose actual money.

There is a dark side to games, and gambling gives people a chance to sense it. Personally, I don't like playing games for money at all; however, a lot of people love it. Everyone has their limits, though.

For some, gambling games are at their best when the amounts involved actually hurt if you lose them; for others, it's the amounts that can be won that make the difference. The point of playing a gambling game from the perspective of this list is to gain an appreciation of the *morality* of games. When something stops being "just a game" and starts to take over the player's life, that's potentially a bad thing. Unless you've seen this kind of obsession in someone, you're never going to understand that fully. Gambling games let you do that. **Warning:** you run a big risk with this if it turns out *you're* the one who gets hooked, so if you do try it and you do get hooked, don't blame me. That's just in case you were thinking of suing me for bad advice and then spending the money you win in damages betting on horse races.

For me, I used to play *Poker* with my friends over lunch when I was 17 or 18. We played for Tic-Tac mints. This was before *Texas Hold 'Em* got big, so we'd play mainly *Draw Poker*, *5-Card Stud*, *7-Card Stud*, or, occasionally, *Montana Red Dog*. We stopped playing when one of my friends, who consistently lost, had to borrow money to buy more Tic-Tacs; I decided things had gone far enough and called the lunchtime sessions off. From that point on, there was *no way* I would design a game that deliberately tried to addict someone to it, and I was mindful of possible accidental addiction, too.

The Heart of a Review

When providing a critique of a game, a critic can either assume the player has played the game or assume the opposite. The latter is the *review* format.

The job of a critic is to appraise a game, not merely to describe it. Describing is only useful insofar as it lays out what is being appraised. In a review, it's enough to say, "*Star Wars* concerns the journey of a young man, Luke Skywalker, from farmer's boy to galactic hero." You don't have to go into the details of the storyline; indeed, you shouldn't: there's a reason that such reveals are called "spoilers."

Critiques can be for players, for designers, for academics, or for others. Reviews are normally for players, though, so critics writing them concentrate on the player experience: what's fun and what isn't; why it's fun and why it isn't. They note similarities to and differences from other games, and say what these mean.

Well, the good ones do, anyway. You're a good one, right? So what should the heart of the review concern?

The heart of a game review should almost always concern the gameplay. If everything else is perfect, dud gameplay will still kill a game. Mechanics can be mentioned if they're particularly sweet or sour, but it's gameplay that matters; mechanics merely support the gameplay. The same is true of the story, the graphics, and the interface. All of these can be awful, but the game can still be fun. All of them can be wondrous, but the game can still be awful. The only reason not to put gameplay at the heart of a review is if some other aspect is so bad you don't get far enough to experience the gameplay.

To appraise a game properly, the critic has to understand the game at a number of levels. They have to be objective. They have to remember that they aren't "the player" or "the designer"; they're "the critic". The player is reading the critic's words for the critic's informed opinion. The designer is reading the critic's words for the same reason, but with different intent. Nevertheless, criticism—educated criticism—is useful to both.

When it comes to computer games, everyone's a critic. However, not everyone is a *decent* critic.

Player Type Misuses #2

Some designers knowingly apply Player Type theory beyond its limits. They see an analogy between what they're doing and what Player Type theory says. "Hey, these guys seem to think like achievers. Hmm…"

Sometimes, this does actually seem to be useful. It's only useful *if* you remember that it's just an analogy, though.

As an, er, analogy of the analogy, it's like teaching how electricity works by saying it behaves the same way that water does in pipes. This electronic-hydraulic approach is great for getting across the basics of circuits and valves and cells, and even voltage and amperage. However, if you cut a pipe, then water flows out; if you cut a circuit, electricity does not flow out. The analogy has limits.

With the Player Type model, you can extend it to a different domain if it helps, sure, so long as you remember that you're only in the realm of "works like the model" and not "is the model." You may have killers and achievers in your non-MMO domain, for example, but that doesn't mean they'll interact with the same effects as in an MMO.

Old Ideas

When new designers ask me to look at their projects, well over half of the Fantasy ones have a four-elements magic system as part of it (fire, earth, water, air). Sometimes, if they're really keen, they'll add another one (wood) or another two (life, death).

A good half of the remaining designs are of the "magic returns after nuclear apocalypse" variety.

Don't worry, it's a phase, you grow out of it.

SW:TOR Consular Gear

This is what my Jedi consular looked like in her full Rakata gear (which was the highest tier prior to patch 1.2 in *Star Wars: the Old Republic*).

She may have strange roof tiles on her wrists and shoulders, but she looks pretty classy in that all-white ensemble. The hat is like a Shell petrol logo with added elf ears, which is why I don't show it; nevertheless, it's easy to believe that she's an important, respected, and powerful Jedi wearing an outfit like this.

Here's what she would have looked like if she'd obtained all her Black Hole gear, which is the upgrade introduced in patch 1.2:

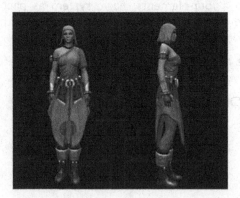

She looks like she's some kind of cavewoman. It's a ghastly, inappropriate statement of an outfit in that most authoritative of colors, sludge brown. Why would anyone remotely interested in their character's story want to swap from the Rakata gear to this? For all I know, it could be deeply-rooted in Star Wars lore, and we're supposed to be impressed by the attention to detail. However, if you want someone to play for *story* reasons, rather than gear reasons, you can't expect them to prefer such an off-the-shoulder abomination over what they had before.

Seeing this, I realized it meant that the developers didn't *expect* players to like it for its look. This in turn meant they didn't see their players as being story-philes, but as being raidingphiles.

My questions as to how this game was going to go in future were thereby all answered, so I didn't need to play it any more.

That's when I cancelled my account.

Making a Point

In *MUD1*, permanent death meant players rapidly learned that attacking one another was a losing strategy: the gameplay promoted co-operation, or at least respect for other players.

I've just spent a chunk of this book arguing that MMO designers are artists: now, I'm challenging them to *do* something with that art.

An MMO that taught pacifists to behave violently would be making an opposite point to *MUD1*—but at least it *would* be making it.

Inversion

MUD was distinct from *Reality*, but bound to it: *Reality* is a place where the world is real but the people false; *MUD* was a place where the world was false but the people real.

You go to a pretend place to find the real you because, in the real world, you're always pretending to be someone else.

Games You Should Have Played #6

A game released in the year you were born.

Most games are built on the foundations of games that went before them, and an appreciation of their history means you appreciate the games themselves more. Games have a *very* long history (indeed, they go back into prehistory), but a modern game is unlikely to quote directly from ancient archetypes. It's more probable that they're going to quote from games from a generation or two before them. Therefore, you should play a bunch of old games to see where the advances were made.

Unfortunately, "old" is a relative term: what *you* think is old might, to me, seem fairly new. What would qualify as old for either of us is something from the year in which we were born (or a year close to that). Play a game from back then and see how things have (or haven't) changed. Bonus: you're almost guaranteed to notice the gameplay more than you do in a (what currently looks) slick, modern game.

For me, the old game would be the board game *Diplomacy*, which was released commercially in 1959 (the year before my birth, but that's near enough). Ah, what a game! It's trapped in its time because it needs seven players and so can only really be played by post. Play-by-email is even more of a niche than play-by-mail was, so it's not a game that is played a lot nowadays.

Lovely mechanics, though!

The MMO Cycle

For MMO designers, creating a virtual world is a journey of the self (in the same way that for players, playing is a journey of the self). When the players *themselves* become designers, that's where the original designer's journey ends (and a thousand new ones begin).

All Very Sad

One of the things about long-term, stuck-in-a-rut griefers is that they will often accuse others of being griefers: "*I* wanted to do something and *you* stopped me, so *you* are a griefer." They'll say this irrespective of your motives and of your awareness of them: it puts the griefer at the center of the universe and objectifies the other players.

Player Type theory tells us that players move between types. Most people who grief will indeed soon grow out of it, but some don't. As in any hero's journey, sometimes it turns out that the protagonist simply isn't a hero.

In the case of serial griefers, what happens is that they get caught up in a feedback loop, in which they grief to show to themselves that they are superior to those whom they are griefing, but in order to do so have to betray a trust or take some other dubious action to get an edge. Afterwards, they feel the elation of victory, sure, but once that wears off they realize that they only "won" because they broke a social norm or picked on someone vulnerable. They're not really better than the other person, they're miserable, and…

So the cycle continues. Eventually, they don't even grief for the fun of it because they extrapolate from their own situation to that of their victims. Rather than empathizing with others, the long-term griefer will project their own lack of empathy onto them. Players become merely another part of the system to be gamed. The griefer retreats into their own little bubble.

Griefers who accuse other people of being griefers can sometimes be doing it as a way of griefing those other people, but more often than not they aren't. They're doing it because they've made so many other people be the victims they feel themselves to be, they think that's simply how things are.

All very sad.

Mulligan vs. Koster

Jessica Mulligan and Raph Koster are two of the five people I had in my list of the most important people in MMO history.

Jess used to author a very influential column she called *Biting the Hand*. In August 2001, she wrote an article which took the point of view that regarding MMO design as an art form was a bad thing. Here's the thrust of her argument[8]:

- Those are *real people* playing your MMO, but they're becoming incidental to its design.

- They sign up to play a game, but designers are making them unwilling participants in performance art!

- They are *not* mere objects to be controlled through the brilliance of the designer's creativity.

- This counter-productive elitism is due to designers' beliefs they are creating art.

In other words, if you treat MMOs as art, then the vision of the designer becomes more important than the experience of the players. Designers should serve players, not the other way round.

Jess being Jess, for the sake of balance she asked Raph to respond in the same column, which he did[9]. Raph's view was this:

- Art subsumes entertainment; it can do many things, of which "entertain" is but one.

- It brings a much-needed emphasis on craft, perfectionism, and ethics.

- Attacking articulations of artistic purpose undermines MMOs' struggle for legitimacy.

In other words, entertaining players is one of the constraints of the medium within which designers of MMOs operate. Designers do serve players because that's part of their art. Besides, you get better MMOs in the end this way.

Is Raph right? Is Jess right?

---

[8]Jessica Mulligan: *Just Give me a Game, Please*. Skotos, 2001. http://www.skotos.net/articles/BTH_07.html
[9]Raph Koster: *The Case for Art*. Skotos, 2002. http://www.skotos.net/articles/BTH_09.shtml

At times, designers *do* treat players as if they were merely an agglomeration of statistics, but then so do plenty of other professions: the people who decide where traffic lights go study traffic flows; they don't care how much you donate to charity or that you have a pet dog called Rufus.

At other times, designers create brilliant pieces of content that players hugely enjoy. Three years after this debate took place, *World of Warcraft* launched and showed exactly how much difference artistry and perfectionism could make. Then again, give any intelligent player $50,000,000 to play with, and they could probably come up with something fairly decent.

An idealist would say that Raph is correct: designers are artists, and creating the conditions for players to have fun is central to that art. A cynic would say that Jess is correct because too few designers actually *are* artists: those who profess artistic pretensions are arrogant or self-obsessed, and ultimately wind up screwing over their players.

Maybe I've spent too long as an academic, but it seems to me that the sooner we can teach would-be designers what being an artist *means*, the sooner we'll get designers who really are artists.

MMO design *is* an art; how could it not be?

What we need is for the people who have the "lead designer" job title actually to *be* designers.

Out and About

Here's a quote from an article in *The Independent* on Sunday, January 8th, 2006:

> "I'd rather my son take a more proactive, less habitual drug like cocaine, than lock himself away and play video games" says Roxanne Richardson, 35, who has a young son, and is expecting another. "It's so lazy. At least with pills and coke you're out and about doing something."

I don't know whether to laugh or cry.

Kind of a Newbie

So, as I mentioned a while back, there are usually two kinds of newbie:

- People who are new to all MMOs (absolute newbies).

- People who are new to this particular MMO (relative newbies).

Of these, the first kind are the best to have because people always adore the first virtual world they get into and will judge all others in the light of their experience there. They are loyal, and they will bring in their friends; they're a joy to have as players, too. Unfortunately, they're also very hard to come by, as there are fewer and fewer seams of them to be mined.

Most newbies are of the second kind. They played some other MMO in the past, they like the look of yours enough to try it, but they still want it to be exactly the same as their first love, and they'll go to the next big shiny if you can't hook them. If you spent a lot of advertising money to attract them from other MMOs, you've got them for just as long as someone doesn't outspend you (because, by definition, these are people whose play can be bought). This is one reason why new MMOs tend to launch with a subscription rather than free-to-play—this way, at least they'll get *some* money out of these people before they leave (if they didn't leave after having sampled the beta).

New products are still aiming to get MMO virgins because of the loyalty problems inherent in trying to lure players from existing MMOs. Where can they find them, though? Well, the hot spot is the casual market, but this means designers have to design worlds that are less intense, less conflicting, and less of what makes MMOs special in the first place. Furthermore, because such newbies will subsequently judge all MMOs to be like this, it means the worlds they play next will also have to be similarly devoid of any real sense of immersion.

Aside: this is one reason I'm not at all happy at the way virtual worlds are being pitched at children: they're going to grow up thinking all virtual worlds are (and, worse, *should be*) like what they play, and we could end up with a future made of weak, wishy-washy, adventure-free, aweless worlds that only exist to sell virtual objects to increasingly skeptical players.

However, I'm not entirely pessimistic, in that I see a new kind of newbie emerging: lapsed players (renewbies).

EverQuest managed to sell well over a million boxes in computer game stores, but it never had a million subscribers. People came, they dipped their toes in the water, and if they didn't like the temperature, they left. They liked the *idea* of MMOs, but they didn't get along with the way that *EverQuest* executed the idea. A good many of those lapsed *EQ* players signed up for *WoW*—and brought along friends and family, too.

It's not just MMOs. How many millions of people have tried *Second Life*? How many thousand are currently playing it? How many of those who were intrigued enough by the thought of virtual worlds to give *SL* a try, but who didn't think it was for them, would be likely to try some new virtual world that took out what they didn't like about *SL* and gave them more of what they did like? I'd expect a reasonable percentage of those millions of people to give it a whirl.

WoW's big innovation was a reversion to allowing solo play, which *EQ* had dropped (earlier textual worlds had featured it) in the belief that, if people were bound to groups, they were less likely to quit; this was true, but people who couldn't get into a group outnumbered them and quit in large numbers.

I wouldn't be at all surprised if the next out-of-nowhere MMO to bring with it a paradigm shift is one that targets lapsed MMO players, not current or virgin players.

Uncritical Separation

Computer games (or, as they're usually referred to in a Psychology context, "video games" or "videogames") are often discussed as a different kind of thing to other kinds of games (such as board games). I agree that they do bring new tools and techniques to the table, broadening the *types* of game you can design, but ultimately games are games.

Is a videogame implementation of *Chess* somehow closer to playing, say, *Assassin's Creed*, than it is to playing the board game version of *Chess*?

Heinrich

Attempts over the years by various authors to connect Player Type theory to existing theories of personality have always come to nothing, mainly because player types are to do with identity, not personality: they're about what players find fun, which (unlike personality) changes in predictable ways over time.

That isn't to say you can't link other aspects of MMOs to personality, though.

In *The Secret World*, one of the regular members of my raid group played under the name Heinrich. He used to be there every week, reliable as clockwork, but early in 2014 announced that he was going to stop playing for a while. He lives in Ukraine and was a supporter of the protest movement there—he called what was going on there a "revolution", which eventually it did indeed turn out to be. He wanted to participate because he felt he couldn't sit idly by and watch events unfold: he had to go out onto the streets and be counted, whatever the cost.

In late summer of 2014, I discovered that thankfully he'd made it through the subsequent upheaval. That's not why I mention this, though. The reason I mention it is that, in the raid group, he was our main tank.

That's what I mean about other aspects of MMOs linking to personality. If you're a tank, you're a tank.

Peace

What if, instead of using the word "war" in their titles, MMOs used the word "peace"? *World of Peacecraft; Guild Peaces; Peacehammer Online; Star Peace: the Old Republic?*

OK, maybe not *World Peace II Online*, but you get the picture.

Dialectics

The Mulligan *vs.* Koster debate comes down to deciding which is more important: entertainment or communication? Are MMOs there simply to entertain, or are they there to communicate some essential truth? Put another way, should designers give the players what the players think they want, or what the designers think they want?

This is an example of a *dialectic*—a contrasting or opposing set of views held by designers, the conflict between which is made manifest through an MMO's design.

Here are some other ongoing dialectics:

- **Direction *vs.* non-direction:** Is this a constrained, theme park world or a sandbox?

- **Responsibility *vs.* liability:** How do players' rights to do stuff stack up against their rights not to have stuff done to them?

- **Commodification *vs.* purity:** Can you spend real money for in-world advantage?

- **Genre *vs.* auteur:** Does the designer or the marketing department call the shots?

- **Social world *vs.* game world:** *LambdaMOO* or *DikuMUD*? *Second Life* or *World of Warcraft*?

When designers have philosophical differences, design differences result. By reading these differences in design, the differences in philosophy can be divined.

A designer makes artistic statements so as to work through internal conflicts. Dialectics arise when the artistic statements of other designers feed into these conflicts.

Designers don't figure out what to say and then say it through their design; they say it through their design and leave others to figure out what it means. This is because their design is *itself* their way of figuring what they're saying. It's the best language they have available to them to express what they want to express.

That's why MMO designers *are* MMO designers and not novelists, movie directors, playwrights, composers, choreographers, sculptors, photographers, librettists, architects, poets, or exceedingly bad rappers.

The Burbs

Here's a picture, *The Burbs*, by Richard Bartle[10]. Dated 2003, it's mixed media, 100cm by 125cm, and it sold for around £3,000.

Sadly for me, it's by a different Richard Bartle.

What's this a picture *of*? What's it *saying*?

Well, I asked Richard Bartle the artist and he *doesn't know*. He knows what the individual components mean (the "words"), but believes it's for others to read and interpret those words.

It's the same with MMOs. Designers have many ways of doing things, but they can only actually *do* one of them. So why choose that particular one? Why not do the same thing some other way?

---

[10]Richard Bartle: *The Burbs*. 2003. http://www.richardbartle.co.uk/

Ultimately, the designer *doesn't know*.

Next time you look at an MMO, try to figure out what the designer is saying through it. What's it *really* about?

Honorable Retirement

At the moment, the top level is in your MMO of choice is, well, let's call it N. Suppose that once you reached it, you kept accumulating XP until you got enough for level $N+1$; at that point, the MMO would ask you if you wanted to retire with honor or to carry on. If you said yes, you did want to retire, then you'd go on the roll of honor, the developer would send you a nice, full-color 3D printout of your character, and that would be that. You could come back to chat with your friends and rerun existing content and stuff, but there'd be no more achievement-oriented play, even if expansions came out. It would be game ended, although not quite game over.

If you said no, you'd carry on as you were.

Given this setup, can you imagine ever taking the retirement option?

If so, and if you could take it right now, would you?

Listening to Players

Ten percent of what players say is the kind of insightful, imaginative, pertinent information that designers want. The other 90 percent isn't. Unfortunately, as with user-created content, every player thinks that their suggestions are in the smaller fraction rather than the larger fraction.

Player opinion is a data stream that designers should respect and consider, but that's all it is. A designer would be have to be foolish or arrogant not to listen to ideas and suggestions, but the day that players dictate rather than inform a designer's actions, is the day that a virtual world loses its soul.

The Covenant

As I mentioned when talking about symbolism, the primary job of the lead designer of an MMO involves the following:

- Setting the fictional **context** of the MMO.

- Providing a set of possible **actions** that the players can do which make sense in this context.

- Offering a range of **goals** for the players, so they want to do what they can do.

- **Connecting** possibilities in such a way as to enable players to make decisions as to which actions they should perform or which goals they should pursue, and why.

So designers give you a fiction, tell you what you can do within it, suggest reasons why you might want to do it, and give several alternatives so you have to make decisions. If you don't think their offering is what you want from an MMO, you don't play it.

This sounds reasonable enough, but there's a problem: part of what people find entertaining about MMOs is anticipatory: *not knowing* quite what will happen in them. The designer therefore *can't* tell players exactly what is expected of them because that would spoil their fun! So how can players decide whether they'll like an MMO in advance of playing it?

Well, designers create a set of general expectations to show where the boundaries of what *could* happen lie. These boundaries concern a number of things, including the genre, gameplay, and ethical attitude. Designers make a covenant with players that what comes up will fall within these boundaries.

For example, if you're told a game is about knitting, you can't complain if it turns out to involve a lot of knitting. You can, however, complain if suddenly you find you're being asked to stab people to death with knitting needles. That's something that should have been mentioned up-front.

People don't like it when the covenant is broken. If you go to watch the fourth movie in a series, the first three of which have been about searching for supernatural artifacts, and it turns out near the climax that this fourth one has been about searching for space alien artifacts, you're going to be annoyed. Yes, Indiana Jones, don't pretend you don't know who I'm glaring at here.

The ethical aspect of the covenant is important. If you know the game is about guns, you can surmise that characters are going to get shot. If you object to that kind of thing, you don't play.

As an MMO example, when you start off as a death knight character in *World of Warcraft*, you're under the influence of an evil power. You can therefore expect to have to do evil things until you can break free. It makes sense in the context, and people who don't want to do evil things ever shouldn't play as death knights.

This doesn't always work, though, because designers don't always get their message across properly. I recall that in *Elder Scrolls IV: Oblivion* I knew there was a chance my character could be turned into a vampire, but that I didn't know it was almost guaranteed if you played the game all the way through, nor that it would be a very distasteful experience.

Designers can put in moral dilemmas for players to wrestle with, which players often like. "Do I feed the villagers or the nomads?" "Do I support the paranoid king or his power-hungry heir?" However, players will feel disturbed if the "correct" solution feels like the wrong one ("I'm supposed to… make a human sacrifice?!"). If the designer doesn't flag this, then the covenant has been broken. When that happens, the players have a hard time trusting the designer again.

You *can* overstep the covenant deliberately in certain circumstances, but you have to flag it. For example, *WoW*'s quest "Zenn's Bidding" has you kill creatures you know you're not supposed to, and then gives you a penitence quest to make up for it: it oversteps a boundary so as to establish it. Likewise, its "Army of the Dead" quest has you role-play the bad guy in order to find out just how bad he *is*.

I talked at length earlier about "The Art of Persuasion" so as to illustrate the importance of this. There is an unspoken covenant between the designer and the players, whereby the players trust the designer to give them a fun experience within certain parameters. If the designer oversteps those parameters, then they have to raise their hand and acknowledge it or the players won't know to give it any leeway. They will think the covenant has been broken. They will feel you have betrayed them.

What's more, you will have.

Ideal Designers

The Digital Games Research Association, DiGRA, is unusual in that it invites actual game designers to give keynotes at its conferences.

The first keynote for the 2009 conference was by Mark Healey, lead designer of *Little Big Planet*, and Kareem Ettouney, who was also deeply involved in the design. What they presented was a magnificent manifestation of what designers *are*. They showed a wide range of cross-disciplinary knowledge (that they didn't seem to be aware *was* a wide range), they explained what they were trying to do and how they did it (and even *why* they did it), and they spoke with a depth of understanding that left no doubt that their *souls* were in that game. Everything I tell people about the ideal designer was there: the imagination, the passion, the desire to articulate something that they couldn't articulate any other way.

Even the "designer-fun" thing was there. I got to pose the last question in the Q&A, so asked if they experienced more fun out of designing, playing, or having people play what they designed. For Kareem, it was the designing: he particularly liked jamming with other designers as a way to help give form to his ideas. Mark said that he didn't usually like playing his games, just designing them, but that he did like *LBP* and couldn't wait to play with it whenever he could. This sounds like a designing-games-for-yourself-to-play argument, which is usually the mark of a lesser designer; however, when he described what he *did* when he played it, it was all to do with using the tools for user-created content. In other words, when he "played," he was playing with designing (which, of course, is the mark of a greater designer).

My own keynote came next, but it wasn't such a success on account of how I managed to insult everyone in the audience indirectly at least once and one person directly to his face (I told him I hoped he went to hell in a handbasket).

5, 10, 20 Years

Over 30,000,000 copies of *The Very Hungry Caterpillar* have been sold. However, people who started out by reading it don't want to read more *Very Hungry Caterpillar*. They want to read more *books*.

Players of today's social games (which is to say games played on social networks—very few of which are actually social) are being educated to play computer games. They're becoming game-literate.

What will they be playing 5, 10, or 20 years from now? Well we don't know. What we can say, though, is that whatever it is it won't be the games they're playing now.

The same applies to MMOs. Today's players *will* want a richer, more sophisticated experience 5, 10, or 20 years from now. All that's holding us up is waiting for enough of them to be educated in the ways of MMOs to make the expense of making such MMOs viable.

To get a critical mass, you need the masses to be critical.

Addiction Problems

Addictiveness itself is not necessarily a problem: technically, we're all addicted to food. Where problems arise from addiction are in the physical, psychological, and social effects that the addiction has. If playing MMOs a lot has no more detrimental an effect on society than watching TV a lot, what does it matter if players are considered to be "addicted" to them?

This is assuming that MMOs *are* in general addictive, of course, rather than merely compelling.

Game Design Mistakes Every Designer Makes #3

Designers don't fully understand the responsibility they have.

There is a moral aspect to game design. The main way this operates is through the covenant that designers have with players. Because designers can't tell players in advance what their experience will be (as that would spoil the game), players have to trust designers not to cross any lines.

As I've mentioned, though, sometimes designers will betray that trust. It can happen through accident, incompetence, ignorance, or general wickedness. Few designers are consciously aware of the covenant—they understand it implicitly. No designer gives it enough thought, though.

Players must be given fair warning of where the boundaries lie before they're reached. Designers can—indeed, should!—cross *design* boundaries, but players have to know where they stand. It's just not *right* if they don't.

An area of responsibility that fell under the spotlight in 2010/2011 was to do with *social games* (that is, games on social sites such as Facebook). Most top social games are exploitative garbage and designers know it. However, "where there's muck there's brass," as we say in Yorkshire, so big-name designers were offered large sums to design such games. This raised an awkward question: how can anyone (least of all a designer, who knows exactly what they're doing) justify creating games that are *deliberately* intended to deceive, trap, and addict people?

I've spoken with pained designers who wrestled with this problem. Some justified it because they felt they could make changes from within—they saw themselves as pro-game fifth columnists. Some justified it because they saw it as merely a passing phase, like training wheels added to help non-gamers who are learning to become gamers. Some justified it in terms of "it's what people want," which is the same argument drug-dealers use. Some justified it as simply a remuneration package too good to refuse. None of these designers were entirely persuasive nor, in my view, persuaded.

So, why is abrogating responsibility a game design mistake?

Well, games are for players and players are people. If you don't treat players as people, you won't make games for people. Therefore, your designs will be lacking in humanity; and therefore, they will be lacking as designs.

Note that shirking responsibilities with respect to games is also a mistake every non-designer makes.

Victory for Art

If a work is not completed, can it said to be a work of art?

This is an important question for MMOs because they're never completed. They're designed with hooks in to add further changes, and when those changes are made, there are more hooks added. There is always more to add to them.

In Portsmouth, you can visit the ship HMS Victory.

You can stand on the very boards that were trod by sailors at Trafalgar. Except, a lot of them aren't those boards: the ship was damaged during the battle and was repaired; she remained in active service for another 100 years, during which period she was maintained; a lot more of the old wood was replaced. The masts aren't the masts that were at Trafalgar; indeed, the masts at Trafalgar probably aren't the ones the ship was built with—she was launched in 1765, 40 years before Trafalgar. Yet is the ship that sits in Portsmouth harbor HMS Victory? Yes, of course it is!

Is the *World of Warcraft* of today, which is different to that of 2004 and will be different from that of 2024, still *World of Warcraft*? Yes, of course it is! It's not "finished," but that's because part of the art of MMO design *assumes* that it will not be "finished," ever.

Note: this is actually the *Ship of Theseus* paradox, which has been known since ancient times. However, I've never been on the ship of Theseus, whereas I have been on HMS Victory…

Not the Players

There's a theory of art that goes something like this.

Art is created by artists. What the artist creates is a statement (a *text*) which those consuming the art *read*. The artist's intellectual ownership of the work is given up once it is finished, passing instead to those whose job it is to interpret it (the readers).

In this view, the reader makes of the artwork what they will. If they interpret it completely differently to what the artist intended or expected, well that's their prerogative. The artist had their say when they finished the work; the reader has it now.

For games, the artist is the designer and the reader is the player.

This point of view works as well for single-player games as it does for paintings, books, sculptures, plays, symphonies, dances, or any other form of expression. The designer expresses through the artwork; the player deals with the artwork on their own terms. This is how I've been approaching the topic in this book so far.

It seems to break down with massively-multiplayer games, though. The difficulty stems from a mistake made by almost all non-players, by many players, and by a good few designers, too. See, who *are* the readers of an MMO? Well, "clearly" the players must be. The problem is, though, *there is no such thing as "the players."* There are many individuals, all of whom are players, but they don't think as one. They think as individuals.

Why is this problematic? A book can have a million readers, each of whom has their own take on what the book is saying. Why can't an MMO mean a million things to a million players, too?

Well, the difference is that an MMO is (by definition) *shared*. If one in a hundred readers of a book finds it hilarious and the rest find it serious, that one reader's laughing isn't going to affect anyone else's reading of it. There *are* some types of art where this would be an issue. For example, in theater, one person laughing throughout *Hamlet* is going to spoil the performance for the rest of the audience who perhaps don't see the play as a comedy.

MMOs go beyond this, though, because they're also (by definition) *persistent*. One person spoiling (for others) the performance of a play or a movie is an inconvenience, but (assuming they're not griefers) they're only there for one performance. They have read the work of art differently, but they *have* read it. With an MMO, they're there reading it indefinitely.

This being the case, there's a permanent clash of viewpoints. Some players will interpret an MMO one way, some another, some yet another, with fine differences extending to the level of the individual. It's all well and good to say that this is "how art should be," and that the meaning of an MMO can be thrashed out by the resolution of a dialectic, but it's a dialectic in the wrong dimension. It's not between designer and designer, or even designer and player: it's between player and player. The conversation may be resolved, but it may well not be. It is especially unlikely to reach a conclusion if one or more sides have no need to listen.

Take, for example, role-playing. Suppose a designer created a game specifically for people who like hard role-playing. Hordes of role-players sign up and have a ball, but a small proportion of the MMO's players don't role-play. They don't see the MMO as being "about" role-playing, or at least not about role-playing by them, personally. This is a legitimate position for them to take, but their attitude can wreck the atmosphere and ruin immersion for those who do role-play. The role-players may outnumber the non-role-players a hundred to one; they may desperately want them to leave, but they have no leverage on them. They can't do anything to annoy them; they can only be annoyed by them. It's an argument that doesn't move. It ends when the role-players look for somewhere else to role-play, whereupon those who don't role-play but who like playing among role-players, follow them. Thus, the story repeats.

So what *should* happen here?

Cahiers

Film is an artistic medium.

Originally, Film's claims to be an artistic medium hung by the thread of its similarity to Theater. Apart from the efforts of a few avant garde film-makers in the silent movie era (when making a movie wasn't so expensive that people couldn't easily experiment), Film's attempts to gain artistic legitimacy were confined to creating adaptations of established forms of art, principally Literature and to some extent Theatre. These were regarded by the art establishment as being worthy, but inferior to the original work upon which they were based; regular, "popular" movies, of the kind being churned out in Hollywood, were deemed low-brow cultural artifacts of little artistic merit.

This attitude persisted through the 1940s. Hollywood movies were slick and had high production values, but they were not regarded as works of art. Government funding for movies was directed either at making documentaries (in the UK), literary adaptations (France), or propaganda (everywhere). When people consciously made films that were intended to be "art," the results were mainly political: art in film-making meant using Film to make an overt point. As is so often the case with artistic forms, entertainment was perceived to be a distraction from the integrity of the message the film-maker wished to convey; art is serious, and entertainment gets in the way of that unless it follows precise (and therefore neutered) conventions.

It wasn't until the 1950s that this way of looking at Film was challenged. The French, who because of the war had been starved of Hollywood movies, were suddenly allowed to see a wave of the best of them. It was clear to a group of French film-makers that these were more intelligent, self-confident, independent, and alive than the staid, high-brow French movies they had been watching for the past decade. They saw that movies did not have to duplicate the art of other forms; they could be art on their *own* terms. The likes of André Bazin, Jean Cocteau, Jean-Luc Godard, Jacques Rivette, and François Truffaut, writing in the magazine *Cahiers du Cinéma*, reevaluated Hollywood-style movies as stand-alone art forms, and in so doing opened up Film to new analyses. Disregarding whatever terms practitioners of other art forms might use to evaluate a Hollywood movie as art, they considered instead the reasons why such a movie might be art in and of itself. Their work finally established Film as a legitimized art form and led to what today we know as Film Studies.

So: games.

Games are art, and game design is an art form. Instead of patronizingly telling us games can be used to make art but aren't themselves art, the art world cognoscenti should be thinking about why games are *intrinsically* art. Instead of trying to read them as Film, people should be trying to read them as Games. As well as writing games to *be* art, people should be examining why the games we have are *already* art. The intersection of art and games isn't "art games" or "game art"—it's *games*. To say that games are only art if they conform to the conventions of other art forms is as out of line as it was for Film.

Start from the premise that a game can be nothing more than a game and yet still be art, and we'll get somewhere.

Why isn't there a *Cahiers des Jeux* when you need one?

No, this isn't just because I bought the cahiersdesjeux.com domain name.

Best of Intentions

Designers should listen to players, of course, but having listened to players, you have to decide what to do about what you hear. You can't simply go along with what players say because they say different things. They also ask for things you can't deliver because it costs too much or is physically impossible (time travel is a common one, for example). Oh, and because there are so many of them, they come up with ideas faster than you can include them.

Thus, even if you were committed to being merely an implementer of player ideas, you'd still have to go through an editing process to decide which of these ideas to implement.

That's unless you ask the whole body of players which ideas to implement, which is *sure* to work out well.

agoraXchange

On the Ides of March, 2004, phase 1 of *agoraXchange*[11] was launched.

So: *agoraXchange* was commissioned by Tate Online in the UK—Tate as in the Tate Gallery and Tate Modern, which are among the nation's leading art establishments. It was created as "an online community for designing a massively multi-player global politics game challenging the violence and inequality of our present political system."

Challenging, yes.

The idea was to use collaborative design to create an online world, and in so doing highlight problems with current forms of government, as well as to help imagine new forms. The team's manifesto featured a long list of existing issues with government; it was very radical and very worthy.

Except, what if the forms of government that the players created were ones that were *worse* than those we have at the moment?

I was at a conference where designer Dave Rickey asked this question of the *agoraXchange* people straight out. They said they hoped MMO players would develop new, fairer forms of government, but he replied that in practice MMO players tend to organize along lines that are anything but fair or democratic. They go for "oligarchies, plutocracies, cults of personalities, tribes, cartels, militaristic feudalism." What if the players of *agoraXchange* chose to implement a fascist state rather than an egalitarian one?

The *agoraXchange* representative said that they wouldn't allow this to happen.

The audience, myself included, broke out into raucous laughter at this point. However, the *agoraXchange* speaker was indifferent to it; she didn't appear to recognize that she even had a problem.

Players are free to create new and dynamic forms of government, casting aside outdated older forms of government, except if she didn't like it? Isn't that itself a very old form of government—the one known as a dictatorship?

Oh well, a heavy dose of irony never did any piece of up-its-own-backside art any harm. They seem to be impervious to it.

On the Ides of March, 2008, phase 2 of *agoraXchange* was launched.

Whatever you think about the developers of *agoraXchange*, you've got to admire their ability to stick to deadlines.

---

[11]Natalie Bookchin and Jacqueline Stevens: *agoraXchange*. Tate, 2003.
http://www.agoraxchange.org http://www.agoraxchange.net

Finding Your Medium

Some MMOs allow players to create original in-world objects themselves; for many social worlds, such as *Second Life*, this is the entire point.

This being the case, the affordances of the client interface may be crucial. For example, if you were creating some outfit to have a particular look, you would want it to have that look for all players. In a graphical world, barring issues such as human hardware problems (e.g., color blindness), this is largely true. However, in a textual world, what people "see" is what their imagination constructs from the object's description.

This doesn't mean a graphical interface is intrinsically better for in-world artists than a textual one; it just means that it's better if you're an artist *for which this is your medium*. Some authors of textual worlds would not wish to create images directly, only to suggest them—their aim is for the players to construct in their minds whatever image is most appropriate for them *individually*. At the other end of the scale, some real-world sculptors would not wish to create anything in *Second Life* because it has no tactile dimension.

If the interface is key to how you express yourself, sure, go with a world that has this interface. It may even be the real world.

Bonus think-as-an-artist advice: ask yourself *why* this interface is the one for you.

Experience Losses

There's a growing tendency among game developers to describe what they do as being the creation of *experiences* rather than being the creation of games. The job of designers is to design said experiences, not to design games, because games are a kind of (or in some views a part of an) experience.

I can see why this idea has gained purchase: modern computer games aren't just about gameplay, they're about the whole package. Players can be put off by bad graphics, bad animation, bad interface, bad music, and bad voice acting; done well, though, all of these can enhance the player's involvement. If developers don't put together the whole experience in an integrated fashion, players will have less fun.

It's in the best interests of developers to promote this view, too. If the team is building an "experience," then it means that everyone's creative input is accorded equal value. It's not all about the lead designer; it's about the whole company. If you have 200 people working on a game, well, all of them deserve credit for the final product. It's true, too: they do. So this is all very egalitarian and good for morale—but as a side-effect, it means you don't get any stars. *This* is what corporate types like. Stars are bad for a development studio because stars want more money. If everyone is a twinkle, no one is a star, and things will run more smoothly. If you want a star, hey, the studio is the star!

Nevertheless, there clearly *is* some direction in game development: the individuals involved don't all work independently, with the product miraculously coming together as a coherent whole at the end. No matter how much companies try to share the love around, non-developers who engage with games (as players, critics, or academics) do notice that some games are better than others—even games from the same studio. Ultimately, one individual has to be responsible for a game's quality. So, who?

If you take the games-as-experience line, you have a problem here. You've said everyone is equally responsible, but few in the real world are buying that. You *can* pin creative control on the lead designer, so long as you make sure you properly downplay your narrative: the designer is just the humble person who is lucky to have their crazy ideas turned into sane product by this supportive team of amazing individuals. This is the honest way to do it if you really *do* see design as being about experiences first and games second—indeed, it's the approach taken by Jesse Schell in his wonderful book on the art of game design[12].

---

[12]Jesse Schell: *The Art of Game Design: A Book of Lenses.* 2nd edition, CRC Press: Boca Raton, Florida, 2014.

However, this is incompatible with projecting your company brand as being the name to trust. You don't want to raise any one creative above the others at all. Unfortunately, *everyone* there is creative, so…

So you say that the game's producer is the person who is most responsible for the player experience. This does make pedantic sense: just as a movie director is the person who most determines what the viewer sees on the screen, you can argue that the producer is most responsible for what the player actually plays. In this view, designers are like screenwriters, not like directors.

I don't accept this. The reason that movie directors get the auteur label is that (in theory) they look at hundreds of screenplays and choose the one that most connects with the kind of movie they want to make. Even in practice, perhaps working with an already-chosen script for a franchise, they get to decide whether a project is right for them or not before taking it on. Producers don't look at hundreds of game designs (either in theory or in practice), and neither do they move around from studio to studio seeking a project they like. Sure, the game industry isn't mature enough yet for that to happen for anyone, but it's hard to imagine its happening ever for producers-as-creative-leads. They don't have creative control.

All this is incidental, though. Personally, I don't think that the view of game design as experience design is accurate in the first place.

My reason for this is that it fails to give proper emphasis to the role of the player. Players don't play experiences, they play games. They *have* experiences, but they are partly the authors of these experiences through their play. Designers therefore don't design experiences, they design *for* players to construct their *own* experiences. A space in which players can author their own experiences is a place of play, but it's not play in and of itself.

Calling games "experiences" suggests that players are more passive than they actually are, and conflates the notion of a play space with that of the play that takes place within it. I don't mind using games-as-experience as a rhetoric to help improve a particular design, but to me it falls short as a stand-alone philosophy.

Conceptualization

I say that MMO design is an art form, and that MMOs are art, but can that art be conceptualized? If MMOs can't be conceptualized as art, can MMOs ever be discussed *as* art?

Well, MMO design can be conceptualized as art. The problem is, this conceptualization is in the language of the medium itself. A high-end game designer can read what a design is saying because they can speak the language. However, they can't express it precisely through words because, if they could, then they wouldn't need the language of game design.

It should be possible for people who don't "get" games nevertheless to be able to write cogently about them if they can access the conceptualization of what a game says in a different form. We have this in other media: a person who has been deaf from birth could still write an essay comparing the music of David Bowie to that of Phillip Glass. The construction and effects of pieces of music can be articulated in words and their technical and emotional content discussed in words, even by people who can't access music directly.

For MMOs, there is no such conceptualization, as yet. Perhaps it will come from designers; more likely, it will come from critics.

Unplanned Consequences

Things happen in MMOs that the designer didn't plan for. Some of these are happy, emergent consequences of rule sets that the designer put in place; others are unhappy such consequences.

Who decides whether these unplanned consequences stay or go? Who *should* decide?

Frames and Boundaries

It's one thing to know why players feel annoyed when a game crosses the boundaries they expected of it, but it raises an additional point to do with the justification that many players invoke when the in-fiction reading of their actions is explained. Usually, if they did something they don't really agree with in real life, they'll dismiss it by saying something along the lines of "it's just a game."

This way of using circumstance to allow you to perform an action you would otherwise have found socially or morally awkward is called *framing*. A frame is a context surrounding a situation that affords some protection from social norms to people operating within that context; it's like a small set of theories that operate in tandem for commonly-encountered sets of circumstances. For example, if you saw a man dressed in Elizabethan costume walking down the street at 9a.m., you might stare: it doesn't fit your "pedestrian" frame. If you saw the same man on stage in a Shakespearean play at 9p.m., you wouldn't think there was anything out of the ordinary at all: it does fit your "acting" frame. Sometimes, the frame can be the norm: if you're dressed in a business suit during Mardi Gras in Rio de Janeiro, *you're* the weird one.

Frames are necessary for the magic circle, but not sufficient: not only do you need to understand where the boundaries lie for a magic circle, but you and all the other players also have to stay within them for it to hold. It doesn't matter how many people in business suits attend Mardi Gras, the frame still protects those in costume; if one competitor gets on a motorbike in a marathon, it breaks the magic circle for all the other runners.

The "it's just a game" attitude exploits the frame aspect of the magic circle: it offers an explanation to those outside of the magic circle for behavior within it. It doesn't affect players because it still falls within the context of the magic circle. Boxers expect to be hit during a boxing match; the frame of the magic circle explains why people don't leap into the ring to separate them.

Can behaviors within a magic circle *ever* be anything other than "just a game"?

Art Games or Games as Art?

The problem I have with "art games" is that the symbolism is in the wrong place.

In general, when people self-consciously create games to be art, they make the same mistakes as do people who self-consciously make games to educate: they latch onto the wrong symbols. They have token A represent *this* concept and token B represent *that* concept, then they marry them using game rules in a way that says, "See how *this* and *that* are connected," This places the symbolism of the game—the part where the artistic payload is delivered—in the components that have least to do with what makes games be games.

Games have tokens (nouns) and rules (verbs governing the nouns; sometimes, the verbs can also be nouns). Interactions between rules create sets of pressures (features): you have to manage resources, reputation, territory, risk, whatever. Interactions between pressures create gameplay: you have to decide whether the resources you hope to capture in a territorial gain and the reputation hit you'll certainly take trying to capture them are going to satisfy your overall goals. Gameplay is what games have that nothing else has: it's here where the symbolism has to lie if you want to talk about games as art. Anywhere else, it's basically games being co-opted as other art. That's why so many created-to-be-art games fail so badly as games: the imposition of symbolism on the tokens and rules fixes the pressures and gameplay that can result. The game ceases to be about the gameplay and becomes being about "let me beat you over the head with this clever metaphor."

It drives me to distraction when people ask questions such as, "Can games be art?" **ALL** games are art (well, all game designs are). They might not be *good* art, but they're all art. People are just looking in the wrong place for that art.

Games are systems for embodying potential experiences which, in the playing, are manifest as a series of events; players construct their own personal stories by selecting the significant (to them) events they have experienced. They get to choose the nature and direction of those personal stories through gameplay. Games are therefore machines for allowing players to create their own, personal stories. If you want to say anything to the players, that's where you have to say it: in the gameplay. It's the only place where games can say something that no other medium can, and it's what makes games be games.

You, as a player, have to make decisions; I, as a designer, get to establish what decisions you will have to make. Those decisions can—indeed *must*—involve questions that I myself either want to ask or want you to answer. The potential and actual consequences of those decisions, both in the game and on you personally, cause you to reflect on them. In that *reflection* is the art that games deliver.

Games You Should Have Played #7

A really bad game.

Some games are just *bad*. The mechanics are all wrong, or they're unfun, or no fun, or the rules are ambiguous, or they drag on and on, or there's a dominant strategy, or well, the list continues. If you play such a game, you can ascertain first-hand what it is that's bad about it; this will enable you to avoid similar games in future and to avoid making similar mistakes in any games you design yourself (see Games You Should Have Played #8). The more you understand about games, the more you'll be able to find the games that are right for you as a designer.

For me, tempting though it is to nominate *Trivial Pursuit* as the game that laid waste to the British board game industry, I didn't actually play that because the very premise filled me with exasperation. I can't therefore count it here. However, my replacement personal pick is one that I'm sure many other people will share, too: *Monopoly*. How many people have been put off playing board games for life because of it?

Reviews of Designers

People review computer games. Why don't they review computer game designers? Film critics routinely talk about a director's style; shouldn't we be affording similar respect to game designers?

We should, but there are three problems.

First, most game designers aren't actually all that good at game design—they're just better than most non-designers. As I mentioned earlier, designers can usually tell when other designers are worse than them, but they can't always tell when other designers are better; this means that only first-rate designers can normally recognize other first-rate designers. There are some designers who are festooned with industry awards who really can't design well at all, it's just there aren't many people around who can see it.

Second, most players aren't good at recognizing good game design. They know what they like, they know whether what they are playing is what they like, so they know what in their view is good design—it's something they like to play. Unfortunately, they don't see beyond that as to how what they like could be so much better—they're not designers. Furthermore, players often judge the ability of designers by the commercial success of the resulting products. This means that so-so games with great marketing and high production values come out better than those brilliant, fun, different, and exciting games that the players never play because they never hear of them. As a case in point, many players take one look at a game's graphics, then pass on playing.

Third, the game industry as a whole is averse to auteur theory. Studios prefer to present themselves as "the developer" in order to build up loyalty to their brand rather than to individual designers (who might leave and take their reputation with them). Players know what to expect from Bioware games, or Bethesda games, or Rockstar games. It's actually rather hard to find out who the lead designer *is* for some games. We're basically in the same situation with games that movies were in during the days of the Studio System (about which more anon).

So, what does this mean for reviews on game designers?

Well, game criticism—as with any form of artistic criticism—is itself an art. You need to find someone capable of reading games and appraising them. That's actually difficult to do for game criticism, but it's nevertheless tractable: there are tens of thousands of highly experienced and cogent players, so there are bound to be *some* among them who have something insightful to say.

If you want reviews of *designers*, as opposed to their games, then you're really cutting down on your pool of available talent. Most players don't understand design in general, so you're basically looking for a designer. Designers do understand design, but few can do justice to better design than they are capable of executing themselves. There *are* designers who do have a full appreciation of what makes good designers, even if they're not great at it themselves—there just aren't many of them. Besides, they have no reason to present their reviews to the public (especially as they can expect to get slaughtered over them if what they write can be perceived as remotely negative in any aspect).

So if we want decent retrospectives of designers' work, we may just have to wait until people who are trained to appraise different media turn their gaze first on games and then on game designers.

It's to be hoped that they *will* focus on designers, and not on studios, producers, or other creatives.

Not a City of Superheroes

Why was *City of Heroes*, an MMO about superheroes, not called *City of Superheroes*?

Marvel Comics and DC Comics jointly have the term "Super Hero" registered as a trademark. *City of Superheroes* would have been close enough to trigger a lawsuit.

Game Design Mistakes Every Designer Makes #4

Designers don't think enough about *who* will play the games they design. Most often, the implicit answer is "me." The more art-theory aware designers might argue that "it's for me to design, for others to interpret." This is fine if those others have a designer aesthetic, but not if they have a player aesthetic.

The thing is, players are an *intrinsic part* of a game's design.

I have a particular interest here owing to the effect of the Player Type model on designer thinking. Wannabe designers see it and believe it means they should address the needs of multiple types of player—which is true; it does mean that (in MMOs, at least). However, they should address those needs in terms *meaningful* to those players: this means you do *not* give people XP rewards for socializing, for example.

Too few designers really get who their players are. Even the best will sometimes reason that some players like X, some players like Y, so if you give them both you'll get all those players who like X *or* Y. Sadly, unless they know their players, they'll often only get those who like both X *and* Y—the intersection rather than the union.

Why is not thinking about who will play your game a design mistake? Well, let's put it this way: if you don't know, you have no business designing games.

Note that not thinking enough about who plays games is also a mistake every non-designer makes.

One-Word Answer

People who work in other media often decry the ability of computer games to convey emotion. The standard question they ask is: "Could anyone ever write a computer game that could make you cry?"

There's a one-word answer to this: *permadeath*.

Merely Players

I used to get asked the same, dopey questions when interviewed by journalists, and on occasion I still do: MMOs and violence, MMOs and addiction, MMOs and addiction to violence, MMOs on anything else bad that they can think of. However, in 2007 I went to a conference in Oviedo, Spain, where I was asked some of the best questions I've ever been asked, before or since. I gave four interviews, and even the one for the local TV station was far more in-depth than what I've ever been asked in the UK. For a start, I didn't have to explain what MMOs actually are.

Of all these interesting questions, the *most* interesting one from a designer's point of view came from a student newspaper journalist: "If Shakespeare were alive today, would he be designing virtual worlds?"

Oh, wow!

Implicit in the question was the statement that *MMO design is an art*. I wasn't asked to argue that perhaps some time in the far distant future it might be regarded as an art, nor to defend it against assertions that only in-world creations such as machinima are truly art, nor to fend off criticism that design is such a collaborative effort that it can't possibly be an art unto itself, nor to plead for its acceptance as the bastard child of some other art. No: the fact that it was art was a given. I was being asked to explain whether MMOs as a means personal expression, of making statements about the human condition, of touching hearts and minds, were the kind of medium that would have suited a dramatist and poet of Shakespeare's caliber.

Some journalists-of-tomorrow, they just *get it*.

Never-Ending Art

Earlier, I asked what should happen when an MMO is being played by a minority who, in the view of those playing alongside them, are playing it wrongly.

"Should" is always a suspect word to use in arguments, as it presupposes that there is a right way to do things. However, to stay true to the original ideal about players interpreting art, the context in which the art (that is, the MMO) was released has to be taken into account. If an MMO is launched as a strict role-playing game and thousands of people sign up to it on that basis, then that is the context within which the players interact. Players who sign up for other reasons, who don't take the role-playing component to heart, *aren't playing the same MMO*. They're like someone who reads over your shoulder then asks you to go back a page because you turned it too soon: it's the same artifact being consumed at the same time, but not under the conditions for which the other consumers signed up to consume it.

I've used role-playing as an example here, but it could be anything. In the past, virtual worlds have been derailed because of a minority's views on PvP, real-money trading, permadeath, gear score, and a host of other differences. Eventually, the developers have either to let matters run their course or to step in and either make gameplay changes or issue bans. That puts them back in the driver's seat, though—which is precisely where, according to the very view of art that they are intervening to defend, they shouldn't be.

Personally, I don't see this as being reconcilable (unless the MMO was consciously designed to have such conflicts between players, which is a valid, if anarchic, position). The majority of players will have signed up to play based on their own interpretation of the designer's vision. When they conflict in a manner that can't be resolved through the adoption of social norms, there can only be one answer to the question of which side "should" be supported: the one that actually does follow the designer's vision because that's the only constant.

Except, of course, it *isn't* constant. The designer's vision can change as a result of the way the MMO is being played. Although it's fashionable to say that this makes MMO design collaborative, I wouldn't put it that way myself—mainly because designers are just as likely to react against the way some players are playing as they are to react for it. In a collaboration, players would have a say (that is, be collectively able to make executive decisions) but (because they are so numerous that individuals can't be heard) no voice; what we have at the moment is more consultative, in which players have (through their collective actions) a voice but (because they don't make the decisions) no say.

Is there a way out of this, theory-wise? Well, yes there is. It does make MMOs somewhat distinct from other forms of art, though.

The answer is that yes, the designer's intellectual ownership of an MMO is indeed given up once the MMO is finished, passing instead to those whose job it is to interpret it (the players). It's just, because the players themselves form part of the designed experience, an MMO never *is* finished. It's merely older.

You knew that anyway, though.

The Real is Imaginary

In the real world there is nothing except subatomic particles. It's only because you view those as collecting to form energy and matter, and interpret particular configurations of energy and matter to be "objects," that you can say a particular thing—a house, for example—"exists" in the real world.

In virtual worlds, objects are emergent consequences of the interaction of computer code and data. People ascribe meaning to these configurations, just as they do to matter/energy in the real world. They recognize that there is a difference between this kind of object and the kind they deal with normally, so they call them "virtual objects."

Ultimately, though, the "objectness" of anything (whether real or virtual) is nothing more than a construct of the mind.

Game Design Mistakes Every Designer Makes #5

The final game design mistake every designer makes (well, the final one I'm going to list, anyway) is that designers think they know what they're doing but they don't.

They *think* they're designing games, but they're not. They're creating art.

Some few do think they're creating art, which of course they are, but actually that's incidental. Ultimately, they're trying to *say* something. Game design merely has the best grammar and vocabulary that they've found for enabling them to say what they want so say.

As for *what* they're trying to say, well they don't know. If they did, they would just say it in words.

Computer games are a medium of expression for their designers. If designers could express themselves in some other medium, well they would—indeed, some do. It's the fact that games allow designers to express things they can't express otherwise that leads them to design. To understand what they're saying, you have to play their games (that's literally, not metaphorically).

Why is a misguided belief in why you're designing games a design mistake? Well, it's because if you're not true to yourself, you can't be true to your players.

Unfortunately, there's a problem here: if you *know* what it is you're saying, you no longer have the need to say it. You've therefore no reason to design games anymore. This means that you can only tell your players the truth about what you're saying when you have nothing left to say!

It's a mistake for designers not to know what they're doing, but it's *also* a mistake if they do know it. This is the paradox behind all art. The better the work of art, the closer the artist is to not being an artist.

The American poet, Emily Dickinson, wrote to the author of an article in *The Atlantic*, Thomas Wentworth Higginson:"Are you too deeply occupied to say if my Verse is alive?" As a brilliant poet, her question was actually its own answer: if she could tell it was alive, then it wasn't; if she couldn't, then it was. She couldn't, therefore it was.

Once you've grokked what you're doing, you no longer find it interesting or exciting. At best, it's a means to an end; at worse, it's a soul trap.

Note that not knowing what game designers do is also a mistake every non-designer makes.

We all make mistakes. We all make mistakes because we *have* to make mistakes: where's the fun otherwise? The best designers just make slightly *different* mistakes.

Miserable Me

When it comes to MMOs, I'm miserable.

What would make me unmiserable is if I were able to create my own large-scale virtual worlds for people to play. However, all I get to do is comment on other people's designs and teach people to design. I'm good at both, and it pays the bills, but there are things I want to say through virtual worlds that can't be said any other way; I'm frustrated at not being able to say them.

That's why I'm miserable.

Lest I'm giving the impression that I resent money being made available to inexperienced designers who don't yet fully understand what it is they're designing, I'd like to stress that I don't. Everyone has to learn their craft somewhere, and we won't get new ideas unless new designers are there to provide them. Where I am disappointed is in the lack of *fight* in designers; they have a glorious opportunity not only to shape virtual worlds but to shape the real world through their actions, yet they don't seem to understand this power they have. Too many are designing what they think people want them to design, rather than what they, themselves, *need* to design. They should trust to their own instincts more.

Hmm, so actually it's my own impatience that's making me miserable.

The Studio System

I said earlier that games were at the same stage as movies were when they had the studio system.

So, the studio system operated in Hollywood from its early days until the mid-1950s. It was the large-scale vertical integration of movie-making and distribution. In the USA (similar systems operated elsewhere), eight studios owned almost all the movie theatres between them. They had under contract all their screenwriters, actors, directors, and anyone else involved in movie-making. People went to see an MGM movie because they knew it would feature big musical set-pieces; they knew a Universal picture would be a western, a melodrama, or a gothic horror. Studios did make a thing of their stars (especially Paramount), and they would occasionally loan them to other studios. However, the studio was the brand, not the actor.

This was not a good system for creativity. What happened was that studios would force cinemas to buy large packages of movies. If they wanted the one movie they knew would bring in the crowds, they had to take the dozens (or even hundreds) more that were nothing special. Sure, they might have cost a million dollars each to make, but they were formulaic, derivative, and unimaginative.

Eventually, the studio system fell apart when the US government ordered studios to sell off their theater chains. It was replaced by a star-driven and director-driven system. Today, most actors and directors are freelance, moving from project to project rather than being stuck with one studio for a decade or more. The same actor can now pop up in a film, a TV show, or on the stage. We get better films, TV shows, and stage plays as a result because actors can now choose what roles best allow them to develop their art, instead of being told what parts they have to play.

The game industry doesn't have actors. It has characters (such as Lara Croft), but these are the intellectual property of developers and publishers, so they're not going anywhere. The game industry does have the equivalent of movie directors, though: game designers. At the moment, they don't change jobs any more than directors of 1930s movies did—but what if they could?

We do have some big-name designers in the game industry, but most had to risk their livelihood by setting up their own studio to obtain this recognition. It's very hard for a quality designer to get noticed while working for a developer in the current climate. It's a studio system.

This is bad for game design. Large, AAA developers will stick with the *status quo* and downplay the voice of designers for as long as they can because it's in their interests to maintain their brand. If they did make stars of their best designers, those designers might be poached.

When asked, the default studio position is that game development involves hundreds of creative people and designers are just cogs in a large machine; to single one out as "the" creator of a game would be a divisive misrepresentation. This sounds reasonable, except that a game's designer *is* "the" creator of the game: they're the person who determines what the player plays. Movies are about seeing, and the director ultimately decides what people see; therefore, movies are ultimately the creation of their director. Games are about playing, and the designer ultimately decides what people play; therefore, games are ultimately the creation of their designer.

Game design is an art form. Is it better to have designers work on projects they feel passionate about, or to work on whatever project they're told to work on? Where will we see the most innovation? Where will the better games we all want come from?

The game industry will eventually have to go the same way as other creative industries—film, music, book publishing, composing—whereby teams come together for one project, only to split up afterwards. Production companies will put these teams together and market the resulting games, and then everyone except the skeleton crew needed for the operation phase will move on to new projects being set up by different prodcos.

We see some of this now, but in negative terms. Developers make a game, overspend, and then have to sack half their workforce to keep afloat. Some of these sacked workers do set up indie studios to make new games, but most don't have the financial wherewithal to do that. Only when it's expected that everyone is freelance and will work only until the end of their contract will the stigma attached to job loss end, and only then will we get a creative jobs market. That's going to take a while.

Dark Room Sex Game

The theme for the annual Nordic Game Jam in 2008 was "taboo." One of the entrants was *Dark Room Sex Game* for the Nintendo Wii. This (now) award-winning two-player game has no graphics, just sounds.

The way it works, players take turns swinging their Wiimote. Each swing, a sound of pleasure is made, as if the players are engaged in a sex act. It's a rhythm game: the idea is to swing your Wiimotes increasingly faster (but not too fast), so that eventually they're close enough to trigger an "orgasm" event, at which point the game ends.

Part of the rationale behind *Dark Room Sex Game* is to push players across boundaries. Normally, the accompanying moans alone are enough to embarrass the players, let alone the fact that these sounds are under their own control. However, the frame of "it's just a game" allows most of them to overcome their reservations. As it happens, much of the enjoyment of the game comes from this naughtiness—it isn't all that compelling in its gameplay.

So *Dark Room Sex Game* does allow people to cross boundaries. However, there *are* still boundaries.

Could two straight men play the game, with one of them having a male-voice controller and the other a female-voice controller? Probably, yes.

What if both voices were male? OK, well some people might drop out at that point, but I'd expect most men would be up for it.

What if one of the voices were that of a donkey, rather than a human? Ah, well we could lose a few more players there. I'd still expect at least half the players to continue, though. After all, it's a bit of a laugh, and it's just a game—you're not *actually* rogering a donkey.

What if one of the voices were that of a human child?

Oh. You would find very few people willing to continue at that point. Suddenly, *Reality* intrudes too much, "it's just a game" or not.

Just because a game gives you *permission* to cross a boundary, that doesn't mean you will choose to cross it.

On Freedom

Right from the beginning, MMOs have always been about freedom.

They're still about freedom, but there's been a gradual decline caused by too much leakage of *Reality* into them, too little understanding on the part of most designers as to what it is they're designing, too many worlds for children that will remove their sense of wonder, too few players who realize quite what's on offer here. At times, I feel as if MMOs are a tropical island being battered by waves that are eventually going to overwhelm them and drag them beneath the ocean's surface.

MMOs offer freedom! Actual, personal *freedom*! You can finally go somewhere and be *yourself*. What an amazing, *glorious* prize! We should be *celebrating* them, urging everyone to join us in this wondrous new future; instead, all the big discussions concern mundanities. We're in real danger of losing the one chance we've ever had throughout all of history for people to have freedom that *means* freedom.

It's not "freedom from," it's "freedom to." Understand that, or it's gone.

Instead?

I was once interviewed in *The Inquirer* by long-standing tech journalist Wendy Grossman, whom I first had the pleasure of meeting at a conference in Singapore (we went round the Night Zoo together). The fact she managed to pull something coherent from our rather wide-ranging conversation explains why she's a journalist and I'm not.

I just wish I'd made myself clearer with the sentiment expressed in the headline, though. It read, "Man who wanted to change the world built virtual ones instead."

There was no "instead" about it.

Oh, Journalists

March, 2015: "I'm an arts, culture, and entertainment journalist currently writing a piece on the increasing demand and appetite of the British public for art in video games."

Sigh.

"Why do you think there's a strong demand and appetite for art in video games?"

No, you misunderstand! Art *in* games is not the art *of* video game design. In game design, the artistic payload is carried by the gameplay, not by the fiction or the setting. "Art games" tend to be woefully self-conscious affairs, speaking primarily through the conventional symbols of other media. Games are dynamic and interactive: the designer speaks to the player through the gameplay, with everything else in support of that. If your idea of "art in video games" involves the narrative, the look-and-feel, or the overt association of philosophical tokens to game tokens, you're missing the point.

Game designers design games (rather than write novels, paint paintings, pen screenplays, compose music, fashion sculpture, choreograph dance, or create boxes full of found objects that speak to the soul) because game design is their medium of artistic expression: they can say things through games that they can't say any other way. The feature that games have that no other medium has is gameplay: *this* is why gameplay is the bearer of the artistic soul of games, and *this* is what so many people who know about art but not games misinterpret the latter.

"Do you think your audience will change and appeal to more people as a result?"

As a result of what? My answering your loaded question a different way?

Game design IS AN ART FORM. If you're not a game designer, OK, well you may not appreciate that point (indeed you may not even if you are!), but it's true.

Suppose that, if instead of talking about this new, cool medium of games, you were talking a hundred years ago about writing screenplays: "Do you think there's a strong demand and appetite for art in movies?" Well yes, of course—movie-making is full of artistic statements. "Do you think your audience will change and appeal to more people as a result?" Well, the question is ridiculous! The implication is that there's no art in movies except when we consciously add it, yet we now know that movie-making is an art form unto itself.

If you try smugly to insert non-movie art into a movie, you end up with a movie about that other art, *not* an "art movie": this is because the movie is ALREADY art. How could it not be? So it is with games today: they're ALREADY art, and if you want to make "art games" by adding art to them, you're using them as a vehicle to explore that other art. This isn't to say it's not meaningful or important to do that, but you're basically in the same camp as those who want to use games for education. Yes, you *can* treat games as an application, but then you're not looking at the games, you're looking at what they're being applied to instead.

"Could games one day achieve the same cultural status as cinemas and photography?"

Yes. All it will take is for people who don't recognize that games are worthwhile cultural artifacts to die off. It took 50 years for the people who said that cinema and photography weren't art forms to die off, plus another 30 or so for the ripples of their views to ebb away. Nevertheless, it happened to them, and it *will* happen to the detractors of games.

Also, why did you pick cinema and photography? My guess is that it's because people still regard these as lowbrow art, rather than the highbrow art of painting, opera, ballet, and so on. You're asking whether computer games can aspire one day to become lowbrow art. Well, big deal!

Even in this day and age, for someone like me who is immersed in the world of games, it can be something of a shock to find out what opinion-formers in the world at large think about them.

The Joy of Design

I once ducked out of a conference in Berlin and went to the Media Design Institute, which runs a games degree. There, I spoke to about 20 of their students for around two hours, giving them my complete theory of why people play MMOs.

That 20 final-year undergraduates had come in to hear me talk on a Saturday morning in a language foreign to them was remarkable (especially given the attitude that many of my own students display with regard to attending my lectures). After lunch (cookies and gummy bears), the German undergraduates split into groups and presented their own ideas for MMOs. There were four of these, but we only had time to listen to three before we were thrown out of the building.

Now these students had only been working on their ideas for about a month, so things were a bit patchy. They'd gone into lots of detail in some places and less detail in others, meaning that often they couldn't see what the consequences of the decisions they'd made in the earlier parts would be for the later parts. As a designer, I could also sense they had conflicts between what they wanted to express and what they were expressing; for example, they might want a sandbox world, implying great freedom, but then impose unnecessary limitations on what the players could do in some specific aspect of play—an obvious tension to me, but one they wouldn't necessarily pick up on themselves until they'd spent lot more time working on it. I suspect this was basically down to their not yet trusting their instincts: all the projects had elements to them which had come from other MMOs, but which were unnecessary. The groups hadn't yet figured that they were allowed not to put those things in if they felt they didn't fit. This lack of self-assurance was just a passing phase, though; they would definitely gain confidence with time.

Oh, and they were all blissfully unaware of the devious, scheming nature of some players, and so of the susceptibility of their designs to griefing. I suggested they might want to consider how they could break their own designs (which is actually a good exercise anyway, because it means you get to understand your designs better). Hmm, maybe I should have asked them to try to break each other's designs too, come to think of it.

If this were all there were to the day, I'd have returned a happy man. When it comes to MMO design, I love talking to people who are willing to listen but also willing to challenge; who can be effortlessly inventive; who become excited by ideas; and who can convey that excitement through their designs.

That wasn't all there was to the day, though. There was something else that was, alone, worth a four-day trip to Germany just to experience. One of the teams had an absolutely beautiful—that's *beautiful* way of handling in-world religion. In the 30 plus years I'd been working on virtual worlds, I'd never come across it before. It was stunningly elegant—I'm almost welling with tears here just thinking about it. It was one of those moments of designer joy that can't be expressed in words, something that perhaps only a few score people in the whole world would fully appreciate, but is just *awesome* if you're one of those few score people.

The students who described it liked it, and knew it was good, but I don't think they knew quite *how* good it was. That's as it should be: they included it because it said something they wanted to say, and the fact that it was a brilliant mechanic was just a bonus. It was there because it needed to be there, but my oh my, it was *sweet*.

Yeah, I know: you want me to tell you what it was that they came up with so you can judge for yourself how good it was. Sadly, I don't feel that I can tell you. In part, this is because if you're not one of the few score people who'll go OH MY GUCKING FOD when you hear it, then you'll either take that as an insult or as evidence that I'm an addled old-timer. However, the main reason I'm not repeating it is because it's *not my idea to repeat*. It would be like telling you how a magic trick works before it was performed. I'd prefer to give the magicians a chance to show you the trick first—they deserve it. I'll take the chance that you suspect I'm making this story up in order to give myself the appearance of being more aesthetically attuned to game design than I really am.

Jeez, though, why has no one thought of it before?

This is why I'm an MMO designer.

Golden Boys and Girls

From Act 4, Scene II of *Cymbeline*, by William Shakespeare:

```
GUIDERIUS
Fear no more the heat o' the sun,
Nor the furious winter's rages;
Thou thy worldly task hast done,
Home art gone, and ta'en thy wages:
Golden lads and girls all must,
As chimney-sweepers, come to dust.
```

It's the first verse of a song sung by Guiderius and Arviragus to honor Cloten, whom Guiderius has just killed in a fight. Don't worry about the plot; all you really need to know here is that, as stepson to the king, Cloten could be considered a "golden lad."

So, earlier in this scene the word "dust" has already been used twice in puns, to refer both to the human body (as a vessel for the soul) and to a point of similarity. Here's the first occasion, where there's some serious word-play:

```
ARVIRAGUS
[To IMOGEN] Brother, stay here
Are we not brothers?
IMOGEN
So man and man should be;
But clay and clay differs in dignity,
Whose dust is both alike.
```

Arviragus really *is* Imogen's brother, but she's disguised as a man so he doesn't know that—he means "brother" in a "brothers-in-arms" sense. Imogen is saying that she and he are the same at a fundamental level (their dust is alike), but she also suggests that the way this stuff of similarity is put together (clay) makes them different.

OK, let's return to the "golden lads" quote.

It's clear that the "dust" that Shakespeare is referring to in this song/poem is the stuff of which people are made. When they die, even the highest-born people in the land take on the same form as does everyone else. The song has three verses, and they all make reference to dust in the last line. As this verse we're looking at is the first, it establishes the tone of the eulogy; the second verse develops it, and the third (which is really rather beautiful) hammers it home.

To illustrate the fact that even the high-born are just the same as everyone else when they die, Shakespeare uses this reference to chimney-sweepers (note: *not* chimney-sweeps; this is important!). People who sweep chimneys are low-born types; they were chosen to contrast with the golden lads because they're grimy (the opposite of golden) and they work with dust—soot—all the time. Shakespeare is using them three times at once: he's contrasting their low-born status with the high-born status of Cloten; he's following through the lustrous metaphor he used for Cloten ("golden") with its antithesis (the matt black-ness of soot); he's saying, in a fairly jestful way, that death is as inevitable as a chimney-sweep's finding soot.

All in two lines: that's pretty classy stuff.

If you don't know what's coming, prepare to be amazed.

A chimney-sweeper can either be a chimney-sweep (the person who sweeps the chimney) or the brush used for their job. The brush bears some resem-blance to a dandelion when it's gone to seed; this is why, in Warwickshire, around Stratford-on-Avon, to this day the locals call them "chimney-sweep-ers." Before the dandelions turn to seed, when they're yellow, they're called "golden boys and girls."

My blood ran cold when I found that out.

A nondescript couplet at the end of the first verse of a song in the middle of a development scene in an over-long play: he *could* have written anything, really, it wouldn't have mattered. But he didn't...

If Shakespeare were alive today, would he be designing virtual worlds?

No, he wouldn't. Anyone who can do *that* has already found his medium.

Maybe ask again a hundred years hence.

So I Did

My dad was a gamer. Most Saturday and Sunday afternoons, my brother and I would pester him to play a board game or a card game with us. He never, ever turned us down. Sometimes, we'd play several different games in one session. I must have spent thousands of hours playing games as I grew up.

My mother was a storyteller. She would make up stories on the fly and tell them to us as if they were out of a book. The ones we liked best were about one Pixie Poppy. We used to beg her to tell us a Pixie Poppy story, and she never, ever let us down. She stopped when we got older and no longer asked; fairytales weren't as appealing any more. However, she went on to tell new Pixie Poppy stories to my children, her grandchildren.

My dad was a gas fitter. My mum was a school meals cook.

We *existed* on a council estate in a coastal town far away from anywhere of any consequence.

We *lived* in our imaginations.

In my formative years, I saw misery and injustice in the world around me. I wanted to make a *better* world.

So I did.

A Breaking Wave

Following *World of Warcraft*, MMO developers took one of basically three approaches:

- They copied *WoW*.
- They said they weren't copying *WoW*, but were so stuck in the paradigm that they copied it anyway.
- They did something wildly different, aiming for a niche success.

Because of the time it takes to develop MMOs, that wave is finally breaking.

What will the crest of the wave following it up look like?

Rationally

In the UK, there are maybe 10,000 graduates actively looking for a computer game industry job, 3,000 of whom have dedicated Computer Game degrees, with another 1,000 fresh Computer Game graduates coming on stream every year. This is in an industry that employs at most 25,000 people total, including those working for companies servicing the game industry.

Rationally, I should be telling my students that they're wasting their time trying to get jobs in the game industry. Each year, though, several do get them. Rationally, I should be telling them that they won't be designing games, they'll be programming tools or working in QA. This is basically correct, but a few short years down the line they could indeed be designing games. Rationally, I should be saying that they're not going to become millionaires by setting up tiny development studios with one another, but each year some of them do set up such companies, and some of those companies do have a paper value of over a million pounds. Rationally, I should be telling them that they would get paid more programming practically anything other than computer games, and that it should matter to them. I do, in fact, tell them this, but it makes no difference.

When they finish their degree, and go out into the big, wide world, they're in a position where they have the skills to make games but not the experience. Incredibly, this lack of experience is what makes it all somehow click. *Because* they don't have experience, they're idealistic; *because* they're idealistic, they'll do things they don't know they're not supposed to be able to do; *because* they try, they sometimes succeed—or they fail, but in so doing learn from their mistakes and bounce back.

This is what keeps me working in academia: the knowledge that what I'm too cynical and jaded to do, some of the people I'm teaching will be overly optimistic and overly enthusiastic enough to attempt.

I'm hoping you'll fall into that category, too.

All I can do is inform and enthuse, driven only by the belief that, in the end, we'll get better games.

That's all I ever wanted from the game industry: better games.

Designers of Games

Learning to design games is like learning a language.

If it's your first language, it's easy.

If it's a second language, it's harder but doable. At first, you'll still think in your first language—writing short stories or screenplays, say—but after a while you'll pick it up. With practice, you'll lose your accent and find yourself speaking like a native. Indeed, because you've had to think about it, you could wind up with a better understanding of the language than do many native speakers.

In both cases, the more you use the language, the more you'll learn, and the more fluent you'll become.

Because so few people have game design as their first language (although the numbers are growing), the subject is usually taught in the way a second language is taught. You're given some basic vocabulary—mechanics—to start you off, then some formal grammar so you can put the mechanics together to create gameplay. Because games haven't been studied for as long as language, the grammar isn't fully understood; nevertheless, you'll learn how some things go together well and other things go together badly. You'll also learn that there are different dialects for different genres, played by different people.

At the end of all this, you'll have all the skills you need to design games; and if you have an aptitude for it, you'll be able to speak game design like a native. So now you're a game designer!

Well, no. Now you're a person who designs games, but that doesn't make you a game designer any more than speaking English makes you English. You might design thrilling games that people really want to play; you may win awards and international recognition. Even so, it's nevertheless entirely possible that you're not a game designer. It's also entirely possible that some inarticulate kid struggling to implement his or her ideas who can barely string a game-design sentence together *is* a game designer.

This is because how well you speak a language is inconsequential if you have nothing to say in it.

Game designers design games to *say* something—something that they couldn't say any other way.

Every other person who designs games, no matter how good they are at it, is just that: a person who designs games.

Reflections

I suspect that this book was not quite what you were expecting.

It sounded as if it ought to be a practical how-to for designing MMOs: where to get ideas, the overall design process, what mechanics are available, design techniques you can apply, how to create an interface, how to embed non-game concepts in games...

I've covered none of this. It's as if you bought a book about learning to paint, but instead I've told you about being an artist. If you've no interest in being a game designer in general or an MMO designer in particular, this will seem a washout. It's not, though.

Were your only aim to use games as a tool, the content of this book could be reduced to one line: "Copy an existing game and repurpose it." If you want to *design* games, though, you have to be a game *designer*.

There is more to game design than meets the eye. Anyone can design games in the same sense that "anyone" can draw or write novels. Sure they can, but would you want to play those games, frame those pictures, or read those books?

It's an ART: you have to put some of your SOUL into it.

Game design is a medium of expression. *This* is what you need to understand. If you're making a game, don't focus on the mechanics or the fiction: focus on what you're trying to *say*. The rest will fall into place as you grasp for processes and metaphors to articulate it.

Games *are* machines, but they're *more*. Games are a *language*. You use them to *say* things. I haven't given you much vocabulary, but I've explained the concepts of nouns and verbs and sentences and grammar. I can't tell you what to say with them, but I *can* tell you that you **can** say things with them—and indeed, that you can't *not* say things with them.

I haven't done it very *well*, but if it's one small step along the way to better MMOs, that's enough for me.

Index

Get the eBook for only $5!

Why limit yourself?

Now you can take the weightless companion with you wherever you go and access your content on your PC, phone, tablet, or reader.

Since you've purchased this print book, we're happy to offer you the eBook in all 3 formats for just $5.

Convenient and fully searchable, the PDF version enables you to easily find and copy code—or perform examples by quickly toggling between instructions and applications. The MOBI format is ideal for your Kindle, while the ePUB can be utilized on a variety of mobile devices.

To learn more, go to www.apress.com/companion or contact support@apress.com.

Printed in the United States
By Bookmasters